The Edinburgh Companion to Virginia Woolf and Contemporary Global Literature

Edinburgh Companions to Literature and the Humanities

Published

The Edinburgh Companion to Virginia Woolf and the Arts
Edited by Maggie Humm

The Edinburgh Companion to Twentieth-Century Literatures in English
Edited by Brian McHale and Randall Stevenson

A Historical Companion to Postcolonial Literatures in English
Edited by David Johnson and Prem Poddar

A Historical Companion to Postcolonial Literatures – Continental Europe and its Empires
Edited by Prem Poddar, Rajeev Patke and Lars Jensen

The Edinburgh Companion to Twentieth-Century British and American War Literature
Edited by Adam Piette and Mark Rowlinson

The Edinburgh Companion to Shakespeare and the Arts
Edited by Mark Thornton Burnett, Adrian Streete and Ramona Wray

The Edinburgh Companion to Samuel Beckett and the Arts
Edited by S. E. Gontarski

The Edinburgh Companion to the Bible and the Arts
Edited by Stephen Prickett

The Edinburgh Companion to Modern Jewish Fiction
Edited by David Brauner and Axel Stähler

The Edinburgh Companion to Critical Theory
Edited by Stuart Sim

The Edinburgh Companion to the Critical Medical Humanities
Edited by Anne Whitehead, Angela Woods, Sarah Atkinson, Jane Macnaughton and Jennifer Richards

The Edinburgh Companion to Nineteenth-Century American Letters and Letter-Writing
Edited by Celeste-Marie Bernier, Judie Newman and Matthew Pethers

The Edinburgh Companion to T. S. Eliot and the Arts
Edited by Frances Dickey and John D. Morgenstern

The Edinburgh Companion to Children's Literature
Edited by Clémentine Beauvais and Maria Nikolajeva

The Edinburgh Companion to Atlantic Literary Studies
Edited by Leslie Eckel and Clare Elliott

The Edinburgh Companion to the First World War and the Arts
Edited by Ann-Marie Einhaus and Katherine Isobel Baxter

The Edinburgh Companion to Fin de Siècle Literature, Culture and the Arts
Edited by Josephine M. Guy

The Edinburgh Companion to Animal Studies
Edited by Lynn Turner, Undine Sellbach and Ron Broglio

The Edinburgh Companion to Contemporary Narrative Theories
Edited by Zara Dinnen and Robyn Warhol

The Edinburgh Companion to Anthony Trollope
Edited by Frederik Van Dam, David Skilton and Ortwin Graef

The Edinburgh Companion to the Short Story in English
Edited by Paul Delaney and Adrian Hunter

The Edinburgh Companion to the Postcolonial Middle East
Edited by Anna Ball and Karim Mattar

The Edinburgh Companion to Ezra Pound and the Arts
Edited by Roxana Preda

The Edinburgh Companion to Elizabeth Bishop
Edited by Jonathan Ellis

The Edinburgh Companion to Gothic and the Arts
Edited by David Punter

The Edinburgh Companion to Literature and Music
Edited by Delia da Sousa Correa

The Edinburgh Companion to D. H. Lawrence and the Arts
Catherine Brown and Susan Reid

The Edinburgh Companion to the Prose Poem
Mary Ann Caws and Michel Delville

The Edinburgh Companion to Virginia Woolf and Contemporary Global Literature
Jeanne Dubino, Paulina Pająk, Catherine W. Hollis, Celiese Lypka and Vara Neverow

https://edinburghuniversitypress.com/series/ecl

The Edinburgh Companion to Virginia Woolf and Contemporary Global Literature

Edited by Jeanne Dubino, Paulina Pająk,
Catherine W. Hollis, Celiese Lypka
and Vara Neverow

EDINBURGH
University Press

Edinburgh University Press is one of the leading university presses in the UK. We publish academic books and journals in our selected subject areas across the humanities and social sciences, combining cutting-edge scholarship with high editorial and production values to produce academic works of lasting importance. For more information visit our website: edinburghuniversitypress.com

© editorial matter and organisation Jeanne Dubino, Paulina Pająk, Catherine W. Hollis, Celiese Lypka and Vara Neverow, 2021, 2025

© the chapters their several authors, 2021, 2025

Edinburgh University Press Ltd
13 Infirmary Street,
Edinburgh, EH1 1LT

First published in hardback by Edinburgh University Press 2021

Typeset in 10/12 Adobe Sabon by
IDSUK (DataConnection) Ltd

A CIP record for this book is available from the British Library

ISBN 978 1 4744 4847 5 (hardback)
ISBN 978 1 3995 4855 7 (paperback)
ISBN 978 1 4744 4848 2 (webready PDF)
ISBN 978 1 4744 4849 9 (epub)

The right of Jeanne Dubino, Paulina Pająk, Catherine W. Hollis, Celiese Lypka and Vara Neverow to be identified as the editors of this work has been asserted in accordance with the Copyright, Designs and Patents Act 1988, and the Copyright and Related Rights Regulations 2003 (SI No. 2498).

Contents

Acknowledgements	vii
Notes on Contributors	viii
List of Abbreviations of Virginia Woolf's Works	xiv
Introduction *Paulina Pająk, Jeanne Dubino and Catherine W. Hollis*	1

Part I: Planetary and Global Receptions of Woolf

1. 'What a curse these translators are!' Woolf's Early German Reception — 25
   Daniel Göske and Christian Weiß

2. The Translation and Reception of Virginia Woolf in Romania (1926–89) — 42
   Adriana Varga

3. The Reception of Virginia Woolf and Modernism in Early Twentieth-Century Australia — 62
   Suzanne Bellamy

4. Dialogues between South America and Europe: Victoria Ocampo Channels Virginia Woolf — 79
   Cristina Carluccio

5. From Julia Kristeva to Paulo Mendes Campos: Impossible Conversations with Virginia Woolf — 96
   Davi Pinho

6. *Three Guineas* and the *Cassandra* Project – Christa Wolf's Reading of Virginia Woolf during the Cold War — 115
   Henrike Krause

7. Virginia Woolf's Literary Heritage in Russian Translations and Interpretations — 132
   Maria Bent

8. Virginia Woolf's Feminist Writing in Estonian Translation Culture — 152
   Raili Marling

9. Virginia Woolf in Arabic: A Feminist Paratextual Reading of Translation Strategies — 166
   Hala Kamal

10. Solid and Living: The Italian Woolf Renaissance — 183
    Elisa Bolchi

11. Tracing *A Room of One's Own* in sub-Saharan Africa, 1929–2019 — 199
    Jeanne Dubino

Part II: Woolf's Legacies in Literature

12. Virginia Woolf's Enduring Presence in Uruguay — 225
    Lindsey Cordery

13. Virginia Woolf's Reception and Impact on Brazilian Women's Literature — 246
    Maria A. de Oliveira

14. English and Mexican Dogs: Spectres of Traumatic Pasts in Virginia Woolf's *Flush* and María Luisa Puga's *Las razones del lago* — 267
    Lourdes Parra-Lazcano

15. A New Perspective on Mary Carmichael: Yuriko Miyamoto's Novels and *A Room of One's Own* — 282
    Hogara Matsumoto

16. Rooms of Their Own: A Cross-Cultural Voyage between Virginia Woolf and the Contemporary Chinese Woman Writer Chen Ran — 297
    Zhongfeng Huang

17. In Search of Spaces of Their Own: Woolf, Feminism and Women's Poetry from China — 314
    Justyna Jaguścik

18. Trans-Dialogues: Exploring Virginia Woolf's Feminist Legacy to Contemporary Polish Literature — 332
    Paulina Pająk

19. Clarissa Dalloway's Global Itinerary: From London to Paris and Sydney — 354
    Monica Latham

20. Virginia Woolf and French Writers: Contemporaneity, Idolisation, Iconisation — 371
    Anne-Laure Rigeade

21. The Dream Work of a Nation: From Virginia Woolf to Elizabeth Bowen to Mary Lavin — 387
    Patricia Laurence

22. Great Poets Do Not Die: Maggie Gee's *Virginia Woolf in Manhattan* (2014) as Metaphor for Contemporary Biofiction — 399
    Bethany Layne

23. The Woolf Girl: A Mother–Daughter Story with Virginia Woolf and Lidia Yuknavitch — 412
    Catherine W. Hollis

Index — 428

Acknowledgements

We, the editors, are grateful, above all, to the contributors. They have worked with us these past four years and have made this project a truly global one.

We thank Jackie Jones, Ersev Ersoy and Sarah M. Hall for their patience and good will through this process, and the anonymous readers for their invaluable comments.

We would like to extend a heartfelt thanks to Jane de Gay, Tom Breckin and Anne Reus, the organisers of Virginia Woolf and Heritage: The 26th Annual International Conference on Virginia Woolf, held in 2016. This conference, with its many participants, panels and discussions, inspired the idea for this project. The first versions of chapters by Jeanne Dubino, Catherine W. Hollis, Paulina Pająk, Anne-Laure Rigeade and Adriana Varga were originally published in *Virginia Woolf and Heritage: Selected Papers from the Twenty-Sixth Annual International Conference on Virginia Woolf*, edited by the organisers. We are indebted to them and to John Morgenstern, Director of Clemson University Press, for giving us permission to republish these papers.

We would also like to thank those who gave us permission to publish the following:

Extracts from papers in the archives at the University of Reading Random House Group Archive. By permission of The Random House Group Ltd.

Extracts from the letters of Alberto Mondadori at the Historical Archive of Arnoldo Mondadori in Milan. By permission of the Mondadori Foundation and the heirs of Arnoldo e Alberto Mondadori.

Extracts from letters of Alessandra Scalero. By permission of the Fondo Scalero, Civica Biblioteca di Mazzè.

Notes on Contributors

Suzanne Bellamy (PhD, University of Sydney) is an Australian artist and writer working on text/image fusions and abstractions, Surrealism, Australian modernism, and Stein and Woolf. Publications include essays in *The Cambridge Companion to To the Lighthouse* (Cambridge University Press, 2015); *Virginia Woolf in Context* (Edinburgh University Press, 2012), *Contradictory Woolf* (Liverpool University Press, 2012), *Virginia Woolf Lesbian Readings* (New York University Press, 1997), *Sentencing* Orlando: *Virginia Woolf and the Morphology of the Modernist Sentence* (Edinburgh University Press 2017), and *Conversas com Virginia Woolf* (Ape'Ku, 2020). Exhibitions of sculptural textboxes: 'Abstract Machines' (Paris 2018; Sydney 2019) and 'Time and Place' (Altenburg 2019). Performance texts and set canvases: 'A Sketch of the Past' (2008) and 'Am I Blue?' (London 2005). Pageant production for *Between the Acts*; and set canvas, 'Woolf and the Chaucer Horse' (Glasgow 2011).

Maria Bent is Assistant Professor of English in the Department of Oriental, Romance and Germanic Languages, Faculty of Eurasia and East, Chelyabinsk State University, Russia. As a graduate student, she spent 2006–7 as a Russian Language Resident at the Oldenborg Center for Modern Languages, Pomona College, California. She teaches undergraduate and postgraduate courses in English, German, translation studies, and academic writing. She studied at Chelyabinsk State University and the Russian State University for Humanities (Moscow). Her research interests and publications are in the areas of literary criticism, women and gender studies, and the history of literature. She is the author of *Metaphor in T. S. Eliot's Poetry of 1920–1930s* ('Entsiklopediya' Publishing House and Sergey Khodov Publishing House, 2014) and a number of papers.

Elisa Bolchi is Marie Curie Research Fellow at the University of Reading, UK, with a project titled *Virginia Woolf and Italian Readers*, which studies the reception of Virginia Woolf in Italy. On this theme she has already published the books *Il paese della bellezza Virginia Woolf nelle riviste italiane tra le due guerre* (Milan, 2007), studying the reception of Woolf in literary periodicals, and *L'indimenticabile artista Lettere e appunti sulla storia editoriale di Virginia Woolf in Mondadori* (Milan, 2015), which tells the background of the first Italian editions of Woolf's novels through unpublished editorial letters. She is founding member and vice-president of the Italian Virginia Woolf Society and has taught English literature at Università Cattolica del Sacro Cuore, Milan, for several years. Other subjects of her research are Richard Aldington, Ian McEwan and Jeanette Winterson, mainly investigating such themes as Italian reception, archival studies, re-writing and ecocritical writing.

Cristina Carluccio completed her PhD in English Literature at the Università del Salento (Lecce) after defending a dissertation which explores the connections between gaze and movement in selected works by Virginia Woolf in the light of Vernon Lee's psychological aesthetics. Her research interests include late Victorian and modernist literature, women's and gender studies, and literary representations of city and space. She has been nominated 'Cultore della Materia' in English Literature at the Università del Salento and is the editor of the Italian Virginia Woolf Society's online bibliography on Woolf. She is currently teaching English language in a school in Milan.

Lindsey Cordery was Associate Professor of English Literature at the School of Humanities and Aggregate Professor of English Cultural Studies and Literary Translation at the School of Translation, Universidad de la República in Montevideo, Uruguay, until she retired in 2019. She is currently Collaborative Professor and Researcher in English Literature at the School of Humanities, Universidad de la República. She studies canonical literary texts from a located, postcolonial, Latin American perspective, and is co-editor of the Coloquios Montevideana series, volume 7 of which is *Virginia Woolf en América Latina. Reflexiones desde Montevideo* (Linardi y Risso, 2013). She also works on Shakespeare, co-editing volume 9 of the series, *Cervantes, Shakespeare. Lecturas refractadas* (Linardi y Risso, 2017). 'Virginia Woolf in South America. Border Reading' was included in *Virginia Woolf and the World of Books* (Clemson University Press, 2018). She has also published on the modernists W. H. Hudson, Conrad, Faulkner, Eliot and Joyce, and on Dickens and Barrett Browning. She is currently studying the marginalia and other notes in Armonía Somers's copy of Borges's translation of *Orlando*, kept in the Biblioteca Pedagógica (Pedagogical Library) in Montevideo.

Jeanne Dubino is a professor of English, Global Studies, and Animal Studies at Appalachian State University, North Carolina. She organised the 1997 Virginia Woolf conference, held in Plymouth, New Hampshire; is a member of the editorial board of the *Virginia Woolf Miscellany* and the *Woolf Studies Annual*; and served as the secretary/treasurer of the International Virginia Woolf Society 2000–5 and 2012–15. Some of her most recent publications include the edited volume *Virginia Woolf and the Literary Marketplace* (Palgrave Macmillan, 2010); and the co-edited *Representing the Modern Animal in Culture* (Palgrave Macmillan, 2014), *Virginia Woolf: Twenty-First-Century Approaches* (Edinburgh University Press, 2014), *Politics, Mobility, and Identity in Travel Writing* (Routledge, 2015); *Virginia Woolf: Critical and Primary Sources* (Bloomsbury Academic, 2020); *Travel and War* (Cambridge Scholars Publishing, forthcoming); and essays, articles, and reviews on Woolf, travel and Animal Studies. She is currently working on a book on stray/street/free-ranging dogs in literature (including Woolf's *Flush*).

Daniel Göske is Professor of American Literature at the University of Kassel, Germany. He was educated at Göttingen, Germany; Canterbury, UK; Pennsylvania State University; and, as Visiting Fellow, at Princeton University. His publications include books on American poetry anthologies and on Herman Melville as well as articles on nineteenth- and twentieth-century poetry and fiction, literary periodicals, translation, the interplay of literature and religion, and the reception of American and British writers in Europe (Poe, Melville, Faulkner, Woolf). Göske has edited annotated translations of works by Melville, Henry James and Joseph Conrad, and has himself translated R. A. Ackerley, Conrad, Melville and Derek Walcott. He is a member of the German Academy of Language and Literature and the Academy of the Sciences and Humanities at Göttingen.

Catherine W. Hollis teaches in the University of California-Berkeley's Fall Program for Freshmen. She recently guest-edited Issue 95 of the *Virginia Woolf Miscellany* which focused on the special topic of book collecting. Her essay, 'Emma Goldman among the Avant-Garde', is included in *Women Making Modernism,* (University of Florida Press, 2020). She is the author of *Leslie Stephen as Mountaineer* (Cecil Woolf, 2010), and has worked as a documentary editor at the Emma Goldman Papers Project. She is the Historian-Bibliographer of the International Virginia Woolf Society (2021–3).

Zhongfeng Huang is an associate professor in Department of English Literature at Beihang University, China, where she teaches English literature. Her research interests include British modernist literature and women's literature. She has published articles on Woolf, Alice Munro and Nathaniel Hawthorne. Her most recent articles are 'The Portrait of a Woman Artist: On Alice Munro's Künstlerroman "Family Furnishings"' (*Foreign Literature*, 2019, in Chinese), 'From "Purified with Fire" to "That Impression of Permanence": Holgrave's Conversion in *The House of the Seven Gables*' (*Papers on Language and Literature*, 2019) and '"Greek literature is the impersonal literature": Virginia Woolf and the Impersonality of Greek Literature' (*Journal of Literature in English*, 2020, in Chinese). Her recent literary research has focused on Virginia Woolf and Alice Munro.

Justyna Jaguścik is postdoctoral research fellow and lecturer in Chinese Studies at the University of Zurich where she teaches premodern and modern Chinese literature. Her research interests include Sinophone women's poetry, workers' literature and the post-socialist transition. She has published essays on Chinese literature and social change in Polish, German and English in journals such as *Studia Socjologiczne, Asiatische Studien/Études Asiatiques, International Communication of Chinese Culture* and *Harvard Asia Quarterly*. Jaguścik is currently revising her dissertation on contemporary Chinese feminist poetry for publication.

Hala Kamal is Professor of English and Gender Studies in the Department of English Language and Literature, Faculty of Arts, Cairo University, Egypt. She studied at Cairo University, the University of Leeds, UK and Smith College, USA. She teaches undergraduate and postgraduate courses in women's writing, autobiography and fiction, and translation studies. Her research interests and publications in both Arabic and English are in the areas of feminist literary criticism, autobiography studies, women and gender studies and the history of the Egyptian feminist movement. She has been engaged in Egyptian civil society feminist activism and gender-education programmes. She has also translated several books on feminism and gender into Arabic; and is co-editor, with Luise von Flotow, of the *Routledge Handbook of Translation, Feminism and Gender* (2020).

Henrike Krause is a PhD candidate at the Peter Szondi Institute for Comparative Literature at the Freie Universität Berlin. Her PhD has been supported by several institutions, including the German Academic Exchange Service (DAAD) and the German Academic Scholarship Foundation (Studienstiftung des deutschen Volkes). Her thesis investigates the reception of Virginia Woolf in the former German Democratic Republic with a focus on the works of Christa Wolf. She was Research Assistant to Professor Claudia Olk and has taught several classes at the Peter Szondi Institute on literary theory as well as English and German literature of the twentieth century.

Monica Latham is a Professor of British literature at Université de Lorraine, France. She is the author of *A Poetics of Postmodernism and Neomodernism: Rewriting* Mrs Dalloway (Palgrave Macmillan, 2015) and *Virginia Woolf's Afterlives: The Author as Character in Contemporary Fiction and Drama* (Routledge, 2021). She is the co-editor of the series Book Practices and Textual Itineraries (Presses Universitaires de Nancy).

Patricia Laurence is a critic, biographer, poet and academic, Professor Emerita, City College of New York. She has published widely on transnational modernism, Virginia Woolf, Bloomsbury studies, and modern women writers. Her publications include *The Reading of Silence: Virginia Woolf in the English Tradition* (Stanford University Press, 1991); *Lily Briscoe's Chinese Eyes: Bloomsbury, Modernism and China* (University of South Carolina Press, 2001); *Julian Bell: The Violent Pacifist* (Cecil Woolf, 2005), and the recent biography, *Elizabeth Bowen: A Literary Life* (Palgrave Macmillan, 2020).

Bethany Layne is Senior Lecturer in English Literature at De Montfort University, UK. She has published widely on biographical fiction in journals including *The Henry James Review*, *Woolf Studies Annual*, *Virginia Woolf Miscellany* and *Adaptation*, and her interviews with David Lodge, Colm Tóibín and Susan Sellers appear in *Conversations with Biographical Novelists: Truthful Fictions across the Globe* (Bloomsbury, 2019). She pioneered the first specialist biofiction module in the UK, and organised a related conference 'Postmodernist Biofictions' at the University of Reading, UK, in 2017. She is the author of the book *Henry James in Contemporary Fiction: The Real Thing* (Palgrave Macmillan, 2020) and the editor of *Biofiction and Writers' Afterlives* (Cambridge Scholars, 2020). In addition to biofiction and James, her research interests include adaptive and appropriative literature, and the works of Virginia Woolf and Sylvia Plath.

Celiese Lypka is a Postdoctoral Fellow in the Department of English, Theatre, Film, and Media at the University of Manitoba, specialising in women's writing, as well as feminist and critical theory. Her current research investigates productive modes of divergent femininity found within modernist texts that reorient anxiety attached to the female body toward a mobilising affect of potentiality and power. She has publications in *Virginia Woolf Miscellany*, *Rhizomes*, *English Studies Canada*, and a chapter in *Deleuze and the Schizolanalysis of Feminism* (Bloomsbury Academic, 2019). She is an editor of the *Virginia Woolf Miscellany* and the Special Issue Editor of *Miscellany* 97, 'Virginia Woolf: Mobilizing Emotion, Feeling, and Affect'.

Raili Marling is Professor of English Studies at the University of Tartu, Estonia. Her main research interests include gender in modernist and contemporary literature and culture, critical affect studies, gender in the postsocialist context and the possibilities of combining affect theory and discourse studies. She has published extensively on these topics in English and in Estonian. She currently leads a research group that studies representations and representability of contemporary crises.

Hogara Matsumoto is Professor of English at Sophia University, Tokyo. She co-edited *Modernist Geo-history: English Culture and Literature between the* Wars (Tokyo: Kenkyusha, 2008), *Post-Heritage Film: Thatcherite England and the New Empire of America* (Tokyo: Sophia University Press, 2010), *Middlebrow Literary Cultures* (Tokyo: Chuo University Press, 2017), and *British Literature and Film* (Tokyo: Sanshusha, 2019). She is currently working on a book on Alice Munro.

Vara Neverow is a professor of English and Women's and Gender Studies at Southern Connecticut State University where she has taught for over thirty years. Her scholarship focuses primarily on Virginia Woolf. She organised the second Annual Conference on Virginia Woolf (1992). She also served as President of the International Virginia Woolf Society for two terms (2000–5) and continues as an ex-officio member of the Society. She has been the editor of the *Virginia Woolf Miscellany* since 2003. Her scholarly work on Woolf includes the co-edited four-volume set, *Virginia Woolf: Critical and Primary Sources* (Bloomsbury Academic, 2020) and the co-edited collection of essays *Virginia Woolf: Twenty-First-Century Approaches* (Edinburgh University Press, 2014). She is currently working on a monograph on Woolf, patriarchy and sexual politics.

Maria A. de Oliveira is a professor at the Federal University of Paraíba. Her dissertation, *Women Representation on Virginia Woolf's Works: A Dialogue between her Political and Aesthetic Discourse*, was published by Paco Editorial in Portuguese in Brazil, in English by Lambert Academic Publishing and in Spanish by Cuarto Propio. She finished her postdoctoral project on Woolf and the Brazilian Women Writers at the University of Toronto. Her recent publication is the co-edited *Conversas com Virginia Woolf* (Ape'Ku, 2020).

Paulina Pająk is a lecturer at the University of Wrocław. Her recent publications include essays in *Woolf Studies Annual*, *Politeja* and *Women's History Review*. She explores memory in Virginia Woolf's oeuvre, Central European modernist networks and modernist legacies in contemporary Polish literature. Her research interests include modernism, memory studies and comparative literature.

Lourdes Parra-Lazcano teaches in the Department of Spanish and Latin American Studies at the University of Aberdeen. Her academic publications are related to Mexican women writers from a combined transcultural, comparative, and Animal Studies approach. She has been co-director of Women's Paths: Rewriting Physical and Discursive Borders, a research group at the University of Leeds about women writers around the world.

Davi Pinho is Professor of English Literature at Rio de Janeiro State University (UERJ). He is the author of *Imagens do feminino na obra e vida de Virginia* Woolf (Appris, 2015) and co-editor of *Eros, Tecnologia, Transumanismo* (Caetés, 2015), *Literaturas de*

Língua Inglesa: Leituras interdisciplinares (Letra Capital, 2017), *CONVERSAS sobre LITERATURA em tempos de CRISE* (Makunaima, 2017), and *Conversas com Virginia Woolf* (Ape'Ku, 2020). He is a member of the International Virginia Woolf Society (IVWS), the American Comparative Literature Association (ACLA) and the Brazilian Comparative Literature Association (ABRALIC).

Anne-Laure Rigeade holds the French 'agrégation' (French selective exam for teaching) and a PhD in comparative literature, and teaches French language and literature at Sciences Po (Reims). She is an associate researcher at CNRS – ITEM (Le Centre national de la recherche scientifique – L'Institut des textes et manuscrits modernes), and works on the manuscripts of Virginia Woolf's reading notes and on Woolf's translation in French. Since 2013, she has been focusing on the French reception of Virginia Woolf and has dedicated many papers to that topic. She contributed to a co-translation in French of a selection of Virginia Woolf's essays, *Rire ou ne pas rire* (Paris: La Différence, 2014), and co-organised an international conference, 'Recycling Woolf', with Monica Latham and Caroline Marie, at Nancy University in 2019.

Adriana Varga is Lecturer in the Department of English at the University of Nevada, Reno. She specialises in twentieth- and twenty-first-century British and world literature and culture, modernism in a transnational context, postcolonial and globalisation theories, gender, race, and identity studies, diaspora and immigration studies, inter-art studies, translation studies and creative writing. She is a Fulbright-Hays Doctoral Dissertation recipient. She is also the editor of *Virginia Woolf and Music* (Indiana University Press, 2014).

Christian Weiß is a research associate in English and American literature at the University of Kassel, Germany. His research interests include modern English-to-German translation, translator studies, publishing history, and the sociology of translation. He is currently working on his PhD project about the Austrian translator and literary agent Herberth Herlitschka.

Abbreviations of Virginia Woolf's Works

AROO	*A Room of One's Own*
BA	*Between the Acts*
CDB	*The Captain's Deathbed and Other Essays*
CE	*Collected Essays* (4 vols)
CR 1	*The Common Reader*
CR 2	*The Common Reader, Second Series*
CSF	*The Complete Shorter Fiction of Virginia Woolf*
D	*The Diary of Virginia Woolf* (5 vols)
DM	*The Death of the Moth and Other Essays*
E	*The Essays of Virginia Woolf* (6 vols)
F	*Flush*
JR	*Jacob's Room*
L	*The Letters of Virginia Woolf* (6 vols)
MB	*Moments of Being*
MD	*Mrs Dalloway*
ND	*Night and Day*
O	*Orlando*
PA	*A Passionate Apprenticeship*
RF	*Roger Fry: A Biography*
TG	*Three Guineas*
TL	*To the Lighthouse*
VO	*The Voyage Out*
W	*The Waves*
WD	*A Writer's Diary*
Y	*The Years*

Introduction: Planetary Woolf

Paulina Pająk, Jeanne Dubino and Catherine W. Hollis[1]

We write this introduction in a time of global crisis, as the Covid-19 pandemic has closed regional and national borders. Almost simultaneously, the Black Lives Matter movement has ignited global protests against racist police brutality. Although the pandemic has separated people physically from one another, while placing the health of first responders and essential workers at risk, the demand for social justice has drawn many people into the streets. From anti-government protests in Hong Kong to the thousands of global demonstrations in support of BLM, the demand for social justice crosses borders and creates activist communities even in the midst of unprecedented global crises. New technologies allow us to create digital communities and new forms of sociability, even in the wake of the many cancelled or postponed in-person events. In difficult times we, as scholars and common readers of Virginia Woolf, turn to her writing to help us make sense of the complexities of the present moment, particularly as we negotiate the relationships between politics and art and between sociability and solitude in our daily lives.

On 11 October 1929, Virginia Woolf wrote:

> & when I wake early I say to myself, Fight, fight. If I could catch the feeling, I would: the feeling of the singing of the real world, as one is driven by loneliness & silence from the habitable world. (*D* 3: 260)

Ninety years later, one can still hear Woolf saying these very sentences in a staccato rhythm, syncopated with characteristic ampersands as rapid breaths. The entry has been insightfully explored by several critics since Mark Hussey's influential book *The Singing of the Real World* (1986) mapped it out among the underlying philosophical patterns of Woolf's oeuvre. This passage is frequently read as juxtaposing the oppositions between the sociable and solitary selves (Mepham 1991: 133), or – as Hermione Lee aptly captures it through *The Waves* – oppositions between 'the lonely mind and the habitable world' that 'are always collapsing and merging' (1999: 569). The artist and scholar Suzanne Bellamy, who opens the door across continents and cultures with her cover for this volume, sees Woolf's 'articulation of the mental landscape when the brain turns within' as 'the peak of her genius and her courage', noting that this 'creative courage . . . led to an explosion of experiments among women artists and writers' (1997: 33) – a surge visible in Bellamy's own chapter on the initial reception of Woolf in Australia.

Brenda R. Silver associates Woolf's popularity in the early 2000s with her 'uncanny ability to cross borders and reveal their arbitrary nature [that] enacts the power of gender to intersect and fracture cultural class' (1999: 72). Today Woolf is a global icon, a transnational symbol. Her voice and art are interwoven in the 'singing of the real world', this imaginary reality explored and created by writers, brought together by solidarities and inequalities in the globalised world. As Madelyn Detloff emphasises, 'Woolf's anti-imperial, feminist, pacifist, and antihomophobic sentiments [draw] new readers to her work' (2016: 100). Yet, Woolf's voice and art are also entangled in prejudices and suppositions of her times. Woolf, a neuro-affectively atypical person herself (Detloff 2016: 114 n.36), created ableist narratives in her fiction (Lyon 2011). She married Leonard Woolf, a Jewish intellectual, but included anti-Semitic and racist statements in her private papers and published works (Marcus 2004), and she asserted that 'literature is common ground' (*E* 6: 278), yet was 'shocked to think' that the domestic worker Nelly Boxall also 'desire[d] the Labour party to win' (*D* 3: 230). Nevertheless, as the present volume shows, generations of Woolf's literary heirs, though occasionally grappling with the writer's contradictory views, have drawn on her democratic, feminist and experimental oeuvre.

The Edinburgh Companion to Virginia Woolf and Contemporary Global Literature is a collection of twenty-three essays that consider Woolf's worldwide impact, as well as the planetary and global responses her work has provoked. The collection originates from 'Virginia Woolf and Heritage: The Twenty-Sixth Annual International Conference on Virginia Woolf' (2016), organised in Leeds, UK, by Jane de Gay, Tom Breckin and Anne Reus. The papers delivered at this hospitable event showed the intricacies of Woolf's East African, Romanian and Russian receptions and revealed that French, Polish and US writers trace their roots back to Woolf. This gathering of Woolfians was followed by time spent together by two of the future editors.[2] During a long trek in the Świętokrzyskie Mountains in Poland, two Woolfians – absentmindedly trespassing a warning board near the legendary mountain of witches' gatherings – were discussing the idea of a volume on Woolf's transnational feminist legacies. Just a month later, in October 2016, the International Women's Strike started, following the Polish 'Czarny protest' (Black Protest) against criminalising abortion and the Argentinian rallies 'Ni una menos' (Not One Less) against gender-based violence. What political urgency drove protest marchers and how do such efforts align with the vision of the Woolfians working on this collection? The inspiring force of pacifist-feminist legacies – including Woolf's *A Room of One's Own, Three Guineas*, and 'Thoughts of peace in an air raid' (Humm 2017) – reverberate and instigate new platforms for marginalised voices; for example, the organisers of the International Women's Strike (International Women's Strike/Paro Internacional de Mujeres) on 8 March in 2018 and 2019 expressed their vision for a better world through protests in more than fifty countries.[3] Around the world, activists and educators inspired by the Black Lives Matter movement ('Global Actions'), which started in 2013, have been looking for new forms of anti-racist and pacifist education, finding inspiration also in Woolf's *Three Guineas*, as visible in the special issue of *Radical Teacher* on teaching Black Lives Matter (Foster et al. 2016).

Two recent paradigms of planetarity and globality overlap and merge both in 'the habitable world' (*D* 3: 260) and on the pages of *The Edinburgh Companion to Virginia Woolf and Contemporary Global Literature*. Characteristic of planetary approaches is – in Susan Stanford Friedman's phrase – the 'consciousness of the earth as a planet, not restricted to geopolitical formations and potentially encompassing the nonhuman as well as the human' (2018: 348). Such ecocritical and posthuman consciousness allows Lourdes Parra-Lazcano to comparatively read the traumatic pasts of dogs in Woolf's and María Luisa Puga's fiction. Yet, planetarity, as envisioned by Gayatri Chakravorty Spivak in *Death of a Discipline*, is also a socio-political gesture of resistance against the domination of the Global North: 'I propose the planet to overwrite the globe. Globalization is the imposition of the same system of exchange everywhere. In the gridwork of electronic capital, we achieve that abstract ball covered in latitudes and longitudes, cut by virtual lines' (2003: 82). In the present volume, this ethical aspect of planetarity is represented by Maria A. de Oliveira's intersectional interpretation of Brazilian women writers in the Global South, including Clarice Lispector and Carolina Maria de Jesus; as a Black woman in search for a room of her own, Jesus found a platform for the gendered voice of the subaltern.

Contrasting with the planetary paradigm, which is deeply engaged with ethical and socio-political debates, globality has been treated as a more neutral choice to 'world literature' dating back to the nineteenth century. However, the word 'global' has been contested since the late 1980s (Moraru 2017: 125). Scholars such as Joseph R. Slaughter (2007) have noted that the global can become synonymous with Euro-US-centrism and even re-colonialism, a recent form of imperial takeover and co-optation. Under the guise of the 'global', the imperial – in this case, the Global North – is forced back to the epistemological centre (2007: 55, 313). The global can also erase and obscure the very differences it is said to encompass. However, as Christian Moraru notes,

> while the objective of the planetary with respect to the global remains emancipatory and thereby oppositional, the planet and the globe do not make up a crude opposition other than rhetorically. . . . The global-planetary connection is somewhat symbiotic. (2017: 130)

As proposed by Eric Hayot and Rebecca L. Walkowitz, 'the "global" is never some fixed centre around which other ideas revolve', but rather it constitutes 'a shifting concept of fixity and centrality, a set of claims made about the world . . . and how it works, whose force depends in every case on the situation and context of its elaboration' (2016: 3) and thus can be viewed as interconnective. In this sense, as Monica Latham observes in this volume, Woolf's Clarissa Dalloway has become a global character transformed by different locations and cultures in the novels of Anne Korkeakivi, Carole Llewellyn and Gail Jones. The present volume also demonstrates that, via transnational modernist networks, Woolf's works have reached and inspired authors and scholarly work in Uruguay as explored by Lindsey Cordery, in Japan through the works of Yuriko Miyamoto as presented by Hogara Matsumoto, and also in China through Chen Ran's novels as discussed by Zhongfeng Huang and Chinese feminist poetry as revealed by Justyna Jaguścik.

The scholars who explore the planetary and/or global dimensions of Woolf's legacies find them further complicated by creative exchanges and tensions between local and world works of literature. Franco Moretti sketches the differences between 'national literature, for people who see trees' and 'world literature, for people who see waves' (2000: 68), explaining that as 'trees need geographical discontinuity (in order to branch off from each other, languages must first be separated in space, just like animal species)', 'waves dislike barriers, and thrive on geographical continuity' (2000: 67).[4] *The Edinburgh Companion to Virginia Woolf and Contemporary Global Literature* offers chapters on how Woolf has been received and transformed in diverse cultures ('for people who see trees') and chapters on how Woolf's works have inspired artists from all over the world ('for people who see waves'). Many contributors combine these two perspectives, situating Woolf's reception in local or national contexts while also exploring her impact within transnational networks. For instance, Cristina Carluccio convincingly argues that Woolf and Victoria Ocampo's relationship was only seemingly asymmetrical, as any geographical hierarchy between Great Britain and Argentina was erased by the writers' shared opposition to patriarchal systems, including its extreme form of fascism.

The volume is inspired by Woolf's persistently planetary and increasingly global presence on the world's stage. The contributors provide background on how widespread her works have become on the global map. The collection shows that Woolf and her oeuvre are widely translated, read, taught, adapted and transformed, and have been since the prime of her writing career in the 1920s and 1930s up through the present day. There are consistent threads that run throughout the twenty-three chapters: feminism and sexuality, ethnicity and nationality, and politics and the environment. The essays address the ways Woolf has been received by writers, translators, publishers, academics, students and reading audiences (including her cherished 'common readers') in countries around the world. This diversity of audiences is particularly mirrored in Elisa Bolchi's chapter on the Italian Woolf Renaissance in the twenty-first century.

The twenty-four contributors – and the countries they write about – hail from nearly all regions of the world, including six continents: Africa, Asia, Australia, Europe, North America and South America. The contributors show how Woolf has inspired people living in different geographical locations and the strategies used by transnational networks of translators, publishers and critics, some struggling with censorship and tense political situations to introduce Woolf's works into diverse cultures. The authors study a range of topics, exploring how Woolf's 'creative courage' inspires generations of her literary heirs, noting her impact on postmodern feminist and queer aesthetics, investigating third- and fourth-wave feminist essayism, and examining cross-genres such as biofiction. This volume in the series of Edinburgh Companions is dialogic and comparative, incorporating both transnational and local tendencies insofar as they epitomise Woolf's planetary reception and global legacy. The collection is designed to disrupt the centre and periphery binary; by including essays that focus primarily on twentieth- and twenty-first-century women and/or queer writers, it offers new models for Woolf global studies and promotes planetary understandings.

The central aspect of this new approach is the multilingual character of *The Edinburgh Companion to Virginia Woolf and Contemporary Global Literature*, which neither attempts to replicate 'the linguistic hegemonies of modernity's imperial legacies' (Friedman 2018: 72) nor presumes that the global English 'will be planetarity's exclusive mode of communication' (Pizer 2015: 17). Along with using English as one of the contemporary lingua francas, 'the singing of the real world' (*D* 3: 260) is heard in Arabic, Chinese, Estonian, French, German, Italian, Japanese, Polish, Brazilian Portuguese, Romanian, Russian and Spanish. Hence, all quotations from texts in world languages are available in the original, translated and transliterated versions (the last in the case of languages using scripts other than Latin).

The collection is divided into two parts. The first part, 'Planetary and Global Receptions of Woolf', moves chronologically from the earliest stages of Woolf's recognition and progresses to the present day. The section focuses on Woolf's reception and translation, showing that Woolf functions differently as a hypercanonical, countercanonical and shadow canonical figure[5] in different cultures of the world. The reception and translation of Woolf's works are often intertwined and integrated, as visible in Maria Bent's chapter on Russia, exploring reception before translations and the following surge in Woolf's publications and scholarship. Adriana Varga elucidates in her chapter not only Romanian translators' struggles with literary censorship but also the role of illustrations in Woolf's *Orlando* – both in the original novel and in translations. As Daniel Göske and Christian Weiß demonstrate in their chapter on the early German translations of Woolf's works, translators – including the intriguing figure of Karl Lerbs – work within specific social and political contexts, as well as constraints such as the demands of publishers and the marketplace. And within those contexts, revealed by the rigorous research in the Goethe- und Schiller-Archiv and the Archives of the Hogarth Press in Reading, Göske and Weiß locate the kinds of choices – aesthetic, personal and ethical – available to translators to convey Woolf's style and themes in their languages. In a similar vein, Hala Kamal's chapter is an insightful contribution to a feminist critique of the strategies used in Arabic translations of Woolf's works, revealing the vital roles of feminist translators as mediators attentive to an ethical translation praxis. Henrike Krause asserts Woolf's relevance for Christa Wolf, a prominent writer of the German Democratic Republic, discovering new materials on Woolf as Wolf's female predecessor in the Archive of the Academy of Arts in Berlin and Christa Wolf's private library.

The chapters in the second part, 'Woolf's Legacies in Literature', are arranged geographically, starting with the Global South, moving to the Global East and ending in the Global North and West. The contributors explore planetary and global legacies of Woolf's oeuvre and life in contemporary literature, particularly in modernist and postmodern biofiction, cosmofeminist texts and multigenre works. Bethany Layne examines the struggles of Angela Lamb in Maggie Gee's novel *Virginia Woolf in Manhattan* and reveals the challenges that contemporary authors of biofiction face when they are measured against Woolf. Anne-Laure Rigeade's chapter focuses on the theory of influence, offering insights into different approaches of French writers – including Nathalie Sarraute – towards Woolf's works. Paulina Pająk explores transtextual dialogues between Woolf and contemporary Polish feminist writers, tracing back the generic fusing of the Nobel Prize Laureate Olga Tokarczuk's 'constellation novels' (2018) to Woolf's hybrid fictional forms.

In many chapters local and global perspectives are – as 'two worlds' in Woolf's diary – 'always collapsing and merging' (*D* 3: 260). The majority of critical perspectives in this volume originated in the 2000s transnational shift and a series of twenty-first-century planetary turns in literary studies, ranging from postcolonial studies (Glissant 1990, 1997; Bhabha 1994),[6] neocosmopolitanism (Walkowitz 2006), world literature (Casanova 1999; Moretti 2000; Damrosch 2003, 2017), ecocritical approaches inspired by comparative ecocriticism (Heise 2017), to exploring 'cosmofeminism' (Friedman 2013) and 'born-translated' works (Walkowitz 2017). Bellamy applies new modernist theory (Mao and Walkowitz 2008; Latham and Rogers 2015) to explore Woolf's presence within early Australian modernism and its transnational circuits. Several of the contributors to this volume draw on the scholarship of Jessica Berman, including Raili Marling and Cristina Carluccio, who follow her interpretation of Woolf's 'cosmopolitan outsider politics' (2015: 438); Pająk, who applies Berman's 'trans critical optics' to explore Woolf's transgressive legacies in Poland (2017); and de Oliveira, who situates the mobility of texts as informed by transnational modernist studies in the centre of Woolf's Brazilian legacies (Berman 2011).

Some of the authors in this collection combine planetary and global approaches with literary perspectives by applying critical theory to transnational readings, as does Davi Pinho in his chapter on Woolf as a modernist signature in the writings of Julia Kristeva and Paulo Mendes Campos. Another interesting critical fusion appears in Catherine Hollis's chapter, which explores the intergenerational dynamic within and between Woolf and Lidia Yuknavitch from the perspective of Girls' Studies and contemporary approaches to biofiction. A comparative space within the collection is also created by the contributors who focus on the reception or translation of Woolf's writings while working within their previously marginalised national, regional or linguistic traditions. For instance, Marling in her chapter discusses the transfer(ability) of Woolf's cosmopolitan feminism into postsocialist Estonian culture as representative of the 'smaller' languages. Patricia Laurence applies a postcolonial perspective to analyse the ways in which Woolf's thinking inspired Elizabeth Bowen and Mary Lavin, taking into account the marginalised position of Irish women and the impact of war. Jeanne Dubino's chapter situates the trajectories of Woolf's absence and presence in sub-Saharan Africa in the global contexts of imperialism, racism and literary production. Returning to Moretti's metaphor, this volume brings together both scholars who see 'trees', or the reception of Woolf within national and regional cultures, and those who view Woolf's works as 'waves' of world literature inspiring her literary heirs. Thus, the geopolitical diversity of the collection corresponds with its methodological versatility and continues long-lasting critical traditions of Woolf studies.

A Snapshot of the Global History of Woolf, 1920–2020

Woolf's global status began when she started to publish and continued after her death in 1941 through the international publication and sales of her books as well as the translations and scholarly work. Woolf's first novels, *The Voyage Out* and *Night and Day*, were published in 1915 and 1919, respectively. George H. Doran, a major US publishing house, approached Woolf in 1919 and a year later reprinted both novels.[7] In 1917 Virginia and her husband Leonard established the Hogarth Press, which became her primary British publisher. Within a few years of acquiring the Press, Leonard and Virginia were marketing its publications abroad, including her short story collection, *Monday or Tuesday* (1921). The Woolfs first approached George H. Doran, but he refused to publish it,[8] so they turned to Harcourt, Brace and Co. Starting in 1921, Harcourt has been the leading US publisher of Woolf's work (Willis 1992: 393) and has, in most instances, made Woolf's oeuvre readily accessible in the United States.[9]

The Woolfs marketed a range of Hogarth Press publications in France. According to John H. Willis, Hogarth Press books – including, presumably, those by Woolf – began to appear in Sylvia Beach's Paris bookshop, Shakespeare and Company, from 1925 onwards (1992: 392, 426 n.24). The Woolfs also marketed Hogarth Press books farther afield; Willis writes that Hogarth Press publications had reached South Africa in 1924 and Tokyo in 1925 (1992: 392) (see also Matsumoto's chapter). In 1929, the Woolfs contracted with an agent in Canada to distribute Hogarth Press books; by the mid-1930s, Hogarth Press publications appeared throughout a large part of the Commonwealth; and by 1936, the Hogarth Press had listing agents in Australia, New Zealand and South Africa (1992: 392).[10]

Translations of Woolf's work began in 1926 and expanded throughout a significant part of the world during her lifetime. The first translations took place in the 1920s, into French,[11] German, Swedish and Czech.[12] Through the 1930s and to the end of Woolf's life, her works were translated into other European languages including Italian, Catalan, Romanian, Spanish (in Spain and Argentina), Latvian, Greek, Hungarian and Danish;[13] they were also translated into Chinese and Japanese.[14]

This overview of Woolf's work and her scholarly reception draws on Thomas Jackson Rice's *Virginia Woolf: A Guide to Research* (1984) and Mary Ann Caws and Nicola Luckhurst's edited volume *The Reception of Virginia Woolf in Europe* (2002).[15] From the 1920s onwards, international writers and academics paid scholarly attention[16] to Woolf's writing. Rice provides an annotated compendium of publications by and about Woolf from 1921 through 1983. According to Rice, Abel Chevalley was the first to write on Woolf outside of Britain; Chevalley praised her as one of 'our great impressionists' in his 1921 *Le roman anglaise de notre temps* [The English Novel in Our Times] (1984: 68). As Pierre-Éric Villeneuve writes, after Woolf was interviewed by Jacques-Émile Blanche in 1927 for the literary journal *Les Nouvelles Litteraire* [Literary News], she became a 'presence' on the French literary scene (2002: 19). That same year, Carlo Linati, in Italy, praised Woolf's writing style (Perosa 2002: 206), and in 1928 he was joined by fellow Italian Umberto Morra, who commended her 'composition' (2002: 206). The first article on Woolf in Germany appeared in 1928: Friedrich Wild's 'Die Englische Literatur der Gegenwart seit 1870' [Contemporary English Literature since 1870], which paired Woolf with James Joyce and Dorothy Richardson as 'principal exponent[s] of the modern English stream-of-consciousness novel' (Rice 1984: 96). The Spanish literary critic and historian Antonio Machilar, in an article about the 'Georgians', included Woolf among them and predicted that this generation's works would be among 'the classics of tomorrow' (Lojo Rodríguez 2002: 248). The following year, Louis Gillet published, in France, 'L'Orlando de Mme Virginia Woolf' (1929), in which he espoused what has now become an old canard – that Woolf was 'thoroughly indebted to the greater genius, Joyce, for her themes and techniques in *Mrs Dalloway*, *To the Lighthouse*, and *Orlando*' (Rice 1984: 75). The handful of short critical pieces about Woolf that were published in the 1920s were followed in the next decade by multiple articles and book chapters that appeared not just throughout Europe but also in South America.[17] Most of these were devoted solely to Woolf but others typically paired her with James Joyce, Aldous Huxley and D. H. Lawrence.

By the 1930s, book-length studies began to be published along with these shorter analyses. The first two monographs devoted entirely to Woolf to appear outside of Britain were published in 1932: Ingeborg Badenhausen's *Die Sprache Virginia Woolfs: Ein Beitrag zur Stilistik Des Modernen Englischen Romans* [Virginia Woolf's Language: A Contribution to the Stylistics of the Modern English Novel] and Floris Delattre's *Le Roman Psychologique de Virginia Woolf* [The Psychological Novel of Virginia Woolf]. *Die Sprache Virginia Woolfs* is a stylistic analysis, and Delattre addresses the influence of Henri Bergson's philosophy on Woolf, her 'intellectual heritage' and her place in contemporary culture (Rice 1984: 40, 43). In 1933, Ilse Finke, in *Virginia Woolfs Stellung zur Wirklichkeit* [Virginia Woolf's Position on Reality], examined 'Woolf's theoretical objections to traditional literary realism, in her critical essays, and her somewhat different and more illuminating presentation of reality in her fiction' (Rice 1984: 45). Two more monographs in German were published in the 1930s: Eva Weidner's *Impressionismus und Expressionismus in den Romanen Virginia Woolfs* [Impressionism and Expressionism in the Novels of Virginia Woolf] (1934) and Gertrud Lohmüller's *Die Frau im Werk Virginia Woolfs: Ein Beitrag zur Psychologischen und Stilistischen Untersuchund des Neusten Englischen Frauenromans* [The Woman in Virginia Woolf's Work: A Contribution to the Psychological and Stylistic Study and the Latest English Women's Novel] (1937). Weidner, according to Rice, 'finds Woolf's transformation into an expressionist beginning in *Jacob's Room* (Rice 1984: 61). Lohmüller examines 'six distinct types of women' in Woolf's work, including 'the romantic woman detached from reality, the erotic woman, the intellectual woman, the stoically reflective woman of late middle-age, the motherly woman, and the artistic woman' (Rice 1984: 51). Ansgar Nünning and Vera Nünning describe German 'effusiveness' over Woolf's writing (Nünning and Nünning 2002: 68, 17); this love of Woolf clearly started from the earliest German translations of her work in the 1920s. In 1938, *Hommage à Virginia Woolf*, was published in France.[18] Consisting of six short biographical and critical articles, *Hommage* was one of the first edited collections on Woolf (Rice 1984: 48–9). The first international dissertations were completed the same year in France, Paul Bizé's *Virginia Woolf as a Literary Artist* (1930), and in the US, Elizabeth McKee Eddy's *A Study of the Style of Mrs Virginia Woolf with Special Emphasis on Her Thought Patterns* (1930). In 1935, *Virginia Woolf: A Study*,[19] a revised version of Ruth Gruber's 1932 dissertation (University of Leipzig) was published as a monograph in English by the German press Tauchnitz.

More international scholarship on Woolf steadily emerged in the decades following her death, starting with Celia Segura's *The Transcendental and the Transitory in Virginia Woolf's Novels* (1943), published in Argentina. Hundreds of articles, review-essays, book chapters and monographs were published in the United States, Canada and Europe, and dozens in Japan, Argentina, India and Israel.[20] Thomas Jackson Rice identifies 256 dissertations written on Woolf outside of Britain between 1930 and 1983.[21] One hundred and seventy-seven of these were written in universities in the United States,[22] where Woolf was far more popular as a subject worthy of study than she was in the United Kingdom, where, according to Rice, only twenty dissertations were written on her during this time.

The steady flow of international scholarship produced upon Woolf's death began to surge in the 1980s. A number of resources that enable the aggregation of information about scholarly publications on Woolf include WorldCat, Google Scholar and the *MLA [Modern Language Association] International Bibliography*. These are the sources used to craft the three tables located at the end of this Introduction. The tables provide valuable data on extraordinarily broad range of websites dedicated to Woolf and the breadth of published and translated work on Woolf globally. These tables, though by no means comprehensive,[23] provide a sense of the sheer wealth of work on Woolf undertaken by scholars writing in languages other than English.

Table 1 is based on data from WorldCat (2020) and provides a sample of the number of editions of Woolf's works that were published in multiple languages between 1926 to early 2020.[24] Table 2 lists the websites devoted to Woolf that are drawn from Google Scholar (2020). Finally, Table 3 includes the international publications that have been compiled by the *MLA International Bibliography* (2020). These tables are useful in that they offer a glimpse of how much scholarship on Woolf has been published outside the United Kingdom, Canada and the United States. The translations reveal how many of Woolf's novels and essays are now in languages spoken across the entire Middle East, including Arabic and Persian (Farsi). Almost all of her publications have been translated into Turkish. In sub-Saharan Africa, it is notable that *Orlando* has been translated into Ndonga, one of many languages spoken in Namibia. The data also indicates that numerous East Asian scholars publish scholarship on Woolf's oeuvre. In short, these tables reveal that Woolf's presence extends far beyond the Global West and North to the Global East and the Global South.

The number of Virginia Woolf societies that have emerged in the last forty-five years further attests to the presence of Woolf across the world.[25] The first Virginia Woolf Society was founded in the United States in 1976. Twenty years later, in 1996, the Society members who hailed at that time from eighteen countries approved the name change to the International Virginia Woolf Society (Neverow 2020: xxvii). While the Virginia Woolf Society of Japan was established in 1977, it took nearly 20 years for a number of other Woolf societies to form. The French Société d'Études Woolfiennes (SEW) [Society for Woolf Studies] was launched in 1996, the Virginia Woolf Society of Great Britain in 1998, the Virginia Woolf Society of Korea in 2003, and the Italian Virginia Woolf Society in 2017.[26] The first of the conferences, symposia and colloquia on Virginia Woolf started in 1974, at the Chateau de Cerisy La Salle (Centre Culturel International) in France. In 1982, three events – two in the US and one in Great Britain – celebrated Woolf's centenary and all three resulted in edited collections of essays drawn from the gatherings. The first annual Virginia Woolf conference was held at Pace University in New York City in 1991 and the selected papers from the conference were published the following year; with the exception of 2020, the conference has since been held every year, primarily in the United States but also in Canada and Britain. Virginia Woolf conferences have also been held in Turkey (1997), Russia (2003), Portugal (2005), as well as in South Korea and Japan (the South Korean and Japanese Woolf societies held a joint conference in 2016).

From 1920 to 2020, Virginia Woolf's international stature has expanded and evolved. The widespread publication and translations of her books, the scholarship and societies devoted to her writing, and the symposia and conferences that have allowed her readers to converge, all indicate her global presence.[27] *The Edinburgh Companion to Virginia Woolf and Contemporary Global Literature* is part of this collective international effort.

Chapter by Chapter

Part I, 'Planetary and Global Receptions of Woolf', moves in roughly chronological order from the earliest reception and translation of Woolf in specific regional and national contexts to the present-day global renaissance of Woolf in translation. Daniel Göske and Christian Weiß in '"What a curse these translators are!" Woolf's early German reception' trace the unique difficulties Woolf's experimental prose caused for her earliest translators into German. Part of the challenge, as Göske and Weiß report, was Woolf herself, as she had little interest in engaging with translators of her work. The Hogarth Press referred all enquiries from independent translators to the Curtis Brown marketing agency (for more on Woolf's attitudes towards translation, see Marling's chapter in this volume). The more daunting task, however, was to find some stylistic equivalent in the German language for Woolf's use of parataxis and free indirect style. This early phase of Woolf's translation into German ended abruptly with the rise of Nazism, a historical moment that highlights the impact of political context on the publication of literature in translation; similarly the political context of Communism shaped the translation of Woolf into Romanian, as Adriana Varga shows in 'The translation and reception of Virginia Woolf in Romania (1926–89)'. Before the Second World War, Woolf was often read in Romania through French translations. Translations of Woolf into Romanian, along with many other Western authors, came to a halt during the period of Romania's communist dictatorship between 1945 and 1963. After Nicolae Ceaușescu came to power in 1965, his determination to reinforce Romania's political and cultural importance on the international scene led to the flourishing of translations of many modernist authors, including Woolf, into Romanian. However, some of the translators of these works, as Varga shows, may have had to engage in covert acts of self-censorship to avoid drawing the official eyes of state censors.

Suzanne Bellamy, in 'The reception of Virginia Woolf and modernism in early twentieth-century Australia', tracks Woolf's reputation over a period of decades, showing how responses to Woolf in Australia reflected cultural politics. The competing influences of cosmopolitanism and nationalism shaped the ebb and flow of how Woolf was read in Australia, as a more nationalistic curriculum in Australian universities in the 1930s prompted a move away from modernism. Previously, Australian literary critics such as Nettie Palmer and Margaret (Margot) Hentze had espoused an internationalism they found reflected in Woolf's work. The 1930s also saw Woolf's early readership in South America shaped by Victoria Ocampo's writings in the journal *Sur*, as Cristina Carluccio writes in 'Dialogues between South America and Europe: Victoria Ocampo channels Virginia Woolf'. Woolf and Ocampo met in person in 1934, and their conversation dwelled on the idea of 'hunger', a desire for cosmopolitanism. Carluccio argues that their shared intellectual hunger should be seen as the epitome of a female desire for borderless circulation and reception in literary circles, such as those enabled by the global trajectories traced by the journal *Sur*.

Davi Pinho imagines a conversation between Woolf, Julia Kristeva and Paulo Mendes Campos in 'From Julia Kristeva to Paulo Mendes Campos: Impossible conversations with Virginia Woolf'. By exploring the signature of Woolf's suicide in 1941 as it resurfaces in Kristeva's writing from Paris in 1974 and in Campos's work from Petropolis, Brazil in 1981, Pinho shows how Woolf's words travel across cultures and contexts to inspire new conversations about writing and creativity. Campos's depiction of Woolf's watery aesthetics in context with her suicide in the river Ouse suggests to Pinho that Woolf's words, like a current, rush through times, contexts, subjectivities and identities, resisting fixation in any of these residences. Henrike Krause develops the idea of a trans-temporal conversation with Woolf, this time with East German feminist author Christa Wolf. In '*Three Guineas* and the Cassandra Project, Christa Wolf's reading of Virginia Woolf during the Cold War', Krause examines Wolf's reading notes in her personal copy of Woolf's *Three Guineas* that emerge in Wolf's Cassandra project. This chapter also shows the channels by which it was possible for East German intellectuals, like Wolf, to gain access to Woolf's works in the 1970s.

Several chapters concern the fate of modernist literature during the Soviet era of socialist realism. In 'Virginia Woolf's literary heritage in Russian translations and interpretations', Maria Bent uncovers Woolf's delayed history of translation into Russian. Although Woolf was known to the Russian intelligentsia in the 1920s and 1930s, the first Russian translation of Woolf was not published until 1976. This delay was due to the state's emphasis on socialist realism over so-called modernist decadence. Although Woolf's modernism was acceptable to post-Soviet Estonia, her feminism was not, as Raili Marling demonstrates in 'Virginia Woolf's feminist writing in Estonian translation culture'. Woolf's modernism was more palatable than her cosmofeminism in a post-Soviet culture uneasy with feminist thought and politics.

In 'Virginia Woolf in Arabic: A feminist paratextual reading of translation strategies', Hala Kamal addresses Woolf's modernism and feminism as she examines Woolf's translations into Arabic through the lens of feminist translation studies. Woolf was first translated into Arabic in 1968, when she was read as a modernist author; it was not until the 1980s that Woolf was contextualised as a feminist writer and critic by her readers in Arabic. Kamal focuses on the politics of translation of *A Room of One's Own* through the gendered usage of pronouns in Arabic and English in translations. Woolf's translation into Italian has been robust since the 1930s translations by the Mondadori publishing company (Bolchi 2015), as Elisa Bolchi shows in 'Solid and living: The Italian Woolf Renaissance'. In this essay, Bolchi focuses on the flourishing of new translations and editions of Woolf in Italy after 2011, when Woolf's works came out of European copyright. Part I of the collection concludes with Jeanne Dubino's 'Tracing *A Room of One's Own* in sub-Saharan Africa, 1929–2019', which tracks Woolf's reception. Dubino's essay initially examines white British women, Woolf's contemporaries, who wrote imperialist romance narratives set against the backdrop of colonial Kenya. Moving to the ongoing influence of *A Room of One's Own* in Africa, Dubino shows that in the context of sub-Saharan African aphoristic culture, the most famous aspect of Woolf's feminist manifesto may be its title. At the same time, some feminists from sub-Saharan Africa are engaging directly with Woolf's written works.

Part II, 'Woolf's Legacies in Literature', examines Woolf's impact on contemporary literature worldwide. Whether Woolf appears as herself in contemporary biofiction or in work inspired by her characters, plots and literary style, the chapters in this section explore how Woolf's life and work continue to inspire cutting edge literature in a variety of languages and cultures. Organised geographically and intended to displace the hegemony of the Global North, this section begins in the Global South before moving counterclockwise to the East, North and West.

Lindsey Cordery opens this section with the chapter 'Virginia Woolf's enduring presence in Uruguay', which examines Woolf's earliest appearance in the Argentine journal *Sur* to her influence on Uruguayan writers like Armonía Somers and Antonio Larreta. Significantly, Cordery shows how Woolf's work continues to inspire a new generation of emerging Uruguayan feminist writers, such as Cristina Peri Rossi and Alicia Migdal. Similarly, Maria A. de Oliveira's 'Virginia Woolf's reception and impact on Brazilian Women's literature' takes a transnational look at how Woolf's work has spread to Brazil and influenced contemporary women's writing there. Essays like de Oliveira's remind readers of the immense amount of literature inspired by Woolf and written in the authors' national languages that remains untranslated into other languages. For example, in 'English and Mexican dogs: Spectres of traumatic pasts in Virginia Woolf's *Flush* and María Luisa Puga's *Las razones del lago*' [The Reasons of the Lake], Lourdes Parra-Lazcano uses the lens of Animal Studies to create a dialogue between Elizabeth Barrett Browning's spaniel and the stray dogs, Novela [Novel] and Relato [Story], in Puga's novel. Parra-Lazcano's analysis of Puga's and Woolf's novels focuses on how animals experience trauma, creating a compelling contrast between London/Florence and Mexico City/Zirahuén through the differing attitudes towards animals in each city.

In 'A new perspective on Mary Carmichael: Yuriko Miyamoto's novels and *A Room of One's Own*', Hogara Matsumoto investigates Japanese writer Yuriko Miyamoto, whose Transeurasian travels brought her to Moscow, Paris and New York, and whose cosmopolitanism is reflected in her novel *Milestone* (1948). Miyamoto's historical survey of Japanese writers, *Women and Fiction* (1948), was directly influenced by Woolf, although Miyamoto argues that Woolf's 'room of one's own' remained a utopian dream for Japanese women. Zhongfeng Huang similarly acknowledges the impact of Woolf's *A Room of One's Own* on Chinese women writers. Her essay, 'Rooms of their own: A cross-cultural voyage between Virginia Woolf and the contemporary Chinese woman writer Chen Ran', shows how Woolf's feminism shaped the novels of Chen Ran, which depict Chinese women's intimate relationships through Woolf's idea of a 'gender-transcendent' consciousness. Justyna Jaguścik further notes that since *A Room of One's Own* was first translated into Chinese in 1983, it has greatly influenced feminist discourse. Her chapter, 'In search of spaces of their own: Woolf, feminism and women's poetry from China', focuses on the poetry journal *Wings*, which she argues offers an imaginary 'room' for poets like Huang Xi and Zhai Yongming to bring a feminist poetics, inspired by Woolf, to Chinese readers.

Paulina Pająk tracks the creative 'trans-dialogues', or transtextual encounters, with Woolf in 'Trans-dialogues: Exploring Virginia Woolf's feminist legacy to contemporary Polish literature'. Following the 1997 translation of *A Room of One's Own* into Polish, Woolf's works have become significant texts for Polish feminist writers, including Olga Tokarczuk. Monica Latham examines the impact of *Mrs Dalloway* on three recent novels inspired by that novel's form and central character in 'Clarissa Dalloway's Global Itinerary: From London to Paris and Sydney'. Two French novels, by Anne Korkeakivi and Carole Llewellyn, pay explicit homage to the character Mrs Dalloway, while a recent Australian novel by Gail Jones reverberates with the experience of temporality from that novel. Anne-Laure Rigeade, in 'Virginia Woolf and French writers: Contemporaneity, idolisation, iconisation', traces Woolf's reception in France through a typology of attitudes displayed by French novelists and literary critics. From Natalie Sarraute, who was Woolf's contemporary, to the feminist 'idolisation' of Woolf by writers like Anne Bragance and Cécile Wajsbrot, to more recent appearances by Woolf in experimental biofiction, French writers have created a distinctively 'French Woolf'. These feminist portraits owe much to Viviane Forrester's defiant 1973 biography of Woolf, which protested Quentin Bell's portrayal of his aunt as a frail genius.

Woolf's idea of the 'outsider' resonates for many people across the globe. In 'The dream work of a nation: From Virginia Woolf to Elizabeth Bowen to Mary Lavin', Patricia Laurence argues that the Anglo-Irish writers Elizabeth Bowen and Mary Lavin embodied Woolf's idea of the outsider, particularly in their respective works responding to the Second World War. The last chapters in this volume travel with Woolf to the United States, quite literally in the case of Bethany Layne's 'Great poets do not die: Maggie Gee's *Virginia Woolf in Manhattan* (2014) as metaphor for contemporary biofiction'. Gee's novel, which depicts Woolf as an outsider in twenty-first-century New York City, offers compelling ethical questions about biofiction as a genre, particularly the way biofictional novels might dwell on those aspects of a writer's biography that could be seen as private or salacious. This chapter and the novel it discusses question our collective fascination with Woolf's private life. Lastly, Catherine W. Hollis in 'The Woolf girl: A mother–daughter story with Virginia Woolf and Lidia Yuknavitch' dwells on the metaphor of Woolf as the foremother 'we think back through' as contemporary women writers. Yuknavitch's experimental work in autobiography and fiction takes up the challenge of representing bodies, violence and creativity in ways that Woolf herself had only begun to develop in her late autobiographical essay, 'A sketch of the past'.

Looking at the global array of essays in this volume, it is clear that Woolf's influence is alive and vital in the twenty-first century. And now we must determine how we can write forward into the challenges of this precarious century, acknowledging all that we have learned from Woolf while we devise new ways of writing about bodies, consciousness, social justice and global community.

Notes

1. The authors of the Introduction wish to thank Vara Neverow and Celiese Lypka, who contributed greatly to it through their keen and generous editing.
2. Paulina Pająk and Jeanne Dubino first began to discuss the project in Summer 2016.
3. The organisers of the International Women's Strike list fifty-four countries in which the protests were held:

    Argentina, Australia, Belgium, Bolivia, Brasil [Brazil], Canada, Cambodia, Chad, Chile, Colombia, Dominican Republic, South Korea, Costa Rica, Czech Republic, China (Hongkong), Ecuador, El Salvador, Fiji, Finland, France, Guatemala, Germany, Honduras, Haiti, Hungary, North Ireland, Republic of Ireland, Israel, Italy, Lithuania, Malta, Mexico, Montenegro, Myanmar, Nicaragua, Pakistan, Panama, Paraguay, Peru, Polonia [Poland], Portugal, Puerto Rico, Russia, Scotland, Senegal, Spain, Sweden, Thailand, Turkey, Ukraine, Uruguay, UK, USA, Venezuela. (International Women's Strike/Paro Internacional de Mujeres)

4. As Moretti writes,

    Now, trees and waves are both metaphors – but except for this, they have absolutely nothing in common. The tree describes the passage from unity to diversity: one tree, with many branches: from Indo-European, to dozens of different languages. The wave is the opposite: it observes uniformity engulfing an initial diversity: Hollywood films conquering one market after another (or English swallowing language after language). Trees need geographical discontinuity (in order to branch off from each other, languages must first be separated in space, just like animal species); waves dislike barriers, and thrive on geographical continuity (from the viewpoint of a wave, the ideal world is a pond). . . . This, then, is the basis for the division of labour between national and world literature: national literature, for people who see trees; world literature, for people who see waves. (2000: 67–8)

5. For recent approaches to canon formation, see David Damrosch (2006: 43–53).
6. The list of colonial and postcolonial approaches to the work of Woolf is long. Readers are encouraged to consult scholarship by Genevieve Abravanel (2000), Tuzyline Jita Allan (1995, 1999), Michelle Cliff (1994), Melba Cuddy-Keane (2003), Madelyn Detloff (2016), Gretchen Holbrook Gerzina (2006, 2010, 2014), Randi Koppen (2018), Jane Marcus (2004), Kathy Phillips (1994), Sonita Sarker (2018), Urmila Seshaguri (2010) and Anna Snaith (2010, 2018).
7. L 2: 401, 403, 418, 419.
8. According to Quentin Bell,

    Monday or Tuesday appeared at the beginning of April, but owing, as Virginia believed, to a blunder by Ralph [Partridge, who worked at Hogarth Press], who had a mistake about the date of publication, the book was inadequately reviewed by *The Times*, Doran (the American publisher of *The Voyage Out*) refused it, and altogether it seemed to have fallen very flat. (1972: 2: 77)

    Anne Olivier Bell and Andrew McNeillie note that what 'Doran refused, Harcourt, Brace and Co. accepted, and *Monday or Tuesday* was published by them on 23 November 1921' (D 2: 106 n.2).
9. From 1920 onwards all of Woolf's novels were reviewed immediately upon their US publication in the prestigious *New York Times* ('First Reviews' 2020).
10. John K. Young writes that in 1929 Leonard invited William Plomer, one of the Hogarth Press authors, 'to serve as Hogarth's book traveller in Japan . . . but Plomer declined' (2012: 132). See also The Modernist Archives Publishing Project (MAPP), 'a critical digital archive of early twentieth-century publishing history' (n.d.).
11. Interestingly, the first translation into French, by Charles Mauron, was of a section of *To the Lighthouse*, 'Time passes', which appeared in 1926 before the novel itself was published in English in 1927. See Chapter 20 by Anne-Laure Rigeade in this volume.
12. From 1926–7, extracts from *Jacob's Room* were translated into French and published in Switzerland; in 1927, extracts from *Jacob's Room* were translated into French and published in France; in 1927, *To the Lighthouse* was translated into German; in 1927, *Jacob's Room* into Swedish; in 1928, *Mrs Dalloway* into German; in 1929, *Orlando* into Czech; and in 1929, *Mrs Dalloway* and *To the Lighthouse* into French. See Mary Ann Caws and Nicola Luckhurst's 'Timeline: European reception of Virginia Woolf' (2002: xxi–xxxvi) for a comprehensive overview of the history of the translations to appear in Europe. See also Kirkpatrick and Clarke for short essays and stories, such as 'The string quartet', that were translated into French in 1929 (1998: 331, 343).
13. See Paul Barnaby (2002: xxi, xxii); *Italian Woolf Project* (2020); Kirkpatrick and Clarke (1998: 307).
14. Shu-mei Shi (2001: 239); Laurence (1995: 10); Shi-Jing Qu (1995: 3); *WorldCat* (2020); Kirkpatrick and Clarke (1998: 309–11, 359–67).
15. B. J. Kirkpatrick and Stuart N. Clarke's superb *A Bibliography of Virginia Woolf* (1998) and Ian R. Willison's helpful *The New Cambridge Bibliography of English Literature* (1972) are also of relevance.
16. While there can be a thin line between an article and a review, the discussion that follows focuses mainly on developed critical work and scholarship.
17. In France (nine), Germany (ten), Belgium (one), Denmark (one), Sweden (one), Spain (one), Italy (six), Greece (three), Poland (three), Russia (one), Argentina (three) and Chile (one).

These figures are not comprehensive. They are drawn from Rice (1984); Kirkpatrick and Clarke (1998); Willison (1972); and Barnaby (2002).
18. This collection seems to have been a special edition of *Impressions: Revue littéraire et artistique*, whose editor at the time was René Debresse.
19. Gruber met with Virginia Woolf in 1933 and added elements from that conversation to her analysis.
20. Following is a sampling of the number of books on Woolf published in each country between 1941 and 1983: Germany (twelve), Italy (five), France (four, plus three collections), Spain (one), Finland (one), Japan (four), Argentina (two more) and India (two). Many articles and review-essays were published in all of these countries, especially in the United States but also in Poland (fourteen), Portugal (five), Sweden (three), Romania (two), Austria (two), Greece (two), Netherlands (two), Serbo-Croatia (one), Chile (one) and Israel (one).
21. One of the first international MA theses written on Woolf outside of Europe and the United States, as Suzanne Bellamy discusses in this collection, was by Nuri Mass from Australia, whose 'Virginia Woolf the novelist' was completed in 1942.
22. Doctoral students also wrote dissertations on Woolf in Germany (nine), France (five), Sweden (one), Spain (one), Ireland (one), Canada (seven) and Israel (one). Again, it must be emphasised that these numbers are incomplete.
23. For example, the Google Scholar chart includes only those sites that are in the dominant languages of the countries listed; most of these countries have many sites on Woolf in English.
24. WorldCat omits many non-English publications. For example, WorldCat indicates that Polish translations of *The Waves*, *To the Lighthouse*, *Mrs Dalloway* and *The Years* were published only once. In fact, according to data from Poland's National Library, there were at least four editions of *The Waves* (1983, 1998, 2003 and 2015), five editions of *To the Lighthouse* (1962, 2000, 2005 and two in 2016), five editions of *Mrs Dalloway* (1961, 1997, 2003, 2008 and 2016) and two editions of *The Years* (1958 and 2006).
25. For an overview of the evolution of Woolf community including the emergence of journals, societies, conferences and selected papers as well as a list of annual conferences on Virginia Woolf, see Vara Neverow (2020: xxv–xxx).
26. See also Sergio Perosa, who writes about the formation of a 'Virginia Woolf University' in Rome in 1977 (2002: 202).
27. Even during the Covid-19 pandemic, Woolfians have been able to gather virtually on platforms like Zoom and stay in touch by email internationally.

Bibliography

Abravanel, G. (2000), 'Woolf in blackface: Identification across *The Waves*', in J. Berman and J. Goldman (eds), *Virginia Woolf: Out of Bounds: Selected Papers from the Tenth Annual Conference on Virginia Woolf*, New York: Pace University Press, pp. 113–19.

Allan, T. J. (1999), 'Civilization, its pretexts, and Virginia Woolf's imagination', in J. McVicker and L. Davis (eds), *Virginia Woolf and Communities: Selected Papers from the Eighth Annual Conference on Virginia Woolf*, New York: Pace University Press, pp. 117–27.

Allan, T. J. (1995), *Womanist and Feminist Aesthetics: A Comparative Review*, Athens: Ohio University Press.

Barnaby, P. (2002), 'Timeline: European reception of *Virginia Woolf*', in M. A. Caws and N. Luckhurst (eds), *The Reception of Virginia Woolf in Europe*, London: Continuum, pp. xxi–xxxvi.

Bell, Q. (1972), *Virginia Woolf: A Biography*, 2 vols, New York: Harcourt Brace Jovanovich.

Bellamy, S. (1997), 'The pattern behind the words', in E. Barrett and P. Cramer (eds), *Virginia Woolf: Lesbian Readings*, New York: New York State University Press, pp. 21–36.

Berman, J. (2011), *Modernist Commitments: Ethics, Politics, and Transnational Modernism*, New York: Columbia University Press.
Berman, J. (2015), 'Modernist cosmopolitanism', in G. Castle (ed.), *A History of the Modernist Novel*, Cambridge: Cambridge University Press, pp. 429–48.
Berman, J. (2017), 'Is the trans in transnational the trans in transgender?', *Modernism/modernity*, 24: 2, pp. 217–44.
Bhabha, H. (1994), *The Location of Culture*, New York: Routledge.
Bolchi, E. (2015), *L'indimenticabile artista. Lettere e appunti sulla storia editoriale di Virginia Woolf in Mondadori* [The Unforgettable Artist. Letters and Notes on the Editorial History of Virginia Woolf in Mondadori], Milan: Vita e Pensiero.
Casanova, P. (1999), *La republique mondiale des Lettres* [The World Republic of Letters], Paris: Éditions du Seuil.
Caws, M. A. and N. Luckhurst (eds) (2002), *The Reception of Virginia Woolf in Europe*, London: Continuum.
Cliff, M. (1994), 'Virginia Woolf and the imperial gaze: A glance askance', in M. Hussey and V. Neverow (eds), *Virginia Woolf: Emerging Perspectives: Selected Papers from the Third Annual Conference on Virginia Woolf*, New York: Pace University Press, pp. 91–102.
Cuddy-Keane, M. (2003), 'Modernism, geopolitics, globalization', *Modernism/modernity*, 10: 3, pp. 539–58.
Cuddy-Keane, M. (2017 [1998]), 'History of the society', International Virginia Woolf Society, <http://sites.utoronto.ca/IVWS/other-societies.html> (last accessed 5 July 2020).
Damrosch, D. (2003), *What is World Literature?*, Princeton, NJ: Princeton University Press.
Damrosch, D. (2006), 'World literature in a postcanonical, hypercanonical age', in H. Saussy (ed.), *Comparative Literature in an Age of Globalization*, Baltimore, MD: Johns Hopkins University Press, pp. 43–53.
Damrosch, D. (2017), 'World literature as figure and as ground', in U. K. Heise (ed.), *Futures of Comparative Literature: ACLA State of the Discipline Report*, London: Routledge, pp. 134–40.
Detloff, M. (2016), *The Value of Virginia Woolf*, Cambridge: Cambridge University Press.
'The first reviews of every Virginia Woolf novel' (2020), *Literary Hub*, 12 May, <https://bookmarks.reviews/the-first-reviews-of-every-virginia-woolf-novel/> (last accessed 21 May 2020).
Foster, J. A., S. M. Horowitz and L. Allen (2016), 'Changing the subject: Archives, technology, and radical counter-narratives of peace', *Radical Teacher*, 105, pp. 11–22.
Friedman, S. S. (2013), 'Wartime cosmopolitanism: Cosmofeminism in Virginia Woolf's *Three Guineas* and Marjane Satrapi's *Persepolis*', *Tulsa Studies in Women's Literature*, 32: 1, pp. 23–52.
Friedman, S. S. (2018), *Planetary Modernisms: Provocations on Modernity across Time*, New York: Columbia University Press.
Gerzina, G. H. (2006), 'Bushmen and blackface: Bloomsbury and "race"', *The South Carolina Review*, 38: 2, pp. 46–64.
Gerzina, G. H. (2010), 'Virginia Woolf, performing "race"', in M. Humm (ed.), *The Edinburgh Companion to Virginia Woolf and the Arts*, Edinburgh: Edinburgh University Press, pp. 74–87.
Gerzina, G. H. (2014), 'Bloomsbury and empire', in V. Rosner (ed.), *The Cambridge Companion to the Bloomsbury Group*, Cambridge: Cambridge University Press, pp. 112–28.
Glissant, É. (1990), *Poétique de la Relation*, Paris: Gallimard.
Glissant, É. (1997), *Poetics of Relation*, trans. B. Wing, Ann Arbor: Michigan University Press.
'Global Actions' (n.d.), Black Lives Matter, <https://blacklivesmatter.com/global-actions> (last accessed 12 July 2020).
Heise, U. K. (2017), 'Comparative literature and the environmental humanities', in Heise (ed.), *Futures of Comparative Literature: ACLA State of the Discipline Report*, London: Routledge, pp. 293–301.

Humm, M. (2017), 'The women's march on London: Judith Butler, John Berger, Virginia Woolf and intersectionality', *Interdisciplinary Perspectives on Equality and Diversity*, 3: 1, pp. 1–14.

Hussey, M. (1986), *The Singing of the Real World: The Philosophy of Virginia Woolf's Fiction*, Columbus: Ohio State University.

International Women's Strike/Paro Internacional de Mujeres, <https://www.facebook.com/womenstrikeus/> (last accessed 8 December 2020).

Italian Woolf Project (2020), <https://www.instagram.com/italianwoolf_project/> (last accessed 21 May 2020).

Kirkpatrick, B. J. and S. N. Clarke (1998), *A Bibliography of Virginia Woolf*, 4th edn, Oxford: Clarendon Press.

Koppen, R. (2018), 'The negress and the Bishop: On marriage, colonialism and the problem of knowledge', in E. Högberg and A. Bromley (eds), *Sentencing Orlando: Virginia Woolf and the Morphology of the Modernist Sentence*, Edinburgh: Edinburgh University Press, pp. 186–97.

Latham, S. and G. Rogers (2015), *Modernism: Evolution of an Idea*, London: Bloomsbury.

Laurence, P. (1995), *Virginia Woolf and the East*, London: Cecil Woolf.

Lee, H. (1999), *Virginia Woolf*, London: Vintage.

Lojo Rodríguez, L. M. (2002), '"A gaping mouth, but no words": Virginia Woolf enters the land of butterflies', in M. A. Caws and N. Luckhurst (eds), *The Reception of Virginia Woolf in Europe*, London: Continuum, pp. 218–80.

Lyon, J. (2011), 'On the asylum road with Woolf and Mew', *Modernism/modernity*, 18: 3, pp. 551–74.

Mao, D. and R. L. Walkowitz (2008), 'The New Modernist Studies', *PMLA*, 123: 3, pp. 737–48.

Marcus, J. (2004), *Hearts of Darkness: White Women Write Race*, New Brunswick, NJ: Rutgers University Press.

Mepham, J. (1991), *Virginia Woolf: A Literary Life*, Basingstoke: Macmillan.

The Modern Archives Publishing Project (MAPP), <https://www.modernistarchives.com> (last accessed 5 July 2020).

Moraru, C. (2017), '"World", "globe", "planet": Comparative literature, planetary studies, and cultural debt after the global turn', in U. K. Heise (ed.), *Futures of Comparative Literature: ACLA State of the Discipline Report*, London: Routledge, pp. 124–32.

Moretti, F. (2000), 'Conjectures on world literature', *New Left Review*, 1, pp. 54–68.

Neverow, V. (2020), 'A chronology of the Virginia Woolf community', in Neverow et al. (eds), *Virginia Woolf: Critical and Primary Sources Volume 1: 1975–1984*, London: Bloomsbury Academic, pp. xxiv–xxix.

Nünning, A. and V. Nünning (2002), 'The German reception and criticism of Virginia Woolf: A survey of phases and trends in the twentieth century', in M. A. Caws and N. Luckhurst (eds), *The Reception of Virginia Woolf in Europe*, London: Continuum, pp. 68–101.

Perosa, S. 'The reception of Virginia Woolf in Italy', in M. A. Caws and N. Luckhurst (eds), *The Reception of Virginia Woolf in Europe*, London: Continuum, pp. 200–17.

Phillips, K. J. (1994), *Virginia Woolf against Empire*, Knoxville: University of Tennessee Press.

Pizer, J. D. (2015), 'Planetary poetics: World literature, Goethe, Novalis, and Yoko Tawada's translational writing', in A. J. Elias and C. Moraru (eds), *The Planetary Turn: Relationality and Geoaesthetics in the Twenty-First Century*, pp. 3–24.

Qu, S.-J. (1995), 'Professor Qu Shi-Jing on Woolfian publications in China', *Virginia Woolf Miscellany*, 45, pp. 2–3.

Rice, T. J. (1984), *Virginia Woolf: A Guide to Research*, New York: Garland.

Sarker, S. (2018), 'Bloomsbury and empire', in D. Ryan and S. Ross (eds), *The Handbook to the Bloomsbury Group*, London: Bloomsbury Academic, pp. 75–93.

Seshagiri, U. (2010), *Race and the Modernist Imagination*, Ithaca, NY: Cornell University Press.

Shi, S. (2001), *The Lure of the Modern: Writing Modernism in Semicolonial China, 1917–1937*, Berkeley: University of California Press.
Silver, B. R. (1999), *Virginia Woolf Icon*, Chicago: Chicago University Press.
Slaughter, J. R. (2007), *Human Rights, Inc.: The World Novel, Narrative Form, and International Law*, New York: Fordham University Press.
Snaith, A. (2010), 'Conversations in Bloomsbury: Colonial writers and the Hogarth Press', in L. Shahriari and G. Potts (eds), *Virginia Woolf's Bloomsbury, Volume 2: International Influence and Politics*, Basingstoke: Palgrave Macmillan, pp. 138–57.
Snaith, A. (2018), 'Case study: Race, empire, and performative activism in late Edwardian Bloomsbury', in D. Ryan and S. Ross (eds), *The Handbook to the Bloomsbury Group*, London: Bloomsbury Academic, pp. 94–108.
Spivak, C. S. (2003), *Death of a Discipline*, New York: Columbia University Press.
Tokarczuk, O. (2018), 'I was very naive. I thought Poland would be able to discuss the dark areas of our history', interviewed by C. Armitstead, *Guardian*, 20 April, <https://www.theguardian.com/books/2018/apr/20/olga-tokarczuk-interview-flights-man-booker-international> (last accessed 30 July 2019).
Villeneuve, P.-É. (2002), 'Virginia Woolf among writers and critics: The French intellectual scene', in M. A. Caws and N. Luckhurst (eds), *The Reception of Virginia Woolf in Europe*, London: Continuum, pp. 19–38.
Walkowitz, R. L. (2006), *Cosmopolitan Style: Modernism Beyond the Nation*, New York: Columbia University Press.
Walkowitz, R. L. (2017), *Born Translated: The Contemporary Novel in an Age of World Literature*, New York: Columbia University Press.
Willis, J. H. (1992), *Leonard and Virginia Woolf as Publishers: The Hogarth Press, 1917–41*, Charlottesville: University Press of Virginia.
Willison, I. R. (1972), *New Cambridge Bibliography of English Literature, Volume 4 1900–1950*, London: Cambridge University Press.
Woolf, V. (1982), *The Diary of Virginia Woolf: Volume 3: 1925–1930*, ed. A. O. Bell and A. McNeillie, Harmondsworth: Penguin.
Woolf, V. (2011), *The Essays of Virginia Woolf: Volume 6: 1939–1941 and Additional Essays 1906–1924*, ed. S. N. Clarke, London: Hogarth Press.
Woolf, V. (1975–80), *The Letters of Virginia Woolf*, ed. N. Nicolson and J. Trautmann, 6 vols, New York: Harcourt Brace Jovanovich.
Woolf, V. (2001 [1929]), *A Room of One's Own and Three Guineas*, London: Vintage.
World Cat (2020), <worldcat.org> (last accessed 21 May 2020).
Young, J. K. (2012), 'William Plomer and transnational modernism', in H. Southworth (ed.), *Leonard & Virginia Woolf: The Hogarth Press and the Networks of Modernism*, Edinburgh: Edinburgh University Press, pp. 128–49.

Part One

The Voyage Out (1915) to A Room of One's (1929)

(Note: these entries are organised from the highest to the lowest number of publications in a country.)

The Voyage Out (1915)	Night and Day (1919)	Jacob's Room (1922)	Mrs Dalloway (1925)	To the Lighthouse (1927)	The Common Reader (1925)	Orlando (1928)	A Room of One's Own (1929)
English (41)	English (38)	English (60)	English (152)	English (128)	English (90)	English (106)	English (96)
Italian (7)	Spanish (6)	Italian (12)	Undetermined (28)	Italian (17)	German (11)	German (38)	Spanish (18)
Undetermined (7)	French (5)	Undetermined (8)	German (23)	Spanish (15)	French (9)	French (18)	Chinese (13)
French (5)	Italian (5)	Spanish (7)	Italian (23)	Undetermined (15)	Undetermined (9)	Undetermined (16)	German (12)
Spanish (5)	Korean (4)	Korean (4)	Spanish (21)	Chinese (11)	Italian (8)	Spanish (14)	Korean (11)
Japanese (4)	Undetermined (4)	Swedish (4)	French (20)	Japanese (9)	Spanish (5)	Italian (11)	Undetermined (11)
Korean (4)	Hebrew (2)	Turkish (4)	Russian (14)	Russian (9)	Russian (2)	Swedish (10)	Italian (9)
German (3)	Hungarian (2)	Chinese (3)	Chinese (13)	Turkish (9)	Turkish (2)	Russian (9)	French (8)
Portuguese (2)	Romanian (2)	French (3)	Korean (13)	German (8)	Arabic (1)	Dutch (9)	Japanese (5)
Russian (2)	Russian (2)	Greek, Modern [1453–] (3)	Swedish (13)	Korean (7)	Chinese (1)	Danish (7)	Danish (4)
Swedish (2)	Swedish (2)	Persian (3)	Greek, Modern [1453–] (7)	French (6)	Croatian (1)	Korean (6)	Hebrew (4)
Turkish (2)	Turkish (2)	Portuguese (3)	Japanese (7)	Portuguese (5)	Japanese (1)	Romanian (5)	Persian (4)
Arabic (1)	Bulgarian (1)	Romanian (3)	Arabic (5)	Greek, Modern [1453–] (4)	Portuguese (1)	Greek, Modern [1453–] (4)	Swedish (4)
Bulgarian (1)	Finnish (1)	Danish (2)	Dutch (5)	Bokmål, Norwegian (4)	Serbian (1)	Portuguese (4)	Turkish (4)
Chinese (1)	German (2)	German (2)	Hebrew (5)	Norwegian (4)		Turkish (3)	Greek, Modern [1453–] (3)
Finnish (1)	Croatian (1)	Croatian (2)	Hungarian (5)	Persian (4)		Catalan (2)	Bokmål, Norwegian (3)
Hebrew (1)	Japanese (1)	Russian (2)	Bokmål, Norwegian (4)	Serbian (4)		Chinese (2)	Polish (3)
Croatian (1)	Macedonian (1)	Bulgarian (1)	Portuguese (4)	Danish (3)		Czech (2)	Arabic (2)
Hungarian (1)	Polish (1)	Dutch (1)	Catalan (3)	Hebrew (3)		Hebrew (2)	Catalan (2)
Polish (1)	Portuguese (1)	Finnish (1)	Danish (3)	Hungarian (3)		Croatian (2)	Dutch (2)
Romanian (1)		Hebrew (1)	Croatian (3)	Romanian (3)		Hungarian (2)	Hindi (2)
Serbian (1)		Hungarian (1)	Persian (3)	Slovenian (3)		Japanese (2)	Norwegian (2)
		Bokmål, Norwegian (1)	Romanian (3)	Vietnamese (3)		Bokmål, Norwegian (2)	Portuguese (2)
		Norwegian (1)	Serbian (3)	Basque (2)		Persian (2)	Thai (2)
		Polish (1)	Bulgarian (2)	Dutch (2)		Polish (2)	Vietnamese (2)
		Slovenian (1)	Norwegian (2)	Finnish (2)		Thai (2)	Albanian (1)
		Vietnamese (1)	Slovenian (2) Turkish (2)	Swedish (2)		Bulgarian (1)	Armenian (1)
			Albanian (1)	Arabic (1)		Estonian (1)	Basque (1)
			Basque (1)	Bulgarian (1)		Finnish (1)	Bengali (1)
			Czech (1)	Catalan (1)		Galician (1)	Bulgarian (1)
			Estonian (1)	Czech (1)		Macedonian (1)	Estonian (1)
			Finnish (1)	Galician (1)		Ndonga (1)	Faroese (1)
			Galician (1)	Croatian (1)		Norwegian (1)	Finnish (1)
			Latvian (1)	Icelandic (1)		Romani (1)	Galician (1)
			Lithuanian (1)	Latvian (1)		Slovenian (1)	Gujrati (1)
			Macedonian (1)	Multiple languages (1)			Croatian (1)
			Polish (1)	Polish (1)			Hungarian (1)
			Slovak (1)	Thai (1)			Indonesian (1)
			Thai (1)				Lithuanian (1)
			Ukrainian (1)				Multiple languages (1)
							Panjabi (1)
							Romanian (1)
							Slovenian (1)
							Serbian (1)
							Ukrainian (1)

Part Two
The Waves (1931) to *Between the Acts* (1941)

(Note: these entries are organised from the highest to the lowest number of publications in a country.)

The Waves (1931)	Flush (1933)	The Common Reader Second Series (1935)	The Years (1937)	Three Guineas (1938)	Roger Fry (1940)	Between the Acts (1941)
English (75)	English (37)	English (30)	English (104)	English (33)	English (28)	English (37)
Spanish (20)	German (19)	German (3)	Undetermined (8)	German (8)	Undetermined (6)	Undetermined (10)
French (7)	French (14)	Italian (2)	Spanish (6)	Undetermined (8)	Italian (5)	Spanish (7)
Italian (6)	Undetermined (12)	Turkish (1)	Italian (5)	French (6)	Spanish (2)	Italian (6)
Undetermined (5)	Russian (8)		French (4)	Italian (3)	French (1)	French (5)
Chinese (4)	Danish (6)		Catalan (3)	Korean (3)	German (1)	Korean (3)
German (4)	Spanish (6)		Korean (3)	Spanish (3)	Japanese (1)	Turkish (3)
Japanese (4)	Italian (5)		Persian (3)	Hungarian (2)	Swedish (1)	Catalan (2)
Turkish (4)	Hebrew (4)		Portuguese (3)	Japanese (2)		Danish (2)
Dutch (3)	Portuguese (3)		Danish (2)	Polish (2)		German (2)
Hungarian (3)	Turkish (3)		Dutch (2)	Swedish (2)		Japanese (2)
Korean (3)	Catalan (2)		Hebrew (2)	Catalan (1)		Portuguese (2)
Persian (3)	Chinese (2)		Hungarian (2)	Chinese (1)		Romanian (2)
Arabic (2)	Czech (2)		Japanese (2)	Danish (1)		Russian (2)
Catalan (2)	Dutch (2)		Swedish (2)	Dutch (1)		Swedish (2)
Greek, Modern [1453–] (2)	Hungarian (2)		Turkish (2)	Greek, Modern [1453–] (1)		Arabic (1)
Russian (2)	Japanese (2)		Bulgarian (1)	Hebrew (1)		Bulgarian (1)
Serbian (2)	Polish (2)		Finnish (1)	Croatian (1)		Czech (1)
Bulgarian (1)	Slovenian (2)		German (1)	Bokmal, Norwegian (1)		Greek, Modern [1453–] (1)
Czech (1)	Swedish (2)		Greek, Modern [1453–] (1)	Persian (1)		Croatian (1)
Danish (1)	Finnish (1)		Croatian (1)	Portuguese (1)		Hungarian (1)
Estonian (1)	Greek, Modern [1453–] (1)		Polish (1)	Romanian (1)		Persian (1)
Finnish (1)	Korean (1)		Romanian (1)	Slovenian (1)		Polish (1)
Galician (1)	Bokmal, Norwegian (1)		Russian (1)	Turkish (1)		Slovenian (1)
Hebrew (1)	Romanian (1)		Slovenian (1)	Ukrainian (1)		
Multiple languages (1)						
Bokmal, Norwegian (1)						
Polish (1)						
Portuguese (1)						
Romanian (1)						
Swedish (1)						

Table 1 WorldCat: Number of editions of Woolf's works in each language

Language	Number of websites on Woolf's work published in each language
Bulgarian	2
Chinese (China)*	2,205
Chinese (Taiwan)	1,210
Dutch	782
French	10,200
German	4,650
Greek	1,086
Italian	4,130
Japanese	1,320
Korean	757
Polish	1,090
Portuguese (Brazil)	1,200
Portuguese (Portugal)	9,630
Spanish	17,400
Turkish	1,180

* Starting in 2010, Google no longer operated in China; thus, this figure is not indicative of the range of websites on Woolf in China.

Table 2 Google Scholar: Number of websites on Woolf's work published in each language

Language	Number of works on Woolf
Afrikaans	1
Arabic	1
Chinese	31
Croatian	14
Danish	6
Dutch	9
Finnish	1
German	87
Hebrew	2
Hungarian	2
Icelandic	1
Italian	65
Japanese	82
Korean	39
Latvian	4
Lithuanian	1
Norwegian	6
Portuguese	23
Romanian	7
Russian	11
Serbo	14
Slovenian	2
Spanish	73
Swedish	7
Turkish	11
Ukrainian	1

Table 3 *MLA International Bibliography*: Number of studies on Woolf's work published in each language

Part I

Planetary and Global Receptions of Woolf

1

'What a curse these translators are!' Woolf's Early German Reception

Daniel Göske and Christian Weiß

'I MUST TELL YOU THAT YOU ARE the idol of the Berlin intelligentsia', wrote Vita Sackville-West from the German capital to Virginia Woolf on 29 February 1928. The 'gros [sic] public', however, she added, 'prefer Galsworthy and – Jack London! who they think is our leading author' (Sackville-West and Woolf 1985: 273). Two weeks later Vita approached Virginia with a proposal:

> there's a woman here called Margaret Voigt-Goldsmith, who is a literary agent and who wrote to you some time ago to ask if she could deal with your books to get them translated into German. You referred her to [the London agency] Curtis-Brown, who sent her an answer which on investigation proved to be inaccurate; i.e. said that Fischer [the German publisher of Joseph Conrad and other English modernists] was doing your books here, which it seems he is not. Would there therefore be any chance of Margaret Voigt getting the handling of your books after all? She is extremely nice, and energetic and intelligent; and incidentally a bosom friend of mine. (1985: 277)

Actually, Voigt, an American writer and the wife of a British foreign correspondent in Berlin, was more than a bosom friend. But Vita did not tell Virginia this. In her attempt to promote Voigt, Vita saucily compared herself to her cousin Eddy Sackville-West's untiring support for Harold Nicolson's German translator and friend, Kurt Wagenseil:

> Really it seems a pity that you should not be translated in German, as they all know about you here; so if you can do anything about Margaret Voigt I think you should. There. (Now I am going on like Eddy about Kurt Wagenseil). (1985: 277)

Over the next five years, Wagenseil and his brother Hans – who tried to establish themselves as agents, scouts and freelance translators – wrote many urgent letters to Virginia Woolf and the Hogarth Press requesting among others translation rights.¹ By the autumn of 1927, however, the agency Curtis Brown had begun to take over the marketing of Woolf's works abroad. From then on, independent translators in Germany or France were regularly informed by Leonard Woolf that 'the [Hogarth] Press dealt only with publishers' (Marcus 2002: 333). Such arrangements were 'very much to the disadvantage of translators, who could not secure the work, as they might well have done if allowed to approach a publisher [or, indeed, an author] themselves. The Press files contain numerous letters from disgruntled translators' (2002: 333).

While some modern English authors like D. H. Lawrence or Joseph Conrad showed a deep interest in the translation of their work, Woolf did not. She was aware of the foreign reception of her work, certainly in the case of French translations, but she did not actively engage in the negotiations. She seems to have been 'remarkably indifferent to what her translators did with her texts, and did to her texts, in any language' (Pellan 2002: 54) and gladly resigned the messy business side of foreign rights, contracts and contacts to her agents, as she wrote Vita in March 1928:

> O what a curse these translators are! Tell your Bosom [sic] friend Mrs Voigt Something or other that all I can say is that I have received a cheque from, and signed a contract with, the Insel Verlag which I understand is the Fischer Verlag by which they are to produce Mrs Dalloway this autumn and The Lighthouse later. But all communications must be through Curtis Brown. (*L* 3: 473)

However, as the Hogarth files suggest, many freelance translators like the Wagenseils continued to write to the author herself, attempting to bypass the agency. Leonard Woolf invariably referred these enquiries to Insel Verlag as the owner of the German rights. His wife may have been indifferent about the ticklish business of translating and publishing her work in foreign languages, yet the form and fate of her fiction abroad was significantly shaped by literary agents, publishers, translators and reviewers, those elusive makers and mediators of world literature. As in the case with other modernists, Woolf's early reception in the sizeable book markets of Germany, Austria and Switzerland is a complex and little-known story. Studies on a writer's foreign or, indeed, global responses usually sidetrack the genesis, quality and context of first translations. Some studies, such as Wilhelm Füger's informative investigation into Woolf's early German reception, at least consider reviews and other ephemeral form of journalistic criticism; most, however, focus on academic criticism that, in Woolf's case, followed in the 'wake of the first translations and journalistic criticism' (Nünning and Nünning 2002: 71). Yet the 'inside narrative' of Woolf's first appearance in German, the question of how her work 'was transferred, translated and sometimes transformed' (Göske 2018: 56), is particularly intriguing. In this essay, we aim to complement and contextualise Füger's, Ansgar and Vera Nünning's, and Laura Marcus's findings for the first phase of Woolf's German reception which virtually ended with the tightened restrictions on literary translation in Nazi Germany and Austria in the late 1930s.

It is important to remember that Woolf's modernist fiction, like James Joyce's or William Faulkner's, presented particular challenges to translators. Like most of their readers, translators were simply not used to techniques like structural discontinuities, abrupt shifts in perspective, free indirect speech or stream of consciousness. And while reviewers and critics can be selective in their focus, translators must grapple with each word, phrase and sentence. In Woolf's case, the meticulous musicality and imagistic density of her prose provided peculiar problems, and her early translators – who could of course not yet resort to helpful criticism, annotated editions, computers or digitised texts – also had to keep the complex web of her dense textures in mind. In the first phase of her reception, translators faced an unusually difficult task. The surviving correspondence with their publishers, who of course wanted to produce books that would sell, attests to the enormous difficulties these translators faced.

After *Mrs Dalloway* had appeared in 1925, Woolf's representation of consciousness and her 'lyric experimentalism' (Goldman 2010: 49) immediately attracted great critical attention in Britain and America. 'To record my books [sic] fates slightly bores me', Woolf noted in her diary, yet she was gratified that even Tauchnitz publishers was interested (*D* 3: 25). Indeed, this famous Leipzig firm, which had specialised in paper-covered English editions for the global market outside of the British Empire and the United States since 1841, brought out both *Mrs Dalloway* and *Orlando* in 1929. By that time, a German-language edition of these novels, published by Insel Verlag in Leipzig, was well under way so that complete German translations of *Mrs Dalloway* (1928) and *Orlando* (1929) preceded not only the French versions but also all other foreign-language versions prior to Woolf's death in 1941.[2] In initiating German-speaking audiences to Woolf's brand of modernist fiction, Insel (and, later, the famous house of Samuel Fischer) played a major role.

Insel Verlag's papers, now held by the Goethe- und Schiller-Archiv in Weimar, do not tell the whole story. But they complement the scant data in Woolf's letters and the Hogarth files by providing fascinating insights into the correspondence between the author, her German publishers and their translators. Archives are indispensable if we want to get a 'greater sense of the comparative and contingent nature of literary production, as well as the wider networks of the marketplace to which author and publisher respond' (Wilson 2014: 85). For Woolf, we are now able to combine several methods that should, ideally, always go hand in hand: the history of the book approach, the study of an author's critical reception and, first and foremost, translation studies. Moreover, we want to suggest here that a serious translation ought to be read as a form of creative interpretation and, indeed, as implicit critique – possibly collaborative, since the publisher's editorial department sometimes has a hand in the final text. Sometimes, as in the case of Woolf's German mediators, we are in the happy position to be able to sketch the publisher's preferences and other contingencies that the translators had to face.

Insel Verlag, founded in 1899 and after 1905 run by Anton Kippenberg (1874–1950) and his wife Katharina (1876–1947), was well known for its handsome editions of Johann Wolfgang von Goethe, Friedrich Schiller, Heinrich Heine or Charles Dickens as well as contemporary writers like Rainer Maria Rilke or Hugo von Hofmannsthal.[3] After the First World War, the Kippenbergs were eager to branch out into recent French literature (e.g. by Paul Valéry, François Mauriac and André Maurois) and, later, into English fiction. In the 1920s they began to publish books by, among others, Sherwood Anderson, D. H. Lawrence, Aldous Huxley and Woolf. The archive suggests that it was Katharina Kippenberg's interest that sparked and shaped the first translations of *Mrs Dalloway* (1928), *Orlando* (1929) and *To the Lighthouse* (1931). Apparently, Woolf's contact with Insel was facilitated by her English friends abroad. Late in 1927, Harold Nicolson, then serving at the British Embassy in Berlin, had been approached for a spare copy of *To the Lighthouse*, and he had asked Woolf to help out. While she did not like the Germans, their interest in her work was not to be despised. On 19 February 1928, she wrote him that she had 'at last found a copy of the Lighthouse and sent it to the Embassy in case', as she put it, 'your Editor still wants it', adding: 'The Germans are apt to be very effusive and very ineffective about translating and writing, but I think Mrs Dalloway will soon appear in German, and any notice is likely to be to my good' (*L* 3: 460).

'Joycean style': *Eine Frau von fünfzig Jahren* – *Mrs Dalloway*

In January 1928, the Kippenbergs had already commissioned the Hamburg translator Theresia Mutzenbecher (1888–1979) to tackle *Mrs Dalloway*. Mutzenbecher had read law at Grenoble and Cambridge in 1912–13 and finished her legal training in 1914 in Hamburg. After her husband's death in 1919 and in the chaotic postwar years, however, she had to fend for herself and her three children by teaching French and translating French and English books. Among them was her German version of Lawrence's *Women in Love* for Insel (1927), though Lawrence later complained that she had given his novel 'a sort of Proustian tone, utterly unreal' (qtd in Göske 2018: 59).

Mrs Dalloway was, of course, a different kind of challenge. Mutzenbecher took her task seriously, but like most little-known translators, she worked under a great deal of pressure. Only six weeks after she had started in early March 1928, Insel pressed her for the manuscript since it was to be published in September. No wonder the translator admitted that she had great trouble in rendering Woolf's 'Joycean style' in readable German (25 April 1928, GSA 50 / 2468).[4] She finally handed in her much-revised manuscript in August. When the Kippenbergs were dismayed because her last-minute revisions had caused extraordinary expenses at the printers, Mutzenbecher confessed that transforming 'this very special style into real German' had been extremely difficult (25 September 1928, GSA 50 / 2468).[5] Indeed, Woolf's use of free indirect speech and the 'continual shifts from an omniscient perspective to one tied to a particular character, shifts that often take us from "actual time" to "mind time"' (Dick 2000: 53), must have posed problems for any translator who was both unfamiliar with what we now call the high modernist style and duty-bound to produce a text that would not alienate German readers. It is no wonder that Woolf's lyrical prose, her metaphorically dense texture, feels more laboured in Mutzenbecher's version. However, this is not so much owing to the translator's lack of time and talent, or her attempts to fill in some details, but to the structures of the German language: its polysyllabic morphology, penchant for compounds and complex, highly subordinated syntax. To cite just one example: Woolf's early evocation of London's hustle and bustle as Big Ben strikes the hour. Mutzenbecher explicates, for her German readers, Big Ben as 'die große Glocke auf dem Turm des Parlaments' (the big bell on the tower of Parliament) and Woolf's mysterious synaesthesia of the 'leaden circles' which dissolve in the air, as 'Die bleischweren Wellenringe' (rings of waves, heavy as lead) (Woolf 1928: 6–7). Clarissa's sprightly musings in idiosyncratic, often colloquial, English are almost impossible to recreate if one pays more attention, as Mutzenbecher usually does, to the semantic content rather than to the brisk, expressive rhythm of Woolf's prose:

> For Heaven only knows why one loves it so, how one sees it so, making it up, building it round one, tumbling it, creating it every moment afresh; but the veriest frumps, the most dejected of miseries sitting on doorsteps (drink their downfall) do the same; can't be dealt with, she felt positive, by Acts of Parliament for that very reason: they love life. (*MD*: 4)

In Mutzenbecher's German, Clarissa's 'frumps' morph into 'die kümmerlichsten alten Schachteln, die kläglichsten Jammergestalten, die da auf den Treppenstufen sitzen und sich an der eigenen Gottesverlassenheit laben' – literally, 'sorry old bags who bask in their own godforsakenness' (Woolf 1928: 7).⁶ This is a curious deviation from Woolf's oblique reference to the public consumption of alcohol in the streets when Britain's adoption of Prohibition was discussed.

If one considers the circumstances, Mutzenbecher's text, if sometimes a little uninspired, can be seen as a reasonably competent rendering of Woolf's radically 'Joycean style'. Printed in traditional gothic type, the handsome volume was published in September 1928. Curiously, the book appeared under the main title *Eine Frau von fünfzig Jahren* [A Lady of Fifty Years], though not without the author's consent. In July 1928, Katharina Kippenberg had explained to Woolf that the original title was 'not advantageous to the German public who will find it difficult to pronounce and remember'; however, if one kept 'Mrs Dalloway' as a subtitle, any possible error would be 'evaded', and German readers would catch the allusion in the main title to Goethe's

> celebrated novel *Der Mann von fünfzig Jahren* [(*The Man of Fifty*)]. So your work will be with respect to the title a sort of conterpart [sic] of it and we hope will be in this way best introduced to the German public. (Insel Papers, 24 July 1928, GSA 50 / 3822)

Goethe's novella, part of his late 1829 novel *Wilhelm Meisters Wanderjahre* (*Wilhelm Meister's Years of Travel*), is about an elderly major's renunciation of his young niece in favour of a mature widow and, hence, a far cry from *Mrs Dalloway*. Yet Woolf, probably unfamiliar with Goethe's work, graciously replied from Monk's House: 'I am quite ready to agree to this and hope that you will find the edition successful' (Insel Papers, 3 August 1928, GSA 50 / 3822). Simultaneous with the book's publication, the publisher's magazine *Inselschiff* introduced Woolf as 'the most famous female writer in contemporary England' ('die berühmteste englische Dichterin unserer Zeit') and praised her novel in glowing terms: 'We see Mrs Dalloway's whole life in the form of impressions, memories, meditations in the burning mirror of the beautiful Now' ('Mitteilungen des Verlags' 1928: 325).⁷ Insel Verlag sent Woolf three copies and announced a visit by Dr Kurt Fiedler, a staff member, in London, to discuss further matters. The meeting must have taken place late in October because Fiedler, on his return to Leipzig, asked Woolf to 'send me some details on your life and on your career' she had promised for marketing 'MRS DALLOWY' [sic] (Insel Papers, 3 November 1928, GSA 50 / 3822).

Katharina Kippenberg acknowledged Woolf's reply of 20 November 1928 (Woolf's letter seems to be lost). She enclosed her essay on Woolf for the *Frankfurter Zeitung* and announced another, to appear in *Inselschiff*, to prepare for new translations. 'Which should you propose to be published first?', she asked. Personally, Kippenberg was 'very fond' of *Orlando* but had not quite finished *To the Lighthouse* yet. She hoped Insel could take both and tried to enlist her beloved author in other matters: 'I should be very much obliged to you if you would be so very kind, to let me have, if you have any spare time, some notes on an English author, whom you consider worth our while' (Insel Papers, 30 November 1928, GSA 50 / 3822). No reply by Woolf has come to light so far. But in December 1928 Insel told Brown that they wanted to acquire the option for *Orlando* and the copyright for *To the Lighthouse* for £60, and on 23 January 1929 they reported that 1,380 copies of the German *Mrs Dalloway* had been sold, for which the agent received 10 per cent of the retail price (23 January 1929,

GSA 50 / 34,1). Apparently, the immediate critical response to the book was meagre. Füger mentions only a review in the Basel *National-Zeitung* of 16 December 1928. It appeared in the Christmas supplement under the heading 'Women's Literature', and the critic questioned whether *Mrs Dalloway*, a 'wise' but not an 'easy' book, was actually a novel, since 'the plot was thin and dominated by soliloquies and aphorisms' (in Füger 1980: 36).[8]

Early in 1929, however, Woolf's fame began to spread, with a little help from her friends and admirers abroad. Translations of André Maurois's authoritative preface for the French version of *Mrs Dalloway* (1929) and Harold Nicolson's essay on 'The Young Generation in England' appeared in various Swiss and German papers in March; and in the *Weltbühne* [World Stage], the radical and influential Berlin weekly, the British writer and musicologist Eric Walter White much preferred the 'cinematic' technique of Woolf's slender city novel to the 'prolonged massiveness' ('Langwierigkeit') of Joyce's *Ulysses* (1929: 19).[9] German reviewers followed suit. In the *Deutsche Allgemeine Zeitung* (Berlin), Kaethe Miethe called Woolf 'in all seriousness a poet' and *Mrs Dalloway* 'one of those rare books which teach you how to read. Slowly, drop by drop, does the world it builds sink in'; and Thomas Mann's son Klaus later praised the book as a new type of novel, 'composed with an exactness that is masterly. It is nothing but a fugue, a fugue of interlocking fates, feelings, tones' (qtd in Füger 1980: 39, 49).[10]

'Excellent wit': *Orlando*

Meanwhile, Insel Verlag kept Woolf informed about the progress of their edition. The publication of *Orlando* was scheduled for September 1929, and Insel had commissioned Karl Lerbs (1893–1946), a 'translator of high reputation, who no doubt will render this book into a corresponding level of German language' (Insel Papers, 12 March 1929, GSA 50 / 3822). Lerbs, the son of a well-known merchant in Bremen, had trained as a bookseller and, after the First World War, become a recognised editor and a prolific author of short stories, anecdotes, comedies and screenplays. He had translated several French and English books for Insel when he took on *Orlando* early in 1929. The files at Weimar contain an extensive correspondence between the translator from Bremen, his publishers in Leipzig, and Woolf in London. They show that the Kippenbergs, hit hard by galloping inflation and the resulting lack of demand, were sceptical about the success of *Orlando*, especially for its stylistically intricate and seemingly plotless form of modernist storytelling. Still, they had offered the book to Lerbs since, as Anton Kippenberg told Lerbs, 'we have to bring it out in order not to lose Virginia Woolf in the future' (29 February 1929, GSA 50 / 2159, 2).[11]

Lerbs was enthusiastic: it was a longish book, but he wanted to make a full translation before considering possible abridgements. Even before he had finished reading *Orlando*, he called it 'doubtless an original novel, told with excellent wit and considerable profundity' (Insel Papers, 25 February 1929, GSA 50 / 2159, 2).[12] Moreover, he planned to 'transpose' Woolf's 'syntax and rhythms' very carefully, and that would take time (27 June 1929, GSA 50 / 2159, 2).[13] In the following months Lerbs stubbornly resisted the cuts that Katharina Kippenberg suggested, particularly with regard to passages near the end of the book (5 June 1929). Significant cuts were quite impossible, Lerbs argued: 'The book is infinitely complex and closely knit, and its charm rests so much on the very idiosyncrasy of its style that larger cuts would utterly destroy its texture' (10 July 1929, GSA 50 / 2159, 2). In the same letter, he detailed (with a clever hint to the Nobel Prize winner of 1929) that omitting extended passages would amount to 'the vain attempt to make cuts in the *Magic Mountain*. This would transform it into a suspense novel but it would no longer be by Thomas Mann'. Woolf's *Orlando*, he emphasised, was 'an infinitely delicate book; every sentence requires a degree of shaping and moulding that I have never yet come across' (10 July 1929, GSA 50 / 2159, 2).[14] Lerbs managed to convince Kippenberg, even though he admitted later that the 'composition' of the book's second part was 'a total failure', especially with all those 'philosophical speculations' towards the end which had given him so much trouble (21 November 1929, GSA 50 / 2159, 2).[15] His insistence on the integrity of the text is a rarely documented case of a commissioned translator risking a rift with his employer in the interest of the translated work.[16]

Lerbs irritated Kippenberg also for other reasons. His careful and rather inventive translation, which had to be sent to the publisher in several instalments to allow the printer to quickly produce the galley proofs, was not completed in time. This may explain why Lerbs did not write the short afterword Kippenberg had requested in order to make the book more accessible (Insel Papers, 17 July 1929, GSA 50 / 2159, 2).[17] Moreover, the translation, now printed in roman type, appeared without Woolf's paratexts (the dedication, preface and index), which complete her parody of the biography genre. Indeed, the German subtitle, *Die Geschichte eines Lebens* [The Story of a Life], seemed to place the book rather in the realm of pure fiction.

There is no space here to do justice to Lerbs's work. Yet it seems fair to say that his version of *Orlando* reads rather well if, occasionally, a bit more ponderously than Woolf's trippingly witty prose, and he seems to have sometimes felt the urge to check her authorial narrator's cheeky playfulness. Occasionally, however, he responded imaginatively to Woolf's blithe briskness in unusual ways. This can even be observed in the 'philosophical speculations' on time and identity in the final chapter. Lerbs stretched German usage as he followed the narrator's speculations about Orlando 'changing her selves as quickly as she drove' ('sie wechselte . . . die Selbste so schnell, wie sie fuhr'), moving from 'the conscious self' ('das bewußte Selbst') to 'nothing but one self' ('Es Selbst'), the 'true self' ('das wahre Selbst'), the 'Captain self' ('Führerselbst') and the 'Key self' ('Schlüsselselbst') (O: 179; Woolf 1929: 318). It is hardly a wonder that Lerbs omitted Woolf's self-reflexive aside to the 'Hogarth Press' (O: 155); he merely mentions an anonymous 'Verleger' (publisher) (Woolf 1929: 273). But when Sir Nicholas asks about 'royalties' and Orlando's premodern mind 'flew to Buckingham Palace and some dusky potentates' (O: 163), Lerbs compensated for the untranslatable pun (royalties) by inventing an aside that can also be read as the tormented translator's sly dig at his penurious publisher: '"Was ist das: Honorar?" fragte Orlando. Sie dachte an etwas ungemein Hohes und Ehrenvolles' (Woolf 1929: 288). A literal back translation would be: 'What is this: royalties? asked Orlando. She thought of something extraordinarily noble and honourable.' Since Lerbs omitted Woolf's funny reference to the Royal Family's guests at Buckingham Palace, Orlando's complaint becomes more generally applicable.

Contrary to Insel's plans, the German *Orlando* appeared only in early December 1929, owing to Lerbs's inspired tinkering with the text and due to delays in the production process. This was too late for the Christmas sales and a 'death sentence', as

Anton Kippenberg angrily told the translator: 'I have made nothing but sacrifices for the translations from the English, and my interest in continuing in that field has dwindled to nothing' (Insel Papers, 18 November 1929, GSA 50 / 2159, 2).[18] The reviews came too late for the important Christmas season, but they were mostly positive. In the influential review *Die literarische Welt* [The Literary World] of 1 February 1930, Dora Sophie Kellner (1890–1964), a feminist author and critic, who was then still married to Walter Benjamin, admired the book as a satirical response to the 'horribly hackneyed and trivialized inquiry into the "essence" of woman'.[19] The *Deutsche Allgemeine Zeitung* of 23 April 1930 printed an enthusiastic praise of Woolf's 'masterly' handling of Orlando's gender switch and repeated Miethe's characterisation of the book as delightful literary slow food (qtd in Füger 1980: 43);[20] in early May, the liberal *Frankfurter Zeitung* emphasised its 'closely knit texture' and Woolf's art of deriving 'psychological meaning' from the tiniest luminous detail (qtd in Füger 1980: 43–4).[21] And in the venerable *Vossische Zeitung* (Berlin) of 15 June, the young Alfred Kantorowicz (1899–1979) admired Woolf's 'cleverness' in creating an enormously 'sensuous' evocation of cultural history, although her 'juggling with symbols', in this book, was of a 'bold yet tiring artificiality' (qtd in Füger 1980: 44).[22] This verdict was echoed later in 1930 in *Der Gral*, a Munich Catholic monthly devoted to the arts; yet the critic also praised Woolf's 'sparkling wit', 'poetic style' and 'metaphysical profundity' (qtd in Füger 1980: 44–5).[23] The Kippenbergs must have sent more reviews and other publication material to Tavistock Square, and Woolf may well have responded. Unfortunately, we have not found a single trace of this in the Insel archive, which was partly destroyed in the fire-bombing of Leipzig in 1944. At any rate, the German publisher continued their campaign on behalf of the English modernist.

'Infinitely ticklish': *Die Fahrt zum Leuchtturm*

Despite Curtis Brown's warning to deal only with them, Anton Kippenberg travelled to London to meet Woolf, as his letter of 21 May 1931 suggests. He announced the publication of the German *To the Lighthouse* and added that he was 'happy and proud' to be her publisher (Insel Papers, 21 May 1931, GSA 50 / 2159, 2).[24] Yet the translation did not turn out a success, even though its quality seems much better than Maurice Lanoire's abridged, 'clumsy, often grossly inaccurate and generally careless' French version of 1929 (Pellan 2002: 55). Like Mutzenbecher's *Mrs Dalloway* and Lerbs's *Orlando*, *Die Fahrt zum Leuchtturm* [lit. The Trip to the Lighthouse] was republished in the 1970s and 1980s when readers in the post-Stalinist German Democratic Republic were finally introduced to Woolf's work.[25]

At first sight, Lerbs had been very sceptical about *To the Lighthouse*. He found the first part, as he told Anton Kippenberg, 'endlessly droll', even 'strangely turbid and lifeless owing to its many repetitions' (Insel Papers, 4 January 1931, GSA 50 / 2159, 2). Though he conceded that a 'sophisticated' writer like Woolf was able to create 'individual effects of great power', he found her 'narrative method' wrongheaded and felt that this novel lacked the 'clarity of composition' of *Orlando* (4 January 1931, GSA 50 / 2159, 2).[26] Two days later, Katharina Kippenberg intervened. She much preferred *To the Lighthouse* to *Orlando*, which was, she maintained, accessible only to readers who were familiar with the situation in England and could appreciate the allusions to Sackville-West, the 'heroine of the novel' (6 January 1931, GSA 50 / 2159, 2).

Kippenberg described *To the Lighthouse* as utterly 'charming' and Woolf's best book, like a 'reflection in the waves' or a 'diaphanous cloud which contracts and evaporates in a series of fleeting moments'; she hoped that the translator would use a 'light and, as it were, airy touch' (6 January 1931, GSA 50 / 2159, 2).[27] Lerbs relented and, having progressed further, had to admit that the novel 'becomes better and more closely knit' (25 January 1931, GSA 50 / 2159, 2).[28] Three weeks later, having finished translating two-thirds of the book, he begged for Kippenberg's opinion, as he had 'polished the text very carefully', trying to render 'all the idiosyncrasies of the original' as best he could (16 February 1931, GSA 50 / 2159, 2).[29] Kippenberg, however, wanted to have the text set up first and then read the galley proofs. Lerbs plodded on and sent weekly instalments of his translation to Leipzig. He completed it by early April 1931 and confessed that tackling Woolf's English, 'richer in shadings than any I know', had been 'infinitely ticklish', asking Kippenberg again: 'How does my text read?' (5 March 1931, GSA 50 / 2159, 2).[30]

When the book appeared in mid-May 1931, Lerbs was pleased. He had taken the job of 'transposing' Woolf's prose very seriously, even rendering Mrs Ramsay's reading of Grimm's fairy tale of 'The fisherman and his wife' and the flounder's verse in the original Low German dialect (Woolf 1931: 80). He also paid attention to the texture of the whole novel: important leitmotifs and intertextual references reappear in surprisingly consistent fashion. Some deviations from the English edition, however, can be seen as attempts to soften the bewildering aspects of its 'highly stylized and playful formal patterns' (Goldman 2015: 30). On the publisher's request, Lerbs had omitted the unusual numbering of Woolf's sometimes tiny subsections. This made the book look more traditional, to be sure, but must have made it more difficult for German readers to perceive, and piece together, the different strands of the novel. The translator's stylistic changes tied in with the publisher's typographical preferences. A clear case of translational transposition is Lerbs's tendency to tone down Woolf's use of free indirect discourse or, more precisely, 'narrated monologue'.[31] One can see this in the passage at the beginning of the third part ('The Lighthouse') where the painter Lily Briscoe sits at the breakfast table and looks out at the distraught widower Mr Ramsay, trying to 'put together', in her mind, an earlier revelatory moment:

> ('Alone' she heard him say, 'Perished' she heard him say) and like everything else this strange morning the words became symbols, wrote themselves all over the grey-green walls. If only she could put them together, she felt, write them out in some sentence, then she would have got at the truth of things. (*TL*: 122)

Lerbs avoids Woolf's metaphor of words writing 'themselves' on the walls but uses the suggestive 'Sinnbilder' instead of 'Symbole' (both mean symbol) to indicate the transformation of aural to visual memory that is so characteristic of Lily. Moreover, he changes Woolf's narrated monologue (past tense, third-person) into the more conventional mode of first-person narration in the present tense:

> ('Allein', hörte sie ihn sagen; 'Unwiederbringlich', hörte sie ihn sagen); und die Worte wurden, wie alles Andere an diesem seltsamen Morgen, zu Sinnbildern, und sie sah sie überall auf den graugrünen Wänden erscheinen. Könnte ich sie nur zusammenfügen, dachte sie, könnte ich sie nur zu einem Satz ergänzen – dann dränge ich zum wahren Wesen der Dinge vor. (Woolf 1931: 205)

In Woolf's text, Lily's memory is suddenly triggered by a tablecloth that 'she had looked at in a moment of revelation', and now she is able to paint 'that picture' which she had left unfinished 'all these years': 'Where were her paints, she wondered? Her paints, yes. She had left them in the hall last night. She would start at once' (*TL*: 122). In Lerbs's version, she resolutely tells herself, in direct speech, to immediately get to work: 'Wo hab ich meine Malgeräte gelassen? dachte sie. Ja, die Malgeräte. Richtig, in die Halle hab ich sie gestern abend gelegt. Ich will sofort anfangen' (back translation: 'Where did I leave my painting tools? she thought. Yes, the painting tools. Right, I put them in the hall last night. I will start at once'). Moreover, Lily's past 'moment of revelation' becomes one of illumination ('Erleuchtung') (Woolf 1931: 206). The final sentences of the novel, that 'last subtle tremble among perspectives' (Levenson 2015: 28), deviate from Woolf's original but with a haunting effect:

> She looked at the steps; they were empty; she looked at her canvas; it was blurred. With a sudden intensity, as if she saw it clear for a second, she drew a line there, in the centre. It was done; it was finished. Yes, she thought, laying down her brush in extreme fatigue, I have had my vision. (*TL*: 170)

> Sie sah die Stufen an: sie waren leer; sie sah die Leinwand an: sie war ein Gewirr. Mit einer jähen und starken Anspannung, als sähe sie für eine Sekunde klar, zog sie eine Linie – da, mitten im Bild. Es war vollbracht; es war beendet. Ja, dachte sie und legte in unsagbarer Müdigkeit den Pinsel aus der Hand: ich habe meine Offenbarung gehabt. (Woolf 1931: 290)[32]

Lerbs achieves this final result employing vaguely biblical diction ('vollbracht' for 'finished', as in Martin Luther's classical translation of John 19: 30, 'Offenbarung' for 'vision') and expressive punctuation, down to the climactic dash that mirrors the enigmatic line in Lily's picture.

Clearly, Lerbs's translation of *To the Lighthouse* meant a lot to him. Repeatedly he asked for the publisher's opinion on his translation and on its fate: did the book sell, were there any reviews? But in the autumn of 1931 it became clear that the sales of *Die Fahrt zum Leuchtturm* were, as Anton Kippenberg complained, 'bad beyond measure' – yet he had not expected anything else (Insel Papers, 28 September 1931, GSA 50 / 2159, 2).[33] The reviews were few, superficial, puzzled and not very encouraging, yet slowly Woolf was referenced as a major voice among Britain's younger novelists (Füger 1980: 51–5). One example of praise comes from a 1932 essay on Woolf and Vita Sackville-West, those 'extravagant Englishwomen', by the young critic Peter Suhrkamp who had just joined S. Fischer Verlag. In 1936, he bought the Berlin part of the publishing house and ran it until he was arrested for high treason by the Gestapo in 1944; after the war he became West Germany's most important publisher. In his essay, Suhrkamp praised the 'new literary method' of *Mrs Dalloway* as more accessible than Joyce's *Ulysses*, but he still preferred Sackville-West's 'witty and ironic gossip' in *The Edwardians* to Woolf's literary impressionism in *To the Lighthouse* (qtd in Göske 2018: 70). Suhrkamp's preference for a less extravagantly inventive form of fiction and his interest in England's aristocracy seems to have reflected the taste of most German readers, not only in the 1930s.

A 'piece of cultural history': *Flush*

The fourth and last of Woolf's books to appear in prewar Germany was the light-hearted *Flush*, 'an attempt to write the life of a dog, Mrs Browning's spaniel Flush', as the blurb on the cover of the English edition had it. The novel was much sought after, judging by the number of individual requests by translators and agents who saw it as an 'attractively translatable text, linguistically and culturally' (Marcus 2002: 333). A story about a dog is always a safe bet, in England as in Germany, where a renowned author like Thomas Mann had had a huge success with his immensely popular *Herr und Hund* (*A Man and His Dog*) of 1919. Moreover, as one of Woolf's least challenging books, *Flush* was especially attractive to publishers, not least because of the relative failure of her earlier translations. This is the gist, at any rate, of a letter to Woolf, written in March 1936 by Herberth Egon Herlitschka (1893–1970), the Austrian translator of *Flush*.

Working from the mid-1920s to the late 1960s, Herlitschka, who had studied in England as a young man, became one of the most prolific translators of major modern authors like William Faulkner, Aldous Huxley, D. H. Lawrence, Thornton Wilder, Woolf and W. B. Yeats. In this period of an increasing internationalisation of national book markets he also took on the role of literary agent and served as reader for various publishers. After the war, he and his wife Marlys 'monopolized the early West German Woolf market' (Wicht 2002: 108) until the late 1970s, when most of Woolf's novels were translated anew for S. Fischer. In the 1930s, however, Herlitschka was still trying to establish himself as a mediator of modern English fiction. On 10 March 1936 he informed Woolf that both the publishing sequence of her books and the quality of the early translations had done her a disservice:

> MRS DALLOWAY came out in a translation which is an abomination. I will not speak of your style being missed – the translation has no style whatever – but nobody could guess from that translation what you really wrote and what it is all about. One needs only to look at the first few pages, particularly beautiful in the original, in order to understand why German readers were frightened off and never asked for a book of yours again. (Correspondence regarding Virginia Woolf translation rights, 10 March 1936, MS 2750/C)

Even if the translation of *Orlando* was better, he added, readers who were introduced to Woolf's oeuvre via *Orlando* were bound to be confused, and after the subsequent disappointment with *To the Lighthouse*, Insel 'lost courage', so Woolf had 'as yet no public over here' (Correspondence regarding Virginia Woolf translation rights, 10 March 1936, MS 2750/C).[34] Herlitschka's letter was, obviously, a sales pitch. Moreover, the denigration of Lerbs's translations as an attempt to curry favour with the author is not unprecedented in Herlitschka's mode of conduct. 'His [Lerbs's] translations', he explained to Woolf, 'are very dry and the flavor is gone. Quite clearly your work does not suit him or rather, the other way round' (Correspondence regarding Virginia Woolf translation rights, 10 March 1936, MS 2750/C). Finally, Herlitschka asked Woolf to arrange with Curtis Brown that he acquire the German rights for *The Years* and any future books. He also wanted her to grant him exclusive translations rights. Herlitschka had approached Lawrence in the same manner, blaming his German publisher, Insel, for their poor selection of 'incompetent translators' and asking Lawrence, and later his widow Frieda, for a word of support with the agency Curtis Brown (qtd in Hayman 2012: 387). Herlitschka's correspondence with his new publisher S. Fischer has apparently not survived, and his translation of *Flush* was less difficult than those by Mutzenbecher and Lerbs. Yet a comparison of the English and German versions is instructive. As in *Orlando*, the English subtitle, 'A Biography', was supplanted by the more general *Die Geschichte eines Berühmten Hundes* [The Story of a Famous Dog], although Fischer did reproduce the paratextual sections on authorities and notes which stress the book's ironic treatment of the biography genre. In contrast to the English blurb, the text on the German cover promoted the book as a 'piece of cultural history' of the 1840s and 1850s.

Flush is stylistically less innovative than Woolf's previous books. Since it is 'all about the sense of smell not sight', it is, of all her works, the 'most remote from the impact of modern visual technology' (Humm 2010: 224). Woolf sometimes belittled the book as a 'freak' (qtd in Marcus 2004: 142), yet the vivid descriptions, subtle ironies and brisk rhythms of her prose are very effective and not easy to render in German. Herlitschka allowed himself some leeway, not least with Woolf's syntax. When Woolf opted for parataxis with full stops instead of semicolons, dashes and commas, he sometimes did the opposite, as in the scene when Flush breaks free and rushes through Regent's Park (*F*: 64 and Woolf 1934: 74).[35] Like many other translators, Herlitschka also liked to expatiate: simple 'basements' (*F*: 30) became manorial kitchens located in the lower level ('im Tiefgeschoß liegende Herrschaftsküchen'; Woolf 1934: 36). Referring to familiar stereotypes, he called England formal and stiff ('das . . . förmlich-steife England'; Woolf 1934: 123) where Woolf had used the more neutral 'conventional' (*F*: 108). One of the most striking deviations from the original, however, occurs at the end of the book, when Flush, about to die, approaches Barrett Browning, who remembers her poem 'Flush or Faunus'. In the English version, the sonnet reads like a eulogy to the dying dog. Strangely, Herlitschka cut the poem altogether and altered the narrative report to cover the traces. Omission can be a useful strategy for translators under pressure. When Herlitschka translated Lawrence's *The White Peacock* in 1936, he omitted 'a considerable number of the allusions to literature, art, and music', with the result that the German reader 'is unable to follow certain more subtle theme and character developments' (Jansohn 2005: 39). In *Flush*, the final omission is rather serious as the 'blurring of boundaries between animal and human' (Marcus 2004: 145) gets lost in the translation.

The German *Flush* received few critical notices (Füger 1980: 57) but, judging by sales figures and later reprints, must have found favour with many readers. Nevertheless, Fischer Verlag's plans to continue its edition of Woolf's works came to a halt. Suhrkamp, the new owner of the Berlin branch, had been anxious to take *The Years* but his letter of 9 August 1937, which has survived in the Hogarth files, darkly hints at the complicated situation and the mentality of the general public in the Reich. Economic reasons must also have played a role as German publishers suffered from increasing restrictions to pay for foreign rights (Marcus 2002: 334). The situation in Nazi Germany, at any rate, worsened, especially for writers, translators and publishers of Jewish origin.[36] With the annexation of Austria by Nazi Germany in 1938, the Herlitschkas, too, were forced to leave their native Vienna. They fled to England where they remained for the next ten years before returning to Switzerland.

The venerable publishing house S. Fischer had split up in 1936, Bermann Fischer first emigrating to Vienna and later to Stockholm and New York, where he continued to publish works by banned authors like Thomas Mann or Hermann Hesse. Soon the war broke out and in 1942, Woolf, like many other foreign writers, was officially banned as an 'enemy author' (Füger 1980: 17). The second phase of Woolf's German reception can be said to have begun in 1946 with the exiled Erich Auerbach's chapter on *To the Lighthouse* in *Mimesis* and, in the 1950s, with the new translations by the Herlitschkas. The emergence of a 'very profitable and prolific Woolf industry' in German (Nünning and Nünning 2002: 68) is, however, another intriguing chapter in her global reception.

Notes

1. On 21 January 1928, Woolf had told Clive Bell that 'Wagenseil has been pestering us for some time – asking for my books and offering his own and never paying – so I haven't much hopes. Mrs Dalloway is coming out in Germany soon – so is the Lighthouse, I think' (*L* 3: 448). On 29 December 1928 she wrote to Vita that she wanted to avoid another meeting: 'Charming, virtuous, accomplished as Wagenseil is, it is to avoid Wagenseil that we come to Berlin' (*L* 3: 569).
2. See B. J. Kirkpatrick (1997) and Peter Barnaby (2002).
3. For more, see Heinz Sarkowski (1999). Hereafter we will quote or translate from letters and other material from the Insel Papers in the Goethe- und Schiller-Archiv (GSA), Klassik Stiftung Weimar, by title, date and file number.
4. 'Diesen Joyce'schen Stil auf Deutsch wiederzugeben, ist wirklich nicht leicht.'
5. 'Es war so überaus schwer, diesen ganz besonderen Stil so zu übertragen, dass wirkliches Deutsch daraus wurde, dass ich trotz gründlichster Durcharbeitung des Manuskripts, – ich habe es zweimal angefertigt und durchgefeilt, – erst im fertigen Satzspiegel eine klare Uebersicht gewinnen konnte.'
6. For more details, see Göske (2018: 60–2). Since all the early translators used the first Hogarth Press editions, we have checked the quotations against the *Cambridge Edition of the Works of Virginia Woolf* or early imprints of the Hogarth edition.
7. 'Wir lernen ihr ganzes Leben als Wirkung, Erinnerung, Meditation, im Brennspiegel des schönen Jetzt kennen.'
8. 'Die Handlung ist spärlich, monologische Aphorismen herrschen vor.'
9. '"Mrs Dalloway" wächst von Seite zu Seite, wie ein Gedicht, wie eine Pflanze. Und die Technik dieser Erzählkunst steht sichtlich unter dem Einfluß des Kinos.'
10. 'Diese Erzählung gehört zu den wenigen Büchern, an denen man eigentlich wieder das Lesen erlernt. Langsam, tropfenhaft sinkt die Welt, die es aufbaut, in einen hinein' (Miethe qtd in Füger 1980: 39). 'In Wahrheit aber ist er mit einer Exaktheit komponiert, die Meisterschaft ist. Er ist nichts anderes als Fuge; Fuge ineinandergreifender Schicksale, Stimmungen, Töne' (K. Mann qtd in Füger 1980: 49).
11. 'Allzu warm urteilen Sie ja über den "Orlando" nicht, aber ich muss ihn doch wohl bringen, um Virginia Woolf für die Zukunft nicht zu verlieren. Als welche Zukunft freilich im Dunkeln liegt [sic].'
12. 'Zweifellos ein origineller, mit ausgezeichnetem Witz und erheblicher Tiefe erzaehlter und gestalteter Roman. Und eine lockende Aufgabe fuer den Uebersetzer. Laengen sind ohne Zweifel vorhanden; ich glaube aber, ueber die Kuerzungen wird man sich erst schluessig werden koennen, wenn man in der Uebertragung steckt. Vielleicht entschliesse ich mich sogar, sie auch dann noch nicht vorzunehmen, sondern mich mit Ihnen nach Ablieferung des Manuskriptes zu verstaendigen.'

13. 'Ich möchte nämlich Satzbau und Rhythmus des Buches wirklich transponieren, und das ist bei Virginias eigenwilligem Stil keine leicht Aufgabe.'
14. 'Das Buch ist so unendlich dicht, und sein Reiz besteht in so hohem Masse in der Eigenwilligkeit des Stils, dass man durch groessere Weglassungen sein Gefuege zerstören würde. Mir kaeme das vor, als wollte man anfangen, den "Zauberberg" zusammenzustreichen. Es wird dann ein spannender Roman daraus, aber er ist nicht mehr von Thomas Mann.... Es ist ein unendlich heikles Buch; jeder Satz erfordert eine Modellierarbeit, die mir bisher noch niemals vorgekommen ist.'
15. 'Nun hakte ich mich zwar in den philosophischen Spekulationen, in die das Buch sich (leider) am Schluss gaenzlich verliert, fest.... Beim "Orlando" wuerde ich mich ueber einen negativen Ausgang, den Sie ja uebrigens selbst schon frueher weissagten, nicht wundern, da ich das Buch in seinem zweiten Teil bei allen Reizen des Einfalls fuer kompositorisch voellig misslungen halte.' This letter was addressed to Anton Kippenberg, who had complained of bad sales.
16. There are, of course, many causes for omissions, for example, a translator's or publisher's preferences or external factors like the constraints of magazine publication. Rather than speculate about them, it is important to gauge the effect of these abridgements. When Borges rendered *Orlando* into Spanish in 1937, for instance, he (or his publisher) deleted numerous passages where Woolf held her writing 'on an unstable gender balance' (Gorla 2012: 94).
17. The Kippenbergs had also asked Mutzenbecher and Herlitschka to provide brief texts for blurbs, advertisements or other promotional material.
18. 'Ich habe nichts als Opfer für die Uebertragungen aus dem Englischen gebracht, und die Lust, auf diesem Gebiete weiterzuarbeiten, ist mir vollkommen vergangen.'
19. Woolf's novel, Kellner wrote, was a brilliant answer to the 'entsetzlich abgeklapperten und banalisierten Frage nach dem "Wesen" der Frau' (Kellner 1930: 5).
20. Orlando's transformation was 'nicht nur ein meisterhaftes Kunststück, sondern zugleich von so hoher Kunst, daß eine aufschlußreiche Tiefenwirkung erzielt wird, wie sie kaum ein philosophisches Werk über die Beziehungen der Geschlechter erreichen kann'.
21. The critic Efraim Frisch praised Woolf's 'unvergleichliche Dichtigkeit der Darstellung' and called her book 'romantisch aus Lebensüberschwang, aus einer Sensibilität, in der das unendlich Kleine seelische Bedeutung gewinnt'.
22. *Orlando* was 'der großangelegte Versuch, Kultur- und Sittengeschichte gleichsam *in abstracto* zu versinnlichen – welches Paradoxon zu konstruieren ihrer überlegenen Klugheit denn auch gelingt ... in der Tat ist dieses Jonglieren mit Symbolen über die Spanne eines umfänglichen Buches hinweg von einer zwar kühnen, aber ermüdenden Künstlichkeit'.
23. *Orlando* was narrated 'mit einer genialen Phantasie, einem sprühenden Witz, in einem ungemein beschwingten, durch und durch poetischen Stil, wenn auch nicht ohne eine gewisse Künstelei und Manieriertheit'. Beneath its comedic lightness, however, lurked 'eine philosophische Tiefsinnigkeit'.
24. 'Lassen Sie mich immer wieder versichern, wie glücklich und stolz ich bin, Ihre Bücher im Insel-Verlag erscheinen lassen zu dürfen.'
25. The 'Woolf project' in the German Democratic Republic had been possible since Insel held the copyright to the old translations, so no royalties had to be paid to the new versions published in West Germany (Wicht 2002: 107).
26. 'Das Buch ist unendlich skurril, mit einer merklichen und bewussten Absicht zur Originalität geschrieben, dabei merkwuerdig wirr und durch Wiederholungen leblos.... Selbstverstaendlich weiss eine Dichterin von solcher Kultur auch in dieser Erzaehlmanier, die ich fuer abwegig halte, einzelne Reize von grosser Kraft zu entfalten; aber es fehlt diesem Buche jede Klarheit des kompositorischen Gefueges, die man bei dem doch auch stark artistischen "Orlando" als Vorzug empfand.' On 23 September 1931 Kippenberg had urged Lerbs to tackle *To the Lighthouse* and hand the translation in by 15 February 1931, as the English publisher had already complained about the delay (Insel Papers, 23 September 1931, GSA

50 / 2159, 2). Since he was busy writing a comedy, however, Lerbs had started only in December 1930.
27. 'Ich muss sagen, ich finde es viel schöner wie "Orlando", der doch eigentlich nur verständlich ist, wenn man die englischen Verhältnisse kennt, und die vielen Andeutungen, die sich auf Rebekka [sic] Sackville-West beziehen, der Heldin des Romans. Eigentlich hätten wir das Buch nicht ohne ein erklärendes Vorwort herausgehen lassen dürfen, und wenn je eine zweite Auflage kommt, so soll das nachgeholt werden. Mir ist es ziemlich unverständlich, dass es ohne diese Hilfen überhaupt relativ so viele Leser gefunden hat, dagegen ist doch "To the lighthouse" jedermann zugängig [sic]. Ich finde es bezaubernd und stimme mit denen überein, die es ihr bestes Buch nennen. Das Ganze ist wie eine Spiegelung in Wellen, die farbig und leicht vorüberhuscht, und so muss es auch genossen werden, als ein durchsichtiges Wolkengebilde, das sich zusammenballt und wieder auseinanderflattert, alles im Verlaufe von Augenblicken. Ich möchte mir wünschen, dass das Buch recht leicht und gleichsam schwebend übertragen würde.'
28. 'Ich muss nun doch auch sagen, dass das Buch im Fortschreiten gewinnt und sich verdichtet. Der sprachliche Stil in seiner – sagen wir einmal: Eigenwilligkeit ist natuerlich ausserordentlich schwer zu treffen, aber an der Kunst der sprachlichen Ausfeilung soll es, wie gesagt, nicht fehlen.'
29. 'Ich habe sprachlich sehr sorgsam geschliffen, aber mich bemüht, alle Eigenarten des Originals soweit nur irgend möglich herüberzunehmen.'
30. 'Die Stilformung des Buches ist unendlich heikel. Das schattierungsreichste Englisch, das ich kenne; ein Schwelgen in Halbtönen und Zwischenwerten. Wie liest sich mein Text?'
31. Cohn (1978: 126). For a detailed analysis of the many 'acts of seeing and telling, interpreting and representing' see Levenson (2015: 19).
32. Woolf (1931: 290). Back translation: 'She looked at the steps; they were empty; she looked at the canvas: it was a maze. With a sudden and strong effort, as if she saw clearly for a second, she drew a line – there, in the middle of the picture. It was finished; it was ended. Yes, she thought and, in unspeakable fatigue, put down the brush: I have had my revelation.' In their new version of 1956, Herberth and Marlys Herlitschka, while adopting parts of Lerbs's reading, offered a closer, if less resonant, rendering:

> Sie blickte auf die Stufe: sie war leer; sie blickte auf die Leinwand: sie war verschwommen. Mit plötzlicher Gespanntheit, als sähe sie es eine Sekunde lang zum erstenmal ganz deutlich, zog sie da, in der Mitte, einen Strich. Es war getan; es war vollendet. Ja, dachte sie, in äußerster Erschöpfung den Pinsel weglegend, ich habe sie gehabt, meine Vision. (Woolf 1956: 255)

33. 'Leider ist der Absatz des "Leuchtturm" über alle Massen miserabel, aber ich hatte schon nicht mehr erwartet.'
34. Permission granted by the Random House Group Ltd.
35. In their version of *Between the Acts* (1963), however, the Herlitschkas followed Woolf's syntax closely, 'expanding and sometimes exploding the capabilities of regular German prose' (Hayman 2012: 395)
36. Since the founding of the Reichskulturkammer in September 1933 all authors, translators and publishers had to join that institution for which they needed an Aryan certificate (Joos 2008: 92); hence, Jews like Herlitschka were excluded.

Bibliography

Barnaby, P. (2002), 'Timeline: European reception of Virginia Woolf', in M. A. Caws and N. Luckhurst (eds), *The Reception of Virginia Woolf in Europe*, London: Continuum, pp. xxi–xxxvi.

Cohn, D. (1978), *Transparent Minds: Narrative Modes for Presenting Consciousness in Fiction*, Princeton, NJ: Princeton University Press.

Correspondence regarding Virginia Woolf translation rights, Archives of the Hogarth Press, MS 2750/C, University of Reading Special Collections.

Dick, S. (2000), 'Literary realism in *Mrs Dalloway*, *To the Lighthouse*, *Orlando* and *The Waves*', in S. Roe and S. Sellers (eds), *The Cambridge Companion to Virginia Woolf*, Cambridge: Cambridge University Press, pp. 50–71.

Füger, W. (1980), *Eine 'Extravagante Engländerin': Untersuchungen zur deutschen Frührezeption von Virginia Woolf* [An 'Extravagant Englishwoman': Studies in Virginia Woolf's Early German Reception], Heidelberg: Universitätsverlag Carl Winter.

Goldman, J. (2010), 'From *Mrs Dalloway* to *The Waves*: New elegy and lyric experimentalism', in S. Sellers (ed.), *The Cambridge Companion to Virginia Woolf*, Cambridge: Cambridge University Press, pp. 49–69.

Goldman, J. (2015), '*To the Lighthouse*'s use of language and form', in A. Pease (ed.), *The Cambridge Companion to* To the Lighthouse, Cambridge: Cambridge University Press, pp. 30–46.

Gorla, P. L. (2012), 'Did Borges translate *Orlando*?', in O. Palusci (ed.), *Translating Virginia Woolf*, Bern: Lang, pp. 85–96.

Göske, D. (2018), 'Virginia Woolf in German: The Hogarth Press, the Insel Verlag, and early translations', *Modernist Cultures*, 13: 1, pp. 55–76.

Hayman, E. (2012), 'English modernism in German: Herberth and Marlys Herlitschka, translators of Virginia Woolf', *Translation and Literature*, 21, pp. 383–401.

Humm, M. (2010), 'Virginia Woolf and visual culture', in S. Sellers (ed.), *The Cambridge Companion to Virginia Woolf*, Cambridge: Cambridge University Press, pp. 214–30.

Insel Papers, Goethe- und Schiller-Archiv, GSA 50 (34,1; 2159, 2; 2468; 3822), Klassik Stiftung Weimar.

Jansohn, C. (2005), '"I never could quote a text from end to end": Cultural borderlines in Herlitschka's translation of *The White Peacock*', *Etudes Lawrenciennes*, 32, pp. 37–54.

Joos, J. C. (2008), *Trustees for the Public? Britische Buchverlage zwischen intellektueller Selbständigkeit, wirtschaftlichem Interesse und patriotischer Verpflichtung zur Zeit des Zweiten Weltkriegs* [British Publishing between Intellectual Independence, Economic Interests and Patriotic Responsibility during the Second World War], Wiesbaden: Harrassowitz.

Kellner, D. S. (1930), 'Virginia Woolf: Orlando', *Die literarische Welt* [The Literary World], 1 February, p. 5.

Kirkpatrick, B. J. (1997), *A Bibliography of Virginia Woolf*, Oxford: Clarendon.

Levenson, M. (2015), 'Narrative perspective in *To the Lighthouse*', in A. Pease (ed.), *The Cambridge Companion to* To the Lighthouse, Cambridge: Cambridge University Press, pp. 19–29.

Marcus, L. (2002), 'The European dimensions of the Hogarth Press', in M. A. Caws and N. Luckhurst (eds), *The Reception of Virginia Woolf in Europe*, London: Continuum, pp. 328–56.

Marcus, L. (2004), *Virginia Woolf*, Tavistock: Northcote House.

'Mitteilungen des Verlags' [News from the publisher] (1928), *Das Inselschiff*, Autumn, p. 325.

Nünning, A. and V. Nünning (2002), 'The German reception and criticism of Virginia Woolf: A survey of phases and trends in the twentieth century', in M. A. Caws and N. Luckhurst (eds), *The Reception of Virginia Woolf in Europe*, London: Continuum, pp. 68–101.

Pellan, F. (2002), 'Translating Virginia Woolf into French', in M. A. Caws and N. Luckhurst (eds), *The Reception of Virginia Woolf in Europe*, London: Continuum, pp. 54–9.

Sackville-West, V. and V. Woolf (1985), *The Letters of Vita Sackville-West to Virginia Woolf*, ed. L. A. DeSalvo, and M. A. Leaska, London: Macmillan.

Sarkowski, H. (1999), *Der Insel-Verlag 1899–1999: Die Geschichte des Verlags* [Insel Verlag 1899–1999: The History of the Publishing House], Frankfurt: Insel.

White, E. W. (1929), 'Virginia Woolf', *Weltbühne* [World Stage], 25: 2, pp. 18–20.

Wicht, W. (2002), 'Intellectual modernism: The reception of Virginia Woolf in the German Democratic Republic', in M. A. Caws and N. Luckhurst (eds), *The Reception of Virginia Woolf in Europe*, London: Continuum, pp. 102–26.

Wilson, Nicola (2014), 'Archive fever: The publishers' archive and the history of the novel', in P. Parrinder, A. Nash and N. Wilson (eds), *New Directions in the History of the Novel*, Basingstoke: Palgrave Macmillan, pp. 76–87.

Woolf, V. (1928), *Eine Frau von fünfzig Jahren – Mrs Dalloway – ein Roman* [A Lady of Fifty Years – Mrs Dalloway – a novel], trans. T. Mutzenbecher, Leipzig: Insel.

Woolf, V. (1929), *Orlando: Die Geschichte eines Lebens* [Orlando: The Story of a Life], trans. K. Lerbs, Leipzig: Insel.

Woolf, V. (1931), *Die Fahrt zum Leuchtturm: Ein Roman* [The Trip to the Lighthouse], trans. K. Lerbs, Leipzig: Insel.

Woolf, V. (1933), *Flush: A Biography*, London: Hogarth Press.

Woolf, V. (1934), *Flush: Die Geschichte eines berühmten Hundes* [The History of a Famous Dog], trans. H. E. Herlitschka, Berlin: S. Fischer.

Woolf, V. (1956), *Die Fahrt zum Leuchtturm* [The Trip to the Lighthouse], trans. H. E. Herlitschka and M. Herlitschka, Berlin: S. Fischer.

Woolf, V. (1977), *A Change of Perspective: The Letters of Virginia Woolf, 1923–1928*, vol. 3, ed. N. Nicolson, London: Hogarth Press.

Woolf, V. (1980), *The Diary of Virginia Woolf: Volume Three: 1925–1930*, ed. A. O. Bell and A. McNeillie, London: Hogarth Press.

Woolf, V. (2006 [1927]), *To the Lighthouse*, ed. D. Bradshaw, Oxford: Oxford University Press.

Woolf, V. (2009 [1925]), *Mrs Dalloway*, ed. D. Bradshaw, Oxford: Oxford University Press.

Woolf, V. (2015 [1928]) *Orlando: A Biography*, ed. M. H. Whitworth, Oxford: Oxford University Press.

2

THE TRANSLATION AND RECEPTION OF VIRGINIA WOOLF IN ROMANIA (1926–89)

Adriana Varga

I BEGAN RESEARCHING THE RECEPTION OF Virginia Woolf's works in Romania with many questions and the assumption that, during the period following the Second World War when most of Woolf's works were translated, I would find heavily censored translations. I thought I would be able to tear the veil of censorship in which, I imagined, Woolf's works must have been shrouded during this period. Instead, I found translations that were, for the most part, faithful to the originals, while the changes that proved unfaithful were important to consider and extremely revealing. Instead of being able to tear apart any veil in order to present the 'truth' about how the Woolfian oeuvre should have been translated, the more I studied these translations and the circumstances in which they appeared, the more I realised that the maze of veils, or, perhaps, levels of understanding that engulfed these translations should not be torn and discarded but instead considered, studied carefully and somehow preserved. They are revealing because they raise questions about the translations, about the contexts in which the translations were created and about the originals themselves. It is useful to also remember that modernism itself, both in Great Britain and on the Continent, developed in a strange and disturbing dialogue with censors and censorship.

In this chapter, I review the history of the reception and translation of Woolf's works in Romania during the interwar period (primarily during the 1920s and 1930s), the early 1940s and the Communist era (from 1945 to 1989), with a special focus on the translation and censorship of *Orlando: A Biography*. I begin with a discussion of the first reviews of Woolf's works and the first Romanian translations of her fiction, pointing out that during the interwar period Romanian critics and reviewers understood Virginia Woolf as one of the young British novelists in a generation interested in exploring similar questions raised by modernism and its experiment. The mid-1920s is the period when Woolf's works were recognised as part of a modernist aesthetic that was just starting to be defined and practised by Romanian authors and literary critics (Finţescu 2003: 34).

Everything changed after 1945, when reviews and translations of Woolf and all other Western authors came to a virtual halt under the newly instituted communist regime and Soviet occupation. By 1968, when translations of Woolf's works resumed, Romania was undergoing a period of liberalisation under its new leader, Nicolae Ceauşescu. The 'liberalisation', however, was a deceptive ploy. In reality, as several political scientists and historians have shown, Ceauşescu was practising a two-faced policy (Troncotă 2006: 182). The system of censorship that had been developed since

1944, and perhaps even earlier (Coborca 2014: 9), began to slowly decline after Ceaușescu came to power and was eventually abolished in 1977. It was, however, replaced by a much more insidious, all-pervasive, 'Orwellian' form of censorship (Coborca 2014: 262). Despite this, it is within this environment that translations of Woolf's works as well as those of other Western authors considered canonical flourished in Romania. I discuss this paradox in the second part of my chapter, explaining that if these translations may be seen as co-opted by the new regime in an attempt to gain legitimacy at home and abroad, they also reveal powerful, if subtle, forms of resistance and questioning of censorship and of the communist totalitarian system itself. The 1968 translation of *Orlando* in particular, demonstrates such forms of subversion.

In the third and final part, I examine interconnections between text and image in *Orlando*. Its 1968 translation into Romanian helps us better understand not only the choices made by a translator working in a heavily censored society but also the very important ways in which Woolf's use of language and image in this novel contributed to questioning and undermining censorship both in Woolf's lifetime as well as within a totalitarian system such as that of pre-1989 Communist Romania.

The Interwar Period (1920s–1930s)

During the first half of the twentieth century, Romanian critics and authors, as well as the general public, were more likely to develop closer literary and cultural connections with France and Germany than with the British Isles. Even so, the volume dedicated to Anglo-Romanian literary relations within the multi-volume *Bibliografia relațiilor literaturii române în periodice, 1919–44* [The Bibliography of the Relations of Romanian Literature in Periodicals, 1919–44] (Brezuleanu et al. 1997) reveals that, during the interwar period, hundreds of articles were published in Romanian periodicals about British literature. Several dozens of these were on Woolf alone – including reviews, studies or translations of her works. Most of these reviews were favourable. For example, the writer Olga Caba began her 1934 review of *To the Lighthouse* in a way that Woolf no doubt would have enjoyed reading had she had access to it:

> More synthetic than Joyce, more profound than Huxley and, no doubt, more artistic than both, Virginia Woolf is a quintessentially British writer. The same nuanced sentimentalism of consciousness, of humour and self-irony, the same fantastic realism rooted in the imaginative that we find in the novels of Sterne and Dickens, embody themselves in a type of sensibility that is absolutely modern in her writings. (1934: 63)[1]

Caba's review is brief but perceptive and powerful. It focuses on the moment when Lily Briscoe struggles to remember a forgotten idea, which finally returns to her, accompanied by the image of the table where she sat when she had the idea. The table follows Lily on her walk, Caba writes, like a quadruped that can sneak around the bushes and climb into trees:

> Beneath any word uttered by [Woolf's] characters hide the history, importance, impressions, memories evoked by that word in the speaker's soul, in such a way that we know simultaneously both lives and temperaments, the wish and resonance

of long years in the echo of the word, which is never a value in and of itself, and therefore inept at dramatizing action. Time is, thus, created not through movement, but rather through a vertical section/dissection underneath the static/stasis of the moment. (1934: 63)[2]

Almost ninety years ago, Caba was commenting on what critics have only recently begun to realise about Woolf's approach to time, memory and language in her fiction. A more or less unknown literary figure, virtually forgotten today, Olga Caba (1913–95) was a Romanian born in Ukraine, who studied literature and philosophy with a specialisation in English at the University of Cluj, Romania. A gymnasium teacher, she wrote prose, including travel journals, and poetry in Romanian and English. Her writings remain almost unknown to the general Romanian public, yet it is tantalising to think of the light in which Caba might have presented Woolf and her fiction to her students.

A more prominent critic, writer and historian was Marcu Beza (1882–1949), a Macedonian Aromanian who spent a considerable time in London as a Romanian diplomat (1909–14, 1920–32 and 1939–46). Beza wrote about Virginia Woolf's works, along with those by Dorothy Richardson, in a volume titled *Romanul Englez Contimporan* [The Contemporary English Novel]. His study was published in 1928, the year when Woolf won the Femina-Vie Heureuse prize for *To the Lighthouse*, but Beza must have decided that she was a representative British novelist long before Woolf was recognised as such by the general public in France. In the spring of 1926, Beza gave a two-part lecture in London titled 'Romancierele Engleze contimporane' [Contemporary British women novelists], dedicated to Woolf (*Mrs Dalloway*) and Richardson (*Pointed Roofs* [1915] and *The Trap* [1925]). The conference was reviewed by the Romanian press in the journals *Universul* (30 April 1926) and *Aurora* (8 May 1926). In 1927, Beza published an article under the same title as his conference in the Romanian journal *Propilee Literare* in September 1927. It is interesting to note that both Caba and Beza came from the margins of Romania. This outsider status may have endowed these critics with a particularly sensitive and accurate way of noticing European literary and aesthetic trends that may have escaped the attention of better-known Romanian critics situated in the capital, at the 'centre' of the Romanian geographical space.

Beza begins *Romanul Englez Contimporan* [The Contemporary English Novel] with a chapter on Samuel Butler, in which he also takes the opportunity to critique H. G. Wells and Wells's criticism of Henry James. He ends the study with a final chapter dedicated to the works of Dorothy Richardson and Virginia Woolf. In his analysis of *Mrs Dalloway*, Beza emphasises the heroine's thoughts of death and war as they reverberate with those of Septimus Warren Smith. He cites the moment when Clarissa notices the motor car carrying 'greatness . . . seated within' (*MD*: 16), and he comments on the destruction of 'greatness' by the passage of time. Although he could not have had access to works such as 'A sketch of the past', the autobiographical essay Woolf began writing in 1939, Beza was able to intuit and point out in his analysis of *Mrs Dalloway* exactly those crucial 'moments of being' that Woolf would later describe as 'the obscure elements in life' that exist alongside 'the shock-receiving capacity [that] makes me a writer' (*MB*: 72).

Questions about reinventing the modernist novel in new, unconventional ways were very important in the context of Romanian literature during the interwar period, when Romanian novelists were responding to the problems posed by the 'new' novel.

If one considers this background, it becomes clear that Marcu Beza as well as another perceptive writer, the poet and lawyer Demostene Botez (1893–1973), were among the Romanian critics who, familiar enough with her works, understood that Virginia Woolf was part of a generation of young British authors who were grappling with problems raised by modernism and the experimental novel that were similar to the ones that he and other Romanian modernists were considering. In a 1929 article titled 'O estetică impresionistă a romanului' [An impressionist aesthetic of the novel], published in the journal *Viața Românească* [Romanian Life], a young Demostene Botez compares André Gide and Virginia Woolf and finds the latter more revolutionary. While Gide's innovation refers more to narrative technique, in Botez's view, Woolf 'affirms a new conception of the novel' (1929: 310).[3] Botez picks up on the conflict between the Edwardians and the Georgians, which Woolf had tried to elucidate in several of her essays. Citing Woolf's essay 'Modern fiction' in French translation (specifically the memorable paragraph in which Woolf affirms that 'life is not a series of gig lamps symmetrically arranged; life is a luminous halo, a semi-transparent envelope surrounding us from the beginning of consciousness to the end' (*E* 4: 160), Botez then paraphrases it for the reader, drawing the conclusion that, according to Woolf,

> the 'matter' of the novel must be different than the conventional one. As small a mixture of references to external facts as possible. A perfect, sincere, and courageous mirroring of the myriad of impressions, banal and fantastic – a rain of innumerable atoms that constitute the life of an everyday person on a day like any other one; and especially the perception of this variation of the changing spirit, unknown and limitless, that emphasizes them, with a varied intensity, today and tomorrow. (1929: 310)[4]

The 'impressionist aesthetic' of the new novel meant, according to Botez – who adopted André Maurois's use of 'impressionist' to refer to the play of light on an object (1929: 310) – that 'a character must not be an object observed and described from the outside'. Rather, Botez sensed along with Woolf that

> you must transpose yourself in the interior, at the centre of the character's very senses and, with them, you must catch and register the myriad of impressions that constitute the interior life of a day, everything that goes through the head of a person in one day, in connection to the exterior life they lead. (Botez 1929: 310)[5]

In a brief study on the reception of Virginia Woolf's oeuvre in Romania, 'Receptarea operei Virginiei Woolf în România', Traian Grigore Finţescu characterises the year 1926 as the beginning of understanding and situating Woolf's works within a modernist aesthetic that was just starting to be defined and practised by Romanian authors and literary critics (2003: 33). Finţescu acknowledges that in the reception of Woolf's works on the Romanian literary scene there was an enormous gap between 'exegesis' and translation: 'literature in the interwar period is no longer concerned with translations. The centre of interest has shifted towards *critical commentary*' (2003: 34).[6] While she was read (often in French translation) and assessed by many Romanian authors and critics, and even though dozens of articles and reviews were published in periodicals, Woolf's works were not translated during the interwar period, with a single exception: the short story 'The lady in the looking-glass' (1929), translated as

'Femeia în oglindă' [The woman in the mirror] by Nora Marian in 1938. *Night and Day* was the first of Woolf's novels to be translated by George Sbârcea in 1942[7] as *Din beznă spre soare* [From Darkness towards Sun].

Reception, Translation, Censorship (1945–89)

Between 1945 and 1963, a period that is categorised as the 'epoch of Proletkult-ism[8] and 'socialist realism' (Finţescu 2003: 34), reviews and translations of Woolf's works, as well as of most other Western authors, came to a halt. The findings of the *Raportul final al Comisiei Prezidenţiale pentru Analiza Dictaturii Comuniste din România* [The Final Report of the Presidential Commission for the Analysis of the Romanian Communist Dictatorship] show clearly that by 1948 connections between Romanian and Western culture and civilisation were destroyed. The country fully reoriented itself towards the Soviet Union, adopting Soviet cultural and political models. This included the Soviet model of state censorship (*Glavlit*) and the purging of all Western forms of expression from books, periodicals and other publications from all public and private libraries, bookshops, used bookstores, schools, universities, institutes, publishing houses, to film and theatre (Tismăneanu et al. 2007: 311). Even though the purge was supposed to target only fascist publications and cultural products deemed hostile to the communist dictatorship, fear of Soviet repercussions led to the overzealousness of the Romanian regional counsellors who, without any exceptions, burned all books published before 23 August 1944. This was the largest destruction of book funds and collections in Romania's history (Coborca 2014: 25). Woolf's works, as well as those of other canonical Western authors, were allowed to return to the Romanian cultural scene only in the late 1960s through a new wave of translations and critical assessments.

Translations of Woolf's works begin to appear in 1968 and to flourish afterwards. In his study, which discusses Woolf's reception from the interwar years to 1968, Traian Grigore Finţescu speaks of the late 1960s as a period when Woolf became a household name in Romanian culture and gained a 'retrospective influence' ('o influenţă retrospectivă') (2003: 34). However, with more caution, I argue that Woolf's influence on Romanian literature and culture was much more subdued at this time. It is true that within just a few decades Woolf's works would be translated into Romanian almost in their entirety and included in university curricula. However, Woolf's direct influence on Romanian writers is rarely felt beyond university circles, and there is little information on how many of her translated volumes were actually bought and read by the Romanian public. Even today, as the reprinting of older translations continues and new translations are commissioned, Romanian publishing houses are reluctant to make public information about the number of volumes printed and sold. As this data is unavailable, those investigating Woolf's reception in Romania have to rely on considering the translations themselves and the circumstances in which they were published in the 1960s. What made it possible for Woolf's works to be rapidly translated starting in 1968? Were these translations faithful to the originals (keeping in mind that 'faithfulness' is a highly debatable concept in translation theory), or were they heavily censored? Romanian political history and literary history suggest answers to both of these questions.

After the death of the first Romanian communist leader, Gheorghe Gheorghiu-Dej, on 19 March 1965, Nicolae Ceaușescu became Secretary-General of the Communist Party of Romania. Ceaușescu proceeded to consolidate his power and gain legitimacy at home by continuing the policies of propagandistic de-Stalinisation that his predecessor had started as early as 1962 (Troncotă 2006: 163). He simultaneously pursued an international policy that affirmed Romania's national independence from Soviet influence (Troncotă 2006: 161). At home, this policy was expressed in nationalistic terms,[9] strengthening Ceaușescu's popularity internally as well as internationally.

Ceaușescu refused to participate in the Soviet-led invasion of Czechoslovakia in 1968 and he openly condemned the Soviet-instigated Warsaw Pact[10] invasion. For a period of time, the West recognised Romania's geopolitical importance and regarded its leader as an anti-Soviet maverick who could create dissension within the Warsaw Pact. In reality, Ceaușescu's dissent was a duplicitous policy and not an actual threat to the Soviet Union (Troncotă 2006: 168, 182). Furthermore, at home, Ceaușescu began to implement neo-Stalinist forms of control, including the censorship of institutions (Coborca 2014: 96), with the aim of transforming a visible, 'state-imposed' censorship into less visible but all-pervasive, ubiquitous Orwellian forms of censorship and self-censorship (Troncotă 2006: 169, 187, 189; Coborca 2014: 262). Foreign publications played an important role in this system, as Liliana Coborca explains: 'under the communist regime the control of foreign publications was one of the most important activities that contributed to maintaining the Iron Curtain and, implicitly, the communist regime' (2014: 125). Clearly, no Western works could be published without first undergoing the merciless scrutiny of the censorship apparatus.

Thus, the image of 'liberalisation' that the communist leader wanted to project should not be misinterpreted: Ceaușescu's pursuit of 'openness' in the 1960s manifested itself very differently inside Romania and did not apply to his domestic policies. Tiberiu Troncotă and many other political scientists and historians have shown that, behind the façade of democratisation and independence from the Soviet Union, measures were taken to control all aspects of cultural and socio-political life and production through propaganda, censorship and a system of institutionalised surveillance that created fear and paranoia. These changes began, ironically, immediately after Ceaușescu openly criticised the 1968 invasion of Czechoslovakia (Troncotă 2006: 188–9, 190). Decrees and laws were passed which limited and violated human rights, women's rights in particular. Two blatant examples are the Decree 770 that was signed into law in 1966 to criminalise abortion[11] and Article 200 of the Penal Code adopted in 1968 criminalising homosexual relationships. The latter remained in force until 2001, when it was finally repealed by Adrian Năstase's government under pressure from the Council of Europe. It is also this context that we must keep in mind when looking at the 1968 translations of Woolf's works.

Considering these domestic policies, it may be surprising that any of Woolf's works were translated at all during this period, especially the highly ambiguous and subversive *Orlando* and *Mrs Dalloway*. In general, however, the translation of Western works that began to flourish at this time can be understood by considering Ceaușescu's determination to reinforce Romania's political and cultural importance on the international scene and his legitimacy at home. The publication of what was considered the twentieth-century Western canon – works by authors such as James Joyce, Samuel Beckett, William Faulkner, Franz Kafka and Virginia Woolf, among others – served as a way to present Romanian literature as one that could resonate and even compete with the great Western tradition.

It is against this deceptive background of internal liberalisation that, alongside other US and Western European canonical and contemporary authors, Virginia Woolf's novels were translated and published for the first time in communist Romania. *Orlando* and *Mrs Dalloway* were translated by Vera Călin and Petru Creția, respectively, and both works were published in 1968 at Editura Pentru Literatură Universală [The Universal Literature Publishing House]. They were followed by *To the Lighthouse* in 1972, translated by Antoaneta Ralian with a preface by Călin; and *The Waves* in 1973, translated by Creția. *Between the Acts* was translated in 1978 by Frieda Papadache; *The Years* in 1983, also by Papadache; and *Night and Day* in 1987 by Veronica Focșeneanu, with an excellent preface by Ștefan Stoenescu. *Jacob's Room*, translated by Mihai Miroiu, appeared just after the collapse of the Ceaușescu regime in 1990. A small selection of Woolf's diaries was also published in 1980 with Leonard Woolf's 1953 preface. *A Room of One's Own* was translated in 1999 by Radu Paraschivescu. After 1990, Woolf's novels were republished more and more often, with only *Mrs Dalloway* and *Orlando* in brand-new translations by Mihai Miroiu and Antoaneta Ralian, respectively. Today's renewed interest in Woolf's works is, arguably, the continuation of a process that began in 1968 with the publication of the translations of *Orlando* and *Mrs Dalloway*.

The Moment: *Orlando* (1968)

The translations that began to appear in 1968 were generally faithful, integral texts that did not show signs of censorship 'mutilation', with a few revealing exceptions. A closer look at the translation of *Orlando* is especially pertinent in this context because it allows for an examination of text, image and text-image relationships as they are affected by both translation and censorship. The one large chunk of text that is immediately noticeable as missing is Woolf's 'Preface' to her mock biography. It is difficult to believe that Călin, the translator, found the author's 'Preface' beside the point. The censors, however, may have perceived the long list of names Woolf showered with lavish, ironic praise and thanks as threatening or at least destabilising. It should not surprise Western audiences that Woolf's metafictional exercise in sarcastic gratitude was unacceptable in a culture whose citizens were supposed to unequivocally worship Romania's totalitarian communist leader and his wife. Also missing from Călin's translation are the photographs that accompanied the first British and US editions of *Orlando*. Although even later Western editions randomly omitted the photographs and paintings Woolf included in the first editions of her works,[12] these illustrations form an important dialogue with the text that should not be ignored or eliminated. I discuss the important role of this dialogue in the last section of this chapter.

Călin's translation is otherwise beautifully done and, with a few (but revealing) exceptions, quite faithful to the original. While translators often argue that faithfulness in translation is impossible, political censorship is a different matter, and Călin managed, for the most part, to save her translation from blatant political censorship. Besides the 'Preface', the illustrations and the index included by Virginia Woolf in the first British and US publications of her novel, no other parts are missing from this translation, not even the crucial moment when Orlando undergoes the famous transformation. However, Călin's 1968 translation does contain small discrepancies which are more difficult to detect but which may show the hand of a censor at work – or perhaps the translator herself, practising the type of self-censorship required by the communist dictatorship. Since Călin died in 2013 and the manuscript proofs and related archival documents are not available, it is not possible to completely understand, at this time, how the censoring process worked in this particular case. However, when asked in a post-1989 interview how the Communist censorship affected authors and texts, Călin clearly stated:

> [Censorship] prevented the publication of anything that was not considered 'useful' to the regime. It eliminated anything which could have been interpreted as hostile or alien to communism and Marxist ideology, and especially anything which could have been taken as irreverent to the person of the dictator. Furthermore, it affected authors and texts by adding a word here and there or a sentence intended to neutralize something that might have sounded ambiguous or could have been interpreted 'the wrong way', or to emphasize something that did not sound explicit enough. The obsession with 'the correct line' – be it political, national, aesthetic, – was a reality every writer had to live with. (Vianu 1998: 25)

Călin goes on to discuss self-censorship as a mechanism of self-protection she considered far more devastating for a writer's creative process than official censorship itself (Vianu 1998: 25). Călin's statements shed some light upon her own translation of one of *Orlando*'s most important moments, the protagonist's change of sex, which Woolf describes in the following way:

> Many people, taking this into account, and holding that *such a change of sex is against nature*, have been at great pains to prove (1) that Orlando had always been a woman, (2) that Orlando is at this moment a man. Let biologists and psychologists determine. It is enough for us to state the simple fact; Orlando was a man till the age of thirty; when he became a woman and has remained so ever since. (O 2006: 103, italics mine)

In Romanian, the text becomes:

> Plecînd de la aceste fapte, mulți oameni au socotit asemenea *metamorfoză* împotriva naturii și și-au dat mare osteneală să dovedească: 1. că Orlando fusese întotdeauna femeie și 2. că Orlando este încă și acum bărbat. Nouă însă ne ajung faptele; anume că Orlando a fost bărbat pîna la vîrsta de treizeci de ani cînd a devenit femeie, ceea ce a rămas pînă-n ziua de azi. (italics mine, O 1968: 134)
>
> [Starting from these facts, many people have considered such *metamorphosis* against nature and they have put great of effort into proving: 1. That Orlando had always been a woman and 2. That Orlando is even now still a man. For us, however, facts are enough; namely that Orlando was a man till the age of thirty when he became a woman, remaining so until today].

In her translation, Călin omits 'Let biologists and psychologists determine' and, more importantly, she translates 'such a change of sex is against nature' as 'such metamorphosis is against nature'. These alterations are important and revealing. Woolf's simple but direct expression, 'change of sex', may have been too queer to print in 1968. And because Woolf does not simply mean that a metaphorical transformation took place but a very literal, physical one that could be scientifically determined, 'let biologists and psychologists determine' also had to be left out of the translation. When *Orlando* was translated again in 2013 by Antoaneta Ralian, it received its author's 'Preface' back, and the lines above were rendered almost literally as in English. The original photographs, however, were still not included (O 2013).

The use of the word 'metamorphosis' introduced by Călin in Woolf's text is important and did not go unnoticed. In 1969, a year after the novel's translation appeared, the literary critic Valeriu Cristea published an article titled 'Experiențele lui Orlando' [The experiences of Orlando] in the journal *România Literară* [Literary Romania], that centred precisely on the word 'metamorphosis'. Relying on this word, Cristea builds an entire interpretation of the novel by drawing a comparison between *Orlando* and Kafka's 1915 novella *The Metamorphosis*: Orlando's sexual transformation is seen through a kind of magical-realist lens similar to the metamorphosis that occurs in Kafka's short story. While philosophically interesting, this interpretation eliminates the difficulty of having to consider an actual sexual transformation and its implications. Cristea concludes that 'beyond the impression of an amorphous reality the hero gives us, there is an essence so profound and unalterable, that not even such a radical modification such as that of sex can change it' (1969: 23). The use of the word 'metamorphosis' in Călin's translation cements an interpretation according to which Orlando's essence remains 'profound and unalterable' (Cristea 1969: 23), despite the sexual transformation. Clearly, in the late 1960s, it was impossible to discuss aspects of this novel in a way that would become possible much later, as for example in 2013:

> *Orlando* remains, in its structural ambiguity, one of the fundamental texts for understanding Virginia Woolf's attitude towards a series of aspects that preoccupied her in the highest degree throughout her entire literary activity: identity, androgynous image, and the relationship between masculine and feminine as it is reflected in Western culture (particularly British!), from the Renaissance to the modern period. (Grigore 2013)[13]

The question still remains: how was it possible to translate and publish Woolf's works at all under a communist, totalitarian dictatorship? As Vladimir Tismăneanu has argued in *Stalinism for All Seasons: A Political History of Romanian Communism* (2003), censorship in Romania after 1968 was no longer an actual institution nor an impenetrable ideological wall. This 'thawing' was calculated and lasted until about 1975, with the old censorship system being gradually replaced by an even more restrictive and elaborate system of control that took effect at various different levels (Coborca 2014: 263). After 1977, and especially in the 1980s, a 'New Censorship' was instituted (Coborca 2014: 264), with all-pervasive forms of control that also relied on fear, paranoia and self-censorship. Furthermore, as discussed above, after gaining power, one of the ways in which Ceaușescu consolidated his rule was through implementing an authoritarian, nationalistic communism that was justified, both domestically and internationally, as a declaration of independence from the Soviet Union.

In this sense, one can think of Woolf's texts, on the one hand, as having been co-opted by a system fighting to gain and maintain legitimacy. On the other hand, the translation of Woolf's works, and of *Orlando* and *Mrs Dalloway* in particular, represented a form of undeniable, if subtle questioning, resistance, even protest against Ceaușescu's repressive policies. Even the explanatory quote, signed by Călin, on the back cover of the 1968 translation of *Orlando*, a book published the same year in which Ceaușescu criminalised homosexuality, advertised the story of a character who is not bound by history and political power, who changes sex, and who does absolutely nothing in terms of bringing praise to the leader of the Romanian Communist party:

> Orlando is an adolescent in the Elizabethan period, loves in the frenetic and licentious age of the Stuarts, changes from man into a woman during a Constantinople ambush, roams through the lively eighteenth century, marries during the puritanical Victorian age, and is 36 years old in 1928. The historical ages crossed by this hero-heroine are just as many hypostases, and represent just as many possibilities [potentialities/alternatives/availabilities] of his/her own conscience, whose flexibility accords his/her passion in Elizabeth's century, frivolity under James I, and matrimonial characteristics during the Victorian age. (Woolf 1968: back cover)[14]

In this context, even more subversive than the story of Orlando's changing from a man into a woman during a Constantinople ambush is the courageous assertion made by Călin on her translation's back cover that consciousness is not fixed, that it has many possibilities, or 'potentialities'.

Orlando's Missing Illustrations: Image, Text, Translation

Another revealing deletion is that of the illustrations Woolf had included in the first editions of her mock biography. When *Orlando* was published in Romania in 1968, none of these illustrations were included with the translation. It is clear why the portrait of the Archduchess Harriet Griselda of Finster-Aarhorn and Scand-op-Boom of Roumania could not be included in the 1968 translated text. The real person that inspired the Archduchess/Archduke is not a Romanian historical figure but Henry George Charles Lascelles, 6th Earl of Harewood (1882–1947) – a suitor whom Vita Sackville-West mockingly rejected. However, *Orlando*'s Harry/Harriet is a rather eccentric and ridiculous character (a man disguised as a woman disguised as a man) and the reference to the 'Roumanian territory' highly ironic.[15] The other illustrations, however, were also left out. When the novel was republished after the fall of the communist regime in 1989, the illustrations were still not included in the text. This may be understandable: including photographs and paintings means having to cover not only additional printing costs but also copyright permissions requests to different manuscript collections and trusts that own the different images included in the first Hogarth Press edition. These are additional financial burdens not only for Romanian publishers struggling to survive in a post-1989 capitalist economy, in which publishing houses are no longer state-controlled and state-subventioned, but also for British and US publishers: several British and US editions of *Orlando* also omit the photographs. However, the omission of the illustrations Woolf intentionally included in *Orlando* raises a series of very important questions about censorship, translation and the relationship between text and image.

With these considerations in mind, I would like to return to the questions I posed at the beginning of this chapter: how can what has been discarded from the original in the process of translation help us better understand the original? How important are the images Woolf included in her mock biography? How crucial is their relationship to this text? Addressing these questions by considering the issue of censorship and its impact on Woolf's text is revealing. A rich critical tradition informs the role and significance of photography and painting in Woolf's works as well as, more generally, the importance of portraiture, photography and painting in Woolf's family, from Julia Margaret Cameron to Leslie Stephen to Vanessa Bell and to Woolf herself.[16] All critics, without exception, affirm the relevance of the image–text relationship in Woolf's works,[17] perhaps no one more strongly than Talia Schaffer, who, when analysing the role of photographs and images in *Orlando*, concludes that 'no reading of *Orlando* can be viable unless it interprets the illustrations, for *Orlando* gets its meaning from precisely the conflicted, complex relation between image and narrative' (1994: 27).

I would like to contribute to this critical tradition by raising the question of censorship – not simply the censorship imposed under a totalitarian state but one that functions at various levels in the so-called 'free' Western world as well. This is a kind of self-censorship writers and publishers practise themselves – one that Woolf was acutely aware of. *Orlando* itself is a work that is, at its very core, both touched by and concerned with questions of censorship. Woolf explored such questions in several of her works, and in her 7 August 1939 diary entry she commented:

> I have been thinking about Censors. How visionary figures admonish us. Thats [sic] clear in an MS I'm reading [the memoirs of the American actress Elizabeth Robins]. If I say this So & So will think me sentimental. If that . . . will think me Bourgeois. All books now seem to me surrounded by a circle of invisible censors. Hence their selfconsciousness, their restlessness. (*D* 5: 229)

In a review of the holograph draft transcribed and edited by Stuart N. Clarke, Hermione Lee explains that, 'for Virginia Woolf, the evolution of writing is closely bound up with ideas about repression and censorship' (1994: 5). In Woolf's own case, understanding the nature and process of writing – or, Woolf's own words, 'how writing was written' (qtd in Lee 1994: 5) – has a great deal to do with self-censorship. Lee argues that Woolf's movement towards a finished text is 'frequently shaped by inhibition or prohibition':

> Very often, in the evolution of her books, she will write in the things people say *en route* to taking them out again. Her cuts can be attributed to a fear of expressing too much emotion, a fear of being laughed at, and a fear of egotism – paradoxical for a writer who is so often accused of writing narcissistically about herself. (1994: 5)

Lee gives a series of examples of what she calls 'dangerous details' – words, fragments or entire sentences – that Woolf crossed out in the holograph version, showing that *Orlando* 'is a work of evasion, an escapade which escapes, through its own "invisible" censorship, the kind of public suppression which *The Well of Loneliness* notoriously encountered in the year of *Orlando*'s publication' (1994: 5). Thus, Lee shows that 'the fantasy and jokiness of *Orlando* form a smoke-screen against self-exposure and confession' (1994: 5).

Viewed from this perspective, the images Woolf included in *Orlando* function not only as reversals of the act of textual self-censorship but also as a kind of resistance to institutionalised censorship.[18] These images reveal, both directly and indirectly, aspects of Woolf's personal life, of her relationship with Vita Sackville-West,[19] of her competitive collaboration with Vanessa Bell, of her views on intimacy, sexuality, gender, gender roles, biography, historiography and, perhaps most importantly, of her views on the art of writing experimental fiction and testing the boundaries of the biography and of the novel. The images that Woolf included in *Orlando* are intrinsically connected with the text of the novel in multiple ways. As Erika Flesher explains, the novel's illustrations, particularly the final one ('Orlando at the present time') form 'Woolf's most dramatic playing with codes of representation to rework notions of identity and femininity' (1997: 45). It is understandable why these particular illustrations provide an additional reason to make a work like *Orlando* powerfully subversive.

In this sense, reading any edition of Woolf's novel (original or translation) that is missing the illustrations Woolf included is like living in a house with no windows. The images Woolf selected (both paintings and photographs) create passageways that help us consider or reconsider aspects of her personal, political and artistic life, even as such aspects could not be expressed openly or directly in the text. Omitting the photographs means losing these intrinsic word–image connections. By definition, translation transforms the word–image relationship because what we lose in the process of translation is exactly the original text – its language. The illustrations themselves, however, do not suffer the same transformation in the process of translation. Paradoxically, by including images, Woolf has created a part of the novel that translation does not affect and can travel across languages – even though, of course, the word–image relationship itself is transformed – as well as the way in which readers in different cultural and linguistic contexts interpret this relationship and the images themselves.

Does cultural relativism render Woolf's illustrations virtually incomprehensible for readers from other cultures? On the one hand, making sense of these images requires a lot of time, effort and study even for native English speakers. Questions must be raised and addressed: why did Woolf select these particular paintings and photographs (and not others) to represent Orlando, Sasha or Archduchess Harriet? Diaries, letters, essays, biographies, critical editions have to be read, and manuscript collections and scholars consulted, in what may sometimes prove to be arduous searches. On the other hand, the images that Woolf included actually diminish the effects of cultural relativism and call attention to the nature of this work as a mock biography. Even a reader who has access to *Orlando* only in translation, with very little knowledge of Woolf's biography, would have to question whether the painting of Orlando as a boy is not very different from the photograph of Orlando upon her return to England or of Orlando on 29 April 1928. Moreover, how is it possible to have a photograph of a seventeenth-century Russian princess as a child? Such questions[20] open up the text as the reader realises that the role of the images Woolf included is highly ironic. The images place a demand on the reader to further engage with the text of *Orlando* and to approach it from different angles. Soon, what begins as an exploration driven by humour, curiosity and irony turns into a serious investigation of the relationship between reality and representation.

I argue that Woolf placed strategically the images she selected for her mock biography. The first UK Hogarth Press trade edition (O 1928), which represents the final text of Virginia Woolf's proofs for the novel (O 2018: lxxxiv–lxxxv), reveals that the chosen illustrations are placed exactly at moments when Orlando either senses the coming of or undergoes important transformations:

1. The portrait of 'The Russian princess as a child' appears in the text on the day when Orlando and Sasha meet for the last time and Orlando senses that 'everything suffered emaciation and transformation' (O 2006: 40).
2. 'The Archduchess Harriet' appears just when Orlando feels both Love's wings beating and Lust the vulture perching disgustingly upon his shoulders (O 2006: 87) and decides to flee for Constantinople.
3. The portrait of 'Orlando as ambassador' appears just before Orlando falls into his transformative deep sleep.
4. The photograph of 'Orlando on her return to England' appears just before the protagonist gains sight of the cliffs of Dover.
5. The photograph of 'Orlando about the year 1840' appears just as Orlando meets Shelmerdine.
6. 'Marmaduke Bonthrop Shelmerdine, Esquire' appears just as he and Orlando are married and Shel sets sail for Cape Horn.
7. The final portrait of 'Orlando at the present time' appears just before Shelmerdine's return, as the clock strikes 4 and Orlando feels she can begin to live again.[21]

The moments and spaces into which Woolf chose to insert these illustrations point to a direct connection between the images themselves and moments of transformation as depicted in the novel. In *Modernist Women and Visual Cultures,* Maggie Humm argues that 'photography is a tool which Woolf and Vanessa Bell used, not simply as a documentary device but as a means of crossing the border between the visual and the unconscious' (2003: iv).[22] The images that Woolf chose to include in *Orlando* create and reinforce border crossings between the visual and the unconscious as well as between gender representations, genres and historical periods – topics that were not up for discussion, and would have been heavily censored in communist Romania. It is understandable, then, why *Orlando*'s illustrations could not be included the 1968 Romanian translation of this work.

Moreover, the images Woolf used in order to visualise Orlando's transformation in Constantinople ('Orlando as ambassador' and 'Orlando on her return to England') parallel the language she uses to describe this transformation, revealing an important word–image connection in this text which is, therefore, lost in the 1968 Romanian translation. At the very centre of the novel, the biographer-narrator makes a pause in the narrative as Orlando, after awakening from his long sleep, discovers he is a woman and 'without showing any signs of discomposure' (O 2006: 102) goes to his bath. It is this particular moment of both change and pause that I want to observe both in English and in the 1968 translation.

Interestingly, even though Orlando is now a woman, Woolf continues to use the pronoun 'he' to refer to her and admires the combination of strength and grace found in the new woman. The Romanian translation faithfully follows this pronoun use:

'The sound of the trumpets died away and Orlando stood stark naked. No human being, since the world began, has ever looked more ravishing. His form combined in one the strength of a man and a woman's grace' (O 2006: 102).[23] This is a crucial moment in the novel, when everything is still undergoing change: not only Orlando's body but also the language that describes this body and the moment of transformation itself. Within a space of two paragraphs, everything becomes unsettled: Orlando, though a woman, is briefly still called 'he' until the narrator finally states that language lags behind and it is time to switch pronouns as well (O 2006: 102). It is at this moment, when time itself seems to have stopped, and when Orlando is both he and she that the narrator introduces the third-person plural 'they', referring still to Orlando. The narrator also urges the readers to pause and reflect for a while, just as the narrator does, on what has happened linguistically as well as physically and perhaps even to relish these transformations:

> We may take advantage of this pause in the narrative to make certain statements. Orlando had become a woman – there is no denying it. But in every other respect, Orlando remained precisely as he had been. The change of sex, though it altered *their* future, did nothing whatever to alter *their* identity. *Their* faces remained, as their portraits prove, practically the same. His memory – but in future we must, for convention's sake, say 'her' for 'his', and 'she' for 'he' – her memory then went back through all the events of her past life without countering any obstacle. (O 2006: 102, italics mine)

Woolf is stretching the limits of the English language in a way that seems natural to us today. However, in the Romanian translation, the departure from the singular he/she/it in order to use the plural 'they' is grammatically, and certainly politically and aesthetically, impossible in 1968. There is ambiguity in the use of the pronoun 'i' (Schimbarea sexului, deși avea să-i schimbe viitorul, nu-i alteră cu nimic personalitatea. Fața a rămas, așa cum arată portretele, în bună măsură aceeași [O 1968: 134]) in the sense that the dative form of the third-person pronoun is gender-neutral in its singular form. This gender ambiguity continues in the following sentence: 'Fața a rămas, așa cum arată portretele, în bună măsură aceeași.' The translator chooses to omit the plural possessive pronoun and noun, 'their faces', altogether and uses instead the impersonal 'the face . . . remained'.

Gender ambiguity is maintained here but in a very different way than in the original, and this difference is important. The editors of the Cambridge Critical Edition of *Orlando* point out an important passage in the holograph draft of *Orlando*, which is missing from the later revisions Woolf made: 'we must beg the reader to remember that Orlando & + the man + Orlanda + the woman + were one & the same person' (O 2018: 407). The use of the pronoun 'they' in this instance helps us understand an important point Woolf is making here – something that third-wave feminists began to discuss several decades later – that English pronouns are clearly divided into he, she and it, and that, at least in English, we do not have the language to express anything that does not fit strictly into these categories.

In the 1968 Romanian translation, such questions and issues that are raised by Woolf's text are obscured in translation. The gender ambiguity is maintained mostly by the grace of the Romanian language, which allows for the dative third-person pronoun to have the same form in feminine and masculine, as explained above. Other words used in the same passage, however, tell a different story. For example, 'Orlando had become a woman' (O 2006: 102) is translated counterintuitively, as 'Orlando se prefăcuse în femeie' (O 1968: 134). Such translation choices obfuscate Orlando's transformation: 'se prefăcuse' is the pluperfect of 'a se preface' [to pretend/transform oneself], a verb that means to transform oneself but also to pretend, convert, act, feign. This transformation is more in the sense of a fairy-tale transformation, which may be temporary and reversible. Călin could have simply used the more literal verb 'devenise': 'Orlando devenise femeie' [Orlando had become a woman]. Instead, 'se prefăcuse' adds a fantastic, fairy-tale-like quality, which goes along with the translator's use of the word 'metamorphosis' a few lines later to refer to Orlando's sex change. Another example is Călin's use of the word 'personalitatea' [(his) personality] instead of Woolf's original 'identity'. Thus, the Romanian translation of this passage becomes, 'His sex change, although it would change his future, did not alter his personality in any way' (O 1968: 134), instead of the original 'The change of sex, though it altered their future, did nothing whatever to alter their identity' (O 2006: 102).

There is yet another textual reference Woolf makes at this point that enhances the linguistic ambiguity she introduced in the text through the use of the pronoun 'they/their' (O 2006: 102). The narrator affirms that even though 'their' sex changed, this did nothing to alter 'their' identity. In order to prove this, the narrator refers to 'their' portraits: 'Their faces remained, as their portraits prove, practically the same' (O 2006: 102). Woolf suggests here a clear connection with the portraits that she placed at crucial, transformative moments in the protagonist's life. The connection is, at the same time, highly inaccurate – and Flesher's discussion of the 'playful fictions inherent in these photographs' (Flesher 1997: 42) comes to mind here. In the 1968 translation, the pronoun 'their' is omitted,[24] and the reference to the portraits, proving that nothing altered Orlando's identity (and the identity of others like her, such as her future husband, Shelmerdine), is an empty reference, since no actual portraits are included in the Romanian text.

Through the illustrations she inserts in her text, Woolf raises questions concerning the relationship between identity, gender, physical appearance and visual as well as linguistic expression. Encompassing all of these issues is the even larger question of representation. The narrator is asking the readers to believe in her arguments by making recourse to fictional but also very real visual, artistic representations: the paintings and photographs. That is, don't take the narrator's word for it, consider the portraits.

The irony of the narrator's arguments is also impossible to miss: the images included in the novel do not represent the characters that populate it. This, in turn, raises the following question: should identities remain as unchanged as the features captured by the artist's camera or brush? The question – or series of questions – is made possible by the very existence of the illustrations Woolf selected and included in her novel. When the illustrations are removed, this layer of meaning is lost. Censorship and self-censorship, rather than translation itself, are the cause of this loss. The movement between past, present and future as well as between the different phases of Orlando's identity is captured through the images Woolf included in her novel in a way that parallels Orlando's moments of transformation. Without the illustrations Woolf included, such questions would never see the light of day. The images themselves remain unchanged in the process of translation, much like Orlando's identity throughout the centuries. These images, along with questioning the limits of language in this novel (illuminated so well in the process of translation), represent the ways in which Woolf herself was challenging the censorship she encountered.

During the interwar period, Virginia Woolf was recognised by several Romanian critics and writers as an innovative author whose works could be situated within a modernist aesthetic that was just starting to be defined and practised in Romania. The system of totalitarian communist repression and censorship instituted after 1944 destroyed such connections that were developing organically between Romanian and English modernisms. The re-emergence of Woolf's works on the Romanian literary scene with the first translations of *Orlando* and *Mrs Dalloway* in 1968, gradually followed by other translations in subsequent decades, did not necessarily restore the connections that had begun to develop during the interwar period. However, examining these translations and the contexts in which they were created provides a wealth of insights and knowledge about not only the art of translation but also the original texts themselves. These translations begin a dialogue that goes back and forth between the source and the target texts and cultures; they open up a space in which we might be able to gain an even deeper, more complex understanding of Woolf's works and perhaps see them in a different light through the eyes of a Romanian reader, translator, writer or critic.

Notes

1. 'Mai sintetică decât Joyce, mai profundă decât Huxley și fără îndoială mai artistă decât amândoi, Virginia Woolf este o scriitoare chintesențial brită. Același sentimentalism nuanțat de o conștiință de umor și de autoironie, același realism fantastic înrădăcinat în imaginative, pe care le găsim în romanele lui Sterne și Dickens, se întrupeaza în varianta unei sensibilități absolut moderne, în scrierile ei.' All translations mine unless otherwise indicated.
2. 'Sub orice cuvânt rostit de personaje, se ascunde istoria, importanța, impresiile, amintirile evocate de acel cuvânt în sufletul vorbitorului, așa încât cunoaștem deodată vieți și temperamente, dorința și rezonanța anilor lungi în ecoul vorbei, care niciodată nu e valoare în sine, deci inaptă pentru dramatizarea acțiunei. Timpul nu e creat deci prin mișcare ci printr'o secțiune verticală sub staticul momentului.'
3. 'afirmă o concepție nouă a romanului'.
4. 'Deci alta trebue să fie "materia" romanului decît cea convențională. Cît mai puțin posibil amestec de fapte exterioare; oglindirea perfect sinceră și curajoasă a miriadelor de impresii, banale, fantastice, – ploae de nenumărați atomi, care constituesc viața unui om obișnuit într'o zi ca toate celelalte; și mai ales sesizarea acestei variații, a spiritului schimbător, necunoscut, nelimitat care le relevă cu variată intensitate, azi, mîni.'
5. 'Un character nu trebue sa fie un obiect pe care să-l observi și să-l descrii din afară, trebue să te transpui în interior, în mijlocul propriilor lui simțuri și cu ele să prinzi și să înregistrezi acele miriade de impresii care consituesc viața interioară de o zi, tot ce-i trece prin cap într'o zi unui om, în legatură cu viața exterioară pe care o duce.'
6. 'literatura din perioada interbelică nu mai este preocupată de traduceri. Centrul de interes se deplasează spre *comentariul critic*.'
7. The translation itself, by Socec publishing house, does not include a year of publication and I have found both 1942 and 1943 as the year of publication in various sources (i.e. Traian Finţescu dates it at 1943). However, a review of this translation, 'Limba traducerilor' ['The language of translations'] published in 1943 in the journal *Viața* [The Life], dates the translation to 1942 ('Limba traducerilor').

8. Proletarskaja kul'tura (proletarian culture).
9. Troncotă explains that Ceaușescu continued and strengthened the political line of an authoritarian nationalist communism begun by his predecessor, Gheorghe Gheorghiu-Dej (2006: 164, 168).
10. A mutual-defence organisation established by the Warsaw Treaty of Friendship, Cooperation, and Mutual Assistance (14 May 1955–1 July 1991) that included the Soviet Union, Albania, Bulgaria, Czechoslovakia, East Germany, Hungary, Poland and Romania.
11. Abortion had been legalised in Romania in 1957, and the communist government believed that this led to a sharp decline in the birth rate. In reality, there were other factors at work in this decline, such as an increasing participation of women in the labour market and a very low standard of living. However, the decrease in population growth was blamed on the 1957 law. As a result, in 1966 Ceaușescu passed Decree 770 attempting to reverse the population decrease by criminalising abortion and contraception. Whereas before 1966 Romania had one of the most liberal abortion policies in Europe, afterwards it adopted one of the most stringent laws, which was strictly enforced. The monitoring and control of all aspects of private and public life were applied to women's reproductive systems in particular.
12. As with all of Woolf's 'illustrated' books (including *Orlando*), subsequent editions randomly omitted the illustrations Woolf originally included. See, among others, Julia Duffy and Lloyd Davis, who write,

    > Apart from *Three Guineas*, Woolf's other books with illustrations are all 'biographies': *Orlando: A Biography*, *Flush: A Biography*, and *Roger Fry: A Biography*. Over the years, reprints and new editions of these works have also randomly omitted the pictures or changed their number or size. Occasionally, later editions have restored the original pictures (for example, the 1973 Harvest edition of *Orlando*) or added extra ones. (1996: 129)

    See also a discussion of the illustrations in *Orlando* in the Cambridge critical edition's 'Publication history' (O 2018: lxi–lxxii).
13. '"Orlando" rămâne, în ambiguitatea sa structurală, unul dintre textele fundamentale pentru înțelegerea atitudinii Virginiei Woolf față de o serie de aspecte care au preocupat-o în cel mai mare grad de-a lungul întregii sale activități literare: identitate, imaginea androginului, relația dintre masculin și feminin așa cum este aceasta reflectată de cultura occidentală (britancă, mai ales!) începând din perioada renascentistă și până în epoca modernă.'
14. 'Orlando e adolescent în epoca elizabetană, iubește în frenetica și licențioasa epocă a Stuarților, devine din bărbat femeie, în timpul unei ambuscade la Constantinopol, străbate vitalul veac al XVIII-lea, se căsătorește în puritana eră victoriană, are treizeci și șase de ani în 1928. Epocile istorice străbătute de acest erou-eroină sînt tot atîtea ipostaze, reprezintă tot atîtea disponibilități ale propriei sale conștiințe, a cărei flexibilitate îi acordă pasiune în veacul Elizabetei, frivolitate sub Jacob Stuart, însușiri matrimoniale în era victoriană.'
15. I further discuss this character in my previous work (Varga 2017).
16. Diane Gillespie discusses Woolf's subversive use of photography in *Three Guineas* (1993), while Erika Flesher shows how Woolf's use of photography in *Orlando*, 'to create a flexible family history' 'allows her to revise [and even undermine] the conventions of her father's more standard biography' (1997: 42, 46). Helen Wussow argues that 'Woolf chose the images [in *Three Guineas*] in order to make the argument that photographs can be manipulated and supposedly hard factual evidence weighted on the side of one's argument' (1994: 2). Maggie Humm reminds us that Woolf herself 'took more than 1,000 domestic photographs' (2010: 7) and analyses *Flush*'s use of photographic tropes and the use of photography in Woolf's companion works 'Aurora Leigh', 'The cinema' and *Three Guineas* 'in terms of modernist photography and Woolf's specific camera expertise', demonstrating 'the significance of the visual in a text usually praised for its olfactory sensuality' and 'the impact of photography on modernist writing' (2010: 7).

17. See also note 18.
18. Critics like Celia Marshik have taken the issue of Woolf's reaction to censorship a step further, arguing that Woolf's sensitivity to explicit representations of sexuality and the breaking of some taboos stemmed in part from her role as a publisher. Although establishing the Hogarth Press in 1917 meant that Woolf was free from other editors and publishers – as she famously wrote in her diary how she felt she was 'the only woman in England free to write what she liked' (D 4: 92) – both she and Leonard Woolf had to anticipate what the authorities would or would not accept. Miscalculations could bring prosecution, court costs and destruction of extant copies. Therefore, 'in publishing her own works, Woolf escaped editors but made her own sense of discretion all the more crucial' (Marshik 2006: 92). Furthermore, in 'Looking for Woolf in the National Archives', Marshik explains that she discovered a handwritten register for correspondence received by the Home Office in 1928, which 'records an anonymous letter regarding *Orlando* and summarizes the authors' point thus: "Considers shd. be suppressed"' (2004: 8). Although the original letter is not extant and not indexed in the catalogue of the National Archives, the existence of this register of correspondence 'does raise the possibility that *Orlando* was closer than many have suspected to suffering the same fate as Radclyffe Hall's *Well of Loneliness*' (O 2018: lxxix).
19. Talia Schaffer also refers to a level of censorship in Woolf's correspondence with Vita Sackville-West: 'Woolf's letters to Sackville-West are highly self-censored – so invitations to photographs had to substitute for more erotic invitations. . . . The photographs forced Sackville-West to disguise herself, as the photographs themselves disguised unwritten desires' (1994: 30).
20. See Flesher for excellent, in-depth discussions of the 'playful fictions inherent in these photographs' (1997: 42) in *Orlando*.
21. For a full description and discussion of the novel's illustrations, see the Cambridge University Press edition of *Orlando*, edited by Suzanne Raitt and Ian Blyth (2018: 305–6, 323–6).
22. In their photo albums and in their art, Woolf and Bell achieved representations of their family and friends that 'were a source of psychic and aesthetic imaginaries. The technologies of modernity – photography and cinema – were then an incentive to, and a medium for, border crossings in this special sense' (Humm 2003: ix).
23. 'Sunetul trîmbițelor se depărta și Orlando stătea gol-goluț. De la facerea lumii, nu s-a văzut ființă omenească mai încîntătoare. În alcătuirea sa se îmbina puterea unui bărbat cu grația femeii' (O 1968: 133).
24. 'Ne putem folosi de acest răgaz pentru a stabili cîteva fapte. Orlando se prefăcuse în femeie – asta nu poate fi tăgăduit. Dar, în toate celelalte privințe, rămase același. Schimbarea sexului, deși avea să-i schimbe viitorul, nu-i alteră cu nimic personalitatea. Fața a rămas, așa cum arată portretele, în bună măsură aceeași' (O 1968: 134). [We can use this respite to establish a few facts. Orlando had disguised as/become a woman – this cannot be denied. But, in all other regards, he remained the same. The sex change, although it would change his future, did not change his personality in any way. The face remained, as the portraits show, in good measure the same.]

Bibliography

Beza, M. (1928), *Romanul englez contimporan* [The Contemporary English Novel], București: Cultura Națională [The National Culture].

Botez, D. (1929), 'O estetică impresionistă a romanului' [An Impressionist aesthetic of the novel], *Viața Românească* [Romanian Life], 6 April, pp. 309–12.

Brezuleanu, A. M., I. Mihăilă, V. Nișcov, M. Schiopu and C. Ștefănescu (eds) (1997), *Bibliografia relațiilor literaturii române cu literaturile străine în periodice (1919–44)* [The Bibliography of the Relations of Romanian Literature with Foreign Literatures in Periodicals (1919–44)], vol. 2, București: Saeculum.

Caba, O. (1934), 'Virginia Woolf', *Pagini Literare*, [Literary Pages], 15 May, pp. 63–4.

Coborca, L. (2014), *Controlul cărții: Cenzura literaturii în regimul communist din România* [Book Control: The Censorship of Literature in the Romanian Communist Regime], București: Cartea Românească.

Cristea, V. (1969), 'Experiențele lui Orlando' [Orlando's experiences], *România Literară, Săptămînal de literatură și artă* [Literary Romania, Literature and Art Weekly], 2: 27 (39), pp. 22–3.

Duffy, J. and L. Davis (1996), 'Demythologizing facts and photographs in *Three Guineas*', in M. Bryant (ed.), *Photo-Textualities: Reading Photographs and Literature*, Newark: University of Delaware Press, pp. 128–40.

Finţescu, T. G. (2003), 'Receptarea operei Virginiei Woolf în România' [The reception of the works of Virginia Woolf in Romania], *Revista Bibliotecii Naţionale a României* [The Magazine of the Romanian National Library], 9: 2, pp. 32–7.

Flesher, E. (1997), 'Mock biography and photography', in D. F. Gillespie and L. K. Hankins (eds), *Virginia Woolf and the Arts: Selected Papers from the Sixth Annual Conference on Virginia Woolf*, New York: Pace University Press, pp. 39–47.

Gillespie, D. F. (1993), '"Her Kodak pointed at his head": Virginia Woolf and photography', in D. F. Gillespie (ed.), *The Multiple Muses of Virginia Woolf*, Columbia: University. of Missouri Press, pp. 113–47

Grigore, R. (2013), 'Orlando: Masculin, feminin, androgyn' [Orlando: Masculine, feminine, androgyne], *Cultura literară* [The Literary Culture], 426, 27 June, <https://revistacultura.ro/nou/2013/06/orlando-masculin-feminin-androgin>(last accessed 4 July 2019).

Humm, M. (2003), *Modernist Women and Visual Cultures: Virginia Woolf, Vanessa Bell, Photography, and Cinema*, New Brunswick, NJ: Rutgers University Press.

Humm, M. (2010), 'The 1930s, photography and Virginia Woolf's *Flush*', *Photography & Culture*, 3: 1, pp. 7–18.

Lee, H. (1994), 'Orlando and her biographer', *The Times Literary Supplement*, 4742, 18 March, p. 5.

'Limba traducerilor' [The language of translations] (1943), Cronica măruntă [The Minute/Minutiae Chronicle], *Viaţa* [The Life], 3: 908, 26 October, p. 2.

Marshik, C. (2004), 'Looking for Woolf in the National Archives', *Virginia Woolf Miscellany*, 65, pp. 7–8.

Marshik, C. (2006), *British Modernism and Censorship*, Cambridge: Cambridge University Press.

Schaffer, T. (1994), 'Posing *Orlando*', in A. Kibben, K. Short and A. Farmanfarmaian (eds), *Sexual Artifice: Persons, Images, Politics*, New York: New York University Press, pp. 26–63.

Tismăneanu, V. (2003), *Stalinism for All Seasons: A Political History of Romanian Communism*, Berkeley: University of California Press.

Tismăneanu, V., D. Dobrincu and C. Vaile (eds) (2007), *Raport final: Comisia Prezidenţială pentru Analiza Dictaturii Comuniste din Romania* [Final Report: The Presidential Commission for the Analysis of the Communist Dictatorship in Romania], București: Humanitas.

Troncotă, T. (2006), *România Comunistă: Propagandă și Cenzură* [Communist Romania. Propaganda and Censorship], București: Tritonic.

Varga, A. (2017), '"A shadow crossed the tail of his eye": The reception of Virginia Woolf in Romania: Heritage transformed', in J. de Gay, T. Breckin and A. Reus (eds), *Virginia Woolf and Heritage*, Liverpool, UK: Clemson University Press, pp. 230–5.

Vianu, L. (ed.) (1998), *Censorship in Romania*, Budapest: Central European University Press.

Woolf, V. (1928), *Orlando: A Biography*, London: Hogarth Press.

Woolf, V. (1938), 'Femeia în oglindă' [The woman in the mirror] ('The lady in the looking-glass'), trans. N. Marian, *Timpul*, 2: 451, p. 2.

Woolf, V. (1942), *Din beznă spre soare* [From Darkness towards the Sun] (*Night and Day*), trans. G. Sbârcea, București: Socec.

Woolf, V. (1968), *Orlando: O biografie* (*Orlando: A Biography*), trans. V. Călin, București: Editura pentru Literatură Universală.

Woolf, V. (1983), *The Diary of Virginia Woolf: Volume Four: 1931–35*, ed. A. O. Bell and A. McNeillie, London: Penguin.

Woolf, V. (1985), 'A sketch of the past', *Moments of Being*, ed. J. Schulkind, San Diego: Harcourt Publishing, pp. 61–160.

Woolf, V. (1994), *The Essays of Virginia Woolf, Volume 4: 1925–1928*, ed. A. McNeillie, Orlando, FL: Harcourt.

Woolf, V. (1993), *Orlando: The Holograph Draft*, transcribed and ed. S. N. Clarke, London: S. N. Clarke.

Woolf, V. (2005), *Mrs Dalloway*, ed. and intro. B. K. Scott, New York: Harcourt Publishing Company.

Woolf, V. (2006), *Orlando: A Biography*, ed. and intro. M. DiBattista, preface M. Hussey, Orlando, FL: Houghton Mifflin Harcourt Publishing Company.

Woolf, V. (2006), *Three Guineas*, ed. and intro. J. Marcus, New York: Harcourt.

Woolf, V. (2013), *Orlando: O biografie* (*Orlando: A Biography*), trans. A. Ralian, București: Editura Humanitas Fiction.

Woolf, V. (2018), *Orlando: A Biography*, ed. S. Raitt and I. Blyth, *The Cambridge Edition of the Works of Virginia Woolf*, Cambridge: Cambridge University Press.

Wussow, H. (1994), 'Virginia Woolf and the problematic nature of the photographic image', *Twentieth Century Literature*, 40: 1, pp. 1–14.

3

The Reception of Virginia Woolf and Modernism in Early Twentieth-Century Australia

Suzanne Bellamy

This exploration of Virginia Woolf's diverse Australian reception in the early twentieth century began with the discovery of an unpublished student thesis by Australian author Nuri Mass (1918–93), completed at the University of Sydney in 1942. Books and articles by Woolf had been circulating in Australia since the 1920s so that by the later 1930s there was a recognisable, if scattered, reception pattern of her work. Under the tutelage of modernist-influenced colonial academics, in the brief period just before the Leavisite dominance took over Australian English departments, Nuri Mass completed what was possibly the first full academic study of Woolf's entire oeuvre.[1] Its failure to be published most likely resulted from the Second World War and distance from European cultural centres, despite Mass's correspondence with and interest from Leonard Woolf. Mass's thesis was written near the end of Virginia Woolf's life and was completed just months after her suicide in 1941, incorporating the news only after most of the research was completed (Mass 1942). The wartime stigma on suicide reinforced an image of Woolf as fragile, perhaps even defeatist, creating some ambivalence over her legacy, as this chapter will show. Moreover, in an era of changing colonial attitudes to Britain and the rise of a vigorous Australian nationalism, the potential impact from a study such as Mass had produced was greatly diminished. Mass published only two small articles on Woolf and left academia, entering the world of publishing as a trainee editor before setting up her own printing press – inspired by the Hogarth Press – which allowed her to publish her own creative work, all while her brilliant research on Woolf lay silent (Bellamy 2007, 2008, 2018).

A major study of Woolf's reception in Australia entails detailed research into areas like library records, sales and book clubs beyond the scope of this essay. In addition to analysing newly digitised Australian newspapers from the period, this chapter also examines work by individual Australian reviewers and writers such as Nettie Palmer (1885–1964), Margaret (Margot) Hentze (1909–47), Christina Stead (1902–83) and Miles Franklin (1879–1954). My aim is to establish Woolf's literary presence among writers, artists, public intellectuals and reviewers in Australia from the 1920s to the later 1940s and to chart the emergence of an engaged reading public. Furthermore, examining the interplay between academic and non-academic responses to Woolf in Australia, as part of the pattern of modernist literary reception, illuminates the role of the Sydney University English Department in the development of literary criticism and the teaching of modernist texts. David Carter argues that Australian universities did not engage formally with Australian culture: 'there was no place within mainstream Australian literary culture where modernism – as a set of ideas, a movement – could be given an intellectual response' (2000: 266). However, this was not true of the young academics – specifically R. G. Howarth and Margot Hentze at the University of Sydney, both of whom taught Mass – though Carter's point emphasises how belated the Australian academic engagement was with Woolf.

New modernist theory (Mao and Walkowitz 2008; Latham and Rogers 2015) considers how early twentieth-century texts, such as Woolf's, moved about the world. My study of Mass's thesis and its contexts (Bellamy 2018) employs this theoretical framework, so that Woolf's work and identity act as a lens for the exploration of early Australian modernism and its transnational circuits. The tension and paradox of Woolf's very English form of modernist creative influence for Australian colonial and postcolonial readers, artists and writers form the larger focus of this chapter. The impact of interconnected networks between Bloomsbury and the colonial intellectual scene, involving publishing cartel politics and new international publication markets, exists within the context of Australian postcolonial debates about the nature of a national literature engaging with modernism and internationalism.

In Europe and the UK, rebellious modernist forms worked more directly against older traditions of the Western literary tradition. In new colonial settings, these influences coexisted with an equally rebellious consciousness working against the imperial dominant culture, which manifested as an emergent longing for a liberating internationalism as well as an ongoing suspicion of the patronising and dismissive attitudes of English literary elitism. These tensions affected the nature of Woolf's critical reception in the Southern Hemisphere through much of the twentieth century: Woolf was both embraced and rejected for her English sensibility, despite her radical feminist perspective and writings. Although Woolf's feminist works were widely reviewed and her novels read in Australia, the impact of the war and her suicide dramatically changed the nature of her reception. Furthermore, when Hogarth Press books began successful distribution in Australia, Australian intellectuals were involved in a complex search for new identities expressed in art and writing that were actively challenging the novelty invoked by British modernism. Encounters with Woolf, and the formalism of Roger Fry's paintings and Clive Bell's art theory, excited some interest in Bloomsbury's experimentalism, but the colonial context in which these encounters occurred put pressure on the centrality of imperial literary culture (Dixon and Kelly 2008; Webby 2000; Modjeska 1981).

Debates about modernism in an Australian literary context reflect that national literatures do not stand alone. Katherine Bode argues that questions of independence, Englishness and colonial dependence were always more nuanced in relation to modernist texts where internationalism was important in both literary and political areas, marking a shift away from a too isolated Australian literary criticism (2008: 184, 190). Indeed, transnational modernist approaches are changing previous perspectives of Australian literary culture as a nation apart and reveal, instead, that Australian literature has always been located in a global context (Bode 2008: 184, 190; Carter 2007). As Leigh Dale argues, 'the history of the teaching and criticism of Australian literature is a narrative of oppositionality to an Anglocentric core: Englishness dominated in curriculum, in appointments, in critical theory – whether

Leavisism or textual scholarship' (1999: 131). In this context, there is a central underlying tension in Woolf's Australian reception: that between the push towards creating a postcolonial national literature and the pull towards placing Australian literature in an international context.

New Readers and New Texts

Finding an Australian reading public for modernist texts depended greatly on sales and distribution, and thus was determined by the interests of international publishers who made decisions governed by costs and distance, colonial book distribution policies and, later, wartime paper shortages. Academics interested in international modernism and other aesthetic issues had always managed through private networks to obtain texts and journals, but the general reading public did not have this same access (Dixon and Rooney 2013). Censorship was a major factor, with 3,000 books banned on moral and political grounds by the mid-1930s. Arguments for protecting Australia from a flood of imported literature were strongly opposed by those advocating internationalism and anti-censorship. Those who believed that a national literature had to be exposed to the world in order to grow objected to tariffs on imported magazines and books, which was seen as a tax on knowledge. Nicole Moore notes that in Australia 'literary modernism had a notably different cast from its European and American models', with strict censorship creating a virtual 'cultural quarantine' (2012: 104). Censorship was an ongoing issue in news media, with the London obscenity trial of Radclyffe Hall's *The Well of Loneliness* (1928) reported on in December 1928 in Adelaide and with Virginia and Leonard Woolf listed among the prominent writers who signed a letter in defence of art and literature of merit (Buckridge and Morecroft 2013). Australian academics were attracted to Woolf's work and to the Hogarth Press booklists in part for their openness to anti-colonial texts and radical ideas.

Nicola Wilson's study of colonial markets for British published books demonstrates how London sought to dominate the international book trade, running a cartel that blocked American publishers from Australia (Wilson 2012, 2016). Contracts show that publishers bought rights 'for England, its Colonies, and Dependencies', with Australia as a major market for receiving cheaply bound colonial editions (qtd in Wilson 2016: 18 n.13). Colonial booksellers received discounts from British publishers, with books often costing less than they did in the UK, while royalties paid on colonial sales were low or non-existent. Hogarth editions of Woolf's works sold in Australia were wrapped in plain covers and stamped Colonial Cloth Editions. British publishers flooded the Empire with relatively cheap British literature, and the Hogarth Press benefited from that trade through the interwar years and beyond (Willis 1992: 287; Wilson 2012, 2016). Leonard Woolf's account books and records of monthly sales (1922–39) list Hogarth Press agents in four Commonwealth countries, including Australia (Willis 1992: 387). The cost of Hogarth Press books, including those by Virginia Woolf, did not change substantially in Australia throughout the 1920s and 1930s, averaging around 7/6d. for each novel. The peak years for sales and distribution of Hogarth Press books were 1927–8, and 1931–2, the same years when books by Woolf were most often mentioned and reviewed in Australian newspapers.

There is little in the Australian press about Woolf's works prior to 1928, the year in which her popularity grew after the Australian release of *To the Lighthouse* (1927). The earliest known Australian review of her work was published in the *Melbourne Herald* in June 1924 by Archibald T. Strong, Professor of English at Adelaide University, in his weekly column on European writers, where he mentioned Woolf's *Monday or Tuesday*:

> The first thing one notices about this book is its hideous and meaningless cover. . . . Some of the sketches within the book are interesting. Best of all, perhaps, is the one entitled An Unwritten Novel, which tells how the authoress invented an imaginary story for a drab-looking woman who sat opposite to her on a train-journey. The story was good and even moving; but as might have been expected, it turned out to be entirely untrue. (1924: 12)

A politically and culturally conservative pro-imperial thinker, Strong's response to the collection of short stories, as well as Vanessa Bell's design for the dust jacket of the UK edition, epitomises the curious ambivalence that marked aspects of Australia's reception of Woolf and Hogarth Press books through the 1920s and 1930s.

At this time, few Australian newspapers carried serious literary book reviews, although they did cover the rising significance of women writers (Dale 2012: 130). For example, in a society column published in Perth in 1924, the novelist Rebecca West is quoted as saying that there are more women than men among the new novelists, noting in particular Virginia Woolf, Stella Benson and Katherine Mansfield. 'They are all over 30. . . . Virginia Woolf, a brilliant woman only now taking the place she deserves in modern literature, is between 40 and 50' (qtd in 'Mainly about people' 1924: 7). West's point about age emphasises that globally Woolf was late to receive recognition as a modern novelist; Woolf was mid-career before she was ever reviewed in the Australian press. However, after *To the Lighthouse* was advertised by Australian booksellers, Woolf received more press references and reviews from perceptive contemporary critics.

Nettie Palmer on Woolf

Nettie Palmer was the most prominent Australian writer and critic of the early twentieth century to comprehensively read and write about Virginia Woolf. A freelance writer, Palmer published wherever she could, often in poorly circulated newspapers, in an effort to contextualise the relevance of Woolf for an emerging, primarily female, Australian readership. In *Modern Australian Literature* (1924), Palmer identified access to European writers and modernist ideas as a critical element for the further development of Australian writers. Lack of discerning literary criticism was a central problem, according to Palmer, since Australian criticism was either too academic or non-existent. Australian writers kept returning to traditional literary forms, which 'young writers of older countries are proudly trying to escape' (N. Palmer 1924: 58). Isolation and lack of originality in Australian writing were linked for Palmer; both presented crucial problems to be overcome by engagement with a wider cosmopolitanism and writers like Woolf (Jordan 1988).

Palmer followed the development of Woolf's essays and fiction through the interwar decades, displaying an interest in European literature and a desire for thoughtful literary criticism. Her work shows the difficulties Australian women writers experienced at that time, foreshadowing the problems and limited publishing choices young writers like Nuri Mass also faced after her university years. Access to public discourse was limited, and yet Palmer published columns in the press and advocated for the fusing of European modes and ideas with Australian literary culture as part of a new national voice (Modjeska 1981: 49). How this new Australian voice might emerge was the vision and hope raised by Palmer's work during the interwar period when it was possible to envisage choices, to travel and to expand on the idea of a modernist context, even with little hope of local publication or engagement with the dominant national culture (V. Palmer 1977; N. Palmer 1988: 282). In exploring the nature of cosmopolitan consciousness, Palmer poses questions about marginality, material choices, women's voices and a dominant masculine culture. Was it even possible for women to inhabit the space of cosmopolitanism? Exile was positive for writers like James Joyce, T. S. Eliot and Gertrude Stein, but theirs were chosen exiles. Australian women writers between the wars were 'exiles at home', in Drusilla Modjeska's term, echoing Woolf's definition of herself as an outsider in *Three Guineas*: '"as a woman I have no country. . . . [M]y country is the whole world"' (Modjeska 1981; Woolf 1938: 197). The idea of not belonging to a specific country in a colonial landscape was a powerful one in the 1930s, reinforced by Palmer's claims of being able to live and work anywhere and of the need for modern ideas and international community (1988: 282).

Enduring divisions between academic critics and creative writers in Australia throughout the period meant that non-academic figures like Palmer played a crucial part in forming literary public opinion. Woolf's essays on modernist literature provided an inspiring model for Palmer, since Woolf was a feminist writer and critic outside of academe who founded her own press. Palmer published two articles on Woolf, 'Virginia Woolf: Modernity in the novel' in the *Brisbane Courier* on 4 August 1928, followed by 'Mr Bennett and Mrs Woolf' in the *Illustrated Tasmanian Mail* on 13 November 1929. It is difficult to assess the influence of Palmer's essays on Woolf's Australian reputation, given their limited circulation, but they demonstrate her nuanced engagement with Woolf in the context of modernist ideas. Neither essay has been reprinted, and this speaks to the larger problem of the lack of interest and availability of research by Australian academic women, since many women like Palmer were only able to publish their work in newspapers. Against the idea that women's research lacked interest and influence, Modjeska (1981) argues that Palmer played a central role in shaping the work of and networks between Australian women writers of the interwar period.

Palmer's essay 'Virginia Woolf: Modernity in the novel' focused on *To the Lighthouse*, which had just won the prestigious Femina-Vie Heureuse prize. Well aware of the celebrity value of the prize, Palmer muses in the essay over how a novel so little known in Australia could win one: 'Perhaps the publicity of the prize will stimulate a moderate "snob sale" as well as an interest among genuine readers' (N. Palmer 1928: 24). In her percipient review, Palmer argued that the novel would not be popular because it demanded too much of its readers. Echoing Woolf's descriptions of Lily Briscoe's painting, Palmer describes *To the Lighthouse* as being like the strokes of a brush in a well-composed painting – where the effect of each paint stroke is blurred until the whole is seen, and all the while the structure lies firmly in place. Palmer also notes that the middle section reads like a despatch, with deaths and war noted in brackets in the immense darkness of time passing. For Palmer, Mrs Ramsay and Lily function as opposites, with Lily's painting holding a permanence that Mrs Ramsay's life cannot. Palmer compares the novel with *Mrs Dalloway*, pointing out how Woolf gives importance to the lives of mature women. She concludes that *To the Lighthouse* 'is a book of women, women from the two sides of Virginia Woolf's finely balanced mind and lightly-moved spirit' (1928: 24).

The title of Palmer's second essay, 'Mr Bennett and Mrs Woolf', refers to Woolf's essay on the modern novel, 'Mr Bennett and Mrs Brown' (1923). Palmer considers how reading Woolf's essay 'left me standing on the modern novel, the really "modern" novel with all its possibilities and uncertainties. What about this very modern novel? Has it done anything; has it come to stay?' (N. Palmer 1929: 4). Woolf's 'brilliant criticism' defines the gap between the writing styles of two different generations: Edwardian authors engaged in realism, like Bennett, and Georgian authors involved in modernist developments, like Woolf. Palmer's interest in the essay, however, lies in interrogating the very term 'modern'. Beyond implying frankness and simplicity, presenting life from a new angle, what does 'modern' actually mean? Palmer asks in her essay. She suggests that a new name is needed for this literary perspective that conveys some inherent meaning beyond its recent composition. For example, Palmer wonders whether Mrs Dalloway, whose observations and impressions are often interrupted, is too diffused as a character. This leads Palmer to posit that art has to do what casual observation cannot do: to make a synthesis; a myriad fragments of a day is not the day itself. In this way, Palmer's essay performs a discursive process, not unlike Woolf's own critical writing style, that twists thoughts back onto themselves for further investigation and encourages readers to examine their own reading practice. Interrogating her own uncertainty with Woolf's claims on modernity, Palmer frames questions about the modernist movement as a whole: 'Is it a clique?' she asks, or a new method of putting into words the stream of thoughts that rise from the unconscious? She concludes by calling on modernists to 'bring forth their inventions, one of them may be a star. Let them attack established writers' (1929: 4). This method of criticism brought to Australian readers interactions with texts regarded by many as too radical. From Woolf, Palmer gained insight not only into modernist texts but also into ways of addressing and engaging common readers, allowing her to assist in building readership of modernist texts despite their difficulty.

While articles and reviews were often not signed, with Palmer's reviews an exception, the late 1920s brought a general widening of interest in literary modernism, as shown in reviews, booklists and advertisements, readers' groups and issues of censorship. *Orlando*, which followed *To the Lighthouse* and was released in London in October 1928, was available for review and purchase in Australia by February 1929. Excitement in Australian press coverage indicated the Hogarth Press's improved marketing efficiency and an expansion of interest in Woolf's work. By the end of 1929, Coles Book Arcade in Sydney was advertising *The Voyage Out*, *Mrs Dalloway*, *Jacob's Room*, *The Common Reader* and other Hogarth Press books. The breakthrough of *To the Lighthouse*, followed by the celebrity success of *Orlando*, increased interest in Woolf's earlier novels, with reviews surfacing of her previously published works. A 1930 review of *The Voyage Out*, *Jacob's Room* and *Mrs Dalloway* acknowledged the demands of reading modern literature: 'In the hands of the modern author and critic the function of the novelist has been stretched beyond recognition, and novel reading has become as complicated as a course in psychology' ('The world of books' 1930: 3). Although Woolf has been labelled as unreadable by some of the reading public for her 'highly individual style' ('The world of books' 1930: 3), the reviewer goes on to praise her for her clever use of irony, stream of consciousness, innovative characterisation and advances in style and technique, and her success as a literary critic. With the publication of A Room of One's Own (1929), Woolf's reputation as a feminist public intellectual and novelist was consolidated in the Australian press.

Enter the University

Adult education courses on Woolf began appearing by the early 1930s, including one run in Perth by the University of Western Australia, with twenty lectures given by members of the English Department on twentieth-century novelists, including H. G. Wells, Aldous Huxley, James Joyce, D. H. Lawrence and Virginia Woolf ('Course notices' 1933). In Sydney, tensions between the university and creative writers were beginning to thaw as the 1930s unfolded. Younger academics founded literary associations and staged debates, amid political ferment on campuses in response to a greater sense of internationalism and a growing awareness of fascism. Access on campus to a wider range of European journals and banned books increased as more writers engaged with international literature. Guy Howarth, who supervised Nuri Mass's thesis on Woolf, was among this group, as were other Australian writers in university publications. Discussions about international literature took place in forums like the Australian English Association.

The first known academic discussion of the work of Woolf at the University of Sydney was at a meeting of the Australian English Association in a lecture given by Margot Hentze in late 1933, later printed as a pamphlet that remained available well into the 1940s (Hentze 1934). Like Mass, whose parents were British and Spanish, Hentze had European parents and completed her MA at Sydney in 1935, followed by a PhD at the University of London in 1938. She returned to Sydney as a lecturer in the History Department and was involved in political and literary life on campus throughout much of the 1930s. Hentze taught European History when Mass was enrolled in that course and was still active on campus in the late 1930s, when schisms over criticism and politics among the faculty were known to undergraduate students. Indeed, Mass later wrote a novel called *The Gift*, not published until 1969, set at Sydney University in the late 1930s. With an autobiographical back story, *The Gift* creates an academic world pressurised by the context of the approaching war. Mass regularly attended meetings of the Australian English Association, where Howarth and Hentze were office holders. Hentze resigned her lectureship in July 1939, determined to make her way to Europe and join resistance to the coming war, dying in 1947 in Belgium (Jacobs 1983).

The continued circulation of Hentze's pamphlet establishes a clear interest in Woolf in the University of Sydney English Department despite the growth of oppositional Leavisite influence, the source of much of the schismatic atmosphere. In the print version of her lecture, Hentze focused on how to assess Woolf's writing as a new form for the novel. She acknowledged a critical impasse in Woolf's Australian reception, given the inadequacy of accepted ideas in academia about literary technique and conventional standards of literary criticism. In so doing, Hentze highlighted a broader debate in Australia about the need for better literary criticism; Woolf's novels were such a complete break with tradition that they demanded a new set of critical values (1934: 3). In Hentze's analysis, Woolf's original point of view had a reflective quality, following the current of everyday thought, with an absence of traditional plot. It was however a method with limitations, possessing just sufficient unity to stop it from drifting into chaos. Reading *Jacob's Room*, *Mrs Dalloway*, *To the Lighthouse*, and a number of Woolf's essays, Hentze praised the imaginative penetration, intense poetry and lyric qualities; however, she also expressed reservations: 'A novel surely must have some kind of structure and symmetry: and if we reduce it to a mere collection of sensations, what possible structure can it have?' (1934: 4). On the other hand, she regarded Woolf's critical essays as miniature masterpieces, more readily accessible and better suited to Woolf's gifts: 'her very weaknesses as a novelist are her strength as an essayist' (1934: 8). The challenge in understanding Woolf's experimental writing style concerned this balance between structure and chaos; was Woolf's work so new as to require a new sensibility and new readership skills, or did it ultimately fall apart? For Hentze, answering this question required new critical literary analysis through an intensive reading of the work.

1930s Debates on Fascism and Responses to *Three Guineas*

Outside academia, the 1930s were a paradoxical mix of dire warnings about the impending rise of the Second World War while Australian life and business went on as usual. Woolf's books continued to be readily available in Australia, with press advertisements for *Flush*, *The Common Reader, Second Series* and 'Walter Sickert: A conversation' (1934), and several reviews of *A Room of One's Own* (McIntyre 1938). The Hogarth Press published a long list of young left-wing writers, postcolonial books and anti-war tracts, but despite this expansion in its publications, it was increasingly seen as aligned with an older conservative politics. An unsigned review of Dmitry Mirsky's *The Intelligentsia of Great Britain* (1935), a text with anti-Bloomsbury attitudes, appeared in the *Sydney Morning Herald* in June ('Current literature' 1935: 10). Mirsky, a Marxist, denounced Bloomsbury liberalism as thin-skinned humanism for enlightened and sensitive members of the capitalist class (1935). The reviewer noticed how Mirsky satirised both Bloomsbury and colonial readership's outmoded responses: Mirsky characterises Bloomsbury intellectuals, including Maynard Keynes, Lytton Strachey, Roger Fry, Clive Bell and Virginia Woolf, as

> intrigued by their own minutest experience. . . . The liberal aestheticism of Bloomsbury reached its season of moulting, lost its feathers. But they are assured, as the colonial and dependent lands take them up, Australia and Tanganyika exclaim over *Queen Victoria* and *Orlando*. ('Current literature' 1935: 10)

Meanwhile, concerns that the roots of fascism were not only foreign but also homegrown gained traction in the Australian media. The *Sydney Morning Herald* printed an article, 'Democracy v dictatorship', that covered news of a public manifesto against the rise of fascism signed by well-known intellectuals in London, including Woolf; her name recognition in the public press by this time was striking ('Democracy' 1934). The article highlighted the failing faith in democracy and defeatist acceptance of dictatorships and noted how even Australia was experiencing the threat of dictatorship and fascism. Although Woolf's *The Years* was written against this political backdrop and several reviews of it appeared in Australia in 1937, it was the publication of *Three Guineas* in 1938 which produced the most varied range of responses across the UK and abroad, as part of this ongoing debate about fascism. The *Hobart Mercury* published a positive review of *Three Guineas* headed 'Distorted Nietzsche: How Hitler seized his philosophy', which stated that war was definitely men's responsibility, since women played such a tiny role in world affairs. This review echoed Woolf's feminist, pacifist and anti-fascist idea that, in terms of education, women were left the ragged ends while men took all the resources ('Distorted' 1938: 8).

The most out-of-context coverage of *Three Guineas* appeared in the popular *Australian Women's Weekly* (Lovel 1938: 2). The article received a full-page spread, using photos similar to those in the first edition of *Three Guineas*, and referred to Woolf by name but never once mentioned the title of the book or any publication details. In addition, Australian material was added to the quirky coverage, with a photo of Australian Prime Minister Joseph Lyons visiting Buckingham Palace, and described these men's 'adventures in splendour' as 'a spectacle' (Lovel 1938: 2). Within the article, the clothes men wore in public were dissected and mocked, but there was no trace of the complex political content of *Three Guineas*' pacifism in the face of fascism and the nature of patriarchal institutions. This apparently whimsical piece of journalism in a women's magazine confirmed Virginia Woolf's celebrity status while also showing how such a controversial book could be depoliticised and cleverly recontextualised for the purposes of satire. Of all the references to Woolf in the Australian press, it stands as the most eccentric response.

The Influence of Modernism on Australian Writers

Virginia Woolf's possible influence on Australian writers was diverse, fragmentary, situational and circumstantial; her very originality formed a challenge to writers and academics, which may have had a lingering influence, even on those who rejected her writing methods and politics. Both Hentze and Palmer appeared to value Woolf the critic as much, if not more, than Woolf the novelist. While Australian novelist Patrick White's early fiction displayed clear Woolfian influences, Australian women novelists were not often stylistically linked with Woolf or modernism, apart from one of Eleanor Dark's earlier experiments. Palmer reviewed White's first novel *Happy Valley* in July 1939, calling it a new form of Australian writing influenced by European modernism, something she had advocated for two decades (N. Palmer 1939: 6). Noting specifically the influences of Woolf and Joyce, Palmer described White's novel as 'the first "stream of consciousness" novel attempted by an Australian writer' (1939: 6), an indication that the literary renaissance she hoped for in Australia was still possible. Indeed, Howarth was the first Australian academic to lecture on White's work (Marr 1991: 33). Though Howarth, Palmer, White and Woolf were connected by modernist aesthetics reaching into Australia, Woolf's direct influence is hard to ascertain.

Eleanor Dark's *Prelude to Christopher* (1934) employs a difficult technique with respect to the handling of time. Influential literary figures Marjorie Barnard and Flora Eldershaw (writing together under the name M. Barnard Eldershaw) found Dark's novel unconvincing and overcrowded, a negative criticism which strongly influenced Dark's future work. They felt that the method did not adequately fit the novel's project as they saw it:

The story is subjective only in that it is related from within the minds of the characters. The minds themselves and the story are conceived in hard objective terms and the stream of consciousness is merely a method of retelling. . . . This brittle objectivity under its thin subjective mask will not quite bear the burden of the novel. (Eldershaw 1938: 196–7)

Barnard and Eldershaw made other critical comments on modernist writers in their *Essays in Australian Fiction* (1938). There, the authors critiqued the use of stream of consciousness and took a contradictory position to Woolf's ideas on the emergence of new literary forms. They described novel writing as 'a recognised feminine profession', arguing that the reason women excelled in the novel was 'psychological' because women novelists did not have to combat a strong literary tradition, an argument very much the opposite of Woolf's in *A Room of One's Own*.

Australian writer Christina Stead arguably engaged with Woolf's modernism without ever naming her as an inspiration. While Stead did not like Woolf's writing or her politics, Susan Carson finds many interesting parallels between Stead's *The Man Who Loved Children* (1941) and Woolf's *To the Lighthouse*, in which 'each sought to represent the thoughts, and voice, of the child in experimental language' (Carson 2016: 1). Helen Groth identifies another link between Stead's *Seven Poor Men of Sydney* (1934) and Woolf's *Between the Acts* (1941) through the exploration of noise and sound, noting that Woolf's use of the gramophone, its rhythm and rhyme, resonates with Stead's use of city soundscapes (2015: 4). Carson refers to the work of Louise Yelin on the vexed matter of Stead's relationship with Woolf's work: 'Stead herself appears to be haunted by the spectre of Woolf, as she herself was haunted by the figure of the Angel in the House' (Carson 2016: 10 n.1). Yelin suggests that what is at play here is what Woolf scholar Jane Marcus described as the repression of Woolf as 'the mother of the enterprise' (qtd in Carson 2016: 10 n.1). Marcus found that this was a recurrent theme in feminist literary criticism, an active denial of Woolf's influence (Yelin 1990; Groth 2015).

Responses to Woolf's Death

News of Woolf's suicide appeared in the Australian press at a time of overwhelming war reports and public sensitivity to any perceived note of defeatism, an uninformed stigma that affected her reputation for some years. Many of Palmer's Australian friends and correspondents responded ambivalently to the news of Woolf's death, in particular novelist Miles Franklin, who had liked *Mrs Dalloway*, *To the Lighthouse*, *Orlando* and *The Waves*. Resolutely anti-war, Franklin read *Three Guineas* in 1939; it showed, she said, that Charlotte Perkins Gilman was right, 'war was the madness of men' (qtd in Roe 2008: 469). In July 1941 however, after hearing of Woolf's death, Franklin wrote:

I have suffered despair to such an extent that had I the pluck of Virginia Woolf I would do as she did, but also had I that pluck I would not do as she did because of that pang to perhaps a few sensitive souls here and there. She hung onto her pacifist views as long as she could. (qtd in Roe 2008: 403)

A more heartfelt testimony was sent to Vanessa Bell by twenty-two-year-old Marcie Collett from Adelaide, who lamented the loss of Woolf and confirmed her admiration of Woolf's life and work. The only known letter to Bell from Australia, it was discovered among the many condolence letters in the University of Sussex Collection of Leonard Woolf's Papers. While most letters in this collection were from literary and political figures, there were a few, such as this letter, from the general public.

> Wattle Park Burnside South Australia
> To Vanessa Bell,
> Whether it may be of any value to the friends of Virginia Woolf to know of the profound sense of loss felt by an unknown person on hearing of her death I cannot decide. And only a dreadfully vague report has dribbled through the press – and that a week ago. Do not doubt that I am aware of the futility of writing this letter; but I regret now tearing up several letters I wrote her in the effort to express my admiration and appreciation of her work. Surely it must have meant something, however many letters you got, to know that for one person – though you were ignorant of her existence – you were the symbol of all she admired in the art she was learning to practice, and as an individual; and that she would have given anything she possessed to have heard you speak or to have seen you? Because I do feel that if I should achieve anything worthwhile as a writer I owe more to her than to anyone else, and even otherwise I shall always have her in my mind as an example of a civilized woman. I won't add more to the melancholy correspondence which must have gathered about you, and I won't apologise either for this letter, because I think you would understand that when your lodestar is suddenly quenched you have to tell someone.
> There is nothing more to say but that
> I am
> yours sincerely
> Marcie Collett. (Oldfield 2005: 183)

A self-educated reader who studied Italian and worked as a translator for the Censorship Department in 1941–5, Kathleen Marcelle Muir (née Collett) found *A Room of One's Own* and *Three Guineas* in the Workers' Educational Association Library in South Australia, texts that supported her own 'feminist and pacifist convictions' (Oldfield 2005: 184). Muir's letter reveals the profound presence of Woolf's writing in her life. As with Mass, Muir was also inspired by Woolf's writing and publishing legacy; Muir found her way into the literary world through writing Australian children's literature and illustrations as well as founding The Wakefield Press. Her letter to Bell in 1941 can stand here as a marker for the unexpressed loss felt by other Australian readers on hearing of Woolf's death.

Leonard Woolf and *Southerly*

Following an article published in the Australian literature magazine *Southerly*, in which Howarth claimed that Woolf's early novel *Night and Day* must have been written before *The Voyage Out* – because he found it less developed and less mature – Leonard Woolf responded at length dismissing the claim (Howarth 1942; L. Woolf 1942: 10–11). This intervention is of note on several counts: Leonard's guardianship of the provenance and legacy of Virginia Woolf's work, his interest in a little magazine on the other side of the world, his attention to detail and his genuine involvement with colonial intellectuals. Leonard's rebuttal of Howarth's article, titled 'A note on Virginia Woolf's *Night and Day*', firmly and politely rejected the argument about the order of composition and publication dates. 'Mr Howarth's article in the April issue is ingenious and interesting but the facts are inconsistent with conclusions', he wrote. 'I feel that it is advisable to put them on record' (L. Woolf 1942: 10–11). With remarkable candour, Leonard wrote of his wife's mental state:

> At the end of 1913 she became seriously ill and had a mental breakdown, with recurring illness through the next few years. The illness from which she suffered all her life was acute neurasthenia, making prolonged strain or fatigue dangerous. By 1916 she began to write *Night and Day*, finishing it in March 1919. (L. Woolf 1942: 11)

Leonard also included a quotation, dated 27 March 1919, in his *Southerly* article from Virginia Woolf's yet unpublished diary, which may be the first-ever published extract from the text.

> In my own opinion N&D is a much more mature and satisfactory book than The Voyage Out; . . . I can't help thinking that, English fiction being what it is, I compare for originality and sincerity rather well with most of the moderns. L. finds the philosophy very melancholy. . . . I don't suppose I've ever enjoyed any writing so much as I did the last half of N&D. Indeed, no part of it taxed me as the Voyage Out did. (L. Woolf 1942: 10–11)

Leonard's surprising use of Woolf's diary in this article, a little more than a decade before his publication of *A Writer's Diary* and almost certainly for the first time after her death, reflected this period of heightened speculation in the years after Woolf's death, when judgements and legacy issues were in full play. That Leonard Woolf published this first diary extract in Australia testifies to his awareness of and involvement with Woolf's reception in Australia.

Roger Fry and the Painters

This chapter has primarily discussed Woolf's influence on Australian writers, critics and academics, but Australian visual artists were also influenced by Woolf and Bloomsbury. A lecture by Mary Cecil Allen to the Melbourne Society of Women Painters in 1935 highlights some of the questions raised by Woolf among women across the arts. Taking *A Room of One's Own* as its frame of reference, Allen advocates for the need of space, resources and time to work, reflecting on how women's lives were split between art and the domestic. She argued that women's paintings compared favourably with men's when they had sufficient independence to devote time to their work and were not forced to fit it in between domestic duties (Allen 1929, 1935).

Three of Australia's greatest modernist women artists, Grace Cossington Smith (1892–1984), Thea Proctor (1879–1966) and Margaret Preston (1875–1963), had encounters with the ideas and practice of Bloomsbury through the Omega Workshops, a design enterprise founded in 1913 by members of the Bloomsbury Group. Post-impressionist formalism offered new theories and ways of seeing, addressing some of the paradoxical dilemmas of colonial creative identity in writing and painting. It is widely claimed that Australia's painters embraced modernist formalism after the First World War, long before the writers, leaving a reactionary and anti-modern Australia for cosmopolitan experiences in Europe. For example, the above-mentioned group of women painters sought to engage with modernist forms by travelling to Europe, either to stay or to come and go in an effort to pass those ideas back home (Williams 1995). Engagement across art forms flourished, in texts and practices, creating links between Woolf, Bloomsbury and Smith, Proctor and Preston, three of the most experimental women painters in Australia.

While questions of influence are nuanced in relation to the visual arts, recent research brings new insight into transnational interactions and patterns of contact. The expansion of transnational modernist studies has opened up new fields of speculation about the influence of Woolf's novel *To the Lighthouse* in the lives of young women artists living thousands of miles away from the centres of London and Paris. In 'Did Grace Cossington Smith read Virginia Woolf?', Christopher Heathcote (2011) suggests linkages and possibilities that Woolf's creation of the fictional artist Lily Briscoe echoes the realities of colonial women artists. Grace Cossington Smith, regarded as the most significant painter of Australian modernism, was one of a group of women painters who shared many characteristics with the fictional Lily Briscoe: unconfident, unsupported and unmarried, but nonetheless desiring access to European ideas and aesthetic experimentation. What we know of Cossington Smith's story comes from the writings of her friend, painter Thea Proctor, who spent eighteen years in Europe from 1903–21 working at the Omega Workshops. On Proctor's return to Sydney, she formed the Contemporary Group, which included Cossington Smith and Margaret Preston (who had also worked at the Omega Workshops). Proctor went on to become an influential teacher in the interwar years, lecturing on modern design.

We see an example of the influence of Bloomsbury in Proctor's 1926 lecture '"Design". Miss Thea Proctor's talk to the students' (given at the Students Club on 21 August), subsequently published in the student magazine *Undergrowth* (Stephen et al. 2006, 160–2; Chanin 2014). Proctor wrote:

> The best definition of art which I know is Clive Bell's. He said: 'Art is not imitation of form, but invention of form'. . . . Art is so much more than representation. Composition is something that is quite mathematical. Every line you place in a certain shape must either conform to that shape or be in opposition to it. If you have a pronounced line going in one direction you must have another in the opposite direction to balance it. You can build up a composition on one pyramid. (Stephen et al. 2006: 160–2)

Proctor's words echo Lily's resolution of her painting in *To the Lighthouse*, making a connection with the line that brings the composition into balance around the triangle that forms the structure. This transmodernist resonance across colonial spaces and between women artists in the real and textual worlds gives extended meaning to the dynamic portrait of Lily Briscoe in Woolf's novel. Proctor and Cossington Smith are thus examples of influence and simultaneity. Speaking in an oral history interview late in her life, Cossington Smith said:

> I wanted to paint from the thing itself. . . . My chief interest has always been colour, but not flat crude colour, it must be colour within colour, it has to shine; light must be in it. . . . Forms in colour is the chief thing that I have always wanted to express. . . . Thea Proctor has always been an encouragement to me. (qtd in Stephen et al. 2006: 758–60)

Under the influence of Proctor, and possibly through the character of Lily Briscoe, Cossington Smith found ideas of composition and colour, of painting 'the thing itself', that would go on to shape her work.

Further material evidence of Australian connections with Woolf, Bloomsbury and Roger Fry have recently come to light through research by Anne Byrne in Ireland, where a previously uncatalogued cache of Cossington Smith's paintings was discovered in Galway, along with Fry's paintings (Byrne 2016, 2017/2018). The Cossington Smith paintings were purchased in Sydney by Irish art collector Gladys MacDermott who spent three years in Australia in 1927–9, becoming part of the Contemporary Art set. MacDermott's collecting taste was greatly influenced by Fry, who was close to the Irish art world and an adviser to several collectors. Following the trail of art in Australia, my research shows that MacDermott actually brought Fry paintings with her to Sydney, exhibiting them to friends and artists in her home. She knew Cossington Smith, Proctor, Preston and Fry and she promoted modernist works in text and painting; thus a wider Bloomsbury network emerges here. Fry's ideas and some of his actual paintings were seen and discussed in Sydney by this network of women artists. The social pages of *The Home*, an art magazine, reported:

> Gladys MacDermott . . . an enthusiastic and practical supporter of modern painting in Sydney . . . has taken away with her more than twenty works by several members of the Contemporary Group. A wide circle of friends had an opportunity of seeing and enjoying the collection of pictures hanging in her house which she brought to Australia with her. The collection included some of the most interesting works that have been seen in Sydney. ('Sydney s'amuse', 1929)

Led by women artists and collectors, these cosmopolitan social networks challenged Australian nationalism by bringing influential Bloomsbury artists and ideas into play at home.

Conclusion

In Australia, the reception pattern of Woolf as writer and public intellectual proceeded through early recognition, informed reviewing, some notoriety for her feminism and pacifism, judgements about her death, and a period of critical demise. As biographical material on Woolf became available in the early and later postwar period, interest in her life pulled focus away from her work. Nonetheless, it remains undeniable that Woolf's literary visibility in Australia can be attributed to the remarkable publishing and marketing skills of the Hogarth Press itself, particularly through Leonard

Woolf's determination during his wife's life and after her death to foster the international spread of modernist ideas (Southworth 2010). As Nettie Palmer had advocated, literary modernism's impact was to prove transformational in Australia, although it remained mixed with the desire for greater political independence. Furthermore, although this cannot be discussed here, the terms colonial and postcolonial remain problematic in a white settler culture which is still not postcolonial for indigenous peoples. Woolf's modernist texts are part of this complex cultural mix.

A writer's legacy pivots on so many points: ideas, timing, quality of work and the confluence of circumstances. Exploring the interrupted moments in the careers of individuals such as Mass, Palmer, Hentze, Dark and Stead allows for a different and more nuanced view of Australian modernism to emerge, one where broken patterns of influence are excavated to reveal their lasting marks. Although Woolf's influence on Australian writing in the first half of the century may have been limited, her feminist and critical texts opened up a crucial space for women writers, artists and academics, developing under the surface until the feminist revival of the 1970s, which is another story altogether.

Acknowledgements

I thank Anne Byrne, at the National University of Ireland, Galway, for information regarding Gladys MacDermott's collection of paintings by Grace Cossington Smith.

Note

1. For more on the impact of the Leavisite English curriculum, please see Chapter 11 by Jeanne Dubino in this volume.

Bibliography

Allen, M. C. (1929), *Painters of the Modern Mind*, New York: W. W. Norton.

Allen, M. C. (1935), 'Women painters', Melbourne Society of Women Painters Report 1935, Box 2/1, Melbourne: State Library of Victoria.

Bellamy, S. (2007), 'Textual archaeology: An Australian study of Virginia Woolf in 1942', in A. Burrells, S. Ellis, D. Parsons and K. Simpson (eds), *Woolfian Boundaries: Selected Papers from the Sixteenth Annual International Conference on Virginia Woolf*, Clemson, SC: Clemson University Digital Press, pp. 1–7.

Bellamy, S. (2008), 'Textual archaeology and the death of the writer', in D. Royer and M. Detloff (eds), *Virginia Woolf: Art, Education, and Internationalism: Selected Papers from the Seventh Annual Conference on Virginia Woolf*, Clemson, SC: Clemson University Digital Press, pp. 131–8.

Bellamy, S. (2018), 'Textual archaeology: A contextual reading of the 1942 Nuri Mass thesis on Virginia Woolf', dissertation, University of Sydney, Sydney eScholarship Repository, <http://hdl.handle.net/2123/18612> (last accessed 27 February 2020).

Bode, K. (2008), 'Beyond the colonial present: Quantitative analysis, "resourceful reading" and Australian literary studies', *Journal of the Association for the Study of Australian Literature (JASAL)*, special issue: 'The colonial present', pp. 184–97.

Buckridge, P. and E. Morecroft (2013), 'Australia's world literature: Constructing Australia's global reading relations in the interwar period', in R. Dixon and B. Rooney (eds), *Scenes of Reading: Is Australian Literature a World Literature?*, Melbourne: Australian Scholarly Publishing, pp. 47–59.

Byrne, A. (2016), 'The Galway Art Gallery collection and Roger Fry's *The Pond* (1921)', *Journal of the Galway Archaeological and Historical Society*, 68, pp. 181–216.
Byrne, A. (2017/2018), 'Roger Fry and the art of the book: Celebrating the centenary of the Hogarth Press 1917–2017', *Virginia Woolf Miscellany*, 92, pp. 25–9.
Carson, S. (2016), 'The children's chorus: Sibling soundscapes in *The Man Who Loved Children*', *Australian Literary Studies*, 31: 6, pp. 1–15.
Carter, D. (2000), 'Critics, writers, intellectuals: Australian literature and its criticism', in E. Webby (ed.), *The Cambridge Companion to Australian Literature*, Cambridge: Cambridge University Press, pp. 258–93.
Carter, D. (2007), 'After postcolonialism', *Meanjin*, 66: 2, pp. 114–19.
Chanin, E. (2014), 'Making Sydney modern', *Modernism/modernity*, 21: 2, pp. 547–56.
'Course notices. Adult education' (1933), *West Australian Newspaper*, April.
'Current literature' (1935), review, *Sydney Morning Herald*, 8 June, p. 10.
Dale, L. (1999), 'New directions: Introduction', *Australian Literary Studies*, 19: 2, pp. 131–5.
Dale, L. (2012), *The Enchantment of English: Professing English Literatures in Australian Universities*, Sydney: Sydney University Press.
'Democracy v dictatorship' (1934), review, *Sydney Morning Herald*, 30 March, p. 6.
'Distorted Nietzsche: How Hitler seized his philosophy' (1938), review, *Hobart Mercury*, 30 July, p. 8.
Dixon, R. and V. Kelly (eds) (2008), *Impact of the Modern: Vernacular Modernities in Australia 1870–1960*, Sydney: Sydney University Press.
Dixon, R. and B. Rooney (eds) (2013), *Scenes of Reading: Is Australian Literature a World Literature?*, Melbourne: Australian Scholarly Publishing.
Eldershaw, M. B. (1938), *Essays in Australian Fiction*, Melbourne: Melbourne University Press.
Groth, H. (2015), 'Modernist voices and the desire for communication in Christina Stead's *Seven Poor Men of Sydney*', *Journal of the Association for the Study of Australian Literature (JASAL)*, 15: 1, pp. 1–14.
Heathcote, C. (2011), 'Did Grace Cossington Smith read Virginia Woolf?', *Quadrant*, 55: 11, pp. 54–9.
Hentze, M. (1934), 'Address on Virginia Woolf', Australian English Association Offprint, 15, from *The Union Recorder*, 5 April.
Howarth, R. G. (1942), 'Dayspring of Virginia Woolf', *Southerly*, April, pp. 18–21.
Jacobs, M. (1983), 'Hentze, Margaret Edith (1909–47)', *Australian Dictionary of Biography*, vol. 9, National Centre of Biography, Australian National University, <http://adb.anu.edu.au/biography/hentze-margaret-edith-6645/text11449> (last accessed 15 July 2014).
Jordan, D. (1988), 'Palmer, Janet Gertrude (Nettie) (1885–64)', *Australian Dictionary of Biography*, 11, National Centre of Biography, Australian National University, <http://adb.anu.edu.au/biography/palmer-janet-gertrude-nettie-7948> (last accessed 7 March 2020).
Latham, S. and G. Rogers (2015), *Modernism: Evolution of an Idea*, London: Bloomsbury.
Lovel, A. (1938), 'Yet men dare to laugh at women's dress', *Australian Women's Weekly*, 6: 23, 12 November, p. 2.
McIntyre, M. E. (1938), 'Women writers', *Launceston Examiner* (Tasmania), 4 May.
'Mainly about people' (1924), *The Daily News* [Perth], 25 November, p. 7.
Mao, D. and R. Walkowitz (2008), 'The changing profession', *PMLA*, 123: 3, pp. 737–48.
Marr, D. (1991), *Patrick White: A Life*, London, Jonathan Cape.
Mass, N. (1942), 'Virginia Woolf the novelist', MA thesis, University of Sydney, Box 6F, Mass Papers, Mitchell Library.
Mass, N. (1969), *The Gift*, Sydney: Alpha Books.
Mirsky, D. S. (1935), *The Intelligentsia of Great Britain*, London: Victor Gollancz.
Modjeska, D. (1981), *Exiles at Home: Australian Women Writers 1925–1945*, Sydney: Sirius.
Moore, N. (2012), *The Censor's Library: Uncovering the Lost History of Australia's Banned Books*, St Lucia: University of Queensland Press.

Oldfield, S. (ed.) (2005), *Afterwords: Letters on the Death of Virginia Woolf*, New Brunswick, NJ: Rutgers University Press.
Palmer, N. (1924), *Modern Australian Literature*, Melbourne: Lothian.
Palmer, N. (1928), 'Virginia Woolf: Modernity in the novel', *The Brisbane Courier*, 4 August, p. 24.
Palmer, N. (1929), 'Mr Bennett and Mrs Woolf', *Illustrated Tasmanian Mail*, 13 November, pp. 4–5.
Palmer, N. (1939), 'Study of a country town', review, *The West Australian*, 15 July, p. 6.
Palmer, N. (1988), *Nettie Palmer: Her Private Journal Fourteen Years, Poems, Reviews and Literary Essays*, ed. V. Smith, St. Lucia, Queensland: University of Queensland Press.
Palmer, V. (1977), *Letters of Vance and Nettie Palmer 1915–1963*, Canberra: National Library of Australia.
Roe, J. (2008), *Stella Miles Franklin: A Biography*, London: Harper Collins.
Southworth, H. (ed.) (2010), *Leonard and Virginia Woolf: The Hogarth Press and the Networks of Modernism*, Edinburgh: Edinburgh University Press.
Stephen, A., A. McNamara and P. Goad (2006), *Modernism and Australia: Documents on Art, Design and Architecture 1917–1967*, Carlton, VIC: Miegunyah Press.
Strong, A. T. (1924), 'Pirates and saints', *Melbourne Herald*, 7 June, p. 12.
'Sydney s'amuse' (1929), *The Home: An Australian Quarterly*, 10: 9, 2 September, p. 10.
Webby, E. (ed.) (2000), *The Cambridge Companion to Australian Literature*, Cambridge: Cambridge University Press.
Williams, J. F. (1995), *The Quarantined Culture: Australian Reactions to Modernism 1913–1939*, Cambridge: Cambridge University Press.
Willis, J. H. (1992), *Leonard and Virginia Woolf as Publishers: The Hogarth Press 1917–1941*, Charlottesville: University Press of Virginia.
Wilson, N. (2012), 'Traces from the archive: Colonial editions and British publishing houses, 1880–1940', symposium paper, University of Reading.
Wilson, N. (2016), 'British publishers and colonial editions', in Wilson (ed.), *The Book World: Selling and Distributing British Literature, 1900–40*, Leiden: Brill, pp. 15–30.
Woolf, L. (1942), 'A note on Virginia Woolf's *Night and Day*', *Southerly*, 3: 3, pp. 10–11.
Woolf, V. (1938), *Three Guineas*, London: Hogarth Press.
Woolf, V. (1953), *A Writer's Diary: Being Extracts from the Diary of Virginia Woolf*, ed. L. Woolf, London: Hogarth Press.
'The world of books' (1930), *The Mercury* [Hobart], 17 January, p. 3.
Yelin, L. (1990), 'Fifty years of reading: A reception study of *The Man Who Loved Children*', *Contemporary Literature*, 31: 4, pp. 472–98.

4

Dialogues between South America and Europe: Victoria Ocampo Channels Virginia Woolf

Cristina Carluccio

When Victoria Ocampo (1890–1979) learned from Aldous Huxley (1894–1963) that Virginia Woolf was to participate in a photographic exhibition held in London, she went there without great expectations. She had heard rumours about how hard it was to meet with Woolf – she 'went out very little' (Ocampo 1946: 250), it was said. Nevertheless, the trip was successful: the two women did meet.[1] In November 1934, the lucky and unforgettable moment arrived, when Ocampo saw that Woolf's 'extraordinary face was already looking' (1946: 250) at hers.

On that occasion, the two women began an intense dialogue that lasted for several years, marked by phases of genuine transnational cooperation. As Ocampo explains, they were 'born in different environments and climates, one Anglophone, another Latin and from America, one attached to a formidable tradition and another attached to emptiness' (1982a: 101–2).[2] Given the emphasis that Ocampo herself placed on some of her divergences from Woolf, their relationship has frequently been described as 'uneven' (Beeber 2015: 22), characterised by a kind of inequality that became accentuated due to their distinct perception of 'what it is like to be a woman writer' (Lojo Rodríguez 2002: 227). Cultural factors have also been variously highlighted by the scholarship as being closely linked to this disparity. For instance, Matthew Beeber explicitly attributes a peripheral position to Ocampo's Argentina. He consequently refers to Woolf's and Ocampo's interaction as involving a 'metropolitan center' and a 'colonized (semi)periphery' (2015: 21). This cartographic approach inevitably leads to a depiction of relationships between countries such as Argentina and Great Britain, and accordingly between Ocampo and Woolf, as being highly asymmetrical. On the contrary, their cultural differences may have acted as a source of a reciprocal fascination for both women: in each there is 'something . . . racially different that the other desires' (Rogers 2012b: 141). Indeed, as Bernice L. Hausman claims, it was precisely by 'asserting her difference from the Englishwoman' that Ocampo managed 'to gain access to Woolf' (1990: 205). In the wake of Hausman's analysis, this chapter will show that any geographical hierarchy apparently influencing Woolf's and Ocampo's relationship was actually erased by their shared struggle against women's subordination to male power, which had become even more threatening during fascism. After all, Ocampo herself seems to have evaluated the actual gap between them in very positive terms, as a potential way of satiating a 'hunger' (hambre) that was otherwise so difficult to satisfy (Ocampo 1982a: 102).

Mariano Siskind appears to be very helpful in exploring this 'hunger' (Ocampo 1982a: 102) that animated the two women's exchanges:

> In Latin America (as in other global peripheries), critical and aesthetic cosmopolitan discourses shared a common epistemological structure that I call *deseo de mundo*, desire for the world. Cosmopolitan intellectuals invoked the world alternately as a signifier of abstract universality or a concrete and finite set of global trajectories traveled by writers and books. (Siskind 2014: 3)

More precisely, the notion of 'deseo de mundo' – or 'desire for the world' – suggests that Woolf's and Ocampo's 'hunger' should be seen as the epitome of a female desire for borderless circulation and reception in literary circles, such as those enabled by the 'global trajectories' traced by the journal – and, later, publishing house – *Sur* [South] (Siskind 2014: 3).[3] Through *Sur* Ocampo provided young writers with an opportunity to publish their works and allowed a Spanish-speaking readership to discover and appreciate texts written in languages other than Spanish, which would have been all but inaccessible without the translations she commissioned. In doing so, *Sur* aligned itself with (and took an active part in) a broader process of modernist trans-circulation.

At the same time, however, Siskind's concept needs to be considered within 'a more expansive framework' (Friedman 2015: x). Siskind clearly acknowledges in Latin America's literary modernism the presence of 'particularistic' and 'cosmopolitan discourses' (2014: 106), and also stresses South America's attitudes towards other cultures, which were more positive than earlier (2014: 104–5). Nevertheless, what most transpires from his account is the exclusion of 'the *modernistas*' world literary discourse' from 'the whole world' (2014: 105).

In fact, as early as 1927, 'Otro horóscopo Victoria (Ocampo)' ['Another Victoria (Ocampo) Horoscope'] by the Argentine painter Xul Solar had shown in a sort of artistic premonition the process of internationalism that Ocampo was to initiate three years later by founding *Sur*. Gorica Majstorovic refers to this canvas by Solar to convey visually – by reference to the 'four encircled spaces' (2005: 171) in the picture – the journal's dual policy of promoting Argentina's involvement in a global literary movement while conserving its local aesthetics (2005: 171). In the light of Ocampo's Argentina-based expansionist project, her relationship with Woolf doubtlessly exemplifies the complexity of the exchanges that impacted twentieth-century cultural geography. As this chapter will stress, not only did Ocampo fulfil her special 'hunger' by talking to Woolf (Ocampo 1982a: 102), but the British writer herself showed an unusual understanding of this need.[4]

Ocampo's 'Carta a Virginia Woolf' [Letter to Virginia Woolf],[5] which may be read as a personal homage, reserves a central place for 'hunger'. This notion permeates the first volume of her *Testimonios* [Testimonies] (1990), described as 'a series of testimonies of my hunger' (Ocampo 1982a: 102).[6] The connection that follows between Ocampo's 'hunger' and Woolf becomes much more evident in the light of Ocampo's decision to use her 'Carta' to open the first volume of *Testimonios*, as though Woolf herself had guided the writing of those essays as a distant mentor.

It was Ocampo who first revealed her 'hunger' – the 'writing impulse' (Lojo Rodríguez 2016: 467) that consumed her – to Woolf, who concurred. In 'Carta a Virginia Woolf', Ocampo confessed to her publicly: 'it was you with whom I talked recently – and in a way that cannot be forgotten – of this richness, which is born from my poorness: the hunger' (Ocampo 1982a: 102).⁷ This shared 'hunger' has also been read as a trope of the letters the two women exchanged (Luckhurst 2002: 7) and hence as a sort of migrating phenomenon, moving between two distant worlds – namely Argentina and Britain – as well as between the different semantics of two languages. On 5 December 1934, after reading the copy of 'Carta' sent by Ocampo, Woolf marked a crucial point in their friendship by sympathetically writing to her: 'I agree about hunger: and agree that we are mostly satiated, or so famished that we have no appetite' (*L* 5: 349). Again, it is the two women's similarities in spite of their differences that may have suggested to Ocampo the unmissable source of intellectual satiation that Woolf represented, and not just for herself.

Indeed, Woolf stood out as being absolutely the right person to support the intellectual plans Ocampo had in mind – and was already actualising via her journal *Sur*. She did this by providing an intellectual form of satiation for the hunger that numerous women may have been feeling, without, however, being able either to sate it or to seek its fulfilment. As if requesting the help of all women, she wrote: 'What each of us realises in her small life has an immense importance, an immense power when lives are added to one another. Let us not forget this' (Ocampo 1936: 68).⁸ While nourishing such beliefs, Ocampo may have truly thought that a kind of global hunger would continue to haunt women, unless ways to feed it were found. Sharing Woolf's ingenious feminist vision – expressed throughout her writing and strongly shaped by her own and others' womanhood – aligned perfectly with this project.

Woolf and Ocampo's view of the female universe as a whole undergirds the desire they both had to cultivate women's dignity and success, thereby giving birth to a form of 'international feminism' (Rogers 2012a: 471) that transcended geographical and cultural factors. Woolf's and Ocampo's alliance thus inaugurated 'an aesthetic fulcrum that played a decisive role in the formation and circulation of transatlantic modernist practices' (Novillo-Corvalán 2017: 35). As such, this alliance joined the large number of other intellectual bonds that were then forming across borders, collectively demonstrating the need for today's scholars to go beyond 'the center/periphery and diffusionist frameworks that still prevail in the field across the disciplines' (Friedman 2015: x)⁹ and 'to arrive at new kinds of comparisons that would go beyond the clichés' (Huyssen 2005: 13) still extensively employed in criticism.

Surpassing categories is also what Melba Cuddy-Keane suggests while simultaneously seeking to address the ambiguities permeating what she calls 'Woolf's global consciousness' (2010: 159).¹⁰ From one point of view, Woolf herself somewhat complicated our understanding of her participation in certain global dynamics. In this respect, her legendary words from *Three Guineas* (1938) are emblematic: 'as a woman, I have no country. As a woman I want no country. As a woman my country is the whole world' (*TG*: 129). As Jessica Berman observes, this 'phrase by Woolf casts her ... as a cosmopolitan outsider' (2001: 115). To clarify Woolf's global views, we need 'both to situate her thinking in relation to that of her contemporaries and to expand our own thinking by viewing her work through multiple eyes' (Cuddy-Keane 2010: 159). In other words, the significance of Woolf's 'global consciousness' will become clearer if we look both '*in and around* Virginia Woolf' (Cuddy-Keane 2010: 160).¹¹

Clearly, an examination of Woolf's interaction with Ocampo requires that we bypass the approach of twentieth-century geography – and, accordingly, of its literature – as structured into a periphery and a centre. This is, after all, what they themselves did when they met. Their 'gaze', albeit 'different' (Ocampo 1982a: 101),[12] more importantly sealed a union that no distance could destroy in the following years.

Women's Desire for Dialogue: Against a Monologic Discourse

Ocampo's trip to Italy, where she met with Benito Mussolini in September 1934, constituted the anguished prelude to her delightful encounter with Woolf in London in November the same year. Meeting soon after that first event, Woolf and Ocampo naturally discussed the Italian dictator, among other topics, at length, revealing to one another their shared anti-fascist ideals.[13] Woolf was anxious for Ocampo to describe her first-hand impressions of Mussolini and took advantage of their first meeting to satisfy her curiosity. In 'Memories of Virginia Woolf', Ocampo reports: Woolf wanted to know 'what . . . Mussolini had said to me about women when I saw him ("The brute!" she exclaimed when I told her)' (Ocampo 1946: 253). Woolf's reaction is not surprising, considering that a few years later she tackled the troubled relationship between fascism and gender in her magnificent *Three Guineas*, although her treatise was concerned with England, an apparently democratic country. In the diary, Woolf also recalled the discussion with Ocampo about this relationship: 'there we stood & talked, in French, & English, about . . . Rome & Mussolini, whom she's just seen' (*D* 4: 263). Woolf adds that, as the dictator heard of Ocampo's 'unhappy marriage', he advised her: 'now go & have a child' (*D* 4: 263).

As expected, Ocampo's conversation with Mussolini could not but touch on her gender at some point. Fascist laws concerning women were very strict. Ocampo's portrait of her visit to the Italian dictator, titled 'Living history' (1990; published originally as 'La historia viva' in 1935), is centred precisely on Mussolini's unwavering belief in the separation of gender roles, which can be condensed in the following imperative: 'the first duty of women is to give children to the State' (Ocampo 1990a: 218). Before meeting Mussolini, Ocampo was aware of what she was allowed to say. As Woolf wrote: 'when a subject is highly controversial – and any question about sex is that – one cannot hope to tell the truth' (*AROO*: 8). Ocampo knew that she could not be completely honest with Mussolini.

With this awareness in mind, the feminist Ocampo found more than one difficulty in talking to Mussolini. Driven by an interest in an empirical approach to history – 'I like living history' (Ocampo 1990a: 217), Ocampo explained in response to the understandable doubts regarding her intention to meet with Mussolini – she nonetheless wished to benefit from her stay in Rome, where the dictator lived. Apparently, their encounter went smoothly: Mussolini 'was simple & kind – on purpose', Woolf comments with sagacious suspicion in her diary, referring to what Ocampo had told her (*D* 4: 263). Although Ocampo had been welcomed by a gentle Mussolini, she could instantly sense the urge to despotism underlying his words: 'His answers were hurled at me as from a catapult' (Ocampo 1990a: 218). By using warlike language Ocampo conveys a convincing equivalence between Mussolini's violent resolve in political and military matters and his aggressive determination in his verbal interaction with her. In contrast, Woolf and Ocampo were able to build a bridge of female complicity against him – and, more broadly, against whatever he represented. As Gayle Rogers argues, both women 'enjoyed belittling Il Duce's apparently fragile ego together' (2012b: 140).

Theirs was a true dialogue, which also sought to mock the monological virility of an egotistical man such as Mussolini. Their discussion of him proves that they were able to immediately create a climate of sympathetic solidarity by sharing a common view of (and against) Fascism's appalling policies. These had worsened women's condition by turning Italy into 'a country for men' (Ocampo 1990a: 220), in line with an absurd logic of grammatical consistency. Since there had to be grammatical coherence with 'State' – a masculine noun in Italian – women were obviously obscured by this 'grammatical rule of agreement' (Ocampo 1990: 220).

Ocampo's report of her talk with Mussolini shows that her own womanhood had influenced his choices on an interpersonal level during their conversation. Both women also knew that such practice had a long history. It was the consequence of a mono-gendered hierarchy of power, rooted in men's ancient belief in women's preconceived inferiority. Hence, when they first met, Woolf and Ocampo reflected on what was really just a sad confirmation of what each of them already knew: Ocampo's talk with Mussolini could never have unfolded as a dialogic form of interaction.

Victoria Ocampo's 'La mujer y su expresión' [The woman and her expression] (1936)[14] ponders such gender-related questions in verbal interaction, in addition to those concerning male and female kinds of writing. In the essay, Ocampo creates an unbridgeable gap between the two genders' form of communication: 'Until now, the monologue seems to have been his preferred mode of expression' (1936: 62). When talking, men merely recite a monologue, and they paradoxically perpetuate this even within their own gender, since 'conversation between men is just a dialogic form of this monologue' (Ocampo 1936: 62).[15] Despite being unable to provide any gratification to women, the monologue has long been preferred as a natural style in the male sphere. Hence, Ocampo proposes a change: she 'promotes dialogue as a way to revise the masculine mirror text' (Hausman 1990: 209). Women's freedom had to be initiated by a clear act of self-assertion, both in writing and in speech; and this had to be strong enough to break the 'mirror' (Hausman 1990: 209) of men's self-referential voices.

As an example pertaining to women's everyday lives, Ocampo recounts a telephone conversation she overheard between a husband and wife. At the end of the account, she comments that, 'for centuries, every conversation between men and women . . . has started with: "do not interrupt me" from the man' (1936: 62).[16] In contrast to men's monologic performances, as a woman Ocampo politely and quite unexpectedly asks of her audience: 'Interrupt me. This monologue does not make me happy. It is to you that I wish to talk, and not to myself' (1936: 62).[17] As Ocampo's request shows, her main suggestion for coping with men's monologues lies in women's brave attempts to 'interrupt' their male interlocutors instead of remaining content with a forced silence. Interruption is therefore conceived as a key step by which, little by little, men could be educated towards a more equal verbal exchange that might finally develop into full respect for their listeners' replies. Ocampo concludes her essay 'La mujer y su expresión' precisely with this hope, namely that, 'from interruption to accepted interruption, [men] may naturally arrive at dialogue' (1936: 69),[18] ultimately including women as active speakers as well.

In her meeting with Mussolini, Ocampo endeavours to remain unaffected by his reflexes in discourse that clearly exemplify the male habit of talking via monologues. Mussolini's ideas were very clear and firm, since his 'precise sentences . . . left no room for any doubt or misunderstanding' (Ocampo 1990a: 218). Given the unpleasant meeting with the dictator in September 1934, Ocampo's dialogic encounter with Woolf in November occurred at a strategic moment. It may, at least, have partly counterbalanced the acrimony of her recent experience in Rome, by offering her a renewed strength and optimism via a fresh and precious friendship. Of course, when Ocampo first saw Woolf, she already knew who Woolf was. Her admiration for Woolf as a woman of letters was part of a broader feminist programme that she had been cultivating ever since the first steps of her career;[19] having read all the works Woolf had published by that time, Ocampo was a true aficionado.[20] What Ocampo discovered during her meeting with Woolf, however, was something that no reading would have unveiled to her. As Ocampo observes, 'Virginia Woolf could talk as marvellously as she wrote' (Ocampo 1946: 254). What is left tacit in Ocampo's account is that Woolf 'could talk . . . marvellously' as a woman. The linkage between womanhood and speech also lies at the very core of Ocampo's depiction of her interaction with Woolf, which portrayed 'two women [who] talk about women' (1982a: 101).[21] This is a very simple description, but their dialogue acted both as the main instrument through which they shared their ideas and as a major weapon they could employ to fight gender inequality.

Curiously enough, although Ocampo sought to persuade women not to be afraid to 'interrupt' in conversation (Ocampo 1936: 62), she felt, when talking with Woolf, 'discomfort . . . in the face of her insatiable curiosity' (Ocampo 1946: 253). This is an intriguing emotion, especially if it is read in light of Ocampo's previous thoughts – and related comments in conversation with Woolf – concerning her talk with Mussolini. Ocampo evidently felt delighted yet helpless in the face of her interlocutor's curiosity: 'Virginia asked me a thousand questions . . . for she wanted to know everything' (Ocampo 1946: 253). This chance to experience the benefits of a truly invigorating exchange composed of pauses and unexpected shifts must have been highly appreciated by Ocampo, given both her wish to finally satisfy her hunger – in this case, thanks to Woolf's 'insatiable curiosity' (Ocampo 1946: 253) – and the gift of 'interruption' that she could apply in their verbal interaction (Ocampo 1936: 69).

What also appears interesting is the terminology that Ocampo uses to describe the overwhelming dialogue she had with Woolf: 'This barrage of questions lasted throughout our conversation' (1946: 253). With its militaristic connotations, the noun 'barrage' recalls the Mussolini's 'catapult' (Ocampo 1990a: 218). Ocampo thus seems to be suggesting a similarity between her encounters with a fascist male dictator and a renowned female novelist. However, this semantic resonance rather accentuates the distance between the two. Ocampo distinguishes the assertions launched by Mussolini's verbal 'catapult' from the 'barrage' made up of Woolf's boundless curiosity. Woolf's 'barrage' represents a mode of expression in opposition to Mussolini's absolute power; namely, a hunger for an infinite possibility of knowledge through dialogue. Significantly, Ocampo wished to make it clear that, in spite of her fervid curiosity, 'Woolf . . . expected and waited for a reply' (1946: 253). Moreover, Ocampo discovered in their conversation that Woolf had learned verbal tricks similar to those Ocampo herself had addressed in 'La mujer y su expresión'. Her encounter with Woolf in London thus proved that she had ultimately found an honest partner in her battle for women's rights, a companion with whom she could finally have an equal exchange.

When Woolf and Ocampo could not meet in person, a form of written dialogue kept the conversation alive. Their private correspondence mirrors a female form of writing, which is confidential and at times conspiratorial, especially if employed against the public voice of male power. Like Woolf, Ocampo was a prolific letter writer. For Woolf, epistolary correspondence also functioned as a valued source of inspiration for her creative writing (Blyth 2012: 357);[22] for Ocampo, it contributed to the refinement of both her personal style and thought, an essential figure being the poet Gabriela Mistral (1889–1957).[23] Similar to what happened with her Mexican friend Mistral, Ocampo's epistolary contacts with Woolf became an arena for an exercise in writing and the construction of a typically female credo via writing.

It is worth noting that Ocampo herself does not seem to associate letter writing with the female gender. In her essay 'Gabriela Mistral in her letters' ('Gabriela Mistral en sus cartas'),[24] Ocampo responded to her friend and colleague Ortega y Gasset by disagreeing with his idea that 'women have a talent for letter writing which men lack' (Ocampo 2003: 296). Moreover, she claimed that many women actually addressed their letters to a wide readership just as men did (2003: 296). Although Ocampo hesitated to attribute epistolary writing to a feminine tradition, her essay nonetheless employs a highly domestic image:

> Gabriela wrote letters in abundance. And she wrote without composing them. They were spoken letters. That's the way Virginia Woolf wrote them, too. . . . Being two writers and two totally different, almost opposite personalities, their command of the language enabled them to use it however they pleased. I mean to say that they used words like they used a comb. Sometimes the comb was made of bone, other times of tortoiseshell, but above all it was what it had to be: a comb. (2003: 297)

Writing letters is an act that awakens in Ocampo's mind an intimate association with a private moment in a domestic female setting, which is cleverly conveyed through the image of the 'comb'.[25] And it is again the epistolary genre that enables Ocampo to construct a direct link between Mistral and Woolf.

In 'Gabriela Mistral in her letters' this connection is embedded in her acknowledgement of the many similarities in Woolf's and Mistral's female authorship revealed through their letter writing. What seems to matter most to Ocampo is the two women's female imprint in a private form of writing, which is also highly dialogic: 'spoken letters' are those that both Mistral and Woolf create by employing 'a comb' (Ocampo 2003: 297). These successful women writers thus offered a model of hope: epistolary correspondence could allow any woman to conquer a degree of freedom, even while enclosed in a state of domesticity. Women just had to be prepared to make their voices and thoughts heard in writing. The 'comb' would do the rest by untangling the knots of their confused thoughts, thus leaving them free to follow the flow of their states of mind and to express them.

A Female Form of Diffusion

While enjoying her personal relationship with Woolf, Ocampo also aspired to show to the world what she herself was learning during her intellectual liaison with her British friend. As mentioned above, her literary activity in the journal *Sur* was emblematic of her wish to inform non-English readers of what was happening in the Anglophone world. To this end, she was able to transmit texts beyond geographical and linguistic barriers, thereby making Woolf's works accessible in Spanish-speaking countries. Her decision to opt for 'the transparent but hard, cold windows of translations' (Ocampo 1946: 249–50) was a demonstration of great intellectual generosity, considering that her proficiency in several languages, including English, enabled her to enjoy Woolf's writings directly. By responding to a vision of 'the novel' which 'looks at the world as a global cultural totality' (Siskind 2014: 38), Ocampo's initiative also proved to be beneficial in another sense. It involved Woolf's writing (as well as other writers' works) in 'the globalization of the novel' (Siskind 2014: 38). In this way, Ocampo's activity took South America to the apex of global literary circulation. The discovery and transmission of distant cultures and texts was not unidirectional though, since both Woolf and Ocampo were reciprocally inspired by and involved in crafting a newer version of the world.

In truth, Woolf already had some knowledge of South America even before meeting Ocampo, as suggested by her novel *The Voyage Out* (1915) (Lojo Rodríguez 2012: 219; Rogers 2012b: 128–31; Parrott 2004: 1). As Patricia Novillo-Corvalán points out, Woolf had become familiar with Ocampo's country as a result of the research assistance she had provided to Leonard Woolf while he was working on *Empire and Commerce in Africa* (1920) (Novillo-Corvalán 2017: 33–4).[26] At the same time, however, it is undeniable that Ocampo's and Woolf's conversations frequently dealt with Argentina, to the extent that once Woolf wrote her friend: 'I still have a dream of your America' (*L* 5: 356).[27] As the possessive adjective conveys, it was the Argentina depicted by Ocampo that populated Woolf's fantasies. Woolf vividly imagined it as 'the land of great butterflies and vast fields' (*L* 5: 365) and wished to know more, repeatedly asking Ocampo, for instance, 'what the country looks like' (*L* 5: 365). As Novillo-Corvalán notes (2017: 35), Ocampo's exchanges with Woolf evidently contributed to arousing in Woolf's mind some 'specific imaginaries of universalism' (Siskind 2014: 38) concerning South Americanness, even though 'Woolf's imaginary excursions to South America' had started before Woolf met with Ocampo (Novillo-Corvalán 2017: 34). Ocampo prompted Woolf to create, in her private and also possibly her public writings, 'narratives of globalization' which were 'usually concerned with lands and peoples far removed from Europe' (Siskind 2014: 38). The two women's interactions may thus have led to the actualisation of the dual manifestation of the global novel: on one level, 'the novelization of the global' through Woolf's representation in her private writings of exotic places lived in by Ocampo and, on another, 'the globalization of the novel' (Siskind 2014: 38) through Ocampo's own requests for translation of Woolf's writings into the language of those same distant lands. In the latter case moreover, Ocampo might have benefited from Woolf's direct support. Woolf was delighted at the idea of having her works translated into Spanish and even offered advice to Ocampo on which choices may have been more congenial.[28] From this point of view, Woolf herself partly participated in Ocampo's endeavours to open up Argentina intellectually. Indeed, the fact that the Spanish translations of Woolf's novels – i.e. the ones that Ocampo commissioned to Jorge Luis Borges – were accessible not only to the Argentine public but also to Spanish readers globally recalibrates the perception that Argentina was peripheral in the distribution of Woolf's – and other writers' – translated works.

What appears peculiar, however, is Ocampo's decision to entrust those translations to Borges.[29] This observation has nothing to do with the quality of Borges's work. His skill in translation is well known as Guillermo Badenas and Josefina Coisson (2011) highlight by analysing the techniques that he specifically employed in his translation of Woolf's *Orlando*. By drawing on the field of feminist translation studies, moreover, Rebecca DeWald even considers the English and Spanish texts of *Orlando* as equals and not as a 'strong' original and a 'weak' derivation (2012: 246).[30] At stake here is something else: the young and talented Borges, who had seemed to endorse *Sur*'s aesthetics (Lojo Rodríguez 2002: 233–4), was a man. Considering the non-neutral role of the translator, Julia Salmerón and Ana Zamorano speculate that 'Woolf could have entered the Spanish literary imagination in a different way had her translators been women' (2006: 56).[31] The paradox the two scholars unveil is undeniable. While Ocampo was succeeding in her dream of promoting widespread distribution of Woolf's oeuvre, she nonetheless allowed Woolf's female voice to be rewritten by a male pen. However, the apparent inconsistency was soon to be solved: Ocampo enriched this form of literary acculturation enacted by a man with an alternative form of criticism written by herself, which crucially displays a kind of 'specular erotica' as well (Arnés 2013: 14, my translation). According to Laura A. Arnés, Ocampo's critical works on Woolf act as a 'mirror' by means of which Ocampo herself 'wishes to be reflected' or rather as an 'image she wishes to reflect' (2013: 14, my translation). As Arnés adds however, the sensuous textual dynamics emerging in Ocampo's manipulation of Woolf's writings were in line with the queer component of *Sur*, which, especially in translations of specific European works, was able to set up 'a sort of sexually deviant canon' (2017: 155, my translation) and, more specifically, 'a lesbian *continuum*' (2017: 158, my translation). The works that Ocampo wrote on Woolf reveal her very personal campaign in South America. These texts sought to raise awareness about what a male mind would struggle to disclose about Woolf as an extraordinary instance of female writing and womanhood.

Borges's translation of Woolf's novel *Orlando* in 1937 was followed a year later by Ocampo's *Virginia Woolf, Orlando y Cía*[32] [Virginia Woolf, Orlando and Co.], where, in imitation of her model Woolf, Ocampo shed her impersonal academic clothes to act as a '"common reader"[33] of the work of Virginia Woolf' (1938: 7).[34] It is worth noting that, unlike English, Spanish grammar permits Ocampo to express the female gender of her readers. In addition, Ocampo's decision to act as a 'common reader' while linking herself to Woolf was also meant to stress her 'humble' (humilde) role 'before a brilliant assembly of literati' (ante una brillante asamblea de literatos) who had assembled for the congress of PEN Clubs in Buenos Aires in 1936 (Ocampo 1938: 45). Her critical analysis continued in the following years.

After Leonard Woolf published some extracts from Woolf's journals as *A Writer's Diary* (1953), Ocampo's counterstroke came in 1954 with *Virginia Woolf en su diario* [Virginia Woolf in Her Diary]. Luckily, since Leonard's selection also included Virginia's comments on her writing, *A Writer's Diary* enabled Ocampo to focus again on Woolf's works. Her analysis is frequently affected by muted frustration at what she saw as unfair treatment of Woolf's writings by her husband at a time when she was no longer able to reply. For instance, Ocampo asks her unknown readership: 'Has Leonard Woolf's censorship intervened in' (1982b: 60)[35] this strange absence of love? Evidently, as Ocampo was reading the extracts collected by Leonard, she could not recognise the Virginia Woolf she had once met. Especially in the first chapter of her *diario*, crucially entitled 'Un diario expurgado' [An Expurgated Diary], Ocampo variously justifies Leonard's choices by pointing to the objective difficulty in managing the large quantity of confessions and commentaries left by his wife. Judging the motivation behind Leonard's editorial work, Ocampo doubts neither his love as a husband nor his admiration as a reader but also observes that 'the two things, unfortunately, do not always go together' (1982b: 11).³⁶ Nevertheless, she cannot help condemning Leonard's numerous omissions, which leave the reader with only the briefest, squinty glance at Woolf's fervid private writing. In this work, Woolf 'sometimes seems . . . on the verge of being dehumanised' (Ocampo 1982b: 18). As a result, Ocampo herself felt the need to reread all the letters Virginia had sent to her before writing about *A Writer's Diary*.³⁷

Intrinsic to Ocampo's goals in *Virginia Woolf en su diario* was the wish to meet again the woman she had once known, that is, the writer and also the woman. Not surprisingly, of the two, Ocampo's plan put the emphasis on Woolf as a woman. Ocampo observes that, whereas men believe that *A Room of One's Own* and *Three Guineas* cannot stand comparison with her novels, the extended essays are precisely the works that most absorb her (1982b: 51); the two works are considered together as 'testimonies of merit . . . in the history of literature' (1982b: 52).³⁸ Though they differ, both texts show how, through the vicissitudes of history, women's persecution has remained constant because of the social inheritance of a despotic patriarchy: 'Our battle, the battle of women against the tyranny of the patriarchal state imposed by them [the despots], is analogous to the battle that they [women] fought against the tyranny of the fascist, Hitlerian state' (1982b: 33).³⁹

A Room of One's Own fascinates Ocampo more than *Three Guineas* as exemplified by the earlier-quoted homage to the former: 'Carta a Virginia Woolf'. The title itself acts as an important signal of female solidarity in and through writing between Ocampo and Woolf. This is a true '[c]arta' – that is, a 'letter' – that Ocampo addressed to Woolf when the latter was still alive, and hence it can be counted among the many actual letters she sent her.⁴⁰ This was no private communication, however. By means of techniques such as direct quotations and constant rewritings, 'Carta' proposes a subtle diffusion of Woolf's female vision as expressed in *A Room of One's Own* by conducting a textual dialogue with it. Such discursive shifts between the two texts – that is, 'Carta' and *A Room* – are however well handled by Ocampo, with no hesitation, as though they were among the 'spoken letters' (2003: 297) that she later praised in Mistral's and Woolf's epistolary production.

In addition, just as the letter writer exposes some part of her own person and thoughts while talking to an addressee, Ocampo also participates actively in the confidential disclosure favoured by the epistolary genre, and this is what happens when she appropriates Woolf's notorious phrase, '*Like most uneducated englishwomen* [sic], *I like reading*' (Ocampo 1982a: 103).⁴¹ As if in response to this, she asserts: '*like most uneducated sauthamerican* [sic] *women, I like writing*' (1982a: 104). She then adds: 'And, this time, the *uneducated* must be pronounced without irony' (1982a: 104),⁴² although this is perhaps not possible, given that Ocampo was in fact very well educated (1982a: 103). Ocampo's strategy of rewriting here aims to convey her personal closeness to Woolf as a woman writer. While contemplating her own intellectual efforts as a woman via an overt association with Woolf, Ocampo is more broadly meditating on women's age-old lack of access to education, a lack which intensified their 'insecurity' (*AROO*: 29) and obscured any talent they possessed. The insecurity denounced by Woolf is rendered as 'an inferiority complex' (un complejo de inferioridad) (1936: 66) in Ocampo, showing her complete agreement with Woolf. Ocampo describes this 'complex' as a trait shared by all women devoted to writing, the legacy of ordinary humiliation made up of exclusion and privation. To explain more clearly what this 'complex' consists of, she provides the example of a famous writer, who is also a friend of hers:

> One of these women, who is one of the most gifted persons I know, a famous novelist with an admirable style, told me: 'I am not truly happy but when I am alone, with a book or looking at a paper and a quill. Beside this world which is so real for me, the other reality vanishes.' However, this woman, who was born in an intellectual environment and whose vocation was uncommonly clear from the very beginning, in her youth lived through years of atrocious torment and uncertainty. Everything conspired to prove to her that her sex was a terrible *handicap* in the profession of letters. Everything conspired to increase in her person what she had inherited, what all of us [women][43] inherit: an inferiority complex. (Ocampo 1936: 66)[44]

That Ocampo is referring to Virginia Woolf is a very likely hypothesis. Writing was not at all an easy affair for women, even privileged women like Woolf. 'Killing the Angel in the House was part of the occupation of a woman writer', Woolf emphasises in her essay 'Professions for women' (*DM*: 238). Contributing to the internalisation of external prejudices concerning their moral conduct, women were constantly pressured to inhibit whatever might appear inappropriate for their gender. When writing too, they had to 'tell lies' in order to silence 'the truth about human relations, morality, sex' (*DM*: 238). Woolf must have inspired admiration and respect in Ocampo, as she had been able to both free herself from the angelic persona she was expected to embody and to share the painful steps by which she had arrived at that murderous act.

In *Virginia Woolf, Orlando y Cía*, Ocampo mentions Woolf among those women writers who had spoken to her of the 'terrible and absurd difficulties they had to overcome, of the upheaval they had to tolerate' (1938: 26).[45] In this sense, Ocampo's 'Carta' truly incorporates the dialogue between the two women, during which, as the essay shows, Ocampo must have usually agreed with Woolf. For instance, in 'Carta' Ocampo writes:

> I am absolutely convinced like you that a woman cannot truly write as a woman unless this preoccupation abandons her, unless her works, by no longer seeking to provide an answer to attacks, disguised or not, aim only to convey her thoughts, her feelings, her vision. (1982a: 106)[46]

Nevertheless, agreement was not a constant. Ocampo felt the need to detach herself from Woolf's ideas at times, sensing in them a trace of experiences that were implausible in Argentina. For example, she explicitly writes that 'the South American woman finds herself in conditions of inferiority in comparison with the woman who lives in certain great countries' (1936: 68).[47] Yet there is some glow of pride in Ocampo's acts of dissent, which appear to be out of step with the subordination that has been identified in her attitude to Woolf. Ocampo has even been described as an exotic object put 'on display for' her British friend who, by contrast, acted as an unwitting 'Old World colonist' (Parrott 2004: 2), glad to instruct her new disciple. The truth is that where necessary, Ocampo was capable of enlarging Woolf's European vision. The temperament intrinsic to her own South American, albeit very cosmopolitan, perspective, prompted her to freely express her feelings, in writing as well as speech.

A case in point is her disagreement with Woolf's reading of Charlotte Brontë's novel *Jane Eyre* (1847) as an instance of the ways in which 'sex' can 'interfere with the integrity of a woman novelist' (*AROO*: 80). Woolf variously praises the novelist Jane Austen, who, like Shakespeare, was able to write 'without hate, without bitterness, without fear, without protest, without preaching' (*AROO*: 74). When it comes to *Jane Eyre*, however, while strongly commending this novel, she argues: 'it is clear that anger was tampering with the integrity of Charlotte Brontë the novelist. She left her story, to which her entire devotion was due, to attend to some personal grievance' (*AROO*: 80). In response to these words, Ocampo openly justifies the anger of *Jane Eyre*. Touched as she is by Brontë's torments, she passionately defends her anger, and asks Woolf, 'don't you believe that this suffering, which torments her books, is translated into a moving imperfection? By defending her cause, it is my own that I defend' (1982a: 105).[48] In the light of the arguably worse situation facing Argentine women who in their 'purely patriarchal society'[49] were subject to more severe restrictions than those experienced by Brontë and even her character Jane Eyre (1982a: 107), Ocampo is of course right to 'defend' Charlotte's 'cause'. Ocampo's words are motivated not by a victim complex, but by an ardent impulse towards sisterhood. 'Carta' shows signs of Ocampo's concordance with Woolf's ideals of equality between genders but also of her own role as the spokesperson of anonymous and silenced women. Referring to women's lives – and not only in Argentina – Ocampo argues that 'the ninety-nine per cent of them will remain obscure and anonymous' (1936: 69).[50] In Argentina, however, unlike what transpired in other countries, including Spain, 'men continue to tell her: "Do not interrupt me"' (1936: 66).[51] Ocampo thus suggests how there was still a long way to go for Argentina in terms of gender equality.

While commenting on the great question of women and writing – Woolf's own 'element' (elemento) – Ocampo specified: 'Virginia Woolf is not just interested in the problems the woman has as a writer. . . . She is interested in the same way in the problems the woman has as a woman, whatever her social class' (1938: 59).[52] Both women hoped that, whatever their lives had in store, they would be widely spoken of one day for the sake of the entire world. This desire is what underpins Woolf's request to women: 'when I ask you to write more books I am urging you to do what will be for your good and for the good of the world at large' (*AROO*: 118). With similar words, perhaps inspired by Woolf herself, Ocampo claimed that 'world literature will be immeasurably enriched' (1936: 67)[53] as soon as a woman begins writing as a woman. Both Woolf and Ocampo hoped that women's lives would be recorded and remembered so as to 'interrupt' (Ocampo 1936: 62) one day the oppression so many of them had suffered for so long. By sharing their hopes in their dialogue on (and across) the distance between them, Woolf and Ocampo embodied an ideal – almost utopian – womanhood, thereby providing an excellent example of what it meant for women to 'interrupt'.

Notes

1. Prompted by Sylvia Beach, Ocampo's first encounter with Woolf had already occurred through *A Room of One's Own* (Lojo Rodríguez 2016: 467).
2. All translations from 'Carta a Virginia Woolf' are mine unless otherwise indicated: 'nacidas en medios y climas distintos, anglosajona la una, la otra latina y de América, la una adosada a una formidable tradición y la otra adosada al vacío'.

3. Although Adrienne Monnier and Sylvia Beach's monthly *Le Navire d'Argent* [The Silver Ship] also seems to have inspired Ocampo (Lojo Rodríguez 2016: 467), *Sur*'s main revolutionary models were Waldo Frank's *The Seven Arts* and Ortega y Gasset's *Revista de Occidente* (Rogers 2012b: 136–9). For further discussion of the interconnections between these three journals and accordingly, between the intellectual centres of Buenos Aires, New York and Madrid, see, among others, Rogers (2012a; esp. 469–72 for Ocampo's *Sur*). Frank's influence on Ocampo is investigated by Gorica Majstorovic (2005), whereas María Teresa Gramuglio (2010) provides insights into the cultural circle around *Sur*.
4. Ocampo believed in the 'American' authenticity of her 'hunger' (hambre . . . americana) (1982a: 102–3). She noted that 'in Europe', in contrast, 'there is everything except hunger' (en Europa . . . parece que se tiene todo, menos hambre) (1982a: 103).
5. Originally published in José Ortega y Gasset's journal *Revista de Occidente* [Western Review] in 1934.
6. '[Son] una serie de testimonios de mi hambre.'
7. '[Pues] con usted fue con quien hablé últimamente – e inolvidablemente – de esta riqueza, nacida de mi pobreza: el hambre.'
8. All translations from 'La mujer y su expresión' are mine unless otherwise indicated: 'Lo que cada una de nosotras realiza en su pequeña vida tiene inmensa importancia, inmensa fuerza cuando las vidas se suman. No hay que olvidarlo.'
9. The introduction to Susan Stanford Friedman's *Planetary Modernisms* also provides an exhaustive account of transnational views within scholarship.
10. As she notes, while Woolf's 'novels are permeated with global movement. . . . [L]iteral global interactions rarely appear. We must turn to her figurative imaginings of geography, peoples and global exchange' (Cuddy-Keane 2010: 158).
11. For instance, Rebecca L. Walkowitz discusses the diversity inherent in Englishness that also affected Virginia's image through the 1917 publication of 'The mark on the wall' in *Two Stories*, together with Leonard Woolf's 'Three Jews'. Because of the association with Leonard's short story, Virginia appeared 'as the wife of a person both British and Jewish, a person of both national and international affiliations' (2006: 126). See the chapter as a whole for a reading of Woolf's evasions in relation to cosmopolitanism (119–44).
12. '[las dos] miradas [son] diferentes'.
13. Among other scholars, Rogers points to Woolf's and Ocampo's 'feminist anti-fascisms' (2012b: 126) – although his observations mostly take into account the Spanish Civil War in his reading of Woolf's *Three Guineas*.
14. Written in 1935 and discussed during a radio broadcast in Argentina and Spain in August 1936, this essay was then published in the collection *La mujer y su expresión* (1936) and finally included in the second series of *Testimonios* (1990).
15. 'Hasta ahora el monólogo parece haber sido la manera predilecta de expresión adoptada por él. . . . [La] conversación entre hombres no es sino una forma dialogada de este monólogo.'
16. 'Creo que, desde hace siglos, toda conversación entre el hombre y la mujer . . . empieza por un: "no me interrumpas" de parte del hombre.'
17. 'Interrumpidme. Este monólogo no me hace feliz. Es a vosotros a quienes quiero hablar y no a mí misma.'
18. 'de interrupción en interrupción aceptada, [el hombre] llegue naturalmente al diálogo'.
19. Her essay 'De Francesca a Beatrice' [From Francesca to Beatrice] (1924), for instance, placed her firmly within a very long tradition of male criticism on Dante Alighieri's *La Divina Commedia* (*The Divine Comedy*).
20. Rogers even uses the verb 'starstruck' (2012b: 142) to convey the effect that Woolf had on Ocampo.
21. 'dos mujeres hablan de las mujeres'.

22. Blyth's essay provides insight into the connections between Woolf's diary and letter writing and their impact on her literary production.
23. The letters Ocampo and Mistral exchanged were translated and collected in Elizabeth Horan and Doris Meyer's *This America of Ours* (Ocampo 2003).
24. Published after Gabriela Mistral's death and included in 1963 in the sixth series of *Testimonios*.
25. Another interesting association between Woolf and Ocampo referencing domesticity is constituted by their own domestic space. This evolution, from childhood to adulthood, was partly reflected in a transformation of texts into literary spaces for women's self-definition (Chikiar Bauer 2016: 16). Besides being crucial to the very act of writing, houses made relations between spaces and gender visible through architecture, which could thus be redesigned by women in terms of 'spaces of resistance to patriarchy' ('espacios de resistencia al patriarcado') (2016: 2).
26. Leonard's work initially was to include other regions such as Latin America in addition to Africa (Novillo-Corvalán 2017: 33–4). Gillian Beer's approach is different, identifying Charles Darwin's *The Voyage of the Beagle* as the main influence for the South American landscape depicted in *The Voyage Out* (1996: 14–16). More recently, Lindsey Cordery has highlighted other sources behind Woolf's novel (2018: 226–32).
27. See *D* 4: 263 and *L* 5: 348–9, 356, 365, 372, 395–6, 405, 438; and Ocampo (1938: 10, 67–8; 1946: 253–4; 1982b: 94–7).
28. In December 1934, she wrote to her:

    > I think the Room is the best to begin on: then perhaps, if you want another, Orlando or The Lighthouse. I heard from your Agent this morning; and oddly enough by the same post got a copy of Mrs Dalloway in a Spanish translation. (Catalan I think) so dont do that. (*L* 5: 358)

29. Borges's first translation was *Un cuarto proprio* (*A Room of One's Own*), published by Editorial Sur (Buenos Aires) in 1936, namely before *Orlando*, which was published in 1937 by the same company.
30. DeWald's conclusions on Woolf's and Borges's *Orlando* are in agreement, albeit on a different level, with scholarly views on the relationship between Woolf and Ocampo, whose cultural positions and roles have long been described through the lens of inequality.
31. The two scholars assert that the majority of Woolf's works were in fact translated by men (2006: 55).
32. *Virginia Woolf, Orlando y Cía* is a revised version of a conference talk Ocampo gave during 'Amigos del arte' [Art Friends] in Buenos Aires (7 July 1937).
33. English in the original.
34. All the translations from this work are mine: '"common reader" de la obra de Virginia Woolf'.
35. All the translations of *Virginia Woolf en su diario* are mine: '¿Ha intervenido en ello la censura de Leonard Woolf?'
36. 'las dos cosas, por desgracia, no siempre andan juntas'.
37. Woolf 'a veces aparece . . . próxima a deshumanizarse'.
38. 'testimonios de un valor [no sobrepasado] en la historia de la literatura'.
39. 'Nuestra lucha, la de las mujeres contra la tiranía del estado patriarcal impuesto por ustedes [los déspotas], es análoga a la lucha que iban a librar ustedes [las mujeres] contra la tiranía del estado fascista, hitlerista.'
40. One can also detect an echo of the epistolary structure of *Three Guineas* in Ocampo's letters.
41. All the terms in English and italics quoted from this work also appear in the original. Ocampo provides the Spanish translation in a note. Another significant instance comes from Ocampo's 'Virginia Woolf in my memory' ('Virginia Woolf en mi recuerdo'), first

published on 20 April 1941 in *La Nación* [The Nation], that is, less than one month after Woolf's suicide. The epigraph of this essay is borrowed from Woolf's dedication of her novel *Night and Day* (1919) to her sister Vanessa Bell. As Ocampo says, nothing can 'express better the difficulty . . . in writing at this moment' (1990b: 235).
42. 'Y, esta vez, el *uneducated* debe pronunciarse sin ironía.'
43. Here Ocampo is referring to all women (Spanish allows the expression of the feminine gender).
44. 'Sin embargo, esta mujer, nacida en un ambiente intelectual y cuya vocación fue, desde el comienzo, singularmente clara, pasó en su juventud años atroces de tormentos e incertidumbres. Todo conspiraba para probarle que su sexo era un *handicap* terrible en la carrera de las letras. Todo conspiraba para aumentar en ella lo que había heredado, lo que todas heredamos: un complejo de inferioridad.'
45. 'terribles y absurdas dificultades que vencer, desgarramientos que soportar'.
46. '[En todo caso,] estoy tan convencida como usted de que una mujer no logra escribir realmente como una mujer sino a partir del momento en que esa preocupación la abandona, a partir del momento en que sus obras, dejando de ser una respuesta a ataques, disfrazados o no, tienden sólo a traducir su pensamiento, sus sentimientos, su visión.'
47. 'la mujer sudamericana se encuentra en condiciones de inferioridad con respecto a la mujer que habita ciertos grandes países'.
48. '¿no cree usted que este sufrimiento que crispa sus libros se traduce en una imperfección conmovedora? Defendiendo su causa, defiendo la mía.'
49. Ocampo is quoting from Woolf's *A Room* (81).
50. 'noventa y nueve por ciento de las cuales permanecerán obscuras y anónimas'.
51. 'Los hombres continúan diciéndole: "No me interrumpas."'
52. 'Virginia Woolf no se interesa sólo por los problemas de la mujer en cuanto escritora. . . . Se interesa igualmente por los problemas de la mujer en cuanto mujer y cualquiera que sea su clase social.' It is also true that Woolf's writing has tended to exclude a certain section of her readership. For instance, 'readers of color or of the working class' are unlikely to be the intended readers of *The Waves* (1931) (Marcus 1992: 138). Jeanne Dubino emphasises Woolf's desire to involve 'a broad cross-section of readers', but notes the contradiction between her 'democratic principles of inclusion' on one hand – exemplified by her depiction of a 'common reader' – and her preclusion of a truly 'mass-market audience' on the other (2010: 9).
53. '[Si lo consigue,] la literatura mundial se enriquecerá incalculablemente.'

Bibliography

Arnés, L. A. (2013), 'Genealogías disidentes en (el) *Sur*' [Dissident genealogies in *Sur*], *Labrys. Etudes Feministes/Estudos Feministas* [Labrys. Feminist Studies], 23, pp. 1–21, <http://www.labrys.net.br/labrys23/libre/laura.htm> (last accessed 1 August 2018).

Arnés, L. A. (2017), 'Afectos y disidencia sexual en *Sur*: Victoria Ocampo, Gabriela Mistral y cia' [Affect and sexual dissidence in *Sur*: Victoria Ocampo, Gabriela Mistral and Co.], *Babedec*, 6: 12, pp. 154–67.

Badenas, G. and J. Coisson (2011), 'Woolf, Borges y *Orlando*. La manipulación antes del manipulacionismo' [Woolf, Borges and *Orlando*. Manipulation before manipulationism], *Mutas Mutandis*, 4: 1, pp. 25–37.

Beeber, M. (2015), 'Virginia Woolf, Victoria Ocampo and the national/transnational dialectic in *Three Guineas*', *Virginia Woolf Miscellany*, 87, pp. 21–3.

Beer, G. (1996), *Virginia Woolf: The Common Ground*, Edinburgh: Edinburgh University Press.

Berman, J. (2001), *Modernist Fiction, Cosmopolitanism, and the Politics of Community*, Cambridge: Cambridge University Press.

Blyth, I. (2012), 'Woolf, letter writing and diary keeping', in B. Randall and J. Goldman (eds), *Virginia Woolf in Context*, Cambridge: Cambridge University Press, pp. 353–61.

Chikiar Bauer, I. (2016), 'Virginia Woolf y Victoria Ocampo: El arte de conjugar modernismo con una domesticidad sin restricciones' [Virginia Woolf and Victoria Ocampo: The art of combining modernism with unrestricted domesticity], *Revista de Literaturas y Culturas Comparadas* [Journal of Comparative Literatures and Cultures], 6, pp. 1–17.

Cordery, L. (2018), 'Virginia Woolf and South America: Border-reading', in N. Wilson and C. Battershill (eds), *Virginia Woolf and the World of Books: The Centenary of the Hogarth Press. Selected Papers from the Twenty-Seventh Annual International Conference on Virginia Woolf*, Clemson, SC: Clemson University Digital Press, pp. 226–32.

Cuddy-Keane, M. (2010), 'World modelling: Paradigms of global consciousness in and around Woolf', in L. Shahriari and G. Potts (eds), *Virginia Woolf's Bloomsbury*, vol. 2, Basingstoke: Palgrave Macmillan, pp. 158–76.

DeWald, R. (2012), '"A dialogue . . . about this beauty and truth": Jorge Luis Borges's translation of Virginia Woolf's *Orlando*', in D. Ryan and S. Bolaki (eds), *Contradictory Woolf: Selected Papers from the Twenty-First Annual International Conference on Virginia Woolf*, Clemson, SC: Clemson University Digital Press, pp. 243–9.

Dubino, J. (2010), 'Introduction', in Dubino (ed.), *Virginia Woolf and the Literary Marketplace*, New York: Palgrave Macmillan, pp. 1–23.

Friedman, S. S. (2015), *Planetary Modernisms: Provocations on Modernity across Time*, New York: Columbia University Press.

Gramuglio, M. T. (2010), '*Sur*. Una minoría cosmopolita en la periferia occidental' [*Sur*. A cosmopolitan minority in the western periphery], in C Altamirano (ed.), *Historia de los intelectuales en América Latina* [The History of Intellectuals in Latin America], vol. 2, Buenos Aires: Katz, pp. 192–210.

Hausman, B. L. (1990), 'Words between women: Victoria Ocampo and Virginia Woolf', in N. Valis and C. Maier (eds), *In the Feminine Mode: Essays on Hispanic Women Writers*, Lewisburg, PA: Bucknell University Press, pp. 204–26.

Huyssen, A. (2005), 'Geographies of modernism in a globalizing world', in P. Brooker and A. Thacker (eds), *Geographies of Modernism: Literatures, Cultures, Spaces*, London: Routledge, pp. 6–18.

Lojo Rodríguez, L. M. (2002), '"A gaping mouth, but no words": Virginia Woolf enters the land of butterflies', in M. A. Caws and N. Luckhurst (eds), *The Reception of Virginia Woolf in Europe*, London: Continuum, pp. 218–46.

Lojo Rodríguez, L. M. (2016), 'Woolf in Hispanic countries: Buenos Aires and Madrid', in J. Berman (ed.), *A Companion to Virginia Woolf*, Oxford: Blackwell, pp. 467–80.

Luckhurst, N. (2002), 'Introduction', in M. A. Caws and N. Luckhurst (eds), *The Reception of Virginia Woolf in Europe*, London: Continuum, pp. 1–18.

Majstorovic, G. (2005), 'An American place: Victoria Ocampo's editorial politics, the foundation of *Sur*, and hemispheric alliances', *Arizona Journal of Hispanic Cultural Studies*, 9, pp. 171–80.

Marcus, J. (1992), 'Britannia rules *The Waves*', in K. R. Lawrence (ed.), *Decolonizing Tradition: New Views of Twentieth-Century 'British' Literary Canons*, Urbana: University of Illinois Press, pp. 136–62.

Novillo-Corvalán, P. (2017), 'Empire and commerce in Latin America: Historicizing Woolf's *The Voyage Out*', *Woolf Studies Annual*, 23, pp. 33–62.

Ocampo, V. (1936), 'La mujer y su expresión' [The woman and her expression], in V. Ocampo, *La mujer y su expresión*, Buenos Aires: Sur, pp. 61–9.

Ocampo, V. (1938), *Virginia Woolf, Orlando y Cía* [Virginia Woolf, Orlando and Co.], Buenos Aires: Ediciones Sur.

Ocampo, V. (1946), 'Memories of Virginia Woolf', *Vogue*, 202, pp. 249–56.

Ocampo, V. (1982a [1934]), 'Carta a Virginia Woolf' [Letter to Virginia Woolf], in V. Ocampo, *Virginia Woolf en su diario* [Virginia Woolf in Her Diary], Buenos Aires: Ediciones Sur, pp. 101–9.

Ocampo, V. (1982b [1954]), *Virginia Woolf en su diario* [Virginia Woolf in Her Diary], Buenos Aires: Ediciones Sur.

Ocampo, V. (1990a [1935]), 'Living history', in D. Meyer, *Victoria Ocampo: Against the Wind and the Tide, with a Selection of Essays by Victoria Ocampo*, trans. D. Meyer, Austin: University of Texas Press, pp. 217–22.

Ocampo, V. (1990b [1941]), 'Virginia Woolf in my memory', in D. Meyer, *Victoria Ocampo: Against the Wind and the Tide, with a Selection of Essays by Victoria Ocampo*, trans. D. Meyer, Austin: University of Texas Press, pp. 235–40.

Ocampo, V. (2003 [1963]), 'Gabriela Mistral in her letters', in E. Horan and D. Meyer (eds), *This America of Ours: The Letters of Gabriela Mistral and Victoria Ocampo*, trans. D. Meyer, Austin: University of Texas Press, pp. 293–313.

Parrott, F. G. (2004), 'Friendship, letters and butterflies: Victoria Ocampo and Virginia Woolf', *Scotland's Transatlantic Relations Project Archive*, pp. 1–7, <https://www.yumpu.com/en/document/view/33860386/friendship-letters-and-butterflies-victoria-ocampo-and-virginia-woolf> (last accessed 26 August 2019).

Rogers, G. (2012a), 'The circulation of interwar Anglophone and Hispanic modernisms', in M. Wollaeger, with M. Eatough (eds), *The Oxford Handbook of Global Modernisms*, Oxford: Oxford University Press, pp. 461–77.

Rogers, G. (2012b), *Modernism and the New Spain: Britain, Cosmopolitan Europe, and Literary History*, Oxford: Oxford University Press.

Salmerón, J. M. and A. Zamorano (2006), 'Virginia Woolf revisited: Intertexts and dissemination in Spanish culture', in A. G. Macedo and M. Esteves Pereira (eds), *Identity and Cultural Translation: Writing across the Borders of Englishness*, Bern: Peter Lang, pp. 55–71.

Siskind, M. (2014), *Cosmopolitan Desires: Global Modernity and World Literature in Latin America*, Evanston, IL: Northwestern University Press.

Walkowitz, R. L. (2006), 'Virginia Woolf's evasion: Critical cosmopolitanism and British modernism', in D. Mao and R. L. Walkowitz (eds), *Bad Modernisms*, Durham, NC: Duke University Press, pp. 119–44.

Woolf, V. (1970 [1942]), 'Professions for women', in V. Woolf, *The Death of the Moth and Other Essays*, San Diego: Harcourt Brace Jovanovich, pp. 235–42.

Woolf, V. (1977 [1929]), *A Room of One's Own*, Hammersmith: Grafton.

Woolf, V. (1979), *The Letters of Virginia Woolf: Volume Five: 1932–1935*, ed. N. Nicolson, asst. J. Trautmann, London: Hogarth Press.

Woolf, V. (1987), *The Diary of Virginia Woolf: Volume Four: 1931–1935*, ed. A. O. Bell, asst. A. McNeillie, London: Penguin.

Woolf, V. (2006 [1938]), *Three Guineas*, annot. and intro. J. Marcus. Orlando, FL: Harcourt.

5

FROM JULIA KRISTEVA TO PAULO MENDES CAMPOS: IMPOSSIBLE CONVERSATIONS WITH VIRGINIA WOOLF

Davi Pinho

I meant to write about death, only life came breaking in as usual.
The Diary of Virginia Woolf, 17 February 1922

I am suspended between life & death in an unfamiliar way.
The Diary of Virginia Woolf, 18 February 1922

IN 1974, PARIS SAW THE PUBLICATION of Julia Kristeva's *Des Chinoises* (*About Chinese Women*),[1] in which Kristeva asserts that the suicides of some modernist women writers pose the question of the impossibility of a truly feminine subject in language. 'I Who Want Not to Be'[2] is the title of Kristeva's fifth chapter, a quote from Marina Tsvetaeva's notes, and it is there that Virginia Woolf's suicide appears as the refusal of the symbolic order by a writer who would, according to Kristeva, have chosen 'to sink wordlessly in the river' (1986a: 157). Two years earlier, Quentin Bell had published *Virginia Woolf: A Biography* (1972), which first shed light on the then unpublished memoirs by Woolf that Jeanne Schulkind would go on to collect in *Moments of Being* (1976). Woolf's last written essay in the collection, 'A sketch of the past', began to unveil what she risked calling a 'philosophy' of her own (*MB*: 72) – that of writing as channelling the shocks of reality into a space that can affirm the continuity of being, a ceaseless return to art as proof of an interminable movement of life, the pattern behind the cotton wool. A little later in Rio de Janeiro, in the early 1980s, Paulo Mendes Campos retired, moved to Petrópolis and resumed his reading and intermittent translations of Woolf, among many others, in order to develop a new project: *Diário da Tarde* [The Afternoon Daily],[3] a newspaper that would never age. In the 'Artigo Indefinido' [Indefinite article] section of his daily, his lyrical essay on Woolf appears, titled '*Orlando* by Virginia Woolf'. The task of this chapter is to bring Kristeva and Campos into coexistence with Woolf's philosophy as presented in 'A sketch of the past' and to make them our contemporaries in an undulant conversation about writing and life, not death. It is interesting that conversation implies coexistence in its etymological roots: *-con* (with) and *-versari* (to turn), which together form the Latin verb *conversare*, to turn round and round and round, and its deponent *conversari*, to live with, dwell together.

As Julia Briggs annotates (2005: 118), the fact that Woolf envisioned her first *Common Reader* (1925) embedded in 'Otway conversation', in reference to Katharine Hilbery's cousins in *Night and Day* (1919), opens interesting critical transits if we bear in mind the etymology of the word conversation.[4] Under the sign of 'conversation', Woolf believed that she 'should mitigate the pomposity & sweep in all sorts of trifles' and that this polyphonic exercise would 'graze nearer'[5] her individual voice as an essayist (*D* 2: 261). Moreover, at the time Woolf chose 'conversation', not 'dialogue', as the frame for her first collection of essays, she had been 'recording conversations in her diary' in order to experiment with the essay as form while also rereading Ancient Greek literature (Briggs 2005: 119). All of these factors indicate that her lexical choice cannot be taken as merely incidental. After all, while Platonic dialogues move towards an authoritative voice through rhetorical questions, Woolf's essays enact an array of voices that are combined without a stable movement towards an alleged truth of the argument. In that sense, as Judith Allen formulates, Woolf's essays resist theoretical stasis, doctrine and any sort of totalising systems (2012: 20). In Allen's words, the 'conversational mode is an awakening and enables critical thinking, "thinking against the current"' (2012: 94).

While conversation is the awakening to a dehierarchised mode of knowledge, it is also a dyschronological form of cohabitation with times past and future. Indeed, T. S. Eliot (1919) argues that, through an acquired historical sense, the true poet contemplates the pastness of the past but also its presence, thus crafting an individual voice in conversations with tradition. If the literature and history of the past still constitute the present, the present can in its turn alter the way one reads the past and frames the future. In this alteration, conversations consciously create possibilities for 'the new' – an imaginative and investigative quality that Geoff Gilbert, reading Robert Musil, construes as modernist 'conscious utopianism' (Gilbert 2004: xii). Through this dyschronological stance, conversation is, therefore, the work of continuous contemporaneity if we think with Giorgio Agamben when he affirms that 'those who are truly contemporary, who truly belong to their time, are those who neither perfectly coincide with it nor adjust themselves to its demands' (2009b: 40).

Reading Woolf against Eliot,[6] with the aforementioned mediations by Gilbert and Agamben, one understands that while Woolf's writing actively responds to the real world around her (Zwerdling 1986), it does so through discontinuous conversations with the past and with an imagined future – as in Judith Shakespeare's imagined historical existence and her messianic return at the end of *A Room of One's Own* (1929). This special form of conversation between times prevents Woolf from fully coinciding either with the male canon of the past (as Eliot does), for hers is not a nostalgic stance by any chance, or with her chronological present, for her vision never accedes to unified beliefs or totalising discourses (be they religious, political or literary), which produces true feminist interventions in the context of the modernist discussion of tradition (Goldman 2004). In fact, dyschronological conversations between 'tradition' and 'the new' – for instance, between Shakespeare's sister and contemporary women writers (*AROO*) or between Antigone and Woolf's fellow outsiders (*TG*) – open Woolf's writings to visions of the future of fiction, women and politics. Thus, etymologically, contextually and thematically, conversation implies a critical mode of contemporaneity and coexistence.

Based on this understanding, this chapter aims at reassessing Kristeva's formulation of Woolf's drowning as 'wordless', which I will instead dub 'wordful' as I invite readers to resort to our own contemporary conversation with Woolf's 'philosophy' in 'A sketch of the past'. This analysis will move from Kristeva to Campos in order to discuss two figurations of the *signature* 'Virginia Woolf'. After all, as Agamben proposes in 'Theory of Signatures', 'all research in the human sciences – particularly in a historical context – necessarily has to do with signatures' (2009a: 76). In his essay, Agamben proposes that signatures, 'which according to the theory of signs, should appear as signifiers, always already slide into the position of the signified, so that *signum* and *signatum* exchange roles and seem to enter into a zone of undecidability' (2009a: 37). Signatures, then, make gestures that open up the traces between the sign and its productions of meaning – between the name as given (as summation of essential traits and/or qualities) and the name as signified over time and space (be it any name or a human being's name). Reading Woolf and Agamben, Maggie Humm observes that Woolf herself writes concurrently with Agamben's theory of signatures, as Woolf 'meditates on the *material* and *historical* conditions of signatures as gestures, rather than on signature as summations' (Humm 2013: 6).

Taking 'Virginia Woolf' as a modernist signature that is signified differently in diverse contexts, this chapter probes its appearance in Kristeva and Campos. First, in *About Chinese Women*, 'Virginia Woolf' appears as a summation of depression and suicide. Then, in *Diário da Tarde*, Woolf's name appears as a gesture of expanded life. In this process of conversing with Kristeva and Campos, I introduce the cultural-historical contexts of their productions in order to trace the signature 'Virginia Woolf'. When Woolf's name appears, I interrupt Kristeva and Campos with references to Woolf's own words, crafting thus our (im)possible conversations. As her words break in, it becomes evident that, in 2020, the signature 'Virginia Woolf' as summation of mental illness and death cannot still engulf Woolf's rather prolific and intensely life-affirming oeuvre.

I make the gesture of reminding readers of Woolf's ultimate choice for the title of her most polyphonic novel, *The Waves* (1931), to signify a wave's trajectory as an eternal conversation with everything it encounters – as it rises, rolls and breaks – only to be absorbed by the whole in different patterns. The undulant movement between texts and their historical contexts that I produce here is deliberately wave-like, a design that I have poetically drawn from Woolf as my own conversational methodology in this chapter. Agamben warns his readers in the 'Preface' to *The Signature of All Things: On Method* that 'method' in the human sciences rarely precedes practical application (2009a: 7–8). It rather stems from interpreting work that has already been produced. Therefore, it is precisely its capacity to be developed that reveals the philosophical element of any work – be it academic or artistic. Interpreting and developing the movement of a wave as a subliminal frame for this chapter, as well as a methodological enterprise of the conversational mode, my text begins its flux in Paris 1974 and rolls to Petrópolis, Rio de Janeiro 1981 to perform these (im)possible conversations with Virginia Woolf.

Virginia Woolf in Paris, 1974

By 1973, as a result of the impasse between her affirmation of Marxist criticism and her break with the French Communist Party (PCF) due to its perceived allegiance to Charles de Gaulle in the context of May 1968, Julia Kristeva had turned to China in search for new Marxist modes of thinking (Moi 1986: 5–6).⁷ As editor of the avant-garde magazine *Tel Quel* [As Is], Kristeva continually associated with Philippe Sollers, Roland Barthes, Michel Foucault, Maurice Blanchot, Jacques Derrida and many other prominent thinkers – all of whom, albeit differently, foster the poststructuralist understanding that history is text and that writing (*écriture*) is its production. Therefore, Kristeva's engagement with Mao Zedong's foundational ideas for the People's Republic of China can be read as an attempt to counter-write liberal ideas of democracy. Between April and May 1974, Kristeva travelled through China in the company of some fellow Telquelians, a trip that resulted in the dedication of the autumn 1974 issue of *Tel Quel* to their Maoist sortie.⁸ But unlike other influential works that originate in this noteworthy political and intellectual exercise known as 'The Chinese experience', Kristeva's *About Chinese Women* questions the structural inequality of the feminine within both Western and Eastern symbolic systems.

In 'My memory's hyperbole' (1983), Kristeva defines the 'Chinese Experience' as a 'more cultural than political' journey that 'definitely inaugurated a return to the only continent we had never left: internal experience' (Kristeva 2002: 19) while she and other Telquelians were in China. Therefore, it is not surprising that, with *About Chinese Women*, Kristeva's main endeavour is to expose the feminine as the negative sphere upon which Western discourses have built all notions of progress. As a woman, unlike her fellow travellers, the feminine as a cultural position constituted as the negative sphere of a binomial was the continent she could not have left behind, as she would later record.

About Chinese Women is one of Kristeva's most controversial works. While Gayatri Chakravorty Spivak (1981) has notoriously defined the book as careless and patronising, Danielle Marx-Scouras (1996) has argued that China appears as a blank slate upon which Kristeva and her fellow Telquelians projected their own cultural preoccupations and intellectual prejudices. Moreover, the political practices of Mao's authoritarian government are now disagreeable with Kristeva's ultimately democratic argument.⁹ While this is an intriguing discussion, my interest lies in the first half of Kristeva's work, 'On this side', before she goes on to describe her impressions of China in the second half of the book, 'Women of China'. It is in the first half of her book that the signature 'Virginia Woolf' appears.

In 'On this side', Kristeva exposes Judeo-Christian culture as the victory of patriarchal monotheism, for it is through the image of Man as God that sexual difference becomes the foundation for metaphysical binomials (body/mind, matter/spirit, nature/reason, immanence/transcendence, etc). If the word is God's, women fall beyond the possibility of the word and its laws, which places them beyond the symbolic realm. In Kristeva's theory, this negative position of the feminine in the private sphere sustains patrilineal progression and is the basis of all oppression, including capitalist exploitation – a point that Woolf had anticipated many years before. For, if one thinks of Woolf's search for a woman's sentence and livelihood (*AROO*) or of her urge for women to subvert their socio-political marginality as a response to men's bellicose institutions (*TG*), she clearly advances viewpoints similar to Kristeva's, though Kristeva never resorts to Woolf's words.

It is only in Chapter 5 of 'On this side', titled 'I who want not to be', that Kristeva summons the signature 'Virginia Woolf', among others. Here, Kristeva investigates the effects of this constant positioning of the feminine in the negative sphere of metaphysical binomials, especially for women who write. She proposes that, in a language that is historically phallocentric, 'to want not to be' was the answer that a woman writer often found when confronted by two tragic invitations. On the one hand, a woman writer would be invited to affirm the alienating identification with the mother, which would ultimately reinforce the mysticism that a matrilineal subject yields in the psychoanalytic tradition: the cyclical and monumental existence of women as mothers of a History that did not include them, as Kristeva would later frame in her experimental 1977 *Tel Quel* essay, 'Stabat mater' (Kristeva 1986b). On the other hand, as a woman of letters, a woman writer would be invited to identify with the father – the centre around whom the symbolic order has historically harboured itself – which would mean an affirmation of the phallocentrism of language, and thus a place as a subject alongside men's time, the time of History.

According to Kristeva, this liminal space between mother and father in their process of subjectification would produce in women of letters the despair of learning that they are Others of the very words they mean to write. 'A call of the mother is not only a call from beyond time, or beyond the socio-political battle', Kristeva affirms, but a call that 'troubles the word' (1986a: 156–7). Since Judeo-Christian monotheism signifies the victory of men over ancient matrilineal societies, Kristeva's point is that men had written themselves as heirs to God's original word and the sole agents of historical time. The word that shapes the world in Genesis, hovering above the amorphous earth and waters, is thus the origin of women's place beyond the word and its historical teleology – always named, never naming; always in service to the maintenance of his word, never heirs to its possession. Here, Woolf's words could have come to Kristeva's aid. After all, to give one example, the crouched woman hidden beyond the horizon in the opening interlude of *The Waves* may be read as an allegory in tune with Kristeva's argument: her hidden figure supports the sun that gives shape to a nebulous world. She is in service to the words/rays of sun that spread out as if fanned over the world.[10]

Building up to the reference to Woolf's name, Kristeva continues by exposing that this general woman who writes – and, therefore, who wants to own the word without a negation of the mother – finds that she is 'without time' and 'with family and history at an impasse' (1986a: 157). Troubled by her impossible existence as a writer of that which she seeks, her own word, she locates the multiple voices as her own, fails to identify with either mother or father and finds hallucinations to be her path towards the inevitable break she would have sought for in writing. 'After the superego, the ego founders and sinks', Kristeva observes. 'Once the moorings of the word, the ego, the superego, begin to slip, life itself can't hang on: death quietly moves in' (1986a: 157).

Signifying death as a devastating way out for women writers, Kristeva contrasts their suicides to that of Fyodor Dostoevsky's character Alexei Nilych Kirillov in *Devils* [*Bésy*] (1871), whose suicide serves 'to prove that his will is stronger than God's' (1986a: 158). According to Kristeva, Marina Tsvetaeva's formula, 'I who want not to be', with which Kristeva titles her chapter, poses an entirely different problem. 'Something entirely different is at stake in Tsvetaeva's suicide', Kristeva affirms: '*not to be*, that is, in the final instance, *to be God*; but to dissolve being itself, to free it of the word, of the self, of God. "I don't want to die. I want not to be"' (Kristeva 1986a: 158). Kristeva suggests that this endeavour, the illusion of a bodiless autonomy in an elsewhere, is what is at stake when a woman writer 'wants not to' and forces life to affirm the final negative. She ends her chapter by implying that women writers' suicides are silent, 'wordless' transgressions of the linguistic games of subjectification and signification that have positioned women in the negative sphere: 'when she is inspired by that which the symbolic order represses, isn't a woman also the most radical atheist, the most committed anarchist? In the eyes of this society, such a posture casts her as a victim. But elsewhere?' (1986a: 158). It is in this sense that Kristeva had earlier summoned 'Virginia Woolf' and her 'wordless' drowning: 'I think of Virginia Woolf, who sank wordlessly in the river, her pockets weighed down with stones. Haunted by voices, waves, lights, in love with colours – blue, green' (1986a: 157).

With this final movement of bringing writers like Virginia Woolf to respond alongside Tsvetaeva to Kirillov's will, Kristeva appraises the symbolic order and its positioning of the feminine in the margins of the word. However, summed up in a uniform group in spite of their significant differences, these women of letters are printed by Kristeva as archetypal examples of women who could only 'be' when they opposed Hamlet, whose immortal soliloquy immediately comes to mind.[11] If 'to be or not to be' ends in an affirmation of life precisely because of the prince's fear of this elsewhere, the unknown, it is towards this unknown 'rub' that women writers heraldically direct themselves through suicide, according to Kristeva. 'I who want not to be' is an impossible statement: women writers do not say 'I don't want to', but rather 'I want not to', as though their desires were equally subsumed by this affirmation of 'not to be'. Rather attuned to Bartleby's formula[12] – 'I would prefer not to' (Melville 1853: 11), which culminates is his aphasic resistance and death – modernist women writers' names become signatures as summations of impossibility, illness and death in 'On this side'.

Thus, in Kristeva's employment of the signature 'Virginia Woolf', the English writer becomes part of a homogenised group of dead woman writers, not a producer of affirmative fictions. This is problematic because if Woolf departed from a similar understanding to Kristeva's, her words always subvert the single word; they always blur the hierarchical boundaries of the symbolic order, especially the ones between the feminine and the masculine as cultural and subjective positions – be it in Woolf's call for women to write their foremothers back into life, as in Judith Shakespeare's final return after the androgynous mind is activated (*AROO*), or in the urge for women to rebuild (rewrite?) the institutions through their difference (*TG*). Kristeva's sudden and isolated reference to the name Virginia Woolf poetically introduces her suicide as a *scene* that engages many in urgent conversations about the impossibility of translations between a woman's self and world in words. However, in 'On this side', the conversation fails to move beyond signature as summation. Precisely because all we have is the scene itself – the writer, the stones, the river, the silence – Woolf's wordless death by water is an element that haunts the language, converses with it, and so it must converse with Woolf's words as well, a stance that deliberately folds death back into life and forgoes any fetishist explanation of her mental illness.

Here, the word scene overrides my text and demands a conversation with Woolf. In one of her many speculative interruptions in 'A sketch of the past', where she sums up scenes from her childhood, Woolf recognises that she is 'a porous vessel afloat on sensation', as if she were trying to solidify the fluidity into words that record and expose some image of a life (*MB*: 133). She keeps on marking these speculations in ways that we may come to understand as textual (im)possibilities, gaps between the scene she crafts and clarifications that she 'will some time try to work out' (*MB*: 133), that she might 'revise', 'rewrite', 'exact' (*MB*: 142). As she marks these gaps, we are guided by the notion that it is life that will work itself out while we follow the stream of scenes framed by (im)possible conversations with their writer. Woolf resumes the image of a 'vessel afloat upon' quiet waters in another attempt to posit what she understands by scene making (*MB*: 142). The scene is not, she says, 'a literary device – a means of summing up and making a knot out of innumerable little threads', because instead of bringing each thread to the surface whole, tied, delivered consciously, she *receives* the scene, marking the past through these mnemonic irruptions (*MB*: 142). It is relevant that, within this same paragraph, Woolf changes 'scene making' to 'scene receiving', as she moves away from the image of the intentional tying of the knot and resumes the image of the writer (and ourselves) as vessels being flooded (*MB*: 142).

The scene bears witness to human crisis if we accept Woolf's notion that 'we are sealed vessels afloat upon what it is convenient to call reality; at some moments, without a reason, without an effort, the sealing matter cracks; in floods reality; that is a scene' (*MB*: 142). She presents us as vessels drifting along a sea of quiet and various manifestations and realities, and asks herself: 'Is this liability of mine to scene receiving the origin of my writing impulse?' Her answer is another (im)possible conversation: 'These are questions about reality, about scenes and their connection with writing to which I have no answer; nor time to put the question carefully' (*MB*: 142). But a suggestion is indeed made in this game of (im)possibility between framing a scene and allowing words to fail at a clarification, and it is this: to write is to record the moment of crisis, the moment the sealing matter cracks as reality breaks in. Here, to explore latent meanings in Woolf's philosophical understanding of scene-writing, I propose that we converse with the multifaceted etymology of 'crisis' (the word that ancient doctors used to describe the decisive moment a patient would either perish or recover), which in its turn comes from the Greek Κρίνειν (to separate, to discern, to delimit, to decide), a verb that will also give us the word 'criticism'. The scene, then, is the moment that reveals Woolf's important notion of writing: the space that contains the potential for our separating, discerning, delimiting and perhaps deciding our presence in language. In other words, Woolf's imagistic philosophy proposes that our enduring crisis comes to a critical moment in the act of writing.

Writers receive the shock of these waters in their moments of being, moments of connection with a larger world and a larger time that destabilise the epistemological limits of those who write (*MB*: 70–3). Concomitantly, writing allows for the flood (since, in Woolf's metaphorical complex, one is flooded by or sinks into reality) and reinforces the sealing matter (since it is precisely Woolf's subjective constitution as a woman and as a writer, her existence within her remembered and expanded reality, that is at stake in her sketching of the past). Confusing as it may sound, writing becomes a space in between our life (what constitutes us) and our death (whatever sinks us) as unified subjects in language. To think of reality as the sea that breaks and floods our intact presence is a commanding metaphor.[13] Here, Woolf sees tragedy as an integral aspect of writing existence: living is tragic, life is what breaks in – one remembers the diary entries intimated in the epigraphs above. As early as 1922, Woolf's endeavour to engage in conversations about death resulted in an irresistible affirmation of life. In her diary, while still recovering from influenza, Woolf inscribes her resistance to allow death to enter her writing as she concludes *Jacob's Room*:

I meant to write about death, only life came breaking in as usual. I like, I see, to question people about death. I have taken into my head that I shan't live till 70. Suppose, I said to myself the other day, this pain over my heart suddenly wrung me out like a dish cloth & left me dead? – I was feeling sleepy, indifferent, & calm; so thought it didn't much matter, except for L. Then, some bird or light I daresay, or waking wider, set me off wishing to live on my own – wishing chiefly to walk along the river and look at things. (D 2: 167–8)

If Woolf means to write about death but life recurrently breaks in, we can only conclude that there is an involuntary life-affirming drive that overpowers her writing and makes it resist to be 'about death', even if death is indeed the question in her mind. The image of the dishcloth as the body that one reads in this diary entry – filled with water when alive, wrung out and dry when dead – may be read as foreshadowing the 'cotton wool' in 'A sketch of the past' (*MB*: 70), written on the verge of Woolf's suicide. As noted above, Woolf's diary entry is in the context of her slow recovery from a prolonged period of illness, so one might wonder whether a damp cooling cloth, perhaps used to break the lingering fever she describes (*D* 2: 170), inspires this figuration of the dishcloth. In any case, Woolf's metaphor of the dishcloth persists. In 1923, she describes mental exhaustion as if her 'brain' were 'like a wrung dish cloth' (*D* 2: 271). And in 1925, in a letter to Jacques Raverat, Woolf allegorises: 'influenza makes me like a wet dish cloth' (*L* 3: 163). The cotton wool, on the other hand, immediately evokes the image of nursing wounds. Both images, then, partake in a metaphorical complex of illness, death and life.

Furthermore, if the dishcloth is clearly a metaphor for the body in a critical state, the 'nondescript cotton wool' (*MB*: 70) is in many ways analogous to the body as well. After all, it is the metaphor Woolf employs in order to describe the actions we perform heedlessly, with no real appraisal of reality, hence naturalising the social fabric as if it were independent of our making and unmaking (*MB*: 70–2). 'This cotton wool, this non-being' (*MB*: 71), phrased thus interchangeably by Woolf, becomes a metaphor for the embodied reproductions of the automatic ceremonies of social and family life – for instance, from 'writing orders' to her servant Mabel (*MB*: 70), to the 'fighting' impulse she recalls from brawling with her brother Thoby Stephen in her childhood (*MB*: 71).

The 'sudden violent shock' (*MB*: 71) operated by moments of being, moments of thinking with one's whole body to the point that they bring 'with them a physical collapse' (*MB*: 72), are moments of awareness of the mechanical reproductions of identities that we perform as bodies in the world. Moments of being fracture time and space and allow for a conscientious recognition of and connection with a larger reality. Metaphorically, they come as if by the removal of the protection of cotton wool (embodied norms), thus revealing a wound. Woolf's image of 'the sledge-hammer force' of the 'blow' of these moments of being reinforce this metaphorical complex of being wounded by awareness – a blow she can only 'blunt' by writing (*MB*: 72). The parallel constructions in Woolf's philosophy – aligning 'cotton wool' and 'we' and 'the whole world' (*MB*: 72) – make being and non-being modes of embodied engagements with reality. The latter reproduces it, the former engages with it artistically, which opens up possibilities of reconstructions – or attempts at 'explanation' in Woolf's words

(*MB*: 72) – of this malleable, liquid reality through writing. Her metaphorical complex culminates in what Woolf feels she 'might call a philosophy':

> From this I reach what I might call a philosophy; at any rate it is a constant idea of mine; that behind the cotton wool is hidden a pattern; that we – I mean all human beings – are connected with this; that the whole world is a work of art; that we are parts of the work of art. *Hamlet* or a Beethoven quartet is the truth about this vast mass that we call the world. But there is no Shakespeare, there is no Beethoven; certainly and emphatically there is no God; we are the words; we are the music; we are the thing itself. And I see this when I have a shock. (*MB*: 72)

Woolf's metaphorical complex hints at human beings as fabricated pieces of absorbent fabric-like material, whose water is reality and language. It is by piercing through the invisible knots that compose our fabric(ated) selves that Woolf finds 'the pattern' that shows that 'there is no' Shakespeare, Beethoven or God (*MB*: 72). Woolf's gesture of invoking their names negatively instates a critique of the illusory unity produced by any name/word. It erases Shakespeare's, Beethoven's and God's presences as mere summations of established meanings in order to frame the potential for our own diverse manifestations: 'we are the words, we are the music, we are the thing itself' (*MB*: 72). In parallel construction, we *are* Shakespeare's *words*, Beethoven's *music*, God/the thing '*itself*'. The stative 'to be' cannot be read as a copula that links 'we' to our own names, our isolated existences or coeval identities. Rather, on the one hand, the verb links 'we' to the possibility of occupying 'words', 'music' and the mysterious 'thing'; and on the other, it poetically indicates that we are in fact constituted (or fabricated) by this very triad that begins with 'words'.

Unlike Kristeva's fatalist interpretation of the name Virginia Woolf in its defiance of the symbolic order, Woolf embraces the possibility of making (and unmaking?) it in her philosophy, as we 'are' it. It is this (im)possible expansion of human life through language – the momentary and dyschronological connections between Woolf and the 'pattern' beyond any illusion of historical progression, essential meaning and fixed identity – that Woolf finds when she feels the shock of a moment of being. In Woolf's words, her artistic delight is 'to put the severed parts together' (*MB*: 72), making past, present and future converse in writing. This tentative philosophical investigation of writing reveals Woolf's painstaking engagement with the deconstruction and reconstruction of reality through words, as she writes in order to capture her instants of discovery (her moments of being) more than her time allowed for.

If Woolf is painfully aware of women's marginal position, which is conversant with Kristeva's psychoanalytic debate, Jane Goldman has shown that it is through programmatically asking 'where is she?' that Woolf relocates women from the position of inert receptacles of the word to that of harbingers of a new culture (see 1998, 2004). Wordfully, then, Virginia Woolf continues to ask 'where is she?', which has become 'where are they?' as new generations are flooded by Woolf and become her contemporaries in the struggle against the literal and symbolic deaths of marginalised bodies and their voices.[14] In the flux of this contemporary understanding, our conversational wave breaks in Petrópolis, in the mountain region of the state of Rio de Janeiro, to find Campos's rejection of the signature 'Virginia Woolf' as summation of mental illness and suicide.

Virginia Woolf in Petrópolis, 1981

When the Brazilian journalist, poet and essayist Paulo Mendes Campos, a keen reader of Woolf, writes *Diário da Tarde* [The Afternoon Daily] (1981), he converses with Woolf's metaphorical complex for writing and scene-receiving in compelling ways. It is important to think of his retirement in 1980, which saw his move from the hubbub of Ipanema in the city of Rio to Petrópolis – a town dating back to Imperial Brazil in the mountains surrounding the metropolis – as a vital condition for this project of a newspaper of a single man: his little avant-garde magazine of sorts – a genre that is perhaps one of the most durable modernist utopias (Sarmatz 2014: 321). There, among vegetables and flowers, Campos wrote, rewrote and collected his texts, producing twenty editorials of *Diário da Tarde* (Bezerra 2013). It is in the 'Artigo Indefinido' [Indefinite Article] section, the 'front page' of his fourth editorial, that his literary essay '*Orlando* de Virginia Woolf' [*Orlando* by Virginia Woolf] appears, a lyrical review of Woolf's novel. We will move to Campos's conversation with Woolf in his essay, but first we will enter into conversation with Campos's times and his retirement project.

In his lifetime, Campos (1922–91) experienced both the fascist turn of Vargas's dictatorship (1937–45), under which he began his career as a journalist and a poet, and the dissipation of all legal rights in the Military Dictatorship (1964–85), which suspended all constitutional guarantees to individual freedoms through its Institutional Act Number 5 (1968). In the context of the exile of fellow Brazilian artists and the disappearance of dissenters into the many torture black sites held by the military, the lyrical literary essay, or *crônica*,[15] translation and literary criticism should be read as important social and political commentary, as well as a means of subsistence in a state of exception. In fact, Campos's constant revision of and engagement with world literature can be considered forms of resistance in this context, for they triggered subliminal discussions that were openly impossible under the adamant surveillance of the dictatorial censorship of the times.

As a young poet, Campos had been identified as part of the Brazilian 1945 generation, which was marked by strong formalist and neo-symbolist tendencies that aimed at an escape from the local (Bosi 1994: 465). This drive marks Campos's production as an essayist even more blatantly than as a poet, for his reading of the past – the lives and art of Walt Whitman, Emily Dickinson, George Bernard Shaw and Virginia Woolf, just to indicate a few of his 'indefinite' conversations collected and rewritten in *Diário da Tarde* (Campos 2014) – informs the life and art of his own times as he writes his *crônicas*. English-language literatures become paradigmatic mediations of the restrictions of his Brazilian reality, which is not surprising considering Campos's marriage to Joan Abercrombie, who was of English descent, and their interest in Anglophone publications throughout their lives. In short, Campos's literary essays draw a curtain around the world – one that 'shuts us in, not out' (*CR 1*: 222), as Woolf herself summarises her aesthetics of the 'The modern essay' (1925), an idea that is on the same wavelength as Campos's retirement project.

Diário da Tarde contains Campos's translations and general impressions on world writers, as well as short aphorisms of his own poetic production. It is a permanent daily, or an 'involuntary volume', as Campos defined it in an interview to *O Globo* [The Globe] newspaper in 1982.[16] If a newspaper usually opens with the News Section, each of Campos's editorials, which are divided into eight sections, are headed instead by an 'Indefinite article' section that opens his daily annotations. His main news, in these opening sections, ranges from literature reviews to poetic musings in the form of lyrical literary essays. In his gesture of giving the front page and headline to rereading and/or rewriting, Campos signifies literature as the production of permanent novelty, one that announces itself as *novus* (novelty/news) through the cracks of time. In this sense, instead of documenting the events of the day, his daily discharges the indefinite time in which writers come to be what they are on the present day. A renowned generalist, Campos forgoes any notion of journalistic documentation in favour of literary conversations that restructure the instant. His 'Indefinite article' section, then, converses with Agamben's understanding of true contemporaneity in 'What is the contemporary?': the urge to break the spine of chronological time and, in that anachronous disjunction, contemplate the shadow of the present as constitutive of the instant (2009b: 41).

When Campos chooses the 'indefinite' work of literature as news of his own time, he methodologically places himself alongside all of the *paradigmatic* texts and writers he rereads in his opening 'Indefinite' *crônicas* – from the Bible, through the aforementioned Anglophone writers, to Fernando Pessoa and beyond. Agamben defines a paradigm as that which 'is never already given, but is generated and produced . . . by "placing alongside", "conjoining together" and above all by "showing" and "exposing"' (2009a: 23), meanings he derives from the Greek etymology of the word, *paradéiknymi*. The paradigm is inextricably intertwined with Agamben's understating of contemporaneity, for 'the attention to this "unlived" is the life of the contemporary. And to be contemporary means in this sense to return to a present where we have never been' (2009b: 51–2). Hence, when Campos writes his 'Indefinite article', he is 'producing' himself and the writers he reads, finding the questions that make them his true contemporaries, and thus mediating the desire to escape from the local, which marked his generation, by engaging in these paradigmatic conversations. Through literature, he creates and occupies a desired, if 'unlived', present 'alongside' these writers – a present that disrupts and expands his own.

It is in the 'Indefinite article' section of Campos's daily that 'Orlando by Virginia Woolf' appears, an essay that makes Woolf a paradigmatic figure in *Diário da Tarde*. His text opens with the question that broadly popularised Woolf's name in Brazil after the adaptation of Edward Albee's play into film in 1966: *Who's Afraid of Virginia Woolf?* (Campos 2014: 65). 'Everybody' is his answer. Quoting from Osbert Sitwell's autobiographies, Campos writes that even Woolf's contemporaries were afraid of her. This fear, he implies, came from their discomfort under Woolf's gaze, as if she were always aware of the shadows that fell beyond the halo of a person's performance (2014: 65). If his first answer is that everybody was and continues to be afraid of Woolf, Campos goes on to assert that this dread of her piercing sight also seems to produce some form of love in everyone who has experienced it, even if anachronously through her texts. Campos's text continues from this conversation between her life and work: 'I only risk thinking that she possessed in high amount all of our weaknesses and all of the qualities that we too would like to possess' (2014: 66).[17] And he ruminates:

> Beyond all this, she was beautiful. Not of some beauty fallen from the sky by neglect, but of beauty that is conquered through solitude, contemplation, through rhythm; a beauty that develops from the inside out and stamps itself on angular bones and

unexpected lines. A beauty in spite of others. Contradictory and almost irritating. A beauty made of imagination in movement, not of reflection, a beauty of water. So quick that friends never reached an agreement about Virginia's eyes, only that they were beautiful. Grey eyes, says the poet Stephen Spender. Hematite, black and blue, says the painter Jacques Émile Blanche. Green for David Garnett. Through these indefinitely iridescent eyes, Virginia saw a world in perpetual mutation of colours and forms. Sight, in the physical and symbolic senses, is her sign. . . . She was a soul situated in the instant, present therefore in the infinitude of experiences, but without precise residence or known address. (Campos 2014: 66)[18]

His qualification of her eyes as 'indefinitely iridescent' above only shows how dominant her mode of seeing is to the design of *Diário da Tarde*, one that, as discussed, favours 'indefinition'. Here, as a central interlocutor of his indefinite project, 'Virginia' is analogous to the very act of writing, a force that deconstructs human identities and 'desubjectifies' the English writer. When Campos attempts to write biographical and physical descriptions of Woolf, which he scatters all through the essay, his strategy is to equivocate, to allegorise and to avoid definitions, as in the quote above. He asserts that her subjectivity, or any notion of her identity, should not interest her readers: 'VW spent her whole life writing about this, about the absence of identity or consistency of the soul or, if you will, about the absence of personality' (Campos 2014: 68).[19] Inscribed in his description of Woolf is Campos's own urge to escape from the local and to resist cultural fixation – the urge to be 'without precise residence or known address'.

Woolf's 'beauty of water', as Campos phrases it in the quotation above, rushes through times, contexts, subjectivities and identities, resisting fixation in any of these 'residences'. Feeding his readers with the suggestion that T. S. Eliot recognised precisely this quality when he recommended that she read Michel de Montaigne (Campos 2014: 68), Campos finds a way to refute the fear that the name Virginia Woolf produces, the fear with which he had opened his essay by reproducing Albee's question. As if inviting readers to move beyond his first answer – everyone was and continues to be afraid of Virginia Woolf – he candidly affirms that one should accept 'the high frequency of [her] undulating and fleeting character' and repeats, assuming a solemn tone, 'we must learn how to be unafraid of Virginia Woolf' (2014: 68).[20] I like to think that this notion – it is our human necessity not to fear 'Virginia Woolf' as a signature that liquefies identities, decentres subjectivities and gestures towards life beyond all of our purportedly fixed identifiers – reveals that Campos sees in her life-work a sort of revelation of ourselves as fluid events that can be negotiated through language.

Here, I turn to Woolf, for Campos is in tune with one of the most pressing questions in Woolf's oeuvre: how to write without imitation, hatred or mere laughter in the effort to reverse the social and historical limits of the subject who imitates, hates or laughs (*AROO*). This question proposes constant dislocation of the self and, consequently, an errant identity through writing. As Kristeva affirms, Woolf does recognise the phallocentrism of language as a deadly impediment to women of letters, but she never deserts words in the effort to liquefy this very phallocentrism. 'I have the feelings of a woman, but I have only the language of men' (1979: 67), Woolf quotes Thomas Hardy's Bathsheba[21] in her 1920 review of Léonie Villard's *La femme Anglaise au XIXème Siècle et son Évolution d'après le Roman Anglais Contemporain*, which has been collected as the essay 'Men and Women'. The impending question for writers, who must record the critical moment reality breaks in, is 'to try the accepted forms, to discard the unfit, to create others that are more fitting' (Woolf 1979: 67).

To discard unfit forms and create others, Woolf suggests that women (and men) who write need to sink into the vast ocean of reality in order to destabilise the masculine sentence – and here, it is of the utmost importance that we inscribe the ambivalence of the word 'sentence': both the linguistic materiality of combined words and their verdict, their potential to discern performance. What's more, to Woolf, writing is a space that works towards the confusion of the purely masculine or feminine sentences, if we think of the androgynous turn (*AROO*). Her question then is: how to break our names, our identities, and our very words by rewriting, reorganising, resealing new vessels or producing new marriages of words as she suggests in 'Craftsmanship', part of the BBC series of interviews symbolically titled *Words Fail Me* (1937). Writing, to Woolf, is to record the indefinite work of words overtime, actively engaging with the search for 'more fitting' forms and undoing the old (self/identity/reality) in the process.

Campos seems to have recognised Woolf's urge to recreate reality as he read *Orlando*. To the Brazilian writer, 'with Orlando, VW became some sort of Diana the Huntress: the piece she hunts in intricate woodlands is the human identity, the continuous self, the whole personality' (Campos 2014: 72).[22] His poetic transmutation of Woolf into Diana reveals his understanding that if Woolf departs from the limited position of a woman of her time, as she appears in conversation with Kristeva, her writing imprints the impulse of undoing this very identity in search for new 'human', 'continuous' and 'whole' 'identities', 'selves' and 'personalities'. These hunted alternatives are no less transformative, if always temporary, in the moment of being, for in writing them one opens up the possibilities of one's and others' momentarily becoming them, be it in literature or in life. Reading Woolf's and Vita Sackville-West's letters, Rosi Braidotti identifies a similar search when she observes that 'becoming has to do with emptying out the self, opening it out to possible encounters with the "outside". Virginia Woolf's intensive genre is exemplary here' (2011: 152).

Indeed, the intensive genre of *Orlando* and its eponymous character – continuously (un)genred and (un)gendered between biography and novel, man and woman, as Braidotti suggests (2011) – seems conducive for Campos's attempts to interrupt his brief biographical comments on Woolf by resorting to her writing. In his interruptions, Campos transforms Woolf into Diana, as noted above, and she in turn becomes Orlando: 'the hunt serves to show that the prey does not exist: instead of an integral I, we find the effacement of personality' (Campos 2014: 72).[23] Hinting at the Platonic understanding that love, Eros, is the renewed search for that which one has not (not the object of desire, but the search itself),[24] Campos proposes that Woolf's novel is not a poetic, scientific or a mythological fantasy about androgyny but 'a poem about time, rather, about the flight of being and the projections of being in time' (2014: 72–3).[25] With this in mind, Campos asserts that Woolf's most important characters in *Orlando* are 'Time' and 'Zeitgeist'. While Time whistles the continuous 'music of human destiny, the *fatum*, the *fado*' (2014: 73),[26] Orlando negotiates it to the demands of his/her cultural and historical moments, the Zeitgeist of each time, becoming who s/he becomes in these renewed negotiations. *Orlando* is about being and non-being; if we bridge Campos's reading and Woolf's philosophy in 'A sketch of the past', then it is a novel about human potentiality – or 'flight of being', in Campos's words – and the socio-historical castrations that limit this very flight – 'non-being' in Woolf's phrasing. Negotiating between being and non-being, Time and Zeitgeist, one comes to be what one is, we can interpret from their conversation.

'We can say that Orlando as a character is the very rhythm of the book. The rhythm of water. . . . The tragic appeal of the waters . . .' (Campos 2014: 74),[27] Campos concludes as he bridges what he had earlier coined as Woolf's 'beauty of water' to Orlando's quest in time. Here, 'the tragic appeal of the waters' followed by an ellipsis hints at both the end of Woolf's career and of his essay. Since his lyrical *crônica* creates a parallel between Woolf's life and art, writing a note on how Virginia Woolf died seems to become inevitable for Campos. Earlier, he had wondered if Woolf indeed came 'to be, as she said in the end, the freest of women in England' and evaded an elaborate answer by stating that 'at least she lived and killed herself for it' (2014: 70),[28] immediately moving on to his reading of *Orlando*. Now, avoiding any form of long discussion of her suicide again, he does not follow up on the cue that 'the tragic appeal of the waters' opens up for a specific discussion of Woolf's suicide scene. Instead, right after vaguely affirming that Woolf 'searched for' death in the waters of a river (2014: 74), he discontinues the logical sequence and interrupts his text as it moves towards death. Leaving the scene behind, he goes back to *Orlando* in the following sentence and allows life to break in again: '*Orlando* might yet be a novel about life' (2014: 74). At the word 'life', Campos immediately turns to Woolf's 'Modern fiction': 'life is a luminous halo, a semi-transparent envelope surrounding us from the beginning of consciousness to the end' (*CR 1*, qtd in Campos 2014: 74). He closes his text in Woolf's words as he reproduces her suicide letter to Leonard Woolf. However, he cuts and edits it freely as he translates Woolf's poignant text into Brazilian Portuguese within quotation marks:

> 'I feel certain I am going mad again. I begin to hear voices, and I can't concentrate in my work. I have fought against it, but I can't fight any longer. I owe all the happiness of my life to you. You have been incredibly good to me. I can't go on spoiling your life.' (Campos 2014: 74)[29]

Campos's rewriting of Woolf's letter could be read as another case of his recurrent use of interruption as a narrative strategy to defer meaning. He does not discuss the letter but rather leaves it there, at the end of his own text, to converse with what came before. In that sense, Woolf's letter becomes a return rather than an end. Cutting and editing here are a methodological interpretation that develops the philosophical element of Woolf's writings from *Orlando* to her suicide note and back again in endless conversations. Moreover, the fact that his rewriting ends her letter and his essay with the word 'life' seems to educe the conversation with Woolf that this chapter has produced. Even when death is at the heart of a sentence ('I can't go on'), life is its final word.

Campos's affirmation, in direct conversation with Woolf in 'Modern fiction', is that only art can document the halo and the gig lamp, expanding its light elsewhere. Not an 'I who want not to be' but rather an 'I who always is, who wants to be persistently'. If Woolf sinks 'wordlessly' in Kristeva, here she wordfully floods in Campos. Words might be an impure medium, as one of the voices in Woolf's *Walter Sickert: A Conversation* (1934) affirms, but they are still a human medium for this artistic endeavour to become no one and, in that sense, everyone. Or, as Hélène Cixous would later phrase it, to turn from the masculine economy of the *Propre*, the self-proper, to that of *Personne*, a feminine no one/anyone,[30] the writer of *écriture féminine* who operates writing as the limit between one's self and all the multiple selves who live in the inexhaustible potentialities of literature.[31] Woolf's life continues elsewhere in this interruption, be it in her political engagement against oppression that still inspires readers in our tyrannical times, in the poetic singularities that incessantly invite new interpretations and contextualisation or in the individual chord her words strike in so many different sorts of readers. And indeed, there is still so much life to be found in Woolf: 'All this writing – what a deluge of words I've let loose' (*D* 6: 342).

Notes

1. Translated by Anita Barrows for Marion Boyars, London.
2. As it appears in Seán Hand's translation especially commissioned for *The Kristeva Reader* (1986), edited by Toril Moi.
3. All translations from Brazilian Portuguese to English are mine.
4. Woolf also chooses 'conversation' to subtitle essays, such as 'Mr Conrad: A conversation' (1923) and *Walter Sickert: A Conversation* (1934).
5. For a discussion of 'conversation' as a methodological principle for getting closer to an individual voice through the collective task of conversing and allowing oneself to be grazed or scratched by other voices, see Pinho (2020).
6. Jane Goldman annotates that Woolf's relation to a new historical sense, the ability of altering history and literature through new fictional perspectives, even if in sync with Eliot's methodology in 'Tradition and the individual talent', differs in significantly feminist ways (2004: 72). Woolf, for instance, never writes a defence of one method of experimentation. In fact, as Goldman suggests, it is perhaps in response to Eliot's defence of James Joyce's 'mythical method' presented in 'Ulysses, order and myth' (1923) as the only one worth experimenting with that Woolf adds the following parenthetical lines to 'Modern fiction', her 1925 revision of 'Modern novels', 'nothing – no "method", no experiment, even of the wildest – is forbidden, but only falsity and pretence' (1925: 164).
7. For a discussion of the wider historical context of the student-led demonstrations, occupations, strikes and general protests against capitalist, colonialist, gendered and racialised politics, see chapters 10 and 11 in Eric Hobsbawn (1994). Also, when Toril Moi (1986) outlines the development of Kristeva's thought, she does not let us forget the context of the May 1968 demonstrations and the break of Left intellectuals, including Kristeva, with the French Communist Party (PCF). This shift happens in the wake of the Party's efforts to mollify the powerful alliance between students and workers by 'locking factory gates and sending workers home in order to prevent sit-ins and occupations' (Moi 1986: 5). By choosing to undermine the revolutionary methods of May 1968, the PCF was perceived to be in agreement with Charles de Gaulle's decision to dissolve the National Assembly and to call for immediate parliamentary elections, thus solidifying Gaullist social conservatism and the liberal agenda in establishing French sovereignty in the Cold War years.
8. To read more about the diverse responses by Julia Kristeva, Roland Barthes, Philippe Sollers, Marcelin Pleynet and François Wahl, see Danielle Marx-Scouras's *The Cultural Politics of Tel Quel* (1996).
9. Kristeva's overall political substance is marked by ambiguity. In fact, in 2018 the Bulgarian Government claimed that she had worked as a communist spy under the codename Sabina from 1971–3, which has sparked intense debates over her defence of democratic values. At stake in these discussions is the critical interpretation of the intricate political landscapes that a Bulgarian immigrant in Paris would have had to negotiate between the affirmation

of Marxist theory and her urge to escape from an authoritarian communist regime. See Schuessler and Dzhambazova (2018) and Jones (1984).
10. See Goldman (1998) for an in-depth analysis of this interlude and other examples of feminist interventions in Woolf's oeuvre.
11. See William Shakespeare's *Hamlet*: 'To be, or not to be, that is the question – / Whether 'tis nobler in the mind to suffer / The slings and arrows of outrageous fortune, / Or to take Arms against a Sea of troubles, / And by opposing end them. To die, to sleep – / No more; and by a sleep, to say we end / The heart-ache, and the thousand natural shocks / That Flesh is heir to – 'tis a consummation / Devoutly to be wished. To die, to sleep – / To sleep, perchance to dream. Ay, there's the rub, / For in that sleep of death, what dreams may come, / When we have shuffled off this mortal coil, / Must give us pause' (1600–1: 3.1.56–68).
12. See Melville's 'Bartleby, the scrivener: A story of Wall Street' (1853). See also Deleuze, (1997) and Agamben (1999).
13. Woolf wrote the 'sealed vessels' section on 11 October 1940. As Hermione Lee annotates, by 2 November this metaphorical complex would match 'what [Woolf] could see out of her window', since a bomb had 'exploded in the river bank, the bank gave way, there was a very high tide and gale, and the river burst its bank' (1999: 735), hence flooding Rodmell.
14. Under the theme of 'Virginia Woolf and social justice', Drew Shannon organised the Twenty-Ninth Annual International Conference on Virginia Woolf (2019), which revealed how her writing refuses to stagnate in time. A quick look through the programme attests to new queer, decolonial and South American afterlives of Virginia Woolf, for instance. As Madelyn Detloff puts it, 'Woolf's value is part of a complex dynamic relationship between her work and her readers' (2016: 99), one that seems to update Woolf's words from time to time.
15. With themes that range from football matches and bar reviews to philosophical investigations on existence, Campos became one of the most relevant voices of the Brazilian *crônica*, the lyrical literary essays that he published in his active years as a journalist, on his columns in the most prestigious newspapers of the time from 1945 until his death, and which were at one point performed by notable Brazilian actor Paulo Autran in the series organised by Murilo Miranda for the Ministry of Education Radio Station in the 1960s. This series featured Carlos Drummond de Andrade, Cecília Meireles, Dinah Silveira de Queiroz, Fernando Sabino, Manuel Bandeira and Rubem Braga and was published in book form by Editora do Autor in 1962.
16. Thanks to the Moreira Salles Institute (IMS, Brazil), a new edition of Paulo Mendes Campos's newspaper was rescued from obscurity and gained a new edition in tabloid format in 2013. Writing about the volume for the IMS blog, Elvia Bezerra unearthed the interview Paulo Mendes Campos gave to Edilberto Coutinho, *O Globo*, in which the Brazilian poet and essayist defined the Project as the following: 'a panel of the hubbub of my curiosities, which was not designed, but which resulted from these multiple attentions that have always arisen in my life and are reflected in this involuntary volume' ('Um painel da barafunda das minhas curiosidades, que não foi projetado, mas resultou dessas atenções múltiplas que surgiram sempre na minha vida e estão refletidas neste volume involuntário') (Bezerra 2013).
17. 'Arrisco apenas a pensar que ela possuía em alto teor todas as nossas fraquezas e todas as qualidades que também gostaríamos de possuir.'
18. 'Além disso era linda. Não de uma beleza caída do céu por descuido, mas de uma beleza conquistada através da solidão, da contemplação, do ritmo, uma beleza que se desenvolve de dentro para fora e se estampa em ossos angulares e linhas inesperadas. Uma beleza apesar dos outros. Contraditória e quase irritante. Uma beleza feita de imaginação em movimento, não de reflexão, uma beleza de água. Tão rápida que os amigos jamais chegaram a um acordo sobre os olhos de Virginia, a não ser que eram belos. Olhos acinzentados, diz o poeta

Stephen Spender. Cor de hematita, negros e azuis, diz o pintor Jacques-Émile Blanche. Verdes para David Garnett. Com esses olhos indefinidamente irisados, Virginia viu um mundo em perpétua mutação de cores e formas. A visão, no sentido físico e simbólico, é o seu signo. . . . Era uma alma situada no instante, presente portanto na infinitude das experiências, mas sem residência certa ou endereço conhecido.'

19. 'VW passou a vida toda a escrever sobre isso, sobre a falta de identidade ou de consistência da alma ou, se quiser, sobre a falta de personalidade.'
20. 'Quanto T. S. Eliot a levou à leitura de Montaigne, devia o poeta ter sentido a alta frequência do caráter ondulante e fugidio da jovem escritora. É preciso aprender a não ter medo de Virginia Woolf.'
21. *Far from the Madding Crowd* (1874).
22. 'Pois, com Orlando, VW se fez uma espécie de Diana Caçadora: a peça procurada no bosque intrincado é a identidade humana, o ser contínuo, a personalidade íntegra.'
23. 'A caçada serve para mostrar que a caça não existe: em vez de um eu integral, encontramos o esmiuçamento da personalidade.'
24. As narrated by Socrates, recollecting and transmitting the words of a woman, his teacher Diotima, in Plato's *The Symposium*. Socrates's retelling of Diotima's lesson corrects all previous speeches, including the one delivered by comic playwright Aristophanes, in which 'androgynous' appears as one of the original genders. See Plato (1989).
25. 'Orlando é um poema sobre o tempo, melhor, sobre a fugacidade do ser e das projeções do ser dentro do tempo.'
26. 'a música do destino humano, o *fatum*, o fado'.
27. 'Pode-se dizer ainda que o personagem de Orlando é o próprio ritmo do livro. . . . O trágico apelo das águas.'
28. 'Chegou a ser, como disse no fim, a mulher mais livre da Inglaterra? Pelo menos viveu e se matou para isso.'
29. '"Tenho a impressão de que vou ficar louca. Ouço vozes e não posso concentrar-me em meu trabalho. Lutei contra isso, mas não posso continuar lutando. Devo-te toda a felicidade de minha vida. Foste impecavelmente bom para mim. Não posso continuar estragando tua vida."'
30. *Personne*, a pronoun translated as 'no one' or 'anyone', is also a feminine noun in French, 'persons'.
31. See Cixous's 'Prediction' to *Prénoms de Personnes* [The First Names of No One] (1994), as well as the epoch-making 'Sorties: Out and out: Attacks/ways out/forays' in *The Newly Born Woman* (Cixous 2001).

Bibliography

Agamben, G. (1999), *Potentialities*, trans. D. Heller-Roazen, Stanford, CA: Stanford University Press.

Agamben, G. (2009a), *The Signature of All Things: On Method*, trans. L. Disanto and K. Attell, New York: Zone Books.

Agamben, G. (2009b), *What is an Apparatus? and Other Essays*, trans. D. Kishik and S. Pedatella, Stanford, CA: Stanford University Press.

Allen, J. (2012), *Virginia Woolf and the Politics of Language*, Edinburgh: Edinburgh University Press.

Bezerra, E. (2013), 'Diário da Tarde: O volume involuntário (I)' [The afternoon daily: The involuntary volume], *Blog do IMS*, 14 November, <https://blogdoims.com.br/diario-da-tarde-o-volume-involuntario-i-por-elvia-bezerra> (last accessed 3 September 2018).

Bosi, A. (1994), *História concisa da literatura brasileira* [Concise History of Brazilian Literature], São Paulo: Editora Cultrix.

Braidotti, R. (2011), *Nomadic Theory: The Portable Rosi Braidotti*, New York: Columbia University Press.

Briggs, J. (2005), *Virginia Woolf, an Inner Life*, Orlando, FL: Harcourt.

Campos, P. M. (2014 [1981]), 'Orlando de Virginia Woolf' [Orlando by Virginia Woolf], In P. M. Campos, *Diário da Tarde* [The Afternoon Daily], São Paulo: Companhia das Letras, pp. 65–74.

Cixous, H. (1994 [1974]), 'Prediction', trans. D. Cowell, in H. Cixous, *The Hélène Cixous Reader*, ed. S. Sellers, London: Routledge, pp. 25–33.

Cixous, H. (2001 [1975]), 'Sorties: Out and out: Attacks/ways out/forays', in H. Cixous and C. Clément, *The Newly Born Woman*, trans. B. Wing, Minneapolis: University of Minnesota Press, pp. 63–134.

Deleuze, G. (1997), 'Bartleby; or, the formula', in *Essays Critical and Clinical*, trans. D. W. Smith and M. A. Greco, Minneapolis, University of Minnesota Press, pp. 68–90

Detloff, M. (2016), *The Value of Virginia Woolf*, Cambridge: Cambridge University Press.

Eliot, T. S. (1932 [1919]), 'Tradition and the individual talent', in T. S. Eliot, *Selected Essays, 1917–1932*, New York: Harcourt, Brace and Co., pp. 3–11.

Gilbert, Geoff (2004), *Before Modernism Was: Modern History and the Constituency of Writing*, New York: Palgrave Macmillan.

Goldman, J. (1998), *The Feminist Aesthetics of Virginia Woolf: Modernism, Post-Impressionism, and the Politics of the Visual*, Cambridge: Cambridge University Press.

Goldman, J. (2004), *Modernism, 1910–1945: Image to Apocalypse*, New York: Palgrave Macmillan.

Hobsbawn, E. (1994), *The Age of Extremes: 1914–1991*, London: Abacus

Humm, M. (2013), 'Multidisciplinary Woolf / multiple Woolfs?, in A. Martin and K. Holland (eds), *Interdisciplinary/Multidisciplinary Woolf: Selected Papers from the Twenty-Second Annual International Conference on Virginia Woolf*, Liverpool: Liverpool University Press, pp. 2–12.

Jones, A. R. (1984), 'Julia Kristeva on femininity: The limits of a semiotic politics', *Feminist Review*, 18, pp. 56–73.

Kristeva, J. (1974), *Des Chinoises*, Paris: Pauvert.

Kristeva, J. (1986a [1974]), 'About Chinese women', trans. S. Hand, in J. Kristeva, *The Kristeva Reader*, ed. T. Moi, Oxford: Blackwell Publishers, pp. 138–59.

Kristeva, J. (1986b [1977]), 'Stabat mater', trans. A. Goldhammer, in J. Kristeva, *The Kristeva Reader*, ed. T. Moi, Oxford: Blackwell Publishers, pp. 160–87.

Kristeva, J. (2002 [1983]), 'My memory's hyperbole', trans. A. Viscusi, in J. Kristeva, *The Portable Kristeva*, ed. K. Oliver, New York: Columbia University Press, pp. 3–22.

Lee, H. (1999), *Virginia Woolf*, New York: Vintage.

Marx-Scouras, D. (1996), *The Cultural Politics of Tel Quel*, University Park: Pennsylvania State University Press.

Melville, H. (1998 [1853]), 'Bartleby, the scrivener: A story of Wall Street', in H. Melville, *Billy Budd, Sailor, and Selected Tales*, ed. R. Milder, Oxford: Oxford University Press, pp. 3–41.

Moi, T. (1986), 'Introduction', in J. Kristeva, *The Kristeva Reader*, ed. T. Moi, Oxford: Blackwell Publishers, pp. 1–22.

Pinho, D. (2020), 'A conversa como um "método" filosófico em Virginia Woolf', in D. Pinho, M. A. de Oliveira, N. Nogueira (eds), *Conversas com Virginia Woolf*, Rio de Janeiro: Ape'Ku, 2020, pp. 11–34.

Plato (1989) *The Symposium*, Indianapolis: Hackett.

Sarmatz, L. (2014), 'Posfácio, colecionador de si mesmo' [Afterword, a collector of himself], in P. M. Campos (ed.), *Diário da Tarde*, São Paulo: Companhia das Letras, pp. 321–30.

Schuessler, J. and B. Dzhambazova (2018), 'Bulgaria says French thinker was a secret agent. she calls it a "barefaced lie"', *New York Times*, <https://www.nytimes.com/2018/04/01/arts/julia-kristeva-bulgaria-communist-spy.html> (last accessed 30 July 2018);

Shakespeare, W. (2003 [1600–1]), *Hamlet, Prince of Denmark*, ed. P. Edwards, Cambridge: Cambridge University Press.

Spivak, G. C. (1981), 'French feminism in an international frame', *Yale French Studies*, 62, pp. 154–85.

Woolf, V. (1934), *Walter Sickert: A Conversation*, London: Hogarth Press.

Woolf, V. (1970 [1937]), 'Craftsmanship', in Woolf, *The Death of the Moth and Other Essays*, London: Harcourt Brace Jovanovich, pp. 198–207.

Woolf, V. (1979 [1920]), 'Men and women', in Woolf, *Women and Writing*, ed. M. Barrett, London: Harcourt, pp. 64–8.

Woolf, V. (1979–1985), *The Diary of Virginia Woolf*, ed. A. O. Bell, 5 vols, New York: Penguin Books.

Woolf, V. (1980), *The Letters of Virginia Woolf: Volume Three, 1923–1928*, ed. N. Nicolson and J. Trautmann, London: Harvest/HBJ.

Woolf, V. (1985), 'A sketch of the past', in Woolf, *Moments of Being*, ed. J. Schulkind, London: Harcourt Brace and Company, pp. 64–159.

Woolf, V. (2000 [1929/1938]), *A Room of One's Own and Three Guineas*, Oxford: Oxford University Press.

Woolf, V. (2003 [1925]), 'The modern essay', in Woolf, *The Common Reader*, vol. 1, London: Vintage, pp. 211–22.

Woolf, V. (2003 [1925]), 'Modern fiction', in Woolf, *The Common Reader*, vol. 1, London: Vintage, pp. 146–54.

Woolf, V. (2015 [1931]), *The Waves*, Oxford: Oxford University Press.

Zwerdling, A. (1986), *Virginia Woolf and the Real World*, Los Angeles: University of California Press.

6

Three Guineas and the *Cassandra* Project – Christa Wolf's Reading of Virginia Woolf during the Cold War

Henrike Krause

Christa Wolf (1929–2011) is one of the most prominent writers of the former German Democratic Republic (GDR). Soon after the Second World War she and her husband, Gerhard Wolf, supported the ideas and ideology of a new socialist state and became members of the Socialist Unity Party. While her first two novels, *Moskauer Novelle* [Moscow Novella] (1961) and *Divided Heaven* (*Der geteilte Himmel*, 1963) are strongly influenced by the aesthetics of socialist realism, her third novel *The Quest for Christa T.* (*Nachdenken über Christa T.*, 1968) already testifies to principles which guided her thinking and writing in the following decades: that literature not only reflects social reality – as socialist realism dictates – but must unfold an individual life and inner subjectivity before the eyes of the reader. Thus, Wolf understands literature as a medium to strengthen empathy within society and to influence social processes.

The Quest for Christa T. was Wolf's immediate response to the eleventh Plenum of the Central Committee of the Socialist Unity Party in 1965, when officials accused writers and artists of undermining the socialist state. Christa Wolf gave an unplanned speech in which she strongly emphasised the writer's right to be subjective, which was harshly criticised by members of the Central Committee. While Wolf's international reputation was growing during the 1970s, her position against the GDR regime became more critical. Even though she still believed in the idea of a socialist state, she also realised that the actual society was suppressing individual self-fulfilment. This inner conflict inspired many of her novels, such as *No Place on Earth* (*Kein Ort. Nirgends*, 1979), *Cassandra* (*Kassandra*, 1983) and *What Remains* (*Was bleibt*, 1990).

After a phase of détente at the beginning of the 1970s, when Richard Nixon, the president of the United States, and Leonid Brezhnev, the leader of the Soviet Union, agreed to establish a new policy of peaceful coexistence, the conflict between the East and West Bloc states increasingly intensified towards the end of the decade. From a German perspective, the NATO Double-Track Decision in December 1979 and the deployment of Pershing II missiles in West Germany put both German states in an alarming situation. If a Soviet nuclear strike occurred, it would first target West Germany and simultaneously destroy East Germany.

During this period of elevated tension, the West German peace movement was founded. Christa Wolf strongly supported the movement's idea of non-violent civil resistance, which she demonstrated through a lecture series delivered in Frankfurt am Main in 1982. These *Lectures on Poetics* and the accompanying novel *Cassandra*, which were later referred to as the *Cassandra* project, testify to her conviction that violence and conflicts are products of power structures that have their roots in language, culture and literature. For Wolf this means first and foremost the suppression of women's experience and writing.

While Christa Wolf prepared the *Lectures on Poetics* and started to write *Cassandra*, she turned her attention to a text which was also written under the threat of an upcoming war: Virginia Woolf's book-length essay *Three Guineas* (1938). In a letter from 29 January 1980 to a German editor she describes in great detail her sustained fascination for Woolf's life and works:

> This [Virginia Woolf's oeuvre] was one of my most essential literary discoveries ever (I think I read *Mrs Dalloway* first) and it generated a burning and sustained interest in this author, in every detail of her life, her family, her friendships, her marriage, her illness, her death. . . . I was captivated and captivated by the immense ability of this woman to imbue her environment with her intellectual atmosphere, and I was fascinated by the manner of this atmosphere and her courage towards the experiments that she carried out with herself through writing. (Wolf 2016: 394)[1]

In the letter she does not mention *Three Guineas*, but newly discovered material at the Archive of the Academy of Arts in Berlin and Christa Wolf's private library indicates that she was intensively involved with Woolf's essay at that time.

The connection between Christa Wolf and Virginia Woolf did not gain much attention in the last decades, with the exception of a small number of studies. Joyce Crick's article 'Christa Wolf and Virginia Woolf' (1989) offers an illuminating discussion about some of the major characteristics of the oeuvre of both writers, and Anne Herrmann's monograph *The Dialogic and Difference* (1989) concentrates on the relationship between the two women writers and their female fictional characters.[2] Indebted to these previous studies, this chapter traces the affinities between the two writers but more emphatically sets out to introduce evidence that reveals that Christa Wolf saw Virginia Woolf as a feminist predecessor for her writing. Also, taking into consideration Woolf's *A Room of One's Own* (1929), I will show how both writers put feminist community-building at the centre of anti-militarism and were both convinced that writers have a social responsibility and that literature can bring about a change in thinking.

Christa Wolf's Reception of Virginia Woolf

In a letter from 29 September 1983 to Hans-Joachim Hoffmann, the Minister for the Arts and Culture (1973–89) of the German Democratic Republic (GDR), Christa Wolf makes a rather bold suggestion:

> Dear Comrade Hoffmann,
> I am pleased to follow your request to name some titles which would in my opinion enrich the offerings of the GDR's publishing houses . . .
> Virginia Woolf: To the Lighthouse
> The Years
> Between the Acts
> Stories and Essays

I think the time has come that this author should be represented in our country with her complete works, not only one of her books every few years. In West Germany, her works have experienced a renaissance – with every right. Also in our country there would be a very large community of readers for her. (Wolf 2016: 457–8)[3]

What makes this suggestion bold is that ever since the expatriation of the singer and songwriter Wolf Biermann in 1976, artists and intellectuals in the GDR were facing a policy of restraint. Christa Wolf, her husband Gerhard Wolf and other prominent writers had signed a protest letter to the political leadership which had far-reaching consequences for most of them (Emmerich 2009: 254–6).[4] To many writers and intellectuals 'a state incapable of tolerating criticism appeared necessarily moribund' (Paul 2009: 189). Intellectuals and artists had left the GDR already before 1976, but the exodus which followed Biermann's expatriation was without precedent (Emmerich 2009: 257). Those who stayed were pessimistic about 'communism's potential for reform' (Paul 2009: 189).

While writers critical of the GDR were harassed with house searches, imprisonment and expatriation, the publishing market of the 1970s showed 'a curious juxtaposition of official tendencies ... and cautious but determined deviations from dogmatism' (Wicht 2002: 104). Since George Lukács's disapproval of modernist writers in his criticism of the 1950s and the development of socialist realism as the GDR's dominating aesthetic programme,[5] literary modernism had a poor chance of publication. However, in the context of the GDR's cultural policy of the 1970s, Wolfgang Wicht points out that modernist texts were discovered and re-discovered by 'courageous editors in publishing houses, not to speak of the reading public, [who] felt that the essentialist conception of realism had to be subverted' (2002: 104).

During the 1970s, *Mrs Dalloway* (1977) and *To the Lighthouse* (1979) were first published in East Germany by Insel Verlag Leipzig.[6] When Christa Wolf complained in her September 1983 letter to Hans-Joachim Hoffmann that only 'every few years' one of Virginia Woolf's books were published in the GDR, she touched a sore spot in GDR's publishing policy. Although modernist writers such as Thomas Mann, Virginia Woolf and James Joyce[7] were published, the GDR's Ministry of Culture limited their availability with small print runs that gave the general reading public only limited access to their texts. Wolf's wide knowledge of writers who had only been published in West Germany testifies to her familiarity with the West German literary market. By mentioning them, she implicitly acknowledged that she was disregarding the censorship of the GDR. Paradoxically this was no secret for the political officials in the Ministry of Culture, who gave her – of course not publicly – their tacit approval.

This incident is exemplary for the GDR's cultural policy, which moved backwards and forwards between liberalisation and communist ideology. As one of the GDR's best-known intellectuals, Christa Wolf enjoyed certain privileges, one of which was a special authorisation to order literature and magazines that were not available at the GDR via her West German publishing house Luchterhand at Darmstadt, as her biographer Jörg Magenau describes it (2002: 307). Wolf's letters to Luchterhand, in which she ordered new books, are held in the archive of the Academy of Arts at Berlin.[8] Furthermore, the private library of Christa and Gerhard Wolf gives an illuminating insight into her literary interests and confirms her deep interest in Woolf and her entire oeuvre.[9]

The library holds almost all obtainable German translations of Woolf's works. Upon examining the holdings, it becomes evident that Wolf discovered Woolf in German translations and possessed most of Woolf's texts in the editions by the West German publisher S. Fischer. However, two books from her collection that are not published by S. Fischer are particularly interesting: *Three Guineas*, translated by Anita Eichholz (1978) and published by Verlag Frauenoffensive in Munich, and *A Room of One's Own*, translated by Renate Gerhardt (1978) and published by her small publishing house Gerhardt Verlag in West Berlin. Eichholz's *Three Guineas* and Gerhardt's *A Room of One's Own* are not only the first translated into German, but their publication coincided with a general trend in German Woolf criticism, which focused on Woolf as a feminist intellectual (Nünning and Nünning 2002: 82). Christa Wolf obviously had a profound interest in Woolf's works when she bought both essays, which were printed only in a small number of copies.

Wolf's copies of *A Room of One's Own* and *Three Guineas* show significant usage and many passages of *Three Guineas* are underlined with pen and pencil, indicating her intense engagement with this book. Considering her writing projects from 1978 onwards, it is likely that she read *Three Guineas* and *A Room of One's Own* while preparing her lectures and writing *Cassandra*.

The *Cassandra* Project and *Three Guineas* – In Search of a Literary Form under the Threat of War

At the end of the 1970s when the conflict between the United States and the Soviet Union was increasing and a nuclear war became possible, Christa Wolf received an invitation to one of the most prestigious guest lectureships in West Germany, the series *Lectures on Poetics* (Wolf 2016: 364). In January 1979, Wolf started to prepare the lecture series and was occupied by the question of how literature could intervene in the conflict. Wolf was convinced that contemporary literature had to come into action as 'peace research',[10] as she proclaimed in her acceptance speech for the award of the Georg Büchner Prize for Literature one year later. Wolf understands literature as 'peace research' in terms of its ability to offer viable alternatives to the rearmament hysteria of the Cold War. In order to develop these alternatives, Wolf sees it as her responsibility to place women's lives and experiences in the centre of her literature.

While searching for a literary form for her *Lectures of Poetics* that could correspond to this notion, Christa and Gerhard Wolf undertook a journey to Greece in Spring 1980 during which she decided to make the mythological figure Cassandra her central character and to explore the roots of Western culture and literature through Cassandra's story through a female point of view. Wolf developed a plan to rewrite the legend of Cassandra from her adolescence as a Trojan princess to her exile in Mycenae until the moment shortly before her death through the hand of Mycenae's queen, Clytemnestra. Wolf further planned a series of four lectures that would reveal the conditions under which she had rewritten Cassandra's story. Wolf considered these lectures as important as the novel and decided to give them three different autobiographical forms: the first two lectures are travel reports of Wolf's journey to the Greek mainland and to the island of Crete ('Travel Report, about the Accidental Surfacing and Gradual Fabrication of a Literary Personage' and 'The Travel Report Continues, and the Trail Is Followed'); the third lecture is a work diary covering the period between May 1980 and August 1981 ('A Work Diary, about the Stuff Life and Dreams are Made Of') and is written as a letter to another women writer in which Wolf discusses German literary history and the role of women writers ('A Letter, about Unequivocal and Ambiguous Meaning, Definiteness and Indefiniteness; about Ancient Conditions and New View-Scopes; about Objectivity').[11]

It seems significant that under the threat of an approaching war, both Woolf and Wolf found a generically heterogeneous form best suited to bring about a change in thinking. Woolf at first tried to interweave the essay and the novel in one text, *The Pargiters*, but separated them into *The Years* and *Three Guineas* during the process of writing. After *The Years* was published in 1937, Woolf adhered to the plan for an essay which would contain material she had meticulously collected since 1931[12] and was sure to have 'enough powder to blow up St. Paul's' (D 4: 77). Her first idea for the book was to write 'a sequel to *A Room of One's Own* – about the sexual life of women' (D 4: 6), but as Elena Gualtieri notes, *Three Guineas* differs in its sarcastic tone and repeating structure very much from the playfulness, irony and rich imagery of *A Room of One's Own* (2000: 82). The change in tone and form corresponds with the different approaches both texts apply to the topic of female subjectivity. But the difference also draws from Woolf's reaction towards the general situation of intellectuals under the influence of enormous political changes in Europe during the 1930s, when Nationalism in Germany and Fascism in Italy were on the rise and the Spanish Civil War was raging.

While Woolf's self-image as a writer of the 1920s was partly formed through her opposition to the earlier generation of authors such as Arnold Bennett, H. G. Wells and John Galsworthy, she found herself in the position of the old guard in the 1930s. A new generation of writers such as her nephew Julian Bell, as well as W. H. Auden, Louis MacNeice, Stephen Spender and Christopher Isherwood were more concerned with political issues than with questions of aesthetics. As Gualtieri has pointed out, Woolf had to face the accusation that she represented 'a dying ruling class whose beliefs and principles appeared to be totally ineffectual in the fight against Fascist brutality and violence' (2000: 83).

Considering the writing projects Woolf undertook and her commitment to several political organisations during the 1930s, the younger generation's reproach seems inaccurate.[13] Since 1931, Woolf had thought of a book which should implicate the 'nature of patriarchy in its public and private guises' (Hussey 1995: 291). Looking more closely at the different titles Woolf considered for the essay which would become *Three Guineas*, the change from a mainly feminist-oriented concept ('Professions for Women' [D 4: 6]; 'Men are like that' [D 4: 77]) to a stronger emphasis on war becomes evident ('The Next War' [D 4: 346]; 'What are we to do' [D 4: 348]), as does the decision for it to take the form of a letter ('Answers to Correspondents' [D 5: 3]; 'Letter to an Englishman' [D 5: 18]; Hussey 1995: 291; Wood 2013: 73–4).[14]

There are several factors which influenced Woolf's decision to write *Three Guineas* in the form of a letter. As the situation in Europe worsened, the Woolfs received almost weekly petitions from all sorts of committees, societies and interest groups. Thus, Virginia Woolf felt the need for opposition, not 'to sit silent and acquiesce in all this idiotic letter signing and vocal pacifism when there's such an obvious horror in our midst' which 'finally made my blood boil into the usual ink spray' (L 6: 250), as she describes it to Margaret Llewelyn Davies in 1938. With *Three Guineas*, Woolf performed the public statement which the 1930s generation of Julian Bell and his fellow writers had demanded. However, as Randi Saloman has argued, the pamphlet does not 'arrive at a plan for eliminating war' but is rather concerned with the question 'of how we are to understand one another[,] ... how a writer can communicate with a reader and how people with different experiences may seek to come to terms with one another' (Saloman 2012: 94, 98).

The question 'of how we are to understand one another' also guided Christa Wolf's *Lectures on Poetics* nearly fifty years later. In choosing autobiographical forms for the lectures – travel report, work diary and letter – she accentuated the sincerity of this undertaking and followed an aesthetic programme that she called 'subjective authenticity' and elaborated in an interview with Hans Kaufmann in 1973 (Wolf 1999: 401–31). The term 'subjective authenticity' means for Wolf that truthfulness and personal experience inform her creative process. In many of Wolf's texts 'subjective authenticity' is linked to an autobiographical writing impulse and often, in a process of second order observation, she describes her own involvement with the text and the effects which the writing process had on her.[15]

In her introduction to the lecture series, Wolf explains that she did not want to construct a straightforward analysis but rather a texture, a 'fabric which ... did not turn out completely tidy' (Wolf 1985: 142), which emerged mainly from the working process itself when she first had 'to master the material' (Wolf 1985: 142). To present the concept for her lectures as a work in progress is part of Wolf's programme of 'subjective authenticity'. She points out that the concept derived from her awareness of a 'tension between the artistic forms within which we have agreed to abide and the living material, ... which has resisted these forms' (Wolf 1985: 142). To resist these forms meant also to resist unequivocal explanations, to question causalities and to mistrust teleology; it even meant to mistrust common language and the meaning of words. Naturally, the question emerged of how to tell stories despite this mistrust in the techniques of storytelling.

In the third lecture, the work diary, Wolf discusses the assumption of some historians that ancient cultures, which did not have a writing system, had to remember their history through narratives with 'vivid and vital, ideal figures' (Wolf 1985: 262). For Wolf, this also affects historiography and classical literature with their plots of battles and heroes that can easily be remembered by a cultural community. Inevitably the complexity of phenomena must be reduced to 'a few symbolic acts' (Wolf 1985: 262). Related to Cassandra's story as Aeschylus has introduced it, this means for instance that Cassandra has violated the agreement with the god Apollo and is inevitably punished for breaking her word. Wolf questions if monocausal narratives are indispensable or if there are other ways to imagine alternative forms of narration. Interestingly she addresses literary texts, which, in her opinion, evade these structures:

> What meaning does this observation have for a literature which no longer wants to create large-scale, vital, ideal figures; no longer wants to tell coherent stories held together by war and murder and homicide and the heroic deeds which accrue to them? What kind of memory does the prose of Virginia Woolf require and endorse? Why should the brain be able to 'retain' a linear narrative better than a narrative network, given that the brain itself is often compared with a network? What other way is there for an author to tackle the custom (which no longer meets the needs of our time) of remembering history as the story of heroes? (Wolf 1985: 262)

It seems reasonable that Christa Wolf saw Virginia Woolf's style of narration as an appropriate alternative to a monocausal way of storytelling and therefore as a literary model for following generations of writers like herself. Considering Wolf's image of a network-like storytelling, Virginia Woolf's novels *Mrs Dalloway* and *To the Lighthouse* come to mind, where different perspectives and different temporal levels intermingle. The novels give us 'no plot, no comedy, no tragedy, no love interest or catastrophe in the accepted style' (*E* 4: 160), as Woolf anticipated in 'Modern fiction' (1925).

Virginia Woolf continuously thought of new ways of melding together different forms. In February 1927 she sketches in her diary while pondering over her first ideas for *The Waves*, how the work would be: 'Away from facts: free; yet concentrated; prose yet poetry; a novel & a play' (*D* 3: 128). Compared to the circumstances under which Christa Wolf wrote her novels, Woolf's experimental novels *Jacob's Room*, *Mrs Dalloway*, *To the Lighthouse*, *Orlando* and *The Waves* demonstrate greater freedom in content and also testify to her conviction that literary form needs to change with the needs of its readers, as she famously explains in 'Character and fiction' (1924). She claims that 'on or about December 1910 human character changed' (*E* 3: 421) and concludes, that '[t]he writer must get into touch with his reader by putting before him something which he recognises, which therefore stimulates his imagination' (*E* 3: 431). This does not only affect the representation of characters but also the form in which their thoughts, feelings and emotions unfold in the text. Regarding the question of form, Virginia Woolf comes to a conclusion that is very similar to the view Christa Wolf endorses decades later: 'At the present moment we are suffering . . . from having no code of manners which writers and readers accept as a prelude to the more exciting intercourse of friendship' (*E* 3: 434).

Both Christa Wolf's and Virginia Woolf's writings were strongly influenced by questions of politics and the threat of war. Both shared the conviction that only new forms in literature could address 'the needs' (Wolf 1985: 262) of their audiences and readers in times of political upheaval. I suggest that when Wolf discovered *Three Guineas*, she found common convictions and perspectives which she could integrate in her own work. Following the traces of Wolf's reading of *Three Guineas* provides further insight into her conversation with this text.

Antigone's and Cassandra's Cry – Asking for Peace

Christa Wolf's underlining with different pens in her copy of *Three Guineas* indicates how she closely followed the text's arguments. She underlined or marked with crosses words, phrases and whole passages. Those passages are for the most part elements of Woolf's discussion of pacifism in correspondence with feminist ideas: that is, the exclusion of women from public institutions and positions, the unequal distribution of household work without financial compensation and the question of how work, capitalism and war are intermingled. The paragraph in which Woolf unfolds her idea of a utopian college – 'a place where society was free' and to which '[p]eople who love learning for itself would gladly like to come' (*TG*: 156, 155) – is heavily marked. As the text moves on, the underlining decreases (especially in Chapter Three), but on the last pages, one paragraph is noticeably marked:

> As we listen to the voices we seem to hear an infant crying in the night, the black night that now covers Europe, and with no language but a cry, Ay, ay, ay, ay. . . . But it is not a new cry, it is a very old cry. Let us shut off the wireless and listen to the past. We are in Greece now. . . . Pictures and voices are the same to-day as they were 2,000 years ago. (*TG*: 269–70)

This allusion to ancient Greece is the fourth time that Woolf refers to Sophocles's *Antigone* (*TG*: 206–7, 258, 266, 269) and it is significant that Wolf underlined the name 'Antigone' in her copy of *Three Guineas* whenever it comes up. In *Three Guineas* Antigone's opposition to Creon is given as a literary example of non-violent resistance. Antigone distinguishes 'between the laws and the Law' (*TG*: 206), emphasising that she puts her own moral convictions over the law of the state, respectively the law of Creon.[16] But the conclusion that Woolf draws from Antigone's fate is rather daunting: Creon shuts Antigone 'not in Holloway or in a concentration camp, but in a tomb' and also 'brought ruin on his house, and scattered the land with the bodies of the dead' (*TG*: 269–70). The 'old cry' – 'Ay, ay, ay, ay' – represents both the cry of Creon's victims and Antigone's cry from her tomb, symbolising the voice of female self-determination. It is noteworthy that Christa Wolf also chose the 'old cry' as her main theme for *Cassandra*.

The Trojan princess Cassandra is mentioned in Homer's *Iliad* and *Odyssey*, but it is Aeschylus who creates a mythological background for Cassandra's gift of prophecy in his *Oresteia* and explains it by referencing her pact with Apollo and the resulting punishment: to make prophecies that are truthful, but which no one believes to be true. Still today people whose warnings are not heard are called Cassandra (a similar idiomatic phrase exists in German: the 'Kassandra-Ruf', which means 'Cassandra's cry'), so it seems to be no coincidence that Christa Wolf's first encounter with Cassandra through Aeschylus's tragedy is accompanied by a cry:

> I witnessed how a panic rapture spread through me, how it mounted and reached its pinnacle when a voice began to speak:
> > Aiee! Aiee!
> > Apollo! Apollo!
> Cassandra. I saw her at once. She, the captive, took me captive. . . . [S]he took possession of me. . . . It worked at once. I believed every word she said. . . . Three thousand years – melted away. (Wolf 1985: 144–5)

Woolf and Wolf chose the motif of a cry and emphasised its literary tradition and origin in ancient Greek literature. However, Wolf also seized upon Woolf's idea of a fictional female precursor like Judith Shakespeare and retold it as the tale of Cassandra. Consequently – to take the metaphor further – Wolf transfers the ancient cry to her own time and fulfils Woolf's idea 'that history shall be re-written' (Woolf 1992: 70). While Virginia Woolf criticised the discrepancy between female characters in the works of fiction and the historical reality that women had to face (*AROO*: 39–40), Christa Wolf turned back to the sources of that myth by asking: 'Who was Cassandra before anyone wrote about her?' (Wolf 1985: 273). Wolf tries to expose the power structure in the institutions of literature and historiography that had shaped Cassandra as a part of Western cultural tradition.

Cassandra's cry in Wolf's novel, or her 'fits' as Georgina Paul categorises them (2009: 203–5), functions as a crucial leitmotif in the novel. On the one hand Cassandra's fits testify to her relationship to the gods and thus place her in the social class of priests and priestesses. On the other hand, her fits mark her struggle between realising the political situation at the palace and her sense of duty as the daughter of the king. As the story progresses, Cassandra is continuously drawn to a world outside the palace at the river Scamander, where women of the lower classes are living in harmonious community.[17] Taking a closer look at the development of the characters and the story in *Cassandra*, two of Woolf's major arguments in *Three Guineas* become apparent.

Woolf's conviction, that without 'free speech' in private 'there can be no public freedom' (*TG*: 246), finds its literary equivalence in the general tendency of Wolf's depiction of Troy's prewar society, where fear and hatred are systematically triggered through censored and manipulated language. Christa Wolf had marked those paragraphs in her copy of *Three Guineas* and her retelling of the Trojan War suggests that the outbreak of war is the result of a society which is deeply divided by mistrust and anger.

After Cassandra has fallen out of favour at court and must flee the Trojan palace, she seeks refuge at the river Scamander. The idyll of communal life – 'We did not stop learning. Each shared his own special knowledge with the other' (Wolf 1985: 132)[18] – calls to mind Woolf's utopian college, 'a place where society was free' (*TG*: 156). A longer passage of the text describes the women's hopes for the generations coming after them – 'repair our omissions, rectify our mistakes' – and the question of whether these generations 'would still know who we were' (Wolf 1985: 132). Because the women at Scamander do 'not know any script to write in' to leave a message for future generations, they decide to press their 'hands side by side into the soft clay' and call it 'immortalizing our memory' (Wolf 1985: 133).

The reference and imagination of a matriarchal tradition not only alludes to Woolf's famous sentence in *A Room of One's Own* – 'For we think back through our mothers if we are women' (*AROO*: 69) – but also to *Three Guineas* when Woolf invokes the macabre image of the mothers laughing out of their graves: '"It was for this that we suffered obloquy and contempt! Light up the windows of the new house, daughters! Let them blaze!"' (*TG*: 208). The daughters of these mothers start to 'dance round the new house, the poor house' and sing '"We have done with war! We have done with tyranny"' (*TG*: 208). In Wolf's *Cassandra*, the Amazons, who had fought with the Trojan army, also dance in ecstasy after the death of their queen Penthesilea (Wolf 1985: 121–2).

It is interesting that both Woolf and Wolf used similar images for their discussion of matriarchal tradition. In this regard it seems possible that Christa Wolf drew much of her inspiration for the novel *Cassandra* and the lectures from *Three Guineas* and – as we will see in the following section – from *A Room of One's Own*.

A Room of My Own – Creating New Traditions

Returning to the compositional and conceptual aspects of Christa Wolf's project, a few issues are still pending – primarily the question of why Wolf chose Cassandra as her key figure in ancient Greek literature. One possible explanation is again linked to Cassandra's gift of prophecy, her 'seeing'. As Wolf explains in her third lecture Cassandra's ability 'to see' is synonymous with woman's writing:

> For women, writing is a medium which they place between themselves and the world of men. . . . The inevitable moment when the woman who writes (who 'sees' in Cassandra's case) no longer represents anything or anyone except herself; but who is that? (Wolf 1985: 232)

Again, the similarities to Woolf's ideas are striking. Not only does this paragraph draw on Woolf's conviction that men and women experience reality differently – 'Though we see the same world, we see it through different eyes' (*TG*: 133) –, but it also refers to one of Woolf's main arguments that women should not follow the career path of their male contemporaries and try to assimilate into male institutions because the patriarchal system inevitably leads to war (*TG*: 191). The 'daughters of educated men' should rather think and act the opposite way: only as outsiders can they establish alternative concepts and ideas which help to prevent war (*TG*: 272). Christa Wolf expresses the same conviction, strongly emphasising women's writing as an act of resistance and autonomy:

> To what extent is there really such a thing as 'women's writing'? . . . To the extent that they stop wearing themselves out trying to integrate themselves into the prevailing delusional system. To the extent that, writing and living, they aim at autonomy. (Wolf 1985: 259)

However, the question of representation remains: Who is the writing woman, if she leaves familiar paths and 'no longer represent[s] anything or anyone except herself' (Wolf 1985: 232)? As Carola Opitz-Wiemers has pointed out, a person who claims to represent only herself must also necessarily know who she actually is (2016: 176).

The narrator of *Three Guineas* knows very well who she is: she gives a constant account of her identity as the 'daughter of an educated man', yet the frequent repetition of this formula not only indicates the narrator's awareness of her social status as a daughter within a patriarchal society but also shows her continuing search for her own identity. Furthermore, the narrator speaks right from the beginning more often in the first-person plural ('we') than in the first-person singular ('I'). Nóra Séllei has observed that the function of this 'first-person plural subject' can be identified as an indicator of 'an inclusive group that opens up the boundaries of the "I"' (2017: 234). To support her own authority in speaking for this inclusive group of women, the narrator quotes another woman writer at the beginning of her letter – the explorer and travel writer Mary Kingsley (1862–1900) 'to speak for us' (*TG*: 118). In Woolf's quote Kingsley explains that her German lessons were all the paid-for education she had, whereas £2,000 was spent on her brother's education. This contrasts starkly with Kingsley's achievements in the fields of ethnology and anthropology at the end of the nineteenth century, especially because she was an autodidact. It does not come as a surprise that Virginia Woolf chose Mary Kingsley as an example since Woolf felt the lack of a formal education to be a disadvantage all her life.

To call upon other women writers as authorities is a rhetorical strategy used throughout *Three Guineas* and in a slightly different way by Christa Wolf in her fourth lecture. While the work diary gives the reader an insight into Wolf's daily thoughts, ideas and impressions, the fourth lecture is presented as a letter to another writing woman, called 'A.'. The letter unfolds longer arguments based on examples from German literary history, where Wolf discusses Ingeborg Bachmann (1926–73) and Marieluise Fleißer (1901–74) (Wolf 1985: 274–7, 295), two of the best-known women writing in German in the twentieth century. The strategy is quite similar to Woolf's in *Three Guineas*: Christa Wolf calls upon other women writers to create a sense of community between herself and her addressee – her friend A.

While both the diary and the letter of *Lectures on Poetics* foreground the writer's subjectivity, this intimate letter to A. also seeks intersubjectivity. As Anne Herrmann has noticed, Woolf and Wolf use the 'female' connotated genre of the letter very consciously to emphasise the communicational and literary tradition in letter writing which women have built over centuries (1986: 178).[19] Keeping in mind Wolf's strong rejection of conventional literary forms in her introduction to the lecture, the fourth lecture paradoxically takes up this literary tradition and finds in it not only freedom of thought but also intersubjective community:

> Dear A.: . . . Recite all the great names of Western literature, forget neither Homer nor Brecht, and ask yourself with which of these mental giants you, as a woman who writes, could identify. We have no authentic models; this costs us time, detours, mistakes; but it does not have to be purely a disadvantage. Few, very few women's voices have reached our ears since Sappho sang circa 600 B.C. (Wolf 1985: 295)

Even though Woolf and Wolf use the fictional letter in similar ways, the tone, the implied addressee and communicational discourse differ. As Herrmann has pointed out with reference to Mikhail Bakhtin, the writer must imagine an interlocutor in the communicational situation of the letter (1986: 166–7). In *Three Guineas*, Woolf imagines a middle-aged barrister, a treasurer of a women's college and another treasurer from a society that helps women to enter the professions. Her polemical tone implies a certain opposition between the fictional recipients of the letter and the argument of her essay. In contrast, Christa Wolf's imagined addressee is a writing woman who seems to be rather sympathetic to Wolf's own case. By communicating via letter, Wolf creates a sense of intimacy as well as intersubjectivity. As mentioned above, addressing her friend A. in the first-person plural strengthens the group identity of writing women. And considering that this intimate letter is given as a public lecture in a university theatre, Wolf uses this intimacy as a rhetorical strategy. The intimate letter invites the audience to be part of a dialogue and gives readers the opportunity to understand one another. Besides, it is also a powerful performative act for Wolf in which she defines herself as a woman who writes and turns each member of the audience into a 'witness' (Wolf 1985: 142) of that process.

Wolf does so by opening her sources for inspiration to the audience; starting the letter with a description of her arrival at her summer house; and listing several books she is unpacking, to give an 'idea of the remarkable blend which has made up my reading for the last year' (Wolf 1985: 273). The list contains twenty-three titles of mainly feminist literature published in the late 1970s.[20] Presenting only the titles (or in some cases only short titles) and leaving out the authors' names, the list gives more the impression of keywords connected to the *Cassandra* project than of a proper bibliography. Yet in the German edition of the *Cassandra* lectures, *Conditions of a Narrative* (*Voraussetzungen einer Erzählung*, 1983), the text is supplemented with a bibliography.[21] Comparing this bibliography with the list in the 'lecture letter', a curious disproportion emerges: of the twenty-three titles which Wolf names, only nine are listed in the bibliography at the end of the printed lectures, six cannot be identified and eight identifiable titles do not turn up in the bibliography. This last category contains Luce Irigaray's *This Sex Which Is Not One* (*Ce Sexe qui n'en est pas un*) (1977), Hélène Cixous's selected essays in *Weiblichkeit in der Schrift* (1980) [Womanhood in

Letters][22] and a book called *A Room of My Own* – not *A Room of One's Own*.[23] In the German original this obvious confusion seems to be at first glance minor, because the reflexive pronoun, which has to be used instead of the English possessive determiner ('one's', 'my'), changes only through one letter: from *sich* to *mich* (*Ein Zimmer für sich allein* – *Ein Zimmer für mich allein*) (Wolf 2008: 173). The English translation by Jan van Heurck does not represent this instance adequately, because the 'mistake' has been tacitly corrected (Wolf 1985: 273). But it can be stated that this is the only obvious 'mistake' Wolf made in her list and considering that she had a copy of Renate Gerhardt's 1978 translation of *A Room of One's Own* in her library it is doubtful that she confused the title.

Whether this change of title was made intentionally or unintentionally must stay unresolved. What is more important to notice is the setting in which these books are unpacked: in her workroom, a room 'I love best – a room that smells of wood' (Wolf 1985: 272). It is indeed a room completely of her own: a room with her desk 'on a wooden platform' and with a view 'which I would like to see in the hour of my death' (Wolf 1985: 272-3). This passage contrasts with and refers to Woolf's discussion of the struggles of woman writers in previous centuries when having 'a room of her own, let alone a quiet room . . . was out of the question' (*AROO*: 48). But Christa Wolf is a woman writer of the twentieth century who has 'money and a room of . . . [her] own' (*AROO*: 97), which is furnished for her needs and a lovely place for work and contemplation. The 'misquoted' title *A Room of My Own* together with the emphasis on her own workroom leads to the conclusion that Christa Wolf saw herself as part of a new generation of woman writers indebted to the work of predecessors such as Virginia Woolf.

Still, the question remains why Wolf neither referred to Woolf's *A Room of One's Own* nor to *Three Guineas* in her bibliography. The *Cassandra* project was not only conceived as a lecture for a West German university but was also meant for publishing in East Germany. The West German audience was already acquainted with Virginia Woolf through the popular reception of her work in the 1970s. Thus, Wolf was so familiar with Woolf that she might not have considered it necessary to mention her as a source. This explanation is consistent with the fact that a generalised disapproval of Western feminist ideas prevailed in the GDR. Western feminism was considered to undermine the Marxist idea of class conflict, which envisaged women and men fighting together against the enemy of the people and not against each other (Bridge 2002: 26-30; Karl 2016: 210-11). It is noteworthy that one of the first reviewers, Wilhelm Girnus, who responded to Wolf's advance publication of the fourth lecture by the East German magazine *Sinn und Form* in January 1983, criticised not only Wolf's inadequate translations from ancient Greek texts but also disqualified the whole idea of women's writing in connection with the retelling of ancient literature as being 'unsocialist' (Jankowsky 1989: 405-6).

Publishing *Cassandra* and Woolf's Legacy

When Christa Wolf delivered her lectures in May 1982, she could not have wished for a bigger audience or more public attention. The theatre of the University of Frankfurt am Main was crowded with over 1,000 people and the lectures were broadcast on TV. By November she had revised the texts. While the novel *Cassandra* and the four lectures were published in West Germany in March 1983, publication in East Germany was initially thwarted. The Office for Book Trade and Publishing Houses at the Ministry of Culture had reservations about Wolf's political statements in the third lecture and refused publication unless Wolf deleted those paragraphs (Hilzinger 2000: 437). A compromise was finally made by omitting the paragraphs and at the same time making the omissions visible through ellipsis. This was the very first time in the publishing history of the GDR that omissions – and through this censorship – were perceptible to the reader. The censored edition was published by Aufbau Verlag in January 1984 and it was not until 1989 that the complete edition was published in the GDR (Hilzinger 2000: 439–40).

The heated debate which accompanied the process of publication in East and West Germany led to high sales figures: in West Germany, 90,000 copies of the lectures and 150,000 copies of the *Cassandra* novel were sold during the first year of publication, whereas in East Germany illegal copies of the West German edition circulated (Hilzinger 2000: 437–8). Based on these numbers alone it is very probable that Wolf's *Cassandra* lectures also increased the popularity of Woolf in both German countries. However, it is not easy to identify specific indicators for Woolf's reception in the GDR after Christa Wolf's *Cassandra* project.[24]

Nevertheless, Virginia Woolf's ideas of a society without fear, where literature has political value in its own right and where women find their own language and literary forms, could and did circulate through Christa Wolf's lectures. In this context one of Woolf's statements in her 'Letter to a young poet' from 1932 sounds like direct advice to Christa Wolf: 'Think of yourself as . . . a poet in whom live all the poets of the past, from whom all poets in time to come will spring' (*E* 5: 309). The poet (like the novelist) writes in a literary tradition that, Woolf argues, has at its core the understanding of oneself and one's understanding of humanity – 'now . . . why should [poetry] not once more open its eyes, look out of the window and write about other people?' (*E* 5: 315). Thus, it is humanity that gives literature its genuine political value.

As I have discussed in this chapter, Woolf's and Wolf's writings were strongly influenced by their reflections on politics under the threat of war. Both writers searched for innovative literary forms that involved their audiences and readers with their arguments in order to promote new ideas. They drew their attention to female protagonists from ancient mythology and brought Antigone's and Cassandra's stories into communication with their own questions during intense and pressing political contexts. Finally, Christa Wolf's intellectual encounter with Virginia Woolf continued throughout her life. Two years before her death in 2011, Wolf bought the last of Virginia Woolf's books, a copy of *Between the Acts* in German translation, which shows an adhesive label dated 2009.

Notes

1. 'Es war nun aber eine meiner wesentlichsten literarischen Entdeckungen überhaupt (ich glaube, *Mrs Dalloway* las ich zuerst), und sie erzeugte ein brennendes, anhaltendes Interesse für die Autorin, für jede Einzelheit ihres Lebens, für ihre Familie, ihre Freundschaften, ihre Ehe, ihre Krankheit, ihren Tod. . . . Mich fesselte und fesselte die immense Kraft dieser Frau, ihre geistige Atmosphäre ihrer Umwelt aufzuprägen, und mich faszinierte die Art dieser Atmosphäre und ihr Mut zu den Experimenten, die sie da, schreibend, mit sich anstellt.'

2. On the comparison of Woolf's and Wolf's use of the form of the essay, see Herrmann (1986). On the comparison of particular works of Woolf and Wolf, see Anna Fattori (1988), Evelyn Westermann Asher (1992), Marie-Luise Gättens (1993), Donna K. Reed (1995) and Hannes Krauss (1997).
3. 'Lieber Genosse Hoffmann, Gerne folge ich Deiner Aufforderung, einige Titel zu nennen, die nach meiner Meinung das Buchangebot der DDR-Verlage bereichern würden . . . Virginia Woolf: Die Fahrt zum Leuchtturm
   Die Jahre
   Zwischen den Akten
   Erzählungen und Essay
   Ich halte es für an der Zeit, daß diese Autorin bei uns mit ihrem Gesamtwerk präsent ist, nicht nur alle paar Jahre mit einem ihrer Bücher. Sie hat im Westen eine Renaissance erlebt, mit Recht. Auch bei uns gäbe es für sie eine sehr große Lesergemeinde.'
4. Apart from the Wolfs, ten more writers signed the protest letter: Jurek Becker, Sarah Kirsch, Günter Kunert, Stephan Hermelin, Volker Braun, Heiner Müller, Stefan Heym, Rolf Schneider, Franz Fühmann and Erich Arendt.
5. In *The Meaning of Contemporary Realism* (1958), Lukács strengthens the opposition between 'avant-garde' literature and literary realism. To Lukács works such as Joyce's *Ulysses* are mainly concerned with style and literary techniques, whereas '[i]t is the view of the world, the ideology or *weltanschauung* underlying a writer's work, that counts' (Lukács 1969: 19). For Walter Ulbricht's disapproval of modernism and the GDR's cultural policy of the 1960s, see Wicht 2002: 103–4.
6. The publication of *Mrs Dalloway* and *To the Lighthouse* were possible only because of old licences that Insel Verlag had held on to since the time of Weimar Republic (Wicht 2002: 102).
7. On the reception of James Joyce in the GDR, see Wicht (2015).
8. See, for instance, her letter to Hans Altenhein, 6 December 1977, in which Wolf orders the German translation of Quentin Bell's Woolf biography, in the Christa Wolf Archive (CWA) at the Academy of Arts, Berlin (CWA 2282).
9. The library is not open to the public. I am very grateful to Gerhard Wolf and his kind permission to examine the library.
10. See Wolf (2000). For a further discussion of Christa Wolf's aesthetics of resistance, see Anna K. Kuhn (2015).
11. The capitalisation used here follows the Virago Press edition of Wolf's *Cassandra: A Novel and Four Essays* (Wolf 1985).
12. For the genesis of *Three Guineas* and Woolf's reading notes see Brenda R. Silver (1983: 22) and Alice Wood (2013).
13. For Woolf's involvement with anti-fascist organisations and her commitment to the London and National Society for Women's Service, see Anna Snaith (2012: xlv–xlviii).
14. The capitalisation used here follows Woolf's orthography in her diary entries.
15. For further discussion of Wolf's 'subjective authenticity', see Carol Anne Costabile-Heming (2005: 287–8).
16. In a footnote to the example of Antigone and Creon, Woolf points out that literature should not be used as 'anti-Fascist propaganda' (*TG*: 302). For a discussion of this argument, see Gualtieri (2000: 88).
17. Even though Scamander is the world of women, men are not excluded. Accordingly, as Georg-Michael Schulz points out, the utopian quality of this place can be seen in its ability to overcome the dualism between male and female and to create a third, harmonious condition (2016: 153).
18. For a contemporary reader it seems odd that Wolf uses the masculine personal pronoun. She often does so in order to express something fundamental, for example, when she addresses the abstract position or role of the writer.
19. For further discussion of Wolf's search for female traditions, see Christiane Zehl Romero (1989: 119–22).

20. Wolf had mixed feelings regarding radical feminist claims. She gives an account of her views when discussing the relation between archaeology and a repressed matriarchal culture with her friends in the second travel report (Wolf 1985: 200).
21. The English edition of Virago Press unfortunately excludes the bibliography from the book.
22. There is neither a French nor an equivalent English edition. Jan van Heurck has translated the title into English as *Womanhood in Letters*. The collection *Weiblichkeit in der Schrift* (1980) contains Cixous's essays 'Poesie e(s)t politique?' (1979), 'Femme écrites, femmes en écriture' (1977), 'Qui chant? Qui fait chanter? Qui est chante? Qui (s')appellee (Orphee)?' (1979) and 'Vivre l'orange' (1979).
23. Karen H. Jankowsky has discussed Christa Wolf's relationship to contemporary feminist theories and gives an account of Wolf's critical attitude towards French feminism but does not mention the reception of Virginia Woolf (1989: 400–1).
24. From the list of Woolf's published works which followed the *Cassandra* project and Christa Wolf's letter to Hans-Joachim Hoffmann, it is evident that only books which seemed to be apolitical were printed: *Orlando* (1983), the essay collection *Die schmale Brücke der Kunst* (1986) [The Narrow Bridge of Art: Selected Essays], and *The Waves* (1988). The last publication of Virginia Woolf in the GDR was *A Room of One's Own* and *Three Guineas* as a single edition paperback in 1989, shortly before the fall of the Berlin Wall.

Bibliography

Bridge, H. (2002), *Women's Writing and Historiography in the GDR*, Oxford: Oxford University Press.

Cixous, Hélène (1980), *Weiblichkeit in der Schrift* [Womanhood in Letters], West Berlin: Merve Verlag.

Costabile-Heming, C. A. (2005), 'Where public and private intersect: The intermingling of spheres in Christa Wolf's *Ein Tag im Jahr*', *Orbis Litterarum: International Review of Literary Studies*, 60: 4, pp. 278–92.

Crick, J. (1989), 'Christa Wolf and Virginia Woolf: Selective affinities', in M. S. Fries (ed.), *Responses to Christa Wolf: Critical Essays*, Detroit, MI: Wayne State University Press, pp. 91–107.

Emmerich, W. (2009), *Kleine Literaturgeschichte der DDR* [Short History of GDR's Literature], 4th edn, Berlin: Aufbau Verlag.

Fattori, A. (1988), 'Schreiben als Identitätssuche in Christa Wolfs *Selbstversuch* im Hinblick auf Virginia Woolfs *Orlando*' [Writing as search for identity in Christa Wolf's *Self-Experiment* considering Virginia Woolf's *Orlando*], *GDR Monitor*, 19, pp. 1–26.

Gättens, M.-L. (1993), 'Language, gender, and fascism: Reconstructing histories in *Three Guineas*, *Der Mann auf der Kanzel* and *Kindheitsmuster*', in E. Martin (ed.), *Gender, Patriarchy, and Fascism in the Third Reich: The Response of Women Writers*, Detroit, MI: Wayne State University Press, pp. 32–64.

Gualtieri, E. (2000), *Virginia Woolf's Essays: Sketching the Past*, Basingstoke, UK: Palgrave Macmillan.

Herrmann, A. (1986), '"Intimate, irreticent and indiscreet in the extreme": Epistolary essays by Virginia Woolf and Christa Wolf', *New German Critique*, 38, pp. 161–80.

Herrmann, A. (1989), *The Dialogic and Difference: 'An/other Woman' in Virginia Woolf and Christa Wolf*, New York: Columbia University Press.

Hilzinger, S. (2000), 'Entstehung, Veröffentlichung und Rezeption' [Genesis, publication and reception], in C. Wolf, *Werke* [Works], ed. S. Hilzinger, Munich: Luchterhand, vol. 7, pp. 429–46.

Hussey, M. (1995), *Virginia Woolf A to Z: A Comprehensive Reference for Students, Teachers, and Common Readers to Her Life, Work, and Critical Reception*, New York: Facts on File.

Jankowsky, K. H. (1989), 'New sense or nonsense? Christa Wolf's *Kassandra* and "weibliches Schreiben" in the GDR', in M. Knapp and G. Labroisse (eds), *Frauen-Fragen in der deutschsprachigen Literatur seit 1945* [Women's Questions in German Literature since 1945], Amsterdam: Rodopi, pp. 397–414.

Karl, M. (2016), *Die Geschichte der Frauenbewegung* [The History of the Feminist Movement], Stuttgart: Reclam.

Krauss, H. (1997), 'Rückzug in die Moderne: Christa Wolf und Virginia Woolf' [Retreating into modernity: Christa Wolf and Virginia Woolf], in R. Adkins and M. Kane (eds), *Retrospect and Review: Aspects of the Literature of the GDR 1976–1990*, Amsterdam: Rodopi, pp. 164–75.

Kuhn, A. K. (2015), 'Christa Wolf's aesthetics of resistance', in R. T. Goodman (ed.), *Literature and the Development of Feminist Theory*, Cambridge: Cambridge University Press, pp. 155–71.

Lukács, G. (1969 [1958]), *The Meaning of Contemporary Realism*, London: Merlin Press.

Magenau, J. (2002), *Christa Wolf: Eine Biographie* [Christa Wolf: A Biography], Reinbek/Hamburg: Rowohlt Taschenbuch Verlag.

Nünning, A. and V. Nünning (2002), 'The German reception and criticism of Virginia Woolf: A survey of phases and trends in the twentieth century', in M. A. Caws and N. Luckhurst (eds), *The Reception of Virginia Woolf in Europe*, London, New York: Continuum, pp. 68–101.

Opitz-Wiemers, C. (2016), 'Weibliche Deutung des Mythos – Zivilisationskritik' [Female interpretation of the myth – critique of civilisation], in C. Hilmes and I. Nagelschmidt (eds), *Christa Wolf-Handbuch: Leben – Werk – Wirkung* [The Christa Wolf handbook: Life – Oeuvre – Influence] Stuttgart: J. B. Metzler Verlag, pp. 164–93.

Paul, G. (2009), *Perspectives on Gender in Post-1945 German Literature*, Rochester, New York: Camden House.

Reed, D. K. (1995), 'Merging voices: *Mrs Dalloway* and *No Place on Earth*', *Comparative Literature*, 47: 2, pp. 118–35.

Saloman, R. (2012), *Virginia Woolf's Essayism*, Edinburgh: Edinburgh University Press.

Schulz, G.-M. (2016), *Christa Wolf*, Marburg: Tectum Verlag.

Séllei, N. (2017), 'Power and female subjectivity in Virginia Woolf's *Three Guineas*', in D. Flothow, M. Oppolzer and S. Coelsch-Foisner (eds), *The Essay: Forms and Transformations*, Heidelberg: Universitätsverlag Winter, pp. 229–40.

Silver, B. R. (1983), *Virginia Woolf's Reading Notebooks*, Princeton, NJ: Princeton University Press.

Snaith, A. (2012), 'Introduction', in Virginia Woolf, *The Years*, ed. Snaith, Cambridge: Cambridge University Press, pp. xxxix–xcix.

Westermann Asher, E. (1992), 'The fragility of the self in Virginia Woolf's *To the Lighthouse* and Christa Wolf's *Nachdenken über Christa T.*', *Neohelicon*, 19: 1, pp. 219–47.

Wicht, W. (2002), 'Installing modernism: The reception of Virginia Woolf in the German Democratic Republic', in M. A. Caws and N. Luckhurst (eds), *The Reception of Virginia Woolf in Europe*, London, New York: Continuum, pp. 102–26.

Wicht, W. (2015), 'James Joyce und die Unterminierung des kulturellen Dogmatismus in der DDR' [James Joyce and the undermining of cultural dogmatism in the GDR], in P. Goßens and M. Schmitz-Emans (eds), *Weltliteratur in der DDR. Debatten – Rezeption – Kulturpolitik* [World Literature in the GDR. Discussions – Reception – Cultural Policy], Berlin: Christian A. Bachmann Verlag, pp. 129–44.

Wolf, C. (1977), Letter to Hans Altenhein, 6.12 [6 December] 1977, Christa Wolf-Archiv, Wolf-Christa 2282, Akademie der Künste, Berlin.

Wolf, C. (1985), *Cassandra: A Novel and Four Essays*, trans. J. van Heurck, London: Virago.

Wolf, C. (1999 [1974]), 'Subjektive Authentizität. Gespräch mit Heinz Kaufmann' [Subjective authenticity. Interview with Heinz Kaufmann], in Wolf, *Werke* [Works], ed. S. Hilzinger, Munich: Luchterhand Verlag, vol. 4, pp. 401–37.

Wolf, C. (2000 [1980]), 'Von Büchner sprechen. Darmstädter Rede' [Speaking of Büchner. Darmstadt acceptance speech], in C. Wolf, *Werke* [Works], ed. S. Hilzinger, Munich: Luchterhand Verlag, vol. 8, pp. 186–201.

Wolf, C. (2008 [1983]), *Voraussetzungen einer Erzählung: Kassandra*, Frankfurt am Main: Suhrkamp Verlag.

Wolf, C. (2016), *Man steht sehr bequem zwischen allen Fronten. Briefe 1952–2011* [It's Quite Comfortable Being Caught in the Middle. Letters 1952–2011], ed. S. Wolf, Berlin: Suhrkamp Verlag.

Wood, A. (2013), *Virginia Woolf's Late Cultural Criticism: The Genesis of* The Years, Three Guineas *and* Between the Acts, London: Bloomsbury Academic.

Woolf, V. (1975–80), *The Letters of Virginia Woolf*, ed. N. Nicolson and J. Trautmann, 6 vols, London: Hogarth Press.

Woolf, V. (1977–84), *The Diary of Virginia Woolf*, ed. A. O. Bell and A. McNeillie, 5 vols, London: Hogarth Press.

Woolf, V. (1986–2011), *The Essays of Virginia Woolf*, ed. A. McNeillie and S. N. Clarke, 6 vols, London: Hogarth Press.

Woolf, V. (1992 [1928–9]), *The Manuscript Versions of* A Room of One's Own, ed. S. P. Rosenbaum, Oxford: Shakespeare Head Press.

Woolf, V. (2000 [1929/1938]), *A Room of One's Own / Three Guineas*, ed. M. Barrett, London: Penguin Books.

Zehl Romero, C. (1989), '"Remembrance of things future": On establishing a female tradition', in M. S. Fries (ed.), *Responses to Christa Wolf: Critical Essays*, Detroit, MI: Wayne State University Press, pp. 108–27.

7

Virginia Woolf's Literary Heritage in Russian Translations and Interpretations

Maria Bent

Introduction

IN 2013 THE RUSSIAN PUBLICATION OF *Night and Day* appeared, the last among Virginia Woolf's novels to be translated into that language. The history of Woolf's translations into Russian dates back to 1976 when Vladimir Kharitonov translated Erich Auerbach's *Mimesis*, which contains an excerpt from *To the Lighthouse*.[1] The first full translation into Russian, however, was Elena Surits's 1984 translation of *Mrs Dalloway*. The complete novel was printed in the April issue of the journal *Inostrannaya Literatura* [Foreign Literature], under the section titled 'Literary Heritage'. Woolf's first essay to be translated into Russian was 'Lewis Carroll'; it was included in the 1978 Nauka publishing house edition of *Alice in Wonderland*, and both the novel and the essay were translated by Nina Demurova (Woolf 1978). While other European countries have been admiring Woolf's work since the late 1920s, it took nearly sixty years for *Mrs Dalloway*, her best-known novel, to be translated into Russian and over ninety years for all of her novels to be published in Russia. This is a substantial amount of time in comparison to other countries in which her works have also had to be translated.

Why was Woolf briefly mentioned in Dmitry Svyatopolk-Mirsky's 1934 volume *Intelligentsia* and all but forgotten until the late 1950s? Even then, when Woolf's name did appear, it was not on the cover of her own novel but buried deep in in an academic coursebook, *Istoriya angliyskoy literatury* [The History of British Literature], issued by the Gorky Institute of World Literature of the USSR Academy of Sciences in 1958. The text situated Woolf as Leslie Stephen's daughter, the leader of the Bloomsbury Group and a '"theorist" of decadence' (*Istoriya angliyskoy literatury* 1958: 360). The answer to this relative silence on Woolf lies in Russian history, dating back to the 1920s when Woolf was first publishing her work.

In 1921 a young woman with 'the blue eyes of Natasha Rostova' (Genieva 2010)[2] walked into one of the most elegant buildings of the tsarist Russia, the former rental building of the Rossiya Insurance Company on Sretensky Boulevard, where the People's Commissariat for Education (Narkompros) was situated. The young woman was there, amid the tumult of civil war,[3] appealing to establish a library for foreign literature. In her memoir, she recalls that people told her, 'Don't you know, girl, these are cold and hungry times we're living through. Not many know how to read or write in

Russian, while you are nagging about foreign books!'⁴ Yet she persisted, answering: 'We've got the office, the books and the hands. We shall carry on with the library' (Rudomino 2005).⁵ The woman was Margarita Rudomino, the founder and first Director (1922–73) of the All-Russian State Library for Foreign Literature in Moscow. After visiting Narkompros every day for two months, Rudomino forced the officials to yield, and in October 1921 the Neophilological Library was established.⁶ In the 1920s, the library held a monopoly over subscriptions to foreign literature from abroad, and it was to develop into the only source of foreign literature in Russia for many years. Streams of people poured into the library, including the future maîtres of translation from English, most of whom first came across contemporary English literary works in the library. In 1929 the library organised the Translators' Bureau, which was later succeeded by the Association of Translation of Fiction as part of the Union of Soviet Writers. Thus, the Neophilological Library laid the foundation for translating foreign works into Russian, including Woolf's writings.

The second development in Woolf's Russian translations was inspired by Anatoly Lunacharsky (1875–1933), whose office was on the second floor of Narkompros. He was the People's Commissar for Education (1917–29) and the individual to whom a great deal of credit in the liberalisation of culture must go. Unlike Vladimir Lenin, Lunacharsky did not view art and literature predominantly as a Soviet propaganda outlet; in his opinion, creative people needed freedom of development, and no artistic movement should be given priority over the other. He repeatedly pleaded for the writers who were considered hostile to the current regime – for example, the Russian writer Ivan Bunin (1870–1953) was saved from execution by Lunacharsky's intervention. Having studied philosophy and natural sciences at the University of Zürich, Lunacharsky had a good command of foreign languages and was a literary critic, translator and dramatist. He penned several classic works, including *Istoriya zapadno-evropeyskoy literatury v ee vazhneyshih momentah* [The History of Western European Literature at Its Crucial Moments] (1924), in which he considered contemporary authors from the point of view of proletarian historicism. Lunacharsky promoted Maxim Gorky's initiative concerning the establishment of the Vsemirnaya Literatura publishing house, which operated from 1919 to 1924 and specialised in new and revised translations of classic literary texts. Established Russian writers and poets in the 1920s were engaged in translations, among them Alexander Blok, Korney Chukovsky, Yevgeny Zamyatin, Nikolay Gumilyov and others; they translated works by many of their contemporary British authors, including Joseph Conrad, Oscar Wilde, H. G. Wells and George Bernard Shaw, all published by Vsemirnaya Literatura. In November 1927, Lunacharsky chaired the first conference of the International Centre for Revolutionary Literature, which took place in Moscow and resulted in establishing *Vestnik Inostrannoy Literatury* [The Magazine of Foreign Literature] with its first issue printed January 1928. Over two decades later, the magazine was transformed into the journal *Inostrannaya Literatura*, established in 1955 as the managing executive committee of the Union of Soviet Writers and became instrumental (if not vital) for Woolf's Russian translations. It was in this journal that five of Woolf's novels were published, including the first translation of *Mrs Dalloway*.

The Soviet Russia of the late 1920s to early 1930s offered an exceptionally favourable atmosphere for new translations and studies in world literatures. It was during this period that the country situated itself as open to foreign influences, and two memorable visits from British writers occurred. H. G. Wells visited in 1920 and wrote a series of articles, collected in *Russia in the Shadows* (1920), in which he set imperialist Russia against Soviet Russia and characterised his meeting with Vladimir Lenin as an encounter with 'the dreamer in the Kremlin' (1920: 123). In his turn, Shaw visited Russia in 1931 and called it a great country conducting an enormous experiment that would create the new fair world order on which all the hopes of humanity hung (Vorontsova 2003). During this period, complete or partial translations of works by James Joyce, Aldous Huxley, D. H. Lawrence and T. S. Eliot were carried out. Such relative freedom from censorship over which text could be translated can explain the prompt and almost instantaneous (in the case of Lawrence) translations of contemporary British literature. Despite the fact that Joyce's *Ulysses* was legally banned in Britain, chapters from the novel were issued in Soviet Russia from the 1920s to the 1930s.[7] *Lady Chatterley's Lover* (1928) by Lawrence was translated into Russian in 1932, and Huxley's *Point Counter Point* (1928) was published in Russia in 1936.

Liberalisation in the cultural and literary domain was brief, lasting only until the well-known First Congress of the Soviet Writers in 1934 and the establishment of the Union of Soviet Writers, when literature was equated with a bayonet.[8] Under the Bolsheviks' power, the First Congress and Union functioned to promote an official literary ideology, undertake censorship of unacceptable texts and mete out punishment for those who did not meet the party requirements. From 1936 to 1938, the period which became known as the Great Terror claimed the lives of at least 1,500 writers, intellectuals, artists, scientists, Red Army officers, political opponents of the regime, the clergy, diaspora minorities and wealthier peasants, with the total number of victims exceeding 1 million people. During this period, one-third of the Congress members (182 people) died in prisons and the Gulag (the Main Administration of Camps), with thirty-eight more who were persecuted but survived.

Translators were not exempt from this persecution. For instance, three of Joyce's translators died tragically after being arrested in 1937. Mirsky died at a camp in 1938, Valentin Stenich (Smetanich) was executed that same year, and Igor Romanovitch starved to death at a camp in 1943. Despite the similarities between Joyce and Woolf's style, there were no translators working on her writings at the time; in fact, as previously noted, it was several decades later that her works began to emerge in Russia. The renowned Woolf scholar Natalya Reinhold (Bushmanova) offers the following explanation of the long silence surrounding Woolf's name in Russia. She cites Mirsky's brief mention of Woolf while giving a description of Bloomsbury and its aesthetic principles in his 1934 volume *Intelligentsia*. Reinhold notes that the words Mirsky used to describe Woolf and the Bloomsbury group eventually came to signify the artists as 'wrapped up in self-contained rhythms and sublimated from the world of reality to a world of aesthetics' (Mirsky qtd in Reinhold 2004b: 4) and argues that this phrasing signalled 'one of the Stalinist ideological bogeys – "art for art's sake", which, once noticed by readers and critics, situated the writer as "a hopeless case"' (Reinhold 2004b: 4). This negligence of Woolf's work was a result of the introduction of Socialist Realism, which became the only officially approved art in the USSR between 1932 and 1988. The main purpose of Socialist Realism was not to reflect the world as closely as possible to how it appeared to the artist; rather, the movement sought to depict an ideal working-class society that had no place for melancholy feelings or leisurely meditation. Instead, everyone had to exude optimism and work towards a common purpose – that is, the promising future of a technologically advanced and classless society. Moreover, characters needed to be shown as either good or bad, with no shades in between. Neither Woolf nor many of her contemporaries complied with these formulations. This seems to be the most probable reason for a two-decade gap before Woolf was mentioned again in Russian literary conversations.

This chapter traces Woolf's sparse early critical reception in Russia up until the 1970s, followed by the first translations of her writings into Russian, which evolved from intermittent ones in the 1980s to complete editions of her novels in the 2000s. It explains the subtle historical, political and social reasons underlying Woolf's obscurity in Russia until very recently as politically motivated rather than just an oversight of an author overlooked in the history of Russian translation, which may yet remain concealed from a non-Russian reader.

First Translations and Critical Reception

Early Critical Reception: 1950s–1970s

Woolf scholarship in Russia started well before her novels were translated. From the 1950s to 1970s, Woolf (like Joyce, Lawrence, Eliot and Huxley) was viewed from the ideological standpoint of whether her writings did anything to support Soviet ideals or serve a practical aim. Soviet literary critic Alexander Anikst (1910–88) was the first one to call modernist writers' works 'decadent literature' (1956: 453),[9] and the term became widely used as a derogative way to speak of the aestheticisation of life and art for its own sake, which was contrary to the approved Socialist realism. Dilyara Zhantieva followed Ankist's approach to literary criticism; reading Woolf's major novels and a selection of her essays (including 'Modern fiction', 'The Russian point of view', 'Phases of fiction' and 'The novels of E. M. Forster'), Zhantieva pronounced *Mrs Dalloway* as Woolf's only book 'in which the protest against the brutal reality is actually expressed, though indirectly' (1965: 95).[10] Septimus Warren Smith's madness in the novel is viewed by Zhantieva as taking a stand against the callous and carefree bourgeoisie, the final word there being used as profanity by most Soviet literary critics. Official Soviet ideology continued to view all art as utilitarian; if an author did not at least try to view the bourgeoisie as a burden on the rest of society, then there was little use in their works. Thus, in *The Years*, Zhantieva found that Woolf 'makes an attempt to face the reality',[11] 'the adversities [and] the injustice'[12] that plague society (1965: 104, 105). However, although the main characters in *The Years* are able to see injustice, none of them does anything beyond dreaming of a better world.

Having called Woolf the head of the 'psychological school' and noting her search for a new literary form, Nina Mikhalskaya nevertheless flatly states, 'Experimenting and psychologism lacking the social basis turn into dehumanisation of the protagonist' (1966: 12).[13] A character living a rich intellectual life but not partaking in the actual fight for the improvement of the existing social structure was barely viable to Soviet censorship. Mikhalskaya also notes that

> in her representation a man is a keen and emotional being acutely responsive to the surrounding reality; however, he is also torpid and passive. Virginia Woolf concentrates on the spiritual life of bourgeois intellectual . . . unnaturally lacking the need to solve real-life problems. (1966: 81–2)[14]

Neither Zhantieva nor Mikhalskaya is apparently free in expressing their judgement: in order to get one's book published, one was supposed to make constant references of the officially approved ideas.

In the early 1970s, sporadic papers on Woolf's work started to appear in or around Moscow. In his 1971 essay titled 'K voprosu ob eksperimentalnom romane: (romany V. Woolf. "Missis Dalloway", "K mayaku")' ['On the Experimental Novel: (V. Woolf's *Mrs Dalloway* and *To the Lighthouse*)'], Oleg Malyugin calls Woolf 'a sophisticated mind of her age', whose individualism was rooted in the political and social turmoil of the interwar years. This period, Malyugin argues, generated 'profound pessimism in their [British intellectuals'] philosophical and cultural views' and seduced them 'into deliberate propagation of "minor themes" and highly specific psychological analysis' (1971: 209).[15] Analysing Woolf's novels, Malyugin positions *Mrs Dalloway* as a successful attempt to show 'a dissolution of being in a stream of consciousness' (1971: 216),[16] while *To the Lighthouse* represents Woolf's failure 'to prove the superiority of [Mrs Ramsay's] irrational world perception' over her husband's scholarly approach (1971: 217).[17] Obviously, there was still no place for such a thing as intuition in the down-to-earth attitude of Soviet criticism.

The first critical receptions of Woolf in Russia were rather cautious to engage in discussions of unsanctioned literature. These considerations began to be published after Joseph Stalin's death in 1953 and during the Khrushchev thaw of the early 1950s to early 1960s, which was marked by the Soviet government opening up to the outside world and alleviating repression and censorship in the USSR. However, scholars were still wary of how their words might be interpreted and dared not praise an unauthorised writer. After Leonid Brezhnev came to power in 1964, a reversion of Nikita Khrushev's liberalisation policy began. While during Khrushev's leadership the number of censors was substantially reduced, under Brezhnev's rule censorship was again in full sway with every work of art having to be approved by the Council of Ministers of the USSR. This time was marked by the oppression of writers and other intellectuals. For example, most translations of foreign authors published at that time were heavily abridged, leaving out whole chapters. Also, an infamous trial was held against Andrei Sinyavsky and Yuli Daniel, who were both sentenced in 1966 to several years in labour camps for publishing their allegedly anti-Soviet writings abroad. Woolf's criticism in 'Modern fiction' of the widely-read – and more importantly, officially praised in the Soviet Union – British realist authors such as H. G. Wells, Arnold Bennett and John Galsworthy left no chance for her writings to be considered for publication at the time. Soviet censorship simply could not stimulate an interest in the work of a writer who spoke against realism. At best, translators and researchers would have wasted their effort; at worst, they would have been persecuted. Based on the unstable social climate of literary circles in Russia, what's surprising about Woolf's presence here is not the fact that she was mentioned infrequently. In fact, it is a wonder Woolf was mentioned at all.

First Translations of Woolf's Essays and Other Works: 1970s–1990s

The translation of Woolf's essays began, as previous noted, with 'Lewis Carroll' in 1978. However, critics paid little attention to Woolf's essays until the late 1990s, when her work became the object of close reading by Russian scholars, which may have been due to the fact that most of Woolf's essays were scattered about in various anthologies and collections of works across different regions of Russia. The choice of essays in these collected works was quite predictable. 'Modern fiction', for example, was mentioned in the 1960s' restrained receptions of Woolf's work; by including them in full, translators offered readers a chance to see for themselves why Woolf's ideas were considered weak and unacceptable by Soviet standards decades earlier. For obvious reasons, essays focusing on Russian literature were not overlooked; in 1983, the journal *Voprosy Literatury* [Literary Issues] produced a selection of Woolf's essays on Russian literature (Woolf 1983b). These included essays on Fyodor Dostoevsky, Sergey Aksakov, Anton Chekhov, Leo Tolstoy and Ivan Turgenev. Other essays were chosen to accommodate the common reader of Soviet Russia, who would have been familiar with Jane Austen and the Brontë sisters but would have known nothing of Joseph Addison or Thomas De Quincey.

An important role in issuing Woolf's essays belongs to Progress Publishers, which ran from 1931 until the early 1990s. This press focused on original and translated versions of foreign literature, and starting from the 1980s until their dissolution, they printed four volumes that included, among other authors' work, Woolf's essays. One of these, the compilation *Pisateli Anglii o literature. 19–20 vv.* [The British Writers on Literature. Nineteenth and Twentieth Centuries] (1981), included Woolf's 'Modern fiction', 'The Russian point of view' and '"The sentimental journey"', while 'How should one read a book?' appeared in the 1983 anthology *Chelovek chitayushiy. HOMO LEGENS. Pisateli 20 veka o roli knigi v zhizni cheloveka i obshestva* [HOMO LEGENS. Twentieth-Century Writers on the Role of Books in the Life of Man and Society] (Woolf 1983a). Ksenia Atarova translated these collections and later added Woolf's 'David Copperfield' to the 1990 anthology *Tayna Charlesa Dickensa* [The Mystery of Charles Dickens] (Woolf 1990).

Another important figure in the history of Woolf's Russian translations was Ekaterina Genieva, who served for over twenty years (1993–2015) as the General Director of the Margarita Rudomino All-Russian State Library for Foreign Literature in Moscow. Genieva compiled several volumes of Woolf's work and authored forewords to Woolf's Russian translations in both journals and book editions. In 1984, after the translation of *Mrs Dalloway* in the journal *Inostrannaya Literatura*, Woolf's original English text of the novel along with twelve essays ('"The sentimental journey"', 'Jane Austen', 'Sir Walter Scott', '"David Copperfield"', '"Jane Eyre" and "Wuthering Heights"', 'Lewis Carroll', 'The novels of Turgenev', 'The Russian point of view', 'Modern fiction', 'Mr Bennett and Mrs Brown', 'On re-reading novels' and 'How it strikes a contemporary') were printed in Moscow as a separate volume with an introductory note and comments by Genieva (Woolf 1984). Shortly after the publication of Genieva's collection, Inna Bernstein translated three of these essays along with five others[18] never before printed in *Izbrannoe* [Selected Works] (Woolf 1989), which included a foreword by Genieva. In 1992, Genieva compiled a volume of essays *Eti zagadochniye anglichanki* [Those Mysterious British Women], which offered critical works by four British women writers: Virginia Woolf, Elizabeth Gaskell, Muriel Spark and Fay Weldon (Genieva 1992). In this volume, *A Room of One's Own* (translated by Natalya Reinhold, under the name Bushmanova) was first published in Russian. In her foreword, Genieva analyses Woolf's essayistic manner and goes as far as to say, 'In her essays Virginia Woolf is a torch-bearer who aspires to reveal to a contemporary reader the everlasting importance and vitality of the British and world classics' (1992: 18).[19] Genieva is speaking here about *The Common Reader* series and Woolf's attention to the aesthetic and moral problems that writers face and which make their work relevant to the future generations of readers.

Apart from the book editions, some of Woolf's essays were translated by Natalya Reinhold and published in journals. In 1986, the journal *Literaturnaya Uchyoba* [Literary Study] issued Woolf's 'A letter to a young poet' (Woolf 1986b), while in 1987 the newspaper *Literaturnaya Rossiya* [Literary Russia] published a compilation titled 'From Virginia Woolf's diaries and essays' (Woolf 1987). With all this translation of Woolf's essays, over two decades the total number still amounted to fewer than twenty pieces. There seemed to be a great probability that Woolf's essays would continue to be neglected; however, after 1984 the translations of her novels began and stirred up interest in her critical writings as well. As the account of the publication of Woolf's novels will show, publishers demonstrated shrewdness and foresight in accepting an obscure author, and this may have been one of the portents of the coming *perestroika*[20] which transformed the literary and social milieus.

The First Translations of Woolf's Novels and Their Reception: 1980s–1990s

Until the 1980s, few people in Russia were familiar with Woolf's name, let alone read her works. However, Progress Publishers' decision in 1976 to issue Edward Albee's *Who's Afraid of Virginia Woolf?* (translated by Natalia Volzhina) encouraged curiosity and popular interest in Woolf. The play was staged in 1984 by the Moscow Sovremennik Theatre and two years later by the Saint Petersburg Memorial Lenin Komsomol Theatre. In 1992, the stage version performed by Sovremennik was made into a film play, which became one of the theatre's best-known productions. Woolf's name resounding from stage and TV screens posed a challenge to those who knew nothing or very little about her. Because of this surge in familiarity with her name and interest in her work, Woolf's first Russian translations fell on fertile ground.

As previously stated, *Inostrannaya Literatura* was essential in the recognition of Woolf's work in Russia. Since *Vestnik Evropy* [The European Herald] was established, as early as 1802 by the well-known Russian historian and man of letters Nikolay Karamzin (1766–1826), thick journals have played an important role for the Russian readership and even formed a specific aesthetic, social and cultural phenomenon. The country's vast size and shortage of books made journals – which encompassed the latest literary works, current political debates and encyclopaedic knowledge – especially welcome outside Moscow and St Petersburg. As a result *Inostrannaya Literatura*, to use its editor-in-chief Alexander Livergant's words, became a symbol of 'non-existent liberalism' (2015);[21] though there was still state censorship, the journal published the same writers whose work was not published as separate editions because they were considered ideologically hostile to the Soviet regime. For Soviet readers, the journal was the only chance to read major Western writers' works and in the 1970s its circulation reached almost 700,000 copies; in addition, there were waiting lists fot the new translations. Then, after Mikhail Gorbachev came to power in 1985, *perestroika* began. It brought 'glasnost' (openness and transparency), which in terms of translation meant free access to foreign-language texts from Special Storage Sections (Spetskhran) in Soviet libraries and archives. However, *perestroika* also brought financial instability and inflation because of which the circulation numbers dropped from 390,000 in 1990 to 67,000 in 1994. These numbers dropped drastically by the early 2000s to 10,000 copies; and by 2018 the circulation plummeted even more, only reaching 3,500 copies. This last decrease can be largely attributed to the rise of the internet in Russia which began in mid-2000s.

Woolf was one of the authors to be actively translated and published in *Inostrannaya Literatura*. Elena Surits, Woolf's first (and major) translator into Russian, was responsible for her vast number of publications in the journal. Surits's translation activity is closely linked with *Inostrannaya Literatura*, which produced her translations of the following: *Mrs Dalloway* (1984, No. 4), *Orlando* (1994, No. 11; which received the journal's Inolit prize for best translation that year), *The Waves* (2001, No. 10) and *Between the Acts* (2004, No. 6). In 1986 Izvestiya Publishers together with *Inostrannaya Literatura* printed a separate volume of *Flush: Rasskazy. Povest* [Flush: Short Stories. A Novel] (Woolf 1986a). Surits translated the novel, while short stories from *A Haunted House and Other Short Stories* were translated by Dmitry Agrachev, Larisa Bespalova, N. Burova, Natalya Vasiliyeva, Maria Loriye as well as Surits. Two years later, the journal *Noviy Mir* [The New World] issued Surits's full translation of *To the Lighthouse* (1988). Surits scarcely ever grants interviews or delivers speeches, and forewords to her translations are fairly non-existent; by and large she, who translated five out of Woolf's nine novels, thinks that the 'translator's role is a humble one' (Lysaya pevitsa 2016: 5).[22] Apart from translations by Surits, *Jacob's Room* was translated by Maria Karp[23] and published by the journal *Inostrannaya Literatura* in 1991 (No. 9); this translation won the journal's annual prize that year.

As soon as the first translations of Woolf were published in Russia there was an almost immediate critical response. In 1985 the journal *Literaturnoye Obozreniye* [Literary Review] issued an essay 'Roman bez tainy. Virginia Woolf. Missis Dalloway' [A no-mystery novel. Virginia Woolf's *Mrs Dalloway*] by literary critic Vladimir Dneprov (Volf Reznik). Dneprov began by stating, 'Virginia Woolf's novel embodies the conservative spirit, which is breathing in every cell of creatively depicted existence' (1985).[24] He goes on to argue that it is Woolf's 'controversial moderation'[25] – that is, her combining the excesses of earlier writers (Henry James, Marcel Proust and Leo Tolstoy) – that allows her to create a new style, one that 'produces a specifically British prose mode based on "acute sensibility"'.[26] Speaking of Woolf's creative style, Dneprov describes it as 'darting'[27] from one narrative element to another. For the Russian reader, who was used to linear narration and not yet familiar with stream of consciousness novels, the fact that events and people scattered about in the beginning would come together as a whole was a revelation.

In 1989 *Inostrannaya Literatura* printed an essay 'Apellyatsiya talanta k talantu: O romane V. Woolf "Na mayak"' [A talent's appeal to talent: On V. Woolf's *To the Lighthouse*] by the journalist and literary critic Alexander Nilin. In Nilin's opinion, Woolf's novel, while having nothing in the way of ordinary plot, is expressive 'because of muteness suffered almost to a raving state and then merely recorded in words' (1989: 231).[28] The novel's form shows 'the continuity of the author's idea of life in general' (1989: 234)[29] that is not viewed within the limited form of this particular novel but is continued into the present moment. In a way, our future is 'foreseen' (1989: 234)[30] by Woolf, *To the Lighthouse* having no set boundaries between the space of the novel and real life.

In 1995 *Noviy Mir* printed the essay '"Sestra Shekspira"' ['"Shakespeare's sister"'] by literary critic Vladimir Vakhrushev as a response to Karp's translation of Woolf's *Jacob's Room* (1991) and Surits's translation of *Orlando* (1994). According to Vakhrushev, in *Jacob's Room*, 'owing to hints and "blunt" strokes, a young British intellectual's image of the early twentieth century is vivid and recognizable';[31] in his opinion, the protagonist 'remains a mystery to the writer herself' because, like any artistic creation, Jacob unintentionally slips out of the author's grasp and starts living a life of his own; thus even Woolf cannot fathom the depths that his image can reach (1995).[32] In contrast, Vakhrushev finds *Orlando* representative of both the implementation of contemporary Western feminist ideas – he reads the novel as being a story about Shakespeare's sister in parallel to *A Room of One's Own* – and the continuity of Renaissance and Shakespearian tradition depicted by the name and heroic spirit of the main character, as well as the comicality of the cross-dressing scenes.

It seemed as though reading Woolf's translated works was bound to arouse a genuine interest in the author; however, apart from critical reviews and several theses,[33] no other research of her work was done. A truly active study of Woolf began in the 2000s, although there were a few papers written in the late 1990s. Political and economic instability in the country might have been to blame for Woolf's late introduction to Russia since from the late 1980s to early 1990s, with *perestroika* underway and wages unpaid for months, the majority of teachers and researchers, like most professionals, had to find alternative work for a living, and few rarely returned to research since there was little possibility of publishing.

After the Year 2000: A Massive Surge of Interest

Further Translations and Critical Reception

The early 1990s were marked by an unprecedented publishing boom in Russia, with numerous publishing houses emerging and book copies increasing rapidly. All this was made possible by lifting the censorship ban imposed by the USSR on the mass media in 1990 and, one year later, rewritten for the new Russia. The severe economic crises hitting Russia in 1994 and 1998 kept pushing the clock back. With Progress Publishers collapsing at the time (it was later reorganised into three separate publishing houses) and the circulation of *Inostrannaya Literatura* steadily decreasing since 1990, new publishers needed to take the lead.

After the situation somewhat stabilised in the 2000s, the translation baton of Woolf's novels was handed over to Text Publishers, founded in 1988 and specialising in publishing world classics and contemporary authors that previously had not been translated into Russian. The press published the rest of Woolf's novels in Russian: *The Voyage Out* (2002)[34] and *The Years* (2005) were translated by Artyom Osokin, while *Night and Day* (2013), translated by Nina Usova, was issued one year later by the Nauka publishing house (and later translated by Reinhold in 2014 as part of the Literaturniye Pamyatniki series). Critical reviews again were quick in coming. In 2006, the journal *Oktyabr* [October] printed literary critic Fyodor Ermoshin's review 'Proza kak vyazanie (Virginia Woolf. Gody)' [Fiction as knitting (Virginia Woolf's *The Years*)] in response to Osokin's first Russian translation of the novel the previous year. Ermoshin declared *The Years* to be one of the most important novels for Woolf, adding that

> this tedious chronicle is not about pursuing the result (as in a brick-shaped unpolished male novel); it is about a fragile attempt to live within the novel while writing it. She is the one who needs the text in the first place; her readers are served on a second-priority basis. (2006: 37)

Ermoshin is suggesting here that for Woolf writing was a means of subduing her loneliness, 'the result' (that is, the physical printed work) being only secondary. This loneliness, in his opinion, is manifested throughout the novel by the author's omission of inverted commas around the characters' spoken words, thus disguising them as her own.

As for Woolf's non-fiction, there were two major publications. In 2009 *A Writer's Diary*, with a foreword by Genieva, was published by the All-Russian State Library for Foreign Literature publishing house, sponsored by the British Council. The book included Woolf's 1918–41 diaries and her letters to Lytton Strachey (1906–30), all translated by Lyudmila Volodarskaya. In 2012, the Nauka publishing house (Literaturniye Pamyatniki series) issued *The Common Reader* and *The Common Reader Second Series* (Woolf 2012a). Two years after these publications, Irina Kabanova notes that the full translation of the first and second series of *The Common Reader* gives scholars 'a chance to do Woolf justice as a literary historian, or to be more specific, to place her as a theorist' (2015: 397).[35] Furthermore, Kabanova speaks about a kind of 'Russification' of Woolf's *The Common Reader* series: 'Instead of adopting the authorial reserve – or British understatement – N. Reinhold assumes Russian largesse'. Kabanova further continues, 'all of these are rich and expressive, but take Woolf from the British library or drawing-room space into the simulated and archaic Russian cultural space' (2015: 398).[36] Despite a certain incongruity between the original text of *The Common Reader* series and its Russian versions, Kabanova argues that the main purpose of Woolf's essays is achieved because 'Reinhold's translations give the readers intellectual delight' (2015: 398).

Nauka also published in 2012 Woolf's essays on Russian authors (previously listed), and her three principal essays 'Mr Bennett and Mrs Brown', 'A letter to a young poet' and *A Room of One's Own* were translated by Reinhold as a follow-up to her Russian journal translations two decades earlier. Up to this time, this is the largest-scale work among Woolf's essay translations into Russian. Less noticeable, but no less important, were Maria Lukashkina's translations of Woolf's essay 'I am Christina Rossetti', appearing in *Inostrannaya Literatura* in 2012, which also introduced a selection of Rossetti's poems (Woolf 2012b). In 2014, the volume *The Cinema* was published, containing six of Woolf's essays: 'Three pictures', 'The cinema', 'Middlebrow', 'Evening over Sussex: Reflections in a motor car', 'Street haunting: A London adventure' and 'Thoughts on peace in an air raid', all translated by Svetlana Silakova.

The majority of responses to Woolf's translations were laudatory; however, there were also some openly vitriolic pieces such as two of Nikolay Melnikov's essays: 'Gamburgskiy schet k missis Woolf' ['Mrs Woolf's Hamburg score'] (2003) and 'Koprolit epohi modernisma: Nechitabelniy shedevr V. Woolf' ['Modernist coprolite:

V. Woolf's illegible masterpiece'] (2004). In the first essay, Melnikov brands Woolf as 'some sort of Bloomsbury ghost'[37] due to her sparse translations into Russian and their resulting unavailability (2014: 288). Melnikov further describes Woolf's overall style as 'dull lyrical prose with incoherent phrases and endless beading together of compound sentences' (2014: 293).[38] In his second essay, Melnikov declares *Jacob's Room* 'a freaky genre mutant which preserved its market label of a "novel" only mechanically' (2014: 296).[39]

From being read and discussed by a limited audience in the 1980s, Woolf's work became accessible to a wide audience with no fewer than nine editions of her collected novels by different publishers and at least fifteen separate editions of them issued and reissued after the year 2000. More criticism was becoming available and less restricted, since anyone was at liberty to read her works and make their own assessment of her style and themes.

2003–4: A Landmark Conference and Two Important Volumes

Until the year 2000 only sporadic essays and papers on Woolf's work were printed in Russia. However, the early twenty-first century brought with it a massive surge of interest in Woolf's work as part of both academic and popular volumes. A landmark in the history of studying Woolf's writing began in 2003 owing to two factors. First, Stephen Daldry's film *The Hours* (2002), based on Michael Cunningham's 1998 novel of the same title, was released in Russia on 3 April 2003. A few years prior to that, *Inostrannaya Literatura* published Cunningham's *The Hours* (2000, translated by Dmitry Vedenyapin). Although most likely only a few read the novel, based on the journal's circulation numbers, the film reached a larger audience, effectively transferring Woolf's name from closed intellectual circles into a household name.

Second, and even more importantly for academia, the Russian State University for Humanities and Leo Tolstoy Estate Museum Yasnaya Polyana (Tula Region) held the international symposium 'Woolf across cultures' on 27–29 June 2003. The symposium welcomed scholars from Britain, Canada, Japan, South Korea, the Netherlands, Portugal, Russia and the USA. It was the first (and so far only) Russian conference devoted specifically to Woolf's work. A year later selected papers from the conference were collected in *Woolf Across Cultures,* edited by Natalya Reinhold and published by Pace University Press.[40] Reinhold authored the preface and the introduction titled 'Virginia Woolf's work in Russia: A success story of 2.5 million copies'. In the introduction Reinhold notes, 'Simple counting produced the total number of 2.5 million copies of Russian translations of Woolf's work issued from 1978 to 2002, with about two million copies published under *perestroika* between 1988 and 1993' (2004b: 1).

In 2004, Vladimir Greshnykh and Galina Yanovskaya produced the first monograph dedicated to Woolf's fiction: *Virginia Woolf: Labirinty mysli* [Virginia Woolf: Trains of Thought]. They point out several currents in Woolf studies: her aesthetic principles, her critical and public work as well as the innovative features in her writing and her creative method. The book pays close attention to three of Woolf's novels; however, analysis of *Mrs Dalloway* is the central part of their research. Greshnykh and Yanovskaya speak of the 'lack of form' (2004: 34)[41] and the 'fundamental lack' (2004: 36)[42] of beginning and ending in the novel, noting that the whole text 'is motivated by the energy of incompleteness' (2004: 44).[43] The latter is manifested in such techniques as 'creative idea moving from consequence to cause; cause which is farthest [in terms of time] and closest in terms of narrative; shifting narrative into another person's consciousness; exact or loose mirroring; . . . a character's emotional present response to a situation of the past; . . . break in the narrative' (2004: 44).[44] The 2003 'Woolf across cultures' symposium and volume and *Virginia Woolf: Labirinty mysli* played a pivotal role in the future of Woolf scholarship. The conference, in Reinhold's words, let the participants discuss their papers 'at leisure' in an informal setting (Reinhold 2004a: x), which was certainly new for Russia with its highly regulated and formal style of plenary meetings and panel sessions that are generally overcrowded with presenters who hardly have time left after the presentations for brief clarifying questions, let alone unhurried discussions. For Woolf scholars in Russia, the conference was a chance to build academic ties with colleagues from other countries and look at Woolf's work from different perspectives. From the interest generated by this scholarship, Woolf studies in Russia firmly established itself as part of mainstream literary studies, and research papers and theses began to increase steadily. Still, there remain specific issues which may be overlooked by the scholars for a number of years yet.

Scholarship on Woolf *2004–Present*

With the lack of original English texts by Woolf and a newly emerging readership, Russian Woolf studies had to be built from scratch, which of course meant drawing upon global scholarship. For example, following Western scholarship practices, Woolf is often studied in her relation to the inner circle of the Bloomsbury group and the general modernist history, as well as in her connection to a female literary tradition; her identity as an artist; her ideas about life, death and time; interactions between her literary texts and painting and music; and the political and pacifist views in her work. However, there are some topics which, though growing increasingly popular with Western scholars, have not been considered by Russian scholars. These include approaches that consider Woolf's family history, the houses she lived in, her letters and diaries, her interpretation of classical literature, queer and lesbian readings and her affiliation with feminist organisations. It is worth noting that from the 1990s to the early 2000s Woolf's creative work was scrutinised from the point of view of poetics and literary theory, as opposed to the late 2000s through the 2010s when attention shifted towards specific aspects of language study, namely linguistic world view,[45] concept, syntax and gender. Common topics include problems of psychologism, time and space; the artists and their work; metaphor; and gender-related issues.

According to Alexander Livergant, 'Woolf did a lot to promote Russian literature' (2018a),[46] and this is the general view maintained by the majority of Woolf scholars in Russia; therefore it is natural that one of the first aspects addressed in this chapter is the Russian theme in her novels and essays. According to Reinhold's 'Russkaya tema i obraz Rossii v tvorchestve V. Woolf' [The Russian theme and the image of Russia in V. Woolf's work] (2007) and Natalia Vladimirova's 'A. Chekhov s russkoy tochki zreniya V. Woolf' [A. Chekhov from V. Woolf's 'Russian point of view'] (2009), the Russian theme is mainly situated as Woolf's pursuit of a new creative form that she did not find in British literature from the turn of the twentieth century.

However, Reinhold suggests other sides to studying the Russian theme in Woolf's work, such as from the point of view of the history of literature, namely 'within the context of literary and cultural links of the 1910s through the 1930s between Britain and Russia' (2007);[47] Woolf's attitude to Russian literature as a literary critic; and Woolf's translations from Russian together with Samuel Koteliansky and others. *Orlando*, in Reinhold's opinion, bids farewell to the Russian theme in Woolf's work, 'the ship with the Russian Princess on board . . . [being] a metaphor . . . [of] some sort of an allegory of Russia, loaded with certain historical, political, and cultural allusions' (2007).[48] Regarding the Russian theme in *Orlando*, Elena Solovyova also notes that while describing the Russian embassy, Woolf lets the national stereotypes about the wild, uncivilised men prevail: 'The writer cannot be bothered with Russian history; she creates an exotic image worthy of astounding the refined Englishman' (2008).[49]

As previously mentioned, the 2000s were not only marked by new translations of Woolf's work but also by constant reprinting of existing ones. Literary scholar and writer Andrey Astvatsaturov authored several introductory notes to the reprintings of existing translations, including those published in *Mrs Dalloway* and *Orlando* by Azbuka publishing house in 2000, as well as in *To the Lighthouse* and *Between the Acts* by Azbuka-klassika (formerly Azbuka publishing) published in 2004. Furthermore, in 2007 Astvatsaturov wrote *Fenomenologiya teksta: Igra i repressiya* [Phenomenology of Text: Play and Repression], which includes a chapter titled 'Virginia Woolf: The metamorphoses of disembodied energy'. In this chapter, Astvatsaturov gives a brief overview of Woolf's 'Modern fiction' and 'Mr Bennett and Mrs Brown' and then attempts to sum up Woolf's basic poetic principles by analysing her five major novels (*Jacob's Room, Mrs Dalloway, To the Lighthouse, Orlando* and *Between the Acts*). According to Astvatsaturov, the main method of Woolf's writing 'makes the reader look at the world through the eyes of . . . a character' (2007: 64),[50] leading to 'the feeling of complete immersion' (2007: 69).[51] He also uses the expression 'disembodied energy' (2007: 65)[52] to characterise the coming into being of the human self, which is evolving together with the world and is temporarily manifested in 'objects, ideas, emotions, [and] people' (2007: 65).[53] In this sense, argues Astvatsaturov, Clarissa Dalloway is 'an "ideal" heroine placed between two worlds. . . . Her body is engulfed by exohuman disembodied energy. At the same time Clarissa . . . intuitively retains her ties with the human sphere' (2007: 71).[54]

Reinhold carries on with her Woolf studies well into the 2000s. Apart from her paper 'Readingskiy buvar s pismami Bunina' [The writing case with Bunin's letters in Reading] (2006), which details to readers her discovery of the correspondence between Bunin and the Hogarth Press, Reinhold has published two monographs: *Mosty cherez La Manche. Britanskaya literatura 1900–2000-h* [Bridging the Channel. The British Literature of 1900s–2000s] (2012) and *Istoriya literatury 20 veka. Angliyskaya literatura modernizma: Istoriya, problematika* [Literary History of the Twentieth Century. British Modernist Literature: History and Problems] (2017). The first book includes Reinhold's essay '"Znat, dlya kogo pishesh", ili Pochemu boyatsya Virginii Woolf' [To know whom to write for, or why everyone is afraid of Virginia Woolf], as well as translated excerpts from *Three Guineas*. In her essay, Reinhold speculates about the difference between Woolf's reception in Russia and in the UK. In Russia, among 'traditionalist specialists in English philology[,] Woolf has a reputation [as] an impressionist',[55] while Woolf scholars esteem her as a 'respected maître, the author of intellectual fiction' (Reinhold 2012: 88, 89).[56]

However, in the Western world Woolf is considered to be one 'part subjective impressionist, highbrow British woman, unapproachable and boring to death' and another 'part ardent advocate of women's rights and all but a pioneer of Anglo-American feminism of the twentieth century' (Reinhold 2012: 90).[57] Reinhold notes the following about Woolf's critical writings: 'almost all critics put their essays into a book' (Reinhold 2012: 92) but not all of them produce a principal work of their time,[58] something which Woolf also excelled at through her two *Common Reader* volumes. Reinhold's second volume is a textbook on British modernism that gives a general overview of its historical and cultural context and chronological details, as well as dwelling upon its main images and expressive means. It also includes original principal British modernist texts, among them three of Woolf's essays: 'Mr Bennett and Mrs Brown', 'Modern fiction' and 'The cinema'.

The first scholarly dispute over Woolf in Russian conversation emerged in 2014, when the journal *Philologiya and Kultura* [Philology and Culture] issued a paper 'Esse "Svoya komnata". Romannoe myshlenie V. Woolf' [*A Room of One's Own*. V. Woolf's novelistic thought] by Tamara Selitrina. The author engages in debate with Reinhold regarding her predominant view of Woolf's essays as inheriting the traditions of the classical British novel from the seventeenth and eighteenth centuries. Selitrina, however, maintains that in the '1910s–1920s the classic British essay in a number of cases has become fictionalised, bridging the gap between creative writing and journalism' (2014: 260).[59] She even goes as far as to offer viewing *A Room of One's Own* as 'a novella with all appropriate elements: a narrator, social, time and space dimensions, characters, situations, portraits, and scenery' (2014: 260).[60]

While Woolf scholarship was steadily on the rise during the post-Soviet era, until recently there have been no attempts to enliven Woolf's image for Russian readers and show her as a human rather than ethereal writer. On 8 October 2018, the biography *Virginia Woolf: 'momenty bytiya'* [Virginia Woolf: 'Moments of Being'] by Alexander Livergant published earlier that year was unveiled in the Reading Club of the All-Russian State Library for Foreign Literature in Moscow. Livergant, heavily relying on Woolf's biographies published in English, presented the first Russian view that considered the intermingling of the writer's life with work. The readers' note asserts the book not only as Woolf's biography but also as a general portrayal 'of the most prominent figures in the British literature of the 1920s–1940s in the context of the turbulent literary and social phenomena in the first half of the twentieth century' (Livergant 2018b).[61] Hopefully this biography will pave the way for future works about Woolf in Russia, which, now that all her novels have been translated and are widely accessible, should not take long.

Notes

1. The fifth chapter from 'The window' in *To the Lighthouse* is included in the chapter titled 'The brown stocking' of *Mimesis*.
2. 's golubymi glazami Natashi Rostovoy'. 'с голубыми глазами Наташи Ростовой'. (All translations mine unless otherwise indicated.) A central character of Leo Tolstoy's *War and Peace*, Natasha Rostova had black eyes; this quotation signals the open and sincere expression in them.
3. The Civil War marking the end of the Russian Empire, immediately after the February and October Revolutions of 1917.

4. 'Devochka, ty poymi, chto u nas seychas golodnoe, kholodnoe vremya. Lyudi ne znayut russkoy gramoty, a ty s inostrannymi knigami pristaesh!' 'Девочка, ты пойми, что у нас сейчас голодное, холодное время. Люди не знают русской грамоты, а ты с иностранными книгами пристаешь!'
5. 'Ved est pomeshenie, est knigi i est ruki. Davayte prodolzhim rabotu biblioteki.' 'Ведь есть помещение, есть книги и есть руки. Давайте продолжим работу библиотеки.'
6. The successor of the Neophilological Institute, which had been functioning from February to August 1921.
7. In 1925 in the almanac *Novinki Zapada* [Latest Books from the West]), in 1929 in the newspaper *Literaturnaya Gazeta* [Literary Paper], in 1934–5 in the journal *Zvezda* [The Star]) and in 1935–6 in the journal *Internatsionalnaya Literatura*.
8. This comparison was originally used by Vladimir Mayakovsky in his 1925 poem 'Homewards': 'I wish that the quill is equal to the bayonet.' 'Я хочу, чтоб к штыку приравняли перо.' The poet was an ardent supporter of the Soviet authorities; however, the circumstances of his suicide caused many controversies, with government pressure being supposedly one of its causes.
9. 'dekadentskoy literatury'. 'декадентской литературы'.
10. 'gde, hotya i v kosvennoy forme, vse zhe vyrazhen protest protiv zhestokoy deystvitelnosti'. 'где, хотя и в косвенной форме, все же выражен протест против жестокой действительности'.
11. 'delaet popytku viyti navstrechu realnoy deystvitelnosti'. 'делает попытку выйти навстречу реальной действительности'.
12. 'bedstviya, nespravedlivost'. 'бедствия, несправедливость'.
13. 'Eksperimentatorstvo i lishenniy sotsialnoy osnovy psikhologizm oborachivaetsya obeschelovechivaniem geroya.' 'Экспериментаторство и лишенный социальной основы психологизм оборачиваются обесчеловечиванием героя.'
14. 'V ee izobrazhenii chelovek – sushestvo tonko chuvstvuyushee, emotsionalnoe, ostro reagiruyushee na okruzhayushee, no bezdeyatelnoe i passivnoe.' 'В ее изображении человек — существо тонко чувствующее, эмоциональное, остро реагирующее на окружающее, но бездеятельное и пассивное.'
15. '"sophisticated mind" svoey epokhi; glubokiy pessimism v ikh filosofskikh i literaturnykh vozzreniyakh; na put soznatelnogo kultivirovaniya v svoem tvorchestve "malykh tem" i uzkopsikhologicheskogo analiza'. '"sophisticated mind" своей эпохи; глубокий пессимизм в их философских и литературных воззрениях; на путь сознательного культивирования в своем творчестве "малых тем" и узкопсихологического анализа'.
16. 'rastvoreniye bytiya v potoke soznaniya'. 'растворение бытия в потоке сознания'.
17. 'dokazat prevoskhodstvo irratsionalnogo poznaniya mira s pomoshyu intuitsii'. 'доказать превосходство иррационального познания мира с помощью интуиции'.
18. 'Jane Eyre and Wuthering Heights', 'Jane Austen', 'Sir Walter Scott', 'Montaigne', 'A terribly sensitive mind', 'Notes on D. H. Lawrence', 'Professions for women' and 'The novels of Turgenev'.
19. 'V esse Virginia Woolf – prosvetitel, stremyashiysya otkryt chitatelyu-sovremenniku neprekhodyashuyu vazhnost i zhivuchest angliyskoy i mirovoy klassiki.' 'В эссе Вирджиния Вулф – просветитель, стремящийся открыть читателю-современнику непреходящую важность и живучесть английской и мировой классики.'
20. The term *perestroika* denotes major political changes within the Soviet Union during the 1980s, which led to more openness in inner policy and, eventually, to the dissolution of the USSR.
21. 'nesushestvuyushego liberalizma'. 'несуществующего либерализма'.
22. 'rol perevodchika vesma skromnaya'. 'роль переводчика весьма скромная'
23. Karp has resided in London since 1991. She worked for BBC Russian Service from 1991 to 2009; one of her broadcasts was 'Bloomsbury's Russian translator Koteliansky' (1993).

24. 'Roman Virginii Woolf – voploshenie dukkha konservatizma, kotoriy zhivet v kazhdoy kletke khudozhestvenno zapechatlennogo bytiya.' 'Роман Вирджинии Вулф – воплощение духа консерватизма, который живет в каждой клетке художественно запечатленного бытия'.
25. 'ostro podannaya umerennost'. 'остро поданная умеренность.'
26. 'sozdaet svoeobrazno angliyskiy variant prozy, osnovannoy na "povyshennoy vospriimchivosti"'. 'создает своеобразно английский вариант прозы, основанной на "повышенной восприимчивости"'. The latter term was introduced by the Russian writer Ivan Bunin.
27. 'broski'. 'броски'.
28. 'ot nemoty, vystradannoy pochti do gallutsinatsiy i potom prosto "zaprotokolirovannoy" slovami'. 'от немоты, выстраданной почти до галлюцинаций и потом просто "запротоколированной" словами'.
29. 'nepreryvnost avtorskoy mysli o zhizni voobshe'. 'непрерывность авторской мысли о жизни вообще'.
30. 'predugadannoye'. 'предугаданное'.
31. 'blagodarya namekam i "pryamym" shtrikham obraz yunogo anglichanina-intellektuala nachala 20 veka poluchilsya zhivym i uznavaemym'. 'благодаря намекам и "прямым" штрихам образ юного англичанина-интеллектуала начала ХХ века получился живым и узнаваемым'.
32. 'ostaetsya zagadkoy i dlya samoy pisatelnitsy'. 'остается загадкой и для самой писательницы'.
33. In 1987, Cholpon Dzhamankulova defended a PhD thesis on the Bloomsbury Group's aesthetics, in which Woolf is mentioned after Roger Fry and Clive Bell.
34. With an afterword by Stuart N. Clarke, who also rendered assistance in producing the Russian edition.
35. 'poyavlyaetsya vozmozhnost otdat dolzhnoe Woolf kak istoriku literatury, tochnee opredelit ee mesto kak teoretika'. 'появляется возможность отдать должное Вулф как историку литературы, точнее определить ее место как теоретика'.
36. 'vse eto sochno, vyrazitelno, no perevodit Woolf iz prostranstva angliyskoy biblioteki ili gostinoy v uslovnoe, arkhaizirovannoe prostranstvo russkoy kultury'. 'все это сочно, выразительно, но переводит Вулф из пространства английской библиотеки или гостиной в условное, архаизированное пространство русской культуры'.
37. 'chem-to vrode bloomsburiyskogo prividenija'. 'чем-то вроде блумсберийского привидения'.
38. 'vyalaya liricheskaya proza s putanoy frazoy i beskonechnym nanizyvaniem slozhnosochinennykh predlozheniy'. 'вялая лирическая проза с путаной фразой и бесконечным нанизыванием сложносочиненных предложений'.
39. 'strannogo zhanrovogo mutanta, lish po izdatelskoy inertsii sokhranivshego rynochnuyu etiketku "roman"'. 'странного жанрового мутанта, лишь по издательской инерции сохранившего рыночную этикетку "роман"'.
40. In 2003 the same publisher produced Volume 9 of *Woolf Studies Annual* with Reinhold's paper 'Virginia Woolf's Russian Voyage Out'.
41. 'besformennost'. 'бесформенность'.
42. 'printsipialnom [ego] beznalichii'. 'принципиальном [его] безналичии'.
43. 'motivirovana energiey nezavershennosti'. 'мотивирована энергией незавершенности'.
44. 'dvizheniye khudozhestvennoy mysli ot sledstviya k prichine; otdalennaya i blizhayshaya v povestvovatelnom otnoshenii prichina; perekhod povestvovaniya v zonu soznaniya drugogo personazha; priem tochnogo ili netochnogo zerkalnogo otrazheniya; <...> emotsionalnaya reaktsiya personazha v moment nastoyashego na situatsiyu, proizoshedshuyu v proshlom; <...> kompozitsionniy razryv ...'. 'движение художественной мысли от следствия к причине; отдаленная и ближайшая в повествовательном отношении причина; переход повествования в зону сознания другого персонажа; прием точного или неточного зеркального отражения; <...> эмоциональная реакция персонажа в момент настоящего на ситуацию, произошедшую в прошлом; <...> композиционный разрыв ...'.

45. The term originates from Leo Weisgerber's 'sprachliche Weltbild' (literally 'language world view') used to denote that every language implies a unique 'world view' which may lead to sustained cultural differences.
46. 'Woolf mnogo sdelala dlya populyarizatsii russkoy literatury.' 'Вулф много сделала для популяризации русской литературы.'
47. 'v kontekste anglo-russkikh literaturnykh i obshekulturnykh svyazey 1910–1930-h gg'. 'в контексте англо-русских литературных и общекультурных связей 1910–1930-х гг'.
48. 'korabl s russkoy knyazhnoy . . . – eto metaobraz, [predstavshiy u Woolf] nekim inoskazaniem o Rossii, nagruzhennym opredelennymi istoricheskimi, politicheskimi i kulturnymi alluziyami'. 'корабль с русской княжной . . . – это метаобраз, [представший у Вулф] неким иносказанием о России, нагруженным определенными историческими, политическими и культурными аллюзиями'.
49. 'Russkaya istoriya malo interesuet pisatelnitsu, ona sozdaet ekzoticheskiy obraz, dostoyniy porazit voobrazhenie utonchennogo anglichanina.' 'Русская история мало интересует писательницу, она создает экзотический образ, достойный поразить воображение утонченного англичанина.'
50. 'zastavlyaet chitatelya smotret na mir . . . glazami svoego personazha'. 'заставляет читателя смотреть на мир . . . глазами своего персонажа'.
51. 'chuvstvo polnogo pogruzheniya'. 'чувство полного погружения'.
52. 'bestelesnaya energiya'. 'бестелесная энергия'.
53. 'predmety, idei, emotsii, lyudi'. 'предметы, идеи, эмоции, люди'.
54. '"Idealnoy" geroiney, stoyashey na grani dvukh mirov, . . . okazyvaetsya Clarissa Dalloway. [. . .] Ee telo vovlecheno v potok vne-chelovecheskoy bestelesnoy energii. No v to zhe vremya Clarissa . . . intuitivno sokhranyaet svyaz s chelovecheskim . . .'. '"Идеальной" героиней, стоящей на грани двух миров, . . . оказывается Кларисса Дэллоуэй. [. . .] Ее тело вовлечено в поток вне-человеческой бестелесной энергии. Но в то же время Кларисса . . . интуитивно сохраняет связь с человеческим . . .'.
55. 'anglistov traditsionnoy shkoly Woolf slyvet impressionistkoy'. 'англистов традиционной школы Вулф слывет импрессионисткой'.
56. 'uvazhaemiy maître, avtor intellektualnoy prozy'. 'уважаемый мэтр, автор интеллектуальной прозы'.
57. 'chastyu subyektivnaya impressionistka, vysokolobaya anglichanka, nepristupnaya i skuchnaya do togo, chto skuly svodit; chastyu – goryachaya storonnitsa zhenskogo voprosa, chut li ne pionerka anglo-amerikanskogo feminisma 20 v'. 'частью субъективная импрессионистка, высоколобая англичанка, неприступная и скучная до того, что скулы сводит; частью – горячая сторонница женского вопроса, чуть ли не пионерка англо-американского феминизма XX в'.
58. 'pochti kazhdiy kritik sobiraet svoi statyi v knigu . . . no daleko ne u kazhdogo poluchaetsya sozdat programmnoe dlya svoego vremeni proizvedenie'. 'почти каждый критик собирает свои статьи в книгу . . . но далеко не у каждого получается создать программное для своего времени произведение'.
59. 'v 1910–20-e gody dvadtsatogo veka angliyskoe esse v ryade sluchaev stanovitsya khudzhestvennoy formoy, sushestvuyushey na styke khudozhestvennoy literatury i publitsistiki'. 'в 1910–20-е годы XX века английское эссе в ряде случаев становится художественной формой, существующей на стыке художественной литературы и публицистики'.
60. 'vymyshlennuyu povest so vsemi prisushimi ey elementami: povestvovatelem, sotsialnymi i prostranstvenno-vremennymi parametrami, kharakterami, situatsiyami, portretom i peyzazhem'. 'вымышленную повесть со всеми присущими ей элементами: повествователем, социальными и пространственно-временными параметрами, характерами, ситуациями, портретом и пейзажем'.
61. '["kollektivniy portret"] naibolee zametnykh figur angliyskoy literatury 20–40-kh godov, danniy v kontekste burnykh literaturnykh i obshestvennykh yavleniy pervoy poloviny

20 veka'. '["коллективный портрет"] наиболее заметных фигур английской литературы 20–40-х годов, данный в контексте бурных литературных и общественных явлений первой половины XX века'.

Bibliography

Anikst, A. (1956), *Istoriya angliyskoy literatury* История английской литературы [The History of British Literature], Moscow: Uchpedgiz.

Astvatsaturov, A. (2007), *Fenomenologiya teksta: Igra i repressiya* Феноменология текста: игра и репрессия [The Phenomenology of the Text: Play and Repression], Moscow: Novoe Literaturnoe Obozrenie.

Auerbach, E. (1976), *Mimesis* Мимесис [Mimesis], Moscow: Progress.

Dneprov, V. (1985), 'Roman bez tainy. Virginia Woolf. Missis Dalloway' 'Роман без тайны. Вирджиния Вулф "Миссис Дэллоуэй" [A no-mystery novel. Virginia Woolf's *Mrs Dalloway*], *Literaturnoe Obozrenie* [Literary Review], 7, <http://md-eksperiment.org/post/20180128-roman-bez-tajny> (last accessed 27 March 2018).

Ermoshin, F. (2006), '*Proza kak vyazanie (Virginia Woolf. Gody)*' Проза как вязанье (Вирджиния Вулф. Годы) [Fiction as knitting (Virginia Woolf's *The Years*)], *Oktyabr* [October], 1, <http://magazines.russ.ru/october/2006/1/er11-pr.html> (last accessed 27 March 2018).

Genieva, E. (1992), 'Zhemchuzhini v korone' Жемчужины в короне [The jewels in the crown], in E. Genieva (ed.), *Eti zagadochniye anglichanki* Эти загадочные англичанки [Those Mysterious British Women], Moscow: Progress, pp. 5–26.

Genieva, E. (2010), 'Intervju' Интервью [Interview], *Teleperedacha 'Shkola zlosloviya'* Телепередача 'Школа злословия' [The School for Scandal Talk-Show], 21 June, <https://www.youtube.com/watch?v=g0n4Mu1PLb8> (last accessed 29 December 2019).

Greshnykh, V. and G. Yanovskaya (2004), *Virginia Woolf: Labirinty mysli* Вирджиния Вулф: лабиринты мысли [Virginia Woolf: Trains of Thought], Kaliningrad: KSU.

Istoriya angliyskoy literatury История английской литературы (1958), [The History of British Literature], vol. 3, Moscow: USSR Academy of Sciences.

Kabanova, I. (2015), 'Virginia Woolf. Obyknovenniy chitatel; Virginia Woolf. Den i noch' Вирджиния Вулф. Обыкновенный читатель; Вирджиния Вулф. День и ночь [Virginia Woolf's *The Common Reader*; Virginia Woolf's *Night and Day*], *Voprosy Literatury* [Questions of Literature], 5, pp. 396–9.

Livergant, A. (2015) 'Flirt s provintsialom' Флирт с провинциалом [Flirting with a countryman], *Nezavisimaya gazeta* Независимая газета [Independent Newspaper], 23 July, <http://www.ng.ru/ng_exlibris/2015-07-23/2_persona.html> (last accessed 30 January 2019).

Livergant, A. (2018a) 'Virginia Woolf' Вирджиния Вулф [Virginia Woolf], *Radioperedacha 'Pora domoy'* Радиопередача 'Пора домой' [Time to Go Home (a radio programme)], 16 January, <http://radiomayak.ru/videos/video/id/1751583/> (last accessed 30 January 2019).

Livergant, A. (2018b), *Virginia Woolf: 'momenty bytiya'* Вирджиния Вулф: 'моменты бытия' [Virginia Woolf: 'Moments of Being'], Moscow: AST.

Lunacharsky, A. (1924), *Istoriya zapadno-evropeyskoy literatury v ee vazhneyshih momentah* История западно-европейской литературы в её важнейших моментах [The History of Western European Literature in its Most Important Moments], vols 1–2, <http://ruslit.traumlibrary.net/book/lunacharskiy-ss08-04/lunacharskiy-ss0804.html> (last accessed 15 April 2017).

Lysaya pevitsa' i drugie perevody Eleny Surits 'Лысая певица' и другие переводы Елены Суриц (2016), ['The Bald Soprano' and Elena Surits's Other Translations], Moscow: Tsentr Knigi Rudomino.

Malyugin, O. (1971), 'K voprosu ob eksperimentalnom romane: (romany V. Woolf. "Missis Dalloway", "K mayaku")' 'К вопросу об экспериментальном романе: (романы В. Вулф. "Миссис Дэллоуэй", "К маяку")' [On the experimental novel: (V. Woolf's *Mrs Dalloway* and *To the Lighthouse*)], Voprosy angliyskoy i frantsuzskoy filologii (*Uchenie zapiski fakulteta inostrannikh yazykov Tulskogo pedagogicheskogo istituta*) Вопросы английской и французской филологии (*Ученые записки факультета иностранных языков Тульского педагогического института*) English and French Philology Issues *(Faculty of Foreign Languages Bulletin, Tula Institute of Education,* 6, pp. 208–22.

Melnikov, N. (2014), *O Nabokove i prochem: Statyi, retsenzii, publikatsii* О Набокове и прочем: Статьи, рецензии, публикации [On Nabokov and the Rest: Essays, Reviews, Papers], Moscow: Novoe Literaturnoe Obozrenie.

Mikhalskaya, N. (1966), *Puti razvitiya angliyskogo romana. 1920–1930. Utrata i poiski geroya* Пути развития английского романа. 1920–1930. Утрата и поиски героя [The British Novel's Development Patterns: 1920s–1930s. Hero Lost and Regained], Moscow: Vysshaya shkola.

Mirsky, D. S. (1934), *Intellidzhentsiya* Интеллиджентсиа [Intelligentsia], Moscow: Sovetskaya Literatura.

Nilin, A. (1989), 'Apellyatsiya talanta k talantu: O romane V. Woolf "Na mayak"' Апелляция таланта к таланту: о романе В.Вулф "На маяк" [A talent's appeal to talent: On V. Woolf's *To the Lighthouse*], *Inostrannaya Literatura* [Foreign Literature], 6, pp. 231–5.

Pisateli Anglii o literature. 19–20 vv. (1981), Писатели Англии о литературе. XIX–XX вв. [The British Writers on Literature. Nineteenth and Twentieth Centuries], Moscow: Progress.

Reinhold, N. (2004a), 'Preface', N. Reinhold (ed.), *Woolf Across Cultures*, New York: Pace University Press, pp. ix–xiv.

Reinhold, N. (2004b), 'Virginia Woolf's work in Russia: A success story of 2.5 million copies', in N. Reinhold (ed.), *Woolf Across Cultures*, New York: Pace University Press, pp. 1–13.

Reinhold, N. (2006), 'Readingskiy buvar s pismami Bunina' Редингский бювар с письмами Бунина [The writing case with Bunin's letters in Reading], *Voprosy Literatury* [Literary Issues], 6, 152–68.

Reinhold, N. (2007) 'Russkaya tema i obraz Rossii v tvorchestve Virginii Woolf' Русская тема и образ России в творчестве Вирджинии Вулф [The Russian theme and the image of Russia in V. Woolf's work], Noviye rossiyskie gumanitarnye issledovaniya Новые российские гуманитарные исследования [New Russian Research in Humanities], 2, <https://elibrary.ru/download/elibrary_14453192_64217202.pdf> (last accessed 16 January 2020).

Reinhold, N. (2012), *Mosty cherez La Manche. Britanskaya literatura 1900–2000-h* Мосты через Ла-Манш. Британская литература 1900–2000-х. [Bridging the Channel. British Literature of the 1900s–2000s], Moscow: RSUH.

Reinhold, N. (2017), *Istoriya literatury 20 veka. Angliyskaya literatura modernizma: Istoriya, problematika* История литературы XX века. Английская литература модернизма: история, проблематика [Literary History of the Twentieth Century. British Modernist Literature: History and Problems], Moscow: RSUH.

Rudomino, M. (2005) 'Knigi moey sudby: vospominaniya rovesnitsy 20 v.' Книги моей судьбы: воспоминания ровесницы XXв. [The books of my life: Memoirs of a woman the same age as the century], <https://www.litmir.me/br/?b=285918&p=20> (last accessed 30 January 2019).

Selitrina, T. (2014), 'Esse "Svoya komnata". Romannoe myshlenie V. Woolf' Эссе "Своя комната". Романное мышление В. Вулф' [*A Room of One's Own*. V. Woolf's novelistic thought], *Filologiya i kultura* [Philology and Culture], 3:37, pp. 260–3.

Solovyova, E. (2008), 'Russkaya tema v romane V. Woolf "Orlando": Istoriya ili mif?' Русская тема в романе В. Вулф 'Орландо': история или миф? [The Russian theme in V. Woolf's *Orlando*: Historical fact or myth?], <https://elibrary.ru/item.asp?id=15230873> (last accessed 30 January 2019).

Vakhrushev, V. (1995), '"Sestra Shekspira"' 'Сестра Шекспира' [Shakespeare's sister], *Noviy Mir* [New World], 5, <http://magazines.russ.ru/novyi_mi/1995/5/bookrev03.html> (last accessed 27 March 2018).

Vladimirova, N. (2009), 'A. Chekhov s russkoy tochki zreniya V. Woolf' А.П. Чехов с «русской точки зрения» Вирджинии Вулф [A. Chekhov from V. Woolf's 'Russian point of view'] Vestnik Novgorodskogo gosudarstvennogo universiteta Вестник Новгородского государственного университета [Novgorod State University Bulletin], 51, pp. 49–52.

Vorontsova, T. (2003), '"V gostyakh u starshego brata"' '"В гостях у старшего брата"' [Visiting 'Big Brother'], *Literatura*, 9, <https://lit.1sept.ru/article.php?ID=200300909> (last accessed 9 December 2019).

Wells, H. G. (1920), *Russia in the Shadows*, London: Hodder and Stoughton.

Woolf, V. (1978), 'Lewis Carroll' Льюис Кэрролл [Lewis Carroll], trans. N. Demurova, in L. Carroll, *Priklucheniya Alisy v strane chudes; Skvoz zerkalo i Chto tam uvdela Alisa, ili Alisa v Zazerkalye* Приключения Алисы в Стране чудес; Сквозь Зеркало и Что там увидела Алиса, или Алиса в Зазеркалье [Alice's Adventures in Wonderland; Through the Looking-Glass, and What Alice Found There], Moscow: Nauka, pp. 248–50.

Woolf, V. (1983a), 'Kak chitat knigi' Как читать книги ['How should one read a book?'], trans. K. Atarova, in S. Belza (ed.), *Chelovek chitayushiy. HOMO LEGENS. Pisateli 20 veka o roli knigi v zhizni cheloveka i obshestva* Человек читающий. HOMO LEGENS. Писатели XX в. о роли книги в жизни человека и общества [HOMO LEGENS. Twentieth-Century Writers on the Role of Books in the Life of Man and Society], Moscow: Progress, pp. 254–65.

Woolf, V. (1983b), 'O russkoy literature' О русской литературе [On Russian literature], trans. N. Bushmanova, *Voprosy Literatury* [Literary Questions], 11, pp. 188–207.

Woolf, V. (1984), *Missis Dalloway. Esse* Миссис Дэллоуэй. Эссе [Mrs Dalloway. Essays], in English, Moscow: Raduga.

Woolf, V. (1986a), *Flush: Rasskazy. Povest* Флаш: Рассказы. Повесть [Flush: Short Stories. A Novel], Moscow: Izvestiya.

Woolf, V. (1986b), 'Pismo k molodomu poetu' Письмо к молодому поэту ['A letter to a young poet'], trans. N. Bushmanova, *Literaturnaya Uchyoba* [Literary Study], 1, pp. 207–13.

Woolf, V. (1987), 'Iz esse i dnevnikov V. Woolf' Из эссе и дневников Вирджинии Вулф [From Virginia Woolf's diaries and essays], trans. N. Bushmanova, *Literaturnaya Rossiya*, 25, pp. 22–3.

Woolf, V. (1989), *Izbrannoe* Избранное [Selected Works], Moscow: Khudozhestvennaya literatura.

Woolf, V. (1990), 'David Copperfield' "Дэвид Копперфилд" [David Copperfield], trans. K. Atarova, in E. Genieva (ed.), *Tayna Charlza Dikkensa* Тайна Чарльза Диккенса, [The Mystery of Charles Dickens], Moscow: Knizhnaya palata, pp. 192–7.

Woolf, V. (2009), *Dnevnik pisatelnitsy* Дневник писательницы [*A Writer's Diary*], trans. L. Volodarskaya, Moscow: Tsentr Knigi VGBIL.

Woolf, V. (2012a), *Obyknovenniy chitatel* Обыкновенный читатель [*The Common Reader*], trans. N. Reinhold, Moscow: Nauka.

Woolf, V. (2012b), 'Ya – Christina Rossetti' Я – Кристина Россетти ['I am Christina Rossetti'], trans. M. Lukashkina, *Inostrannaya Literatura* [Foreign Literature], 12, pp. 218–24.

Woolf, V. (2014), *Kinematograf* Кинематограф ['The cinema'], trans. S. Silakova, Moscow: 'Ad Marginem Press' LLC.

Zhantieva, D. (1965), *Angliyskiy roman 20 veka. 1918–39* Английский роман XX века. 1918–39 [The British novel of the twentieth century. 1918–39], Moscow: Nauka.

8

Virginia Woolf's Feminist Writing in Estonian Translation Culture

Raili Marling

Virginia Woolf today is not just a towering giant of modernist literature but also, more perhaps than her contemporary literary classics, an icon whose work and image transcends the pages of literature textbooks and can be found on coffee mugs and tote bags (Silver 1999). This commodification would probably have horrified Woolf, who was concerned about 'settling into a figure' (D 4: 85). However, the wide dissemination of her image has also attracted generations of 'common readers' – as defined by Woolf in her 1925 collection of the same name – people who read her work for pleasure, as opposed to professional academic readers. Many of these common readers come to Woolf in translation. Woolf was already recognised as a major writer during her lifetime, with research volumes published in several European countries, and her stature has only increased since her death. The transnational Woolf of today speaks in many languages, in diverse cultural inflections, integrated into different receiving cultures and their literary systems, side by side with local literature (Andringa 2006). This contemporary phenomenon has been explored in several collections (for example, Caws and Luckhurst 2002; Reinhold 2004), although the range of countries covered tends to remain limited to major European cultures, such as France and Germany. There is, especially, a gap in scholarship about smaller languages and literatures, of which Estonian is one example.

The different scholarly approaches to Woolf in various cultures call attention to the roadblocks in interpreting the movement of an author's textual corpus across cultural and linguistic boundaries. Geneviève Brassard (2016: 441), for example, notes that translators may feel the need to make Woolf more easily accessible to the target culture by using different strategies of domestication. They above all aim for a 'regularisation' of Woolf's diction, for example, by converting her free-indirect discourse into a third-person narrative or changing the flow of the text by changing the punctuation in the Italian translations or the deletion of textual elements in the Portuguese versions (Brassard 2016: 447). More seriously, Brassard draws attention to how 'key thematic strands have been obscured or elided' in translations into French, German or Spanish (2016: 449). Much is lost in translation because of the difficulty of conveying Woolf's unique style and political stance into other languages. Translation is not just a linguistic and poetic task but also a political one. This can be seen most vividly in certain translations that at times subsume Woolf's feminist notions in androcentric terms, thereby radically transforming the intended message, for example, fixing the gender of Orlando and thus undermining the intended project of gender fluidity in Polish (Terentowicz-Fotyga 2002: 141). Probably the most famous case of such an androcentric translation intervention is the Spanish translation by Jorge Luis Borges who altered Woolf's language according to his own aesthetic criteria that 'privileged the masculine' (Santaemilia 2012: 169; Bengoechea 2011; and Federici and Leonardi 2012 also provide useful insights into the topic). Scholarship on the translation of Woolf demonstrates that this challenge is greatest when it comes to conveying Woolf's critical cosmopolitanism and her feminism, as these two topic areas continue to create friction in many target cultures to this day.

This chapter analyses the transfer(ability) of Woolf's cosmopolitan feminism into the postsocialist Estonian culture. This is not merely a question of the linguistic challenge involved in translating a modernist classic or fitting a foreign text into a local literary system in which translations become a part of the wider 'polysystem' of culture (Even-Zohar 1990).[1] The perhaps greater challenge comes from the need to introduce a sense of feminist agency into a context that has not participated in and perhaps is even opposed to the feminist theory building of the second half of the twentieth century (Koobak 2018). In the case of Estonia, feminism's re-introduction was hampered by the shadow of the Soviet period when gender equality was preached but not practised: women and men were equal in rhetoric but not in reality, and women shouldered a double burden of paid and unpaid labour. This double standard led to a knee-jerk rejection of feminist notions, falsely associated with the vacuous Soviet slogans, in the post-Soviet period. Feminism, in a sense, appears as an intimidating 'Other' against which the post-Soviet nation has constructed itself (Marling 2010).

Yet feminism is increasingly attractive to the younger generations raised in the international information exchange and seeking relevant means of expression in their native language. In the context of a lack of feminist theorising available in Estonian,[2] Woolf as a classic modernist may act as a gateway to a deeper engagement with feminist thought. Biljana Dojčinović-Nešić (2010), speaking from a Serbian perspective, has suggested that the translation of Woolf's *A Room of One's Own* can be viewed as an Eastern European country opening itself to feminist theory. The core of this vision of translation is not linguistic transposition but inspiration. The impact of specifically feminist Woolf has also been noted in Poland (Terentowicz-Fotyga 2002: 143). The Estonian case thus fits into that broader cultural network of Eastern Europe.

This chapter first explores Woolf's relationship with translation and its affective implications. Next, building on my previous work on the paratexts of the published Estonian translations (Põldsaar 2006), I provide an overview of the translation of Woolf's work into Estonian. Third, I will provide a close reading of the translation of *Oma tuba* (*A Room of One's Own*) (1994/1997) for specific translation strategies, including affective ones that engage with the tension of anger and aesthetics. Finally, the chapter will explore the negotiation of Woolf's feminism in the Estonian context that has been, if not explicitly antifeminist, then at least distancing itself from feminist ideas (Marling 2010). The ultimate aim of the chapter is to identify the 'potential cultural work translations can perform' (Brassard 2016: 444). In the Estonian context, this means asking whether Woolf translations can help smuggle in feminist ideas that otherwise may remain foreign.

Woolf and Translation

The present chapter argues that translation deserves attention both as a linguistic-cultural practice and as an expression of Woolf's broader cosmopolitan worldview. As previous research has shown, Woolf was no stranger to translation. She was famously terse with her French translator Marguerite Yourcenar (Brassard and Guénot-Hovnavian 2009) but at the same time she read and appreciated translations such as C. K. Scott Moncrieff's translation of Marcel Proust's *À la recherche du temps perdu* [*Remembrance of Things Past*] (Dalgarno 2012: 99). In 'The Russian point of view', Woolf commented on both the need for and the impossibility of translation (*CR* 1: 177–87). She published translations at Hogarth Press, including works by Fyodor Dostoevsky, Ivan Bunin, Rainer Maria Rilke and, perhaps the most widely read of all, Sigmund Freud, but she also tested her own skills in translation, particularly with Aeschylus's *Agamemnon*. Woolf also collaborated on a translation of a suppressed chapter of Dostoevsky's *The Possessed* (Dalgarno 2012: 3, 6).[3] Dalgarno notes that in her translations from Greek, Woolf used a bilingual edition (2012: 3). Woolf's translation practice when it came to Russian authors was that of collaborative translation; she, like Katherine Mansfield and D. H. Lawrence, worked with the Russian émigré S. S. Koteliansky to arrive at 'an imaginative, expressive leap' between two languages that the collaborators knew to 'a creative space between the two' (Davison 2014: 9). In this process, the word-to-word translation is rendered into idiomatic and poetic English and then checked again by Koteliansky to ensure the appropriateness of the word choices (Davison 2014: 15).

It has been argued that Woolf did not take great interest in the translations of her own works (Marcus 2002: 332). However, Jennifer Raterman (2010) has more recently demonstrated Woolf's heightened awareness of the differences that translations inevitably contain and the reading practices they require. Claire Davison (2014) shows how the dialogic encounter derived from translation enriched Woolf's own creative language. Davison also notes that it is possible to see Woolf 'thinking through translation, double language codes and forms of imperfect bilingualism rather than merely writing about translation' (2015: 78). Moreover, Woolf returns to the broader philosophical issue of translatability in several of her works, most explicitly perhaps in *Orlando* and *The Years*.

This is not merely a writer's attention to how literary works, things 'made of language' to cite Tim Parks (qtd in Walkowitz 2013: 35), inevitably undergo transformation when moving across language boundaries but also a conscious political stance. Woolf's famous refusal of a national identification as a woman in *Three Guineas* echoes her unique cosmopolitan position. In 'The leaning tower' (1940), for example, she writes: 'literature is common ground. It is not cut up into nations; there are no wars there' (qtd in Dalgarno 2012: 7). Rebecca L. Walkowitz (2013: 37–8) sees Woolf's *Three Guineas* as not just accommodating translation but as an encouragement of 'comparative thinking', a precursor to transnational cooperation and solidarity. This, however, is a process rife with tension. As Walkowitz puts it:

> Translation is required: one must acknowledge networks of causation and responsibility, and it is often necessary to imagine larger political frameworks. But translation must be resisted, or at least made visible, in order to make distinctions among agents and among the histories that have divided those agents. (2013: 45)

Jessica Berman links this vision of cosmopolitanism to community building that complicates 'the dichotomy between private and public life, home and away' (2015: 430). As such, this process is deeply invested in identity creation, political as well as personal. Woolf, Berman argues, uses her status as a woman on the margins of British imperialism from which she is excluded to construct 'a cosmopolitan outsider politics, which creates a new community of those who refuse the authoritarian state and its demands for unreal (and unequally repaid) loyalties' (2015: 438). Walkowitz suggests that Woolf's critical cosmopolitanism is characterised by 'an aversion to heroic tones of appropriation and progress, and a suspicion of epistemological privilege' as well as 'reflection about reflection' (2006: 2–3). With the latter, Walkowitz stresses the need to consider critical styles, as well as conventions of writing and thinking.

This outsider politics can also be linked to translation. Davison uses the term 'outlandishness', borrowed from Woolf's *The Voyage Out*, to talk about Woolf's relationship with translation (2015: 72–90). It should be noted here that, as Raterman has observed, translation was for Woolf related to common reading (2013: 170). The common reader is for Woolf also the outsider (Raterman 2013: 177). Translation creates new modes of reading but also new ways of coming together across the limiting national barriers. This notion of translation is not just a linguistic endeavour but also a social phenomenon. Importantly for the present chapter, Walkowitz notes the significance of affect and self-consciousness in critical cosmopolitanism (2006: 27). Affects bubble up in critical discussion of Woolf, especially in connection with politics and Woolf's contradictory statements on strong affects (as in her famous juxtaposition of Austen and Charlotte Brontë [*AROO*: 70]). Scholars have taken particular interest in Woolf's engagement with anger, the affect most frequently associated with her political writing, and have shown, first, a complex interplay of affects in Woolf's political writing and, second, the problems of assuming that only anger can inspire political engagement (Silver 1991; Hsieh 2006; Ziarek 2010).

Thus, the use of affect is not just aesthetic but also political. This chapter focuses specifically on Woolf's feminism and its translation in this broader cosmopolitan context that challenges both 'atomistic individualism' and the view that groups are 'monolithic, consistent, whole' (Berman 2001: 122). One of the group labels that questions the notion of consistent monolithicity is feminism as a belief system and form of activism. Woolf did not always welcome the label 'feminist' because of her overall suspicion of ideological entanglements (*TG*: 137). In her letters, she also expressed her suspicion of preaching; for example, she wrote, 'I never meant to preach, and agree that like God, one shouldn't' (*L* 1: 383). In other words, she rejects the stereotypical definition of feminism, prevalent already in her time, and seeks to construct a different transnational community of outsiders, using modernist narrative strategies that expand the boundaries of political rhetoric as well as feminist fiction with new forms of tonal ambiguity that resists tone-deaf political categorisation (see Hite 2017). Woolf's essays, above all *A Room of One's Own* and *Three Guineas*, are explicitly feminist and her fiction is interpreted as containing feminist narrative strategies (discussed, for example, by DuPlessis [1988]). Woolf's feminism is built on her sense of critical cosmopolitanism, as noted above, and is fused with an expanded sense of 'collective political agency' that embraces cultural diversity (Raterman 2013: 180).

Estonian Woolf

Woolf critics have identified three phases in the academic reception of the author: as a modernist novelist, as a feminist essayist and as a diarist and letter writer (Brosnan 1997: 2). As I have shown in my earlier work (Põldsaar 2006), the Estonian Woolf can be viewed only through the first two lenses for the simple reason that Woolf's diaries and letters have not yet been translated, although Estonian scholars have studied them (for example, Kurvet-Käosaar 2005). Many of Woolf's texts can be read in Estonian: *To the Lighthouse* (*Tuletorni juurde*, translated by Malle Talvet and Jaak Rähesoo, 1983, reissued in 2005); *A Room of One's Own* (*Oma tuba*, translated by Malle Talvet in 1994); *Esseed*, a selection of Woolf's essays (translated by Malle Talvet and Jaak Rähesoo in 1997);[4] *Orlando* (translated by Riina Jesmin, 1997, reissued in 2007 and 2016); *Mrs Dalloway* (*Proua Dalloway*, translated by Riina Jesmin, 1998, reissued in 2007 and 2018); *The Waves* (*Lained*, translated by Riina Jesmin, 1999, reissued in 2008); *Moments of Being* (*Olemise hetked*, translated by Krista Mits, 2013); and a selection of her shorter fiction (*Kirjutamata romaan ja teisi jutte*, translated by Mirjam Parve, 2017).[5] Talvet and Rähesoo have tackled many modernist classics in addition to Woolf: Gertrude Stein in the case of Talvet and Joyce, and William Faulkner and T. S. Eliot in the case of Rähesoo. Similarly, the literary scholar Mits has also translated Djuna Barnes's *Nightwood*, and Jesmin is a very prolific translator from both English and Romanian. However, Woolf is one of the first translations for Parve.

It is interesting to note that Woolf was not translated into Estonian in the 1920–1930s. In the Soviet period, her work was shunned because its modernism did not fit the socialist realist ideological framework. A few of her shorter texts appeared in Soviet-era literary periodicals, including, for example, 'Kew Gardens' in the translation by Inna Feldbach in the literary magazine *Looming* in 1975 and 'Modern fiction' in the translation by Jaak Rähesoo in the same magazine in 1982. This publishing venue is important in the Estonian context, as *Looming* ['Creation' in literal translation] was and still is the monthly magazine of the Estonian Writers' Union. Its monthly supplement, *Loomingu Raamatukogu* ('Library of Creation' in literal translation), mostly publishes translated works by writers from all over the world. The series has been an important place for the publication of translations, especially those considered potentially subversive in the context of Soviet censorship. Translations were subjected to much less heightened scrutiny in the Soviet era than local literature, as long as the writers refrained from open criticism of the USSR (for a broader discussion, see Safiullina and Platonov 2012: 254). As a periodical, *Loomingu Raamatukogu* was able to escape the scrutiny of the Soviet censors more easily than the publishing houses, as has been demonstrated by Anne Lange (2017: 158). This allowed *Loomingu Raamatukogu* to publish Aleksandr Solzhenitsyn's *One Day in the Life of Ivan Denisovich* and Albert Camus's *The Plague* in the 1960s, to name just two texts that diverge from the celebration of the Soviet regime.[6] Woolf's work, because of its modernism, otherwise shunned in the Soviet Union for its formalism, thus could be published in this semi-subversive venue. A similar approach also creates a parallel with Poland where reading modernist authors also was a 'political as well as an aesthetic gesture: a refusal to participate in the official culture of a totalitarian state' (Graff 1999: 5). The Estonian case reflects the general Soviet situation, where some literary journals were on the forefront of introducing important international literature to the readers behind the Iron Curtain, despite censorship.[7]

Woolf presented a problem for Soviet-era censorship for two reasons. Literary production was supposed to promote proletarian, not bourgeois writers, especially because readers flocked to buy the latter. Modernism was specifically singled out for criticism due to its formalism and distance from the prescribed socialist realist canons.

Woolf's feminism posed another dilemma. Soviet ideology declared that was feminism a bourgeois relic since, in propaganda (though not in reality), equality of men and women had been achieved. The 'woman question' was raised in different 'organizational fictions' that assumed the solution of these problems (Chatterjee 1999: 16). Feminist texts could appear only if they critiqued capitalist societies, but the publication of such texts was rare. Simone de Beauvoir could be issued as a fiction writer but not a feminist because she pointed out in *The Second Sex* that the promise of equality had not been fulfilled in the Soviet Union. (When de Beauvoir and Sartre visited Soviet Estonia in 1964, the fact that she had published *The Second Sex* was not mentioned in the local press.) The reception of these twin bans, however, was different among the reading public: while modernism was seen as subversive, and thus read in privately owned illegal copies in defiance of the official censure, feminist texts did not find the same resonance. One possible explanation is that the language of gender equality and women's rights, to a superficial eye, resembled the hollow Soviet slogans of equality and seemed to reiterate official propaganda. If anything, it seemed to many Soviet dissidents that it was men who were the victims of the Soviet regime (Zdravomyslova and Temkina 2012). The situation was no different in Estonia where the suspicion of Soviet equality discourses found the clearest outlet in the anti-Soviet nationalist discourses that, too, were anything but enthusiastic about feminism (Ross 2018). Thus, feminism was silenced both from the side of the official and underground culture. This also explains the paucity of feminist translations even though many other supposedly ideologically suspicious texts found their way to the readers.

The suspicion of feminist texts was not diminished by the fall of the Soviet Union. In Estonia, as in most other Central and Eastern European countries, the post-Soviet period was marked by a desire to return to the nationalist imaginaries of the 1930s or, more prominently in the political arena, to integrate fully and forcefully into the neoliberal global economy. Feminism fitted neither perspective. Western feminists in the 1990s were baffled by the way Estonia, among other former Eastern bloc countries, shunned feminism (Watson 1997). In Estonia, feminism was too reminiscent of the Soviet period's hypocritical equality slogans that had hidden profoundly gendered inequalities. Estonia thus developed a backlash against feminism before it could resurrect the feminist tradition from the years before the Soviet occupation (Marling 2010).

As can be seen in this brief history of translating Woolf into Estonian, Woolf makes the first appearance as an explicitly feminist author in 1994, with the publication of *Oma tuba* (*A Room of One's Own*). My analysis of the paratexts to the Estonian translations has shown that feminism has been present in the Estonian Woolf reception from the first translation. Modernism could not be mentioned explicitly in the paratexts, but feminism could, despite it being shunned in the Soviet period as well (Põldsaar 2006). However, feminism is never made into a political topic but rather is blended into Woolf's aesthetic project. For example, the first edition of Malle Talvet's translation of *A Room of One's Own* mentions Woolf's concern with the position of women writers in the male-dominated world but rushes to add that literary form and style was Woolf's overarching concern (Põldsaar 2006: 466).

The fact that *A Room of One's Own* has been inspirational for feminist activism and feminist literary criticism is not highlighted in the paratexts, most probably because of the stigmatisation of feminism in early post-Soviet Estonia. This can be seen in the 1997 reprint of the translation of *A Room of One's Own* in a selection of Woolf's essays. Jaak Rähesoo's afterword to the collection states: 'For a polemical work, [Woolf's] book is remarkably free of shrillness; there are frequent flashes of irony but it is calm and self-confident'[8] (translation used in Põldsaar 2006: 468). The stereotype of the shrill feminist is evoked, although the afterword otherwise identifies gender as a central concern of Woolf's work and its continued topicality. Rähesoo makes a point of stressing that feminism was the impetus of a 'Woolf boom', although he limits feminist attention to Woolf's two major essays on this topic, *A Room of One's Own* and *Three Guineas*, in his afterword (Rähesoo 1997: 270). Only the former is included in the volume; *Three Guineas* still awaits Estonian translation. The ways in which Woolf's feminism coloured her fiction more broadly are not mentioned and, instead, Woolf is implicitly congratulated for disliking the label of a feminist on the basis of her own words in *Three Guineas*.

In the same afterword, the sexual politics and fluid sexuality in the Bloomsbury group are viewed as an overzealous interpretation by observers affected by the sexual revolution, a perspective, Rähesoo claims, which does not illuminate Woolf's writing. In something of a contradiction, Rähesoo follows this observation with an admission that Woolf herself was 'probably bisexual' (1997: 267–8).[9] This viewpoint, however, is assumed to have no interpretive value in approaching Woolf's work, with the possible exception of *Orlando*, which is described as a fantasy. In the paratext, Rähesoo distances Woolf both from the physical and the erotic (1997: 268). Sexual subversion is just viewed as a regrettable symptom of the gossipy treatment of Bloomsbury in the popular mind, with no reference to fluid gender identities or queer theory that was widely incorporated into literary criticism in Western countries by that time (Põldsaar 2006: 467). This analysis of the interpretation of sexuality in the Estonian Woolf reception of the 1990s is not meant to create a sense of a common progress narrative for feminism or to demonstrate the existence of a temporal lag in the Estonian public reception of feminism but, rather, to indicate that the Estonian public discourse has been reluctant to address feminism and, especially, queer identities (Koobak and Marling 2014).

My analysis of the reception of Woolf in Estonian literary culture was published in 2006. However, the translations that have been published since that date do not alter the gender evasive picture. Krista Mits's 2013 afterword to *Olemise hetked* (*Moments of Being*) focuses on Woolf's biography, with only passing references to Woolf's gender politics. Mits refers to Woolf's turn to more political themes, including women's role in society (Woolf 2013: 117). Also, Mits locates Woolf's text in the context of her broader interest in life writing and biography, conventionally conceived as a form of celebrating great men, and places it in a dialogue with both the fictive biography of *Orlando* and that of Shakespeare's sister from *A Room of One's Own* (Woolf 2013: 118–19). The 2017 volume lacks a fore- or afterword altogether. Overall, the Estonian Woolf, emerging from the paratexts of the translations of her work, is a modernist who takes an interest in gender and feminism, but is by no means primarily a feminist thinker, and blends her political commitments with formal experimentation.

Translating *A Room of One's Own*: Affect and Aesthetic

For two countries, Spain in 1936 and Iceland in 1973, *A Room of One's Own* is the first text by Woolf to be translated (Luckhurst 2002: 10). As discussed above, the text was the second work by Woolf to be published in Estonia and the same translation was issued twice. As I testify on the basis of my own personal experience, both versions are hard to procure on the used book market, suggesting its continued popularity among Estonian common readers. In other words, the lack of a visible feminist movement that would constitute a distinct market segment and the overall conservatism of the Estonian public sphere does not mean that there is no audience for this feminist text. However, the mode in which the audience meets the text needs to be considered. The analysis of paratexts, summarised above, allows me to conclude that, in the Estonian context, the observation made by Silver about Woolf's *Three Guineas* can also applied in the case of *A Room of One's Own*, namely that the authority of the text is reduced 'by denying the authority of [its] anger' (1991: 34). This, as Silver observes, allows the text to be resituated from the context of public debate to that of aesthetics, where Woolf can be praised for her style rather than her political contribution (1991: 348).

The tension between politics and aesthetics is a persistent topic in Woolf studies, as Ewa Plonowska Ziarek argues (2010: 70). This tension takes different forms. Els Andringa, in her longitudinal study of the Dutch literary polysystem, also identifies a divergence between criticism of women's writing, often by women, and the more mainstream discussion of literary innovation in the Dutch reception of Woolf (2006). Although the present chapter only examines one work, *A Room of One's Own*, it can be surmised that a similar tension might emerge in domesticating Woolf into the Estonian target culture in which the modernist reading has prevailed over the feminist one.

This tension is political and also affective. Lili Hsieh believes that Woolf 'tries to theorize a feminist politics and aesthetics *out of* anger' (2006: 20) and hence it is important to consider whether or not a translation can enable readers to experience this anger. The following discussion seeks to identify whether it is possible to trace the highlighting or downplaying of anger and other strong affects in the Estonian translation of *A Room of One's Own*.[10] However, it needs to be stated, as Hsieh has also shown, whether or not the text comes off as angry greatly depends on the eye of the reader – and there are readers for whom a text that raises feminist questions by definition sounds polemical and aggressive (2006: 20).

Because the majority of the international readership will be unable to follow the linguistic nuances of the Estonian translation, the following section will summarise the main findings of the stylistic comparison of the English original and the Estonian translation by Malle Talvet and thus will not bog down the text by long Estonian quotations and their verbatim translations that would be necessary. Instead, I will focus on the affective and political effects of the translation.

The translational strategies used in the Estonian version of *A Room of One's Own* aim at smoothness and elegance of style, in accordance with the translation norms prevailing in Estonia. Even the pricklier passages of the essay are conveyed smoothly, with linguistic dexterity that does justice to Woolf's wit and style. The translator, Talvet, carefully chose rare words to give an extra poetic sheen. In other words, to render Woolf's famous style into Estonian, the translator makes Woolf's language somewhat quainter than it is in the original, no doubt with the best of intentions. This strategy is most evident in the translation of visual images and related adjectival choices, for example, a very unusual verb form 'contourless' ('hahmutud') for 'dim' and a somewhat unusual version of 'hook' ('kida') for 'snag'. There are also instances of diminutions that do not have a parallel in the English original, for instance, 'pretty girl' is replaced by 'pretty girlie' ('kena neiukene'). These choices do not introduce significant semantic shifts and concern rather minor changes, but they embellish the text, calling attention to its verbal surface. This translation norm can be found in Estonian translations of foreign literature, where the local literary custom of avoiding repetition and varying the adjectives may result in adding colour to the source text. This technique can be explained with the 'compensation method' used in the translations of the period, according to which translators had to seek for means 'to compensate for losses in one part of their translation with more pronounced stylistic devices elsewhere if considered appropriate (and where the original itself is using more neutral devices)' (Sütiste and Lotman 2016: 27).

The use of the compensation method may be necessitated by the desire to build an impression of the text for the reader for whom the many cultural, socio-economic and poetic references do not resonate immediately and do not evoke parallels in the Estonian cultural context. The translator has opted not to add many new footnotes that would slow down the reading and also mark the text as academic. Instead, the translation of *A Room of One's Own* preserves the footnotes of the original and adds only references to the translators of poetry excerpts and phrases from languages other than English. For example, in the second section of the text, the original quotes Jean de La Bruyère's 'Les femmes sont extrêmes; elles sont meilleures ou pires que les hommes' and the Penguin Classics edition provides no translation (Woolf 2000: 31), but the Estonian one does in the footnotes. However, the cosmopolitan flavour of the text is maintained by preserving the French in the main body of the text. At the same time, the reader-friendly translation also opens the text's potential to the audience, as proficiency in French is no longer an ordinary feature of a common reader.

Talvet also does an excellent job with conveying Woolf's ironical tone in the key scenes like the one in the British Library that bristles with witty anger, as in the original. Interestingly, here the word stem 'anger' ('viha' in Estonian) remains the same consistently throughout the translation and is not replaced with other, potentially more poetic alternatives that would be expected from the compensation method often used in Estonian translations. This can be in examples like 'I descended the steps in anger' (Woolf 2000: 10), translated as 'vihasena trepist alla astudes' (Woolf 1997: 143). This pattern of unadorned transfer recurs throughout the text. The language is not overwrought in these sections and, perhaps, even erring in the opposite direction from the strategy chosen in the poetic passages, is more colloquial in syntax and lexis. Thus, the Estonian translation does not deny the authority of anger, although it couches it in a somewhat more stylistically elaborate frame than the English original. Therefore, despite the struggle between the desire to establish Woolf as a stylist above Woolf as a polemicist, the translation serves the purpose that Woolf herself also desired, 'to encourage the young women – they seem to get fearfully depressed – and to induce discussion' (Hsieh 2006: 47). As such, it remains true to the tone of ambiguity that Woolf strives for and does not succumb to – as happens in the androcentric translation effects like the Spanish and Italian translations cited above that fixed Woolf to one meaning, preferring the aesthetic to the political. While Borges's translation made Woolf fit the dominant values of the 1930s, at the cost of her narrative style and gender multiplicity (Santaemilia 2012: 169), Talvet gives Estonian readers access to an ironical and at times angry Woolf whose style is enhanced at times but not at the cost of the effectiveness of the message.

Conclusion: Is Estonia Afraid of Woolf's Feminism?

The Estonian translation of *A Room of One's Own* gives precedence to stylistic excellence over political affect but not to an extent that would mute the political intentions of the text. Ziarek's concern about 'the persistent complicity of subversive textual politics with domination' (2010: 70) is confirmed with regard to separating feminist politics from literary innovation. By having been placed in the gilded cage of modernist masterpieces, the anger of the text is muted and hence its potential for political community building is also reduced.

This brief discussion of the Estonian translation shows that, indeed, the literary system's reading of Woolf as a modernist stylist, at least in the 1990s, encourages the translator to overemphasise the style. Davison argues that nineteenth-century French translations tended to first and foremost celebrate the beauty of French (2015: 79). Estonian translation norms have typically required the maximal use of 'the resources of the Estonian language in order to convey both the style and the content of the source text' (Sütiste and Lotman 2016: 29). However, Talvet in her translation also remains attentive to the ambiguous tone of the essay and does not deny the authority of anger. Indeed, the translation retains its simplicity and power in the context of stylistic elaborations.

The formal framing of Woolf into canonical certitudes does not necessarily eliminate the effect of Woolf's critical cosmopolitan community-building strategies. Woolf's *A Room of One's Own* has acquired comparative power in the 2000s due to the new social circumstances where gendered double standards have once again become undeniable in the Estonian social context. This cultural shift sends readers in search of textual interpretations, and they will find Woolf as one of the few feminist texts translated. In Estonia, where English is most people's second language, translations do important cultural work of bringing new questions to the local context and also of helping to make visible the important differences that remain.

The Estonian literary scene has canonised Woolf the modernist but, fittingly in the context described above, the lasting legacy of Woolf for Estonian feminism of the past decade is providing the name for the most popular feminist Facebook group, *Virginia Woolf sind ei karda* [Virginia Woolf is Not Afraid of You]. The group began in order to read and discuss feminist texts and evolved into a larger internet community that has, to this day, pursued its mission of furthering debate on a variety of issues related to gender and thereby fostering a communal sentiment. As such, the 'Woolf Group' (in Estonian, 'Virgina Woolf sind ei karda', usually shortened to 'Woolfi grupp'), as it is informally known in Estonia, seems to meet the Woolfian sense of the critical cosmopolitanism as a form of community building and value ambiguity at the same time. It is this engaged, open and at the same time affectively ambivalent form that works best in domesticating Woolf's contradictory version of feminism for the postsocialist Estonian context. Feminism may still be an intimidating Other (Marling 2010), but one that now has been translated into the Estonian language as well as the Estonian cultural space. These elements have created a truly constructive body of outsiders that has the potential to affect the public discourse more than a successful literary translation.

Acknowledgement

This work was supported by the Estonian Research Council (Grant PRG934, 'Imagining crisis ordinariness: Discourse, literature and image').

Notes

1. Itamar Even-Zohar uses the term 'polysystem' for this complex network of independent systems that act as a structured whole (1990).
2. This is not an exaggeration. Very few feminist classics have been translated into Estonian at the time of this writing: an abbreviated and problematic version of Simone de Beauvoir's *La deuxième sexe* (translated in 1997 by Mare Mauer and Anu Tõnnov as *Teine sugupool*), which among many other things lacks de Beauvoir's dialogue with Woolf; Julia Kristeva's *Pouvoirs de l'horreur* (translated in 2006 by Heete Sahkai as *Jälestuse jõud*); the collection *Feminist Contentions* (translated in 2006 by Merilin Sikk as *Feministlikud vaidlused*), edited by Linda Nicholson and containing essays by Seyla Benhabib, Judith Butler, Drucialla Cornell and Nancy Fraser; a collection of feminist art criticism; and a volume of Evelyn Fox Keller's essays on gender and science. Shorter essays have been published in different periodicals, including the peer-reviewed gender studies journal *Ariadne Lõng*. There is an introductory Estonian gender studies textbook and a keyword-based theory survey, translated from Finnish, as well as an essay collection by a local feminist journalist, to name texts that have been issued as independent volumes.
3. Woolf has in her writings stressed her own lack of proficiency in Greek – most famously in her 'On not knowing Greek' – but she actually studied Greek when she was enrolled in King's College, London (Dalgarno 2012: 2). In her translation of *Agamemnon*, however, she seems to have relied on a bilingual text by A. W. Verrall (Dalgarno 2012: 3). Dalgarno also shows that both Virginia and Leonard Woolf studied Russian with S. S. Koteliansky, whose translations from Russian Virginia also edited (2012: 70). Rebecca Beasley, on the basis of her study of manuscripts and typescripts, has shown how Virginia Woolf domesticated the Russian text for British audiences (2013).
4. The selection of essays appeared in the series by the Hortus Litterarum publisher that published literary classics prior to Woolf, including, for example Henry David Thoreau's *Walden*, a selection of Alexis de Tocqueville's *Democracy in America* and St Augustine's *Confessions*. In addition to *A Room of One's Own* the selection also includes essays from *The Common Reader*, *The Death of the Moth and Other Essays* and *The Moment and Other Essays*. The selections were made by the translators, Malle Talvet and Jaak Rähesoo.
5. The selection is drawn from *The Complete Shorter Fiction of Virginia Woolf* (London: Triad Grafton, 1987) and *The Death of the Moth and Other Essays* (London: Hogarth Press, 1942).
6. Censorship policies varied over years; for example, the translation of John Milton's *Areopagitica* was banned in 1972 and could not be published until 1987, when the Soviet regime was effectively over in Estonia (Lange and Monticelli 2013: 887).
7. In Woolf's lifetime, the editor of the most prominent Soviet journal of the same type, *Internacional'naja Literatura* [Foreign Literature], maintained contact with Woolf to publish her work, but without results (Safiullina and Platonov 2012: 258).
8. The Estonian original reads: 'Tema enda raamat on poleemilise teose kohta hämmastavalt kiledusvaba; siin välgub küll tihti irooniat, aga see on rahlik, enesekindel' (Woolf 1997: 271, translation mine).
9. The full phrase in the original: 'Küll oli temagi loomult nähtavasti biseksuaal, tundis ennast naiste seltsis koguni lahedalmalt, oli elu jooksul mitmesse naisesse tõsiselt kiindunud' (Woolf 1997: 268, translation mine).
10. This chapter uses the second edition of the translation by Talvet (Woolf 1997: 138–257).

Bibliography

Andringa, E. (2006), 'Penetrating the Dutch polysystem: The reception of Virginia Woolf, 1920–2000', *Poetics Today*, 27: 3, pp. 501–68.

Beasley, R. (2013), 'On not knowing Russian: The translations of Virginia Woolf and S. S. Kotelianskii', *The Modern Language Review*, 108: 1, pp. 1–19.

Bengoechea, M. (2011), 'Who are you, who are we in *A Room of One's Own*? The difference that sexual difference makes in Borges' and Rivera-Garretas's translations of Virginia Woolf', *European Journal of Women's Studies*, 18: 4, pp. 409–23.

Berman, J. (2015), 'Modernist cosmopolitanism', in G. Castle (ed.), *A History of the Modernist Novel*, Cambridge: Cambridge University Press, pp. 429–48.

Berman, J. (2001), *Modernist Fiction, Cosmopolitanism and the Politics of Community*, Cambridge: Cambridge University Press.

Brassard, G. (2016), 'Woolf in translation', in J. Berman (ed.), *A Companion to Virginia Woolf*, Malden, MA: John Wiley & Sons, Ltd, pp. 441–52.

Brassard, G. and M. Guénot-Hovnanian (2009), 'Colonizing an anti-imperialist text: Marguerite Yourcenar's rendering of *The Waves* into French', in R. Hackett, F. Hauser and G. Wachman (eds), *At Home and Abroad in the Empire: British Women Write the 1930s*, Newark: University of Delaware Press, pp. 137–53.

Brosnan, L. (1997), *Reading Virginia Woolf's Essays and Journalism*, Edinburgh: Edinburgh University Press.

Caws, M. A. and N. Luckhurst (eds) (2002), *The Reception of Virginia Woolf in Europe*, London: Continuum.

Chatterjee, C. (1999), 'Ideology, gender and propaganda in the Soviet Union', *New Left History*, 6: 2, pp. 11–28.

Dalgarno, E. (2012), *Virginia Woolf and the Migrations of Language*, Cambridge: Cambridge University Press.

Davison, C. (2015), 'Bilinguals and bioptics: Virginia Woolf and the outlandishness of translation', in J. Dubino, G. Lowe, V. Neverow and K. Simpson (eds), *Virginia Woolf: Twenty-First Century Approaches*, Edinburgh: Edinburgh University Press, pp. 73–90.

Davison, C. (2014), *Translation as Collaboration: Virginia Woolf, Katherine Mansfield and S. S. Koteliansky*, Edinburgh: Edinburgh University Press.

Dojčinović-Nešić, B. (2010), 'Translation as border-crossing: Virginia Woolf's case', *TRANS*, 9, <http://journals.openedition.org/trans/417> (last accessed 30 July 2018).

DuPlessis, R. B. (1988), 'Feminist narrative in Virginia Woolf', *Novel: A Forum on Fiction*, 21: 2/3, pp. 323–30.

Even-Zohar, I. (1990), 'The position of translated literature within the literary polysystem', *Poetics Today*, 11: 1, pp. 45–51.

Federici, E. and V. Leonardi (2012), 'Using and abusing gender in translation: The case of Virginia Woolf's *A Room of One's Own* translated into Italian', *Quadrens. Revista de Traducció*, 19, pp. 183–98.

Graff, A. (1999), 'The Polish Woolf', *Virginia Woolf Miscellany*, 54, p. 5.

Hite, M. (2017), *Woolf's Ambiguities: Tonal Modernism, Narrative Strategy, Feminist Precursors*, Ithaca, NY: Cornell University Press.

Hsieh, L. (2006), 'The other side of the picture: The politics of affect in Virginia Woolf's *Three Guineas*', *Journal of Narrative Theory*, 36: 1, pp. 20–52.

Koobak, R. (2018), 'Narrating feminisms: What do we talk about when we talk about feminism in Estonia', *Gender, Place & Culture: Journal of Feminist Geography*, <https://doi.org/10.1080/0966369X.2018.1471048> (last accessed 14 September 2018).

Koobak, R. and R. Marling (2014), 'The decolonial challenge: Framing post-socialist Central and Eastern Europe within transnational feminist studies', *European Journal of Women's Studies*, 21: 4, pp. 330–43.

Kurvet-Käosaar, L. (2005), 'Maternal spaces in the diaries of Aino Kallas, Virginia Woolf and Anaïs Nin', *Interlitteraria*, 10, pp. 260–79.

Lange, A. (2017), 'Editing in the conditions of state control in Estonia: The case of *Loomingu Raamatukogu* in 1957–1972', *Acta Slavonica Estonica*, 9, pp. 155–73.

Lange, A. and D. Monticelli (2013), 'Tõlkelised ebakõlad totalitarismi monoloogis. Järjepidevused, katkestused ja varjatud konfliktid Nõukogude Eesti tõlkeloos' [Translational dissonances in the totalitarian monologue. Continuities, discontinuities and hidden conflicts in Soviet Estonian translation history], *Keel ja Kirjandus*, 56: 12, pp. 881–99.

Luckhurst, N. (2002), 'Introduction', in M. A. Caws and N. Luckhurst (eds), *The Reception of Virginia Woolf in Europe*, London: Continuum, pp. 1–18.

Marcus, L. (2002), 'The European dimensions of the Hogarth Press', in M. A. Caws and N. Luckhurst (eds), *The Reception of Virginia Woolf in Europe*, London: Continuum, pp. 328–56.

Marling, R. (2010), 'The intimidating other: Feminist critical discourse analysis of the representation of feminism in Estonian print media', *Nora: Nordic Journal of Feminist and Gender Research*, 18: 1, pp. 7–19.

Põldsaar, R. (2006), 'Bewitched, bothered and bewildered: The reception of Virginia Woolf's feminist writing in Estonia', *Interlitteraria*, 11: 2, pp. 458–70.

Rähesoo, J. (1997), 'Virginia Woolf: Märksõnade valguses ja varjus' [Virginia Woolf: In the light and shadows of keywords], in *Esseed* [Essays], by V. Woolf, Tallinn: Hortus Litterarum, pp. 258–78.

Raterman, J. (2013), 'The novel of translation: Multilingualism and the ethics of reading', dissertation, State University of New Jersey, Rutgers.

Raterman, J. (2010), 'Reading from the outside: The uses of translation for Virginia Woolf's *Common Reader*', *Translation Studies*, 3: 1, pp. 78–93.

Reinhold, N. (ed.) (2004), *Woolf Across Cultures*, New York: Pace University Press.

Ross, J. (2018), *Aira Kaalust Mari Saadini. Nõukogude Eesti naisarenguromaan ja selle lugemisviisid* [From Aira Kaal to Mari Saat: The Soviet Estonian Female Bildungsroman and Its Reading Modes], Tartu: Tartu Ülikooli Kirjastus.

Safiullina, N. and R. Platonov (2012), 'Literary translation and Soviet cultural politics in the 1930s: The role of the journal *Internacional'naja Literatura*', *Russian Literature*, 72: 2, pp. 239–69.

Santaemilia, J. (2012), '*A Room of One's Own* in Spanish: From Borges to a feminist translation', in O. Palusci (ed.), *Translating Virginia Woolf*, Bern: Peter Lang, pp. 167–80.

Silver, B. (1991), 'The authority of anger: *Three Guineas* as case study', *Signs*, 16: 2, pp. 340–70.

Silver, B. (1999), *Virginia Woolf Icon*, Chicago: University of Chicago Press.

Sütiste, E. and M.-K. Lotman (2016), '"The translator must . . . ": On the Estonian translation poetics of the 20th century', *Interlitteraria*, 21: 1, pp. 17–34.

Terentowicz-Fotyga, U. (2002), 'From silence to a polyphony of voices: Virginia Woolf's reception in Poland', in M. A. Caws and N. Luckhurst (eds), *The Reception of Virginia Woolf in Europe*, London: Continuum, pp. 127–47.

Walkowitz, R. L. (2006), *Cosmopolitan Style: Modernism beyond Nation*, New York: Columbia University Press.

Walkowitz, R. L. (2013), 'For translation: Virginia Woolf, J. M. Coetzee, and transnational comparison', *English Language Notes*, 51: 1, pp. 35–50.

Watson, P. (1997), '(Anti)feminism after communism', in A. Oakley and J. Mitchell (eds), *Who's Afraid of Feminism?*, London: Penguin, pp. 144–61.

Woolf, V. (1953 [1925]), *The Common Reader*, New York: Harcourt, Brace and World.

Woolf, V. (1966 [1938]), *Three Guineas*, San Diego: Harcourt Brace Jovanovich.

Woolf, V. (1977), *The Letters of Virginia Woolf: Volume One: 1888–1912*, ed. N. Nicolson and J. Trautmann, New York: Harcourt Brace Jovanovich.

Woolf, V. (1983), *The Diary of Virginia Woolf, Volume Four: 1931–1935*, ed. A. O. Bell, Orlando, FL: Harcourt & Brace.

Woolf, V. (1994 [1929]), *Oma tuba* [*A Room of One's Own*], trans. M. Talvet, *Loomingu Raamatukogu* [Library of Creation], issues 44–5.

Woolf, V. (1997), *Esseed* [Essays], trans. M. Talvet and J. Rähesoo, Tallinn: Hortus Litterarum.
Woolf, V. (2000 [1929]), *A Room of One's Own*, London: Penguin Classics.
Woolf, V. (2013 [1972]), *Olemise hetked. Märkmed möödanikust* [*Moments of Being: A Sketch of the Past*], trans. K. Mits, *Loomingu Raamatukogu* [Library of Creation], issues 33–5.
Zdravomyslova, E. and A. Temkina (2012), 'The crisis of masculinity in late Soviet discourse', *Russian Studies in History*, 51: 2, pp. 13–34.
Ziarek, E. Płonowska (2010), 'Woolf's feminist aesthetics: On the political and artistic practice in *A Room of One's Own*', *Parallax*, 16: 4, pp. 70–82.

9

Virginia Woolf in Arabic: A Feminist Paratextual Reading of Translation Strategies

Hala Kamal

Introduction

THE FIRST TRANSLATIONS OF VIRGINIA WOOLF'S fiction into Arabic were her novels *To the Lighthouse* and *The Waves*, both published in Egypt in 1968. This interest in Woolf's fiction can be seen as a result of the critical attention that she received in Arabic cultural magazines and journals beginning in the 1960s. In February 1964, the Egyptian monthly *Al-Majalla* [The Journal], in a section titled 'Arab Magazines', published Al-Fiqi and Al-Awani's reviews of a number of literary articles published in different parts of the Arab world (in this case one magazine from Syria and two from Lebanon). In their review, they included a reference to an article by Ayman al-Amir titled 'Dirasa fi adab Virginia Woolf' [A study in Virginia Woolf's literature], published earlier in the Lebanese magazine *Al-Adāb* [Literatures], in which al-Amir provides an overview of Woolf to readers, shifting back and forth between her personal life and writings (Al-Amir 1964: 61–4). The following year, the first article written on Woolf was published in the Egyptian literary magazine *Al-Qiṣṣa* [The Story] within a series of articles on 'Prominent story writers in modern English literature'. Taha Mahmoud Taha's article 'A'lām al-Qiṣṣa fi al-adab al-injlīziyy al-ḥadīth: Virginia Woolf' [Famous figures of the story in modern English literature: Virginia Woolf] (1965) offers a brief literary biography of Woolf, in which he emphasises the similarities between her writing and that of James Joyce, repeatedly insisting that Joyce influenced Woolf. A year later, Ali Shalash published an article in the Egyptian cultural journal *Al-Fikr al-Mu'asir* [Contemporary Thought] titled 'Virginia Woolf and the stream of consciousness story' (1966), an article that similarly focused on her modernist literary technique.

In these writings, Woolf is considered within the framework of literary criticism and modernism; it was not until two decades later that an article acknowledging Woolf's feminism was published in the Syrian journal *Al-Mawqif Al-Adabi* [The Literary Position]. Syrian feminist academic and literary critic Buthaina Shaaban's article, titled 'Bayna al-adab al-nisa'iyy al-arabiyy wa al-adab al-nisa'iyy al-injlīziyy: Ghada Al-Samman wa Virginia Woolf' [Between Arab women's literature and English women's literature: Ghada Al-Samman and Virginia Woolf] (1986), offers a comparative study of the two women writers at a time that preceded the development of feminist critical approaches to literature in the Arab world. Shaaban's article is not only significant in its representation of Woolf's feminism; it also, and perhaps even more importantly, stands out as one of one of the first to discuss the issue of a women's literary tradition, or *al-adab al-nisa'iyy* (women's literature), in early Arabic literary criticism. The point of Shaaban's analysis is her contention that instead of asserting their feminism, both Al-Samman and Woolf seem to embrace androgyny through their emphasis that human beings have elements of both masculinity and femininity – an idea introduced by Woolf and adopted by Al-Samman as a way of asserting their presence in the male-dominated literary mainstream (Shaaban 1986: 66–7). Neither writer was actively involved in feminist protests or political circles, but they both devoted their lives to feminist thought and values in writing and raised questions about the gendered roles of women in their societies. Still, Shaaban's article reveals, at times, her inaccurate knowledge of Woolf's life and writing as she accuses Woolf of failing to establish relationships with women, even though she had many strong connections with women. She further suggests that Woolf's writings were almost totally dominated by her concern with the experience of war, which is a very limited understanding of Woolf, whose writings express her pacifist, anti-fascist views in addition to her feminist ideology and modernist technique.

This chapter, however, is not concerned with the critical reception of Woolf's work in the Arab world; instead it focuses on Woolf's representation through the translation of her writings into Arabic, and, thus, offers a feminist critique of the strategies used in translating Woolf's work into Arabic. The study opens with a historical overview of Woolf's works translated into Arabic followed by a discussion of critical approaches to translated texts from a feminist perspective, with particular emphasis on the significance of paratextual analysis. The last section focuses on Virginia Woolf's *A Room of One's Own* as a case study of the translation of Woolf into Arabic. Finally, I conclude by highlighting the ethical dimensions embedded in translation strategies related to Virginia Woolf and feminist texts more generally.

Virginia Woolf in Arabic: A Historical Perspective

The history of Woolf in Arabic can be defined in terms of two historical periods: the 1960s and the 1990s. Both of these periods mark an interest in a specific aspect of Woolf's writings. In the 1960s, critics and scholars were interested in introducing Woolf to an Arab audience as a modernist writer, which ultimately affected the selection of the texts to be translated and available. This came at a moment when Arabic literature was developing beyond the first generation of the Arabic novel which had emerged at the beginning of the twentieth century and was marked by its realism, depiction of Egyptian society and imitation of the nineteenth-century Western and Victorian form of the novel. The 1960s witnessed the rise of a new phase in Arabic fiction that was characterised by postcolonial and postmodern concerns and techniques. In the 1990s, with the emergence of the third wave of feminism in Egypt, Woolf came to life again in Egypt and the Arab world through the translation of *A Room of One's Own*, as well as the re-translation of some of her novels.

The Waves was Virginia Woolf's first novel to be translated into Arabic. It was published in Cairo as *Al-Amwaj* and translated by Murad Al-Zumur, followed by a later edition in 1968 by the same translator (Woolf n.d.; 1968a). A more recent translation by Atta Abdel Wahab was published in Beirut in 2009. Similarly, *To the Lighthouse* was published in Cairo for the first time in 1968, translated by Girgis

Mansi as *Al-Manar* [The Lighthouse] (Woolf 1968b); it was recently republished in Cairo in 2015 and translated by Izabel Kamal as *Ila al-Fanar* [To the Lighthouse]. Following the early translations of Woolf's novels, her critical articles and literary essays collected in *The Common Reader* were published in Arabic under the title *Al-Qari' al-'Adiyy* (Woolf 1971). The names of three women appear on its front cover, as the text was written by Woolf, translated by Aqila Ramadan and edited by Saheir Al-Qalamawy. The publications of these two novels and the collection of critical essays that explored Woolf's thoughts on literature over time and her modernist manifesto, 'Modern fiction', can be seen as part of an Arabic general interest in Woolf's development of modernist fictional techniques, especially that of stream of consciousness.

The late 1980s and early 1990s were marked by the emergence of the feminist movement in the Arab world and the rise of the third generation of writers in the Arab world, which included the appearance of women writers who have since been defined as the '1990s Generation'. During this period, Woolf was now being revisited and translated not merely as a modernist writer but, more importantly, as a woman writer. It was in this socio-literary context that Woolf's translations were republished, while her other novels started appearing in Arabic. *Flush: A Biography* was translated by Atta Abdel-Wahab and published in Iraq in 1992. This was followed by *Mrs Dalloway*, translated by Abd al-Karim Mahfud and published in Syria (Woolf 1994); another translation by Atta Abdel Wahab was published in 1998 in Lebanon. The most recent translation of Woolf's novels was *Orlando*, which was translated by Tawfiq Al-Asadi and published in 2016 in Iraq, with distributors in Egypt, Lebanon and Syria.

From this publication history, we find that the translation of fictional work has been performed by men, mostly professional literary translators; while on the other hand, as mentioned above, Woolf's critical writings were translated by academic women. This gender division in publication corresponds with the marked separation in Egyptian receptions of her work between those who read and wrote about Woolf the modernist author or Woolf the feminist critic. Only two of Woolf's nonfiction books were translated into Arabic and published in Egypt: *The Common Reader* and *A Room of One's Own*. The former, as previously mentioned, was translated in the context of modernist writing. The polemic *A Room of One's Own*, on the other hand, was introduced in the context of women's and feminist writing within a national translation initiative, translated by Somaya Ramadan and published in Cairo by the Egyptian Supreme Council for Culture in 1999, and then republished commercially in Cairo in 2009 (Woolf 2009b). Another edition of *A Room of One's Own* appeared in Syria in 2017 and was translated by Ahd Subiha; it seems to offer an edited version of Ramadan's translation (Woolf 2017). However, in his translation, Subiha does not include an introduction or preface, unlike Ramadan, who included an introduction in which she situated Woolf as both modernist writer and, more importantly, as a prominent feminist thinker.

The publication of *A Room of One's Own* brought Woolf back to literary discussions in Egypt; thus, over the past two decades, several translations of her books, by different translators, were published by state-owned bodies. However, during this time there were additional translations of her short story collections rather than single short stories, novels and essays. In 2004, *Juyub Muthqala bil-Hijara wa 'Riwaya lam Tuktab Ba'd'* [Pockets Heavy with Stones and 'An Unwritten Novel'], was translated by Egyptian author Fatima Naoot (Woolf 2009c). This publication, however, does not simply offer a translation of one of Woolf's books; alongside her translation of 'An unwritten novel', Naoot includes a long imaginary conversation between herself and Woolf. Naoot also translated *Athar 'ala al-Ha'it* [A Mark on the Wall] in 2009 (Woolf 2009a); this collection included the title short story and a selection of other stories of Naoot's choosing, rather than offering the translation of, for example, *The Mark on the Wall and Other Short Fiction* edited by David Bradshaw (Woolf 2008a). Laila Othman Nagaty produced a translation of Woolf's *Monday or Tuesday* (1921) which appeared in Arabic as *Al-Ithnayn aw al-Thulatha' (Wa Qisas Ukhra)* [*Monday or Tuesday (and Other Stories)*] (Woolf 2008b). The publication does not specify which edition of Woolf's collection was translated, as there have been several editions published in the UK and the USA, all of which include the same eight short stories, six of which appeared in another short story collection entitled *A Haunted House and Other Stories* (1944) (Woolf 2002). Nagaty, in turn, simply adds a selection of Woolf's stories that were neither included in *Monday or Tuesday* nor in *A Haunted House* so that while the original English edition is composed of eight texts, the Arabic version includes eighteen short stories.

This historical overview of Woolf in translation into Arabic carries significant socio-political implications. First, the translation of Woolf's works in Arabic began decades after their original publications and is most likely attributed to the fact that, as part of the Anglophone literary canon, Woolf had only started receiving attention in the Arab world with the rising critical interest in modernist writing techniques. Thus, her books were introduced as part of the literary and critical endeavour to introduce literary modernism to Arab readers.[1] Second, the publications point to the main centres of translation from English into Arabic and publishing in general in the Arab world since the 1970s onwards: Baghdad, Beirut, Damascus and Cairo. This indicates the widespread interest in Woolf's writing across the Arab world and opens up untrodden paths in Arabic literary criticism about the influence Woolf had as a modernist writer on Arabic literature. Lastly, the translation of Woolf's works into Arabic raises questions regarding the roles of translators as mediators, translation strategies, Woolf's representation in these translated versions and more general issues related to the emerging intersection of feminist theory and translation.

A Feminist Approach to Translation Criticism

Feminist Translation

Emerging as an approach in translation studies, feminist translation has been developing since the late 1980s and through the 1990s (e.g. Godard 1988; Flowton 1997), and it marks one of the dimensions of the cultural turn in translation studies. The politics of translation, for instance, can be identified in the power relations between the text and the translation in terms of their respective historical moments and cultural contexts. Furthermore, scholars may consider the dynamics between the author and translator in terms of an act of mediation influenced by the translator's ideology and intentional visibility in the text through the process of translation. Feminist translation theory, however, is not limited to the practice of translation; it is also the praxis where translation processes are informed by feminist theory. Hence the study of feminists in translation, women translators and feminist discourse lies at the heart of feminist translation. In light of the fact that globally few translations of feminist writing (including that of Woolf) have been conducted by feminist translators, which has led to many mistranslations of feminist texts, my concern here is focused on feminist translation as critical practice and analysing translations of Woolf's works into Arabic from a feminist perspective.

Virginia Woolf in Translation

Although feminist translation theory and practice remains a nascent area in Arabic translation studies, there are several discussions of Woolf's work in translation to other European languages. Jorge Luis Borges's translation of *Orlando* into Spanish in 1937 is one of the earliest translations of Woolf's fiction discussed through the lens of gender. Jhonny Alexander Calle Orozco contends that instead of highlighting Woolf's notion of androgyny in the novel, Borges's translation carries his patriarchal attitude in contradiction to the author's text which 'dispels the confrontation between sexes' (Calle Orozco 2013: 448). Borges's translation strategies, for example, include the repeated replacement of the gender-marked pronouns 'he' and 'she' by the proper masculine noun 'Orlando'. In addition, Borges adapted the form of the novel to fit the popular Latin American literary genre of the fantastic (2013: 450–3) by highlighting, for example, the temporal unrealistic shifts in time and place to create a sense of magic-realist descriptions of setting in general. Borges's gender position as a writer and translator can be traced in his other writings which 'are characterized by an exacerbation of ... masculinity, highlighted also by a Creole-macho writing style' (2013: 449). And his anti-feminist position can be specifically identified in his translation of Woolf which 'constitutes a critical commentary on the author, text and context, through open intervention' (2013: 450). This intervention in the translation of *Orlando*, Calle Orozco argues, is 'covert sexism' (2013: 453); instead of expressing his anti-feminist stance in his own writing, Borges manages to reinforce patriarchal ideology indirectly in his short stories – notably in his early writing such as *Ficciones* (1956) and in his later writing such as in *The Book of Sand* (1975) – as well as in his (mis)translation, and hence misrepresentation, of the author's intention.

In their study of *A Room of One's Own*, Eleonora Federici and Vanessa Leonardi seek to identify feminist strategies in three Italian translations of the book. Federici and Leonardi acknowledge the significance of paratextual elements in translated texts and, therefore, focus their analysis on such elements as 'explanatory introduction' and footnotes as a sign of the translator's active presence in the text where they can highlight and explain Woolf's feminism to their Italian readership (2012: 189–90). Their study offers a comparative examination of the linguistic and cultural aspects involved in translating *A Room of One's Own* through selections of lexical items and pronouns. It is worth noting here that the three translations in Italian opt for the same phrasing of the title: *Una stanza tutta per sé*, which maintains the impersonal pronoun 'one' (rather than the personal pronoun she or he); in English, the pronoun 'one' is neutral, while in other languages such as Italian (and Arabic) the impersonal pronoun itself is gendered, taking feminine and masculine forms. Thus, there is variation in the translation of the same pronoun appearing within the text in its three translations into Italian; in some cases the sentences including the word 'one' are restructured in translation whereby words related to this impersonal pronoun take the traditional generic masculine forms instead of the feminine ones (2012: 193). Federici and Leonardi reach the conclusion that the three translations rely on 'traditional or canonical translation strategies', such as using generic masculine forms, instead of neutralising or feminising the translation in a way that corresponds and contributes to the author's feminist intention (2012: 197).

Virginia Woolf in Arabic

Very few studies have been conducted on Woolf in translation into Arabic. This can be attributed to the fact that feminist literary criticism and translation studies as critical practice, let alone feminist translation criticism, are not yet well developed in Arab writing. The earliest is Reuven Snir's short article 'Virginia Woolf in Arabic literature: Translations influence and reception' (1999), in which he is concerned with Woolf's modernist influence on Arabic literature, rather than her feminist impact. Snir comments on the translators' footnotes where they explain literary features, figures and genres (such as the sonnet), as well as their interventions in Arabicising certain words (such as Sirens) and in other features such as combining paragraphs, omitting sentences and adding subtitles within the chapters of the novels (1999: 5–6). A more recent and elaborate study of Woolf in translation is Paola Viviani's '"Acting like a thief": Fatimah Na'ut[2] translates Virginia Woolf in Egypt' (2012), where she states her interest in Woolf 'as a woman and a writer, as a feminist and as a feminist writer', which she follows with a comprehensive list of Woolf's works, fictional and nonfictional, translated and published in Egypt since the 1960s (2012: 147). Viviani outlines how early translations of Woolf in Egypt focused on her work in the context of modernism, while the revival of interest in Woolf's work in Egypt since the 1990s coincides with the development of the Egyptian feminist movement and the emergence of a new generation of writers, known as the 'Generation of the nineties' (2012: 152). The study focuses on Fatimah Naoot's translation of 'An unwritten novel' (1920); apart from her concern with the technical rendering of Woolf's style and literary technique, Viviani suggests that Naoot employs a conscious intervention in the text by establishing a female voice as narrator and allowing the protagonist, Minnie Marsh, to appropriate the narrator's neutral voice in the original text (2012: 155). It is worth noting in this context that while attention has been given to Woolf's modernist literary technique, no one has addressed the process and impact of the translation of Woolf's feminist *A Room of One's Own* and *Three Guineas*. *Three Guineas* is widely regarded as a feminist masterpiece equal to *A Room of One's Own* and has yet to be translated into Arabic.

Paratextual Intersections

With the growth of feminist translation studies, much attention has been directed to the translation strategies used by feminist translators, the most prominent of which have been defined by Luise von Flotow in terms of prefacing, footnoting, supplementing and hijacking (Flotow 1991). Although these practices are recognised strategies in general translation studies, it is through feminist translation theory that these strategies gain significance as they offer space for feminist intervention. This intervention takes many forms as feminist translators make themselves and their translation strategies visible in the text, explaining their choices, elaborating on the feminist concepts and figures mentioned in the text and defining their innovative coinages in translating feminist terminology. Prefacing and footnoting are two powerful spaces for intervention not only in translation but generally in authorship and publication. These translation strategies informed Gérard Genette's attention to paratextual aspects in literary criticism, as explained in his *Paratexts* (1987), translated into English in 1997. Paratextuality, Genette outlines, is a critical approach that

> compris[es] those liminal devices and conventions, both within the book (peritext) and outside it (epitext), that mediate the book to the reader: titles and subtitles, pseudonyms, forewords, dedications, epigraphs, prefaces, intertitles, notes, epilogues, and afterwords ... but also the elements in the public and private history of the book. (1997: xviii)

Although Genette's analysis does not include translations, his final chapter states that translation is one of 'three practices whose paratextual relevance seems undeniable' (1997: 405). Literary critics perceive the translated version of a particular text as a paratext (specifically an epitext) of the original. Critical approaches within translation studies, however, deal with the translated text itself as the main text rather than an epitext of another text. Moreover, those working within translation might possibly consider the original text itself as an epitext in addition to the other paratextual elements (prefaces, footnotes, glossaries) included within the translated version itself.

Kathryn Batchelor's recent edited collection *Translation and Paratexts* (2018) shifts the earlier attention in literary criticism from translation as paratext to studying the paratexts of translation. She argues that 'the most widely studied type of paratext is the translator's preface', which is a 'peritextual' element included within the book, but she also refers to 'epitextual material such as a translator's memoirs', which is an autobiographical account of a translator's experience as a translator (2018: 26). What remains missing throughout Batchelor's collection is a feminist lens in paratextual reading of translated texts. Her analysis does not carry the perspective of a feminist translation critic, nor does she pay attention to Barbara Godard's notion of 'womanhandling', in her groundbreaking article 'Theorizing feminist discourse/translation' (1988). It is here that Godard briefly lays the foundation of 'feminist translation' as theory and practice, and where she identifies it as a practice of 'womanhandling':

> The feminist translator, affirming her critical difference, her delight in interminable re-reading and re-writing, flaunts the signs of her manipulation of the text. *Womanhandling* the text in translation would involve the replacement of the modest, self-effacing translator. Taking her place would be an active participant in the creation of meaning who advances a conditional analysis. . . . The feminist translator immodestly flaunts her signature in italics, in footnotes – even in a preface. (1995: 94)

Godard actively advocates for the feminist translator to leave her mark on the process of translation within the text itself, through italics and footnotes, and in her framing at the beginning of the text in the preface, asserting her visibility and agency.

Feminist translation as praxis (practice informed by theory) is situated at the intersection of feminism, translation and criticism, giving particular attention to the use of paratextual analysis in translation criticism. One of the earliest paradigms of this can be found in Flotow's 'Feminist translation: Contexts, practices and theories' (1991) in which she establishes 'supplementing, prefacing and footnoting, and "hijacking"' as feminist translation strategies' (1991: 74). Flotow shows that supplementing is a common practice in translation and points out its feminist dimension by which feminist translators are 'conscious of [their] political role as . . . mediator[s]' and, as a consequence, how they tend 'to reflect on their [own] work in a preface, and to stress their active presence in the text in footnotes' (1991: 75, 76). She also recognises, conversely, the process of 'hijacking' as a political act of feminisation and appropriation, whereby feminist translators appropriate a non-feminist text and reproduce it in translation to reflect their feminist ideology. These strategies can be closely connected to the notions of visibility/invisibility pertinent to both feminism and translation studies (Venuti 1995), in relation to the translation of feminist discourse.[3] Lawrence Venuti proposed the translator's visibility in the text as a means to reverse earlier attitudes that viewed translation practices as invisible acts meant to maintain the position of the author and marginalise the role of translator as simply mediator and co-producer of meaning in a different language and cultural context. Both Godard and Flotow emphasise the role of the translator as mediator and, more specifically, the role of the feminist translator as mediator of a feminist position. These paratextual paradigms not only offer a prescriptive model for feminist translators, they also provide feminist critics with an analytical approach when they are dealing with feminist texts in translation. This is particularly useful when considering Woolf's translation into Arabic, where my concern is with the extent to which Woolf's feminist thought and discourse have been preserved in translation.

A Room of One's Own in Arabic

A Room of One's Own (1929) was not translated into Arabic until 1999, when Somaya Ramadan published her translation under the title *Ghurfa Takhussu al-Mar' Wahdahu* (Woolf 2009b). It was published by the Egyptian Supreme Council for Culture (Ministry of Culture) under the umbrella of the National Translation Project, which promoted the translation of a number of feminist books.[4] These publications were promoted alongside an international conference on Qasim Amin, the Egyptian thinker and propagator of women's rights, who wrote two books published in Egypt at the turn of the twentieth century – *The Liberation of Women* (1899) and *The New Woman* (1900)[5] – in which he called for women's liberation within the national liberation project. A second edition of Ramadan's translation appeared in 2009, published by the private publisher Madbouly Books. Recently, another translation with identical phrasing of Ramadan's title was published by Ninawa, a private publisher in Syria, translated by Ahd Subiha (Woolf 2017). The remainder of this chapter examines these three translations of *A Room of One's Own* through discussions of the paratextual aspects of each text. I particularly focus on the elements that involve translators' rather than publishers' decisions; namely, the translation of the title of the book, the translators' footnotes and the introductions. The analysis is thus informed by Flotow's feminist translation strategies of supplementing, footnoting and prefacing.

The Title: The Problem with 'One'

Ramadan's translated titled of *A Room of One's Own* in Arabic is *Ghurfa Takhussu al-Mar' Wahdahu* (the literal backward translation[6] is 'A Room Belonging to Oneself Alone'). In its Arabic version, the title sounds odd. Alternatively, Maher Shafik Farid, in his preface to another translation of Woolf's work,[7] refers to *A Room of One's Own* as *Ghurfa Khassa* (Farid 2009: 12), which through backward translation becomes 'A Private Room'. Farid argues that Ramadan's choice of the word 'mar' as an equivalent to the impersonal pronoun 'one' in Woolf's original title is inaccurate since in Arabic this impersonal pronoun is grammatically masculine (2009: 16). Farid's reading of Ramadan's translated title is further supported by the last word in the Arabic title 'wahdahu' (the equivalent of 'own'), which acts as a qualifier of 'mar' (one) that is also grammatically masculine. He adds that instead of a literal translation of Woolf's title, his suggested title reflects the main point in her book: that a 'talented woman needs a private room of her own and an annual income that guarantees her devotion to writing' (2009: 16, translation mine).[8] Despite Farid's valid criticism of the title, it is interesting to note that the third edition of *A Room of One's Own*, translated by Ahd Subiha and published in Syria in 2017, uses the same title as Ramadan's translation. However, before the publication of Ramadan's translation, articles published on Woolf in Arabic hardly make any mention of *A Room of One's Own*;[9] and, as such, Ramadan's phrasing of the title has been established as the common usage in Arabic.

Ramadan herself was obviously aware of the untranslatability of the title of the book. In her 'Introduction' to the translation, she explains her phrasing of the title as a desire to maintain Woolf's intentional ambiguity and generalisation in the English title conveyed through the use of the impersonal pronoun 'one'. The other alternatives that Ramadan considered included a title which would be backward translated as 'My Own Room', which implies that it refers to Woolf only and not to women writers in general (Ramadan 1999: 12–13). Ramadan also explains her insertion of the word 'takhussu' ('belonging') in the title, arguing that by including it in the title, she opted for the more common phrasing in Arabic which emphasises ownership rather than the more canonical literal one, which also adds to the notion of privacy and ownership implied in the English original (1999: 12–13). She further justifies her translation of the impersonal pronoun 'one' as 'mar', which although grammatically masculine in Arabic still remains contextually impersonal and not directly masculine ('his') in common usage; nor does she choose to replace the impersonal pronoun 'one' (which in Arabic implies 'man') with the word 'woman' since Woolf herself did not choose to title her book 'A Woman's Room' (1999: 13). She concludes her point by quoting from the most canonical Arabic language dictionary, *Lisan al-Arab*, which states that 'al-mar' is 'human being' without reference to gender (1999: 13).

It is worth noting, however, that the word 'one' is repeatedly used throughout *A Room of One's Own*. In the long opening paragraph of the text, Woolf writes:

> At any rate, when a subject is highly controversial – and any question about sex is that – *one* cannot hope to tell the truth. *One* can only show how *one* came to hold whatever opinion *one* does hold. *One* can only give *one*'s audience the chance of drawing their own conclusions as they observe the limitations, the prejudices, the idiosyncrasies of the speaker. (*AROO*: 2; emphasis added)

The word 'one', which appears six times in this selected passage, appears only twice in Ramadan's version. Moreover, it is translated in the first instance as 'mar' (identical to the title), whereas it is replaced by 'insān' (human being) in another sentence.[10] If translated backwards, this is how the passage would be phrased:

> At any rate, when a subject is highly controversial – and everything about sex is that – it becomes difficult to hope to tell the truth. One can only express in this case the way (he) reached forming a specific opinion. It becomes only possible for the human being then to give (his) audience the chance of drawing their (masculine) own opinion as they (masculine) observe (his) stylistic prejudices and limitations. (Woolf 1999: 16, back translation mine)[11]

The passage, in this phrasing, raises several issues. First, it is clear here that Ramadan is not fully comfortable with the use of 'mar' as an equivalent of 'one', and therefore resorts to the omission of the word in the Arabic version, employing instead an alteration between 'al-mar' and 'al-insān', without affecting the structure or meaning of her text. When she feels the need for an equivalent phrasing for 'one', she uses 'human being' instead. Second, since Arabic language is gendered, the verbs 'reached' and 'give', the possessive pronoun qualifying the nouns 'audience' and 'style', as well as the pronoun 'their', all require grammatically gendered qualifiers. In this case, because of the use of 'mar' and 'insān', which are masculine words in Arabic, all their qualifiers necessarily take on the masculine form as well. Thus, reading this passage in Arabic (without awareness of the context) implies that the whole situation Woolf is describing concerns a man, not a woman.

In this sense, the gender ambiguity created in Woolf's original text through the use of 'one' is not maintained in Ramadan's translation. On the contrary, instead of suggesting Woolf's notion of androgynous human identity, Ramadan's translation shatters gender ambiguity by grammatically fixing masculinity over femininity. It is important to remember that Woolf wrote *A Room of One's Own* originally as a shorter series of lectures that were given at women's colleges at the University of Cambridge: Newham College and Girton College. And this passage from the opening of the published text was given as part of those lectures; thus, the feminine identity of both speaker and audience is established in the English version. The use of ambiguous words such as 'one' can be easily perceived as referring to women in the context of how Woolf first delivered these words. This context gets lost in the Arabic text, where the sense of orality and the context is removed, thus reinforcing the masculinity inherent in Ramadan's word selection lexically, syntactically and semantically. This is a case of supplementing and omitting in translation studies that ends up taking away rather than adding to the feminism of Woolf's text in Arabic translation. If feminist translation strategies were to be used here, then the supplementation of the feminine would be the norm, whereby the feminist translator would then add a footnote explaining the strategy of choosing feminine word forms to represent gender ambiguity in Woolf's feminist text, and perhaps connect it to the history of the college lectures and Woolf's notion of androgyny.

Footnoting: The Absence of Feminist Annotation

Both Ramadan and Subiha include footnotes to the original text in their translations of *A Room of One's Own*. Ramadan offers two sets of footnotes, as she explains in her introduction, having kept Woolf's original footnotes numbered throughout the text and inserting her own footnotes preceded by an asterisk instead of a number. Subiha, on the other hand, includes both his and Woolf's notes numbered at the bottom of every page without distinction in the numbering sequence, following each footnote with the identity of the writer between brackets: '(Woolf)' or '(the translator)'. It is worth noting that Woolf includes a total of eleven footnotes in the text, mostly identifying the sources of her quotes; both translators, however, add numerous additional footnotes of their own. Ramadan's notes mostly offer information to her Arab audience pertaining to the British names mentioned in the text; for example, she explains the identity of 'Miss Mitford', 'George Eliot' and 'Mrs Gaskell' (Ramadan 1999: 15). In other instances, Ramadan provides, in her footnotes, contextual information, such as the fact that Oxbridge refers to an imaginary university derived from the names of the two 'glorious' universities of Oxford and Cambridge (1999: 16), the function of the Beadle and the identities of the authors of quotes and texts cited in the book. Subiha's translation uses footnotes extensively, including all of Ramadan's original footnotes, as well as additional ones in which he explains the names of places and geographical locations. Yet neither translator uses footnotes to explain the translation problems they face or the choices they make linguistically and grammatically, nor are they used to highlight feminist dimensions in Woolf's text.

In this sense, Ramadan's footnoting follows the conventional use of footnotes in translation and does not engage its potential as a feminist translation strategy. Footnoting as a feminist strategy would have, for example, elaborated on the significance of women writers to the rise of the novel in general and the Victorian novel in particular. It also would have been useful to be as inclusive as possible and provide footnotes for every woman mentioned by Woolf in her text, instead of dropping some less known figures to an Arab readership, such as the writer Rebecca West and Woolf's fictional protagonist Mary Carmichael. It could have also been useful to further explain the conditions of women's education at the turn of the century to Arab readers who most likely do not know when women enrolled in universities in England or the events of the suffrage movement. Another point worthy of commentary would have been Woolf's reflections on gender identity in Chapter 6, where she refers to androgynous minds and formulates the hyphenated identities of the 'man-womanly' and 'woman-manly' (*AROO*: 84–5), which are rendered in Arabic without any further explanation as to what Woolf was suggesting through these constructions.

Prefacing: Feminist Translation Praxis

The first page of Subiha's translation includes the original title of the book, its author and publication date. There is no preface or introduction; instead the translation opens with a one-paragraph biographical note on Woolf, followed by her first footnote from the original text in which she details that this 'essay' is based on two papers, selections of which were read to the students at Newnham College and Girton College in 1928 (*AROO*: 1). The brief biographical note identifies Woolf as an English novelist and essayist, followed by a list of her works with their publication dates and concludes with a statement about her suicidal drowning to save herself from another potential mental breakdown (Woolf 2017: 4). Interestingly, this brief biographical sketch does not carry the translator's name at the end and, thus, could easily be a publisher's rather than translator's note. Ramadan, on the other hand, opens her translation with an 'Introduction' which consists of three sections: 'Virginia Woolf', 'This book' and 'The translation' (Ramadan 1999). Although she keeps the content of her 'Introduction' the same in the second edition, the structure is changed, beginning with 'This book', followed by 'Virginia Woolf in a few lines' (with a slight title change) and concluding with 'The translation' (Ramadan 2009). No explanation is given for this change, nor is any reference made to the earlier edition.

As for the 'Introduction' itself, Ramadan's first edition begins with biographical information under the subtitle 'Virginia Woolf', which details her birth, family, life, work, marriage and writings. The section also provides, for the first time to Arab readers, information about Woolf's support of women's suffrage and her engagement with the emerging feminist movement. It is also the first time that the representation of her cultural life is not restricted to the circle of Bloomsbury or other modernist writers, as Ramadan makes a specific mention of Woolf's presence at Fabian Society gatherings and feminist conferences (Ramadan 1999: 7). It is also the first time where an account of her mental illness[12] is given, and a detailed description of her suicide with an excerpt from her suicide note is included. Thus, unlike most earlier representations of Woolf, Ramadan highlights her feminism and suffering, providing supporting quotations from Quentin Bell's *Virginia Woolf: A Biography* as well as from *The Letters of Virginia Woolf*.

In the next section entitled 'This book', Ramadan gives tribute to Woolf and *A Room of One's Own*, describing it as a 'manifesto of the feminist critical movement in the twentieth century' and linking Woolf to the next generation of feminist critics such as Kate Millet, Germaine Greer, Marilyn French, Julia Kristeva and Hélène Cixous (1999: 9). Ramadan also connects the first wave of the feminist movement to the ideologies of the French Revolution in Europe and the end of slavery in the USA. This wave coincided historically with the decolonisation movement in the Arab world, where the first wave of the Egyptian feminist movement was closely connected to the national struggle for independence from the British occupation.[13] She also refers to Mary Wollstonecraft's *A Vindication of the Rights of Woman* (1792) in an attempt to establish a continuum of women's activism for their rights to education and political representation, among other rights. This section highlights for readers Woolf's main argument about women's writing: her questions about women's life before the eighteenth century, the lack of women's colleges and the scarcity of women's writing; the relationship between women, creativity and madness; and the constructions of masculinity and femininity discussed in her notion of androgyny (1999: 10–11). This reflection by Ramadan reveals the relevance of Woolf's questions today and the importance of providing present-day readers (both women and men) in the Arab world with Woolf's views on feminist criticism, the feminist movement and gender issues. In connecting Woolf's views to Arab contemporary discourses on modernity and coloniality in relation to women's lives and their rights, Ramadan concludes that *A Room of One's Own* can guide Arab and Egyptian feminists towards establishing a history of their own through an investigation of the history of the Egyptian movement since the end of the nineteenth century (1999: 12).

The final section, 'The translation', offers Ramadan's commentary on the translation process itself. She begins with an explanation of the ambiguity in the English title of the book. She then justifies her choices in the translation of the title, as previously detailed above, and clarifies her annotation system, whereby she occasionally inserts a bracketed explanatory word or phrase immediately after a concept that might not be familiar to an Arab reader. However, she also notes that she has avoided using in-text original words in the Roman alphabet between brackets – which has become a convention of Arab translation in cases of untranslatability – except when mentioning titles of works and books that have not been translated into Arabic. Another point that Ramadan addresses in this section is how challenging it is to try to maintain Woolf's style and stream-of-consciousness technique, which involves frequent usage of the passive voice that is difficult to translate into Arabic due to its grammatical conventions (1999: 14).

In both editions, Ramadan's 'Introduction' to her translation of *A Room of One's Own* presents a feminist paratextual intervention and marks the first direct and detailed representation in Arabic of Woolf foremost as a feminist followed by Woolf as a modernist. By including information of Woolf's engagement in the feminist movement and her contribution to feminist literary criticism, Ramadan introduces Woolf not only as a feminist writer and thinker, she also emphasises the existence of a women's literary and critical tradition for Arab readers. Furthermore, Ramadan's 'Introduction' carries a political message that reveals her own feminism and intentional propagation of feminist ideology through translation. As a feminist, she highlights Woolf's feminism over her modernism and situates the global history of feminism along parallel lines, connecting Woolf's reflections on women's history and writing in *A Room of One's Own* with the history of the Egyptian women's movement. Finally, Ramadan's 'Introduction' offers the first discussion of the problematics of translation, something Arabic translators seldom reflect on within the publications of their works. As such, Ramadan is revealed through her supplementary material as an informed translator, whose translation of Woolf unfolds as feminist praxis; and in translating Woolf's feminist manifesto into Arabic, Ramadan can also be seen as being actively engaged in producing a feminist text and knowledge in Arabic.

Conclusion: On the Ethics of Feminist Translation

In his insightful article 'The task of the translator' (1921), Walter Benjamin defines the translator's duty in terms of 'finding the particular intention toward the target language which produces in that language the echo of the original' (2002: 258), whereby the purpose of translation is not to achieve the traditional value of 'fidelity' understood as the 'faithful reproduction' of meaning (2002: 259).[14] Instead, the governing value is that of the 'translatability' of the original text, in the sense of its linguistic clarity (2002: 262). In a more recent discussion of ethical aspects in translation, Andrew Chesterman charts out four fundamental ethical values in translation: clarity, truth, trust and understanding (1997). Both Benjamin and Chesterman, however, are focused on translation as linguistic exercise, whereas the cultural turn in translation studies has shifted the attention from the strict linguistic elements of translation to contextual, cultural and historical considerations. In recognition of the intersectionality of translation practice with cultural studies, literary theory and ethics, Sandra Bermann states the importance of both cultural knowledge and linguistic competency as primary factors in translation ethics. In her introduction to *Nation, Language, and the Ethics of Translation*, Bermann notes: 'Translators have long agreed that the effort to render one language system into another requires a keen awareness of broad cultural as well as specific linguistic values' (2005: 5). Rosemary Arrojo explains the shift from the traditional notions of faithfulness and communication to the contemporary notions of construction, whereby she calls for an 'ethics of difference' in which 'translation can no longer be conceived in terms of an impersonal transportation of stable meaning across different languages, cultures, and contexts, but is recognized, instead, as a form of transformation' (2013: 3). She calls for an acknowledgement of the 'translator's intervention'; hence 'it would actually be unethical and irresponsible for translators to insist on hiding behind claims of neutrality or to wash their hands of the responsibilities involved in the highly complex and influential work they do' (2013: 3–4).

In light of these views on the ethics of translation, and in connection with feminist translation praxis, I conclude with my reflection on feminist ethics of translation based on the three main components of the translation process: the original text, the translated version and the translators themselves. First, concerning the choice of the original text, a feminist ethics would give priority to translating a feminist literary text or a polemic text that would empower women and support the feminist cause. Second, the translated version should reflect feminist translation strategies and abide by the values of clarity and cross-cultural transformation. Third, and perhaps most importantly, feminist translation ethics relies on translators who are informed by feminist theory and aware of their role as mediators. It is therefore imperative for translators to understand the feminist knowledge they are translating and to translate it as clearly and accurately as possible, to reveal their ideological position vis-à-vis the texts they are translating and to assert their visibility in their texts. In this sense, translators' prefaces and introductions offer crucial paratextual spaces for self-reflection, vocal intervention and the assertion of translators' roles as active mediators who are attentive to an ethical translation praxis.

It is worth noting that *A Room of One's Own* is now out of print in Egypt in both editions (1999 and 2009). This stands as a clear indication of the popularity of Woolf's work, especially taking into consideration that in the absence of print editions, several pirated online copies of Woolf's books are available. However, despite this interest in Woolf's work, there remains a gap in the critical consideration of her influence on Arabic literature of the 1960s onwards, and her influence on the Egyptian feminist thought also remains an untrodden path that lies at the intersection of feminist literary criticism, translation studies and Arabic studies. It is through a feminist translation praxis that Woolf deserves to be more fully translated into Arabic and, hence, introduced to the Arab feminist activist, the Arab woman writer in 'a room of her own' as well as 'the [Arab] common reader'.

Notes

1. However, the multiple translations of texts into Arabic also suggest the absence of an organised process of translating her work and the frequent negligence of acknowledging the edition that was translated or including an informative preface.
2. Although previously spelled as Fatima Naoot (the author's spelling of her name in English) in this chapter, this is the spelling of the author's name in Arabic by the non-Arab writer Paola Viviana, who has opted for a traditional transcription of the name rather than using the author's preferred English spelling.

3. For more on the translation of feminist discourse into Arabic, see Kamal (2016b).
4. The feminist books translated for this occasion included the following: Leila Ahmed's *Women and Gender in Islam: Historical Roots of a Modern Debate* (1992), Beth Baron's *The Women's Awakening in Egypt* (1994), Cynthia Nelson's *Doria Shafik: A Woman Apart* (1996), Amira Sonbol's *Women, the Family and Divorce Laws in Islamic History* (1996) and Lila Abu-Lughod's *Remaking Women: Feminism and Modernity in the Middle East* (1998).
5. Feminist scholars have challenged his position as a representative of the Egyptian women's liberation movement; for example, see Ahmed (1992).
6. A backward translation is a translation of a translation back to its original language, which sometimes exposes inaccurate translations in the first account.
7. Having revised the translation, Farid wrote a preface to Naoot's translation of *An Unwritten Novel* in which he introduces both the author and translator.
8. This is my translation into English of Farid's statement in Arabic: 'حاجة المرأة الموهوبة إلى غرفة خاصة بها ودخل سنوي يكفل لها التفرغ للكتابة'.
9. Except for Buthaina Shaaban who mentions *A Room of One's Own* in relation to women's creativity in her article 'Between Arab women's literature and English women's literature' (1986).
10. *Al-Insan* is a synonym of '*Almar*' in the Arabic–Arabic Dictionary just as the word 'one' in English is independent from the word 'person' or the phrase 'human being' yet can also be considered synonymous.
11. Ramadan's Arabic translation of Woolf's words in the earlier quotation is as follows: المرء في هذه الحالة هو الإفصاح عن على كل حال، عندما يكون موضوع ما مثار جدل كبير – وكل ما يخص الجنس هو كذلك – إلى تكوين رأي بعينه. يكون كل ما في وسع الإنسان، حينئذ، هو أن يعطي يستعصي الأمل في قول الحقيقة، ويكون كل ما يستطيعه مستمعيه فرصة تكوين رأيهم الخاص وهم بصدد تأمل انحيازات أسلوبه، ومحدودياته. الكيفية التي وصل بها
12. One of the most compelling studies of Woolf's bipolarity and creativity is Thomas Caramagno's controversial *The Flight of the Mind: Virginia Woolf's Art and Manic-Depressive Illness*, where he integrates 'neuroscience, psychobiography, and literary theory' to establish a connection between Woolf's patterns of creativity and mood swings (1992: 1).
13. For more on the history of the Egyptian feminist movement, see Kamal (2016a) and Kamal (2018).
14. Lori Chamberlain has critiqued the use of fidelity as a metaphor of translation, which she considers a form of 'sexualization of translation', whereby translation is seen as a contact between a woman/translator faithful to her man/author (2008: 307).

Bibliography

Ahmed, L. (1992), *Women and Gender in Islam: Historical Roots of a Modern Debate*, New Haven, CT: Yale University Press.
Al-Amir, A. (1964), 'Dirasa fi adab Virginia Woolf' دراسة في أدب فيرجينيا وولف [A study in Virginia Woolf's literature], *Al-Adab* الأداب [Literatures], 12: 1, January, Beirut, pp. 61–4.
Al-Fiqi, S. H. and A. M. Al-Awani (1964), 'Al-Majallat al-Arabia' المجلات العربية [Arab magazines], *Al-Majalla* المجلة [The Magazine], 86, February, Cairo, pp. 121–3.
Arrojo, R. (2013), 'Translator's code of ethics', in C. A. Chapelle (ed.), *The Encyclopedia of Applied Linguistics*, Oxford: Blackwell Publishing, pp. 1–5.
Batchelor, Kathryn (2018), *Translation and Paratexts*, London: Routledge.
Benjamin, Walter (2002 [1921]), 'The task of the translator', in M. Bullock and M. Jennings (eds), *Walter Benjamin: Selected Writings, Volume 1, 1913–1926*, Cambridge, MA: Harvard University Press, pp. 253–63.
Bermann, S. (2005), 'Introduction', in S. Bermann and M. Wood (eds), *Nation, Language, and the Ethics of Translation*, Princeton, NJ: Princeton University Press, pp. 1–10.

Calle Orozco, J. A. (2013), 'Gender and translation: Spanish translation of Virginia Woolf's *Orlando* by Jorge Luis Borges', *Mutatis Mutandis*, 6: 2, pp. 444–54.

Caramagno, T. C. (1992), *The Flight of the Mind: Virginia Woolf's Art and Manic-Depressive Illness*, California: University of California Press.

Chamberlain, L. (2008 [1988]), 'Gender and the metaphorics of translation', in L. Venuti (ed.), *The Translation Studies Reader*, London: Routledge, pp. 306–21.

Chesterman, A. (1997), 'Ethics of translation', *Translation as Intercultural Communication*, Amsterdam: John Benjamins Publishing Company, pp. 147–57.

Farid, M. S. (2009), 'Preface' تصدير *Virginia Woolf: Juyub Muthqala bil-Hijara wa Riwaya lam Tuktab Ba'd* جيوب مثقلة بالحجارة ورواية لم تكتب بعد [Virginia Woolf: Pockets Heavy with Stones and 'An Unwritten Novel'], trans. F. Naoot, Cairo: National Centre for Translation, pp. 9–17.

Federici, E. and V. Leonardi (2012), 'Using and abusing gender in translation: The case of Virginia Woolf's *A Room of One's Own* translated into Italian', *Quaderns. Revista de Traducció* [Notebooks: Journal of Translation], 19, pp. 183–98.

Flotow, L. V. (1991), 'Feminist translation: Contexts, practices and theories, *TTR: Traduction, terminologie, rédaction*, 4: 2, pp. 69–84, <https://www.erudit.org/fr/revues/ttr/1991-v4-n2-ttr1475/037094ar/> (last accessed 20 January 2020).

Flotow, L. V. (1997), *Translation and Gender: Translating in the 'Era of Feminism'*, Manchester: St. Jerome Publishing.

Genette, G. (1997 [1987]), *Paratexts: Thresholds of Interpretation*, trans. J. E. Lewin, Cambridge, MA: Cambridge University Press.

Godard, B. (1995 [1988]), 'Theorizing feminist discourse/translation', in S. Bassnett and A. Lefevere (eds), *Translation, History and Culture*, London: Cassell, pp. 87–96.

Kamal, H. (2016a), 'A century of Egyptian women's demands: The four waves of the Egyptian feminist movement', *Gender and Race Matter: Global Perspectives on Being a Woman (Advances in Gender Research, Vol. 21)*, Emerald Group Publishing Limited, pp. 3–22, <https://www.emerald.com/insight/content/doi/10.1108/S1529-212620160000021002/full/html> (last accessed 20 January 2020).

Kamal, H. (2016b), 'Translating feminist literary theory into Arabic', *Studia Filologiczne Uniwersytetu Jana Kochanowskiego* [Philological Studies at Jan Kochanowski University in Kielce], 29: 2, pp. 57–73.

Kamal, H. (2018), '"Travelling concepts" in translation: Feminism and gender in the Egyptian context', *Synergy* 14: 1, pp. 131–45.

Ramadan, S. (1999), 'Muqaddima' مقدمة [Introduction], in V. Woolf, *Ghurfa Takhussu al-Mar' Wahdahu* غرفة تخص المرء وحده [*A Room of One's Own*], trans. S. Ramadan, Cairo: Supreme Council for Culture, pp. 7–14.

Ramadan, S. (2009 [1999]), 'Hadha al-Kitab' هذا الكتاب [This book], in V. Woolf, *Ghurfa Takhussu al-Aar' Wahdahu* غرفة تخص المرء وحده [*A Room of One's Own*], trans. S. Ramadan, Cairo: Madbouly Books, pp. 7–21.

Shaaban, B. (1986), 'Bayn al-adab al-nisa'iyy al-arabiyy wa al-adab al-nisa'iyy al-ingliziyy: Ghada Al-Samman wa Virginia Woolf' بين الأدب النسائي العربي والأدب النسائي الإنجليزي: غادة السمان وفرجينيا وولف [Between Arab women's literature and English women's literature, Ghada Al-Samman and Virginia Woolf], *Al-Mawqif al-Adabi* الموقف الأدبي [Literary Position], 16: 186, Syria, pp. 64–89.

Shalash, A. (1966), 'Virginia Woolf wa Qissat Tayyar al-Wa'y' فرجينيا وولف وقصة تيار الوعي [Virginia Woolf and the stream-of-consciousness story], *Al-Fikr al-Mu'asir* الفكر المعاصر [Contemporary Thought], 15, Cairo, pp. 50–9.

Snir, R. (1999), 'Virginia Woolf in Arabic literature: Translations, influence and reception', *Virginia Woolf Miscellany*, 54, pp. 5–6.

Taha, T. M. (1965), 'A'lam al-Qissa fi al-Adab al-Ingliziyy al-Hadith: Virginia Woolf' أعلام القصة في الأدب الإنجليزي الحديث: فرجينيا وولف [Famous figures of the story in modern English literature: Virginia Woolf], *Al-Qissa* القصة [The Story], 2: 13, pp. 23–42.

Venuti, L. (1995), *The Translator's Invisibility*, London: Routledge.
Viviani, P. (2012), '"Acting like a thief": Fatimah Na'ut translates Virginia Woolf in Egypt', in O. Palusci (ed.), *Translating Virginia Woolf*, Bern: Peter Lang, pp. 145–55.
Woolf, V. (n.d.), *Al-Amwaj* الأمواج [*The Waves*], trans. M. Al-Zumur, Cairo: Dar al-Katib al-Arabi.
Woolf, V. (1968a), *Al-Amwaj* الأمواج [*The Waves*], trans. M. Al-Zumur, Cairo: Dar al-Maarif.
Woolf, V. (1968b), *Al-Manar* المنار [The Lighthouse], trans. G. Mansi, Cairo: Dar al-Hilal.
Woolf, V. (1971), *Al-Qari' al-'Adiyy* القارئ العادي [*The Common Reader*[, trans. Aqila Ramadan, Cairo: Al-hay'a al-misriya al-'amma lil-ta'lif wal-nashr [General Egyptian Organisation for Authorship and Publishing].
Woolf, V. (1992), *Flush* فلاش [*Flush*], trans. Atta Abdel-Wahab, Baghdad: Dar al-Shams.
Woolf, V. (1994), *Al-Sayyida Dallaway* السيدة دالاواي [*Mrs Dalloway*], trans. A. K. Mahfud, Homs: Dar Jafra lil-Nashr.
Woolf, V. (1998), *Al-sayyida Dalaway* السيدة دالاواي [*Mrs Dalloway*], trans. Atta Abdel-Wahab, Beirut: Al-mu'assasa al-arabiya lil-dirasat wal-nashr [Arab Organisation for Research and Publishing].
Woolf, V. (2001 [1929/1938]), *A Room of One's Own and Three Guineas*, London: Vintage Books.
Woolf, V (2002 [1944]), *A Haunted House and Other Short Stories*, San Diego: Harvest.
Woolf, V. (2008a), *The Mark on the Wall and Other Short Fiction*, ed. D. Bradshaw, Oxford: Oxford University Press.
Woolf, V. (2008b), *Yawm al-Ithnayn aw al-Thulatha' (Wa Qisas Ukhra)* يوم الاثنين أو الثلاثاء (وقصص أخرى) [*Monday or Tuesday (and Other Stories)*], trans. L. M. O. Nagaty, Cairo: Al-maglis al-a'la lil-thaqafa [Supreme Council for Culture].
Woolf, V. (2009a), *Athar 'ala al-Ha'it* أثر على الحائط [A mark on the wall], trans. F. Naoot, Cairo: Al-maglis al-a'la lil-thaqafa [Supreme Council for Culture].
Woolf, V. (2009b [1999]), *Ghurfa Takhussu al-Mar' Wahdahu* غرفة تخص المرء وحده [*A Room of One's Own*], trans. S. Ramadan, Cairo: Madbouly Books.
Woolf, V. (2009c), *Juyub Muthqala bil-Hijara wa 'Riwaya lam Ttuktab Ba'd'* جيوب مثقلة بالحجارة و" رواية لم تكتب بعد" [Pockets Heavy with Stones and 'An Unwritten Novel'], trans. F. Naoot, Cairo: Al-maglis al-a'la lil-thaqafa [Supreme Council for Culture].
Woolf, V. (2015), *Ila al-Fanar* إلى الفنار [*To the Lighthouse*[, trans. Izabel Kamal, Cairo: Al-hay'a al-'amma li-qusur al-thaqafa [General Organisation for Culture].
Woolf, V. (2016), *Orlando* أورلاندو [*Orlando*], trans. Tawfik Alasadi, Baghdad: Al-Mada.
Woolf, V. (2017), *Ghurfa Takhussu al-Mar' Wahdahu* غرفة تخص المرء وحده [*A Room of One's Own*], trans. Ahd Subiha, Damascus: Ninawa.

10

SOLID AND LIVING: THE ITALIAN WOOLF RENAISSANCE

Elisa Bolchi

IN HER INTRODUCTION TO THE VOLUME *The Reception of Virginia Woolf in Europe*, Nicola Luckhurst poses a stimulating question for scholars of reception studies: 'Is this multiple and iconic Virginia Woolf at the beginning of the twenty-first century the conclusion of the writer's reception in Europe?' (2002: 17). Drawing from this question, this chapter[1] shows how, far from fading with time, Woolf's iconic status in Italy has continued to grow into what I call an 'Italian Woolf Renaissance'. Furthermore, the chapter aims to highlight the relevance of local reception histories by identifying and evaluating those factors and agents which shape the reception of Woolf in non-English-speaking literary traditions: not only professional readers, publishers and scholars, but also common and passionate readers as well, to whom Woolf has been able to address.

The first to examine Virginia Woolf's fortune in Italy in the twenty-first century was Sergio Perosa, with his essay 'The reception of Virginia Woolf in Italy' (2002), in which he made a quick survey of the Italian translations of Woolf and of the Italian literary journals in which her work was discussed. A more specific analysis of the writer's reception in periodicals came out in my own 2007 book *Il paese della bellezza. Virginia Woolf nelle riviste italiane tra le due guerre* [The Country of Beauty. Virginia Woolf in Italian Literary Periodicals between the Two World Wars], which not only analysed her early reception in Italy, but also gathered the transcription of all the articles that had appeared in Italian journals from 1927 – when the first article on Woolf appeared in the *Corriere della Sera* [The Evening Gazette] – to the end of the Second World War. When Alessandra Scalero's Italian translation of *Orlando* was released by mainstream publisher Mondadori in 1933, twelve articles surveying Woolf's novels and essays had already appeared in leading literary periodicals.[2] In this first phase of Woolf reception, her prose was often read by critics with a sense of reverence 'only similar to what one feels in front of ancient beauty',[3] as Umberto Morra wrote (1928: 27). Most interestingly, Italian scholars have continuously focused their attention on three crucial aspects of Woolf's prose: form, character-creation and the psychological aspects of her narration.

The editorial aspects of Woolf's Italian publication were analysed in my 2015 book *L'indimenticabile artista. Lettere e appunti sulla storia editoriale di Virginia Woolf in Mondadori* [The Unforgettable Artist. Letters and Notes on the Editorial History of Virginia Woolf in Mondadori] (Bolchi 2015a). By means of the documents preserved at the Mondadori's Historical Archive, the book examines Woolf's Italian publication up to the 1960s to understand the editorial dynamics which had put her works in the Italian literary marketplace. Her reception actually suffered a contraction in the aftermath of the Second World War, when publishers and readers were more interested in politically engaged fiction with a neorealistic approach. Yet, after this postwar phase, a resurgence of popular interest in her work took place in concomitance with the rise of feminism in Italy.

After a reception characterised by alternating phases, Virginia Woolf has been enjoying a renewed and growing attention in Italy in the last decade, an attention which started when her publication rights expired in 2011, thus allowing greater access for the retranslation and republication of her work. As this chapter will show, once Woolf's works were in the public domain, their publication in Italy was characterised by three main paths: the retranslations of her most important novels by prestigious publishers like Giulio Einaudi Editore, the translations of works that had never been translated before and the appearance of refined editions of her books in the catalogues of small, independent publishers. The competent translators and scholars who edited some of these volumes have helped Italian readers to better understand Woolf's prose, and have ushered in her Italian Renaissance.

Having as its focus the recent popularisation of Woolf icon in Italy, this study does not take into account her critical reception, either in scholarly essays or in periodicals and newspapers, but concentrates instead on the agents who play fundamental roles in the distribution of an author within the marketplace: publishers, translators and, of course, readers. Specifically, the editorial projects that came after the expiration of Woolf's translation rights in 2011 are the focus; interviews were thus the preferred tool of investigation to gather information from publishers and translators, and the recent founding of the Italian Virginia Woolf Society in 2017 has made it possible to tentatively characterise Italian readers of Woolf. In this Italian Renaissance, independent publishing houses such as Nuova Berti, Nottetempo or Racconti edizioni play a role similar to that of the Modern Library series in the United States; in fact, as Lise Jaillant explains, the US series not only widened Woolf's audience but it also allowed her books 'to cross the gap between common and professional readers' (2014: 83).

Readers have indeed played a fundamental role in the Italian Woolf Renaissance. Virginia Woolf herself gave readers a crucial role by claiming that independence is 'the most important quality that a reader can possess' (*E* 5: 573), thus positioning common readers outside the dependency of highbrows' reviews or judgement to read and appreciate a work. As she wrote in 'How should one read a book?': 'the only advice, indeed, that one person can give another about reading is to take no advice, to follow your own instincts, to use your own reason, to come to your own conclusions' (*E* 5: 573). Woolf wrote for, and addressed her essays to, the common reader and, as Jaillant notes, she 'wrote for popular magazines such as *Vogue*, she was published by the commercial publishing firm Harcourt, Brace, and some of her books sold widely to a middle-class audience. In other words, Woolf willingly participated in middlebrow culture' (2014: 94). Yet most scholars have viewed her 'as an archetypical highbrow writer, without questioning a label which dates from the interwar period' (Jaillant 2014: 94). It was Melba Cuddy-Keane who presented Woolf as 'an advocate for both democratic inclusiveness and intellectual education' (2003: 1), a perception that describes the contemporary reception of Woolf in Italy. By means of interviews with recent translators and publishers of Woolf's works and of an analysis of their reception in the Italian cultural network (reading public, web, artistic field), I elucidate the reasons why Italians' fascination for Woolf is growing horizontally among cultural and age groups, social classes, and professional and common readers.

The Mondadori Trust

Although the catalyst for renewed interest in Woolf was the above-mentioned expiration of her publication rights in 2011, a step back is necessary to thoroughly understand how this interest developed. To that end, I discuss the original Italian translations of Woolf by her historic publisher, Arnoldo Mondadori Editore.

The first of Woolf's novels to be translated in Italian was *Orlando* (1933), published as part of the newly created Medusa series. This series, directed by Luigi Rusca for the Mondadori publishing house, was devoted entirely to foreign contemporary fiction, for which they envisaged only 'élite translators' (Scalero 1932a). In 1934, two other novels by Woolf appeared in Italy: Fratelli Treves published *To the Lighthouse* in the Scrittori Stranieri Moderni series, translated by Giulia Celenza with an introduction by the renowned scholar Emilio Cecchi, while Mondadori published *Flush*, again in the Medusa series and translated by Alessandra Scalero. But the translation of Woolf's novels soon had to stop because of the harsh cultural climate of fascism. The Regime's propaganda, exalting manliness and patriarchal ideals, would not have welcomed the publication of novels such as *Mrs Dalloway*, which explores a woman's psyche and portrays a distraught shell-shocked veteran who commits suicide.[4] Towards the end of the Second World War, however, Mondadori hastened to buy the foreign rights for many authors, including Virginia Woolf, whose translation rights he bought with an agreement dated 31 December 1944. The Mondadori Press seemed more interested in acquiring the publication rights, which they considered to be 'the only true wealth of a publisher' (Mondadori 1945a),[5] than in actually publishing the works they had bought. The translator Alessandra Scalero noted this in her first encounter with the publishers and wrote to her sister: 'it seems that Mondadori, with inconceivable arrogance, is buying out all the foreign market; they did unpleasant things, they stepped on other publishers' toes even grabbing the authors, a true *trust*' (Scalero 1932b).[6] Alberto Mondadori's project was ambitious: he wanted to publish the complete works of Woolf in an *Opera Omnia* edited by the renowned scholar Emilio Cecchi, and he wrote to Leonard Woolf claiming to be 'especially interested in the critical books', which he wanted to prioritise (Mondadori 1945b). The difficulties were many, however. First and foremost was the problem of translators, because Italian intellectuals who knew English well enough to translate Woolf were rare at the time and both Alessandra Scalero and Giulia Celenza had died prematurely. Mondadori had to overcome several other obstacles; some of the commissioned translations never came back, for instance, and so these circumstances led to him abandoning his project to publish Woolf's *Opera Omnia*. Those 'critical books' that Mondadori wanted to prioritise were not published until nineteen years after the signing of the agreement, in a significantly reduced edition titled *Per le strade di Londra* [Street Haunting: A London Adventure] (Woolf 1963).[7] What is more, the collection was not published by Mondadori but by the publishing house that Alberto, Arnoldo Mondadori's son, had founded in 1958, Il Saggiatore. Italian readers had to wait until 2012 – when the volume *Voltando pagina* [Turning a Page], edited by Liliana Rampello for Il Saggiatore was published – to read a more exhaustive, although still incomplete, collection of Woolf's essays (Woolf 2012).

A first wave of (re)publication of Woolf started in 1975, when the independent feminist press La Tartaruga bought the rights to *Three Guineas*, and a second wave took place in 1991, when the rights, which lasted fifty years from the death of the author, first expired. The duration of rights was, however, soon extended to seventy years, so that Mondadori once again became the owner of the Italian rights until 2011, when they eventually expired.

Who's Not Afraid to (Re)translate Woolf?

As a matter of fact, Mondadori's monopoly on Woolf rights had ended many years before 2011. Einaudi publishing house had bought the rights to Woolf's diaries and letters in the 1970s, but published only five of the six volumes of letters and never published the diaries; although they were entirely translated by Bianca Tarozzi, only one volume with a selection of pages from 1925 to 1930 was released by the publisher Rizzoli in 2012. In 1992, on the wave of retranslations that followed the first expiration of publication rights in 1991, Nadia Fusini translated *To the Lighthouse* for the publisher Feltrinelli, changing the Italian title from *Gita al faro* [A Trip to the Lighthouse] to the more faithful *Al Faro*, because, as she noted in her introduction,

> that *to* is a preposition that in English does not simply indicate a preposition of movement. . . . It is also a dative: the pole of an offer, of a gift. Virginia Woolf thus writes *for the Lighthouse*: addressing that light. And thanks to that light. And what she writes for that light becomes her present to it. (Fusini 1992: 7)[8]

In 1993 Fusini also translated and edited a new edition of *Mrs Dalloway* for Feltrinelli; in 1995 she made a new translation of *The Waves* for Einaudi, in the prestigious Scrittori tradotti da scrittori [Writers translated by writers] series founded by Italo Calvino; and in 1998 she edited Woolf's works for Mondadori's canonizing series Meridiani.

When the duration of rights was extended from fifty to seventy years, Einaudi and Feltrinelli were forced to stop their projects of retranslating Woolf. They had to wait until 2012, when Einaudi published a new translation of *Mrs Dalloway* by Anna Nadotti, the Italian translator of both A. S. Byatt, a writer with clear modernist influences, and Anita Desai, described by Nadotti herself as a 'very Woolfian writer' (Nadotti 2017). Einaudi also planned to retranslate James Joyce's *Ulysses*, which had been published by Mondadori in 1960 and translated by Giulio De Angelis, and whose rights had expired in the same year as Woolf. However, while Joyce came out in the Letture series, an expensive collection addressing highbrows and scholars more than the 'common reader', Einaudi proposed that *Mrs Dalloway* be published in the Classics section of the Tascabili series, a paperback collection of the texts that was part of the university canon, including authors such as Jane Austen, Robert Louis Stevenson and Leo Tolstoy. Nadotti was delighted with this decision because, she said, 'when I was at university, Virginia Woolf was not part of the canon yet, and the idea of being the person in charge of translating her prose for a canonical collection filled me with pride' (Nadotti 2017). Moreover, the books from this collection were to include authoritative introductions. According to Nadotti, the introduction was especially important for the reintroduction of *Mrs Dalloway* to Italian readers. Nadotti asked the writer and poet Antonella Anedda to introduce *Mrs Dalloway* so that the final editorial product might represent a door through which Italian readers could (re)enter and (re)discover the novel. The translation was published in June 2012; by the end of September it had run out of stock. Einaudi made a first reprint in October, but a third reprint was needed for the annual book fair the following May. Three reprints in under a year for an eighty-seven-year-old novel, already available to the public in several other editions, is a considerable success in a country in which 59.5 per cent of the population have not read a book in one year ('La lettura' [Book reading] 2016). This success led Einaudi to ask Nadotti for a new translation. *To the Lighthouse* was selected, and this novel once again was received with great approval, although it is curious that the 'old' title *Gita al faro* was chosen over the new title *Al faro* that was selected by Fusini in 1992. The novel was another success, as testified by the fact that it was turned into a summer marketing tool: every summer, Einaudi creates a beach towel with an illustrated quote from a classic novel, and in summer 2018 it was the turn of Nadotti's translation of *To the Lighthouse*, which readers could get by buying two novels in the Tascabili series.[9]

While the two retranslations by Einaudi are examples of the publisher proposing a new translation of Woolf to a competent translator, Feltrinelli's new edition of *The Years* represents a different scenario, one in which it was the translator who proposed a republication of the work. The editor-in-chief of Feltrinelli's collection of classics had told the Italian scholar Antonio Bibbò about their need to fill some editorial gaps in their catalogue and asked him to think of some canonical authors to translate. Bibbò proposed five novels, two of which were enthusiastically accepted: Woolf's *The Years* and Daniel Defoe's *Moll Flanders*. Woolf was the first to be translated and published, and *Gli Anni* [The Years] went out at the beginning of 2015, selling more than 3,400 copies in two years. Once again Woolf's iconic status was affirmed by a marketing campaign launched by Feltrinelli. By buying two novels of the Universale Economica (the paperback series), readers could get a throw reproducing the cover design of *Gli anni*. From beach towels to fleece blankets Woolf actually seems to be 'a woman for all seasons'.

Bibbò admitted to feeling 'a debt' towards *The Years*: 'Among Woolf's novels this is the last I have discovered, and a reason for such a delay was the oblivion into which the novel had fallen after the first successful months, not only in Italy' (Bibbò 2017).[10] Bibbò admitted to being both enchanted and frightened by it:

> it seemed to me, and it still does, that it is one of Woolf's most sincere novels, the most human, in which she faces not only the limits of existence, but also some of her most evident limits as a writer, such as that of rarely abandoning the representation of an upper-class London environment. (Bibbò 2017)[11]

Bibbò was afraid of not being able to reproduce the 'never cloying elegance of the novel',[12] noting how

> *The Years* does not have poetic prose like *The Waves*, it is a city novel, often discordant and prosaic; it tries, more than any other of Woolf's texts, to plunge into the filthiness of society while never renouncing careful control of tone and register, which is never vulgar. The internal musicality, the continuous cross-references between the pages and the phrases spoken and played with by different characters are less mechanical than in other more modernist novels; they have the spontaneity of daily speech, of family sayings, and I wanted to render such spontaneity at all costs without the result sounding mechanical. (Bibbò 2017)[13]

Woolf's prose was also held in awe by two other translators, Francesca Cosi and Alessandra Repossi. In 2012 they translated extracts from the early diaries of Woolf, and in particular the pages she wrote while she travelled in Italy, Greece and Turkey, which had never before been translated into Italian. Cosi and Repossi admitted that their translation of Woolf is the one of which they are most proud and they translated her pages with a sort of 'reverential fear' (Cosi and Repossi 2017), given that Woolf had always been one of their personal idols.[14] When asked why they chose to translate her travel journals, although Woolf was certainly not a travel writer, they answered:

> At first we did not think about her travels; in studying the juvenile writings of Woolf in search of unpublished pages, however, we thought that the most interesting texts were these diaries. . . . [T]hey . . . were a true training ground for her writing, extremely rich in reflections on other literary texts, on writing and also, of course, with suggestions deriving from the places she had been visiting. Travelling in these pages is, for Woolf, almost a pretext to test her own talent: she is searching not for descriptive but for evocative writing. . . . It's true that Woolf's name is not commonly associated with travel, but in this case the travel is the stimulus that induces her to find new ways to tell the truth. (Cosi and Repossi 2017)[15]

Probably because of these 'new ways to tell the truth', this collection offered readers the possibility of reading Woolf from a new perspective. The translators at first only envisaged publishing the travel diaries in Italy, Greece and Turkey, but the book was such a success that the publisher asked them to put together other books from Woolf's diaries: *Qui è rimasto qualcosa di noi* [There is Something of Our Own Preserved Here] in 2012, the diaries of her travels in Great Britain, and *Ultimi viaggi in Europa* [Last Travels in Europe] in 2013. The success of these books is demonstrated by the fact that in 2016 they were reprinted in a three-volume paperback edition and titled *Diari di viaggio in Italia e in Europa* [Travel Diaries in Italy and Europe]. The publisher of these diaries, Mattioli 1885, is a small but historical publisher who prints an average of fifty titles per year. Independent publishers like Mattioli 1885 have played the most active role in the Italian Woolf Renaissance, as I go on to show in the next section.

Independent Publishers' Gift to Woolf

Independent publishers benefited the most from the expiration of the publication rights of Woolf's works in 2011 because they were finally able to include her in their catalogues. If these editions played a crucial role in the Italian Woolf Renaissance it is, first of all, because they facilitated more widespread reading of Virginia Woolf. Similarly to what happened with Woolf's participation in the American Modern Library series, her publication in the catalogue of independent publishers exemplified 'her positioning as a democratic writer who wrote for the intelligent common reader' (Jaillant 2014: 84). The appearance in the market of these small volumes, often presenting collections of essays, allowed Italian readers to no longer be afraid of Virginia Woolf because they were allowed to enter into her prose from different, sometimes secondary, doors that might offer easier access. Most of these editions are small but sophisticated volumes in lively handy format – 'solid objects', as in Woolf's short story (Woolf 1977). Many of the translators and publishers I interviewed described their work in terms of a gift from Italian intellectuals to Virginia Woolf. This approach to her prose is also perceived as new by the Italian community of Woolf's readers, who are (re)discovering Woolf through these new editions and through the words of the new editors.

One of these solid objects is the collection *Lunedì o Martedì*, a translation of *Monday or Tuesday* published in 2012 by Nuova Editrice Berti. I interviewed the director of the publishing house Cecilia Mutti, who told me that she had always loved Woolf and that she 'liked the idea of re-proposing her to the Italian public with *Monday or Tuesday*, Woolf's only collection of short stories to be published while she was still living' (Mutti 2017). Mutti was fascinated by the project because it was a 'domestic publishing project of the Hogarth Press, with a cover design by Vanessa Bell and a conspicuous series of typos that made Leonard furious', and she also was amused by this because 'after all, we are a small publishing house too, with an almost domestic dimension' (Mutti 2017).[16]

This volume was followed by a translation of *Granite and Rainbow*. As Mutti explains,

> presented with a graphic design recalling the original one by Vanessa, these essays, in which Woolf moves between solid-as-granite facts and the weightless flash of the rainbow, are tangible proof that a lucid, pleasant-to-read and vivid literary criticism can exist. It is wonderful how this book is also loved by young boys and girls who, even though they are not looking for academic reads, probably fascinated by the title, or by the handy format, buy this book and find themselves with a hidden gem in their hands. (Mutti 2017)[17]

Cecilia Mutti's words are particularly interesting if read in the light of Mondadori's decision not to buy the translation rights of the collection when it was published in 1958 because it was considered by Elio Vittorini to be a 'needless expenditure' (Vittorini 1958), given that these were pages that had been discarded by Leonard Woolf. However, because Mondadori did not want other publishers to issue a volume of essays by Woolf before they had published those already in their possession, they agreed with Leonard that he could sell the rights of *Granite and Rainbow* only after Mondadori had published a collection of essays. The first collection of essays by Woolf was only published in 1963 though, and since no publisher showed an interest in *Granite and Rainbow* in the following years, the collection remained unpublished until 2013. After *Granito e arcobaleno*, Nuova Editrice Berti also published *Anon* and *Reading at Random* as very refined editorial projects: a small and handy format, a matte cover with nineteenth-century illustrations in pale blue and straw-coloured pages, whose layout is enriched by Demetrio Costa's drawings. When Costa was asked to illustrate *Anon*, he discovered that Woolf mentioned Thomas Malory in her essay, and since he had a fascination for Aubrey Beardsley's illustrations of Malory's *Morte d'Arthur*, he took inspiration from Beardsley's style to draw chapter initials, inspired by the Goudy Mediaeval Regular font, which was designed in England in the 1930s. For the decorations he put together Beardsley's illustrations, with their Eastern and Pre-Raphaelite elements, and flowers and plants. 'I read that the idea of writing *Anon* came to Woolf while she was harvesting blackberries, so I made long walks myself, picking blackberries and making jams, thinking about my drawings',[18] Demetrio Costa explains, and in thinking about his drawings he 'tried to imagine the visual worlds which had nourished Woolf's words; those words are images themselves' (2017).[19] The books are translated and edited by Massimo Scotti, whose introductions are essential to guide the reader into Woolf's prose. 'The quality (and peculiarity) of the texts forced me to make an adequate edition', Scotti comments, 'since the book represented an *unicum* also inside

Woolf's authorial macrotext, notes and introduction were fundamental, and I kept taking notes while I translated so I wouldn't get lost' (2017).[20] Scotti dedicated almost a year and a half to the translation of the few pages of *Anon*, equally dividing his time between translation, notes and introduction, and this is the reason why he considers it 'a sincere homage to Virginia' (2017).[21] These uncommon, less canonical texts are helping to present a new portrait of Woolf to the Italian common reader, showing her multiplicity, her flexibility, her ability to be a modernist writer with a strong sense of tradition and, most important, her contribution to forming a new tradition of female writing. The development of her writing skills and of her literary talent is also displayed to the public in the complete collection of short stories, recently published by another independent Italian publishing house, Racconti Edizioni.

The complete short stories had already been translated and published in Italy by the small yet historic publishing house La Tartaruga, which was the first to publish *Three Guineas* in 1975, thus launching Woolf's feminist thought in Italy. The collection of short stories had, however, been out of stock for years, meaning that they were only readable as e-books until 2016. Stefano Friani and Emanuele Giammarco, who had just founded Racconti Edizioni as a publishing house devoted to short stories, felt there was 'an undeniable and compelling call'[22] to reissue Woolf's short-stories (Friani 2017); they were edited by the renowned critic Liliana Rampello, with the suggestive title *Oggetti solidi* [Solid Objects]. Woolf's short stories are the seventh volume in their catalogue and 1,300 copies were printed – a considerable number for a new-born independent publisher in a country in which the publishing market is in crisis. The book was unexpectedly out of stock in two weeks; a reprint ran to 1,000 copies, which also sold out, so that it went through a third reprint in less than a year, becoming their bestseller.

The Italian Woolf Community

Such a proliferation of new editions of Woolf's works proved the existence of a community of Woolf readers in Italy, of people sharing a passion for, an interest in and a knowledge of Woolf. It is a community similar to what Étienne Wenger defined as a 'community of practice', that is 'a group of people who share a concern, a set of problems, or a passion about a topic, and who deepen their knowledge and expertise in this area by interacting on an ongoing basis' (Wenger et al. 2002: 4). It was not until February 2017, when I founded the Italian Virginia Woolf Society together with Nadia Fusini, Liliana Rampello and Iolanda Plescia, that I could fully realise how real and strong such a community of Italian readers and scholars of Woolf existed. As Wenger et al. affirm: 'communities of practice are the ideal social structure for "stewarding" knowledge. . . . [T]hese communities provide a social forum that supports the living nature of knowledge' (2002: 12), and we had this idea in mind when we decided to institutionalise the Italian community of Woolf readers and scholars. As a matter of fact, if it was possible to create an Italian Virginia Woolf Society, it was because a community already existed and just needed an 'intentional and systematic organization about managing knowledge' (Wenger et al. 2002: 6). Proof of this was the fact that the Italian Virginia Woolf Society received membership requests as soon as it was founded, and these have never stopped. Academics, actors, writers and common readers alike soon joined the Society not to be part of an institution, but to share knowledge, concerns and interest in Woolf. 'Though our experience of knowing is individual, knowledge is not' (Wenger et al. 2002: 10), and that is why it was fundamental to base the making of the Society on a multi-way channel: scholars share their knowledge of experts and readers shared their knowledge of passionate apprentice. In three years from its foundation, the Italian Virginia Woolf Society counts 190 members and has a website (Italian 2017), a Twitter profile, an Instagram account and a Facebook page with more than 4,000 followers; and public events have been organised in Rome, Turin, Bologna, Milan and other smaller cities, each attended by hundreds of people.

The web and social networking services have been fundamental in the creation and development of the Society. While during the earliest period of its development the web 'functioned as a reading vehicle, a digital forum where information prevailed and communication was one-way' now it has 'evolved into a socialization platform, which holds a vast store of knowledge deriving from the large amount of research and innovation produced through the talent, imagination, audacity, and intelligence of the network's users' (López-Pérez and Olvera-Lobo 2016: 243). Web users handle information differently than they used to do ten years ago, and this mainly derived from the advent of social media, the so-called Web 2.0, the users of which have grown from 970 million in 2010 to 2.62 billion in 2018 ('Number' 2019). Social media are user-centred, open, participatory, interactive and they are (or should be) places for knowledge sharing. Indeed, thanks to social media the web was transformed into a new public space for citizen participation, and Facebook has become 'one of the most popular tools for sharing, commenting on, and posting new content' (Ciftci and Knautz 2016: 116). Interactivity and the exchange of information are part of social media's nature and therefore represented the perfect 'forum' for our community.

Among the definitions provided by Wenger et al., I particularly cherish the one in which they explain how

> communities of practice do not merely manage knowledge assets. They create value in multiple and complex ways, both for their members and for the organization. . . . '[S]ome . . . of their greatest value lies in intangible outcomes, such as the relationships they build among people, the sense of belonging they create, the spirit of inquiry they generate, and the professional confidence and identity they confer to their members. (2002: 15)

This was the aspect we hoped to enhance by creating an Italian Virginia Woolf Society and this is what we can, proudly, claim to have attained. In cooperation with Raffaella Musicò, the owner of a bookshop significantly called *Virginia e co.*, the Italian Virginia Woolf Society organises 'Il faro in una stanza' [The lighthouse in a room], an annual festival dedicated to Woolf. The festival takes place on the last weekend of November – three days in which writers, scholars and translators are invited to speak on Woolf to a wide audience. Although the first four festivals took place in Monza and Sesto San Giovanni, two towns near Milan, they enjoyed an enthusiastic participation: events were fully booked, with people queuing to buy entrance tickets. Dozens of national newspapers, journals and blogs dedicated articles to the festival and people came from all over Italy to meet and listen to people talking about Woolf. Apart from showing a cultural interest in the writer, the festival contributes to build those relationships among people and that 'sense of belonging' to which Wenger et al. refer.

The aim of the Italian Virginia Woolf Society is also to gather, both physically and virtually, readers, scholars and teachers interested in Woolf for personal or scholarly reasons. A tangible effect of this is the fact that the community can represent a useful tool for surveying Woolf readers in Italy, to discover more about them and their reading habits – for example, how old they are, when they started to read Woolf and which work they started with. I thus created six short questions regarding their gender, their age, the first book they read by Woolf, when they read it, who suggested or recommended it and how many books by Woolf they have read. To test the relevant role social media can have as tools not only to communicate scientific results but also to gather data for research, also at an academic level,[23] the survey was disseminated through the Society's Facebook and Twitter pages on 28 June 2018, and it was closed after twenty days. The survey was completed by 444 people: 85.2 per cent of readers were women, while only 14.6 per cent were men; and their ages were mainly between twenty and thirty-five years, mirroring the average age of Facebook users ('Distribution' 2019). When I looked at this sample in detail, however, I saw interesting aspects.

The first question regarded gender and it was no surprise to have fewer than 15 per cent male readers, given that Woolf has often been considered by Italian public as a writer who mainly addresses women. Interestingly, though, a closer analysis of the data shows that almost 47 per cent of the male respondents had read more than five books by Woolf, and 22 per cent of this 47 per cent had read more than ten books by Woolf. Given that the corresponding percentage of women who had read more than ten books by Woolf was 19 per cent, this percentage is not just very similar, it is slightly higher. It thus proves that, once introduced to readers, Virginia Woolf speaks equally to women and men, and gives rise to an interest in her work regardless of the reader's gender.

In her essay 'Hours in a library', Woolf wrote that 'the great season for reading is the season between the ages of eighteen and twenty-four' (*E* 2: 55). This seems to be partially true for Woolf readers in Italy as well: almost 45 per cent of respondents affirm that they read Woolf for the first time before turning 25, thus confirming Woolf's statement. This is curiously truer in men (55.4 per cent) than in women (42.4 per cent). However, the survey does reveal that readers who discover Woolf before the age of eighteeen are mainly women (32.5 per cent compared to 16.9 per cent of men).

One of the most interesting aspects that emerged from the sample was the fundamental role played by school in introducing Woolf to Italian readers. Those who first read Woolf at school or at university represent the vast majority of Woolf readers (48.7 per cent); interestingly, though, the absolute majority is represented by the 32.1 per cent who first read Woolf at secondary school, whereas only 16.6 per cent were introduced to her at university, exactly the same percentage as those who were introduced to Woolf by friends. The results regarding the role of magazines and newspapers are also interesting because they demonstrate that these media played a slightly more important role than family in introducing Woolf to readers (6.7 per cent versus 6.2 per cent). Surprisingly, fewer than 1 per cent were introduced to Woolf by films (two mention Sally Potter's *Orlando* and only one *The Hours*). If we then compare this data with that of the number of Woolf's books read by each respondent, we discover that more than 50 per cent of those who were introduced to Woolf at school have read one to four books by her, while only 11 per cent have read more than ten books. This percentage increases for those who first read Woolf at university to 18.6 per cent. This seems to suggest that school is valuable for introducing Woolf to Italian readers, but it is not enough to create lifelong Woolf lovers. The highest percentage of people reading more than ten books by Woolf was those who got to her independently, through personal choice.

If we then consider which of Woolf's books are read, in first place we have *Mrs Dalloway* with 28.2 per cent, while *To the Lighthouse* is in third place with 23 per cent. This is easily explained by the fact that they are the texts usually included in school anthologies. In second place we find *A Room of One's Own* with 24.3 per cent. This text is usually included in university programmes, and the high percentage of people for whom it was the introductory text to Woolf confirms the importance of her iconic status as a feminist in Italy.[24] *Orlando*, which was the first novel translated into Italian, comes in only in fourth place in this sample, with 12.7 per cent, followed by *A Writer's Diary* (3.6 per cent) and *The Voyage Out* (3.2 per cent).

Because this chapter mainly focuses on the most recent years of Woolf's status in Italy, specifically the period after 2011, the group of youngest readers (under 20 years old) is particularly worth analysing, even though they represent only 1.8 per cent of the sample, probably because Facebook and Twitter are not the favoured social networks of 'Generation Z' ('Number' 2019). The data shows that there is no clear tendency in this group of readers: considering their young age, one would imagine that almost all of them were introduced to Woolf by a schoolteacher, but only 25 per cent confirm this expectation. The remaining 75 per cent mention a newspaper article, a bookseller or a member of the family. It is also worth noting that, in this group, the first novel to be read was not *Mrs Dalloway* but *To the Lighthouse*, followed by *Orlando*.

New Artistic Impulses

Having concentrated on the reading of Virginia Woolf in Italy, I conclude by mentioning two examples of the re-reading of her works. The interlinguistic one is actually not the only translation of Woolf in Italy; some of her works, like *Orlando*, *Room* and the letters between Woolf and Vita Sackville-West, have been adapted for the stage, and *Room* has also inspired a children's book titled *Una stanza tutta per me* [A Room of My Own] (2017), written by Serena Ballista and illustrated by Chiara Carrer. In 2018, Woolf was the object of two exhibitions that were not simple retellings of her works. In fact, the artists Piera Benetti and Gloria Bertolone used Woolf's novels, specifically *Mrs Dalloway* and *The Waves*, as ingredients to create their own works of art.

From 11 February to 11 March 2018, Spazio Oberdan in downtown Milan hosted an exhibition by the Italian painter Piera Benetti. Titled *Nelle cose* [Inside Things], it represented the First World War on the Italian mountains of Lavarone, Trentino, through the eyes of Septimus Warren Smith and the language of Virginia Woolf. The captions of the abstract paintings were passages from *Mrs Dalloway*. 'We wanted to show Septimus's intimate dialogue, to let it flow parallel to the paintings',[25] the artist told me when I interviewed her:

> He thinks and looks; when he raises his eyes it is the places of war he sees, not Milan, the city seen by Rezia. In the same way the visitors, after having read the

captions (displaying without interruption the pages of Woolf's novel), raise their eyes and see not what Septimus saw in his mind, but what we see today in visiting those places. (Benetti 2018)[26]

One of the most fascinating aspects of the exhibition was the colours of the paintings: bright, light, joyful colours, quite the opposite of what one would expect from an exhibition on the First World War. I asked Benetti the reason for this choice and she answered: 'I chose colour as my language. I could perhaps say that the colour in my paintings is like Mrs Dalloway's flowers, like Rezia's straw hats, what cannot be overlooked, what cannot be postponed, what we should start from' (Benetti 2018).[27] The artist Gloria Bertolone, by contrast, used photos, texts and videos for her exhibition *Sulle onde. I Fell in Love with Virginia Woolf*. Inspired by *The Waves*, it took place in Genoa, at the Theatre-museum Commenda from 26 July to 9 September 2018. The project was the result of the artist's deep passion for the novel and it is the realisation of many years of study. As Bertolone explains:

> the works follow the pace of Virginia Woolf's text and develop in the time frame between the first and the tenth interlude; in the middle, the immensity and the charm of soliloquies. Renouncing for the first time the representation of the human body, I completely abandoned myself to the visions of the landscapes of the soul that the writer gave us and that have rested in me. ('*Sulle onde*' 2018)[28]

Such an adaptation of Virginia Woolf by Italian artists to portray Italian landscapes and feelings is indeed indicative not only of the iconic status that the writer has reached in the Peninsula, but of her active role in inspiring and encouraging new artistic productions. And is there a better symbol of Renaissance than a new drive for artistic development and expression?

Notes

1. The writing of this article was supported by funding from the European Union's Horizon 2020 research and innovation programme under the Marie Skłodowska-Curie grant agreement No. 838658.
2. For example, Carlo Linati presented her in the pages of *Il Corriere della Sera* on 24 January 1927 and reviewed *A Room of One's Own* in the journal *Leonardo* in 1930; and Umberto Morra, who, along with writing a long article in the journals *Il Baretti* in 1928 and *La Cultura* in 1931, reviewed *Orlando* in *Solaria* in 1929 and *The Waves* in *Pègaso* in 1932. The renowned writer Sibilla Aleramo reviewed *Orlando* in the journal *L'Italia Letteraria* in 1931.
3. 'Simile solo a quello che si prova davanti alla bellezza antica.' All translations mine unless otherwise indicated.
4. Evidence for this is provided in letters that Rusca wrote to Woolf's translator, Alessandra Scalero (Rusca 1940); see Bolchi (2015b).
5. Alberto Mondadori wrote in a memo for the President: 'I diritti restano e sono l'unica autentica ricchezza dell'editore.'
6. 'Pare che Mondadori, con una boria da non dirsi, si stia accaparrando tutto il mercato straniero, hanno fatto delle cose poco simpatiche, pestando i piedi agli altri editori accaparrandosi gli autori addirittura, un vero trust.' Alessandra Scalero used the word 'trust'

in English. The two sisters often used foreign words (German, French, English) in their correspondence when they thought they were more 'emphatic' or meaningful in a language other than Italian.

7. The collection presented twenty-one essays: four from the *First Common Reader*, four from the *Second Common Reader*, seven from *The Death of the Moth*, five from *The Moment and Other Essays*, plus *A Room of One's Own*.
8. 'Quel *to* è preposizione che in inglese non indica semplicemente un moto a luogo. . . . È anche un dativo: il polo di un'offerta, di un dono. Virginia Woolf scrive per il Faro, dunque: rivolta a quella luce. E grazie a quella luce. E ciò che scrive per quella luce, anche glielo dona.'
9. The quote is taken from 'The window' at the end of Chapter 10: 'Girandosi, guardò al di là della baia, e laggiù, certo, scivolando a intervalli regolari sulle onde, prima due lampi veloci, poi uno lungo e durevole, c'era la luce del Faro. L'avevano acceso.' [Turning, she looked across the bay, and there, sure enough, coming regularly across the waves first two quick strokes and then one long steady stroke, was the light of the lighthouse. It had been lit.]
10. 'È il romanzo di Woolf che ho scoperto più tardi e mi sono reso conto che uno dei motivi di questa mia tardiva scoperta è stato proprio il sostanziale oblio nel quale questo romanzo è caduto dopo i primi trionfali mesi, non solo in Italia.'
11. 'mi sembrava, e mi sembra tutt'ora, che sia uno dei libri più sinceri di Virginia Woolf, uno dei più umani, in cui la scrittrice non solo affronta i limiti dell'esistenza, ma anche alcuni dei suoi più evidenti limiti di scrittrice, come quello di uscire raramente dalla rappresentazione di un certo ambiente londinese benestante e alto-borghese'.
12. 'l'eleganza mai stucchevole del romanzo'.
13. 'Y non ha una prosa poetica come W, è un romanzo cittadino, spesso stridente e prosaico, cerca, più di altri testi di Woolf, di affondare nel basso corporale e nel sudiciume della società ma sempre senza rinunciare a un controllo molto attento sul tono e sul registro, che non è mai volgare. La musicalità interna, i continui rimandi tra le pagine e tra le frasi simili pronunciate e masticate da personaggi diversi sono meno meccanici che in altri romanzi più volontariamente modernisti; hanno la naturalezza delle parole quotidiane, degli scambi del lessico familiare e volevo a tutti i costi rendere quella naturalezza senza risultare meccanico.'
14. In addition to my interview with them in June 2017, see Lucius Etruscus (2011) for part of the story of the Italian translation of Woolf's travel diaries.
15. 'All'inizio non avevamo in mente il viaggio; studiando gli scritti giovanili di Woolf alla ricerca di inediti, però, ci è sembrato che i testi più interessanti fossero proprio questi diari: . . . erano delle vere e proprie palestre di scrittura, ricchissime di riflessioni su altri testi letterari, sulla scrittura stessa e anche, ovviamente, di suggestioni dei luoghi attraversati. Il viaggio in queste pagine è per Woolf quasi un pretesto per mettere alla prova il proprio talento: è alla ricerca di una scrittura che non descriva ma che evochi. . . . È vero che il nome di Woolf non è comunemente associato al viaggio, ma in questo caso il viaggio è lo stimolo che la induce a trovare nuovi modi di raccontare la realtà.'
16. 'un progetto editoriale nato in famiglia, alla Hogarth Press, con la copertina disegnata dalla sorella Vanessa e una serie incalcolabile di errori tipografici che avevano fatto infuriare il marito Leonard, mi divertiva molto: in fondo anche noi siamo una piccola casa editrice, con una dimensione quasi famigliare'.
17. 'sono la dimostrazione tangibile che possa esistere una critica letteraria viva, e lucida, e piacevole da leggere. È bello che questo libro sia molto apprezzato anche dai ragazzi più giovani, che, pur non essendo in cerca di letture accademiche, forse affascinati dal titolo, o dal formato esile privo di apparati, si trovano per le mani una perla sconosciuta'.
18. 'Ho letto che l'idea di scrivere *Anon* era venuta a Virginia Woolf mentre andava in cerca di more, quindi ho fatto anch'io lunghe passeggiate, molte raccolte di more e molte marmellate, pensando a come avrei fatto i miei disegni.'

19. 'cercavo di immaginare quale fosse il mondo visivo che aveva nutrito le sue parole; quelle parole stesse sono immagini'.
20. 'si tratta in qualche modo di un *unicum* anche all'interno del macrotesto autoriale woolfiano; introduzione e note erano irrinunciabili, e prendevo appunti mentre traducevo, per non disperdermi'.
21. 'Un sincero omaggio a Virginia.'
22. 'era una chiamata irresistibile e irrinunciabile'.
23. As asserted by Lourdes López-Pérez and María Dolores Olvera-Lobo (2016), Johanna Ross (2012), and Gemma Nández and Ángel Borrego (2013), among others.
24. It would, however, be intriguing to discover what role the publication of *A Room of One's Own* in the very economic series '1000 lire' by the publisher Newtown Compton played in this.
25. 'Abbiamo pensato di mostrare il dialogo intimo di Septimus a di farlo correre parallelamente ai quadri.'
26. 'Lui pensa e guarda, quando alza lo sguardo vede i luoghi della guerra, non vede Milano, la città che vede Rezia. Così il visitatore dopo aver letto le didascalie (che riportano senza interruzione due intere pagine del romanzo della Woolf) alza lo sguardo e vede. Non quello che vedeva nella sua mente Septimus ma quello che oggi si vede visitando quei posti.'
27. 'Ho scelto il colore come linguaggio. Il colore nei miei quadri potrei forse dire che è come i fiori di Mrs Dalloway, come le pagliuzze di Rezia quello da cui non si può prescindere, quello che non si può mettere dopo ma con cui forse sarebbe meglio cominciare.'
28. 'le opere seguono a stralci l'andamento del testo di Virginia Woolf e si sviluppano nell'arco di tempo compreso tra il primo e il decimo interludio, in mezzo, l'immensità e la malia dei soliloqui. Rinunciando per la prima volta alla raffigurazione del corpo umano mi sono abbandonata totalmente alle visioni dei paesaggi dell'anima che la scrittrice aveva regalato e che mi erano restati dentro.'

Bibliography

Aleramo, S. (1931), 'Orlando inglese' [English Orlando], *L'Italia letteraria*, 42, pp. 8–9.
Ballista, S. (2017), *Una stanza tutta per me* [A Room of My Own], Cagli: Settenove.
Benetti, P. (2018), email interview, 19 March.
Bibbò, A. (2017), email interview, 9 June.
Bolchi, E. (2007), *Il paese della bellezza. Virginia Woolf nelle riviste italiane tra le due guerre* [The Country of Beauty. Virginia Woolf in Italian Literary Periodicals within the Two World Wars], Milan: EDUCatt.
Bolchi, E. (2015a), *L'indimenticabile artista. Lettere e appunti sulla storia editoriale di Virginia Woolf in Mondadori* [The Unforgettable Artist. Letters and Notes on the Editorial History of Virginia Woolf in Mondadori], Milan: Vita e Pensiero.
Bolchi, E. (2015b), '"La Woolf è scrittrice difficile e ci vuol dei traduttori coscienziosi". Le vicende traduttive delle prime edizioni italiane di Virginia Woolf' ['Woolf is a difficult writer and we need diligent translators'. The background of the Italian translations of Woolf], *Testo a fronte*, 53, pp. 87–106.
Ciftci, T. and K. Knautz (2016), 'Information literacy levels of Facebook users', in Knautz and K. S. Baran (eds), *Facets of Facebook. Use and Users*, Berlin: De Gruyter, pp. 115–45.
Cosi, F. and A. Repossi (2017), email interview, 21 June.
Costa, D. (2017), 'Illustrazioni per un Anonimo' [Illustrations for *Anon*], *Giacomo Verri libri*, 20 March, <https://giacomoverri.wordpress.com/2017/03/20/6574/> (last accessed 18 January 2019).

Cuddy-Keane, M. (2003), *Virginia Woolf, the Intellectual, and the Public Sphere*, New York: Cambridge University Press.
'Distribution of Facebook users worldwide as of October 2018, by age and gender' (2019), *Statista*, <http://www.statista.com/statistics/376128/facebook-global-user-age-distribution/> (last accessed 29 January 2019).
Etruscus, L. (2011), 'Francesca Cosi & Alessandra Repossi', *Thriller Magazine*, 7 November, <http://www.thrillermagazine.it/11660/francesca-cosi-and-alessandra-repossi> (last accessed 31 July 2018).
Friani, S. (2017), email interview, 6 June.
Fusini, N. (1992), 'Introduzione' [Introduction], in V. Woolf, *Al faro*, Milan: Feltrinelli, pp. 7–30.
Italian Virginia Woolf Society (2017), <http://www.itvws.it> (last accessed 2 June 2019).
Jaillant, L. (2014), *Modernism, Middlebrow and the Literary Canon: The Modern Library Series, 1917–1955*, London: Pickering and Chatto.
'La lettura in Italia' [Book reading in Italy] (2016), Istituto Nazionale di Statisca (Istat), <https://www.istat.it/it/archivio/178337> (last accessed 2 June 2019).
Linati, C. (1927), 'Virginia Woolf', *Il Corriere della Sera*, 24 January, p. 3.
Linati, C. (1930), 'Virginia Woolf – A room of one's own', *Leonardo*, 3, pp. 175–6.
López-Pérez, L. and M. D. Olvera-Lobo (2016), 'Social media as channels for the public communication of science: The case of Spanish research centers and public universities', in K. Knautz and K. S. Baran (eds), *Facets of Facebook: Use and Users*, Berlin/Boston, MA: De Grutyer, pp. 241–64.
Luckhurst, N. (2002), 'Introduction', in M. A. Caws and N. Luckhurst (eds), *The Reception of Virginia Woolf in Europe*, London: Bloomsbury, pp. 1–18.
Mondadori, A. (1945a), 'Memo for the President', *Miscellanea Arnoldo Mondadori*, B. 12 f. 5 (Esilio Svizzera), Fondazione Arnoldo e Alberto Mondadori, Archivio Storico Arnoldo Mondadori Editore. Milan: not dated (but probably June 1945).
Mondadori, A. (1945b), 'Letter to Leonard Woolf', *Virginia Woolf*, Fondazione Arnoldo e Alberto Mondadori, Archivio Storico Arnoldo Mondadori Editore. Milan: 15 November 1945.
Morra, U. (1928), 'Virginia Woolf', *Il Baretti*, 5, p. 27.
Morra, U. (1929), 'Virginia Woolf – *Orlando: A Biography*', *Solaria*, 5, pp. 50–6.
Morra, U. (1931), 'Il nuovo romanzo inglese. Virginia Woolf' [The new English novel. Virginia Woolf], *La Cultura*, 1, pp. 34–51.
Morra, U. (1932), '*The Waves*', *Pègaso*, 3, pp. 377–80.
'Most popular social networks worldwide as of October 2018, ranked by number of active users (in millions)' (2019), *Statista*, <http://www.statista.com/statistics/272014/global-social-networks-ranked-by-number-of-users/> (last accessed 29 January 2019).
Mutti, C. (2017), email interview, 7 June.
Nadotti, A. (2017), phone interview, 10 June.
Nández, G. and A. Borrego (2013), 'Use of social networks for academic purposes: A case study', *The Electronic Library*, 31: 6, pp. 781–91.
'Number of social media users worldwide from 2010 to 2021' (2019), *Statista*, <https://www.statista.com/statistics/278414/number-of-worldwide-social-network-users/> (last accessed 30 January 2019).
Perosa, S. (2002), 'The reception of Virginia Woolf in Italy', in M. A. Caws and N. Luckhurst (eds), *The Reception of Virginia Woolf in Europe*, London: Bloomsbury, pp. 200–17.
Ross, C. (2012), 'Social media for digital humanities and community engagement', in C. Warwick, M. Terras and J. Nyhan (eds), *Digital Humanities in Practice*, London: Facet Publishing, <https://blogs.ucl.ac.uk/dh-in-practice/chapter-2/> (last accessed 28 January 2019).
Rusca, L. (1940), 'Letter to Alessandra Scalero', ref. 6.01.03, Fondo Scalero, Civica Biblioteca di Mazzè. Mazzè: 5 November.

Scalero, A. (1932a), 'Letter to Liliana Scalero', Fondo Scalero, Civica Biblioteca di Mazzè. Mazzè: 1 December.

Scalero, A. (1932b), 'Letter to Liliana Scalero', Fondo Scalero, Civica Biblioteca di Mazzè. Mazzè: 28 November.

Scotti, M. (2017), email interview, 6 June.

'*Sulle onde*': *Alla Commenda la mostra ispirata al romanzo più rivoluzionario della* Woolf ['On the Waves': An exhibition inspired by Woolf's most revolutionary novel at the Commenda Theatre] (2018), *Goa Magazine*, 25 July, <http://www.goamagazine.it/sulle-onde-alla-commenda-la-mostra-ispirata-al-romanzo-piu-rivoluzionario-della-woolf/> (last accessed 30 January 2019).

Vittorini, E. (1958), 'Note for the head director', *Virginia Woolf*, SEE 77/43, Fondazione Arnoldo e Alberto Mondadori, Archivio Storico Arnoldo Mondadori Editore. Milan: 11 July.

Wenger, E., R. McDermott and W. M. Snyder (2002), *Cultivating Communities of Practice: A Guide to Managing Knowledge*, Boston, MA: Harvard Business School Press.

Woolf, V. (1963), *Per le Strade di Londra* ['Street Haunting: A London Adventure'], trans. L. Bacchi Wilcock and J. R. Wilcock, Il Saggiatore: Milan.

Woolf, V. (1977 [1944]), *A Haunted House and Other Short Stories*, Harmondsworth: Penguin.

Woolf, V. (1986–2010), *The Essays of Virginia Woolf*, ed. A. McNeillie (vols 1–4) and S. N. Clarke (vols 5–6), 6 vols, San Diego: Harcourt.

Woolf, V. (2012), *Voltando Pagina* [Turning a Page], ed. L. Rampello, Il Saggiatore: Milan.

11

Tracing *A Room of One's Own* in Sub-Saharan Africa, 1929–2019

Jeanne Dubino

Introduction

On 28 June 2016, the *New York Times Book Review* published its first short story ever: 'The arrangements: A work of fiction' by Chimamanda Ngozi Adichie (1977–). The original short story had been commissioned to cover 'anything' about the 2016 US election season (Williams 2016). Adichie chose to retell Virginia Woolf's *Mrs Dalloway*, with Melania Trump featured as Mrs Dalloway. Thus it happened that a retelling of Woolf's narrative spanned three continents, when one of her most famous novels set in London was adapted by a Nigerian novelist living in the United States to address one of its most important presidential elections.

Adichie is not the only sub-Saharan African expatriate to engage with the writing of Virginia Woolf. Fiona Melrose (1973–), who hails from South Africa and now lives in London, wrote the novel *Johannesburg* (2017), which is closely based on *Mrs Dalloway*; even its cover page looks like it could have been designed by Vanessa Bell. Born in Nigeria, the British writer Helen Oyeyemi (1984–) now resides in Prague and has been compared to Woolf (Scutts 2018), whom, Oyeyemi said, she reads and rereads:

> Virginia Woolf's got that way of pouring out sentences like long, cool cocktails – here's one I noted during my last reread of *Mrs Dalloway*: 'He thought her beautiful, believed her impeccably wise; dreamed of her, wrote poems to her, which, ignoring the subject, she corrected in red ink.' (2014)

NoViolet Bulawayo (1981–), a Zimbabwean writer who spent her young adulthood in the US, emerged onto the global literary scene with *We Need New Names* (2013). In his review of this novel, Ikhide R. Ikheloa writes: 'Here comes Virginia Woolf ululating out of the shadows, chasing men away from the playground' (2013).

In the works of Adichie, Melrose, Oyeyemi and Bulawayo, all of whom have relocated, to one degree or another, from sub-Saharan countries to Western nations, we can see how some contemporary diasporic African women writers are engaging with Woolf's oeuvre. However, *within* sub-Saharan Africa itself, Woolf's presence is growing more slowly. She is being read, to be sure: Nigerian novelists such as Ben Okri, A. Igoni Barrett and Jude Dibia[1] count her among their favourite writers.[2] At most, however, when Woolf is known at all, it is generally through the title of *A Room of One's Own*. By examining the historical context of Woolf's essay from the date of its publication to the present day one can understand why Woolf is, except through the memorable title of one of her most famous works, largely absent in sub-Saharan Africa. The historic trajectory of this chapter starts with the final decades of the British Empire's colonial rule in sub-Saharan Africa, with a focus on Kenya (1929–59); continues through the half-century of the postcolonial era (1960–2010); and rounds back to the present day, to the age of globalisation (2011–). As I will show, colonialism and its institutional legacies militate against her broader appeal to sub-Saharan Africa-based writers.

Colonial Era, 1929–59

The Reference to a 'Negress' in A Room of One's Own *– 1929*

When Leonard Woolf began what would be his lifelong work on anti-imperialism in the 1910s, Virginia Woolf assisted him in his research for *Empire and Commerce in Africa, A Study in Economic Imperialism* (1919).[3] Woolf rarely mentions sub-Saharan Africa in her own work. One of the few instances occurs when a Black woman fleetingly appears in *A Room of One's Own* (1929): 'It is one of the great advantages of being a woman that one can pass even a very fine negress without wishing to make an Englishwoman of her' (52).[4] The face-to-face racial encounter takes place, it would seem, on the street, and is portrayed from the perspective of a white woman walking past a Black woman. In her role as a *flâneuse* on the streets of London, Woolf, a white woman, did direct her gaze upon people of colour, including Black women and men. She would have seen British colonials, African-Americans, Haitians, Congolese and more; drawing people from all over the world, London has long been a cosmopolitan city. Woolf would have seen Black Britons,[5] many of whom could trace their families and heritage in Great Britain for many generations. Sub-Saharan African people were present in the Britain at least since the arrival of Roman armies in the second and third centuries ('Early Black British' n.d.).

Whatever encounters Woolf did have with people of colour took place within a racist milieu. Frank Füredi writes that racist thinking was seldom questioned before the Second World War: '[e]ven radical critics of imperialism were reluctant to criticise the racist justification for national expansion' (1998: 6). Edmund Morel (1873–1924), a renowned activist who steadfastly worked to bring down the reign of the notorious King Leopold II in the Congo (see Hochschild 1999), referred in 1920 to Africans as 'black savages' and 'primitive . . . barbarians' (Fryer 2018: 317). For many white Britons, Danell Jones writes, Africans were viewed as 'people . . . on a low rung of the evolutionary ladder, without rational thought, moral integrity, or comprehensible language' (2018: 2).

Many white critics have perceived the unnamed white woman in *A Room* to be everywoman, who represents all women who choose to be united in their opposition to oppression in all forms.[6] However, these scholars do not take into account the way the white woman turns the Black woman into an Other. Like her fellow critics, Alice Walker recognises *A Room of One's Own* as a feminist manifesto; at the same time, she critiques Woolf by contrasting the fictitious sister of William Shakespeare, the aspiring writer Judith Shakespeare, with the life of the enslaved African-American poet Phillis Wheatley (1753–84):

Virginia Woolf wrote further, speaking of course not of our Phillis, that 'any woman born with a great gift in the sixteenth century [insert 'eighteenth century', insert 'black woman', insert 'born or made a slave'] would certainly have gone crazed, shot herself, or ended her days in some lonely cottage outside the village, half witch, half wizard [insert 'Saint'], feared and mocked at'. (Walker 1994: 404; all brackets and their insertions are Walker's).

As Tuzyline Jita Allan notes, 'Walker inserts black womanhood in the spaces of Woolf's text to make room for her own voice' (1993: 131). Allan herself is particularly interested in the emergence of the 'repressed African history' in Woolf's writing, noting that Woolf was aware of 'the dominant ideas about Africa's culture of savagery that barraged British society at the dawn and height of Empire' (1999: 123). Allan writes that Woolf 'endorsed the huge elements of that story that dealt with the uncivilized state of the racial other'; sometimes, however, Woolf 'queried' this story (1999: 122).

By the early 2000s, US-American white critics had become more aware of the racial tensions evoked by Woolf's manifesto. Jane Marcus contends that there is an indelible separation between the white Englishwoman and the 'negress', who is 'locked into her role as the representation of slavery ... [and] cannot then be included in the figure '"woman"' (2004: 25). Christine Froula, responding to Marcus, suggests that there are actually two distinct ways of perceiving the narrator. One option is that the narrator 'imagines the non-European woman *ethnographically*, as an autonomous subject of another civilization on whom she has no imperialist designs'; in contrast, writes Froula, Marcus argues that the narrator sees the non-European woman '*ethnocentrically*, as a postcolonial subject whose emancipation depends on the Eurocentric concept of rights'. Continues Froula, Marcus accuses Woolf of 'restricting' her characterisation 'to white Englishwomen' (Froula 2005: 31; italics mine). Froula acknowledges that, although Woolf[7] may display 'egregious blindness to her own complicity with imperial domination', the word 'But' – the first word of A Room – 'invites objection and dialogue', encourages all readers to consider a range of positions and statements made throughout the essay and invites them to 'speak on equal terms, unveiled and unmarked' (2005: 32).

In her 1994 essay-poem, Jamaican-American author Michelle Cliff highlights the racial and imperial underpinnings in the writing of Woolf. Though she is not specifically referring to A Room, Cliff addresses the ways Woolf, 'in much of her writing' (1994: 102), exposes Empire and its foundation to reveal the brute exploitation of 'dark people':

> Dark people are the subtext of Empire.
> The subordination, othering, ordering of those people.
> In the beginning was the slave trade.
> The basis of Empire was the traffic in human beings. (1994: 96)

Cliff writes,

> I have adjusted my gaze as I have taught myself the real history of color on the European landscape. Ever since, with my own adjusted gaze, I have noticed how *present* race is, in books where I was taught race was absent, if it was mentioned at all. (1994: 100)

Woolf herself had, as Jane Garrity writes, 'a racial blindspot', particularly in 'her difficulty in thinking outside polarized notions of the primitive and the civilized' (2003: 59).[8] While Woolf demonstrated great creativity and curiosity about the lives and art of the obscure white Britons she writes about over the course of her life, she does not quite make that imaginative leap with the art she sees by African artists. We know, for instance, that Woolf attended the Chelsea Book Club exhibition of 'Negro art' in 1920; she describes the carved statues that she saw as 'impressive' yet also 'sad' (D 2: 30).[9]

Ten years before the Chelsea Book Club exhibition, Virginia Stephen infamously participated in the 1910 *Dreadnought* hoax, concocted to mock the British navy. This public performance in blackface has received and continues to garner much critical attention and, increasingly, criticism. Peter Stansky calls the *Dreadnought* hoax 'disrespectful' (1997: 18); Kevin Young, 'exoticist' (2017); and Natasha Frost, 'racist' (2017).[10] Allan speculates that this 1910 prank may be echoed some two decades later in *A Room*; is the *Dreadnought* hoax, Allan asks, 'a drama waiting to be reconceived as Judith Shakespeare's Revenge, whose main act is the recuperation of repressed African history?' (1999: 123). African history is not recuperated in *A Room* – at most, it may be fleetingly figured as a Black woman – but the Judith Shakespeare envisioned by *A Room*'s narrator is re-imagined by Allan as one who will reprise 'repressed African history'.

'Kenya Novelists' and Kenya Memoirists – 1920s–50s

Woolf, through her narrator, asserts that (white) Englishwomen do not have the same urge as their white brothers to possess and to convert someone into imperial property. At the time she wrote this claim, there were real-life white European women who were walking by Black women in Kenya. These white counterparts were, like Woolf, professional women who made their living by writing. As white women hailing from the European metropole, what was their relationship to the women and men among whom they lived? It is worth testing Woolf's declaration about white women's lack of propensity to recreate others in her own image. To that end, I examine four romances set in Kenya by two British women who were contemporaneous with Woolf and whose work has been long forgotten, Nora K. Strange (1884–1974) and Florence Riddell (1885–1960). Strange worked as a secretary in Nairobi from 1913–19 and returned for a tour of the country in 1932. Riddell ran a private school for European settler children, also in Nairobi, around 1918–22 and never returned after that. Riddell did make a few short visits to individual farms while she was there. I also briefly touch upon three famous European-born writers, Isak Dinesen (1886–1961), Beryl Markham (1902–86) and Elspeth Huxley (1907–97), all of whom wrote memoirs about their lives in Kenya.

Before I consider how these five white writers 'saw' the Black women and men whom they encountered, I want to urge those who read Woolf to also read works written by and read by her contemporaries. Even if Woolf did not read romances set in Kenya, such as those by Strange and Riddell – and I have not yet found evidence that she did – she surely must have known about them. She was familiar with the genre of the romance novel, and even wrote some reviews on it, including *The Glen o'*

Weeping by Marjorie Bowen (1885–1952) (*E* 1: 138–9).[11] Woolfian critics have now made a host of cases for why we need to look at multiple strands of writing, including the lowbrow and highbrow, and those set in the metropole and the periphery – the global context of literary production. For example, Susan Stanford Friedman focuses on 'feminist geopolitical literacy' (1998: 109); Sonita Sarker on 'feminist whiteness studies' (2012: 119); Melba Cuddy-Keane on the ways literary modernism has been inflected by geopolitics and globalisation, and vice versa (2003: 543); and Andrea Lewis on 'overlapping histories' (1995: 107). While not a Woolfian critic, Ngũgĩ wa Thiong'o's notion of 'globalectics' also offers an approach for reading world literature holistically:

> Globalectical reading means breaking open the prison house of imagination built by theories and outlooks that would seem to signify the content within is classified, open to only a few. This involves declassifying theory in the sense of making it accessible . . . a means of illuminating the internal and the external, the local and the global dynamics of social being. (Ngũgĩ 2012: 61)

While Ngũgĩ is particularly interested in breaking out of the prison house of theory, his emphasis on world literature, accessibility, interconnections, and the local and global happens to mesh with geopolitical literacy, feminist and whiteness studies, and overlapping histories. To that end, it is illuminating to consider how the imaginary white *flâneuse* woman writer in *A Room of One's Own* compares to the real white settler women writers in Kenya.

Strange and Riddell[12] wrote what is referred to as the 'Kenya novel', a subgenre of romance fiction set in the white highlands of Britain's Crown Colony Kenya. Like Harlequin and Mills & Boon today, two of the leading brands of romance fiction, the 'Kenya novel' is formulaic: it is the Cinderella plot told over and over again. A white British female settler, typically from the lower-middle classes, moves to Kenya and meets an inscrutable British-born male settler from the middle to the upper classes. After following a path strewn with adventures and misunderstandings, the couple declare their eternal love for each other and look forward to a long life together in Kenya.[13]

Kenya and its animals and people form the backdrop of these novels and become an occasion for the writers to wax political. These 'Kenya novelists' tended to be unabashed white supremacists who used their texts to promote a racist ideology. They were also professionals who wrote to make a living. Given the high circulation of their novels,[14] they were successful at both earning money and conveying 'the white settler view of Kenya to British readers' (1991: 432). Against the background of Kenya, Strange wrote *Kenya Calling* (1928) and *Courtship in Kenya* (1932), and Riddell wrote *Kismet in Kenya* (1927) and *Castles in Kenya* (1929). In *Kismet in Kenya*, a representative example, the main heroine is named Virginia Stanhope, who, interestingly (given that romance heroines are often diminutive), is tall and brown and repeatedly called a 'man-woman' (Riddell 1932: 125, 136, 137, 175, 181).[15] Virginia comes to Kenya, along with other Stanhopes, to lay claim to an inheritance of a relative, who sets up a plot of progressive elimination. The Stanhope who stays for all of two years gets to inherit the plantation. Virginia does, and she also gets to marry the farm manager, Christopher Carey. The plots of the other three novels follow circuitous paths as well; however, rather than trace those, I want to examine the racist representations of the Black Kenyans who appear in all four books.

Black Kenyans are consistently stereotyped above all as lazy in these novels.[16] In one scene, from *Courtship in Kenya*, the coffee pickers, 'on the approach of the headman ... would put forth strenuous efforts to fill their baskets with ripe, rich cherry, but as soon as his back was turned, their activity was restricted to their tongues' (Strange 1932: 37). In *Kismet* Black Kenyan adults are characterised as children (Riddell 1932: 221), and in *Courtship* they are characterised as children 'with, in many cases, grown-up vices' (Strange 1932: 84) such as stealing (104–5) and drunkenness (137). They are also 'savage' (Strange 1932: 56, 137). The Kikuyu are called 'Kukes' (Strange 1932: 69),[17] and writers like Strange occasionally use the N-word (107). 'Native' women are represented as 'swarm[ing]' (Strange 1932: 86). They are 'insensible to pain' (Strange 1932: 88).

Some of the male African characters are named and granted a degree of individuality – even as they generally conform to the above stereotype. The Black male character Juma in *Kismet* may be jolly. At the same time, he steals from the white Stanhope family and sells the goods at the market (Riddell 1932: 264–7). The exception proves the rule in *Kenya Calling* when the white romantic hero Major Carew indicates that he 'would infinitely prefer to put ... in charge' the Black worker O'Molo rather than the white and 'haphazard' assistant Boyd (Strange 1928: 223).

The Black women African characters, on the other hand, are very rarely granted individuality. If these novels are any indication, when white Kenyan women writers 'passed' Black women, they hardly saw them at all. What they did 'see' were Black '*bibis*' – which in Swahili means ladies or women – who are not talking; instead, they are 'chattering' (Riddell 1932: 48, 223, 301) and almost always as a group, rarely solo (Riddell 1929: 55). Their 'chattering' is typically described as 'shrill' (Riddell 1929: 53, 94). The sound the women make at work becomes a part of nature, of a piece with the animals around them:

> the noises of full-born day began: the shrill chattering of the *bibis* as they weeded the parallel red paths between the coffee bushes, the *kee-kee* of a hawk soaring hungry-eyed above the plains, the cry of a vulture spying from afar the remains of a lion's meal. (Riddell 1929: 94; see also Riddell 1932: 310)

Black Kenyan women work in other capacities too, as ayahs or nursemaids, whose presence is almost always incidental to the scene (Riddell 1929: 150, 171, 215, 240, 260). Occasionally, we see the ayahs capable of feeling; at the very least, from the colonising writers' perspective, Black women have a maternal instinct. Riddell writes in *Castles in Kenya* about the 'worshipping *ayah*' who, along with all the 'simple black folks[,] invariably adore white babies' (1929: 166). When a Black Kenyan woman is singled out for attention from an undifferentiated whole, she is portrayed as derelict in her duties, like the servant Ishivina in *Kismet*, who, for example, rapidly spreads gossip about her employers (Riddell 1932: 118, 120, 124).

Infrequently, white women characters will try to make Englishwomen out of the Black Kenyan women they meet, but to no avail. The message that writers like Riddell try to transmit to their audience is that white Englishwomen should *not* try to do so. This message is conveyed forcefully in Riddell's *Kismet in Kenya* and Strange's *Courtship in Kenya*. In *Kismet*, one of the first things the newly arrived white fusty British woman

Rebecca Stanhope (one of the relatives clamouring for the inheritance) does when she reaches Kenya is to clothe the 'naked young breasts of one of the native ladies' (Riddell 1932: 55). She finds 'the way these native women run about the farm half-naked . . . positively disgusting! . . . [and] degrading to us all' (Riddell 1932: 57–8). However, the 'bust-bodices' that Rebecca sews for the women are instead found 'artistically swathed' around the head of the main servant Juma and functioning as a 'dinky door-curtain' (Riddell 1932: 55–6, see also 262–4). Rebecca's sister Susan Stanhope attempts to make Englishwomen out of the Kenyan women by 'Christianizing' them (Riddell 1932: 266, see also 106); however, her efforts prove fruitless too. She is told,

> Can't you see that the average native is satisfied with his own queer gods. He hasn't got either the intellect or education to digest our strange new ideas yet. Those who pretend to let you Christianize them are only falling in with your suggestion in order to find new methods of doing you down, Susan. They're willing to accept a surface smattering, that's all! (Riddell 1932: 266)

The white British woman Charlotte Walker in Strange's *Courtship in Kenya* visits Kenya for the purpose of investigating and critiquing 'the affairs of the Protectorate' (Strange 1932: 98). Over the course of her stay, Charlotte is 'enlightened' (Strange 1932: 147): she comes to see that British settler rule in Kenya is just and reasonable, especially as it is embodied in the figure of the eminently fair (and suave) government official Gilbert Selden.

Euro-Kenyan Memoirists – 1930s, 1940s, 1950s

As a product of 1920s and 1930s settler culture, the 'Kenya novel' attempted to justify British colonial rule in East Africa. From the 1930s through the 1950s, more novels and autobiographies emerged out of, or about, Kenya. Some of these are classics, including *Out of Africa* (1937) by Isak Dinesen, *West with the Night* (1942) by Beryl Markham and *The Flame Trees of Thika* (1959) by Elspeth Huxley. All three of these memoirs are nostalgic for a 'pristine Africa marked by adventure, freedom, and power' (Knipp 1990: 3) – or, the imaginary Kenya that is represented in the 'Kenya novels'. While Black Kenyans are portrayed in these three texts with more sympathy – and even love – than they are in the 'Kenya novel', they are still often of a piece with the landscape, as is evident in the following description by Isak Dinesen:

> The Natives were Africa in flesh and blood. The tall extinct volcano of Longonot that rises above the Rift Valley, the broad Mimosa trees along the rivers, the Elephant and the Giraffe, were not more truly Africa than the Natives were, – small figures in an immense scenery. All were different expressions of one idea, variations upon the same theme. . . . We ourselves, in boots, and in our constant great hurry, often jar with the landscape. (1972: 21)[18]

Dinesen waxes lyrical upon the landscape and the people who inhabit it. Westerners 'jar' this oneness and, with their boots, seem to trample upon it. In her quest to portray a kind of Platonic ideal of oneness, Dinesen erases not only individuality, but she also essentialises 'Natives' as undifferentiated from 'Nature'.[19]

Like Dinesen, Markham romanticises Africa and its people, whom she writes about as a whole:

> Competitors in conquest have overlooked the vital soul of Africa herself, from which emanates the true resistance to conquest. The soul is not dead, but silent, the wisdom not lacking, but of such simplicity as to be counted non-existent in the tinker's mind of modern civilization. Africa is of an ancient age and the blood of many of her peoples is as venerable and as chaste as truth. What upstart race, sprung from some recent, callow century to arm itself with steel and boastfulness, can match in purity the blood of a single Masai Murani whose heritage may have stemmed not far from Eden? (1983: 7)

In 'the tinker's mind of modern civilization', the soul of Africa is so simple as to be non-existent. In Markham's mind, Africa's soul is 'vital', resistant to conquest and ancient, outside of modernity and, it would seem, history. The young Maasai warrior is pure of blood and of the most aristocratic class possible, with his lineage traced as far back as Eden. In her desire to elevate the African soul and the Africans, Markham essentialises and reverts to stereotypes. The Maasai, in the European imagination, were the 'noble savages of Kenya' and frequently stereotyped 'like Native Americans, noble but doomed' (Shaw 1995: 184, 191; see also Kotowicz 2013).

Huxley, in contrast, describes the Kikuyu she and her family walked by when they first arrived in Kenya in terms that are far from ennobling:

> we found ourselves face to face with a Kikuyu who stood transfixed, just like an antelope pierced by the instinct to bolt, and then stepped aside to let us pass. But the women uttered high-pitched squeals like those of piglets, and scattered into the grass as if they had been partridges, their loads and babies swaying on their backs. (20)[20]

This encounter took place when Huxley was a six-year-old girl, just after her arrival in Kenya with her parents; her memoir was written decades later. She chooses to remember the Kikuyu as animals, with a Kikuyu man slightly more dignified and portrayed in the singular as a frightened antelope and the women as a foolish and language-less chattering collection of piglets, partridges and starlings. Micere Githae-Mugo notes that Huxley grouped the African characters in her writing into types and gave them labels. For example, the Kikuyu 'are on the whole, a troublesome lot, clannish and treacherous by nature, untrustworthy, "disputatious and difficult", but cunning' (1978: 18). Over the course of her life, Huxley took the 'the most adamant' position of the white Kenyan settler (Githae-Mugo 1978: 19; see also 39–51).

How did Black Kenyans themselves who lived during this period see the white settlers?[21] Near the end of the twentieth century, the African-American anthropologist Carolyn Martin Shaw recorded some of the life histories of Kikuyu men and women who had memories of the early part of the century. While 'the colonialists saw themselves as gods', the Africans saw them as purveyors of disease and infection (Shaw 1995: 11). Shaw emphasises that '[g]etting a sense of what Africans thought of the early colonialists is not easy' (1995: 10). We have already seen what six white European women writers living during the colonial era – Woolf in London and five of her real-life counterparts some 10,000 kilometres away in Kenya – thought when they saw Black people. With the postcolonial era, we can see the written reaction – with the acclaimed *Things Fall Apart* (1994) by the Nigerian novelist Chinua Achebe (1930–2013) as one of the most famous global examples – against hegemonic colonial rule and against the racism that is especially egregious in the 'Kenya novels' and is also present in the memoirs of writers like Dinesen, Markham and Huxley. What, specifically, was the response to the modernist writer Virginia Woolf, who largely protested colonial rule? To understand how Woolf was 'seen' in sub-Saharan African universities and the publishing industry, one must consider the curriculum.

Postcolonial Era – 1960–2010
Decolonisation and the Rise of Universities

The year 1960 opened up with the British Prime Minister Harold Macmillan's 'Wind of change' speech in which he announced that he would not block sub-Saharan African territories that were under British colonial rule from declaring independence (Macmillan 2011: 31). Indeed, 1960 marks the great era of decolonisation and is called the 'Year of Africa': seventeen African countries gained independence from three European colonisers, and more followed in the course of the decade.[22] Nation-building in African included development of the educational infrastructure, with universities taking pride of place.[23] Some universities, based on colonial models (Ndlovu-Gatsheni 2013: 191), had already been established near the end of the colonial era, including the Universities of Ghana (1948) and Nairobi (1956). Others, such as Makerere (1963),[24] were expanded. Initially, these, among the nearly eighty universities throughout sub-Saharan Africa – fifty in Anglophone countries, twenty-six in Francophone and two in Portuguese-speaking – were modelled on British, French and Portuguese patterns.[25] 'For many years', writes Bert N. Adams, 'there was strong sentiment that the African university was one of the best achievements of colonial policy' (1975: 51). By building on these successful institutions, 'it was possible for African students to gain educational parity with students in the metropolitan countries' (1975: 51), namely, those in the nations that had colonised theirs.

Quickly, however, the colonially based African university came to be seen as 'a mixed blessing, if not a problem' (Adams 1975: 51). Sabelo J. Ndlovu-Gatsheni writes that '[p]ostcolonial Africa possessed universities in Africa rather than African Universities' (2013: 189). In 1964, Kofi Abrefa Busia (1913–78), who later became a prime minister of Ghana (1969–72), reflected that 'over the years, as I went through college and university, I felt increasingly that the education I received taught me more and more about Europe, and less and less about my own society' (qtd in Adams 1975: 51). Africans like Busia came to perceive higher education 'as one of the technologies of subjectivation' that alienated Africans from 'their societies and cultures' (Ndlovu-Gatsheni 2013: 177).

It was in this atmosphere that Ngũgĩ wa Thiongo, Henry Owuor-Anyumba and Taban Lo Liyong proposed, in 1968, the abolition of the English department:

> if there is a need for a 'study of the historic continuity of a single culture', why can't this be African? Why can't African Literature be at the centre so that we can view other cultures in relationship to it? (qtd in Ngũgĩ 1986: 89)

Even before this call, in 1962 the student newspaper of Uganda's Makerere University 'appealed (fruitlessly) for "a revision of the present examination system", which otherwise "would cling to the new African university like the musty black crepe of an outworn Victorian fashion"' (qtd in Sicherman 2008: 19). Through the 1960s and 1970s and into the present day (Ndlovu-Gatsheni 2013: 182–3), the quest throughout much of sub-Saharan Africa has been to 'Africanise' the university and promote Indigenous cultures.[26]

Leavisism

Thus, during the postcolonial era, the writing of Virginia Woolf would have been resisted. Even in Anglophone universities where British literature dominated the curriculum, Woolf's work was not taught. Why? In Britain, as well as sub-Saharan Anglophone Africa (and Australia, as Suzanne Bellamy notes in her chapter), the English Department curriculum was dominated by Leavisism, the writing and ideas of F. R. Leavis (1895–1978) and Q. D. (known as Queenie) Leavis (1906–81). F. R. Leavis was renowned for his deep engagement with the concept of the university (Storer 2009: 104) and, for a time, his ideas, especially as they are crystallised in his *Education and the University* (1943), had a significant impact on the shaping of universities in post-war Britain. In the 1980s, Leavisism was in full bloom. Terry Eagleton wrote in 1983, 'English students in England today are "Leavisites" whether they know it or not' (31; see also Ortolano 2002: 624). Morris Freedman insists, 'it would be impossible to overstate the importance of F. R. Leavis. In the company of Johnson, Arnold, Eliot, and Trilling, he belongs on a Mount Rushmore of literary lawgivers' (2001: 99).

Given the ways that Anglophone African universities were modelled on British ones in the 1960s and onwards, it is hardly a surprise that their English Departments were characterised by Leavisite reading lists, approaches to literature and ideas about 'what literature is for' – in short, as Ngũgĩ writes, 'the Leavisite selected "Great Tradition of English Literature"' (1986: 90; see also Sicherman 1995: 15–17). The Leavises endorsed stalwarts like Edmund Spenser, William Shakespeare and John Milton and also included the male modernists James Joyce, T. S. Eliot, D. H. Lawrence and Joseph Conrad (Ngũgĩ 1986: 90; Gregor 1985: 439).[27] Lawrence and especially Conrad had a deep impact on Ngũgĩ's own writing (Sicherman 1995: 16–17). Yet, as Michaela Bronstein writes, Ngũgĩ's 'use of European literature shows not an African novelist trailing behind a European vanguard but an African novelist turning the tables on colonialism and repurposing the resources of the center for the benefit of the periphery' (2014: 414). And, as Peter J. Kalliney writes,

> one of the major legacies of Leavisite thinking is the tendency in postcolonial theory to regard English literary studies both as contaminated by its association with imperialism and also as the field of thought most capable of articulating resistance to metropolitan domination. (2013: 111)

The Leavis postcolonial legacy is a paradoxical one, and Kalliney explains how postcolonial thinkers used F. R. Leavis's ideas about to literature to forge a connection between their own nations and narrations.

The Publishing Industry and Libraries

The writing of Virginia Woolf was not part of the Leavises' 'Great Tradition', and they scorned her. Q. D. Leavis relegated Woolf to the status of a minor writer, minor thinker and minor human being, most infamously in 'Caterpillars of the Commonwealth unite!' (1938), her scathing review of *Three Guineas* and of Bloomsbury, where she calls 'Mrs Woolf's proposals' (one of which, writes Leavis, is 'to penalize specialists in the interests of amateurs' [208]) a series of 'babblings' (209). Nor was Woolf's writing widely published in sub-Saharan Africa. There are several reasons why, but it is important to begin with a caveat; as Hans Zell, one of the leading scholars on publishing in Africa, writes, Europeans tend to generalise the African publishing industry and to see it as a whole. Quoting Raphaël Thierry, Zell continues, 'Do we ever speak of European publishing as a whole, American or Asian publishing as a whole?' (2019: 27). With these words in mind, the section offers a general overview of the very complex reception of Woolf's work in sub-Saharan Africa. Among the many who have written about the publishing industry in sub-Saharan Africa,[28] Mukoma wa Ngugi describes how colonialism made educational publishing the model for the book industry (2018: 157) and points out that '[t]he colonial cultural machinery had not been interested in cultivating African literary culture or reading for pleasure' (2018: 148). Even now, 95 per cent of all books published in sub-Saharan Africa are educational (M. W. Ngugi 2018: 151, 157; see also Makotsi and Nyarki 1997: 4). The costs of importing books from foreign publishers to sub-Saharan Africa are also high (le Roux 2012: 260); with the rise of Amazon and e-books, however, this is changing. Non-educational books thus did not appear in great numbers unless they were 'dumped' by Western countries – that is, discarded as so much waste and, like waste, not wanted.[29]

All this is not to say that Woolf's work was entirely absent. Some of her books were sold by the Hogarth Press to bookshops in South Africa, including *The Years* (in 1939, eighteen copies), *Three Guineas* (in 1939, five copies) and *Flush* (in 1934, one copy), and in time one may unearth more sales of her books ('Modernist Archives Publishing Project' 2019), but these numbers are small. Other possible reading sites include, of course, libraries. However, libraries throughout much of sub-Saharan are typically poorly managed, underfunded (Makotsi and Nyariki 1997: 54) and 'starved' for books (Olden 1995: xi). Gertrude Kayaga Mulindwa, the director of the National Library of Uganda, notes that students tend to be the main users of libraries, and mainly as places to do their homework (2015: 74). Furthermore, according to Mulindwa, the very purpose of libraries is not made clear to the populace at large, and so they do not understand what they are to gain by frequenting them (2015: 76).

Postcolonial Writers and Woolf

In spite of the general absence of Woolf in the curriculum, publishing houses, bookstores and libraries, there were some postcolonial writers in Africa who must have had access to Woolf's texts. Nobel Prize-winner Doris Lessing (1919–2013), who spent most of the first three decades of her life in Zimbabwe (formerly Rhodesia), was an avid reader, though she may not have read work by Woolf until she moved to London. The contributors to the collection *Woolf and Lessing: Breaking the Mold* (1994), edited by Ruth Saxton and Jean Tobin, explore the affinities and resonances between the authors' writings.[30] Nadine Gordimer (1923–2014), also a Nobel Prize-winner, said in several interviews that Woolf was a significant 'influence' on her as a writer.[31] Ama Ata Aidoo cites passages from *A Room* in her essay, 'To be an African woman writer' (1988: 156, 163). Marjorie Macgoye (1928–2015), the great Kenyan writer, seems not to have engaged with Woolf. Other canonical women writers whose origins are in sub-Saharan Africa, including Flora Nwapa (1931–93, Nigerian), Bessie Head (1937–86, Botswanan) and Buchi Emecheta (1944–2017, Nigerian) do not demonstrate a writerly connection to Woolf.

At least one male postcolonial sub-Saharan African writer, Ngũgĩ wa Thiongo, does indicate that he had read Woolf or at least knew the title of *A Room*. He captures its spirit and its resistance to imperial authority in *Decolonising the Mind* (1986), where he writes about his year in prison, when he was kept in chains, underwent the torture of solitary confinement and was dehumanised and detained without having been charged for any crime:[32]

> I was in cell 16 at Kamĩtĩ Maximum Security Prison as a political detainee answering to a mere number K6,77. Cell 16 would become for me what Virginia Woolf had called *A Room of One's Own* and which she claimed was absolutely necessary for a writer. Mine was provided free by the Kenya government. (1986: 64)

It was while he was in Cell 16 that he wrote one of his masterpieces, *Devil on the Cross* (1980, 1982), and, significantly, in a language of his own – namely, in his mother tongue, Gikuyu. *Decolonising the Mind* is a polemic on the vital importance of Kenyan writers 'return[ing] to the sources of their being in the rhythms of life and speech and languages of the Kenyan masses' (qtd in Ngũgĩ 1986: 73). Ngũgĩ's observation resonates of the advice Woolf gives to women writers:

> Above all, you must illumine your own soul with its profundities and its shallows, and its vanities and its generosities, and say what your beauty means to you or your plainness, and what is your relation to the everchanging and turning world. (*AROO*: 93–4)

Global Era – 2011 to Present

A Virtual Room of One's Own

Before his reference to Woolf in 1986, Ngũgĩ had lived for eight years throughout Europe. Whether he had heard about Woolf while he was in Britain or Germany, or before when he was still living in Kenya, it is evident that Woolf was clearly, at the very least, in the air. By 2000, she was in a specific form of air – in the cloud, the ether, the internet. In sub-Saharan Africa, Woolf appears virtually, online,[33] through the title of one of her most famous works. Writing about Woolf's 'virtual' room of one's own, Tegan Zimmerman considers the new kind of room that is frequented online. He sees this virtual room as 'a free psychic and utopian space of the imagination' (2012: 49) and adds that 'Woolf continues to this day, in the era of virtual rooms and e-feminism, to engage and encourage women to wander, muse, and most importantly, to write' (2012: 50).

A Workshop of One's Own

It is from online references to *A Room of One's Own* that one can see how Woolf's idea of a room is transformed throughout regions of sub-Saharan Africa into a writers' workshop. If Woolf's name is popularly known in the US by the title of Edward Albee's play *Who's Afraid of Virginia Woolf?* (1962),[34] she may be known in sub-Saharan Africa as the writer who advises writers to find, above all, rooms of their own. In her reference to 'a room of one's own', the writer Aminatta Forna said in an interview that 'African writers have the greatest challenge' in finding a literal space to write

> because of the economic problems and extended family demands. . . . [B]eing able to gather writers for two weeks and let them share experiences and aspirations is a valuable thing. The greatest gift to any writer would be a stipend and a year off. But in the absence of that, a 2-week workshop is a pretty good gift. (Umez 2010)

E. Kim Stone notes, 'Gender inequities in many countries in Africa still make it difficult for women to have what Virginia Woolf wanted for British women writers in 1929 – money and a room of one's own' (2010). About her time at the Ebedi Writers' Residency in Lagos, the Kenyan teacher Gloria Mwaniga writes, after quoting 'A woman needs money and a room of her own if she is to write fiction', that the 'idea of a room of my own and time to write appealed to me' (2018). The introduction to a report by the Nigerian writer and poet Tolu Ogunlesi in the Kenyan publication *Kwani?* about a writing workshop includes the following reference to *A Room*: 'Over the last few years, African writers have found something larger than "a room of one's own" . . . in a . . . space shared between alike types from across the continent' (2012). This writer's workshop, like the one attended by Gloria Mwaniga, functions as this space: 'Normally held for a week, in some corner of Africa, the continental creative workshop, hosted by different institutions, has become a fixture in the African contemporary Lit and Cultural calendar' (Ogunlesi 2012). And yet, of course, other writers also long for a room in which to write as well, including the Zimbabwean novelist Tsitsi Dangarembga, who said in an interview, 'Virginia Woolf's shrewd observation that a woman needs 500 and a room of her own in order to write is entirely valid' ('Her politics' 2010). For the Nigerian playwright and Caine Prize winner Rotimi Babatunde, 'A room of one's own, in its literal and figurative implications, is all one needs to write, as Virginia Woolf brilliantly observed' (Specht 2013). And, he adds, it does not matter where: 'Any country that provides that is fine enough for me' (Specht 2013).

Aphorisms in Sub-Saharan Africa

There may be another way to approach the frequent presence of *A Room of One's Own* in sub-Saharan Africa. Proverbs and aphorisms are an integral part of many sub-Saharan African cultures.[35] Quotations from Woolf are quotable 'orts, scraps and fragments' (*BA*: 188, 189), especially those most relevant to the lives of contemporary sub-Saharan African writers across the gender spectrum. This literary tradition is a long and rich one (Monye 1996). Jeylan W. Hussein writes, 'Proverbs are the most widely and commonly used in the continent's long-standing tradition of oral arts . . . [and] the African proverbs have been facilitating the transmission of knowledge and conventions from generation to generation' (2005: 59). Chinua Achebe writes, 'proverbs are the palm-oil with which words are eaten' (1994: 7; see also Finnegan 2012).[36] One can see the frequent quotation of a room of one's own as a creative appropriation of Woolf, and one grounded in sub-Saharan literary and oral storytelling practices.[37]

The slogans derived from *A Room* appear often; however, Woolf's novels and other writings are rarely read. There may be other factors at work, however. Sub-Saharan African university libraries have, at best, limited access to conventional journals and serials (Suber: 2012). In terms of overall literacy, rates in sub-Saharan Africa are rising, but they are the lowest in the world (*Literacy Rates* 2017; Roser and Ortiz-Ospina 2018).[38] In the online journal *Wajibu*, Justus Mbae exclaims, 'reading is an alien culture to us, one that does not come naturally to most Kenyans' (n.d.).[39] Adaobi Tricia Nwaubani makes the same point:

> At almost every Nigerian literary event I have attended, the topic of the country's lack of reading culture has come up. The falling standard of education, increasing culture of materialism, poverty, and online distractions are given as reasons for this alleged loss of interest. (2015)

Margaret Baleeta attributes the lack of development of a 'reading culture' to the education system in general and 'the all-consuming emphasis placed on test scores' in particular (2005: 305, 313). Ruth L. Makotsi and Lily Nyariki write about the way that 'very little effort has been made by publishers and the [Kenyan] Government to develop a book reading culture' (1997: 2). On the other hand, as Kate Wilkinson reports, there may be more of a book-reading culture in South Africa than is claimed but that not enough studies had been done in this area (2017; see also Matsinde 2017).[40]

A Room of One's Own *as a 'How-for-Do' Book*

The reading culture (or lack thereof) does not militate against all books. Self-help or motivational books are globally popular, particularly in sub-Saharan Africa (Blum 2018: 1100, 1103). Elizabeth le Roux agrees: African readers have 'a significant preference for self-help books rather than fiction' (2012: 262). Motivational books, also called 'how-for-do' books (Blum 2018: 1102), are widespread in Nigeria (Nwaubani 2015). The 'self-help hermeneutic' does not just apply to self-help books, Beth Blum writes; she explains how British mission schools 'trained pupils to mine literature for a moral message' (2018: 1103). Students in the Global South even read texts that are 'not strictly considered part of the self-help canon' for the 'purposes of self-betterment' (2018: 1100).

A Room of One's Own can be considered as one of those 'how-for-do' texts. It is true that Woolf would not have wanted to be considered an author of a self-help manual (Blum 2018: 1111); along with other modernists, Woolf disassociated herself from Victorians like Samuel Smiles, renowned for his *Self-Help* (1859), which 'quickly became an international sensation' (Blum 2018: 1105). And yet, Woolf often gave advice. For example, in 'A letter to a young poet', she adjures young poets to stay in contact with 'the common objects of daily prose' (*E* 5: 310); and in 'How should one read a book?', she advises her audience to re-read and even write novels themselves to understand novels better (*E* 5: 579–80, 574). Though she evidently eschews the persona of a self-help guru and though her essay is slightly ironic, she endeavours to empower her readers, as one can see in the opening of 'How should one read a book?':

> In the first place, I want to emphasise the note of interrogation at the end of my title. Even if I could answer the question for myself, the answer would apply only to me and not to you. The only advice, indeed, that one person can give another about reading is to take no advice, to follow your own instincts, to use your own reason, to come to your own conclusions. (*E* 5: 572–3)

A Room of One's Own functions as a self-help book on how to write a book.[42] Its aphoristic qualities and its emphasis on the material conditions necessary for writing appeal as well to the Anglophone sub-Saharan reading public. While *A Room* is a feminist manifesto and a model of essay writing, it also cuts across races, history, nationalities and genders. Even if readers do not get beyond the title or the first few pages, they can, according to Blum, selectively appropriate 'the wisdom literature from the past' (2018: 1099). In the age of the internet, these and all readers have access to *A Room* online. Yet, as globalisation continues to reshape the lived experience of sub-Saharan Africans, Woolf's writing will function as more than a guide: it will become widely appealing within the continent just as it is outside of it, to diasporic writers like Chimamanda Adichie and Helen Oyeyemi, who, one might argue, are not trapped inside the figuration of the Black woman whom the white narrator of *A Room* encountered on the streets of London but, rather, become writers with voices and worlds of their own.

Chapter acknowledgment

I would like to thank Vara Neverow, who generously read many drafts of this chapter and provided invaluable suggestions and ideas. With thanks also to Paulina Pająk, Catherine Hollis, Celiese Lypka, Ziba Rashidian and Andrew Smyth.

Notes

1. See Okri (2014), A. I. Barrett (2016) and Evan Mwangi (2014).
2. That said, reviewers have not (yet) drawn connections between Woolf's work and theirs.
3. See Wayne A. Chapman and Janet M. Manson (1998), AnneMarie Bantzinger (2007), Dubino (2013) and Luke Reader (2017). Michèle Barrett writes that 'Woolf's extensive reading and research contributed to the distinctive factual ambition' of Leonard's *Empire and Commerce* (2013: 86; see also Froula 2005: 31).
4. This representation may not be 'African' as such, and that point will be addressed below.
5. See especially Jeffrey Green (1998). See also Susan Okokon (1998), Deborah J. Rossum (1997), Jane Marcus (2004: 43–4), Caroline Bressey (2010) and Michael Diamond (2007: 168).
6. Naomi Black, who, like many white Anglo-American scholars, views *A Room of One's Own* as a feminist tract (2004: 74), argues for the concept of the narrator as an everywoman.
7. Froula refers to 'Mary/Woolf' to indicate how it can be challenging to separate out the three Marys (Mary Beton, Mary Seton and Mary Carmichael), or the unnamed narrator, from Woolf herself (2005: 29, 31). In this chapter I will occasionally use 'Woolf' in place of one of *Room*'s variably named narrators.

8. Several passages from her diaries and letters evince this polarised thinking; for example, in a diary entry on 30 October 1935, she writes that she saw, at a peace conference, 'several baboon faced intellectuals; also some yearning, sad, green dressed negroes and & negresses, looking like chimpanzees brought out of their cocoanut groves to try to make sense of our pale white platitudes' (D 4: 349). No matter where in the world the Black attendees hail from, their place is in the jungle ('cocoanut groves').
9. Cliff remarks how Woolf was 'at once touched, and removed' (1994: 100), and Lois J. Gilmore notes that, overall, with regard to 'ethnographic exhibition culture', 'Woolf's response to the primitive is arbitrary, ambivalent, troublesome, and largely ironic, embodying notions of the primitive' (1999: 128).
10. See Peter Stansky (1997: 17–46) for a full account of this hoax. See also Genevieve Abravanel (2000), Gretchen Gerzina (2006), Danell Jones (2013), Georgia Johnston (2009), Steve Putzel (2012: 51–2) and Allan (1999: 123–4). For a discussion of the connections among Woolf, the *Dreadnought* hoax, blackface scandals in the US in 2019 and the use of the word 'Nigs' by early twentieth-century US and British writers, see the Woolf listserv discussion 5–12 February 2019.
11. She knew of the work of bestselling romance novelists, including those by Mrs Humphry Ward (1851–1920) (E 1: 15), and at the end of her life she even wrote an essay defending one of the most famous romance novelists, Marie Corelli (1855–1924) (D 5: 260 n.13).
12. Others include Florence Kilpatrick (1888–1968), Margaret Peterson, Mrs Horace Tremlett (1875–1948), Eleanor Mordaunt (1876?–1942), Jane Rodner, Julie Peters (pseudonym of Flora Hilda Day; 1900–34) and Elsie M. Sanders.
13. See Dubino (1993: 103–4).
14. For example, as C. J. D. Duder notes, the serial version of Riddell's *Kenya Mist*, published in 1924, appeared in the *Daily Express* when its circulation was over 750,000 (1991: 434)
15. One might be tempted to see Virginia Stanhope as Virginia Woolf's idea of an androgyne.
16. Non-British ethnicities, including Jewish and Irish, fare only a little better. Jewish people are 'swarthy Hebraic' though to be admired for their business acumen (Strange 1928: 45–6), and the Irish have a 'dislike of anything approaching really hard work' (Riddell 1929: 106).
17. This is a highly disparaging term. See Daniel J. Goldhagen (2009: 329) and Caroline Elkins (2005: 49).
18. Colonialism continues in the movies. Writes Duder about the 1985 film *Out of Africa*, 'Robert Redford and Meryl Streep have combined to produce an image of white Kenya at least as romantic, inaccurate and as popular as the "Kenya novels" of the 1920s' (1991: 438) in which, again, Black women blur into the background. *Nowhere in Africa* (2001), a German movie also set in Kenya, repeats this image of Kenya, as the reviewer Stephen Holden writes: 'The native Kenyans . . . fit a little too snugly into a stock National Geographic stereotype of gentle, noble tribespeople living harmoniously with nature and viewing the European arrivals with an affectionate amusement' (2003).
19. For further discussion on *Out of Africa*, see Abdulrazak Gurnah (2000: 283–8), Dubino (2007), Simon Lewis (2000) and Judith Thurman (1982: 282–5). See also Sidonie Smith, who writes about the way Dinesen aligns herself with Black Africans as a way to distance herself from bourgeois, patriarchal philistinism. However, as Smith writes, as 'class disidentification encourages her to align difference along a certain axis, it also leads her to participate in a mystifying essentialism' (1992: 428).
20. *The Flame Trees of Thika* was turned into a seven-part series that, like *Out of Africa*, was bathed in a nostalgic glow. Writes Lesley Smith, who questioned the wisdom of the remake of this 1981 series into a DVD in 2005,

> the exoticism of this mini-series raises the ongoing question of the place of Africa in the Western imagination. In *Flame Trees* Africa functions as a fantasy land, a tabula rasa designed to teach European adventurers to be more resilient, more enterprising,

and more successful individualists. Africa is a spark to the imagination rather than an inhabited continent with millennia of history and cultures. (2005)

21. While there may be little written documentation on how sub-Saharan Africans perceived Europeans during nineteenth- and twentieth-century colonial rule, there is abundant evidence of African resistance; for one history, see Adam Hochschild (1999: 164, 314). In Kenya, the most sustained period of resistance is the Mau Mau rebellion from 1952–60; among other accounts, see Elkins (2005).
22. Currently there are fifty-four recognised nation-states in Africa; all but four of them were European colonies in the 1950s. By the 1950s, the European colonisers were Britain, France, Belgium and Portugal. Focusing mostly on Kenya, this chapter broadly addresses Anglophone sub-Saharan African countries. The Anglophone sub-Saharan African countries that gained independence from Britain in the late 1950s and through the 1960s are Botswana, Gambia, Ghana, Kenya, Malawi, Nigeria, Sierra Leone, Uganda and Zambia. South Africa gained independence in 1910 and was under apartheid rule until 1994. Zimbabwe, formerly Rhodesia, became self-governing in 1923 and gained nation-status in 1965. It was under de facto apartheid rule until 1980. Sudan, now two countries, Sudan and South Sudan, is geographically located in Northern Africa; both are also often regarded as part of sub-Saharan Africa. South Africa, Zimbabwe, Sudan, and South Sudan are Anglophone countries, though, as is true of all sub-Saharan Africa, are also multilingual.
23. See Emmanuel A. Ayandele for the challenges that most of Africa faced in its attempt to provide higher education for its citizens in record time (1982: 168, 175).
24. The University of Nairobi is the largest university in Kenya. Makerere University is the largest public university in Uganda.
25. See Ayandele (1982: 168), Bert N. Adams (1975: 51), Carol Sicherman (1995: 15; 2008: 19).
26. See also Nobantu L. Rasebotsa (1997: 178–80), Ndlovu-Gatsheni (2013: 177, 182), Beverley Thaver (2009: 29), and Lynn Quinn and Jo-Anne Vorster (2017: 131).
27. The Leavises also included Jane Austen and George Eliot in their canon, but these writers are not mentioned in the Leavis-informed curricula in sub-Saharan African English departments.
28. See, above all, Henry Chakava (2005), widely known the 'father of African publishing'. For more on Chakava, see Chris Wanjala (2016), Ruth Makotsi and Lily Nyarki (1997) and le Roux (2012).
29. The question of book donations is a complicated one. Sub-Saharan Africa is a major target for donations. For some of the issues that arise, see le Roux (2012: 260) and especially Hans Zell and Raphaël Thierry (2016: 51).
30. See also Anne E. Fernald (2006: 163).
31. See Gordimer (1990: 37, 129, 139, 140, 145, 215); Gordimer (1983); Andrew Vogel Ettin (1993: 18–20, 56).
32. See his *Wrestling with the Devil: A Prison Memoir* (2018), for a powerful and full account of this year.
33. For current statistics on how widespread the internet is in Africa, see 'Internet penetration in Africa' (2019).
34. See Brenda R. Silver, who writes 'it would be hard to overstate the importance of *Who's Afraid of Virginia Woolf?* in constructing and securing Virginia Woolf's name recognition and the persona attached to it' (1999: 102).
35. Aphorisms are of course not limited to Africa; they are global, now more than ever. For a short critique on how, with Instagram, 'This should be the golden age of the aphorism', but in fact is not, see Jessa Crispin (2019: 9; see also Adam Gopnik [2019]).
36. See Patrick Ibekwe (1998) for a sampling of African proverbs from around the world.
37. In the twenty-first century, in the age of virtual space, one might see, as John Miles Foley writes, about what he calls the 'Pathways Project', 'fundamental similarities and correspondences between humankind's oldest and newest thought-technologies: oral tradition and the Internet' (Foley 2012: 5).

38. Book lovers around the world bemoan the ways that people do not read for pleasure (Blakemore 2015; Brown 2017).
39. In 2018, Fareeda Abdulkareem asked, 'Nigeria has produced some of the world's best authors – so why is its reading culture so poor?' (2018).
40. See also le Roux, who writes, 'Widespread reading and literacy . . . have a relatively short history in Africa. Reception studies have a shorter history still, and there is still a great deal of work to be done in this field' (2012: 261).
41. For a full discussion on the voice that Woolf takes in 'How should one read a book?', see Beth R. Daugherty (1997).
42. Interestingly, a new 'self-help' movement, seemingly inspired by Woolf, has arisen in the US. It is called 'What would Virginia Woolf do?' (Collins 2018); on her blog Paula Maggio posted a response: 'What would Virginia Woolf do? Not this' (2018).

Bibliography

Abdulkareem, F. (2018), 'Nigeria has produced some of the world's best authors – so why is its reading culture so poor?', *Quartz Africa*, 14 May, <https://qz.com/africa/1276791/nigeria-has-produced-some-of-the-worlds-best-authors-so-why-is-its-reading-culture-so-poor/> (last accessed 21 May 2019).

Abravanel, G. (2001), 'Woolf in blackface: Identification across *The Waves*', in J. Berman and J. Goldman (eds), *Virginia Woolf: Out of Bounds: Selected Papers from the Tenth Annual Conference on Virginia Woolf*, New York: Pace University Press, pp. 113–19.

Achebe, C. (1994 [1959]), *Things Fall Apart*, New York: Anchor Books.

Adams, B. N. (1975), 'Africanizing the African university', *Africa Today*, 22: 3, pp. 51–9, <https://www-jstor-org.proxy006.nclive.org/stable/pdf/4185521.pdf?refreqid=excelsior%3Aecf54448d31fc02a26e4c3085980a220> (last accessed 19 May 2019).

Adichie, C. N. (2016), '"The arrangements": A work of fiction', *New York Times Book Review*, 28 June, <https://www.nytimes.com/2016/07/03/books/review/melania-trump-in-chimamanda-ngozi-adichie-short-story.html> (last accessed 4 May 2019).

Aidoo, A. A. (1988), 'To be an African woman writer – an overview and a detail', in K. H. Petersen (ed.), *Criticism and Ideology: Second African Writers Conference, Stockholm 1986: Seminar Proceedings No. 20 from the Scandinavian Institute of African Studies*, Uppsala: Scandinavian Institute of African Studies, pp. 155–72.

Allan, T. J. (1993), 'A voice of one's own: Implications of impersonality in the essays of Virginia Woolf and Alice Walker', in R.-E. Boetcher Joeres and E. Mittman (eds), *The Politics of the Essay: Feminist Perspectives*, Bloomington: Indiana University Press, 1993, pp. 131–47.

Allan, T. J. (1999), 'Civilization, its pretexts, and Virginia Woolf's imagination', in J. McVicker and L. Davis (eds), *Virginia Woolf and Communities: Selected Papers from the Eighth Annual Conference on Virginia Woolf*, New York: Pace University Press, pp. 117–27.

Ayandele, E. A. (1982), 'Africa: The challenge of higher education', *Daedalus*, spec. issue: 'Black Africa: A generation after independence', 111: 2, pp. 165–77, <https://www-jstor-org.proxy006.nclive.org/stable/pdf/20024790.pdf?refreqid=excelsior%3Af2e2d2e237bf2f6142c11edf7f280067> (last accessed 19 May 2019).

Baleeta, M. (2005), 'Barriers to reading: Cultural background and the interpretation of literary texts', in K. Perry, S. Andema, L. Tumusiime (eds), *Teaching Reading in African Schools*, vol. 1, Newark, DE: International Reading Association, pp. 305–13.

Bantzinger, A. (ed.) (2007), 'Leonard Woolf: Special topic', *Virginia Woolf Miscellany*, 72 (whole issue).

Barrett, A. I. (2016), 'Good minds suggest: A. Igoni Barrett's favorite books about transformation', *Goodreads*, 29 February, <https://www.goodreads.com/interviews/show/1107.A_Igoni_Barrett> (last accessed 15 May 2019).

Barrett, M. (2013), 'Virginia Woolf's research for *Empire and Commerce in Africa* (Leonard Woolf, 1920)', *Woolf Studies Annual*, 19, pp. 83–122.

Black, N. (2004), *Virginia Woolf as Feminist*, Ithaca, NY: Cornell University Press.

Blakemore, E. (2015), '27 percent of U.S. adults didn't read a single book last year', *Smithsonian.com*, 23 October, <https://www.smithsonianmag.com/smart-news/27-percent-american-adults-didnt-read-single-book-last-year-180957029/> (last accessed 21 May 2019).

Blum, B. (2018), 'The self-help hermeneutic: Its global history and literary future', *PMLA*, 133: 5, 1099–1117.

Bressey, C. (2010), 'Looking for work: The Black presence in Britain 1860–1920', *Immigrants and Minorities: Historical Studies in Ethnicity, Migration and Diaspora*, 28: 2–3, pp. 164–82, <https://doi.org/10.1080/02619288.2010.484245> (last accessed 19 May 2019).

Bronstein, M. (2014), 'Ngũgĩ's use of Conrad: A case for literary transhistory', *Modern Language Quarterly*, 75: 3, pp. 411–37, <https://read.dukeupress.edu/modern-language-quarterly/article-pdf/75/3/411/443002/MLQ753_04Bronstein_FF.pdf> (last accessed 30 December 2018).

Brown, B. (2017), 'The ultimate guide to global reading habits (infographic)', *Global English Editing*, 12 May, <https://geediting.com/world-reading-habits/> (last accessed 21 May 2019).

Bulawayo, N. (2013), *We Need New Names*, New York: Reagan Arthur Books.

Chakava, H. (2005), *Publishing in Africa: One Man's Perspective*, Oxford: Bellagio Publishing Network.

Chapman, W. K. and J. M. Manson (eds) (1998), *Women in the Milieu of Leonard and Virginia Woolf: Peace, Politics, and Education*, New York: Pace University Press.

Cliff, M. (1994), 'Virginia Woolf and the imperial gaze: A glance askance', in M. Hussey and V. Neverow (eds), *Virginia Woolf: Emerging Perspectives: Selected Papers from the Third Annual Conference on Virginia Woolf*, New York: Pace University Press, pp. 91–102.

Collins, N. L. (2018), *What Would Virginia Woolf Do? And Other Questions I Ask Myself as I Attempt to Age without Apology*, New York: Hatchette Book Group.

Crispin, J. (2019), 'Why isn't Instagram more witty?', *New York Times*, 2 June, Sunday Review, p. 9.

Cuddy-Keane, M. (2003), 'Modernism, geopolitics, globalization', *Modernism/modernity* 10: 3, pp. 539–58, <https://muse-jhu-edu.proxy006.nclive.org/article/46433/pdf> (last accessed 14 May 2019).

Daugherty, B. R. (1997), '"Readin', writin', and revisin'": Virginia Woolf's "How should one read a book?"' in B. C. Rosenberg and J. Dubino (eds), *Virginia Woolf and the Essay*, New York, St. Martin's, pp. 159–75.

Diamond, M. (2007), *'Lesser Breeds': Racial Attitudes in Popular British Culture, 1890–1940*, London: Anthem, 2007.

Dinesen, I. (1972 [1937]), *Out of Africa*, New York: Vintage.

Dubino, J. (1993), 'The Cinderella Complex: Romance fiction, patriarchy, and capitalism', *The Journal of Popular Culture* 27: 3, pp. 103–18.

Dubino, J. (2007), 'The source, the movie, and the remake: Imperial nostalgia in Isak Dinesen's *Out of Africa*, Sydney Pollack's *Out of Africa*, and Melinda Atwood's *Jambo, Mama*', in M. Helmers and T. Mazzeo (eds), *The Traveling and Writing Self*, Newcastle upon Tyne: Cambridge Scholars Publishing, pp. 35–60.

Dubino, J. (2013), 'Globalization, inter-connectivity, and anti-imperialism: Leonard Woolf, the Hogarth Press, and Kenya', in A. Martin and K. Holland (eds), *Interdisciplinary/Multidisciplinary Woolf: Selected Papers from the Twenty-Second Annual International Conference on Virginia Woolf*, Clemson, SC: Clemson University Digital Press, pp. 231–6.

Duder, C. J. D. (1991), 'Love and the lions: The image of white settlement in Kenya in popular fiction, 1919–1939', *African Affairs* 90: 360, pp. 427–38.

Eagleton, T. (1983), *Literary Theory: An Introduction*, Minneapolis: University of Minnesota Press.

'Early Black British' (n.d.), *Black Past*, <https://www.blackpast.org/blog/early-black-british> (last accessed 16 May 2019).

Elkins, C. (2005), *Imperial Reckoning: The Untold Story of Britain's Gulag in Kenya*, New York: Henry Holt.

Ettin, A. V. (1993), *Betrayals of the Body Politic: The Literary Commitments of Nadine Gordimer*, Charlottesville, VA: University Press of Virginia.

Fernald, A. E. (2006), *Virginia Woolf: Feminism and the Reader*, New York: Palgrave Macmillan.

Finnegan, R. (2012), *Oral Literature in Africa*, Cambridge, UK: Open Book Publishers, <https://books.openedition.org/obp/1202?lang=en> (last accessed 20 May 2019).

Foley, J. M. (2012), *Oral Tradition and the Internet: Pathways of the Mind*, Urbana: University of Illinois Press.

Freedman, M. (2001), 'The oracular F. R. Leavis', *The American Scholar*, 70: 2, pp. 93–9, <https://www.jstor.org/stable/41213151> (last accessed 20 January 2019).

Friedman, S. S. (1998), *Mappings: Feminism and the Cultural Geographies of Encounter*, Princeton, NJ: Princeton University Press.

Frost, N. (2017), 'When Virginia Woolf dressed up as an "African" prince to fool the Royal Navy', *Atlas Obscura*, 29 August, <https://www.atlasobscura.com/articles/dreadnought-hoax-virginia-woolf-navy-racism-prince> (last accessed 15 May 2019).

Froula, C. (2005), *Virginia Woolf and the Bloomsbury Avant-Garde: War, Civilization, Modernity*, New York: Columbia University Press.

Fryer, P. (2018 [1984]), *Staying Power: The History of Black People in Britain*, London: Pluto Press.

Füredi, F. (1998), *The Silent War: Imperialism and the Changing Perception of Race*, New Brunswick, NJ: Rutgers University Press.

Garrity, J. (2003), *Step-Daughters of England: British Women Modernists and the National Imaginary*, Manchester, UK: Manchester University Press.

Gerzina, G. H. (2006), 'Bushmen and blackface: Bloomsbury and "race"', *The South Carolina Review* 38: 2, pp. 46–64.

Gilmore, L. J. (1999), 'Virginia Woolf, Bloomsbury, and the primitive', in J. McVicker and L. Davis (eds), *Virginia Woolf and Communities: Selected Papers from the Eighth Annual Conference on Virginia Woolf*, New York: Pace University Press, pp. 127–35.

Githae-Mugo, M. (1978), *Visions of Africa: The Fiction of Chinua Achebe, Margaret Laurence, Elspeth Huxley, Ngugi wa Thiongo*, Nairobi: Kenya Literature Bureau.

Goldhagen, D. J. (2009), *Worse than War: Genocide, Eliminationism, and the Ongoing Assault on Humanity*, New York: PublicAffairs.

Gopnik, A. (2019), 'Brevity, soul, wit: The art of the aphorism', *The New Yorker*, 22 July, pp. 67–9.

Gordimer, N. (1983), 'Nadine Gordimer, the art of fiction no. 77', interview, *The Paris Review*, 88, <https://www.theparisreview.org/interviews/3060/nadine-gordimer-the-art-of-fiction-no-77-nadine-gordimer> (last accessed 19 May 2019).

Gordimer, N. (1990), *Conversations with Nadine Gordimer*, ed. M. T. Bazin and M. D. Seymour, Jackson: University Press of Mississippi.

Green, J. (1998), *Black Edwardians: Black People in Britain 1901–1914*, Abingdon, UK: Frank Cass Publishers.

Gregor, I. (1985), 'F. R. Leavis and "The Great Tradition"', *The Sewanee Review*, 93: 3, pp. 434–46, <https://www.jstor.org/stable/27544482> (last accessed 20 January 2019).

Gurnah, A. (2000), 'Settler writing in Kenya: "Nomenclature is an uncertain science in these wild parts"', in H. J. Booth and N. Rigby (eds), *Modernism and Empire*, Manchester, UK: Manchester University Press, pp. 275–91.

'Her politics did not end in books' (2010), *The Zimbabwean*, 14 June, <http://www.thezimbabwean.co/2010/06/her-politics-did-not-end-in-books/> (last accessed 20 May 2019).

Hochschild, A. (1999), *King Leopold's Ghost: A Story of Greed, Terror, and Heroism in Colonial Africa*, New York: Mariner Books.

Holden, S. (2003), 'Film review; a shallow snob at the beginning, transformed by exile to Africa', *New York Times*, 7 March, <https://www.nytimes.com/2003/03/07/movies/film-review-a-shallow-snob-at-the-beginning-transformed-by-exile-to-africa.html> (last accessed 31 December 2019).

Hussein, J. W. (2005), 'The social and ethno-cultural construction of masculinity and femininity in African proverbs', *African Study Monographs*, 26: 2, pp. 59–87, <https://doi.org/10.14989/68240> (last accessed 20 May 2019).

Huxley, E. (2000 [1959]), *The Flame Trees of Thika: Memories of an African Childhood*, New York: Penguin.

Ibekwe, P. (1998), *Wit & Wisdom of Africa: Proverbs from Africa & the Caribbean*, Trenton, NJ: Africa World Press.

Ikheloa, I. R. (2013), [untitled review], *The New Black Magazine*, 6 May, <http://www.thenewblackmagazine.com/view.aspx?index=3112> (last accessed 15 May 2019).

'Internet penetration in Africa' (2019), *Internet World Stats: Usage and Population Statistics*, 18 May, <https://www.internetworldstats.com/stats1.htm> (last accessed 21 May 2019).

Johnston, G. (2009), 'The Dreadnought Hoax', *Woolf Studies Annual*, 15, 1–45.

Jones, D. (2018), *An African in Imperial London: The Indomitable Life of A. B. C. Merriman-Labor*, London: C. Hurst & Company.

Jones, D. (2013), 'The Dreadnought hoax and the theatres of war', *Literature and History*, 22: 1, pp. 80–94.

Kalliney, P. J. (2013), *Commonwealth of Letters: British Literary Culture and the Emergence of Postcolonial Aesthetics*, New York: Oxford University Press.

Knipp, T. R. (1990), 'Kenya's literary ladies and the mythologizing of the White Highlands', *South Atlantic Review*, 55: 1, pp. 1–16, <https://www-jstor-org.proxy006.nclive.org/stable/pdf/3199869.pdf?refreqid=excelsior%3Acf982bdd8aa171336f31a185ba6c786b> (last accessed 15 May 2019).

Kotowicz, A. M. (2013), 'Maasai identity in the 21st century', Master's thesis, University of Wisconsin-Milwaukee, <https://dc.uwm.edu/cgi/viewcontent.cgi?article=1720&context=etd> (last accessed 18 May 2019).

Leavis, F. R. (1979 [1943]), *Education and the University*, Cambridge: Cambridge University Press.

Leavis, Q. D. (1938), 'Caterpillars of the Commonwealth unite'!, review of *Three Guineas* by V. Woolf, *Scrutiny* September, pp. 203–14.

le Roux, E. (2012), 'Book history in the African world: he state of the discipline', *Book History*, 15, pp. 248–300, <https://www.jstor.org/stable/23315050> (last accessed 27 January 2019).

Lewis, A. (1995), 'The visual politics of Empire and gender in Virginia Woolf's *The Voyage Out*', *Woolf Studies Annual* 1, pp. 106–19.

Lewis, S. (2000), 'Culture, cultivation, and colonialism in *Out of Africa* and beyond', *Research in African Literatures* 31: 1, pp. 63–79.

Literacy Rates Continue to Rise from One Generation to the Next (2017), UNESCO Institute for Statistics, Fact Sheet No. 45, September, <http://uis.unesco.org/sites/default/files/documents/fs45-literacy-rates-continue-rise-generation-to-next-en-2017_0.pdf> (last accessed 21 May 2019).

Macmillan, H. (2011 [1960]), 'Wind of change', 'Great speeches of Africa's liberation', *African Yearbook of Rhetoric*, 2: 3, pp. 27–39, <http://www.africanrhetoric.org/pdf/J%20%20%20Macmillan%20-%20%20the%20wind%20of%20change.pdf> (last accessed 18 May 2019).

Maggio, P. (2018), 'What would Virginia Woolf do? Not this.', *Blogging Woolf* 5 April, <https://bloggingwoolf.wordpress.com/2018/04/05/what-would-virginia-woolf-do-not-this/> (last accessed 22 May 2019).

Makotsi, R. L. and L. K. Nyariki (1997), *Publishing and Book Trade in Kenya*, Nairobi: East African Educational Publishers.

Marcus, J. (2004), *Hearts of Darkness: White Women Write Race*, New Brunswick, NJ: Rutgers University Press.

Markham, B. (1983 [1942]), *West with the Night*, San Francisco: North Point Press.

Matsinde, T. (2017), 'Challenging the statement that Africans don't read', Shoko Press, 2 March, <http://www.shokopress.com/challenging-the-statement-that-africans-dont-read/> (last accessed 21 May 2019).

Mbae, J. G. (n.d.), 'Kenya: A reading nation?', *Wajibu: A Journal of Social and Religious Concern*, 19, <http://africa.peacelink.org/wajibu/articles/art_4487.html> (last accessed 21 May 2019).

Melrose, F. (2017), *Johannesburg*, London: Corsair.

'Modernist Archives Publishing Project' (MAPP) (2019), <modernistarchives.com> (last accessed 7 June 2019).

Monye, A. A. (1996), *Proverbs in African Orature: The Aniocha-Igbo Experience*, Lanham, MD: University Press of America.

Mulindwa, G. K. (2015), 'National libraries in Africa: Refocusing their work to ensure delivery of services', *Library Trends*, 64: 1, pp. 72–83, <https://muse-jhu-edu.proxy006.nclive.org/article/601975/pdf> (last accessed 19 May 2019).

Mwangi, E. (2014), 'Nigerian writer who fell in love with Binyavanga', 3 August, <https://mobile.nation.co.ke/lifestyle/Jude-Dibia-Binyavanga-Wainaina-Homosexuality-Africa/1950774-2235606-format-xhtml-3cdpmo/index.html> (last accessed 15 May 2019).

Mwaniga, G. (2018), 'Lots of "peppe" and fermented food: Diary of a visitor to Lagos', *Daily Nation*, 9 February, <https://www.nation.co.ke/lifestyle/weekend/Diary-of-a-visitor-to-Lagos/1220-4298460-j0itu4z/index.html> (last accessed 20 May 2019).

Ndlovu-Gatsheni, S. J. (2013), *Empire, Global Coloniality and African Subjectivity*, New York: Berghahn Books.

Ngugi, M. W. (2018), *The Rise of the African Novel: Politics of Language, Identity, and Ownership*, Ann Arbor: University of Michigan Press.

Ngũgĩ w. T. (1986), *Decolonising the Mind: The Politics of Language in African Literature*, Nairobi: East African Educational Publishers Ltd.

Ngũgĩ w. T. (2012), *Globalectics: Theory and the Politics of Knowing*, New York: Columbia University Press.

Ngũgĩ w. T. (2018), *Wrestling with the Devil: A Prison Memoir*, New York: The New Press.

Nwaubani, A. T. (2015), 'The secret of Nigerian book sales', *The New Yorker*, 1 October, <https://www.newyorker.com/business/currency/the-secret-of-nigerian-book-sales> (last accessed 21 May 2019).

Ogunlesi, T. (2012), 'Unlearn, un-know & then maybe write', <http://www.kwani.org/editorial/report_essay/21/unlearn_unknow__then_maybe_write.htm> (last accessed 20 January 2019).

Okokon, S. (1998), *Black Londoners 1880–1990*, Stroud, UK: Sutton Publishing.

Okri, B. (2014), 'A mental tyranny is keeping black writers from greatness', *Guardian*, 27 December, <https://www.theguardian.com/commentisfree/2014/dec/27/mental-tyranny-black-writers> (last accessed 15 May 2019).

Olden, A. (1995), *Libraries in Africa: Pioneers, Policies, Problems*, Lanham, MD: Scarecrow Press.

Ortolano, G. (2002), 'Two cultures, one university: The institutional origins of the "Two Cultures" controversy', *Albion: A Quarterly Journal Concerned with British Studies*, 34: 4, pp. 606–24, <https://www.jstor.org/stable/4054671> (last accessed 20 January 2019).

Oyeyemi, H. (2014), 'What motivates author Helen Oyeyemi: "Perversity . . . keeps me writing"', interview by T. Cowan, *The Globe and Mail*, 11 April, <https://www.theglobeandmail.com/

arts/books-and-media/what-motivates-author-helen-oyeyemi-perversity-keeps-me-writing/article17941117/> (last accessed 5 May 2019).

Putzel, S. D. (2012), *Virginia Woolf and the Theater*, Lanham, MD: Farleigh Dickinson University Press.

Quinn, L. and J.-A. Vorster (2017), 'Connected disciplinary responses to the call to decolonise curricula in South African higher education', in B. Carnell and D. Fung (eds), *Developing the Higher Education Curriculum: Research-Based Education in Practice*, London: University College London (UCL) Press, pp. 131–44.

Rasebotsa, N. L. (1997), 'Teaching African literature in the Department of English, University of Botswana', *Women's Studies Quarterly*, spec. issue, 'Teaching African literatures in a global literary economy', 25: 3/4, pp. 178–87, <https://www.jstor.org/stable/40003382> (last accessed 21 December 2018).

Reader, L. (2017), '"An alternative to imperialism": Leonard Woolf, the Labour Party and imperial internationalism, 1915–1922', *The International History Review*, 41: 1, pp. 157–77.

Riddell, F. (1929), *Castles in Kenya*, Philadelphia, PA: J. B. Lippincott.

Riddell, F. (1932), *Kismet in Kenya*, Philadelphia, PA: J. B. Lippincott.

Roser, M. and E. Ortiz-Ospina (2018), 'Literacy', *Our World in Data*, 20 September, <https://ourworldindata.org/literacy> (last accessed 21 May 2019).

Rossum, D. J. (1997), '"A vision of Black Englishness": Black intellectuals in London, 1910–1940', *Stanford Electronic Humanities Review* 5: 2, <http://stanford.edu/group/SHR/5-2/rossum.html> (last accessed 2 June 2016).

Sarker, S. (2012), 'Woolf and theories of postcolonialism', in B. Randall and J. Goldman (eds), *Virginia Woolf in Context*, Cambridge: Cambridge University Press, pp. 110–28.

Saxton, R., and J. Tobin (eds) (1994), *Woolf and Lessing: Breaking the Mold*, New York: St Martin's Press.

Scutts, J. (2018), '*Orlando* is the Virginia Woolf novel we need right now', *Vulture*, <https://www.vulture.com/2018/10/why-virginia-woolfs-orlando-feels-essential-right-now.html> (last accessed 1 June 2020).

Shaw, C. M. (1995), *Colonial Inscriptions: Race, Sex, and Class in Kenya*, Minneapolis: University of Minnesota Press.

Sicherman, C. (1995), 'Ngũgĩ's colonial education: "The subversion . . . of the African *mind*"', *African Studies Review*, 38: 3, pp. 11–41.

Sicherman, C. (2008), 'Makerere's myths, Makerere's history: A retrospect', *Journal of Higher Education in Africa / Revue de l'enseignement supérieur en Afrique*, 6: 1, pp. 11–39, <https://www-jstor-org.proxy006.nclive.org/stable/pdf/jhigheducafri.6.1.11.pdf> (last accessed 19 May 2019).

Silver, B. R. (1999), *Virginia Woolf Icon*, Chicago, IL: University of Chicago Press.

Smith, L. (2005), '*Flame Trees of Thika* (1981)', popmatters.com, 25 May, <https://www.popmatters.com/flame-trees-of-thika-dvd-2496240704.html> (last accessed 18 May 2019).

Smith, S. (1992), 'The other woman and the racial politics of gender: Isak Dinesen and Beryl Markham in Kenya', in S. Smith and J. Watson (eds), *De/Colonizing the Subject: The Politics of Gender in Women's Autobiography*, Minneapolis: University of Minnesota Press, pp. 410–35.

Specht, M. H. (2013), 'Interview with playwright and fiction writer Rotimi Babatunde', *Necessary Fiction*, 29 July, <http://necessaryfiction.com/writerinres/InterviewwithRotimiBabatunde> (last accessed 23 May 2019).

Stansky, P. (1997), *On or about December 1910: Early Bloomsbury and Its Intimate World*, Cambridge, MA: Harvard University Press.

Stone, E. K. (2010), 'African fiction in America today: Five questions for postcolonial literature scholar E. Kim Stone', *Encyclopædia Britannica*, 1 November, <http://blogs.britannica.com/2010/11/african-fiction-in-america-today-five-questions-for-postcolonial-literature-scholar-e-kim-stone> (last accessed 20 May 2019).

Storer, R. (2009), *F. R. Leavis*, New York: Routledge.
Strange, N. K. (1928), *Kenya Calling*, London: Stanley Paul.
Strange, N. K. (1932), *Courtship in Kenya*, London: Stanley Paul.
Suber, P. (2012), *Open Access*, Cambridge, MA: MIT Press, <https://openaccesseks.mitpress.mit.edu/> (last accessed 21 May 2019).
Thaver, B. (2009), 'Transforming the culture of higher education in South Africa', *Academe*, 95: 1, pp. 28–30, <https://www.jstor.org/stable/40253294> (last accessed 21 December 2018).
Thurman, J. (1982), *Isak Dinesen: The Life of a Storyteller*, New York: St Martin's Press.
Umez, U. P. (2010), 'Reminiscences: Interview with Aminatta Forna', *Sentinel Literary Quarterly: The Magazine of World Literature*, 4: 1, October–December, <http://www.sentinelpoetry.org.uk/slq/4-1-oct2010/interviews/uche-peter-umez.html> (last accessed 20 May 2019).
Walker, A. (1994 [1972]), 'In search of our mothers' gardens', in A. Mitchell (ed.), *Within the Circle: An Anthology of African American Literary Criticism from the Harlem Renaissance to the Present*, Durham, NC: Duke University Press, pp. 401–9.
Wanjala, C. L. (2016), 'Going down memory lane with doyen of publishing', *Daily Nation*, 25 March, <https://www.nation.co.ke/lifestyle/weekend/Going-down-memory-lane-with-doyen-of-publishing/1220-3133954-10yykwk/index.html> (last accessed 19 May 2019).
Wilkinson, K. (2017), 'Do only 14% of South Africans read books?', *Africa Check*, 8 September, <https://africacheck.org/reports/14-south-africans-read-books/> (last accessed 21 May 2019).
Williams, J. K. (2016), 'Adichie on Mrs Trump', *New York Times Book Review*, 28 June, <https://www.nytimes.com/2016/07/03/books/review/adichie-on-mrs-trump.html> (last accessed 15 May 2019).
Woolf, V. (1957 [1929]), *A Room of One's Own*, New York: Harcourt, Brace and World.
Woolf, V. (1969 [1941]), *Between the Acts*, San Diego: Harcourt Brace Jovanovich.
Woolf, V. (1977–1984), *The Diary of Virginia Woolf*, ed. A. O. Bell, 5 vols, New York: Harcourt Brace Jovanovich.
Woolf, V. (1986–2011), *The Essays of Virginia Woolf*, ed. A. McNeillie and S. N. Clarke, 6 vols, San Diego: Harcourt; London: Hogarth Press.
Young, K. (2017), 'The time Virginia Woolf wore blackface', *The New Yorker*, 27 October, <https://www.newyorker.com/books/page-turner/the-time-virginia-woolf-wore-blackface> (last accessed 15 May 2019).
Zell, H. (2019), *Publishing and the Book in Africa: A Literature Review for 2018*, <https://www.academia.edu/38243661/Publishing_and_the_Book_in_Africa_-_A_Literature_Review_for_2018> (last accessed 19 May 2019).
Zell, H. M. and R. Thierry (2016), 'Book donation programmes for Africa: Time for a reappraisal? Two perspectives', *African Research & Documentation. Journal of SCOLMA (the UK Libraries and Archives Group on Africa)*, 127, <https://www.academia.edu/13165497/Book_Donation_Programmes_for_Africa_Time_for_a_Reappraisal_Part_I> (last accessed 27 May 2019).
Zimmerman, T. (2012), 'The politics of writing, writing politics: Virginia Woolf's "A [Virtual] Room of One's Own"', *Journal of Feminist Scholarship* 3: 3, <https://digitalcommons.uri.edu/cgi/viewcontent.cgi?article=1034&context=jfs> (last accessed 20 May 2019).

Part II

Woolf's Legacies in Literature

12

Virginia Woolf's Enduring Presence in Uruguay

Lindsey Cordery

It is intriguing for people in Uruguay to come across the country's name in a work by Virginia Woolf. In a scene from 'Kew Gardens', an elderly man's confusion triggers 'spirits of the dead' (Woolf 1989: 93) in his mind and the sight of beautiful flowers immerse him in a distant, romantic time of a quasi-magical land, which he calls Uruguay. Why did Virginia Woolf think of Uruguay for this moment in 'Kew Gardens'? What was she reading; or, perhaps, what had she been looking at? The sumptuous art in the Marianne North pavilion in Kew Gardens – which houses the work of the English Victorian biologist and botanical artist, who had travelled widely in South America – might easily conjure up 'forests . . . tropical roses, nightingales, sea-beaches' and, perhaps even, the imagery of 'mermaids and women drowned at sea' (*CSF*: 37). By the time she published 'Kew Gardens', Woolf had read W. H. Hudson's *The Purple Land* (1904), almost entirely set in Uruguay, which is evoked as an arcadia-like landscape. Charles Darwin's *The Voyage of the Beagle* (1839), with his descriptions of Uruguay, were also known to Woolf, as she writes a note in her diary on 24 March 1940 stating that she must write an essay on *The Voyage of the Beagle* (D 5: 274). And perhaps Joseph Conrad's Viola from *Nostromo* (1904), who had fought on the battlefields of Uruguay alongside Giuseppe Garibaldi, is echoed in Evelyn M.'s romantic yearning for Garibaldi in *The Voyage Out*. Yet, despite these various connections between Woolf and descriptions or evocations of Uruguay, it is unlikely that we can come to any verifiable conclusion as to why she chose this country as the name of an imagined place in 'Kew Gardens'. However, we might marvel at the rightness of the description of a place that to Woolf was mere fantasy: that blend of nostalgia, loss and death set against a backdrop of natural beauty that is so peculiarly Uruguayan.

Several years after 'Kew Gardens' was published, Uruguayan readers were introduced to Woolf through the literary journal *Sur*, founded by Argentinian Victoria Ocampo (1890–1979) in 1931. Two years later, Ocampo founded Sur publishing house and then in 1939, with a group of Argentinian and Spanish writers, founded Sudamericana, also a publishing house. New European and North American works in translation brought out by these specifically southern-hemisphere Spanish-language publishers were strongly influential not only in the River Plate but throughout Latin America.[1] In Spain, under Franco's dictatorship (1936–75), several publishing houses closed down or relocated to Buenos Aires or Mexico Distrito Federal with these cities becoming important publishing centres. Ocampo's editorial projects were unique in that they were both local and led by a woman.

In *Sur*, Ocampo presented reviews and translations of European and American contemporary writers she valued, such as Woolf, Carl Jung, André Malraux, Martin Heidegger, E. M. Forster, Henry Miller, Vladimir Nabokov and Graham Greene, among others. And it was through the journal that she carried out her personal literary vocation: that is, writing as a woman, experimenting with different forms freed of masculine structures of thought and expression that Woolf also believed would have to be left behind if an authentic female literature were to be born. Ocampo discovered Woolf in 1929 when her friend Sylvia Beach gave her *A Room of One's Own* to read; eventually Ocampo met Woolf, even visiting her at her home and corresponding with her for a time. For Ocampo, Woolf and the Hogarth Press were her inspiration for *Sur*, which was published regularly from 1931 to 1966 and then more sporadically until 1996, becoming the most important and influential literary journal in Spanish-speaking America. Ocampo's journal and its major role in the Spanish-speaking world have been examined in numerous studies that testify to *Sur*'s paramount importance in introducing English and French literature in translation to River Plate readers.[2] Thanks largely to Ocampo's enthusiasm for Woolf's writings, they were read in Uruguay in translation soon after their original publications in Britain.

The importance of *Sur*, especially in its early years, cannot be overestimated. It was through four instalments printed in *Sur* (1934–5) that readers in both Buenos Aires and Montevideo were introduced to Woolf's *A Room of One's Own*, translated by Jorge Luis Borges as *Un cuarto propio*. Importantly, Borges's translation was read as a call for feminism by Uruguayan women in the 1960s;[3] an outcome of this movement in Montevideo was the *Centro de Comunicación Virginia Woolf – Cotidiano Mujer* [Virginia Woolf Communications Centre and Women's Daily], founded in 1985. Ocampo rightly hailed *A Room* as opening up new directions for women and for women's writing in Latin America. Prior to this, only the 'Time passes' section of *To the Lighthouse* had been translated into Spanish, anonymously in 1931, thus anticipating the translations that would be published in Buenos Aires in the 1930s (see Lázaro [2000]). Two years after his translation of *A Room*, Sur published Borges's translation of *Orlando* [*Una biografía*] (1937), which was received enthusiastically – although it was primarily read as fantasy, its feminist aspect was lost in Borges's translation.[4] Ocampo discussed all of Woolf's work in her literary criticism, including *A Writer's Diary*, and continued to publish on the author after her death (see Salomone [2006]); and Ocampo's *Testimonios* (published between 1935 and 1977). In Montevideo, Woolf's works in English were read by a relatively small but growing English-speaking public and, from 1934, were widely available as library books.

In this chapter, I trace nearly ninety years of reading and writing on Woolf in Uruguay, focusing first on her early critical reception and then on distinguished Uruguayan writers who either explicitly or implicitly dialogue with Woolf's life and works. I demonstrate how early engagements with Woolf's works focused initially on translations of *Orlando* and later on *A Writer's Diary*, although *Mrs Dalloway* and *To the Lighthouse* received critical attention too. Later, Stephen Daldry's 2002 film *The Hours* kindled major interest in Woolf studies, leading many to re-read *Mrs Dalloway* and her other works. Among contemporary Uruguayan writers, references to Woolf may be less explicit, but her works nonetheless permeate the texts of those I discuss here. This is true of Alicia Migdal, a self-styled 'womanly writer' (Pérez 2013: 107), who writes in her own recognisably feminine voice, in the tradition founded by

Virginia Woolf and Marguerite Duras.[5] Finally, with my mind on the opening lines of Cristina Peri Rossi's poem 'Virginia Woolf, etc.' that positions previous women writers as her 'sweet foremothers' (1986: 115), I spoke to two young women writers whose work I see as embodying the 'foreign tongue' of Migdal's feminine sentences, Fernanda Trías and María Sánchez, who acknowledge Woolf's impact.

The Cultural Context for the Reception of Woolf in Uruguay

In the early twentieth century, Montevideo was a city with a distinctly Francophile cultural outlook. Europe in general was seen by Montevideans as the centre of culture and art, with Paris specifically as the epitome of high culture; while the British, and the English language itself, were more often associated with commerce. This changed after the First World War as Britain's allies in South America took increasing interest in its language and literature, which Britain readily encouraged. In 1934, the British ambassador to Uruguay, Sir Eugene Millington-Drake, and several prominent Uruguayans founded the Anglo-Uruguayan Cultural Institute (AUCI), which played a fundamental role in the country's shifting cultural scene, which was slowly turning from Francophilic to Anglophilic. This role was further enhanced by the British Council opening an office in Montevideo, which contributed to the expansion of the AUCI's library, making it the largest English language library in South America. Among the first books entered in the library's catalogue were *Mrs Dalloway*, *To the Lighthouse* and *The Waves*. The AUCI also had its own magazine *Cultura* (1945–7), which published reviews and articles on both local and British authors as well as translations from English, such as Virginia Woolf's 1930 'Street haunting: A London adventure', translated as 'Una aventura en Londres'. The magazine's overall aim was more ambitious, however, as the project sought an in-depth immersion in British culture for the general public; this included social events and conferences on British literature, both in English and in Spanish.

Wider in scope and readership than *Cultura*, the weekly journals *Marcha* (1939–74) and *Número* (1949–55, 1963–4) were highly influential in Montevideo, both before and after *Sur* was founded. *Marcha* and *Número* were closely connected to *Sur*, with some critics writing for both the Montevideo and Buenos Aires journals. *Marcha* was founded by Carlos Quijano, a lawyer, politician, essayist and journalist, and Juan Carlos Onetti, who went on to become one of Latin America's most notable writers. Quijano and Onetti were considered senior members of the so-called Generación del 45, a Uruguayan intellectual and literary movement that also included the founders of *Número*. *Marcha* influenced a change in the cultural and political outlook of the country by critically engaging with world politics and cultural topics from a Latin American perspective. Towards the end of the 1960s, after the Cuban revolution and in the pre-dictatorship days of CIA infiltration in Uruguay, *Marcha* took a leading role in the ongoing political debates throughout Latin America until the journal was shut down in 1974 by the Uruguayan military dictatorship (1973–85)[6] and its leading contributors were forced to seek exile.

Edited by Emir Rodríguez Monegal (henceforward Monegal) and Idea Vilariño, *Número* was especially important in introducing to Montevideo new works by authors from the English-speaking world in translation and through critical studies of their work. Monegal, one of the most distinguished intellectuals of his time, continues to be regarded as one of the twentieth century's most influential Latin American literary critics.[7] A friend of Ocampo and great admirer of Borges – his *Jorge Luis Borges: A Literary Biography* was published in New York in 1978 – Monegal shared their interest and admiration for contemporary English literature, advocating strongly for the publication of translations into Spanish. Like Ocampo and the *Sur* group, Monegal believed in the 'democratic role' of translation as it was later described by Patricia Willson (2017: 273); that is, foreign language texts being made available to single-language (Spanish in this case) readers. For *Marcha*, Monegal wrote a column on English literature, as Borges had for *Sur* in the 1930s, and briefly edited the literary section of the journal; like Borges, Monegal was a true Anglophile. By mid-century, Montevideo was notable for fertile intellectual debates in literary journals; after the Cuban revolution, these debates were increasingly divisive as they became more political and ideological rather than purely literary.

One of the most ardent battles was about the role of foreign literatures in a Latin American context. Monegal and his intellectual rival Ángel Rama, a renowned academic, literary critic and member of the Generación del 45, disagreed over the direction to be taken by what was commonly known as the nation's 'aesthetic project'; that is, whether to align politically and culturally with Latin America rather than with so-called imperialist nations, a debate which included defining the role and place of foreign literatures. This debate led to a polarisation of Uruguayan culture and intellectuals in general, with Rama's position (as a 'Latinamericanist') prevailing in the 1960s and 1970s, and *Sur* now being regarded with suspicion by some members of the so-called anti-US and anti-imperialist intelligentsia. However, Pablo Rocca's study of foreign writers read in Uruguay at this time reveals that the most popular texts came from authors writing in English: James Joyce, Henry James, H. G. Wells, William Faulkner, Ernest Hemingway, Katherine Anne Porter, Katherine Mansfield, Virginia Woolf, Joyce Cary, Graham Greene, T. S. Eliot and Evelyn Waugh (Rocca 2006). It is undeniable that interest in new literature in English, in what was once a strongly Francophile culture, was due largely to the work of Ocampo and Borges through *Sur*, as well as *Marcha* and *Número*.

The Early Critical Reception of Woolf in Uruguay

In the 1950s, however, the 'Latin America versus imperialist countries' polarisation was yet to come. In 1952, *Número* published an article by George Pendle, 'Virginia Woolf, née Stephen',[8] which he wrote after reading Noel Annan's *Leslie Stephen: His Thought and Character in Relation to His Time* (1951). Pendle was deeply impressed by Virginia Stephen, more so than by her father, although she figures only briefly as a writer in Annan's study. Pendle sees Woolf as the inevitable literary descendent of her Stephen forbears, known for their generations of clear, lucid thinking, referring specifically to her father. In his essay, Pendle states that

> it was the pressure of her Stephen predecessors that led Woolf to develop and perfect a literary style which we recognise today as her own. . . . In Virginia Woolf the talents and aspirations of the Stephen family were conjoined; the Stephens, however, lacked one quality: the poetic vision. And this was her own personal and decisive contribution: she added the sudden outburst of beauty which occasionally illuminates life. (1952: 160)[9]

However, Leslie Stephen's shadow as a renowned man of letters loomed large on the Montevideo literary scene, so it was not surprising that Woolf's comment on her father – 'His life would have entirely ended mine' (*WD*: 135) – caused a stir among reviewers and readers alike when it was published posthumously in *A Writer's Diary*. Woolf and her father's complex literary and filial relationship was further revealed later that same year when Ocampo, to coincide with the translation of *A Writer's Diary* (*Virginia Woolf: Diario de una escritora*), wrote several articles for the daily Buenos Aires newspaper *La Nación*, which were later collected and published as *Virginia Woolf en su Diario* [Virginia Woolf and Her Diary] (Ocampo 1954). Monegal's review of Ocampo's book for *Marcha* on 9 July 1954 was titled 'De Virginia a Victoria' [From Virginia to Victoria], referencing Ocampo's 'Carta a Virginia Woolf' [Letter to Virginia Woolf] (1934), included in the collection as an appendix, as well as underscoring Ocampo's autobiographical presence in the book. For Monegal, the book was more than just a study of Woolf; it was also a study of Victoria Ocampo.

Monegal subsequently wrote a long essay for *Marcha* (1955) titled 'Vanidad, creación y muerte en el *Diario* de Virginia Woolf' [Vanity, Creation and Death in Virginia Woolf's *Diary*]. The essay begins by reflecting on the fact that Leonard Woolf's editing of the diaries Virginia left behind presents only a partial picture of the author. Monegal, in agreement with Leonard, finds that a diary can always be seen as a 'caricature' (*WD*: viii); however, he also finds this

> fragment of Virginia Woolf's self, tendentious and specialised and so, by definition, incomplete, how irresistible and revealing! How absorbing ... and how through what she obstinately hides and involuntarily reveals we can reach out to other fragments, and other visions. . . . [H]ow can one resist the temptation to reconstruct (bearing in mind what is presented here) the rest of her partially hidden personality ... through the vibrant, intense notes to be found within the pages of the book. Even if one knows that one may be mistaken, and that the picture will be only partial. (1955: 20)[10]

He then moves on to discuss Woolf's 'vanity' in connection with her anxiety about possible reactions to her works as they go into publication, and the torture she experiences in solitude as she awaits critics' comments; he calls this section the '*superficie* [surface] of this *terrible diario* [terrible diary]' (1955: 20). In the second section dealing with Woolf's creation, Monegal marvels at what he describes as 'an extraordinary testimony of literary creation: one of the most extraordinary in Western literature since Flaubert's letters. . . . Virginia Woolf belongs to the great renovation of the contemporary novel, which attempts to capture other realms of reality' (1955: 21). Monegal's final section contemplates the figures of death and dying, of endings, that accumulate towards the end of Woolf's diary: the threat posed by fascism; the refugees from Bilbao, Munich, Danzig, war; Leonard and Virginia's suicide pact in the event of an invasion; and the completion of *Between the Acts*. All of these elements converge in her suicide: 'The tension to live, and the tension to create became too great. . . . [H]er sensibility, the quality which made her such a magnificent creator, left her utterly vulnerable to the world' (1955: 21).[11] Monegal closes his essay with a quotation from Woolf's *Diary*, which perfectly portrays the tension between the life and death that he observed. Written just days before her suicide, Woolf attempts to organise her life – 'observe . . . spend this time to the best advantage' – but immediately after this she writes: 'I will go down with my colours flying' (*D* 5: 358). ('Me hundiré con todas las banderas desplegadas', Monegal translates.) 'And that was what she did so magnificently' (1955: 21),[12] he concludes.

Monegal's critical attention to Woolf (and to writers such as Edgar Allan Poe, Rudyard Kipling and G. K. Chesterton) underscores his conviction that English culture was the liveliest and the best suited to fertilise local Latin American culture. Moreover, Monegal undoubtedly, and rightly, perceived himself as the key player in this process. Rama, the other notable critic, and Monegal were rivals from the time they both wrote for *Marcha*; this rivalry became clearly political after the Cuban revolution. Rama took a Latin Americanist position, establishing his anti-USA and anti-CIA position, as well as critically examining, almost exclusively, Latin American literature. Monegal, on the other hand, deepened his Anglophilic position (he was already inclined towards being pro-USA) and stopped writing for *Marcha*; the journal he started, *Mundo Nuevo* (1966–8), was attacked by Rama for its alleged pro-USA sympathies.[13] During the dictatorship, both critics lived abroad: Monegal as professor of Latin American contemporary literature at Yale University from 1969 to his death in 1985, while Rama lived in exile in Venezuela, where he founded the Biblioteca de Ayacucho, until his death in 1983. After their deaths, all of Woolf's published work was available in translation. However, for many Spanish-language readers, the most interesting and original of Woolf's books was *Orlando*, which they would read in Borges's translation. Certainly, this was the book that Armonía Somers was to find most inspiring.

Armonía Somers (1914–94)

Somers's legal name was Armonía Etchepare, and under this name she was known as a prominent pedagogue specialising in adolescent education. She represented Uruguay at international conferences and was appointed to positions of leadership in international organisations; she published several pedagogical works and received awards and distinctions for her contributions to the field. Armonía Somers grew up in the reformed welfare state of President José Batlle y Ordóñez (1903–7 and 1911–15), where women earned the right to vote as early as 1917. Despite the fact that Batlle y Ordóñez reformed and modernised society through legislation far in advance of other parts of the world – among many other reforms, making Uruguay a secular state – the influence of the Catholic church and its control over social conduct, especially concerning the roles of women, remained as powerful and puritanically repressive as ever. Armonía Somers kept her two careers quite apart from one another: Armonía Etchepare was the name she used as a pedagogue, and Armonía Somers – the name she is most commonly known by today – was the pseudonym for her anti-Catholic, sexually explicit, counter-establishment fiction.

In 1950, Somers published her first novel, *La mujer desnuda* [The Naked Woman][14] in *Clima* (nos 2–3), a short-lived literary journal. The novel caused a tremendous scandal for its sexually explicit content and strong criticism of social and religious matters. Published under her new name, critics believed that the pseudonym was used to hide the identity of some well-known male writer. Years went by before the novel received critical attention, and even then it was only after Somers had established her reputation as a short story writer. Rama considered Somers's work unique in the history of Uruguayan literature, finding everything in her writings 'strange, disconcerting and repulsive while at the same time astonishingly fascinating' (1963: 30). Somers has been considered with Onetti, Clarice Lispector and María Luisa Bombal;[15] and, more recently, following the translation of *La mujer desnuda* into English, Somers's first novel is being promoted on the internet in connection with Angela Carter and Djuna Barnes. Initially, Somers's work was read as fantasy writing, as *Orlando* was, especially when considered in the context of the regional or cosmopolitan realism of its time. Innovative, subversive, irreverent and surreal, Somers's work is now also regarded as feminist. Perera San Martín contextualises *La mujer desnuda* as 'one of the first feminist manifestos. . . . The novel denounces, in rather dramatic narrative terms, the sexist basis of social organisation' (qtd in Blixen 1996: 195).[16]

There are several striking echoes from Woolf's *Orlando* that run throughout Somers's novel. *La mujer desnuda* is the story of Rebeca Linke, who one day looks into a mirror and sees a beautiful face (her own) and decides to leave her life as a prisoner of bourgeois society. She does so by buying a large house surrounded by fields and a river, making sure, unlike Orlando, to keep the title deeds in her possession. She travels to her new home by train, naked under her overcoat, on her thirtieth birthday. Once in the house, she picks up a book she finds on the bedside table that has a small, beautifully wrought dagger bookmark inside. The book is more than bedside reading: it is a 'libro de cabecera' (Somers 1994b: 10), which means a favourite book, read frequently, for guidance. I suggest that this book could be *Orlando*, Somers's very own 'libro de cabecera', one she read throughout her life, as proven by her final texts that I will later discuss. There are further similarities between Somers's novel and *Orlando*; for example, Rebeca's radical and empowering decision to leave is taken at the same age that Orlando undergoes a change from male to female, though this is a consequence of the times rather than of Orlando's own volition. Furthermore, Rebeca takes up the dagger from the 'libro de cabecera' and slices off her head, which rolls down her body like a heavy fruit, signalling that she is severing social and religious manacles (as in William Blake's poem 'London') that are forged in the mind of the society she lives in; she later forces it firmly back onto her neck, like a helmet. While Orlando is first seen slicing at the head of a Moor, Rebeca slices off her own.

Orlando's clothes proclaim his or her sex; Rebeca is naked and will remain so throughout the story: 'the history of Orlando's sexual and social identity is inescapable from his, then her, attire' (DiBattista 2006: lxiii). Rebeca sheds her social identity with her clothing and flaunts her sexual self: 'She would never more relapse into the ancient mating of the two contradictory halves of herself' (Somers 1994b: 11). In this new state, 'Rebeca Linke, aged thirty . . . left her personal life behind on a strange memory-lacking frontier' (1994b: 15) and walks away from her house through tall grasses and the woods into the home of a sleeping woodcutter and his wife. She lies by the man, touches him and then leaves. But her presence in the community causes a commotion among the men in a small village, arousing them all to a sexual frenzy, even the priest. They rape their wives, and among various incidents we read of a woman whose husband forces her to tell him of a long-ago relationship she had with another girl, with whom she shared an innocent kiss, reminiscent of *Mrs Dalloway*. Rebeca selects one man she desires, Juan, and they make passionate, explicit love in the open air, echoing the passion of Orlando and Shelmerdine. When the incensed villagers begin to close in around them, Juan persuades Rebeca to leave him; unwillingly, she agrees to make her way back to her house. In a final turn, Somers evokes Woolf's death as Rebeca drowns in the river.

Although Somers was reluctant to comment on possible influences on her work (Dalmagro 2013: 23), *Orlando* is clearly the strongest intertext in *La mujer desnuda*. Somers's final work, which she completed and prepared for publication just before her death, stages her personal farewell and finally declares her literary allegiance to, and admiration for, both Borges and Woolf. The book jacket for *El hacedor de girasoles. Tríptico en amarillo para un hombre ciego* [The Sunflower Maker. Yellow Triptych for a Blind Man] (Somers 1994a) uses a well-known line drawing of Borges's hands resting on his walking stick to represent the blind man in question. The triptych of stories is composed of the title work, plus 'Un cuadro para El Bosco' [A painting for Hieronymous Bosch] and 'Un remoto sabor a cal' [A remote taste of lime]; the book also includes a speech Somers gave in 1993 upon accepting a literary award and a final self-interview.[17] Álvaro Risso, her friend and editor, published the book just a few months after her death. In the 'Editor's note', he enigmatically states that although Somers completed the stories before her death, she had wanted to consult an edition of *Orlando* before publishing. This desire to consult Woolf's work, which was thwarted by Somers's death, becomes clear to the reader in the story 'A remote taste of lime', where there is a reference to *Orlando*. The story is subtitled 'Desencuentro en dos actos' [A failed meeting in two acts] and is dedicated to 'la genia V. W. en algún lugar de Inglaterra' ('the brilliant V. W. somewhere in England') as well as to 'la araucaria del Cementerio Británico de Montevideo' ('the monkey-puzzle tree in the British Cemetery, Montevideo') (Somers 1994a). 'Desencuentro' is an ambiguous word in Spanish: a failed meeting, or a failure to coincide, it refers to the two characters in the story, but may also refer to Woolf and Somers. The dedication to 'V. W.' and the *araucaria* at the British Cemetery in Montevideo where Somers is buried close to the tree mark this story as her poetic testament.

Throughout the text, Sommers cites Woolf, both directly and indirectly, and addresses her in imagined dialogues. The characters in the story move between the year 1932 (from near the date of *Orlando*'s publication, incorrectly dated as 1929 by Somers) to the present moment, 'over six decades since . . . Orlando tripped up the prudish people of the day' (Somers 1994a: 25).[18] In the first act of the story, dream time and real time flow into one another: an elderly woman pauses while organising her will and recalls a dream: a young workman hired to whitewash the walls with lime lies with her in bed. On awakening, she can feel his wet tears on her face and the first act ends with her agonised question: 'Why, Virginia . . . have we the inescapable obligation to grow old, and even, inevitably, to die?' (1994a: 30).[19] There follows a short 'Interlude in broad daylight' when the actual moment of the narrator's death (or is it Somers's?) and burial are narrated, including what she calls the mysterious beginning of non-being, which is also the resolution of the 'Great Enigma' (1994a: 32).

The second act takes place in the present at the British Cemetery and opens with a conversation between the same woman and two gravediggers who ask her why she goes there so often: she and the *araucaria*, she replies, understand one another well. The gravediggers mention to her that a young man, as lovely as a girl, comes regularly too. When an elderly man approaches, the woman is overcome by a taste of lime in her mouth, reminding her of the young workman who lay with her so many years before in a dream. The woman has an overwhelming desire to kiss the man, the very kiss she found she could not give him long ago – not even in her dream, so strong were the moral and social mores of the time that such an act was prohibited by social rules. The old man, who is in fact the same young workman from her past, tells her he has been coming to the cemetery since 1932, for over fifty years, waiting for her to come. Almost immediately, the old man dies and the woman lies by him, weeping on his face as he stiffens (the sexual implication is clear) into his own funereal monument. Through metempsychosis, the woman tells the astonished gravediggers, she is simultaneously transformed into both her young self and the young man, becoming a youthful androgynous Orlando-esque figure. Woolf's Orlando changes from young man to young woman in mid-novel, but Somers is constructing both persons, both sexes, in one youthful body as a means of echoing and conflating Woolf's own concerns with ageing, death and androgyny.

Near the end of the second act, the narrator directly addresses Woolf one more time:

> And what of you Virginia, where are your delicate bones of ivory now? I would remove them from their absurd prison, you would guide my hand, as if I were illiterate, and then I would write the strange novel. . . . Come, lovely woman, let us leave this place. (1994a: 35)[20]

This final proclamation of allegiance to Woolf, especially to the 'strange' fantasy novel *Orlando*, signals a way to approach Somers's own 'strange' novels (Rama 1963: 30). What was once seen as strange and fantastic was, perhaps, the remote taste not of lime but of the inspiring role of Woolf upon Somers's writing.

Antonio Larreta offers a different tribute to Virginia Woolf. Rather than allegiance or influence, his own life itself appears to resonate with Woolf's in the following texts I examine.

Antonio Larreta (1922–2015)

When Antonio, or 'Taco', Larreta died in 2015, the obituary in the daily *El País* for 20 August carried a headline hailing him as 'el último intelectual renacentista del Uruguay' ('Uruguay's last renaissance intellectual'). With an impressive trajectory as a distinguished man of letters, actor, playwright, director, critic, novelist, short-story writer, film and television scriptwriter, Larreta was one of the last surviving members of the Generación del 45. He achieved renown as an actor and playwright and wrote as a film critic for *Marcha* and the daily newspaper *El País*. He first lived in Montevideo and Buenos Aires, and later in Spain where he was forced to seek exile during the military dictatorship. He is remembered for the groundbreaking Brechtian version of Lope de Vega's *Fuenteovejuna* (1619) he directed and adapted in 1969. Conservative critics were scandalised that Larreta had interfered with a canonical text (something he would do again with Woolf), inserting speeches of his own into the original text, so that the play would resonate meaningfully in those darkening, censorship ridden pre-dictatorship days. Other playwrights, such as Antonio Mediza's *King Lear* or Alberto Restuccia's *Hamlet* (both staged in 1969), also modified classical texts to bring out their potential to raise public awareness of the dangers of an imminent military coup while at the same time eluding censorship.

In 2002, Larreta published the first, and ultimately only, volume of an autobiography he planned to write. *El jardín de invierno* [The Winter Garden] details his childhood in a privileged, upper-class and culturally open-minded Montevideo family. His memoir in many ways is reminiscent of Woolf's 'A sketch of the past'. The book is about his family, at first wealthy and then nearly ruined, and of their emblematic house, Sarandí; and Larreta tells of a lifelong close relationship with his sister and of their free access and uncensored reading in their father's large library. This short book also sketches the lives of his forebears and relatives, and, fast-forwarding occasionally to his life as an adult, records the enduring bond between the siblings, both of whom went on to become actors. The memoir ends in 1940, when Larreta is seventeen, on a sombre note: 'Germany was winning the war . . . and Sarandí was sold' (2002: 79).[21] Larreta's closing words resonate strongly with Woolf's diary entry for 17 December 1939, after the Battle of the River Plate: 'the Graf Spee is going to steam out of Montevideo today into the jaws of death . . . and the British captain has been given a KCB' (*D* 5: 251).

A few years after this memoir, Larreta published *El sombrero chino. Virginia. 2 cuentos, 2 actos* (2005) [The Chinese Hat. Virginia. 2 Stories, 2 Acts], as a tribute to Woolf. But the collection also constitutes, at a slant, something akin to one of the announced but unwritten volumes of his autobiography. As an elderly gay man re-reading Woolf, Larreta found he was both fascinated and haunted by Woolf's life. Possibly her same-sex relationships resonated with his, the varied literary and artistic milieu frequented by both, and strong family ties, especially with a sister and, in Larreta's case, a niece (in Woolf's it was her nephew Julian); however, he never made any explicit comments relating to these connections. Certainly, his perceptive readings draw on and explore what he sees as the strong presence of Eros and Thanatos (love and death) in Woolf's life which he foregrounds through his play and two stories. *El sombrero chino* addresses attraction and sensuality within the family; same-sex seduction; love, long-lasting and sexual; and death. From the vantage point of his nearly eighty years, Larreta appears to identify poetically with his character.

El sombrero chino, a work of fiction, is organised so that the stories come before the play, though the play was written first. The book opens with a 'Preamble' where Larreta explains how he came about writing it:

> I still have with me the first Sudamericana [publishing house] edition of *Mrs Dalloway* with my full name inscribed on the first page, and the date, now also amazing to me, of 1939. It was then that I also read *To the Lighthouse*, *The Waves*, *Orlando*, and, later, the essays. . . . And one day in 1941 as Hitler hurled himself onto England, we read that Virginia Woolf had committed suicide. (2005: 7)[22]

He goes on to 'confess' that sixty years went by before he re-read her work, inspired to do so after watching Stephen Daldry's film *The Hours,* based on Michael Cunningham's novel of the same title (1998):

> I confess that sixty years went by before I re-read it, and that it was the cinema (Daldry's film, Cunningham's novel) that sent me to find the green book, its Sudamericana colour well-preserved. This was a second revelation, or the real revelation. At 17 I was a snob as a reader. At over 80 I am a virgin reader. And I have now spent almost an entire year with Virginia Woolf. (2005: 7)[23]

The year he spent with Woolf proved fruitful: he then wrote the play *Virginia*, but when the opening of the play had to be postponed, he continued to be haunted by Woolf and wrote the two short stories, perhaps as an act of self-exorcism.

The text of the play, the third and longest section in the book, is preceded by an acknowledgements page where Larreta indicates that of the books he consulted the most important were a Spanish edition of Quentin Bell's *Virginia Woolf: A Biography* (1972) and Jane Dunn's *A Very Close Conspiracy: Vanessa Bell and Virginia Woolf* (1990). The first Larreta identifies as rich in information, the second in psychological insight (2005: 63). Larreta's first story, 'El sombrero chino', is clearly inspired by Woolf's memoir of Julian Bell, written in 1937 and published as an appendix in Quentin Bell's biography. In the memoir, Woolf recalls Julian turning up at her house, wearing a great sun hat and that, as he was leaving, they 'half-kissed' (Bell 1972: 498). Like Daldry's film, which Larreta found inspirational, 'El sombrero chino' is also structured around kisses.

'El sombrero chino' is presented as the secret diary Woolf kept just before her death, a private 'suicide diary' as she calls it, which she is going to 'drown' together with herself (Larreta 2005: 11). It is an intimate diary, intended for no one to see; nonetheless, it is recovered (with the eponymous straw hat she was wearing when she drowned) from the Ouse and restored by Leonard. This information appears as an 'editor's note' at the end of Larreta's imaginative retelling of Woolf's diary and final days. The editorial note goes on to detail that Leonard could never make up his mind whether to publish the 'suicide diary'; after his death, the diary passed into the hands of Vanessa Bell; eventually her son Quentin Bell publishes this final diary with Vanessa's permission. A second note states that Quentin also kept the Chinese hat from which Leonard had never parted (2005: 44).

The story opens with Virginia closing her regular diary and starting a new one, her suicide diary. She begins by recalling Thomas Chatterton's suicide described to her, at the age of eight, by her father, and then goes on:

> This morning I closed my diary forever. . . . This is another diary, written to register only three days for only one reader: myself. But at this crucial moment. . . . I can't stop writing. . . . Yes, this is it. This is my suicide diary. (Larreta 2005: 11)[24]

On 23 March 1941, three days before her planned walk into the Ouse (Larreta gets this date wrong), Woolf records a delightful walk down to the river on a beautiful morning in March. Ruminating on the word March, she is suddenly greeted by the March Hare from *Alice's Adventures in Wonderland*, who accompanies her part of the way along her walk. When she arrives at the river, she sees someone appear on the other side – a young man, standing in the dazzling sunlight. He wears Andalusian trousers and a broad, sensuous smile lights up his face. It is Julian, whom Woolf believes to be an amazing gift from the March Hare.

She looks again and sees him wearing a large, yellow straw hat, the one she thinks he brought back from China. Then, moments later,

> he was swimming towards me, his green eyes smiling at me, and I shivered with cold, as if I too had flung myself into the river, as if it were already three days later. . . . I waited for Julian. For he had surely come to fetch me. (Larreta 2005: 18)[25]

She then imagines feeling a kiss and her body responds sexually to Julian's, but the voice panting in her ear is Leonard's familiar voice: 'And then I felt, for the first time in many years, that rapture of love which is the deepest and most indescribable experience I have ever felt. . . . It is the only thing in this life that seems truly sacred' (2005: 19).²⁶

It is Leonard and not Julian who makes love to her; or rather, the vision of Julian who is embodied in Leonard. They make love on the grass by the river and reach, at exactly the same time, a psychical and spiritual orgasm. The next day she goes down to the river again and once more Julian appears, now completely nude, like David, 'his genitals so lively, so droll',²⁷ just like the Chinese hat he is wearing again, she thinks (2005: 24). Julian walks over to Woolf, who is now also naked, puts the Chinese hat on her head, picks her up in his arms and flies her through the air over the Ouse, over Sussex and over England. This clearly signals a physical orgasm, though Leonard isn't present this time: 'I was woken up by the warm flow between my thighs I had heard spoken of so often' (2005: 24).²⁸

On the next day, the day of her suicide, Leonard brings her a surprising and mysterious gift from London: a Chinese hat, bought on the Portobello Road. The diary ends with a long comment on Leonard, Julian and the two hats, followed by a reflection on their mutual interconnection: 'I was very moved . . . especially when [Leonard] put the hat on me, just like Julian. . . . Everything is ready. I have put the hat on. And now . . . what shall I do with this diary?' (2005: 44).²⁹ Thus, Larreta's imaginative story fills the blank space between Woolf's last actual diary entry and the day of her suicide with a fantasy of three days of joyous fulfilment for Woolf. She consummates her unconscious, forbidden desire for Julian, which allows the perfect consummation of her love for Leonard. Woolf then goes to her death wearing Leonard's Chinese hat: 'like a piece of Leonard',³⁰ she says, 'I will hurt him terribly in an hour's time, but I know he will understand' (2005: 43).³¹

The second story, 'El regalo de Violet' [Violet's gift] is about Violet Robson, a wealthy widow from Edinburgh (possibly based on Violet Dickinson) who visits Virginia at her house just after the death of Leslie Stephen. Violet brings Virginia a beautiful dress from Fortuny's, which was bought in Italy years before in the company of Virginia as a future gift for the young woman she admired and was attracted to. Larreta has Virginia use her two powerful weapons of seduction, her beauty and her storytelling, to enthrall and then enrage Violet, driving her into a frenzy of slapping, kissing and touching Virginia. This episode is referred to again in Larreta's play when Virginia talks about the women who have been in love with her (2005: 138).

Larreta's play *Virginia* opened in 2006, directed by Gabriela Iribarren, who also played the title role: the other characters are Vanessa Stephen, Clive Bell and Leonard Woolf. It features a number of detailed stage directions for the stage technicians. Their difficult job was to handle the complex scene-shifts, a variety of musical and lighting effects, and slides projected on both the stage and the actors' clothing and faces as they moved in a multi-purpose acting space defined by colour and light more than by any specific structure. Also on stage are a few significant pieces of furniture: on one side sits Virginia's desk, on the opposite side is Vanessa's easel. Within the play, moments of total darkness occur several times and some scenes are played out entirely in silence, with eloquent images expressing the drama of the moment more powerfully than words projected onto the stage (Larreta 2005: 65, 66).

The timeline of the play spans 1904–41; an early scene in the play depicts a mature Vanessa reflecting on her sister twenty years after her death, answering a reporter's questions about sibling rivalry during a retrospective exhibition of her work in London. The sequence of events in the play is not linear; instead, a chain of luminous '*moments of being*', as defined in *Moments of Being*, explore the theme of untimely death. Early in the play, Clive tells Virginia that the part that interested him most in her novel *Mrs Dalloway* was Septimus's suicide; he has Virginia read him a paragraph from the novel, and as she does so, she is overcome with grief. I read Larreta's note for the actor playing Virginia in the stage direction as his own response to the novel: he sees Virginia herself in the mutilated Septimus and also in the raving Lucrezia (2005: 91).

No posthumous papers of Larreta's have been published so, for the time being, we cannot know if there are any verifiable connections between Larreta's life and his version of Woolf in *Virginia*. Sex – tragic and joyful, incestuous and polymorphous – and death structure the narrative of his *Virginia*. Significant, too, are the liberties Larreta takes with Woolf's biography, such as locating the time of Julian's death closer to Virginia's suicide, a poetic proximity between the two that he explored in 'El sombrero chino'. Larreta identified closely with Virginia Woolf and was moved to write what, at times, appears to be an exploration of his own self with Woolf as a kind of alter ego. It is an intriguing speculation, one that might lead us to wonder whether we might not hazard paraphrasing Gustave Flaubert from *Madame Bovary*: 'Virginia Woolf, c'est moi'.

'Virginia Woolf, etc. / *dulces antepasadas mías*'

Woolf continues to inspire, as author Cristina Peri Rossi (1941–) makes clear when she traces the roots of her literary family tree back to 'Virginia Woolf, etc. / sweet foremothers of mine' (Peri Rossi 1986: 115).[32] I take Peri Rossi's poetic statement as the title of this final section, applying it to both her own writing and to other contemporary Uruguayan women writers. But rather than point out Woolfian influences or dialogues I prefer to follow Verónica D'Auria, who uses Gérard Genette's richly suggestive concept of 'reverberations' to link the works of contemporary Uruguayan women writers to Woolf. This discontinuous and even possibly contradictory relationship among texts, rather than one of contiguity or of similarity, may be termed reverberations'; that is, 'a poetically-charged illustrative metaphor . . . evoking a preexisting text without necessarily referring to it or quoting it, but without which the new texts would not easily be understood in their full poetic dimension' (D'Auria 2013: 134).[33] It is in this sense that I shall briefly refer to Peri Rossi, as well as Alicia Migdal and Fernanda Trías; Woolf continues to reverberate in their work. Peri Rossi's writing could function as a transition point between the earlier writers considered in this chapter and those who, like her, are actively engaged in innovative writing at the present moment. Her work explicitly invokes Woolf while reverberating with Woolf's texts.

Peri Rossi's poetry, short stories and novels have been translated into many languages to critical acclaim; she is considered one of the leading post-boom Latin American writers. Her genre-fluid, ironic, lesbian works have been read in connection with, among others, Armonía Somers (Ulla 1995: 81–91), as well as through their explicit dialogue with Woolf (Acosta and Rodríguez 2017). A radical and outspoken political writer, Peri Rossi fled to Spain during the military dictatorship, never returning to Uruguay. Many contemporary female Uruguayan writers lived through those dark days; some began publishing towards the end of the dictatorship as conditions eased. Among them, Peri Rossi's poetic tribute to Woolf resonates strongly:

> Virginia Woolf, etc.,
> Sweet foremothers of mine
> drowning in the sea
> or committing suicide in imaginary gardens
> locked up in castles with lilac-coloured
> arrogant walls
> splendid women challenging
> the elemental biology
> which reduces women to parturition machines
> before being really women
> superb in solitude and in the little scandal
> of their lives
> they have a place in the herbarium
> beside the rare specimens
> of variegated nervure (1986: 115)[34]

Another poem, 'La historia de un amor' [The history of a love] notes the milestones in Peri Rossi's family history – as well as carefully selected significant political, historical and literary moments – that made it possible for her to love a woman.[35] One of the verses that make up this long poem states,

> So that I might love you
> Virginia Woolf had to write *Orlando*
> and Charles Darwin
> travel to the River Plate. (2009)[36]

which neatly connects Woolf to the River Plate via Charles Darwin. Woolf is therefore the acknowledged literary foremother of Peri Rossi in the poem quoted above and, also, a referent in the genealogy of her personal love story.

Alicia Migdal (1947–) is a highly regarded novelist, poet, literary and film critic who began publishing towards the end of the military dictatorship and whose work has been analogised to Woolf's.[37] Her first novel, *La casa de enfrente* [The House Opposite] was published in 1988. Early criticism of her work recognised her search to find a language of her own and connected it to that of Woolf, Katherine Mansfield, Marguerite Duras, Christa Wolf and Clarice Lispector, each of whom sought to write in a distinctly woman's voice (see Peyrou 1993).[38] In 'Alicia Migdal: Escribir en un cuarto propio' [Alicia Migdal: Writing in a room of her own] (1997), Carina Blixen analyses Migdal's importance as a writer who began publishing fiction at the end of the dictatorship, her relationship with the Generación del 45, her role as an intellectual, her Jewish family history and her literary relationship with *Marcha* editor Onetti. Although Onetti was a powerful figure all young writers were measured against, Migdal, in Blixen's words, 'feminises the implacable *machismo* of Onetti's world' (1997: 40).[39]

Migdal's *En un idioma extranjero* [In a Foreign Tongue] (2008), brings together three earlier novellas and a final so-called 'Abstacto' [Abstract]. The short texts are interconnected and include, together with the title story, *La casa de enfrente*, *Historia quieta* [A Still Story] (1993) and *Muchachas de verano en días de marzo* [Summer Girls in March Days] (1999). Ortiz writes that

> Migdal works with feminine writing as an expansion, not as a limitation. She generates her own locus of enunciation, which pays no attention to the demands of the ego of intimate-diary writing. . . . [W]riting appears at times as her salvation, as a safe place, but at other times, as a crime of self-defense, both sentence and suicide. (2009)[40]

This collection of stories, which I translate as 'In a Foreign Tongue', alludes to Woolf's statements about the differences in men's and women's sentences, referencing the gendered language spoken of in *A Room of One's Own* and gesturing towards Hélène Cixous's notion of *écriture feminine*; that is, like Woolf, Cixous (1981) believes that women should write about themselves and other women, bring other women to writing, and realise the fundamental importance of language for understanding the self. Thus, Migdal writes in a language that is not the customary Spanish sentence that male writers (such as Onetti) might use but instead in a new, distinctly female language.

Woolfian scenarios, such as walking in the city streets or spending time in the privacy of houses, are present throughout Migdal's texts: in *The House Opposite*, the city a woman walks in or hearkens back to, specifically Montevideo, has Woolf's London as its counterpart. Through this landscape, the narrator explores her various selves, her houses and the men who left her, as she simultaneously thinks back through her foremothers, sifting through memories of her mother and grandmother and providing a genealogy of strong women. Although the story is written in the first person, the memories are mostly related in the third person, ultimately blurring the narrator's first-person 'I'. Her narrative, which is plotless in a strict sense, constructs her self as a woman who has found her woman's voice – a voice that is permeated with intimate, womanly descriptions of smells; for example, of babies' mouths or her own odour, reminiscent of Elaine Showalter's 'female phase' in women's writing. The titled 'house opposite' is one of several houses in Migdal's texts, with the female associations of 'house' augmented in Spanish, as the noun '*casa*' is feminine. Her sense of otherness, of being an outsider, is in her opening statement, which raises the feminine house as a metaphor for writing: 'I always live in the house opposite' (Migdal 2008: 11),[41] the narrator declares. The house as domestic space and, traditionally, literary space needs to be reinvented, Migdal seems to be saying, to be considered from a different perspective, which is a hard task: 'To really look at houses one needs courage, courage which won't destroy us, and also patience to allow us to invent them from the outside' (2008: 11).[42] The narrator thus alerts readers that she is embarking on something different, in form and content, from the likes of male writers like Onetti.

By *A Still Story*, the narrator says: 'The house opposite was going to be refurbished' (Migdal 2008: 75).[43] Migdal's female speaker is now able to discover (and expose) her self, celebrating the *jouissance* of writing (as per Cixous). Blixen comments: 'At a time of crisis, when traditional ways of thinking grow weary, or new openings are tried out, Migdal presents her writing proposing the topography of the body, feelings and loved ones, as a site for reflection' (1997: 35).[44] Throughout the stories in *In a Foreign Tongue*,

Migdal's texts reverberate with resonances from Woolf's works – from *Mrs Dalloway* to the monologues in *The Waves* – as the woman-narrator modulates differences to articulate in her 'foreign tongue' the subtle polyphony of voices that shape her various selves. The 'foreign tongue' is the language Migdal and her narrators have learned from Woolf: how to shape a woman's sentence using her own voice. Whereas Armonía Somers's novels were initially critiqued by male critics as strange and fantastic, Alicia Migdal's female critics respond to and joyfully recognise her 'foreign tongue'.

In the contemporary Uruguayan literary landscape, a younger generation of women writers have appropriated this 'foreign' language, a language made up of women's sentences narrated by women protagonists, inspired by *A Room of One's Own*, as their mother tongue. I would like to briefly mention Fernanda Trías (1976–), who has published three novels and one short story collection, *No soñarás flores* [You Will Not Dream Flowers], all of which have received awards and distinctions both in Uruguay and abroad. Her works feature young women in cities, going through traumatic situations. The novel *La Azotea* [The Rooftop], for example, delves into the protagonist Clara's loneliness and her desire to experience her father's love, which leads her to submit to him sexually. As a result of this incestuous relationship, Clara gives birth to a daughter with whom she shares a distorted bond, and the novel chronicles the slow and subtle process of her inability, ultimately, to relate to anyone. In an interview, Trías cited Lispector and Woolf as authors she read regularly; and, in an email exchange with me on the subject of influences and reverberations, Trías wrote,

> I don't think that Woolf's influence on my work stands out immediately. However, I must say that *Mrs Dalloway* was one of the books that led me to reflect on the treatment of madness, mental ill-health and suicide, and also on paranoid discourse. My story 'No soñarás flores' connects with *La Azotea*, and (like *Mrs Dalloway*) shows suicide as the only possible way of escape.[45]

Finally, I would like to close by citing the poet María Sánchez, who, perhaps unknown to her, echoed Peri Rossi's acknowledgement of Woolf as her literary foremother while also endorsing both Woolf's and Peri Rossi's blurring of poetry/prose genre divisions. In 2018, Sánchez brought out an anthology of hitherto unpublished Uruguayan women poets, entitled *Cuerpo, Palabra y Creación* [Body, Word and Creation]. When she presented me with a copy of her beautifully edited book, she smiled and said, 'These are poems. But of course, Virginia is here, in all of them.'

Notes

1. It is important to bear in mind the long-standing connection between the two River Plate capitals, Buenos Aires and Montevideo, a connection which links the two cities more closely to one another than to the rest of their respective countries. In colonial times they were part of the Viceroyalty of River Plate; in later colonial and nation-forming times, they alternated as enemies, rivals and allies. In times of dictatorships in Argentina and in Uruguay, both Buenos Aires and Montevideo in turn harboured their counterparts' political exiles. It is possible to speak of 'River Plate' history and culture, and even a 'River Plate' variety of spoken Spanish, differing from other parts of Argentina and Uruguay.
2. See for example, Salomone (2006).

3. Ironically, in an interview by Osvaldo Ferrari, Borges stated that he had given *A Room* to his mother to translate because he wasn't interested in a text that was 'merely a statement for feminism' but that he was, nevertheless, a feminist. What he did not like, he said, was that Woolf had turned herself into a missionary for feminism, and he could do without missionaries (see Borges and Ferrari [1985: 305]).
4. The translations of specific works especially relevant for this chapter, such as Borges's translation of *Orlando*, have been discussed by Leah Leone (2012) and Patricia Wilson (2017) among others.
5. 'literatura escrita por mujeres que han logrado conformar una voz propia y reconocible como femenina. Bajo esta noción inscribe la narrativa de Migdal en la tradición fundada por Virginia Woolf y Marguerite Duras, por ejemplo' (Ortiz 2009; see also Labraga de Mirza [2011] for references to Duras).
6. As in other South American countries, the Uruguayan military coup led to a traumatic twelve-year dictatorship. Thousands of Uruguayan intellectuals were detained and imprisoned, tortured, killed, forced into exile, or, at best, lost jobs and positions as journals were quashed. These losses to Uruguayan culture were devastating, and even today, forty years on, wounds remain unhealed.
7. See Rocca (2006) for an in-depth study of Monegal.
8. First published in English (London, 1951). Translated into Spanish, probably by Monegal, the translation was published in *Número*.
9. 'la fuerte presión de sus antepasados . . . impulsó a Virginia Woolf a desarrollar y perfeccionar un estilo literario que reconocemos hoy como típicamente suyo. En Virginia Woolf los talentos y las aspiraciones de la familia Stephen se cumplieron. Los Stephen habían carecido de una cualidad: la visión poética. Y esa fue la contribución personal y decisiva de Virginia: ella agregó el súbito estallido de belleza que ilumina ocasionalmente la vida.'
10. All unattributed translations from Spanish are my own. 'un fragmento tendencioso y especializado, incompleto (por definición). Pero qué irresistible y qué revelador. Qué absorbente y dominante. . . . Y cómo a través de él, . . . de lo que obstinadamente calla e involuntariamente revela, se pueden alcanzar otros fragmentos, otras visiones . . . cómo resistir a la tentación de reconstruir (con la parte emergente a la vista) el resto de esa personalidad sumergida, . . . de las notas (algunas notas) que tan vivas e intensas yacen todavía entre las páginas de ese libro. Aún sabiendo que es posible equivocarse y que la imagen ofrecida es parcial. Es caricatura.'
11. 'Pero es, por encima de todo, un extraordinario testimonio sobre la creación literaria: uno de los más extraordinarios que posea la literatura occidental desde las cartas de Flaubert.' 'Y Virginia Woolf pertenece precisamente a ese gran impulso de renovación de la novela contemporánea que intenta apresar otras zonas de la realidad.' 'La tensión de crear y la tensión de vivir eran demasiado.'
12. 'Y eso fue lo que supo hacer.'
13. See Rocca (2006) for an in-depth study of the two critics; and Claudia Gilman, who also points out the importance of both on an international level (2009).
14. It was published by the Feminist Press in 2018 and translated into English by Kit Maude.
15. See for instance an overview in Rodríguez and Szurmuk (2016: Chapters 14–16).
16. 'uno de los primeros manifiestos feministas. . . . La narración denuncia en términos narrativos algo dramáticos, los fundamentos sexuales de la organización social.'
17. See Dalmagro (2004: 10–11).
18. 'más de seis décadas después, que . . . Orlando hiciera trastrabillar a la pacata gente de entonces'.
19. 'Por qué, Virginia . . . la ineludible obligación de envejecer y, hasta como corolario, morir?'
20. 'Y qué será de ti, Virginia, dónde estará tu dulce esqueleto de marfil? Lo sacaría de su absurdo encierro, tú me llevarías la mano como a un analfabeto, y yo escribiría la extraña novela. . . . Vamos hermosa, salgamos de aquí.'
21. 'La Guerra la estaba ganando Alemania . . . entonces se vendió Sarandí.'

22. 'Conservo todavía la primera edición de *Mrs Dalloway* con mi nombre real y la fecha de 1939. Y un día de 1941 cuando Hitler se lanzaba sobre Inglaterra, leíamos que Virginia Woolf se había suicidado.'
23. 'Confieso que dejé pasar 60 años sin releerla, y que fue el cine (la película de Daldry, el libro de Cunningham) que me hizo buscar el libro verde de Sudamericana. Fue una segunda revelación, o la verdadera revelación. A los17 años yo era un lector snob. A los 80 y pico soy un lector virgen. Y ahora he pasado casi el año entero con Virginia Woolf.'
24. 'Esta mañana cerré definitivamente mi diario. . . . Este es otro diario, destinado a registrar sólo tres días y un solo lector: yo misma. Pero en este momento crucial . . . no puedo dejar de escribir. . . . Este es el diario de mi suicidio.'
25. 'venía hacia mí, nadando . . . los ojos verdes sonriéndome, y entonces me estremecí de frio como si me hubiera echado al río yo también, como si fuera tres días más tarde . . . esperé a Julián. Que sin duda había venido a buscarme.'
26. 'Entonces sentí . . . ese arrebato del amor que es la experiencia más honda y más indescriptible que he sentido nunca. . . . Es lo único en esta vida que me parece verdaderamente sagrado.'
27. 'sus genitales tan vivos, tan graciosos como el sombrero chino'.
28. 'Y entonces me desperté ese flujo cálido entre los muslos del que tanto había oído hablar.'
29. 'Yo estaba conmovida . . . sobre todo en el momento en que me puso el sombrero, igual a Julián. . . . Me he puesto el sombrero . . . y ahora, qué hago con el diario?'
30. 'como un trozo de Leonard'.
31. 'Lo voy a herir gravemente dentro de una hora, pero sé que me comprenderá.'
32. Translated by Kate Flores.
33. 'Se trata de una metáfora ilustrativa con una carga poética que corresponde . . . sería el caso de textos derivados de otro preexistente que lo evocan sin necesariamente hablar de él y citarlo, pero sin el cual difícilmente serían comprendidos en toda su dimensión poética.'
34. 'Virginia Woolf, etc.,
Dulces antepasadas mías
ahogadas en el mar
o suicidadas en jardines imaginarios
encerradas en castillos de muros lilas
y arrogantes
espléndidas en su desafío
a la biología elemental
que hace de una mujer una paridora
antes de ser en realidad una mujer
soberbias en su soledad
y en el pequeño escándalo de sus vidas.'
35. She cites the conquest of America, her Italian grandparents' emigration to Uruguay, the Spanish Civil War and her own forced exile to Spain, along with Catullus, Lesbia, Karl Marx, Pablo Neruda, Giuseppe Garibaldi, Francisco Franco, Federico García Lorca, Ingrid Bergman and Pier Paolo Passolini, among others.
36. 'Para que yo pudiera amarte / Virginia Woolf tuvo que escribir Orlando / y Charles Darwin / viajar al Río de la Plata.'
37. See Julia Ortiz (2019).
38. 'Narradoras como Virginia Woolf, Mansfield, M. Duras, como Christa Wolf o Clarice Lispector, han logrado . . . una voz que es reconociblemente femenina a nivel de la escritura.'
39. 'Feminiza el implacable machismo del mundo onettiano.'
40. 'Migdal ejerce la literatura femenina como expansión y no como limitación. Genera un lugar de enunciación propio, que desoye los reclamos del ego de sumisión al diario íntimo. . . . [L]a escritura se le muestra a veces como salvación, como lugar seguro, pero otras veces como "crimen en defensa propia", como condena y como suicidio.'

41. 'Vivo siempre en la casa de enfrente.'
42. 'Para mirar de verdad las casas se necesita un coraje que no nos destruya, una paciencia nos permita inventarlas desde afuera.'
43. 'La casa de enfrente iba a ser reformada.'
44. 'En un momento de crisis, en que las vías tradicionales de pensamiento flaquean, o se revisan y tantean nuevos caminos, Migdal propone una literatura que es un lugar de reflexión a partir de una topografía del cuerpo, las emociones, los afectos.'
45. 'Yo no creo que en los textos que te voy a mencionar se observe una influencia de V. W. que salte a la vista. Sin embargo, si me preguntás por mi percepción, puedo decir que Ms Dalloway fue uno de los libros que me hizo reflexionar sobre el tratamiento de la locura, la enfermedad mental y, en menor medida, el suicidio. . . . Estoy pensando en dos textos míos, *La azotea*, novela breve que se publicó por primera vez en 2001, y luego un cuento largo, "No soñarás flores" y es el que da título al libro de cuentos El cuento retoma algunos temas de *La azotea*, pero desde otro ángulo bastante distinto, y toca el tema del suicidio como única escapatoria posible' (Fernanda Trías, email to the author, 3 August 2018).

Bibliography

Acosta, M. and V. Rodríguez (2017), 'La morada del lenguaje de las extranjeras: La búsqueda de un espacio otro en la poesía de Alejandra Pizarnik y Cristina Peri Rossi' [The abode of the language of the foreign women: The search for another space in the poetry of Alejandra Pizarnik and Cristina Peri Rossi], *Tenso Diagonal* [Diagonal Tension], 3, pp. 47–60.

Bell, Q. (1972), *Virginia Woolf: A Biography*, 2 vols, New York: Harcourt Brace Jovanovich.

Blixen, C. (1996), 'Armonía Somers: Fantasía mito y escritura' [Armonia Somers: Fantasy myth and writing], in H. Raviolo and P. Rocca (eds), *Historia de la literatura uruguaya contemporánea. La narrativa del medio siglo* [The History of Contemporary Uruguayan Literature. The Narrative of the Half Century], Montevideo: Ediciones de la Banda Oriental, pp. 191–211.

Blixen, C. (1997), 'Alicia Migdal: Escribir en un cuarto propio' [Alica Migdal: Writing in a room of one's own], in C. Blixen (ed.), *Papeles de Montevideo. Aproximaciones a la narrativa uruguaya posterior a 1985* [Montevideo Papers. Approaches to Uruguayan Narrative after 1985], Montevideo: Trilce, pp. 34–52.

Borges, J. L. and O. Ferreri (1985), *En diálogo* [In conversation], Barcelona: Seix Barral.

Cixous, Hélène (1981) 'The laugh of the Medusa', trans. K. Cohen and P. Cohen, in E. Marks and I. de Courtivron (eds), *New French Feminisms: An Anthology*, New York: Schocken, pp. 245–64.

Cosse, R. (ed.) (1995), *Cristina Peri Rossi, papeles críticos* [Cristina Peri Rossi, Critical Papers], Montevideo: Linardi y Risso.

Cunningham, M. (1998), *The Hours*, New York: Farrar, Straus and Giroux.

Dalmagro, M. C. (2004), 'Ficcionalización del yo en las entrevistas de Armonía Somers' [Self-fiction in Armonía Somers's interviews], Universidad Nacional de Mar del Plata II 'Congreso Internacional CELEHIS de literatura' [Centre for Hispanic Literature international conference article], <http://anaforas.fic.edu.uy/jspui/handle/123456789/38387?mode=full> (last accessed 17 March 2020).

Dalmagro, M. C. (2013), 'Uruguay, un cuento de Somers y un remoto sabor a Woolf' [Uruguay, a story by Somers and a remote taste of Woolf], in E. Basso and L. Cordery (eds), *Virginia Woolf en América Latina. Reflexiones desde Montevideo* [Virginia Woolf in Latin America. Reflecting on Woolf from Montevideo], Montevideo: Linardi y Risso, pp. 117–28.

D'Auria, V. (2013), 'Las reverberaciones de Woolf en la prosa poética de Sabela de Tezanos y Silvia Guerra' [Woolf's reverberations in the poetic prose of Sabela de Tezanos and Silvia

Guerra], in E. Basso and L. Cordery (eds), *Virginia Woolf en América Latina. Reflexiones desde Montevideo*, Montevideo: Linardi y Risso, pp. 129–40.

DiBattista, M. (2006), 'Introduction', *Orlando*, New York: Harcourt Brace Jovanovich, pp. xxv–lxvii.

Gilman, C. (2009), 'El factor humano y una rivalidad histórica: Angel Rama y Emir Rodríguez Monegal' [The human factor and a historical rivalry: Angel Rama and Emir Rodríguez Monegal], in *Episodios en la formación de redes culturales en América Latina* [Episodes in the Formation of Cultural Networks in Latin America], Buenos Aires: Prometeo, pp. 1–19, <https://www.academia.edu/1020237/_El_factor_humano_y_una_rivalidad_hist%C3%B3rica_Angel_Rama_y_Emir_Rodr%C3%ADguez_Monegal_> (last accessed 24 February 2020).

Labraga de Mirza, M. (2011), 'El sujeto de la escritura y el yo extranjero. Alicia Migdal y Marguerite Duras' [The subject of writing and the foreign self. Alicia Migdal and Marguerite Duras], *Revista de la Biblioteca Nacional del Uruguay* [Journal of the National Library of Uruguay], 4–5 ('Escrituras del yo') [Scriptures of self], pp. 287–99.

Larreta, A. (2002), *El jardín de invierno* [Winter Garden], Montevideo: Ediciones de la Plaza.

Larreta, A. (2005), *El sombrero chino. Virginia. 2 cuentos, 2 actos* [The Chinese Hat. Virginia. 2 Scenes, 2 Acts], Montevideo: Fin de Siglo.

Lázaro, A. (2000), 'Luchando contra la marea: Virginia Woolf y la censura española' [Fighting against the tide: Virginia Woolf and Spanish censorship], <https://core.ac.uk/display/58907309?recSetID=> (last accessed 25 August 2020).

Leone, L. (2012), *Orlando de Virginia Woolf, en la traducción de Jorge Luis Borges (1937)*, [Virginia Woolf's *Orlando* in Jorge Luis Borges's Translation (1937)], Alicante: Biblioteca Virtual Miguel de Cervantes.

Migdal, A. (2008), *En un idioma extranjero* [In a Foreign Tongue], Montevideo: Rebeca Linke Editoras.

Ocampo, V. (1954), *Virginia Woolf en su Diario* [Virginia Woolf in Her Diary], Buenos Aires: Sur.

Ortiz, J. (2009), 'Recopilaciones femeninas' [Feminine compilations], *La Diaria* [The Daily], 15 December, <https://ladiaria.com.uy/articulo/2009/12/recopilaciones-femeninas> (last accessed 8 September 2020)

Pendle, G. (1952), 'Virginia Woolf, née Stephen', *Número* [Number], 2, pp. 159–63.

Pérez, C. (2013), 'Un beso inesperado: Woolf, Somers, Migdal. Palimpsestos de la androginia' [An unexpected kiss: Woolf, Somers, Migdal. Palimpsests of androgyny], in E. Basso and L. Cordery (eds), *Virginia Woolf en América Latina. Reflexiones desde Montevideo*, Montevideo: Linardi y Risso, pp. 103–16

Peri Rossi, C. (1986), 'Virginia Woolf, etc.', in A. Flores and K. Flores (eds), *Hispanic Feminist Poems from the Middle Ages to the Present: A Bilingual Anthology*, New York: Feminist Press, CUNY, p. 115.

Peyrou, R. (1993), 'Algo más que una historia de amor' [Something more than a love story], *El País Cultural*, 10 September, p. 12.

Rama, Á. (1963), 'La insólita literatura de Somers: La fascinación del horror' [Somers's unusual literature: the fascination of horror], *Marcha* [March], 1118, 27 December, p. 30.

Rocca, P. (2006), *Ángel Rama, Emir Rodríguez Monegal y el Brasil: Dos caras de un proyecto latinoamericano* [Ángel Rama, Emir Rodríguez Monegal and Brazil: Two faces of a Latin American Project], Montevideo: Ediciones de la Banda Oriental.

Rodríguez, I. and M. Szurmuk (eds) (2016), *The Cambridge History of Latin American Women's Literature*, New York: Cambridge University Press.

Rodríguez Monegal, E. (1954), 'De Virginia a Victoria' [From Virginia to Victoria], *Marcha* [March], 9 July, p. 15.

Rodríguez Monegal, E. (1955), 'Vanidad, creación y muerte en el "Diario" de Virginia Woolf' [Vanity, creation and death in the 'Diary' of Virginia Woolf], *Marcha* [March], 22 April, pp. 20–1.

Salomone, A. (2006), 'Virginia Woolf en los Testimonios de Victoria Ocampo: Tensiones entre feminismo y colonialismo' [Virginia Woolf in the testimony of Victoria Ocampo: Tensions between feminism and colonialism], *Revista Chilena de Literatura* [Chilean Journal of Literature], 9, pp. 69–87.

Sánchez, M. (ed.) (2018), *Cuerpo, Palabra y Creación. Antología de poetas uruguayas* [Body, Word and Creation. An Anthology of Uruguayan Poets], Montevideo: Editorial Encuentros.

Somers, A. (1994), *El hacedor de girasoles. Tríptico en amarillo para un hombre ciego* [The Sunflower Maker. Triptych in Yellow for a Blind Man], Montevideo: Linardi y Risso.

Somers, A. (1994), *La mujer desnuda* [The Naked Woman], Montevideo: Tauro.

Trías, F. (2010), *La Azotea* [The Rooftop], Caracas: Punto Cero.

Trías, F. (2017), *No soñarás flores* [You Will Not Dream Flowers] Montevideo: Hum.

Ulla, N. (1995), 'Discurso ficcional y discurso crítco en dos cuentos de las escritoras uruguayas Armonía Somers y Cristina Peri Rossi' [Fictional and critical discourses in two stories by the Uruguayan writers Armonía Somers and Cristina Peri Rossi], in R. Cosse (ed.), *Cristina Peri Rossi. Papeles críticos* [Cristina Peri Rossi. Criticism], Montevideo: Linardi y Risso, pp. 81–91.

Wilson, P. (2017), *La constelación del sur. Traductores y traducciones en la literatura argentina del siglo XX* [The Constellation of the South: Translators and Translations in Twentieth-Century Argentine Literature], Buenos Aires: Siglo XXI.

Woolf, V. (1930), 'Street Haunting. A London Adventure', fragment trans. as 'Una aventura en Londres' [An adventure in London] (unknown translator), in *Cultura*, 20, April 1947, 'Páginas selectas de la prosa inglesa [Selected Pages of English Prose], COL445, Biblioteca Nacional (The Public Library), Montevideo.

Woolf, V. (1954), *Virginia Woolf: Diario de una escritora* [Virginia Woolf: Diary of a Writer], trans. J. Coco Ferraris, Buenos Aires: Sur.

Woolf, V. (1981 [1953]), *Virginia Woolf: A Writer's Diary*, New York: Harcourt Brace Jovanovich.

Woolf, V. (1985), *The Diary of Virginia Woolf: Volume 5: 1936–1941* eds. A. O. Bell and A. McNeillie, Harmondsworth: Penguin.

Woolf, V. (1989 [1919]), 'Kew Gardens', *The Complete Shorter Fiction of Virginia Woolf*, ed. S. Dick, New York: Harcourt Brace Jovanovich, pp. 90–5.

13

Virginia Woolf's Reception and Impact on Brazilian Women's Literature

Maria A. de Oliveira

Virginia Woolf's growing presence in Brazil makes it possible to talk about multiple Brazilian Woolfs. The initial access to Woolf was created by her first translators, who homogenised her innovative language. The second Woolf appears after 2012, when the copyrights expired and many new translations emerged, works which finally take into account her experimental language. The third Woolf is the one who inspired the Brazilian writers I discuss below: Tetrá de Teffé (1897–1995), Lucia Miguel Pereira (1901–59), Clarice Lispector (1920–77), Carolina Maria de Jesus (1914–77), Ana Cristina Cesar (1952–83), Lygia Fagundes Telles (1923–), Hilda Hilst (1930–2004), Sônia Coutinho (1939–), Adriana Lunardi (1964–) and Hilda Gouveia de Oliveira (1946–).

For this chapter, I concentrate on the third iteration Woolf to show how she impacted these Brazilian women writers. I connect Woolf to them through a transnational and transcultural perspective. By doing so, I think back through Woolf's essays 'Women and fiction' (Woolf 1979) and *A Room of One's Own*, and I reflect upon the following questions: how have women advanced? How has literature evolved? Given that there is a global system of patriarchal oppression, what would be a transnational strategy to fight back using the production of art and women's creativity?

Focusing on these Brazilian women writers, I address how they negotiate Woolf's aesthetic and political discourse, her feminist modernism and the Brazilian literary traditions that struggled with the influence of European modernism. I consider Woolf's legacy, which in this case means her contributions to modernism, contributions that also permeate her literary criticism and feminist criticism. Woolf's literary criticism is now read more widely in Brazil since most of her essays have been translated (including *Three Guineas*), and *A Room of One's Own* remains a fundamental text for Brazilian feminist critics. By reading Woolf transnationally, I am thinking about Brazilian women writers who are inspired by her and her feminist ideas, bearing in mind Woolf's argument '[f]or we think back through our mothers if we are women' (*AROO*: 69). I also use Woolf's gaze into the future to understand the past and, crossing the boundaries of time and space, to think back through Woolf in connection to Brazilian women writers in a global environment.

Women Writers: Transnational and Transcultural Approaches

As a theoretical framework, I rely on a transnational approach drawing on such works as Jessica Berman's *Modernist Commitments: Ethics, Politics and Transnational Modernism* (2011), Chandra Talpade Mohanty's 'Under Western eyes: Feminist scholarship and colonial discourse', Gayatri C. Spivak's 'Can the subaltern speak?' (1988) and Pelogia Goulimari's edited collection *Women Writing across Cultures* (2017). To better comprehend the origins and influence of Woolf's popularity in Brazil and how her writings have been read and adapted in other artistic media, I also refer to Brenda R. Silver's *Virginia Woolf Icon* (1999).

The notion of transnational modernism helps to reveal the mobility of texts, whether it be Woolf's texts travelling to Brazil or the texts of Brazilian women writers moving around the world. This optic allows readers to comprehend how Woolf has been read in Brazil and how she has been transformed by contemporary Brazilian readers and writers. This mobility corroborates Berman's idea that reading beyond the original context is a transformative matter. Berman's argument also helps readers to understand Woolf in relation to Brazilian women writers and how they were navigating Woolf's feminism and their own national and cultural boundaries.

In terms of a transnational approach, Goulimari's *Women Writing across Cultures* depicts Woolf at this intersection of books, authors and different cultures. The book reflects not only on a transnational perspective but also on a transtemporal connection between past, present and future that considers female agency and subjectivity and especially on women writers' role in the construction of history, beyond the 'official' history. Morag Shiach (2017) analyses Woolf's pronominal tensions and ambiguities and considers *Orlando* not only as a transcultural and transnational work but also as a transtemporal one, since it crosses centuries, cultures and nationalities. Woolf represents a quasi-historical figure based on Vita Sackville-West's family lineage, who travels in time from the Elizabethan era, through Turkey, where Orlando is changed into a woman in the 1700s. Orlando then travels with the gypsies for a time but eventually returns to England where, on 11 October 1928 at thirty-six years of age, she greets her husband when his aeroplane lands.

Berman calls attention to the cultural, communal and geopolitical contexts of works as multiple by following their activity as they move beyond their immediate contexts and become fresh in new contexts according to where and how they are read (2011: 30). A transnational mode of reading implies different forms of alliances, coalitions and new approaches that negotiate and trespass national, ethnic and cultural boundaries. Similarly, Mohanty argues that a transnational feminist practice should rely on the construction of unified strategies to fight a global system of patriarchy by implementing feminist solidarities that extend beyond the fragmentations of place, identity, class, work and religion. In this difficult global moment for political democracy, Berman and Mohanty's ideas are more important than ever.

Mohanty (1988) analyses 'women' as a category, and she questions how we can understand women writers as a non-identical group, with different interests and desires, taking into consideration their class, ethnic and racial location. Following Mohanty it can be said that not all women from the Global South are ignorant, poor, uneducated, traditional-bound, religious or domesticated. On the contrary, many of them, as it will be demonstrated here, are educated and modern, often have control over their own bodies and sexualities and have freedom to make their own decisions. Mohanty's essay also calls attention to the urgent political need for women to form strategic coalitions across class, race and national boundaries.

Mohanty suggests that when women cannot represent themselves, they end up being represented, as demonstrated in Spivak's 'Can the subaltern speak?' (1988). Both Mohanty and Spivak address the way that 'Third World' subjects are misrepresented within Western discourse. I want to explore how these representations can be understood in the books of these ten Brazilian women writers in relation to Woolf and how they move from the condition of objects to subjects of their historical process. How do the texts of the Brazilian women writers analysed here represent the position of women in patriarchal society, and how do they reflect on their own position in the society in relation to family, to their sexuality, to other women, to the workplace, to the process of ageing and to the way they are affected by some institutions? How do they politically locate themselves? Is sisterhood across cultures and among women writers, as in the intersectional solidarity proposed by Mohanty, possible?

Woolf's Popularity in Brazil

In Brazil, during the 1940s, Virginia Woolf was read only by a minority of people from the cultural elite. At this time, education was not available for everybody: even the right to speak a language other than Portuguese was not in the basic education curriculum. Then came the first translations, which appeared in the 1940s and made Woolf more accessible to readers, but generally only to intellectuals. In the 1960s, her image started to be associated with Edward Albee's play *Who's Afraid of Virginia Woolf?*, an important factor in Woolf's reception in Brazil. Brenda Silver in *Virginia Woolf Icon* (1999) argues that Albee made Woolf a household name related to fear, creating the image of a threatening writer. The name of the play links Virginia Woolf to dread and Silver explores Albee's rhetorical question: who should be afraid of Woolf and why? In which contexts is Woolf presented or perceived as frightening? Silver states:

> once Albee made Virginia Woolf a part of the popular, once she had become a household term whose naturalized, descriptive meaning was inseparable from fear, she became subject to articulations and rearticulations that not only track the ups and downs of feminism, but indicate the power of popular representations to shape cultural meanings. (1999: 116)

In her work, Silver tracks Woolf's popularity and how her image has been changed or manipulated in the media. Silver (1999: 76) perceives Woolf as a boundary-dwelling and border-disrupting figure who escapes and persistently returns under different facades. Maintaining that Woolf became a multifaceted star in the intellectual media and in the popular culture, Silver contends that the multiplying images of Virginia Woolf have transformed the author into a powerful cultural icon whose image appears constantly in debates about art, politics, sexuality, gender, class, the canon, fashion, feminism, race, anger and fear (1999: 3).

Woolf's popularity in Brazil coincided with a process of a wider democratisation, both in terms of politics and education, which would last until the military coup in 1964; Woolf was read in universities and she appeared in mass culture. In the following years, there were several plays inspired by Woolf's writings. *Não tenha medo de Virginia Woolf* [Don't Be Afraid of Virginia Woolf] (1990) is a direct response to Albee's play. Directed by Elias Andreatto and starring Ester Goes, the play functions as an invitation to explore Woolf's texts, avoiding the stereotypes and fear associated with Albee's play. Another example is the play *Orlando* (1989), an interpretation of

Woolf's faux biography adapted by Sérgio Sant'Anna and directed by Bia Lessa, with Fernanda Torres in the role of Orlando and Júlia Lemmertz as Sasha.

At the same time that images of Woolf were appearing widely in the media in Great Britain and in the United States, Brazilian newspapers were also publishing her picture; her image was being reconstructed and reinvented in different artistic modes. Her vision appeared in books, magazines, newspapers, television, plays and digital media, and in recreations and adaptations of her novels in theatre, dance spectacles, music and paintings. Many iterations of Woolf's image have emerged over the years, allowing Woolf scholars – both national and international – and common readers alike to explore a multiple, plural, diverse and contradictory Woolf globally. Woolf's dialogical texts, her multivalent writing and the proliferating images of her, of her novels and of her essays, are all testaments to her plurality. While such factors have spread around the world and beget multiple readers, her impact on the artistic life of Brazil has been particularly intense and compelling and is manifest in many ways, including stream of consciousness and her fragmented narrative techniques, as well as in her 'global vision'.

The Waves of Feminism in Brazil

Constância Lima Duarte, in 'Feminismo e literatura no Brasil' [Feminism and literature in Brazil] (2003), points out four waves of the Brazilian feminist movement, starting respectively in 1830, 1870, 1920 and 1970. The first movement began with the publication of *Direito das mulheres e injustiça dos homens* [Rights of women and injustice of men] (1832) by Nísia Floresta Brasileira Augusta (1810–85), one of the founding texts of feminism in Brazil, based on *A Vindication of the Rights of Woman* (1792) by Mary Wollstonecraft. Nísia Floresta fought for women's education and raised awareness about injustices against women in a time when only a few women were educated and few knew how to read or write. At this time, a woman who wanted to write was certainly subversive because she was fighting against the mainstream, and so writing was strongly related to feminism. Duarte (2003) suggests that for Nísia Floresta the progress of a nation could be estimated by the importance given to women. The second wave came in 1870, when a large number of feminist newspapers emerged and women started to advocate for the vote. Duarte mentions some of them, observing that most were mainly created in São Paulo and Rio de Janeiro, for instance, *O Sexo Feminino* [The Female Sex], directed by Francisca Senhorinha da Mota Diniz, during the period of 1887 to 1889. Later on, its name would change to *O Quinze de Novembro* [15th November] from 1890 to 1896 and its success is evident in the number of copies sold, which reached 4,000. It advocated for women's right to work and education. Another example was the newspaper *Echo das Damas* [Lady's Echo] edited by Amelia Carolina da Silva Couto from 1875 to 1885; *Echo das Damas* defended women's equality, their right to education and women's achievements abroad. *O Domingo* [Sunday] and *O Jornal das Damas* [Ladies' Newspaper] appeared in 1873; both promoted women's independence, highlighting women's access to university, proprietorship rights and professional work. Finally, Duarte refers to the newspaper *A Família* [The Family], which was directed by the journalist Josefina Álvares de Azevedo. Azevedo, who also created the play *O Voto Feminino* [The Female Vote] in 1878, was a tireless feminist activist who fought for women's and men's emancipation and franchise, and for women's right to an education.

By the third wave in 1920, women were actively fighting for the right to vote and to enter universities and the workforce; they did not want to be only teachers but also doctors, lawyers, judges and politicians. Women in Brazil achieved the right to vote in 1932, less than fifteen years after Great Britain in 1918 and the United States in 1920. Key figures in the movement for women's suffrage, advancement and education in Brazil were Bertha Lutz (1894–1976) and Maria Lacerda de Moura (1887–1945). Lutz fought for women's suffrage while Moura was an anarcho-feminist who founded the League against Illiteracy.

It is crucial to emphasise that, early on, Brazilian modernism rejected European models in the search for a national identity. After the Second World War, modernists plunged into existentialism, reflecting upon universal themes and embracing international authors. In the forties, there was a revolution in language undertaken by the writers Guimarães Rosa and Clarice Lispector. Studies by Elódia Xavier (1998), Luiza Lobo (1998) and Helena Parente Cunha (1998) demonstrate that the writings of a few Brazilian women writers reflected a shift from the dominating authoritative patriarchal voice to a more flexible one as the country, in the 1950s, was undergoing significant change. As widescale industrialisation started, there was migration from rural to urban areas and from the North to the South. Overall, though, as Cunha notes, until the 1960s the narratives of Brazilian women writers reveal a general commitment to traditional patriarchal models. While the 1950s represented a period of more experimentation in Brazil, the 1960s and 1970s were the severe years of dictatorship, and consequently political writing became more necessary than ever. Except for Clarice Lispector, most women writers did not question the situation of women nor did they break with literary standards during the 1940s through the 1960s. After the 1960s, for women writers there was a struggle between compliance with traditional patriarchal standards and an urgent need for freedom. Brazilian women writers at the time depict this strong conflict between the demands of the patriarchal society and women's desire to win independence and reclaim their own bodies and voices.

The fourth and largest wave of Brazilian women's activism occurred in 1970s, when the United Nations declared International Women's Day in 1975, which led to a large number of meetings and conferences about bringing more visibility and political awareness to bear on improving women's conditions. During the 1970s, women were obliged to fight against the dictatorship (1964–85), and for democracy, amnesty and human rights for those who were tortured or persecuted. The newspaper *Brazil Mulher* [Woman Brazil] was founded in 1975 and was linked to the movement 'Women for Amnesty', while in 1976 the journal *Nós Mulheres* [We Women] introduced a feminist feature. Both of these newspapers discussed important and polemic issues such as amnesty, abortion, maternal mortality, women in politics, women in the workforce and prostitution. The debates presented in these publications also grappled with racial and sexual discrimination and women in literature, the theatre and the cinema. In literature women made great strides in the 1970s when, in 1977, Rachel de Queiroz (1910–2003), a writer, journalist and communist, prevailed over a room full of men in the competition for the Brazilian Academy of Letters and became the first woman to be accepted. Among many women who could be mentioned here, Rosie Marie Muraro was a great authority on feminist studies and was responsible for inviting Betty Friedan, whose trip to Brazil in 1977 was considered as a paradigm-shifting feminist tsunami (Duarte 2003: 165). Women were liberating themselves from domestic spaces to occupy positions of authority in universities, newspapers and companies; of course, there was a direct positive impact on their writing.

It is important to position these 1970s writers within the historical context of Brazilian feminism. During the 1970s, the main theme in literature by women was the search for identity and an emerging desire to free women from the domestic realms and constraints of the patriarchal family. Luiza Lobo (1987) argues that, in the 1960s and 1970s, Brazilian women writers experienced an increasingly favourable position in the literary scene despite the dictatorship, possibly because their texts were not as politically explicit compared to those of male writers and censors could not detect the subtleties of women's discourses. Lobo defines five tendencies in Brazilian women's writing of this period: existential strategy, experimentation, political allegory, humour and eroticism.

Woolf's Reception through Brazilian Women Writers

Woolf's political essays and novels impacted the writings of Brazilian women writers from the 1930s until now. In spite of their differences and the distances of time and place that separated them, Woolf and Brazilian women writers shared a common ground: the creation of literature that depicts the experience of a woman struggling to overcome the boundaries defined by a patriarchal society.

From the 1930s to 1960s
Tetrá de Teffé (1897–1995)

In the subsequent analysis of Woolf's reception among Brazilian women writers, I explore how Woolf has been read and interpreted since the 1930s, how these writers were referring to Woolf, which texts they were reading and what kinds of conversations are evident within this historical context. As my research in the digital database of the National Library of Rio de Janeiro shows, the first known reference to Woolf occurred in 1937, when the Brazilian writer Tetrá de Teffé mentions Woolf in 'Ver em abstracto' [To see in the abstract]. Teffé's real name was Tetrazzini de Almeida Nobre. She was born in Rio de Janeiro and she played an important role in the Brazilian social, political and cultural life in the first decades of the twentieth century. Gabriela de Lima Grecco (2018) argues that Teffé was almost completely excluded from Brazilian literary history, although she won the Machado de Assis prize in recognition for her masterpiece, *Bati à Porta da Vida* [I Knocked on Life's Door] (1940), which conveys the bourgeois society of Rio de Janeiro through the representation of three sisters: Dorinha, a young modern woman; Heloísa, an austere widow; and Marta, a disenchanted divorcee. Lima Grecco points out that Teffé presents an analysis of the psychological life of her female characters. Lima Grecco explains how the novel expresses major feminist perspectives in its treatment of subjects such as marriage, divorce, betrayal, women's emancipation and abortion. Men are secondary characters; they are weak, unfaithful and cowardly. The writer presents women struggling against men's oppression, and she brings female subjectivity to the political arena.

In 'Ver em abstracto' [To see in the abstract], Teffé discusses the differences between men's and women's writing:

Today, however, in this pseudo-feminist century, writers pretend to ignore the wonderful development, in the field of literature, of writers such as Virginia Woolf . . . whose novels portray iconic female characters and who deserve to be awarded international literary prizes – including the Nobel. They will certainly be recognized by future nations. (1937: 130)[1]

It is important to point out two facts here: first, Teffé mentions Woolf's feminism and her political argument; second, she was reading Woolf in English, since there were no translations of her books at that moment and Portugal relied on Brazilian first translations of Woolf's novels. In her familiarity with Woolf's feminism, Teffé, a Brazilian woman writing in the 1930s, stood out. Although the Constitution of 1934 advocated that education should be provided by the government for all citizens, it was, in fact, a privilege for the elite. Few people would have read in English. Furthermore, Brazilian modernists rejected European writers, concentrating on national literature and regional elements.

Lucia Miguel Pereira (1901–59)

Lucia Miguel Pereira is one of the major contributors to the rise of Woolf in Brazil. During the 1940s, Pereira wrote several articles on Woolf for the newspaper *Correio da Manhã* [The Morning Mail]; most of them were later organised and edited by Luciana Viégas in the collection *Escritos da Maturidade* [Writing from Maturity] (1994). In 1944 Pereira devoted four articles to Woolf. In 'Dualidade em Virginia Woolf' [The duality of Virginia Woolf], Pereira starts by comparing Woolf's language in her novels and essays, as if the reader was dealing with two different writers, one more lyrical and fluid and the other more logical and incisive. Then, she analyses Woolf's novels and Woolf's relation with time. Pereira argues that, while in *Mrs Dalloway*, time represents only one day in the life of the main character, in *To the Lighthouse* and *The Years,* time itself is the central theme, indicating 'lost time' and 'found time' similar to Marcel Proust's famous work *In Search of Lost Time*. Pereira perceives *The Waves* as the expression of time through the lives of six characters while she suggests that *Orlando* is the negation of time. Pereira finishes her work by stating that Woolf's obsession with time represented her obsession with death, quoting a passage from *The Waves*: 'What enemy do we now perceive advancing against us, you whom I ride now, as we stand pawing this stretch of pavement? It is death. Death is the enemy' (1994: 228).

In her short essay, 'O Big Ben e o Carrilhão Fantasista' [Big Ben and the fanciful carillon] (1994), Pereira again discusses time, focusing on *Mrs Dalloway* and *To the Lighthouse*. Pereira opens her article by comparing two diverse stages of the narrative. On the one hand, there is the solemn and majestic sound of the Big Ben as the powerful tower related to important men, laws and duties. On the other hand, the fanciful and ordinary carillon refers to the meaningless things, confusing thoughts, worries, doubts, and fragmented memories of Clarissa Dalloway, who tries to insert her domestic narrative into the public life of important men. By doing so, Mrs Dalloway's chromatic carillon represents her ideals, her imagination and her utopian desire to change the order of things. Woolf's literary technique is to find the harmony between the two sounds of Big Ben and the carillon in both narrative plans of *Mrs Dalloway*: the patriarchal order and the female subversive plot. Woolf's task, according to Pereira, is to create 'harmony between the ephemeral and the eternal, the consciousness and subconsciousness, reason and instinct, solidity and fluidity, unity and plurality' (1994: 102).[2]

In 'Assombração' [Haunted], Pereira examines Woolf's short stories in *The Haunted House*; for her, 'The mark on the wall' is the best and contends that Woolf's power lies in her ability to lead the reader to think beyond what is described. She grasps in Woolf's stories something that transcends reality towards infinity: 'Woolf's short stories represent a silent world of transmitted thoughts, of premonitions, intuitions, mute antagonisms and comprehensions' (1994: 113).[3] Finally, in 'Crítica e feminismo' [Criticism and feminism], she starts from Woolf's first *Common Reader*, observing Woolf's position as a reader, someone who has a great sense of humour, reads for pleasure and travels to unknown places through the words on a page. Pereira compares Woolf to other critics, including T. S. Eliot and Edmund Wilson, but they cannot compete with her literary talent. For Pereira, Woolf's criticism is precise, acute and erudite; it is not dogmatic or arrogant. At the end Pereira discusses *A Room One's Own*, where she focuses on Woolf's irony and her intellectual honesty. She ends her text by arguing that 'freedom of thinking and a minimum of material conditions do not belong to feminist conquests; they are essential rights of human beings, men or women, artists or workers' (1994: 101).[4]

Lucia Miguel Pereira read Woolf's novels and political essays intensively in the original, as the translations of the novel did not begin until 1946. Elizabeth Vieira Camara (2011) undertakes a comparative study between Woolf's *Mrs Dalloway* and *To the Lighthouse* and Pereira's *Amanhecer* [Dawning], exploring how both authors deal with temporality in the construction of the novel, and considering Woolf's aesthetic proposal and Pereira's critical point of view. Camara perceives more psychological depth in Woolf's characters than in Pereira's. Woolf's time is more fragmented both in *Mrs Dalloway* and in *To the Lighthouse*, while there is linearity in Pereira's novel, which is chronologically divided into sequential chapters. I should also add that both *Mrs Dalloway* and *Amanhecer* deal with the developmental process of female characters to show how they adapt, adjust or subvert the order of patriarchal society until the moment of their awakening about themselves and the reality around them.

Clarice Lispector (1920–77)

Clarice Lispector comes from a very different cultural and ethnic background than Woolf; she was born to a Jewish family in Ukraine and emigrated with her family to Brazil when she was three years old.[5] During her life, she used different names: Chaya, Nina, Clarice, Clara, Clarinha, Clarice Gurgel Valente and finally, only Clarice Lispector. She was a divorced mother struggling to survive and care for two children. She was a journalist and writer, and wrote under the pseudonyms Tereza Quadros, Helen Palmer and Ilka Soares. Lispector launched her career as a novelist, short story writer and journalist in her mid-twenties. She divorced officially in 1964 and kept writing until her death in 1977.

Lispector lived in Britain in from 1950 to 1951 and then moved to Washington, DC. During this period, she worked for the newspaper *Comício* [Rally] under the pseudonym of Quadros. Her column was titled 'Entre Mulheres' [Between women] and her task was to select texts, translate some and give advice to women, in a conversational tone. In 1952, she published in *Comício* a free translation of Woolf's depiction of Judith Shakespeare in *A Room of One's Own* (Lispector 1952; republished in 1977).

Mariângela Alonso in *O Jogo de Espelhos na Ficção de Clarice Lispector* (2017) [The Game of Mirrors in Clarice Lispector's Fiction] explains that Lispector's appropriation of Woolf's ideas depicts Lispector's own attention to the gender problems her readers were facing in social and family environments.

Aparecida Maria Nunes in *Correio Feminino* [Women's Mail] organised and republished Lispector's journalistic work for the Brazilian press, offering readers a different Clarice Lispector, one who is more focused on the day-to-day and less introspective than the Lispector we know from her novels (Lispector 2006). However, Nunes also argues that Lispector used the disguise of her pseudonym Tereza Quadros to initiate her female readers to other literary texts and thus did more than offer advice on what women should eat, dress or behave in her work as a journalist. Nunes writes:

> The female seduction play – what is shown and what is hidden, the spoken and the non-spoken – demarcates the territory where the interlocutor of these pages should walk, and also highlights the choices of Clarice Lispector's prose and the disguises she created – Tereza Quadros, Helen Palmer and Ilka Soares – to write to women who, possibly, would not be Clarice Lispector's readers. (Lispector 2006: 12)[6]

Clarice Lispector has been compared to Virginia Woolf, especially in terms of their shared modernist language and techniques. Álvaro Lins in *Os mortos de sobrecasaca: Ensaios e estudos* [The Dead in Overcoats: Essays and Studies] (1963) was the earliest critic to compare the language of Lispector's first book to Woolf.

However, Lispector denied that she had ever read Woolf at the point when she published her first novel in 1943. Benjamin Moser quotes Lispector's statement:

> I do not like when people say I have affinities with Virginia Woolf (I only read her, by the way, after finishing my first book): it is that I do not forgive her for committing suicide. The terrible duty is going until the end. (2009: 205)[7]

But by the 1960s Lispector was certainly familiar with Woolf's novels. When Helena Collett Solberg interviewed Lispector for the newspaper *Mundo Ilustrado* [The Illustrated World] (1960), she asked Lispector what she thought about Woolf. Lispector confessed great admiration for Woolf's work and talked about how she was affected by her novels, especially *Mrs Dalloway*. It can be understood why Lispector would have denied any comparison to Woolf at first – it was a way of reaffirming and reassuring her own identity as a writer. But, in the later years, when her career was established, thinking back through Woolf and the literary image of Judith Shakespeare was a way for her to create a community of literary sisters, although there is no evidence that she wrote about Judith Shakespeare beyond the 1952 *Comício* translation.

Lispector's texts do have many similarities with Woolf's writing, both in terms of technique and content. Both writers deal with the limits of the language to express the emotions of the body and of the mind; they struggle to convey different levels of consciousness; their writings depict a strong conflict in expressing rational knowledge and the unknown; and, finally, their novels are not simple representations of life, but rather offer extensive inquiries into the uncertainties of life. As a result, their narratives express the fragmented lives of their characters and the existential condition of human beings in a chaotic world.

Rita Terezinha Schmidt, in 'Crossing borders: Clarice Lispector and the scene of transnational feminist criticism' (2018), observes that – due to the migrations, disseminations and translations of Lispector's works across different geographies – her writings have achieved an international cross-cultural status. Such international recognition refers to the fact that feminist criticism has (re)signified Lispector's fiction in terms of female identity, experience, difference and writing in and beyond the context of Brazilian patriarchal culture. Schmidt's text is fundamental to Lispector's reception in Brazil and overseas; in Brazil, Schmidt relocates Lispector in the national scenario, reviewing the early criticism on the author and noting how common it was for male critics to underestimate the value of women writers' work. Schmidt's analysis maps the translations and the most significant criticism on Lispector. Schmidt's work is also a milestone because she places Lispector on the scene of transnational feminist criticism. On the one hand, emphasis should be given to the fact that Lispector never considered herself a feminist; like Woolf, she avoided labels. On the other hand, feminist critics found rich materials for their approaches because of Lispector's ambivalent female characters, typically depicted as unsatisfied with the social structures of patriarchal societies and fighting to find meaning in their lonely, aimless and repetitive routines.

From Schmidt's perspective, feminist criticism has always had to rely on relations, intersections, translations, migrations and different registers according to the specificities of geographical and political locations (2018: 260). The travels of Lispector's texts across geographical and national borders have promoted a polyphony of voices that converge in a transnational critical network of affiliations and differences, leading to outcomes attuned with the greatness of her literary accomplishments. This transnational perspective enhances the impact of Lispector's texts travelling the world, such as when she was discovered by Hélène Cixous who, subsequently, transformed and reinvented Lispector's writing through her interpretations of it. Correspondingly, Lispector's writing impacted Cixous's creativity, which became so similar to Lispector's that it was difficult to discern who was writing. The transnational movement of Lispector's texts also resembles Woolf's books travelling to Brazil and meeting a large Latin American audience, which allows us to call her a South American Woolf, who is multiple, plural and contradictory.

Carolina Maria de Jesus (1914–77)

In the 1960s, Carolina Maria de Jesus, who is perhaps the best example among Brazilian women to illustrate Woolf's argument in *A Room of One's Own*, began to publish her work. Jesus makes it clear that to be a writer, a woman needs to have financial autonomy, as well as personal and private space. Born poor and black, Jesus was a writer in search of a room and a voice of her own. A single mother with three children and living in the favelas, the Brazilian slums, Jesus intended to leave and to buy a house of her own using revenue from her writings. Following Woolf's argument, Jesus was aware that she needed a proper house and a worthy salary in order to write, but even though she did not have enough privacy, she wrote at night after work and when her children were sleeping. Jesus was conscious that she needed money of her own to support her children and her writing, so during the day she made a living by collecting garbage. Having a husband was not in her plans because she knew that no man would allow her to spend her time writing. By rejecting societal norms, it is possible to say that Jesus was embracing Woolf's feminism while she was also breaking the boundaries of the Brazilian literary tradition. I consider her a marginal voice condemning the system and resisting being part of it.

Quarto de Despejo: Diário de uma Favelada [Dumping Room: Diary of a Female Slum-Dweller], was published in 1960 and was translated into English as *Child of the Dark* in 1962. It was very successful, as Robert M. Levine writes in 'The cautionary tale of Carolina Maria de Jesus': 'in three days' time, the initial print run of ten thousand copies sold out in São Paulo. Six months later, ninety thousand copies had sold' (1994: 60). Soon, it was translated into more than thirteen languages and was published in forty countries. After that, Jesus left the slums to live in a brick house in a middle-class neighbourhood. But her dream became a nightmare when her second book, *Casa de alvenaria: Diário de uma ex-favelada* [Brick House: Diary of an Ex-Slum Dweller] (1961), had a very different reception and success vanished as fast as it came. The book was harshly received because she criticised politicians and middle-class people, and with extremely severe language. Jesus realised she was not part of the slums any more but neither could she identify with her middle-class neighbours, who ostracised her. The writer searched for seclusion in a ranch forty kilometres from the city, where she could write and make a living by cultivating the land, but, despite the revenue from the first book's sales, she died in poverty at the age of sixty-three.

Lesley Feracho, in *Linking the Americas: Race, Hybrid Discourses, and the Reformulation of Feminine Identity*, proposes an analysis of Jesus's first book, observing that the author was aware of her miserable conditions and writing about it gave her some distance to reflect upon and overcome it. Feracho divides the themes of the Jesus's diary into six different subjects: Jesus's personal routine; observations and emotions about life in the favela; social commentary; plans for herself and her family; and political denouncements (2005: 20). Feracho poses two main questions: what was the cause of Jesus's incredible success? And, given her immense initial success, why did Jesus die in poverty? For Feracho, Jesus's success can be understood in relation to the historical context in which she was writing. In the second rhetorical question, Feracho explores a complex mix of racial, gender-based and class prejudice, adding that Jesus refused to conform to social norms and publication standards. Addressing the first query, I can infer that there was a certain objectification and exotification of the misery and of the poor black woman who was raised in the favelas.

José Carlos Sebe M. Meihy and Robert M. Levine (1994) view Jesus's *Quarto de despejo* as a social product that denounces the extreme inequality between rich and poor, the impossibility of ascending socially, and the relentlessness of poverty in the country. The political and economic contexts of the 1960s were not favourable for the poor; the government believed that first the country had to grow economically in order to distribute its wealth later. However, this distribution was never made and the poor kept getting even poorer and the rich, richer. For Feracho, reading Jesus's diary makes it possible to understand questions of race, class and the acquisition of power both in Latin America and in Brazil. Jesus's writing represents not only a means of channelling the daily suffering she experienced and a means of acquiring a status that would set her apart from other slums dwellers but also a form of resistance against social and cultural forces that oppressed her (2005: 39).

Jesus was a female working-class voice who countered a patriarchal middle-class tradition; she was also a poet, and her 'ugly' poetry was not in harmony with the traditional *belle lettres* of the previous decades. She was expressing a raw reality of life in the favelas in her poetic unique language, with her broken sentences, fragmented syntax and lack of norms. Her language reveals not only the cries of the poor, the hunger for justice, the need for survival and the call for a better education; through her verse she offers a gaze at the poor, in the same terms that Paulo Freire proposes in his *Pedagogia dos Oprimidos* [Pedagogy of the Oppressed] (1968). In this sense Jesus's voice is also similar to the African-American activist bell hooks (2015) and her yearning for justice. Jesus has to shout for attention; she demands to be heard from her subaltern position, from the guts and the garbage of the slums and the great inequalities that divide the country.

In *Quarto de despejo*, Jesus denounces the corruption of the system and shows the relation of powerless women struggling to survive in a hostile world of men. The novel reveals the cruel life of the slums, where powerless and oppressed women relate to powerless, oppressed and absent men, some of whom are *machos* who kill women who do not follow their own rules. In her work, men's representations have shifted from the patriarchal figure to the absent one in families where women are the heads.

Regina Dalcastagné (2005) asserts that Carolina Maria de Jesus's life illustrates Spivak's argument in 'Can the subaltern speak?' (1988). Dalcastagné observes that Spivak's essay is not only about being able to speak but also about the possibility of speaking with authority and of being heard. The harsh political moment of the 1960s was not favourable enough for Jesus's political criticism, when Brazilian democracy was being stolen by the dictatorship and she was forgotten. However, in the 1990s, Jesus's work was rediscovered, and now many studies explore her history and writings. As of 2013, the archival collection, titled Acervo Carolina Maria de Jesus, is now in Arquivo Público Municipal Cônego Hérmogenes Cassimiro de Araújo Brunswick and was organised by the scholars Sergio da Silva Barcelos and Eliana Garcia Vilas Boas in the city of Sacramento, in Minas Gerais, where Jesus was born.

Other 'Carolinas' are emerging today both in Brazil and globally, with Conceição Evaristo as one example. Evaristo started her literary career in 1990. Today she is a visiting professor at Federal University of Minas Gerais, an activist advocating for Black rights, and a writer whose works address race, gender and class. Another example is Djamila Ribeiro, a feminist writer who was inspired by Spivak's article and has recently published the book *O que é lugar de fala?* [What Is the Place of Discourse?] (2017). Ribeiro addresses the question of who has the right to speak and focuses not only on individuals, both men and women, but also on the social conditions that allow marginalised people to develop their citizenship or, alternatively, prevent them from doing so. These Carolinas are beginning to exercise their right to speak, and readers who concur with Chandra Talpade Mohanty's vision of communities of feminist solidarities, where Carolinas can live in a space of their own ready to express their creativity and their vision of the world.

Considering again Woolf's argument about women writers: 'For we think back through our mothers if we are women' (*AROO*: 69), it is clear that Jesus has inspired her own successors and has generated a tradition of black female writers, who are thinking back through their mothers and about a better future, where Jesus would have had a different future. In keeping with Woolf's vision of a room of one's own and £500 a year, Jesus through her writing acquired a house of her own, and she became a professional writer with an income of her own, although it was not an easy task to negotiate between Woolf's feminism advocated in *A Room of One's Own* and the Brazilian classist and patriarchal literary traditions.

The 1980s and 1990s
Ana Cristina Cesar (1952–83)

The 1980s and 1990s represent a very important time in the politics of Brazilian society. The dictatorship ended in 1985. During the period, the number of published women writers increased dramatically; these writers were invested in liberating their texts and their bodies from the limitations and repressions of patriarchal restraints as well as from traditional and conventional modes. In this context, Ana Cristina Cesar (1952–83), a poet who studied and translated Katherine Mansfield, Emily Dickinson and Sylvia Plath, emerged as a key figure. Cesar was mainly a poet, but she also wrote several essays; during 1975–7 she worked as a journalist for newspapers like *Jornal do Brasil* [Brazil Newspaper], *Correio Brasiliense* [Brazilian Mail] and *Folha de São Paulo* [São Paulo Mail Folha]. In her book-length work *Escritos no Rio* [Written in Rio] (1993), Cesar defends the idea of a woman writing as a woman, as opposed to the androgynous writer she perceived in Woolf's depiction of women authors in *A Room of One's Own*. As Cesar emphasises, 'it is not necessary to connect to Lampião[8] or become androgynous (as Woolf wanted) to make great literature' (1993: 176).[9] *Escritos no Rio* was eventually incorporated into *Crítica e tradução* [Criticism and Translation], published in 2016. The collection includes most of her other books, such as *Escritos da Inglaterra* [Writings from England] and *Literatura não é documento* [Literature Is Not a Document]. Her works were fragmented, unfinished and scattered in part due to her unexpected death in 1983 when she took her own life. Aside from the obvious similarity in the choice of suicide, there are many ways that Woolf and Cesar connect through their poetic texts. Although Woolf wrote only two poems (neither of which she intended for publication), it could be said that her poetic prose permeates Cesar's work. I compare them as women poets writing with their bodies for a collective group of women reading through their poetic veins. I think of Woolf as more a poet of the soul, though she was very aware of the importance of the body in capturing all the perceptions and transferring them to consciousness, the locus of her prose writing in her novels such as *The Waves* as well as in short stories and essays, while Cesar is more a poet of the body in search of her soul in most of her poems.

Although I understand Cesar's criticism on Woolf's androgyny, I cannot agree completely with it. In *A Room of One's Own*, Woolf says that a woman writer needs a room of her own and £500 a year to be able to speak her mind (*AROO*: 85). *A Room of One's Own* was originally published in 1929, but even though women had been writing for centuries, despite the constraints of a patriarchal society it was still too soon to define women's writing. On the one hand, Woolf herself was the first one to stimulate and inspire many Latin American women to write, as she encouraged Victoria Ocampo, through personal contact and letters, to write her autobiography in Argentina.[10] In 'Virginia Woolf and Victoria Ocampo: A Brazilian perspective', I analyse the dialogue between the two writers and how Woolf is depicted in Ocampo's writing (M. A. de Oliveira 2016). On the other hand, Woolf herself was stimulated by women writers as can be seen in *A Room of One's Own*. Woolf, in turn, inspired a community of women to write across cultures; through their writing Woolf herself is inscribed in transnational feminism. A further example of this transnational relationship among women writers is Woolf's correspondence with the Chinese writer Ling Shuhua. Patricia Laurence (2003) investigates the connections between them in *Lily Briscoe's Chinese Eyes: Bloomsbury, Modernism and China*. Julian Bell, Virginia Woolf's nephew, had an affair with Ling Shuhua when he was teaching at the National Wuhan University during the years of 1935–7. Woolf corresponded with Ling during the period, and Laurence examines this complex network and illustrates how both women writers shared their feelings during the Second World War and talked about the social limitations because of their female condition. Although her autobiography was written in English, Woolf encouraged Ling to write in her language, expressing her own culture. Hua Jiang in 'Virginia Woolf and Ling Shuhua: Writing and practicing transnational feminism' discusses this epistolary encounter of women writers across nations and argues that both had to reflect on their own position while facing the problems of war. She declares:

> Woolf was led to examine her own positioning through gender and nationhood in the imperial system and to make her stand against imperialist patriotism, while Ling was enabled both to critique sexism in the Chinese patriarchal system and to subvert the official ideology of nationalism. (2008: 236)

This transnational dialogue among women writers was crucial to establishing literary communities, where they could discuss the political and aesthetic aspects of their work. Such transnational movement is an instance of transgressive action and transformative power. Ocampo's construction of a transnational community among Argentina, England, France and other Spanish-speaking countries is one way of alleviating the isolation of their inhabitants and building intellectual bridges among them. Ling's autobiography was also a transgressive act in a time when women did not have much of a voice in China. By using a young girl's point of view, especially in 'Childhood in China', she could expose the corruption of the society (Laurence 2003: 285).

Lygia Fagundes Telles (1923–)

Lygia Fagundes Telles was one of several Brazilian women inspired by Woolf. Telles was elected for the Brazilian Academy of Letters in 1987. As of 2020, she is ninety-six years old and her last book was published in 2012. Telles's first book *Ciranda de Pedras* [Circle of Stones] was published in 1954. The main character, Virginia, tries to break the boundaries of a patriarchal family, but she has to suffer the consequences of it. In 1991, Telles in 'Na viragem do século' [At the turn of the century] thinks back to Woolf but reflects as well on Brazil's process of colonisation. She addresses Brazilian modernism:

> I believe that since colonial times we have never been so dependent and so colonised as in these days of such decadent manners and habits. It is necessary, yes, to repeat until exhaustion that we have sixty million illiterates. And many more living in poverty. . . . There has never been such an acute desire for evasion, for fleeing. And such a desire to cling to the myths and gods of other lands, other people. Forget the past, minimise, especially, the Letters and Arts, and oh woe to you, oh literature, mirror of our society and of our time. Cover fast this mirror with other images, other names, oh Virginia Woolf, oh Proust, oh James Joyce. (1991: 3)[11]

In this passage, Telles is advocating for national literature, for more recognition of Brazilian authors; she says that our fight in literature has to be undertaken on national ground and in our own language. It is interesting to notice the great contrasts of Brazil where, while a small elite holds the power, millions of people are illiterate and in poverty. That is why Telles is speaking on behalf of social justice and for decolonising people's minds. In an interview with *Jornal do Brasil* [Brazil Newspaper] (1980), Telles proclaims her admiration for Woolf. Although her writing style is not like Woolf's, she declares that she and Woolf are part of the same family of writers who influence one another. On this relation between books and writers, Woolf herself states: 'masterpieces are not single and solitary births; they are the outcome of many years of thinking in common, of thinking by the body of the people, so that the experience of the mass is behind the single voice' (*AROO*: 59).

Telles in *As Horas Nuas* [Naked Hours] (1989) has used elements of Woolf's political essay *A Room of One's Own* to create a counter-narrative. In the novel, the presence of the husband who was tortured during the harsh years of the dictatorial period is as secondary as the presence of the cat that narrates the story. But the second level – that of the husband's – is the most important part of a novel that obliquely calls attention to the politics of that time. Published during the dictatorial period when few noticed its subversive aspect, the novel depicts how the torture of intellectuals affected their lives and how the system erased the university faculty. Because the book was written by a woman, censors would suppose it was a poetic narrative told from the perspective of a cat talking about the decadent life of an actress; it was not suppressed because the censors did not recognise its dissident aspects. Either they could not grasp the meaning of the novel or they underestimated the poetic power and politics of a woman's writing. *As Horas Nuas* can be compared to Woolf's *Orlando*, which was considered a fantasy and a faux biography that was also not censored in spite of its subversive traits between the lines, while Radclyffe Hall's *The Well of Loneliness*, published the same year, was prohibited because of the explicit representation of lesbianism.

Telles's novel *As Meninas* [The Girls], published in 1973, traces the unfolding lives of three young women, Ana Clara, Lorena and Lia. Lia is a feminist, communist and writer who embodies the testimonies of those tortured during the dictatorship; her story epitomises the ideological content of the novel. As is true of *As Horas Nuas*, *As Meninas* survived censorship due to the subtlety of its technique. Offering readers multifaceted perspectives, *As Meninas* features not only an omniscient narrator but also the observations of the three girls. By creating four distinct voices that overlap, Telles makes it is difficult for a reader to determine who is speaking. Moreover, Ana Clara's discourse is blurred because of her mind being altered by the use of drugs, giving the impression of the confused imagination of a young woman. Telles, like Woolf, used the techniques of stream of consciousness, fragmented narrative, broken sentences and multiple points of view as strategies to confuse and fend off censorship.

Hilda Hilst (1930–2004)

Hilda Hilst, a controversial and irreverent writer, was also inspired by Woolf. With wit and humour Hilst deals with questions about God, sex and women's liberation. Her first book of poems was *Presságio* [Presage] (1950). Part of her archive is at the University of Campinas and part is at the Hilda Hilst Institute, which used to be her home, Casa do Sol [House of the Sun], where she lived with her sixty abandoned dogs and wrote more than forty books before her death. One of the most important critics of Hilst, Leandra Alves dos Santos (2006), analysed Hilst's poetry, drama and prose. Most of her chronicles, articles and essays written for the newspaper *Correio Popular de Campinas* [Popular Campinas Mail] were organised into a collection, *Cascos e Carícias* [Casks and Caresses] (1998), in which she addressed not only daily subjects, but also human frailties, the sacred and profane, and joy, misery and violence. Her provocative writing relates to politics, human anxiety and financial matters; her poetry is about love, the mysteries of life, the search for identity and the need for connection with nature and God, while her drama deals with social injustices, human cruelty and atrocities, especially when she is portraying the political scene of dictatorship during the 1960s and 1970s. In a community of writers who inspired one another, Hilst was fascinated by Woolf's faux biography *Flush*. When mentioning authors who inspired her, Hilst declared in one interview ('Obscena Senhora' [Mrs Obscene] 1995) that she, like Woolf, wrote a book through a dog's perspective: *Com meus olhos de cão* [With my dog's eyes] (1986).[12] Hilst deliberately uses *Flush* in her experiments with perspective and narrative voice. By using animals' points of view, she is able to integrate humour and sarcasm into her work and also to question both the rational philosophical system and the logos of the 'Father' that underpin patriarchy.[13]

Sônia Coutinho (1939–)

While Ana Cristina Cesar questions Woolf's androgynous view, Sônia Coutinho in *O jogo de Ifá* [Ifá's game] (1980) embraces Woolf's androgyny to create the character Renata/Renato and brings African traditions to the narrative, in which the character Ifá, like Orlando, has many lives. Ifá is a divine entity from Africa; he is a guide, a counsellor, the one who shows people their fate. Coutinho's narrative is self-reflexive; in each chapter she explains to her readers the next feature of the plan. For instance, Coutinho writes in chapter eleven, 'Game and maze':

> I intend my book to be a kind of game . . . and at each throw of dice, the central character, hero/heroine, as Virginia Woolf's Orlando, wins the right to advance or is obliged to return. Each move is a passage of his/her life. (1980: 24)[14]

Sometimes the author writes about Renato and then changes to Renata's plot, not entirely like Orlando, who, as noted, is a man who changes into a woman. Coutinho's character is more like two faces of the same coin. Renato/Renata lived until he/she was twenty-seven years old, tormented by prejudices of the provincial city.[15] When Renato/Renata leaves for Rio de Janeiro, he/she starts a job as a journalist and divides her time with literary activities. However, after being emotionally suffocated in the busy city, Renato/Renata decides to return home in search of his/her lost identity while planning to write a fictional book about the existential crisis of being asphyxiated in a small city, then enduring the pressures of a huge city and coping with love, divorce, broken families and his/her broken heart.

Adriana Lunardi (1964–)

Adriana Lunardi in *Vésperas* (2002) mixes fiction and biography to depict the lives and deaths of nine women writers: Virginia Woolf, Dorothy Parker, Katherine Mansfield,

Colette, Sylvia Plath, Clarice Lispector, Ana Cristina Cesar, Zelda Fitzgerald and Júlia da Costa. Lunardi connects Brazilian women writers with authors they were familiar with. For instance, Lispector read Woolf and Mansfield, and Cesar wrote about Plath and translated Mansfield. The first chapter is about Ginny – Virginia Woolf – who decides to write her last letter to her husband and goes towards the river where she picks up a stone, puts it on her pocket and walks into the water. Lunardi states: 'The desperate efforts of Virginia ignore the reactions of her body. The voices in her head prevent her from thinking clearly. She is in a nightmare, as if she is running without moving' (2002:18).[16] The book is not only about death but also throws some light on how these women writers lived on a daily basis.

Hilda Gouveia de Oliveira (1946–)

Hilda Gouveia de Oliveira is a prolific writer who has written extensively on Virginia Woolf. In her book, *Imagens e criatividade no lirismo de Virginia Woolf* [Images and Creativity in Virginia Woolf's Lyricism] (2007), she explores Woolf's poetics and techniques in four of her novels, *Jacob's Room, Mrs Dalloway, To the Lighthouse* and *The Waves*. Oliveira's book *Mrs Dalloway – uma unidade estrutural* [Mrs Dalloway – A Structural Unity] was published in 1979 and analyses three narrative categories in the novel: time, space and the main character, Clarissa Dalloway. Oliveira presents three different graphics which illustrate the waves in these narrative categories. According to Oliveira, Clarissa Dalloway is the element linking the structural patterns and the waves represent the relation between the main character and time and space. The first graphic depicts a map of London representing different scenes related to Clarissa Dalloway. The second graphic portrays the main character in relation to time and space, showing scenes in Westminster. The third graphic features Clarissa in Westminster, Septimus in the park, Lady Bruton in Mayfair, Miss Kilman in Clarissa's house and visiting the stores, and Elizabeth on the bus. Oliveira's *O Sentido Recriado* [The Recreated Meaning] (2005) is a collection of essays on literature and criticism. In one of these essays, 'O romance inglês do século XIX e a questão da mulher' [The English novel in XIX century and the question of women], the author follows Woolf's example in *A Room of One's Own* and discusses English women writers including Jane Austen, Charlotte and Emily Brontë, George Eliot and Elizabeth Gaskell. She also discusses women's confinement, self-sacrifice, the solitude of the Angel in the House, the repressive mother figure, the Cinderella complex and the archetypal father.

Final Considerations

As indicated in this chapter, there is so much more to say about the works of Clarice Lispector, Lygia Fagundes Telles and Ana Cristina Cesar. Contemporary women writers will continue to address Woolf's feminism and other aspects of her creative writing. The texts by Brazilian women writers discussed here represent women in a patriarchal society, reflecting on their position in relation to family, their sexuality, other women, men, the workplace, the process of ageing and the way they are affected by institutions. The writing of Lispector and Telles, for instance, is populated by women: they are housewives, maids, professionals, artists, mothers, wives, grandmothers and daughters, all of them conveying their experiences in relation to patriarchy. Lispector's *Laços de família* [Family Ties] (1983), a collection of short stories, represents women in the realm of family relationships. Telles's *As Meninas* and *As Horas Nuas* locate women in the harsh years of the dictatorship and show not only how many women were involved in the political arena but also how many of them, particularly from the middle class, were not touched by it, as if it they were blinded by the system.

Once Lispector's work relating to Woolf started to be published, Woolf's oeuvre began to inspire Brazilian women writers and many have followed her writing practices. Some like Ana Cristina Cesar problematised her androgynous approach; others like Telles questioned the devotion to foreign writers such as Woolf, Proust and James Joyce while reflecting on Brazil's colonised mentality.

Brazilian women writers have had to navigate between Woolf's feminist modernism and Brazilian conservative literary traditions. At first, Brazilian women writers had to conform to these conventions; yet, after the 1960s, they started to play with language, transforming writing in mischievous ways, with more humour and eroticism, as if by liberating their writings, they were also freeing their bodies from patriarchal constraints and finding their voices.

Going back to where I started and following a transnational and transcultural perspective, there are some answers for the questions proposed in this chapter. When Woolf's writing travels to Brazil and encounters such a multicultural context, it is enhanced by not only a transnational and transcultural perspective but also by a transtemporal one. Woolf has had an enduring impact on Brazilian women writers, and now their own texts are travelling together with Woolf's books. Consequently, these works too will leave their 'original' context and they will be read and transformed by the readers in a global environment. As Silver notes, Woolf's image became more and more popular during the 1980s and 1990s. By the twenty-first century, Woolf's work had become truly global. Woolf died almost eighty years ago, but her texts are still alive: as she herself said, 'great poets never die' (*AROO*: 102), and neither do great novelists and essayists. Woolf is still moving and inspiring other women today, to the point that we can talk about a multiplicity of Woolfs.

Notes

1. 'Hoje, porém, neste pseudo século feminista, fingem os escritores ignorar o desabrochamento maravilhoso, no campo da literatura, de romancistas, como Virginia Woolf ... cujas personagens idealizadas em livros, que merecem os maiores prêmios conhecidos, tais como o Internacional e o Nobel, serão certamente, um dia outros tantos símbolos para as nações futuras.'
2. 'A harmonia entre o passageiro e o eterno, entre o consciente e o subconsciente, entre a razão e o instinto, entre a solidez e a fluidez, entre a unidade e a pluralidade.'
3. 'É o mundo silencioso das transmissões de pensamento, das premonições, das intuições, dos mudos antagonismos e compreensões mudas.'
4. 'Liberdade de pensamento e um mínimo de bem-estar material – não pertencem às chamadas conquistas feministas. São direitos essenciais da pessoa humana, homem ou mulher, artista ou operário.'
5. The best reference to understand Clarice Lispector's life is Nádia Battella Gotlib's *Clarice: Uma vida que se conta* [Clarice: A Life that Tells Itself] (2011). This biography is based on Lispector's letters, photographs, historical documents and friends' testimonies.

6. 'O jogo da sedução feminina – daquilo que se mostra e daquilo que se esconde, do dizer e do não dito – demarca o território por onde a interlocutora dessas páginas deve caminhar, mas também deixa evidente as escolhas da prosa de Clarice Lispector e dos disfarces que criou – Teresa Quadros, Helen Palmer e Ilka Soares – para escrever a mulheres que, possivelmente, não seriam as leitoras de Clarice Lispector.'
7. 'Não gosto quando dizem que tenho afinidade com Virginia Woolf (só a li, aliás, depois de escrever o meu primeiro livro): é que não quero perdoar o fato dela se ter suicidado. O horrível dever é ir até o fim.' All subsequent translations are mine unless otherwise indicated.
8. Virgulino Ferreira da Silva, better known as Lampião (1898–1938), was a renowned figure from the north-east who took his fight for justice into his own hands. He sought to revenge his father's death at the hands of the police.
9. 'Não é preciso atrelar-se a Lampião ou androgenizar-se (Como queria Virginia Woolf) para fazer grande literatura.'
10. Her dialogue with Woolf can be found in *Against the Wind and the Tide: Victoria Ocampo* (Meyer 1990).
11. 'Creio que desde os tempos coloniais nunca fomos tão dependentes, tão onformadamente colonizados como nestes dias de tamanha decadência dos nossos usos e costumes. É preciso, sim, repetir até a náusea que temos sessenta milhões de analfabetos. E mais outro tanto vivendo em estado de pura pobreza. . . . Nunca foi tão agudo o desejo de evasão, de fuga. Tanta vontade de se agarrar aos mitos e deuses de outras terras, outras gentes. Esquecer o passado, minimizar principalmente as letras e as artes. Ai de ti, ó literatura! Espelho de nossa sociedade e do nosso tempo. Cobrir depressa esse espelho com outras imagens, outros nomes, ó Virginia Woolf, ó Proust, ó James Joyce!'
12. Lygia Fagundes Telles, in *As Horas Nuas* [The Naked Hours] (1989), also employs an animal's perspective, but in her case, part of the story is narrated through the eyes of Raul, a cat.
13. *Obscena Senhora D.* (2016) can also be considered as a parody of *Mrs Dalloway*, with Senhora D [Mrs D] as an obscene version of Mrs Dalloway. In another interview for the newspaper *Nicolau* (1993), the journalist, referring to Virginia Woolf, asked Hilst about her aim in her writing. Hilst responded that she searches for an originary state – one that is prohibited; the unspeakable.
14. 'Pretendo que meu livro seja uma espécie de jogo. . . . E, a cada lance de dados, o personagem central, herói/heroína, qual Orlando de Virginia Woolf, ganha o direito de avançar ou é obrigado a recuar. Cada jogada é uma passagem de sua vida.'
15. The provincial city is in the state of Bahia, but it is not specified in the work.
16. 'O esforço desesperado de Virginia ignora as reações do corpo. As vozes não permitem que ela calcule seus avanços. É como um sonho ruim, em que se sente correr sem sair do lugar.'

Bibliography

Alonso, M. (2017), *O jogo de espelhos na ficção de Clarice Lispector* [The Game of Mirrors in Clarice Lispector's Fiction], São Paulo: Annablume.

Berman, J. (2011), *Modernist Commitments: Ethics, Politics, and Transnational Modernism*, New York: Columbia University Press.

Camara, E. V. (2011), 'A forma do ensaio e a construção do tempo ficcional em Lucia Miguel Pereira e Virginia Woolf' [The form of the essay and the construction of fictional time in Lucia Miguel Pereira and Virginia Woolf], dissertation, São Paulo: Universidade de São Paulo.

Cesar, A. C. (1999), *Escritos no Rio* [Written in Rio], São Paulo: Brasiliense.

Coutinho, S. (1980), *O jogo de Ifá* [Ifá's Game], São Paulo: Ática.

Cunha, H. P. (1998), 'Becoming whole: One woman's words', in S. Coelsch-Foisner, H. Wallinger and G. Reisner (eds), *Daughters of Restlessness: Women's Literature at the End of the Millennium*, Heidelberg: Universitätsverlag Winter, pp. 227–38.

Dalcastagné, R. (2005), 'A personagem do romance brasileiro contemporâneo: 1990–2004' [Character in the contemporary Brazilian novel: 1990–2004], *Revista Estudos de Literatura Brasileira Contemporânea* [Journal of Contemporary Brazilian Literature Studies], 26, pp. 13–71, <http://seer.bce.unb.br/index.php/estudos/article/viewFile/2123/1687> (last accessed 5 April 2018).

Duarte, C. L. (2003), 'Feminismo e literatura no Brasil' [Feminism and literature in Brazil], *Estudos Avançados* [Advanced Studies], 17: 49, pp. 151–72, <http://www.scielo.br/pdf/ea/v17n49/18402.pdf> (last accessed 25 December 2018).

Feracho, L. (2005), *Linking the Americas: Race, Hybrid Discourses, and the Reformulation of Feminine Identity*, Albany, NY: State University of New York Press, <https://ebookcentral.proquest.com/lib/appstate/detail.action?docID=3407705> (last accessed 20 December 2019).

Freire, P. (1968), *Pedagogia do oprimido* [Pedagogy of the Oppressed], Rio de Janeiro: Paz e Terra.

Gotlib, N. B. (2011), *Clarice – uma vida que se conta* [Clarice – A Life that Tells Itself], São Paulo: Edusp.

Goulimari, P. (ed.) (2017), *Women Writing across Cultures: Past, Present, Future*, London: Routledge.

Hilst, H. (1986), *Com meus olhos de cão* [With My Dog's Eyes], São Paulo: Globo.

Hilst, H. (1993), 'Hilda Hilst: Um coração em segredo' [Hilda Hilst: A heart in secret], interviewed by I. Mafra, *Nicolau*, Paraná, 51: 7, p. 5.

Hilst, H. (1995), 'Obscena Senhora' [Mrs Obscene], *Jornal do Brasil* [Brazil Newspaper], Rio de Janeiro, 00164, p. 39.

Hilst, H. (2016), *Obscena Senhora D.* [The Obscene Mrs D.], São Paulo: Folha de São Paulo.

hooks, b. (2015 [1990]), *Yearning: Race, Gender, and Cultural Politics*, New York: Routledge.

Jesus, M. C. de (1960), *Quarto de Despejo: Diário de uma favelada* [Dumping Room: Diary of a Female Slum-Dweller], São Paulo: Francisco Alves.

Jesus, M. C. de (1961), *Casa de alvenaria: Diário de uma ex-favelada* [Brick House: Diary of an Ex-Slum Dweller], São Paulo: Paulo Azevedo Editora.

Jiang, H. (2008), 'Virginia Woolf and Ling Shuhua: Writing and practising transnational feminism', in F. A. Durão and D. Williams (eds), *Modernist Group Dynamics: The Politics and Poetics of Friendship*, Newcastle upon Tyne: Cambridge Scholars, pp. 219–40.

Laurence, P. (2003), *Lily Briscoe's Chinese Eyes: Bloomsbury, Modernism, and China*, Columbia, SC: University of South Carolina Press.

Levine, R. M. (1994), 'The cautionary tale of Carolina Maria de Jesus', *Latin American Research Review*, 29: 1, pp. 55–83, <http://www.jstor.org/stable/2503644> (last accessed 26 September 2016).

Lima Grecco, G. de (2018), 'Levemos a mulher à Academia Brasileira de Letras! Tetrá de Teffé, a primeira romancista premiada pelos imortais' [Taking women to the Brazilian Academy of Letters! Tetrá de Teffé, the first novelist awarded by the immortals], *Revista Travessias*, 12: 1, pp. 177–92.

Lins, A. (1963), *Os mortos de sobrecasaca: Ensaios e estudos* [The Dead in Overcoats: Essays and Studies], Rio de Janeiro: Civilização Brasileira.

Lispector, C. (1952), 'A irmã de Shakespeare' [Shakespeare's sister], *Comício*, 22 May, Rio de Janeiro, p. 18.

Lispector, C. (1983), *Laços de Família* [Family Ties], Rio de Janeiro: Nova Fronteira.

Lispector, C. (2006), *Correio Feminino* [Women's Mail], ed. A. M. Nunes, Rio de Janeiro: Rocco.

Lobo, L. (1987), 'Women writers in Brazil today', *World Literature Today*, 61: 1, pp. 49–54.

Lobo, L. (1998), 'Beyond realism and towards the imaginary: Latin-American women writing at the end of the millennium', in S. Coelsch-Foisner, H. Wallinger and G. Reisner (eds), *Daughters of Restlessness: Women's Literature at the End of the Millennium*, Heidelberg: Universitätsverlag Winter, pp. 297–306.

Lunardi, A. (2002), *Vésperas* [The Day Before], Rio de Janeiro: Rocco.

Meihy, J. C. S. B. and R. M. Levine (1994), *Cinderela negra: A saga de Carolina Maria de Jesus*, Rio de Janeiro: UFRJ.
Meyer, D. (1990), *Against the Wind and the Tide: Victoria Ocampo*, Austin: University of Texas Press.
Mohanty, C. T. (1988), 'Under western eyes: Feminist scholarship and colonial discourses', *Feminist Review*, 30, pp. 61–88, <http://www.jstor.org/stable/1395054> (last accessed 17 October 2017).
Moser, B. (2009), *Clarice, uma biografia* [Clarice, A Biography], São Paulo: Cosac Naify.
Oliveira, H. G. X. (1979), *Mrs Dalloway – Uma unidade estrutural* [Mrs Dalloway – A Structural Unity], Rio de Janeiro: Catédra.
Oliveira, H. G. X. (2005), *O sentido recriado* [The Recreated Meaning], São Paulo: Scortecci.
Oliveira, H. G. X. (2007), *Imagens e criatividade no lirismo de Virginia Woolf* [Imagery and Creativity in Virginia Woolf's Lyricism], São Paulo: Scortecci.
Oliveira, M. A. de (2016), 'Virginia Woolf and Victoria Ocampo: A Brazilian perspective', in J. Vandivere and M. Hicks (eds), *Virginia Woolf and Her Female Contemporaries*, Clemson, SC: Clemson University Press, pp. 122–8.
Pereira, L. M. (1994), *Escritos da maturidade* [Writing from Maturity], ed. L. Viégas, Rio de Janeiro: Graphia Editorial.
Ribeiro, D. (2017), *O que é lugar de fala?* [What Is the Place of Discourse?], Belo Horizonte: Letramento, Justificando.
Santos, L. A. dos (2006) 'Hilda Hilst: Amor, angústia e morte – passagens grotescas de uma arte desarmônica' [Hilda Hilst: Love, anguish and death – grotesque passages of a disharmonious art], MA thesis, Faculdade de Ciências e Letras de Araraquara (FCL-Ar), Universidade Estadual Paulista, Araraquara, Brazil.
Schmidt, R. T. (2018), 'Crossing Borders: Clarice Lispector and the scene of transnational feminist criticism', in E. F. Coutinho (ed.), *Brazilian Literature as World Literature*, London: Bloomsbury Academic, pp. 243–64.
Shiach, M. (2017), 'On or about December 1930: Gender and the writing of lives in Virginia Woolf', in P. Goulimari (ed.), *Women Writing across Cultures: Past, Present, Future*, London: Routledge, pp. 279–88.
Silver, B. R. (1999), *Virginia Woolf Icon*, Chicago: Chicago University Press.
Solberg, H. C. (1960), 'Os dois mundos de Clarice: Livros e filhos' [The two worlds of Clarice: Books and children], *Mundo Ilustrado* [Illustrated World], Rio de Janeiro, p. 40.
Spivak, G. C. (1988), 'Can the subaltern speak?', in C. Nelson and L. Grossberg (eds), *Marxism and the Interpretation of Culture*, London: Macmillan, pp. 271–313.
Teffé, T. (1937) 'Ver em abstracto' [To see in the abstract], *Aspectos* [Aspects], 1, p. 130.
Telles, L. F. (1973), *As Meninas* [The Girls], São Paulo: Círculo do Livro.
Telles, L. F. (1980), 'A literatura é disciplina' [Literature is discipline], *Jornal do Brasil* [Brazil Newspaper], 235, p. 42.
Telles, L. F. (1989), *As Horas Nuas* [The Naked Hours], São Paulo: Círculo do Livro.
Telles, L. F. (1991), 'Na viragem do século' [At the turn of the century], *Nicolau*, 41: 3, p. 3.
Woolf, V. (1979), 'Women and fiction', in *Women and Writing*, ed. M. Barrett, London: Women's Press, pp. 43–52.
Woolf, V. (1993 [1929/1938]), *A Room of One's Own and Three Guineas*, ed. M. Barrett, London: Penguin Books.
Xavier, E. (1998), 'The family in Brazilian literature at the end of the 20th century: A social-literary analysis', in S. Coelsch-Foisner, H. Wallinger and G. Reisner (eds), *Daughters of Restlessness: Women's Literature at the End of the Millennium*, Heidelberg: Universitätsverlag Winter, pp. 265–72.

14

ENGLISH AND MEXICAN DOGS: SPECTRES OF TRAUMATIC PASTS IN VIRGINIA WOOLF'S *FLUSH* AND MARÍA LUISA PUGA'S *LAS RAZONES DEL LAGO*

Lourdes Parra-Lazcano

The specters of traumatic pasts emerge in dreams, compulsive actions, or inadvertent reenactments, out of that shadowy realm we call the unconscious, that outside of deliberate signification that is curiously inside.

    Jean M. Langford, 'Toward a hauntology for the other-than-human' (2015)

The dog is sprawled out on the floor with a back leg twitching and his lip curling. . . . The dog lets out a scary nasal white howl which causes us both to jump up. I spill scalding hot coffee all over myself. . . . 'I told you he was having a nightmare', she says.

    Ellis Butcher, 'What is our dog having nightmares about?' (2014)

IN THE FIRST EPIGRAPH ABOVE, Jean M. Langford writes of the ways in which the unconscious reappearance of traumatic events can become, in a metaphorical sense, spectral presences. The origins of a trauma cannot be seen any longer by the individual once the traumatic event passes, but the former trauma still has an impact on the mind and everyday activities of some humans and nonhuman animals. In the second, Ellis Butcher tells the story of how she and an anonymous woman see the corporeal reaction of a dog affected by a nightmare. Both examples show that traumas can have a long-lasting effect. Currently, humans cannot communicate with dogs to decipher what they are dreaming about or why they have developed particular compulsive actions or inadvertent re-enactments. Still, humans can try to interpret what non-human animals could be experiencing and establish a closer relationship with them. Literature can contribute to a better understanding of the sensory world of animals; it can also cause humans to provide proper care for and form relationships with their non-human animal counterparts. This chapter carries out a comparative reading of Virginia Woolf's *Flush: A Biography* (1933) and María Luisa Puga's *Las razones del lago* [The Reasons of the Lake] (1991).[1] I compare the spectres of traumatic pasts of the dog Flush with those of the dogs Novela [Novel] and Relato [Story].[2] *Flush* and *Las razones del lago* were published nearly sixty years apart and are set in different cultures – *Flush* in London and Italy in the 1840s and *Las razones del lago* in a Mexican town in the late 1980s. Although Woolf died in England in 1941, three years before Puga was born in Mexico, both authors raise questions about spectres of traumatic pasts in their specific contexts. In their novels, the dogs show traumatic behaviours present in their 'dreams, compulsive actions, or inadvertent reenactments' (Langford 2015: 1). I argue that there are differences in terms of the origin of their traumas based on their social and cultural contexts.

Woolf's *Flush* is the biography of a cocker spaniel living in Victorian England. The eponymous dog begins his life in the idyllic Three Mile Cross, at the home of Mary Russell Mitford. Once Mitford gives him as a gift to her friend Elizabeth Barrett[3] in London, he stays with her for the rest of his life. Flush's adventures include his life with the writer Elizabeth Barrett in London while she was ill, his kidnapping, his escape with Elizabeth Barrett Browning and her husband Robert Browning to Italy, his return to London, his second departure to Italy and his death. In Woolf's story, several dreams reveal Flush's traumatic past, particularly after he is stolen and travels to Italy. Puga's *Las razones del lago* concerns the lives of two semi-stray dogs in the Mexican town of Zirahuén, their two-month trip to Mexico City with human companions and their return to Zirahuén. The main human characters are a couple, an unnamed man and woman in their forties, and Damián, a nineteen-year-old man who feels like an outsider in his town and is hired by the couple to build their house in Zirahuén. While roaming in this Mexican town, Novela and Relato develop a relationship with Damián, having known him since he was a child, and through him they come to know the couple. When the couple need to travel from Zirahuén to Mexico City to obtain money for the construction of their home, Damián moves with them to take a workshop in plumbing, and the couple also bring the dogs. Throughout the novel, an unnamed third-person omniscient narrator in a frame story provides context to the narration of the canines. After Novela and Relato witness the deaths of humans and dogs in Zirahuén as well as experiencing life in confinement in Mexico City, their actions express the traumas that continue to haunt them.

Woolf's modernist writing aesthetics and feminism have been analysed prolifically. In particular, *Flush* has been investigated from these two approaches. On the one hand, based on human-centred problems, this dog biography has been studied in relation to the politics of gender and sexuality (Squier 1985; Vanita 1993; Eberly 1996), its status in the literary canon (Caughie 1991), an ethical representation of a servant (Caughie 2013), Woolf's anti-fascist writing (Snaith 2002), a critique of Victorian empiricism (Faris 2007), women's education and a new kind of masculinity (Knauer 2011), and disability studies (Colón Vale 2016). On the other hand, based on nonhuman animal-centred issues, *Flush* has been studied in relation to its exclusion from the literary canon (Smith 2002), 'an ethical sense of community' between human and animals (Wylie 2002: 128), the human and animal world and nonhuman animal consciousness (Johnson 2013), a canine epistemology of smell (Feuerstein 2013), human–animal relations (Ittner 2006; Ryan 2013), and an evolutionary perspective based on species interactions (Dubino 2016). In this chapter, *Flush* is studied from this second approach that takes into account a nonhuman animal-centred perspective by incorporating the notion of trauma. In *Virginia Woolf and Trauma: Embodied Texts*, edited by Suzette Henke and David Eberly (2007), chapters by Patricia Cramer, Karen DeMeester, Jane Lilienfeld, Clifford Wulfman, Claire Kahane, and Patricia Moran address the notion of trauma in Woolf's writings. Reina van der Wiel (2014) pays attention to the manner in which Woolf depicts her traumatic emotions through her writing style. However, not enough attention has been given to the animals themselves as subjects of trauma; thus, this chapter explores the animals' various traumatic experiences.

The Mexican writer María Luisa Puga (1944–2004), who published in Spanish and whose works have not been translated into English, has been studied from several different thematic approaches. For example, scholars have considered nostalgia (Reckley 1985), alterity (Acevedo-Leal 1992; Bradu 1992), cultural marginality (Castillo 1992), dystopic worlds (Franco 2004), the recurrent topics in Puga's oeuvre (Pfeiffer 2006), cultural encounters through the gaze (Pitman 2009) and her notion of nomadism (Lindsay 2010). Irma M. López (1996) has analysed most of Puga's body of work. Puga herself also talked about her literary production and influences in interviews (De Beer 1999; Domenella 2006; Hind 2003). *Las razones del lago* has been analysed for its representation of nature (Mejía-Pérez 2008); López (1996) relates the voices of animals to the representation of the people's voices of Zirahuén. In this chapter, the voices of the dogs are read not as an allegory but rather as a consideration of canine traumatic experience and their links with humans. The influence of Woolf's *Flush* on Puga's writing is evident in this novel, though at the same time, Puga underlines her own concerns about the human–canine bond. In an interview with Emily Hind, Puga declared, 'Virginia Woolf is always present in my narrative, but I wouldn't know how to imitate her. What I want is for my writing to sound as I truly feel' (Hind 2003: 180).[4] In pursuit of this homage to Woolf and in search of her own literary voice, before *Las razones del lago*, Puga wrote *Antonia* (1989). In that novel, Puga's narrator seeks but fails to live in the same parts of London where Woolf lived. However, she acknowledges the new experiences she underwent in her failed quest to inhabit these spaces. In her autobiography, *De cuerpo entero: El espacio de la escritura* [Full Body: The Space of Writing] (1990), Puga also recognises Woolf's influence on her work and life. She mentions how enriching it was for her to live in various writers' rooms, recalling Woolf's *A Room of One's Own*. *Flush* and *Las razones del lago* thus lend themselves to a comparative analysis.

This chapter comprises four parts. The first section introduces the notion of spectres of traumatic pasts in nonhuman animal studies. The second establishes a comparison between Flush as a pet and Novela and Relato as semi-stray dogs to show how in each story a traumatic past of confinement has impacted the dogs' lives. The next section discusses how the dogs' spectres are associated with their violent past experiences, and the final one addresses the traumatic pasts in their human–animal bond.

Spectres of Traumatic Pasts in Animals

Trauma is an overwhelming experience caused by an external agent that may have a lasting mental impact. According to Roger Luckhurst, trauma 'derives from the Greek word meaning wound' (2010: 191). It was first used as a medical term to address bodily injuries, but after the late nineteenth century, it also became associated with mental problems (Luckhurst 2008: 3). Sigmund Freud – a leading figure in opening the discussion about trauma – developed different theories by relating trauma to sexuality and anxiety. About anxiety Freud writes, 'a danger-situation is a recognized, remembered, expected situation of helplessness. Anxiety is the original reaction to helplessness in the trauma and is *reproduced later on* in the danger-situation as a signal for help' (qtd in Sletvold 2016: 470, my emphasis). Jean Laplanche elaborated on how anxiety is related to the later reproduction of a trauma sign. He singles out the 'afterwardsness' in trauma to underline 'the odd temporality of an event not understood as traumatic until its return' (qtd in Luckhurst 2008: 8–9). In the same vein, taking into account this notion of the 'return', Lyotard identifies trauma as a problem of our time: 'A past that is not past, that would signal itself even in the present as a specter' (1997: 11). In sum, trauma describes a reiterative process that denotes the necessity of acknowledging the sign of the repetition and can be read in a metaphorical sense as a spectre. Dealing with the notion of a returning trauma or spectre, Jacques Derrida mentions that its return shows that 'things are going badly' and that something must be done 'under the name or in the name of justice' (2006: 26, 27). The circumstances and nature of a trauma that is haunting like a spectre might change, but its repetitive message remains a sign that needs to be heard and healed. Yet all the above discussed theories were created with strictly human problems in mind.

In 'Toward a hauntology for the other-than-human', Langford provides a different approach to the notion of the spectre by examining this concept in light of nonhuman animals' behaviours that are related to their previous traumas. For her, spectres are not only a metaphor to explain human social problems but also a mean of naming a past trauma that reappears in the unconscious mind of some nonhuman animals and affects their everyday behaviour. Langford writes:

> The question arises as to whether nonhuman animals themselves might be, at times, haunted, particularly those once-wilder animals who have been displaced from habitats or ways of life, who have experienced extreme abuse or confinement, or who have been so immersed in cross-species sociality with humans that they have difficulty affiliting with their own kind, or being comfortable in their own skin. (2015: 1)

Examples that she provides are a cockatoo that bites because he hears an external noise that he associates with an explosion that occurred in his violent past, and a chimp that screams and faints because he associates anaesthesia for a medical examination with the dart gun that knocked him down when he was an experimental subject in a lab (2015: 1).

Dogs have coevolved more closely to humans than almost any other species (Haraway 2003), and this is one of the main reasons to study them in relation to human-based trauma theories. This approach is particularly useful if we consider that there are 'embodied, relational and affective aspects of the dog–human relationship as well as the human and animal actions that construct this companionship through mutual interaction' (Satama and Huopalainen 2019: 5). Furthermore, the notion of the 'apparition of the spectre' (Derrida 2006: 57) can be helpful for taking the literary representation of the dog 'seriously' as a human-animal character who claims empathy and respect (Ryan 2013: 3). Ryan bases this claim on Cary Wolfe's understanding that animals are 'not just "out there", among the birds and beasts, but "in here" as well, at the heart of this thing we call human' (2009: 570). For these reasons, it is valuable to study works that locate canines at the core of their narration, such as those by Virginia Woolf and María Luisa Puga.

The Restriction of Movement for a Pet Dog and Two Semi-Stray Dogs

After living in relative freedom at Three Mile Cross with Elizabeth Barrett's friend Mary Russell Mitford, Flush becomes Barrett's pet. In the beginning of the story, he is confined in London because Barrett is ill and consequently does not go out that often.

For Flush, the contact with nature and the restricted mobility of his home in London contrasts with his life in two other places. The first is Three Mile Cross, where he lived as a puppy and 'throve[,] . . . enjoy[ing] with all the vivacity of his temperament most of the pleasures' and felt '[t]he cool globes of dew or rain [break] in showers of iridescent spray about his nose' (F: 7). The second contact takes place later in Italy, where he escapes with Elizabeth Barrett Browning and her husband. During this 'voyage of discovery' (F: 81), he is able to engage in 'escapades' outside his house, 'to enjoy something . . . denied him all these years' (F: 78). When Flush is back for a time in London after Italy, he returns to the human restriction that is imposed over his movements, and this has an adverse effect on his behaviour. The narrator says:

> The confinement, the crowd of little objects, the blackbeetles by night, the bluebottles by day, the lingering odours of mutton, the perpetual presence on the sideboard of bananas – all this, together with the proximity of several men and women, heavily dressed and not often or indeed completely washed, wrought on his temper and strained his nerves. He lay for hours under the lodging-house chiffonier. (F: 93)

Although this way of living is justified by the social norms of his time, in terms of being considered a pet with a particular breed and owner, his confinement to the house has an impact on his wellbeing. His everyday activities are disrupted by his stress and, as a consequence, he prefers isolation to human contact.

Likewise, his dreams show the impact this restriction has on him. For instance, in one dream, 'He was in Spain; he was in Wales; he was in Berkshire; he was flying before park-keepers' truncheons in Regent's Park. Then he opened his eyes. There were no hares, and no partridges' (F: 38).[5] Although Flush is recalling the experiences of his ancestors, this dream portrays how constrained his movements are and how his freedom is determined by his mistress. He has an overriding desire to run and move beyond his 'locked' (F: 93) door, as his progenitors did. Flush's spectres appear in the form of anxieties and dreams as a result of his confinement as a pet. However, Elizabeth Barrett also protects Flush by restricting his movements because London is a dangerous place for him, due to the value that a cocker spaniel represents for kidnappers.

In contrast, the dogs Novela and Relato in *Las razones del lago* are semi-strays: for periods they are adopted and fed by human characters, but most of the time they roam in Zirahuén, unattached to any specific human owner. They are mongrels, living in a socio-economically distressed town, and thus few people even note their existence. As opposed to Flush, Novela and Relato hold no economic value to the people of Zirahuén. While the first ancestors of Flush are situated in Spain, Novela and Relato reclaim a non-eurocentric past in the current territory of Mexico, prior to Spanish colonisation. The dogs hear from human characters who are nostalgic for the past: 'Before[,] . . . it wasn't like this. Before, here, it was a paradise. Before, it was meaningful, but there were enemies as well. . . . This before was before the Spanish came to this place. There was a kingdom here [in Zirahuén]' (Puga 1991: 48).[6]

Beyond this idealistic notion of 'paradise', it is true that things were different prior to colonisation, for humans as well as dogs. Although Indigenous populations pre-dated the Native American dog *Xoloitzcuintli* (Cortés 1843: 39), these dogs also 'had important symbolic and ritual roles such as . . . accompanying the souls of the dead to the Underworld' (Sandoval-Cervantes 2016: 172). In contrast, 'European dogs were used to launch surprise attacks on populations' (2016: 171). Later, there was an eradication of Native American dogs, followed by a 'proliferation of European dogs' (2016: 172) and a multitude of 'street dog[s] in an urban landscape' who still prevail (Mauleón qtd in Sandoval-Cervantes 2016: 172).

Novela and Relato are the result of this postcolonial time, yet the story they overhear about Zirahuén prior to Spanish colonisation interests them because it offers a glimpse into another possible way of living. In particular, based on an account they had heard of the period, the dogs are haunted by spectral thoughts of how life was for other canines before them and the question of whether an acknowledgement of humaness in dogs is possible. In a critical moment, the dogs try to recuperate the time prior to the Spanish colonisation they hear about, narrated in the dogs' own voices:

> All together we go and lie down around here, very vigilant for buses. It is when we try to imagine that 'before' they talked about with so much admiration. How would the wind or the afternoon light have been? The early morning? The hunger? The lake, to start with? (Puga 1991: 54)[7]

Although the dogs try to rest, they cannot do so entirely for fear that, if they did, they could be hit by buses. As a consequence, Novela and Relato reminisce of less violent circumstances by recalling the calmer past. This is analogous to the way Flush reminisces about his ancestors when he wants to break free from his own confinement in Elizabeth Barrett's home (*F*: 38, 93).

In comparison with the humans, Novela and Relato are concerned less with the historical process of colonisation and more with its consequences for the ecosystem and their way of life. The fact that the ecosystem is more directly relevant for the dogs leads to an idealisation of a better past, a pre-Hispanic time that is more natural. Besides this essentialist claim in favour of the past, this yearning allows the dogs' narrative voices to express their wish to live in a peaceful manner – for example, to be able to lie down without fear of being killed by buses. In reality, in this part of the story, the dogs are trapped between their idealisation of the past and their current circumstances. They are, after all, semi-stray dogs excluded from protected places, such as houses, and unable to rest when they want or need. They are also not safe on the street, which can be a violent place for them. Thus, they are haunted by recent spectres of traumatic pasts of anxiety and stress.

As noted earlier, Novela and Relato take a trip to Mexico City and stay there for two months with the young Damián and the unnamed man and woman. During this trip, these humans try to adopt them temporarily as pets, but the dogs complain about 'immobility' (Puga 1991: 141) and compare the humans' house to a 'prison' (1991: 145). Nobody walks them and they are confined to the residence, lying beside Damián when he is at home, just as Flush did in London when Elizabeth Barrett was ill. Similar to Flush in London, they are constrained and imprisoned while living in Mexico City. As Sandoval-Cervantes states, 'In Mexico in general, dogs do not have ample space to stay active' (2016: 175–6). Likewise, people living in cities can have long working shifts and commutes, which means less time to walk their dogs. In the case of Damián, he studies and in his free time prefers to watch news in his room. As a consequence, Novela and Relato tend to be confined indoors because Damián prefers to have them inside the house, not necessarily because they live in a small space.

Following their experience in Mexico City, Novela and Relato return to Zirahuén with Damián and the couple. Back in the town, the dogs like to be 'covered with dirt and mud' (Puga 1991: 149). In this case, the dirt and mud denote mobility as once again they can move freely between the streets and the couple's house in the town. At the same time, the dogs' desire to cover themselves in dirt and mud implies the manner in which they try to cover their past trauma in Mexico City. It can be said that the lack of proper mobility and their experiences there continue haunting them once they are back in their hometown. The dogs prefer to go 'to the street' and run 'towards the lake' (1991: 149).[8] In other words, attempts to treat Novela and Relato as pets in the city fail; nobody has time for them. Though they prefer life in Zirahuén, the freedom they experience there also presents difficulties since most of the time their food and shelter are not secure.

Despite the differences between Flush and Novela and Relato, all three prefer close contact with nature to indoor confinement. Flush aligns his life in Three Mile Cross and in Italy with nature, while Novela and Relato associate nature with a precolonial past and their hometown. Flush sees Italy as a paradise, and Novela and Relato prefer their albeit less-than-idyllic lives in Zirahuén to being in confinement.

Dreams of Death and Dogs that Witness Violence

Flush's dream of death and the occasions in which the dogs of *Las razones del lago* witness the deaths of other animals demonstrates how these dogs' spectres are related to their traumatic past. As previously mentioned, Flush's dreams are a path that connect him with nature; but the old trauma resurfaces with Flush's final dream just before his death. In this dream, he recalls his experience of being stolen in London – 'the most terrible experience of his life' (*F*: 53). Flush was, the narrator recalls, 'stolen three times', though the three thefts were 'compressed into one' (*F*: 109). In his last dream, Flush

> slept as dogs sleep when they are dreaming. Now his legs twitched. . . . And now he yelped, quickly, softly, many times in succession. . . . And then he lay for a time snoring, wrapt in the deep sleep of happy old age. Suddenly every muscle in his body twitched. He woke with a violent start. Where did he think he was? In Whitechapel among the ruffians? Was the knife at this throat again? Whatever it was, he woke from his dream in a state of terror. (*F*: 104–5)

In this description, Flush recalls a violent memory with which he never comes to terms. He, like other dogs of his time, such as Jane Carlyle's dog Nero,[9] experienced trauma after being 'stolen' (*F*: 93, 114). Flush's spectres are present because he has not overcome his terror of being kidnapped and as a result his distance from Elizabeth Barrett Browning increases as he declines. She becomes more interested in Spiritualism, and often 'she looked through him as if he were not there' (*F*: 102). They no longer gaze 'at each other' (*F*: 15) as often as they did in the beginning, and he experiences a sense of disconnection that echoes his previous physical distance from her when he was kidnapped. Thus, at the end of his life, Flush encounters the unconscious reappearance of traumatic events in his dreams, through which he relives the trauma of his past.

Puga's *Las razones del lago* does not describe the dreams of Novela and Relato but rather discusses their experience of violence from humans and their exposure to the deaths of other animals. At the beginning of the story, the dogs lament,

> There are so many of us that it is not noticed when one of us disappears. We are in a group and we strive not to be noisy, so nobody looks at us. Kids and adults enjoy kicking us, throwing stones. We grow up with these people but they don't see us. They don't realise that we are also alive and, like them, we feel pain and hunger. (1991: 16)[10]

In contrast to the lifestyle that Flush enjoys in Italy where he has freedom of mobility but also secure food and shelter, Novela's and Relato's narrative voices show how they wish to avoid the spectres that arise from their anxiety due to the death of other animals in Zirahuén – including humans – and the violence that humans direct towards the dogs, in particular when the humans consume alcohol in excess. In this regard, the dogs' narrative voices tell that the majority of dogs die in Zirahuén due to drunk drivers who run over them 'to have fun' (1991: 72).[11]

In *Las razones del lago*, very few humans pay attention to the dogs and many abuse them:

> Our life is not easy, as can be deduced by the vast numbers of dead dogs everywhere, in particular on the regional road. It can be said that they like to smash us. Perhaps for drivers, this is a sport . . . and our bodies stay there, rotting as carrion for vultures. (1991: 16)[12]

The fact that dogs are killed in traffic, their bodies mangled and unmourned, demonstrates how their lack of a fixed abode makes them vulnerable, since no human claims their bodies and almost no human is concerned about their deaths. For this reason, Relato and Novela's spectres are associated with the deaths occurring in the town. They are anxious about being the next victims in a world where violence and lack of social and economic development are problems that affect both humans and dogs.

In terms of the social and economic conditions in Woolf's depiction, there is an opposition between the humans living in Wimpole – the safe, upper-class neighbourhood – and Whitechapel – the poor, dangerous neighbourhood. This difference in London also has an impact on the way Flush lives: as a pedigree dog of an upper-class family, he needs to be protected by Elizabeth Barrett. His mobility is restricted in Wimpole to avoid encountering further dangerous situations in Whitechapel. In comparison, Puga writes in more detail about Zirahuén, which has economic and social problems, such as alcohol abuse in the streets and at dancing events, the emigration of young people to the cities or the US, drug trafficking and social class divisions (1991: 72, 103, 107). There is only one wealthy person in the town, as well as a middle-class intellectual couple and some other relatively secure characters, like a butcher and an owner of a convenience store. However, most of the humans in the novel struggle with financial problems and alcoholism, and the dogs are similarly affected by these problems as they are neglected by the humans.

The Dogs and the Writers

Both *Flush* and *Las razones del lago* include the voice of a writer, who narrates the relationships that the characters have with the canines of the novels. In *Flush*, the focalisation is that of the eponymous dog. However, the biography also includes excerpts from Elizabeth Barrett Browning's life and letters, in which her dog is present. *Las razones del lago*, as noted earlier, includes the narrative voices of the dog protagonists and of an unnamed third-person omniscient narrator in a frame story. Although not clearly specified in the narration, according to López (1997: 80), this narrator could presumably be associated with the unnamed woman in the couple and her writing in italics could be associated with her journal notes.

Through Barrett's letters, Woolf offers information that Flush would presumably not understand from his point of view but that the reader does. For instance, we learn of the fondness that Barrett feels for her dog and, most importantly, come to realise that certain spectres of Flush's traumatic past also haunt the poet. For example, in the beginning, Barrett is ill and Flush lies beside her sofa. She writes, 'Flushie . . . is my friend – my companion – and loves me better than he loves the sunshine without' (*F*: 22). She believes that Flush is devoted to her; but as seen above in the first section, his spectres related to his restriction of movement haunt him. After Elizabeth Barrett meets her future husband Robert Browning, she begins to pay less attention to Flush (*F*: 46). However, when Flush is kidnapped by a thief from Whitechapel, Barrett is afraid of losing him, in particular because she knows he is likely to encounter discomfort, privation and abuse.

Inspired by her shared memories with Flush, Barrett decides to follow her own instincts rather than taking the advice of those who suggest not paying for the dog's rescue. She writes, 'But Flush, poor Flush, who has loved me so faithfully; have I a right to sacrifice *him* in his innocence?' (*F*: 60–1). For Anna Snaith, Flush's kidnapping exemplifies 'the complex hierarchies of power in the Barrett home to distinct areas of London' (2002: 620). Laila Colón Vale argues that this passage shows more than a social class discussion; it reveals the empowerment of a disabled woman 'demanding to be seen and heard' (2016: 60). From a viewpoint more centred in the human–dog relationship, Jamie Johnson argues that Barrett's reaction is a recognition of her 'ethical responsibility for the other' (2013: 36). In spite of Barrett's empowerment and responsibility towards Flush, she is not able to prevent him from recalling this kidnapping as a traumatic event throughout the remaining years of his life.

Later in the novel, Barrett Browning becomes concerned about Flush once again when he has fleas in Florence. She writes letters to people in London to find a remedy (*F*: 88) because she and her husband find it 'intolerable' (*F*: 89) to see other people mock Flush and point at him in the street. When they decided to shave him, Flush 'felt emasculated, diminished, ashamed' (*F*: 89) in front of the mirror but in the end he heals. Due to the care that Elizabeth Barrett Browning and her husband provide to Flush, Italy remains a good place for him. In Italy, Flush 'was the friend of all the world now. All dogs were his brothers. He had no need of a chain in this new world; he had no need of protection' (*F*: 77). Flush may feel safe in Italy because he has the option to return to a familiar home for food and a place to stay overnight. In this manner, his 'personhood' is more acknowledged and the traumatic spectres from his kidnapping in London and the problem he later encountered with the fleas are less present.

While the relationship between Flush and Elizabeth Barrett Browning shows close proximity and care in crucial moments for the dog, *Las razones del lago* demonstrates how the couple and, in particular, the omniscient narrator in the frame story prefer to maintain a physical distance from the dogs throughout the novel. Damián has the closest relationship with Relato and Novela, yet the information about the dogs is provided by the narrative voices of the dogs and the narrator. The connection between Damián and the dogs is not based on a notion of care but of empathy due to their mutual social exclusion. For a while, Damián does not know what to do with his life and feels that nobody in the town understands him. Later, the writer-narrator describes Novela and Relato as having been present at crucial moments for Damián – such as the day on which his alcoholic uncle moved into his house (Puga 1991: 81). Damián feels 'confident' when the dogs 'gaze at him, waiting, trying to understand him' (1991: 85),[13] and when he is sad in Mexico City, he feels able to speak to them 'in silence' and cry in their company (1991: 135).[14] In this story, a close human–animal relationship is established among those who are excluded and share similar spectres related to their social exclusion.

Furthermore, when Novela and Relato develop fleas and are expelled from various houses, utterances such as 'Look at this dog with fleas! Go away, go!' (Puga 1991: 121) are constant refrains.[15] When the narrator describes this situation, she labels it as something 'common' (1991: 116). Novela and Relato reflect the living conditions of the majority of Mexican dogs, 70% of whom live on the street, neither vaccinated nor dewormed ('México' 2018). The situation of Novela and Relato worsens when they travel to Mexico City. Here, the dogs are confined in the house without proper mobility and they are suffering from fleas (Puga 1991: 141, 144); unlike Flush, they barely receive attention concerning their health from any human character. The couple and Damián mainly care about the dogs' food, which was inconsistent before their trip to Mexico City. Thus, the human characters of *Las razones del lago* do not acknowledge that fleas may also have an impact on the dogs. Although the dogs show evident discomfort from their flea infestation, scratching themselves incessantly, people do not address their health but instead reject them by pointing and pushing them away or not allowing them to enter their houses. In this sense, the fleas become a traumatic event that continues to haunt Novela and Relato as spectral presences in the Mexican town as well as during their trip.

A further connection between humans and animals established in the novel concerns the barking of the dogs. When the narrator acknowledges in her journal notes the continual barking, she questions the society in which they are living: 'It is hunger that is ringing in their barks, solitude, helplessness. Or fatigue at so many injustices, arbitrariness, overbearingness. Their barks acquire a steady pace at times' (Puga 1991: 165).[16] This narrator notes that the dogs' behaviour is a message that has no recipient. Thus, she asks, 'When will they listen to those barks?' (1991: 165).[17] These barks become a claim that she introduces to raise a voice in favour of the human–animal bond, urging listeners to pay attention to the spectres that the barking recalls. At the end of the novel, this prolonged barking also brings some hope, at least for Novela and Relato, who are left with the possibility of a better future. They come back from Mexico City to Zirahuén with the couple, who plan to live on a permanent basis in the town, and Damián, who is newly married and now has a sense of direction in life. These changes in the human characters may also benefit the dog protagonists in terms of allowing them to have easier access to food than at the beginning of the story while still maintaining their desire for mobility and freedom.

Final Thoughts

Woolf was interested in animals' perspectives and in the human–pet relationship of an upper-class English family. Puga, on the other hand, offers up the perspective of semi-stray dogs by acknowledging and foregrounding animals in a Mexican town facing economic struggles.

This chapter considers the relevance of applying the notion of spectres of traumatic pasts not only to human concerns but to nonhuman animals, in particular, canines' problems. For Flush, Three Mile Cross and Italy represent an idyllic freedom that he does not have in London, where his spectres of house confinement are constant and affect his temper making him nervous. In comparison, Novela and Relato discover in the pre-Hispanic past a peace that they cannot find either in their town or in a city. In the former, since they are semi-stray dogs, they are not entirely welcome in a particular house or on the street. In the latter, their house confinement with no space for roaming makes them more anxious. For that reason, Flush experiences more wellbeing in regard to his freedom and general contentment, whereas the lives of Novela and Relato are full of adversity and violence.

This chapter also shows the impact that the kidnapping has on Flush; it creates a spectre that stays with him across his life and makes him more anxious when he lives in London. On the contrary, Novela and Relato encounter the deaths of other animals on the road, and this witnessing leaves a trace of the reiterative spectres associated with violent memories that does prevents them from lying down in peace. The last analysis exhibits the relation that exists between humans and dogs. There is a shared suffering between Elizabeth Barrett Browning and Flush about his kidnapping and his fleas. For Novela and Relato, the closest relationship is with Damián, a socially excluded character, until the very last section of the story. Thus, the bonding is less about a notion of care and more about social empathy towards problems.

In the end, the constant barking becomes the last claim for justice that the Mexican dogs ask for in their lives. In the case of Flush, Elizabeth Barrett Browning's care is more evident; while for Novela and Relato, the human–animal bond is never entirely fulfilled, though the novel's open ending leaves hope that this may change. In both cases, most of the time, the dogs' lack of mechanisms for coping with their traumatic memories is underlined. Overall, these novels show the necessity of heeding canine traumas and suffering and also explore the human–animal connections and empathy in contemporary societies.

Notes

1. The novel was published in Spanish and has not been translated into English.
2. According to Irma M. López (1997: 81) and Carlos Urrutia (2005: 68), María Luisa Puga herself had dogs named Novela [Novel] and Relato [Story], as well as others named Coma [Comma], Punto [Period] and Cuento [Short story].
3. As Simon Avery and Rebecca Stott indicate in 'A note on names' from *Elizabeth Barrett Browning*: 'Any writer on Elizabeth Barrett Browning has to decide what name to use when referring to her' (2014: vii). Avery and Stott use 'Elizabeth Barrett' in their references to her life prior to her marriage to Robert Browning and 'Elizabeth Barrett Browning' after her marriage. Avery and Stott validate their decision by referring to Dorothy Mermin, who has argued: 'this is a poet who clearly recognises the importance of names and naming in her poetry and the imposed or self-elected identities which this signifies. . . . It seems only

right, therefore, to be exact when referring to the poet herself' (Avery and Stott 2014: vii). In keeping with this format, I have chosen to use Barrett when discussing her early relationship with Flush depicted in Woolf's biography and Barrett Browning both when she had married and in all general discussion of her work.

4. 'Virginia Woolf siempre está presente en mi narrativa, pero no sabría cómo imitarla. Yo lo que quiero es que lo que escribo suene a lo que verdaderamente siento.' All translations are mine unless otherwise indicated.
5. As Jeanne Dubino notes, this dream of his ancestors, human and spaniel, 'recalls Darwin's famous "Tree of Life" diagram . . . and foreshadows the domestic, and class-defined, world' (2016: 146).
6. 'antes . . . no era así. Antes esto era el paraíso. Antes tenía sentido, aunque también tenía enemigos. . . . Este antes era antes de que llegaran los españoles. Aquí había un reino [en Zirahuén].'
7. 'En bola nos vamos y nos echamos por ahí muy pendientes de los camiones. Es cuando tratamos de imaginarnos ese "antes" del que hablan con tanta admiración. ¿Cómo sería el viento o la luz de la tarde? Las madrugadas. El hambre. El lago, para no ir más lejos.'
8. 'A la calle' and 'Hacia el lago'.
9. The dog Nero is considered the pet of the character Jane Carlyle who is a friend of Elizabeth Barrett Browning in *Flush*. According to the narrator, among the possible motivations for Nero jumping from the top floor of his home was an intent to commit a canine suicide caused by the trauma of being stolen. Another reason could have been that he became tired of living with his family or that he was simply chasing a bird. However, as this happened after he had been stolen, the parallels with Flush's spectres of his traumatic past seem relevant and suggest that this was an act of recurring trauma. The narrative voice also explains that other valuable dogs were stolen during that time period (F: 113–14).
10. 'Somos muchos, por eso ni se nota cuando desaparece alguno. Andamos en bola y procuramos no hacer ruido para que no se fijen en nosotros. Niños o grandes se divierten dándonos de patadas, arrojándonos piedras. Crecemos con esta gente, pero no nos ven. No se acaban de dar cuenta de que también vivimos y, como ellos, sentimos dolor y hambre.'
11. 'por divertirse'.
12. 'Nuestra vida no es fácil, como podrá deducirse por el gran número de perros muertos en todas partes, pero sobre todo en la carretera. Se diría que les gusta apachurrarnos. A lo mejor entre los choferes es un deporte . . . y nuestros cuerpos se quedan ahí pudriéndose como carroña para zopilotes.'
13. 'lo miren esperando, buscando entenderlo'.
14. 'en silencio'.
15. '¡Mira, pues, ese perro pulguiento, ¡sáquese de aquí, ándele!'
16. 'Es el hambre que retintinea en sus ladridos; la soledad; la impotencia. O el cansancio ante tanta injusticia, arbitrariedad, prepotencia. Adquieren un ritmo machacador por momentos.'
17. '¿cuándo van a atender a esos ladridos?'

Bibliography

Acevedo-Leal, A. (1992), 'El reconocimiento de la realidad a través de la alteridad en *Las posibilidades del odio*' [The acknowledgment of reality through alterity in *The Possibilities of Hate*], *Monographic Review/Revista Monográfica*, 8, pp. 223–8.

Avery, S. and R. Stott (2014), *Elizabeth Barrett Browning*, Abington, UK: Routledge.

Bradu, F. (1992), *Señas particulares: Escritora. Ensayos sobre escritoras mexicanas del siglo XX* [Particular Signs: Women Writers: Essays on Twentieth-Century Mexican Writers], Ciudad de México: Fondo de Cultura Económica.

Butcher, E. (2014), 'What is our dog having nightmares about?', *The Westmorland Gazette*, 23 January, <https://www.thewestmorlandgazette.co.uk/news/10954168.what-is-our-dog-having-nightmares-about/> (last accessed 3 December 2019).

Castillo, D. A. (1992), *Talking Back: Toward a Latin American Feminist Literary Criticism*, Ithaca, NY: Cornell University Press.

Caughie, P. (1991) '*Flush* and the literary canon: Oh where oh where has that little dog gone?', *Tulsa Studies in Women's Literature*, 10: 1, pp. 47–66.

Caughie, P. (2013), 'Dogs and servants', *Virginia Woolf Miscellany*, 84, pp. 37–9.

Colón Vale, L. (2016), 'Flush, the sickroom, and the heroine', *Virginia Woolf Miscellany*, 89/90, pp. 59–61.

Cortés, H. (1843 [1520]), 'Second letter of Hernando Cortés to Charles V', *Early Americas Digital Archive*, 8 October, <http://eada.lib.umd.edu/text-entries/second-letter-of-hernando-cortes-to-charles-v/> (last accessed 14 April 2019).

Cramer, P. M. (2007), 'Trauma and lesbian returns in Virginia Woolf's *The Voyage Out and The Years*', in S. Henke and D. Eberly (eds), *Virginia Woolf and Trauma: Embodied Texts*, New York: Pace University Press, pp. 19–50.

De Beer, G. (1999), *Escritoras mexicanas contemporáneas: Cinco voces* [Mexican Contemporary Women Writers: Five Voices], Mexico City: Fondo de Cultura Económica.

DeMeester, K. (2007), 'Trauma, post-traumatic stress disorder, and obstacles to postwar recovery in *Mrs Dalloway*', in S. Henke and D. Eberly (ed.), *Virginia Woolf and Trauma: Embodied Texts*, New York: Pace University Press, pp. 77–93.

Derrida, J. (2006 [1993]), *Spectres of Marx: The State of the Debt, the Work of Mourning and the New International*, trans. P. Kamuf, New York: Routledge.

Domenella, A. R. (2006), 'María Luisa Puga, del testimonio postcolonial al cuerpo del dolor: Un camino reflexivo a través de la escritura' [María Luisa Puga, from the postcolonial testimony to the body of pain: A reflexive path through writing], in A. R. Domenella (ed.), *María Luisa Puga. La escritura que no cesa*, Toluca, Mexico: Tecnológico de Monterrey, campus Toluca/Fondo Nacional para la Cultura y las Artes/Universidad Autónoma Metropolitana, pp. 25–36.

Dubino, J. (2016 [2011]), 'Evolution, history, and *Flush*; or, The origin of spaniels', in K. Czarnecki and C. Rohman (eds), *Virginia Woolf and the Natural World: Selected Papers of the Twentieth Annual International Conference on Virginia Woolf*, Liverpool, UK: Liverpool Scholarship Online, pp. 143–50.

Eberly, D. (1996), 'Housebroken: The domesticated relations in *Flush*', in B. R. Daugherty and E. Barrett (eds), *Virginia Woolf: Texts and Contexts: Selected Papers from the Fifth Annual Conference on Virginia Woolf*, New York: Pace University Press, pp. 21–5.

Faris, W. B. (2007), 'Bloomsbury's beasts: The presence of animals in the texts and lives of Bloomsbury', *Yearbook of English Studies*, 37: 1, pp. 107–25.

Feuerstein, A. (2013), 'What does power smell like? Canine epistemology and the politics of the pet in Virginia Woolf's *Flush*', *Virginia Woolf Miscellany*, 84, pp. 32–3.

Franco, J. (2004), *Las conspiradoras: La representación de la mujer en México* [The Conspirators: The Representation of Woman in Mexico], Mexico City: Fondo de Cultura Económica.

Haraway, D. (2003), *The Companion Species Manifesto: Dogs, People, and Significant Otherness*, Chicago, IL: Prickly Paradigm Press.

Henke, S. and D. Eberly (eds) (2007), *Virginia Woolf and Trauma: Embodied Texts*, New York: Pace University Press.

Hind, E. (2003), *Entrevistas con quince autoras mexicanas* [Interviews with Fifteeen Mexican Authors], Madrid: Iberoamericana/Frankfurt am Main: Vervuert Verlag.

Ittner, J. (2006), 'Part spaniel, part canine puzzle: Anthropomorphism in Woolf's *Flush* and Auster's *Timbuktu*', *Mosaic: A Journal for the Comparative Study of Literature*, 39: 4, pp. 181–96.

Johnson, J. (2013), 'Virginia Woolf's *Flush*: Decentering human subjectivity through the nonhuman animal character', *Virginia Woolf Miscellany*, 84, pp. 34–6.

Kahane, C. (2007), 'Of snakes, toads, and duckweed: Traumatic acts and historical actions in *Between the Acts*', in S. Henke and D. Eberly (eds), *Virginia Woolf and Trauma: Embodied Texts*, New York: Pace University Press, pp. 223–46.

Knauer, E. (2011), 'Of dogs, daughters, and the "Back Bedroom" School: Woolf's *Flush* (1933) and women's education', *CEA Critic*, 73: 2, pp. 1–20.

Langford, J. M. (2015), 'Toward a hauntology for the other-than-human', conference paper, *Ghost, Haunting, and the Subject of the Culture: Toward an Anthropological Hauntology*, Meeting of the Society for Psychological Anthropology, <http://www.academia.edu/download/43606827/Hauntology_Other_Human.pdf> (last accessed 13 October 2018), pp. 1–4.

Lilienfeld, J. (2007), '"Could they tell one what they knew?" Modes of disclosure in *To the Lighthouse*', in S. Henke and D. Eberly (eds), *Virginia Woolf and Trauma: Embodied Texts*, New York: Pace University Press, pp. 95–122.

Lindsay, C. (2010), *Contemporary Travel Writing of Latin America*, New York: Routledge.

López, I. M. (1996), *Historia, escritura e identidad: La novelística de María Luisa Puga* [History, Writing and Identity: The Novelistic Art of María Luisa Puga], New York: Peter Lang.

López, I. M. (1997), 'Autobiografía interminable: La novelística de María Luisa Puga' [Endless autobiography: The novelistic art of María Luisa Puga], *Texto crítico: Nueva época*, 4–5, pp. 73–82.

Luckhurst, R. (2008), *The Trauma Question*, London: Routledge.

Luckhurst, R. (2010), 'The trauma knot', in R. Crownshaw, J. Kilby and A. Rowland (eds), *The Future of Memory*, New York: Oxford, pp. 191–206.

Lyotard, J.-F. (1997 [1988]), *Heidegger and 'the Jews'*, trans. A. Michel and M. Roberts, Minneapolis: University of Minnesota Press.

Mejía-Pérez, M. (2008), *Return to Nature: An Ecocritical and Ecofeminist Reading of María Luisa Puga and Leonardo da Jandra*, Santa Barbara, CA: ProQuest Dissertations Publishing.

'México, país con más perros callejeros en A[mérica] L[atina]' [Mexico, the country with the most stray dogs in Latin America] (2018), *El Universal*, 27 July, <https://www.eluniversal.com.mx/nacion/sociedad/mexico-pais-con-mas-perros-callejeros-en-al> (last accessed 14 October 2018).

Moran, P. (2007), 'Gunpowder Plots: Sexuality and Censorship in Woolf's Later Works', in S. Henke and D. Eberly (eds), *Virginia Woolf and Trauma: Embodied Texts*, New York: Pace University Press, pp. 179–204.

Pfeiffer, E. (2006), 'María Luisa Puga, una conciencia descentralizada' [María Luisa Puga, A decentralised consciousness], *Anuario de Letras*, 44, pp. 271–90.

Pitman, T. (2009), 'Postcolonial compañeras? The desire for a reciprocal gaze in two Mexican women's accounts of Africa', *Journal of Transatlantic Studies*, 7: 3, pp. 376–88.

Puga, M. L. (1989), *Antonia*, Mexico City: Grijalbo.

Puga, M. L. (1990), *De cuerpo entero: El espacio de la escritura* [Full Body: The Space of Writing], Mexico City: Universidad Nacional Autónoma de México/Corunda.

Puga, M. L. (1991), *Las razones del lago* [The Reasons of the Lake], Mexico City: Grijalbo.

Reckley, A. (1985), 'Looking ahead through the past: Nostalgia in the recent Mexican novel', dissertation, University of Kansas.

Ryan, D. (2013), *Virginia Woolf and the Materiality of the Theory: Sex, Animal, Life*, Edinburgh: Edinburgh Scholarship Online.

Sandoval-Cervantes, I. (2016). 'Semi-stray dogs and graduated humanness: The political encounters of dogs and humans in Mexico', in M. P. Pręgowski (ed.), *Companion Animals in Everyday Life: Situating Human-Animal Engagement within Cultures*, New York: Palgrave Macmillan, pp. 169–81.

Satama, S. and A. Huopalainen (2019), '"Please tell me when you are in pain": A heartbreaking story of care, grief and female-canine companionship', *Gender, Work and Organization*, 26: 3, pp. 358–76.
Sletvold, J. (2016), 'Freud's three theories of neurosis: Towards a contemporary theory of trauma and defense', *Psychoanalytic Dialogues*, 26: 4, pp. 460–75.
Smith, C. (2002), 'Across the widest gulf: Nonhuman subjectivity in Virginia Woolf's *Flush*', *Twentieth Century Literature* 48: 3, pp. 348–61.
Snaith, A. (2002), 'Of fanciers, footnotes, and Fascism: Virginia Woolf's *Flush*', *MFS: Modern Fiction Studies* 48: 3, pp. 614–36.
Squier, S. M. (1985), *Virginia Woolf and London: The Sexual Politics of the City*, Chapel Hill: North Carolina University Press.
Urrutia, C. (2005), 'María Luisa Puga: Heroine of writing', *Voices of Mexico*, 73, pp. 65–72, <http://www.revistascisan.unam.mx/Voices/pdfs/7316.pdf> (last accessed 18 March 2020).
van der Wiel, R. C. (2014), *Literary Aesthetics of Trauma: Virginia Woolf and Jeanette Winterson*, New York: Palgrave Macmillan.
Vanita, R. (1993), '"Love unspeakable": The uses of allusion in *Flush*', in V. Neverow-Turk and M. Hussey (eds), *Virginia Woolf: Themes and Variations: Selected Papers from the Second Annual Conference on Virginia Woolf*, New York: Pace University Press, pp. 248–57.
Wolfe, C. (2009), 'Human, all too human: "Animal Studies" and the humanities', *PMLA* 124: 2, pp. 564–75.
Woolf, V. (2015 [1929/1938]), *A Room of One's Own and Three Guineas*, ed. A. Snaith, Oxford: Oxford University Press.
Woolf, V. (2016 [1933]), *Flush*, London: Penguin Random House.
Wulfman, C. E. (2007), 'Woolf and the discourse of trauma: The little language of *The Waves*', in S. Henke and D. Eberly (eds), *Virginia Woolf and Trauma: Embodied Texts*, New York: Pace University Press, pp. 157–77.
Wylie, D. (2002), 'The anthropomorphic ethic: Fiction and the animal mind in Virginia Woolf's *Flush* and Barbara Gowdy's *The White Bone*', *ISLE: Interdisciplinary Studies in Literature and Environment* 9: 2, pp. 115–31.

15

A New Perspective on Mary Carmichael: Yuriko Miyamoto's Novels and *A Room of One's Own*

Hogara Matsumoto

Yuriko Miyamoto (1899–1951), the renowned Japanese novelist and critic, is regarded as a feminist and a communist writer committed to 'Democratic Literature', a left-wing literary movement launched in postwar Japan (Kang 2014: 71). Critics tend to focus on Miyamoto's works written before the Second World War, when she was actively engaged in the Proletarian Cultural Movement (Karlsson 2011: 29; Cullen 2010: 65), but recently the Democratic Literature she wrote after the war has started to attract attention. Though some critics have paid attention to the representation of Koreans in *Banshū Heiya* [The Plains of the Banshu] (1946), a novel which illuminates Miyamoto's implicit condemnation of Japanese imperialism and her ambivalence towards American imperialism during the Occupation Era (Ikeda 2015; Kang 2014), her works have mainly been read in the context of the national literary culture as part of the Democratic Literature movement.

Miyamoto, however, was not merely a nationalist writer. She was a cosmopolitan intellectual who had experienced life as a student in America and had gone on a two-year trip from Japan to France, Britain and Russia (Dobson 2016: 486–7). Well-read in British literature, Miyamoto wrote modern novels and also compiled a literary history of Japanese women writers in her essay 'Fujin to Bungaku' [Women and fiction] (1939–40, 1948), which analyses Virginia Woolf's writings, specifically *A Room of One's Own* (1929). Seeing Woolf as a forerunner of women writers that Asian women writers should take as a model, Miyamoto simultaneously regarded Woolf critically as an upper-middle-class Western woman writer. This chapter examines how Miyamoto develops the representation of Asian women characters in her novel, *Dohyo* [Road Signs] (1948–51), by analysing her discussion of Mary Carmichael in Woolf's *A Room of One's Own*, and by considering the similarities and differences between Woolf's imaginary modern Western writer, Mary Carmichael, and the contemporary Asian women characters Miyamoto delineates.

Indeed, Miyamoto seems to explore the representation of the contemporary Asian women characters by treating Woolf's discussions of women characters as a model and yet critically reconsidering them at the same time. The unexpressed voice of Asian women which Miyamoto presents in 'Fujin to Bungaku' further resonates in *Dōhyō*, in which the protagonist's sense of subjectivity is explored through a meta-historical, international view of feminism. This paper examines the Asian voice of a woman figure in Miyamoto's texts. Through a creative reading of the figure of Mary Carmichael in Woolf's *A Room of One's Own* (1929) – as an ambivalent figure who raises complex issues concerning class, gender and imperialism – Miyamoto depicts the protagonist of *Dōhyō* as a modern woman who sojourns in Western cities such as Moscow, Berlin, Paris and London; observes unequal power structures within British society and between Western and Eastern societies; and searches for an alternative way to represent the lives and political beliefs of contemporary women. Finally, this chapter sheds new light on Miyamoto's *Dōhyō* by showing that the protagonist can be construed as a modern Transeurasian woman who, through an acute observation of disparate modernities among Western and Asian nations, explores an alternative relationship between Asian women whose very existence is hidden and whose desires have yet to be fulfilled.

Woolf's Mary Carmichael, Miyamoto's Modern Woman and Disparate Modernities

Born the daughter of an architect in an upper-middle-class family in Tokyo, Yuriko Miyamoto enrolled in the Tokyo Women's Higher Normal School in 1911.[1] Her career as a novelist began at the age of seventeen, when her novella *Mazushiki Hitobito no Mure* [A Horde of the Poor] was published in 1916 in the prestigious literary journal *Chūō Kōron* [The Central Review] under her birth name, Yuriko Chūjō. The novella was highly praised for the ironic manner in which the narrator's limited understanding of the rural poor and her sense of complacency as a 'humanistic, middle class woman' are exposed (Miyamoto 2000–4, vol. 17: 224–5). For this work, Miyamoto gained celebrity as a rising novelist studying at an elite girls' school. In 1918, she accompanied her father on a business trip to New York; while there, she audited classes at Columbia University.[2]

Her life in New York was described in her first autobiographical novel, *Nobuko* (1924). The novel depicts the modern protagonist, Nobuko Sassa, as she encounters a new world in New York, falls in love and marries a Japanese man in a strange city. When Nobuko and her husband move to Tokyo, the marriage collapses just as the protagonist's sense of autonomy and awareness of desire are awakened. Like Nobuko, Miyamoto married a Japanese man in New York, divorced him in Tokyo, and set out for the Soviet Union in 1927 with her lesbian partner, Yoshiko Yuasa (1896–1990), a Russian literature scholar. They built friendships with a number of Russian artists, such as Sergei Eisenstein, and travelled back to Japan via Paris and London in November of 1930 (Aoyama 2015: 123–7).

This Transeurasian journey afforded the material for Miyamoto's second autobiographical novel, *Dōhyō* [Roadsigns], serialised in 1948–51 in the highbrow journal *Tenbō* [The Prospect]. Long before the novel's publication, however, between 1930 and the end of the Second World War in 1945, Miyamoto's life had taken a new direction. After the Transeurasian journey, she broke up with Yuasa, joined the Proletarian Culture Movement, formed an intimate relationship with Kenji Miyamoto, a leader of the movement, and married him while he was in prison for committing ideological offenses (Aoyama 2015: 127). It should be noted that *Dōhyō* was written after all these changes in her life and at a time when constitutional democracy was introduced in postwar Japan, following Japan's unconditional surrender to the Allied powers.[3]

The Second World War fractured Japanese people's sense of historical continuity, and *Dōhyō* needs to be considered within this complex historical context.

Dōhyō reprises Nobuko Sassa, the protagonist from Miyamoto's *Nobuko* who is now a writer, and depicts her arrival in Moscow with her partner Motoko Yoshimi on a winter day in 1928.[4] While Motoko attends university classes, Nobuko walks around the city, takes in Russian plays and meets a variety of cosmopolitan artists and scholars. Nobuko's publishers have given her a generous advance to report on Moscow and write a new novel. She also wants to experiment with new writing styles. But changes in her view of Western society and in her relationship with Motoko occur after the two women explore European cities such as Berlin, Paris and London. Upon returning to Moscow after having travelled for a year in Western Europe, Nobuko suffers from liver disease and undergoes emergency hospital treatment. The Russian nurse tending to her is expecting a baby, and Nobuko discovers that the Soviet Union has an advanced welfare system that grants women maternity leave and a child-rearing allowance. Deeply impressed by the communist system, in which women enjoy favourable working conditions, she attempts to learn more about it. At the same time, her relationship with Motoko starts to cool. As Motoko prepares to return to Tokyo, Nobuko considers whether she should stay, as she has received an offer to work in Moscow as a correspondent. Nobuko wavers but, in the end, decides to return to Tokyo to write a novel, effectively ending her three-year Transeurasian journey.

Scholars are now starting to pay attention to the issues of imperialism, European modernity and high modernism in Miyamoto's works. For example, Jill Dobson focuses on the role that the discourse of Russian avant-garde cinema, such as that relating to montage theory, functions in Miyamoto's essays 'Mosukuwa Inshōki' [A record of Moscow impressions] (1928) and 'London 1929' (1930) (Dobson 2016). Dobson also discusses Miyamoto's experiences of and writings about Soviet socialism and modernity, contending that *Dōhyō* 'foregrounds the advanced status of women in the Soviet Union as a powerful motivator for the protagonist Nobuko's "conversion"' (2017: 814).

As noted earlier, my chapter proposes a historicisation of the growing awareness of disparate modernities among women and the possibility of the emergence of international feminism that *Dōhyō* represents. Miyamoto was well aware that there were great differences among the processes of modernisation that occurred in the East, West and the Soviet Union as 'modernity as a historical phenomenon [emerged] around the globe at different times in history' (Friedman 2005: 246). By juxtaposing Miyamoto's discussion of Mary Carmichael in Woolf's *A Room of One's Own* and Miyamoto's *Dōhyō*, this chapter examines how Miyamoto elaborates the representation of the contemporary Asian women characters by considering and reconsidering Western highbrow models.

To analyse the representation of the modern woman in *Dōhyō*, it is essential to look at Miyamoto's metahistorical and internationalist approach to feminist issues. Miyamoto published the aforementioned 'Fujin to Bungaku' as a serial in 1939–40 in the monthly literary journal *Bungei* [*Literature*]. This essay was significantly revised and published as a book in 1948. In this later version, Miyamoto added references to Woolf. An analysis of these references reveals her ambivalent attitude towards the English woman writer and Western modernity. The title suggests that Miyamoto is paying homage to Woolf's *A Room of One's Own* and 'Women and fiction', an essay published in *The Forum* in March 1929 while Miyamoto's analysis of *A Room of One's*

Own betrays her discomfort with Woolf's class consciousness as an upper-middle-class woman writer from the British Empire.[5]

Miyamoto's essay, which somewhat follows Woolf's style, reflects on the literary history of Japanese women writers. Her main interest lies in how a woman character can be constructed by Japanese women writers as a modern, autonomous individual in Japanese novels where a woman is still expected to be feminine, attractive, yet strong so that male critics would find her plausible and enduring enough to survive in a patriarchal culture (Miyamoto 2000–4, vol. 17: 244–5). Considering that a literary history of English women writers supplies a model for the development of Japanese women writers and their representation of a modern woman character, yet lamenting the fact that Japanese women novelists have not yet written a 'good' novel because they have not discovered a self under the pressures of conventional patriarchal society and the Western economy (Miyamoto 2000–4, vol. 17: 312–13), Miyamoto introduces Woolf as a literary critic who argues that British women writers 'may be beginning to use writing as an art, not as a method of self-expression' (*AROO*: 72). According to Miyamoto, however, unlike British women writers, Japanese women writers adopt a writing style Miyamoto describes as 'coquettish' and 'mimicking femininity to get favourable attention of the male audience' (2000–4, vol. 17: 244–5, 273, 288, 301–6, 312–13).[6] Disdainfully calling them popular 'feminine' women writers, Miyamoto turns to retracing the 'uncoquettish' lineage of modern women writers such as the 'New Woman' Toshiko Tamura (1884–1945) and the socialist-feminist Kikue Yamakawa (1890–1980). Miyamoto suggests that Tamura and Yamakawa are the women writers the current generation should follow and, in a sense, grafts onto them the Western feminist ideas of Mary Wollstonecraft (1759–97), the Swedish educationalist Ellen Key (1849–1926) and Woolf. However, Miyamoto believes that Japanese male critics who laud Japanese male writers by linking them to the lineage of British Romantic poetry or German Romanticism have failed to properly evaluate 'New Woman' writers like Tamura and Yamakawa (2000–4, vol. 17: 311–12) because they did not like the 'New Woman' or the progressive, modern woman. Miyamoto contended that her references to Woolf and other Western women writers enabled her to regard them as the forerunners of Japanese women writers and trace a new lineage for the young generation.

Although Miyamoto refers to Woolf's *A Room of One's Own* as a model for the future of Japanese women writers, she simultaneously regards Woolf critically as an upper-middle-class Western woman writer. Addressing Woolf's famous claim in *A Room of One's Own* that 'it is necessary to have five hundred a year and a room with a lock on the door if you are to write fiction or poetry' (*AROO*: 94), Miyamoto believes that, according to Woolf, literary works are created out of one's financial security and cultured, leisured lifestyle (2000–4, vol. 17: 313–14):

> If it is grievously the case that the wealthy and leisured are the only people who are entitled to enrich literature and the whole of humanity with their valuable contributions, all Japanese writers, male or female, must suffer a deep sense of despair over a bleak prospect for their future lives and the future literary tradition. There is no woman writer in Japan who meets the conditions that Woolf specifies. Or, suppose that there is a woman who enjoys immense wealth and comfortable circumstances, it is highly likely she is so conservative as not to pursue a life as a woman writer. Wealth and conservatism are thus inextricably entwined in Japan. (Miyamoto 2000–4, vol. 17: 314)[7]

Miyamoto offers in the passage above a seemingly deliberate misreading of Woolf. For example, Woolf does not believe that 'the wealthy and leisured are the only people who are entitled to enrich literature'. Miyamoto's misreading of Woolf will be thrown into relief more sharply when I later explain how Woolf characterises the figure of Mary Carmichael in *A Room of One's Own* as an imaginary woman writer who, though still wearing 'the shoddy old fetters of class on her feet', will go 'in the spirit of fellowship, into those small, scented rooms where sit the courtesan, the harlot and the lady with the pug dog' (*AROO*: 80). As Woolf tells Mary Carmichael, 'All these infinitely obscure lives remain to be recorded' (*AROO*: 81), and, as such, writers like Mary Carmichael are expected to cross class boundaries and unearth the lives of these unknown, 'unrespectable', underclass women.[8]

From Miyamoto's viewpoint, however, Woolf's argument seems to indirectly marginalise the non-Western parts of the world, as there is a great disparity between the processes of modernisation occurring in the East and West. This is not just to say that a room of one's own and an unearned income are beyond the reach of most Japanese women. Even after universal suffrage was granted to women in Japan on 17 December 1946, a variety of pressures and limitations, such as the conventional notion of femininity and the traditional images of housewife and mother, continued to be placed on women in all areas of Japanese society (Miyamoto 2000–4, vol. 17: 313). Although Miyamoto deliberately overemphasises Woolf's class consciousness in *A Room of One's Own*, her indication of Woolf's seeming unawareness of women in non-Western countries forecasts the advent of postcolonialism and third-wave feminism.[9]

In fact, Gayatri Chakravorty Spivak (1942–) posits that another imaginary figure in *A Room of One's Own*, Mary Beton – who could be the nameless narrator (*AROO*: 4) or the narrator's 'aunt' (*AROO*: 33) – is complicit with imperialism. The first-person narrator, who is not exactly the speaker of the lecture, but 'somebody who has no real being', could be called 'Mary Beton, Mary Seton, Mary Carmichael or by any name' (*AROO*: 4). Spivak thinks it is possible to see Mary Beton as the figure who enables the narrator to regard 'money as a better alternative to democracy' (2003: 40); when Mary Beton 'died by a fall from her horse when she was riding out to take the air in Bombay' (*AROO*: 33), she left £500 a year to the narrator in her will (*AROO*: 34). Like Spivak, Miyamoto seems to be irritated that Woolf, insisting on the importance of the material and social circumstances of women, such as 'five hundred a year' and 'a room with a lock on the door' (2000–4, vol. 17: 60–1, 85, 94), only briefly mentions the colonial money that Mary Beton bequeaths to the narrator and never alludes to the impoverished state of Indian women, leaving the rest to the insight and imagination of the reader. Having insight into the fact that Western economy and the geopolitics of the world are driven by the colonialist and capitalist motives of Western nation-states, Miyamoto claims in 'Fujin to Bungaku' that Japanese women writers 'have not discovered a self under . . . the pressure from the Western economy' (2000–4, vol. 17: 312–13).[10]

The contradictions in Woolf's writings disturb Miyamoto. Presenting a unique definition of Woolf as 'an aesthetic writer who introduced surrealism into English literature' (2000–4, vol. 17: 314), Miyamoto questions why the 'writer who dips into the subconscious and turns away from the world of reality' retains the conventional ideas of the British middle class and contends that literature is created out of one's financial security and cultured, leisured lifestyle (2000–4, vol. 17: 314). Miyamoto suggests that

Woof overlooks the power of creative energy, although it could be said that the values of a new society – postwar Japan – have to be recognised by its citizens so that a writer can achieve the emotional, spatial leeway and sense of freedom to muster the imagination (2000–4, vol. 17: 313–15).

This is likely the reason Miyamoto focuses on the fictional character of Mary Carmichael in *A Room of One's Own* and imaginatively describes the potential and desire of this figure:

> Woolf presents an imaginary, new type of woman writer named Mary Carmichael. Is Mary Carmichael supposed to start her literary career by recognising the importance of favourable conditions? Or does she just start writing, driven by an irresistible urge, reaching out for what women do not possess, or what they desire to possess?
>
> What is essential in the case of Carmichael is that a generation or an individual, entertaining new ideas about one's society, aspires to what she/he does not possess. . . . Romanticism is embraced in the essential part of a human being, and it signifies our high-minded aspiration and struggle for a society with brilliant intelligence, which subsumes complexities that the present human society has not embraced. (Miyamoto 2000–4, vol. 17: 315–16)[11]

In her interpretation of Mary Carmichael, Miyamoto counters Woolf's emphasis on the material and social circumstances of women and focuses on the power of desire within this imaginary figure who lacks the means to give herself leisure to write and a room of her own. Following the passage quoted above, Miyamoto discusses Fumiko Hayashi (1903–51), a renowned woman writer who penned autobiographical novels about the poverty of lower-class women. In *A Room of One's Own*, Miyamoto seems to find a link that could connect the East to the West.

In fact, through Miyamoto's critical yet creative reading of *A Room of One's Own*, Mary Carmichael could be reinterpreted as a figure in which the unfulfilled potential of the dispossessed in the East could be envisioned. Miyamoto discards realism; as will be discussed later, through a Transeurasian cultural network connecting Miyamoto, Woolf and other subaltern women are hypothetically imagined. But before going into the discussion of Miyamoto's Mary Carmichaels, it is necessary to examine the spatial metaphors which play crucial roles in *A Room of One's Own*, as when Woolf's Mary Carmichael – the author of the novel *Life's Adventure*, which the narrator takes from the shelves at the beginning of Chapter 5 – is imaginatively represented (*AROO*: 72–85).

The first-person narrator of *A Room of One's Own* views Mary Carmichael from two viewpoints: as an adventurer and a writer. As an adventurer, Mary Carmichael is expected to explore several kinds of unknown spaces: strange, unknown areas of London where harlots and match-sellers reside, and the 'depths' of the soul or the 'dark place at the back of the head' that will be illuminated anew by Carmichael's own adventures (*AROO*: 80–2, 84). As a writer, she is expected to step into a new textual space of literature that only 'aspiring and graceful female novelists' can reach by taking a 'jump' and going beyond 'fence' after 'fence' (*AROO*: 85).

The problems of space in *A Room of One's Own* have been discussed widely by critics. As Anna Snaith points out in her discussion of the connections between the geographical space and suffrage, 'Woolf's arrival in Bloomsbury heightened her awareness of the politics of the area' (Snaith 2000a: 27). The politics of domestic space, especially the importance of the room in A Room of One's Own, have also been scrutinised (Gan 2009: 68–9; Stevenson 2014: 113). As to the textual space, although feminist critics in the 1980s argued that Woolf writes fiction to disavow the essayist's patriarchal authority (Marcus 1987: 148, 172) or to construct a feminine textual space that allows constant interruptions (Kamuf 1982: 17–18), a more recent critic finds 'unresolved contradictions' between the public/domestic and masculine/feminine spaces by focusing on the complex narrative frame of the book (Wall 1999: 184–5). The argument of my chapter, however, lies in the modern imperialist geopolitics of the textual space of A Room of One's Own. The narrator's representation of an imaginary woman writer, Mary Carmichael, can be reinterpreted as an attempt to create a new transgressive textual space that is not realised in the period of modern imperialism and capitalism. The narrator imagines that Mary Carmichael will learn to write 'as a woman', while '[forgetting] she is a woman', by cultivating a quality in which 'sex is unconscious of itself' (AROO 84). With this freedom from gender constrictions, Mary Carmichael would in turn have the power to grant her readers a vision: to make them feel as if they 'had gone to the top of the world and seen it laid out, very majestically, beneath' (AROO 84). It might take 'another hundred years' (AROO: 85) for this vision to happen, the narrator says. Mary Carmichael is a figure of the present but she is also a projection of the future – of the world in 100 years' time. Only then might Mary Carmichael create this textual space, which surpasses but also includes Britain. To provide a variation on Frederic Jameson's 'utopian enclave', this space, with the possibility of the realisation of a meta-worldly vision, might be regarded as an 'imaginary enclave' for women that is situated 'within real social space' (Jameson 2005: 15). This enclave, in short, made possible by women writers and experienced by all readers, could, by extension, be seen as a transgressive and utopian space.

The Representation of Modern Asian Women in Dōhyō

The global, critical view of the world as an enclave seen in A Room of One's Own seems to be expanded in scale and somewhat realised in Miyamoto's Dōhyō. Woolf's Mary Carmichael has the potential to write a novel that enables readers to envision an extensive, global view of the world, one that seems to transgress the viewpoints of traditional highbrow male writers. As writers and adventurers, modern Asian women, living in the 1940s world in Dōhyō – Miyamoto's Mary Carmichaels – explore a newer, more autonomous subjectivity with an ardent desire to shop and to write in the West. As I will show, the relationships between Asian women are refashioned in a postwar Asian textual space.

Dōhyō represents a modern Asian woman's encounter with European modernity in Paris and London and with Soviet modernity in the Soviet Union, her recognition of the seeming backwardness of Japanese society and culture, and her determination to commit herself to envisioning an alternative relationship between culture and society in postwar Japan. In other words, Nobuko is a transgressive adventurer who becomes liberated from traditional gender norms after experiencing Western modernity. At the same time, she critically compares the state of the West to that of the East, and through intellectual speculation she attempts to write a new novel as a modern woman writer. As she gradually realises what she should do as a writer, she learns to analyse Japan, China, the West and post-revolutionary Moscow from a higher, broader perspective – just as Mary Carmichael in *A Room of One's Own* conveys a meta-worldly vision in a new textual space. Nobuko thus in a sense becomes Miyamoto's version of Mary Carmichael, a modern Asian woman.

Nobuko's experiences in the West serve her well as she becomes a modern Asian woman. Her encounter with the western modernity of Eastern Europe begins with her shopping experience in pre-revolutionary Moscow. While walking past the Moscow Art Theatre with Motoko, Nobuko is fascinated by the shop windows and enters a hat shop. She takes a fancy to a hat and tries it on, only to realise that it does not suit her because of her long hair (Miyamoto 2000–4, vol. 7: 45). Nobuko immediately has her hair bobbed and purchases the hat (2000–4, vol. 7: 46). In this way, her life in Moscow begins with her attraction to a sense of freedom from gender norms and the allure of consumer spectacle. With her new hat, Nobuko walking the streets as a *flâneuse* is an image of a modern woman.

She feels liberated. Stimulated by the energy of the city, her spirit is rejuvenated and she finds a new sense of self arising from within:

> It was as if a bottle, a suffocating object lying at her core, melted away in Moscow, where the heat is excessively high. Nobuko discovered herself anew: she was feeling so happy to see things, enjoying the feeling, and having fun getting to know things. It was as if she were going back to her childhood with her heart exposed, and she embraced herself and Moscow. . . . In Moscow, the old and the new were mixed in a strange way, exposing human life as historical and three-dimensional. The old and the new activated Nobuko's knowledge and senses significantly, letting loose the pleasure of living. (Miyamoto 2000–4, vol. 7: 57–8)[12]

Nobuko's modernness is clear from her bodily sensations and awareness of 'pleasure' (2000–4, vol. 7: 58). Her sense of liberation, however, dissipates when a shocking incident makes Nobuko realise the duplicity of Western modernity. Nobuko and Motoko are invited to a party at the house of a Russian couple. There, a large man takes an interest in Nobuko and drunkenly attempts to rape her in one of the bedrooms (2000–4, vol. 7: 133–4). The violent image of the incident evokes a strong awareness of imperialist domination: a large Russian man exploits the small body of an Asian woman. The large Russian body also symbolises an immense economic and military power as an uncontrollable sexual desire as the small size of Asian bodies and the large size of Western bodies were often mentioned in postwar Japanese journalism.[13]

Nobuko realises that the disparity between the economic and military powers of the West and East works to exploit an Asian woman who is aspiring to Western modernity. Nobuko criticises another form of modernity – capitalism in Western Europe – when she visits London with her family. She walks around the city and takes a bus from East London via Hyde Park to Kensington Gardens. Comparing people in East London to those in West London, she observes that capitalism divides the British people into 'two races' (Miyamoto 2000–4, vol. 7: 105) and that British writers, such as George Bernard Shaw (1856–1950) and John Galsworthy (1867–1933), take the gap between the rich and poor for granted (2000–4, vol. 7: 105). Nobuko also mentions that the Ramsay MacDonald administration (1924, 1929–35) has suppressed the miners' strikes, and she is critical of the lectures offered at Toynbee Hall for workers and the Workers' Educational Association, stressing that professors sent down from Oxford and Cambridge do not truly sympathise with the workers' cultural aspirations (2000–4, vol. 8: 106–7). Bitterly disappointed about witnessing the structural, spatial problems of modern capitalism at work alongside the British class system, Nobuko remembers the phrase, 'Let all the workers possess learning', put up under the dome of Moscow State University (2000–4, vol. 8: 107). She returns to Moscow, determined this time to observe an alternative modernity in the Soviet Union – the successful implementation of the first Soviet five-year plan, that is, the final stage of history in communist ideology.

Nobuko's encounter with communism is a turning point. She rejects Western modernity and starts to adopt a belief in Soviet modernity. Nobuko learns to attach importance to the daily lives of ordinary working people and the insights they gain from culture. Raymond Williams discusses these concepts in his definition of the word 'culture': 'the independent noun, whether used generally or specifically, indicates a particular way of life, whether of a people, a period, a group, or humanity in general' (Williams 1988: 90). In the 1920s, in the period of high modernism, ordinary people were familiar with the word 'culture', indicating 'the independent and abstract noun which describes the works and practices of intellectual and especially artistic activity' (1988: 90). As will be discussed later, Miyamoto, like Williams, places importance on overcoming the cultural divides between high culture and ordinary people's lives, seeing 'culture' as 'a whole way of life' (Williams 1977: 18) and stressing that '[c]ulture is ordinary' (Williams 1989: 5).

After experiencing Soviet modernity in the perceptible changes in ordinary workers' lives who enjoy the benefits under welfare system, Nobuko ends her journey by celebrating Soviet society for its attainment of 'socialism that realises the people's struggle for revolution' (Miyamoto 2000–4, vol. 8: 431), and she decides to become an artist-worker. By choosing Soviet modernity rather than that of the West, a bourgeois Japanese woman commits herself to writing about workers and writing as a worker herself. Yet, the conclusion of the text is curiously ambivalent, as the protagonist seems to only have Japanese workers in mind:

> The season of the white night is beginning in Moscow. 'What should I do?' Nobuko started to think she should go back to Japan. Not to the Japan that she had left with Motoko, but to the Japan that had started to assume a new significance after she had spent three years in Moscow. That was the Japan the Sassa families [Nobuko's parents and siblings] were not familiar with. That was the Japan that had a million unemployed people, a mass of people who kept fighting against power. Nobuko would return to it as a newcomer. . . . She would find a song of her life that she would commit herself to. Nobuko kept standing in front of her desk, pressing her hands. She would go back. However, it terrified her to speak this declaration out loud. (2000–4, vol. 8: 437–8)[14]

At the end of the novel, the protagonist is determined to become an international writer who represents ordinary people. Yet Nobuko's intention to return home, her 'terrified' state and her aims as a writer appear inconsistent. On the one hand, her journey to the West – both to the Soviet Union and to Britain – makes Nobuko and her sense of world a global one. On the other hand, at the end of the story, she intends to go back home and thereby become national and local while confessing that voicing that decision makes her 'terrified'.

Though it appears slightly contradictory, this is the point at which *Dōhyō* and Western late modernism intersect. Whereas in Britain, the modernism of the 1920s is usually regarded as international and cosmopolitan in character, the late modernism of the 1930s, having witnessed a 'nativist and culturalist turn' (Esty 2003: 9), is considered to have turned inward and fetishised English national culture (2003: 1–8).[15] It is clear that Miyamoto did not turn nativist or culturalist, but in Esty's view, the worldwide recession of the 1930s propelled artists in Britain and America to turn inward and think nationally and communally.[16] Just like other nations, Japan suffered from the recession and the economic and administrative chaos after its defeat in the Second World War, which resulted in mass unemployment. As Nobuko links her interest in 'a million unemployed people, a mass of people who kept fighting against power' in Japan to 'the reality of her own life' she would find among them (Miyamoto 2000–4, vol. 8: 437–8) through her own writing, *Dōhyō* projects onto Nobuko an interest in building a community of working-class people in this country devastated by the war. *Dōhyō* depicts the modern protagonist's conflicts between different political frameworks, as well as a resolution of her conflicts through her experiences of Soviet modernity; at the same time, Miyamoto's text, as if to reveal its own political unconscious, seems to become part of global late modernism, ironically showing the protagonist's national turn.

To see an opposition between the West and the Soviet Union in the story of Nobuko – the modern woman – and place *Dōhyō* in the historical context of European late modernism, however, screens off another implicit yet important possibility: Western and Soviet imperialism in Asia. In other words, analysing Nobuko's story as the resolution to her vacillation between Soviet communism and Western civilisation risks displacing attention from the problems of Western and Soviet imperialism in Asia. The protagonist's seemingly nationalistic turn has to be reinterpreted as a reconsideration of the geopolitics and space of Asia being dominated by Western imperialist nations.

A figure in *Dōhyō* who points to this cultural blindness in the text is a Chinese woman, Dr Lin, who teaches law at a university in Moscow. Nobuko is immediately attracted to Dr Lin, who talks about 'the great, immense potential in Chinese people' and 'the women students at Sun Yat-sen University' (Miyamoto 2000–4, vol. 7: 89). Dr Lin's words resonate mysteriously, somewhere deep in Nobuko's mind:

> In Dr Lin's bosom are embraced, if you open it, hundreds and thousands of Chinese people and women students with bobbed hair. In contrast, if I unbutton my blouse, what would I find there? First, myself. Second, my family in Japan. How would they be connected to hundreds and thousands of people's destinies? (2000–4, vol. 7: 90)[17]

Nobuko believes that Dr Lin is far more mature than she is. During her three-year stay in Russia and Europe, Nobuko is reminded of Dr Lin's words a few times and thinks that she and Dr Lin 'have something essential in common' (2000–4, vol. 7: 266). Calling up her memories of Dr Lin, Nobuko attempts to broaden her own vision as a writer. Nobuko's interests lie in how to 'connect' herself to 'hundreds and thousands of people's destinies'. What is noticeable is that the Japanese word for 'connection' in this context evokes a sense of collective responsibility for those 'hundred and thousands of people' and a possibility of forming social solidarity with them. What is more, Nobuko uses the word 'people', not 'the Japanese', though she mentions Dr Lin's connection with 'Chinese people and women students'. Through her respect for Dr Lin, Nobuko thinks of taking on a collective responsibility with other Asian women. Therefore, it is possible to interpret that she, as an Asian woman in this textual enclave, imaginatively attempts to form a Transeurasian cultural network. This network connects Woolf to Miyamoto and other subaltern women in Asia.

A connection formed between China and Japan in a modernist text, however, is complicated and ambivalent. Shu-Mei Shi contends that it is important '[t]o better explicate the literary and political relations in modernist crossings across the transnational terrain', adding that one needs to understand 'the changing role "Japan" played in Chinese cultural imaginary and "China" in Japanese cultural imaginary' (Shi 2001: 17):

> Throughout all of this, Chinese intellectuals nevertheless saw Japan as a model of successful modernization/Westernization. The logic of this contradictory perception of Japan as both aggressor and exemplar operated thus: Japan was able to defeat Russia and conquer parts of China due to its program of Westernization. By emulating the ways Japan learned from the West, China could also become Westernized and strong. During the Republican era, until the outbreak of the Sino-Japanese War in 1937, an intellectual could become influential in literary circles through knowledge of modern Japanese literature, as did the critic Xie Liuyi (1898–1945), or by importing Western modernism via Japan and appropriating Japanese modernism, as did the writers Yu Dafu (1896–1945), Liu Na'ou (1900–39), and many others. (2001: 17)

Chinese intellectuals had traditionally held an 'ethnocentric prejudice' against the Japanese, but 'Japanese cultural products and mediated presentations of Western culture were . . . deemed necessary for China to understand the West and "Asianize" it for Chinese use' (2001: 17–18). Japan's view of China was 'equally contradictory' (2001: 19).

Likewise, in the case of *Dōhyō*, the protagonist envisions the possibility of a transnational bond between Chinese and Japanese women by acknowledging yet putting aside their respective images towards each other. During the Second World War, the Japanese Empire invaded China, attacking it violently, ruthlessly exploiting the country and using Chinese women as sex slaves (Hicks 1997: 11–26). While Miyamoto was writing *Dōhyō*, it was not clear how Japan would apologise for these acts and honour the corresponding liabilities. Miyamoto, however, affirms in her aforementioned 'Fujin to Bungaku' that what the Japanese Empire did in China was an 'invasion' (2000–4, vol. 17: 292–3). More importantly, Miyamoto contributed an article, 'Three kinds of democracy: On the standpoint of the Women's Democratic Club', to the first issue of *The Women's Democratic Club Newspaper*, published on 22 August 1946, which discussed different types of democracies around the world. According to Miyamoto, there are three kinds: the bourgeois democracy of the United States, Britain and France;

the socialist democracy of the Soviet Union; and the new democracy to be established in China and Japan (2000–4, vol. 16: 288). Miyamoto defines 'the new democracy' as a third way, an alternative created out of the relationship between a 'bourgeois-dominated democracy' and a 'proletariat-dominated democracy', because the identities of both the bourgeois and the proletariat have remained undeveloped in Asia (2000–4, vol. 16: 289). It is highly likely, then, that the characterisation of Dr Lin and Nobuko's desire to form an alliance with her in *Dōhyō* evolve from the author's metahistorical conception of the postwar order and the role of women in Asia.

Though Miyamoto is regarded as a leading member of Democratic Literature movement, her attitude is far from nationalist or inward-looking. Indeed, she has a pan-Asiatic vision in which a protagonist, a returnee from the Soviet Union, wishes to realise the unforeseen, new, democratic, feminist workers' bond by forging a loose transnational alliance with modern Chinese women from a metahistorical viewpoint. In other words, *Dōhyō* envisions a relationship of modern Transeurasian women which bridges the gap between the Japanese middle-class and international working-class women and what is yet to come.

Conclusion

In conclusion, Yuriko Miyamoto's ingenious, creative reading of Woolf's 'Women and fiction' and *A Room of One's Own* paved the way for the emergence of a tie linking modern women in Asia. Inspired by Woolf's tracing of the lineage of women writers back a few generations, Miyamoto critically rewrites a literary history of Japanese women writers. Although Miyamoto senses a touch of bourgeois Eurocentrism in Woolf's argument that women writers should have an annual income of £500, an encounter with Woolf's imaginary character Mary Carmichael enables Miyamoto to conceive of her own transnational network of modern women. Her literary aspiration, kindled by Woolf, is realised in *Dōhyō*, an autobiographical novel published in postwar Japan. The novel delineates how a modern woman develops her sense of identity as a worker and writer by making observations of the interrelationships between art, social systems and ordinary people's lives in Moscow, Berlin, Paris and London. At the end of the novel, with the protagonist's decision to become an international writer who represents ordinary people, is a vision of a new, democratic, modern women's bond, a vision that foresees an as yet unformed network between Chinese and Japanese women. With a title that means 'road signs', *Dōhyō* represents Yuriko Miyamoto's 'turn' to modernising Japanese women's novels by generating a new textual space for modern Asian and Transeurasian women writers.

Notes

1. For more on Miyamoto's life, see her diary in vols 26–9 of *The Complete Works of Yuriko Miyamoto* (Miyamoto 2000–4). All translations are mine unless otherwise indicated.
2. From Miyamoto's description of Nobuko's life in New York in *Nobuko*, it is generally assumed that Miyamoto audited courses in English literature and sociology.
3. Miyamoto says that the novels written after the Second World War, such as *Banshū Heiya* and *Dōhyō*, reflect a new democratic society (Miyamoto 2000–4, vol. 17: 330).
4. For a lesbian reading of Miyamoto's works, see Tomoko Aoyama (2015).

5. A translation of Woolf's *A Room of One's Own* was published in Japan in 1940 by Aoki Shoten under the title 'Women and literature'. A translation of *Orlando: A Biography* (1928) was published by Shun-Yodo in 1931. Woolf's novels had been available in Tokyo in the 1920s, and Japanese scholars of English introduced Woolf's works in *Eigo Seinen* [The Rising Generation], a periodical for English literature scholars and high school English teachers, starting from the 1930s onwards.
6. 「ところで、ここに問題なのは、その文学の中に女心を装っている婦人作家たちが、今日男に「かえっていとおしく」思われる効力を自覚しないで、無心に、鏡に向って余念なく化粧する女のようなこころで、女心をその作品のうちに装っているであろうか、ということである」。
7. 「富裕な教養的有閑というものだけが、人間を発展させ文学を展開させる唯一の『厳粛な事実』であるならば、私たち現代の日本の婦人作家どころか、文学者全体が、一人のこらず人間生活と文学の発展について絶望に陥らなければならない。何故なら、ヴァージニア・ウルフの云うような程度で富裕な婦人作家はおそらくただの一人もいないであろうから。仮にもしそれだけ金銭的に裕福な境遇というものがあれば、彼女をゆたかにしているその境遇の諸条件が、殆ど決して彼女を曲りなりにも一人の作家として生活させないほど、日本の富と保守とは結びついている」。
8. Though Woolf was regarded as a highbrow writer, she was not unaware of the fact that lowbrow and middlebrow women read her works. Some of them sent letters to Woolf, and Ella Ophir argues that Mary Geraldine Ostle, inspired by Woolf's *A Room of One's Own*, published *The Note Books of a Woman Alone* in 1935 by editing the notebooks of Evelyn Wilson, a London working woman (Ophir 2014). For Woolf's interest in, and dialogue with, 'common readers', see also Anna Snaith (2000b) and Beth R. Daugherty (2006).
9. Rebecca Walker is credited with coining the term 'third wave' in her January 1992 article in *Ms.* Magazine entitled 'Becoming Third Wave'. For recent discussion on Third Wave Feminism, see Johanna Oksala (2016).
10. 「それにもかかわらず、日本の挫かれた社会と文化の事情で、（中略）封建性と近代経済の二重の圧力によって、婦人作家は「女心」の擬態から自身を近代的に解放出来ずにいる」。
11. 「彼女が婦人作家の新しいタイプとして認めているメアリー・カーマイクルの文学の世界は、メアリーが女性としてこの社会に既に獲ている有利な諸条件の認識から出発しているであろうか。それとも、女性が、まだ獲ていないものについて、獲たいと願うものについて新しい認識が生れていて、そこから彼女の創造がうながされたものだろうか。カーマイクルの現実がそうであったように婦人と文学との歴史の過程で重大なのは、寧ろまだ獲ていないものに対して、その世代及び個人がどういう評価と認識をもって、獲て行こうとしたかという点である。（中略）人間精神の本質に横わるロマンティシズムというものは、このようにしていまだ人間社会が到達していないより複雑な、より智慧の輝いた社会への私たちの雄々しい憧れとその努力でなくて何であろう」。
12. 「息苦しい存在の壁のようなものが熱量の高いモスクワ生活でとけ去って、観ることのこんなにもうれしい自分、感じることがこんなにも愉しい自分、知ってゆくことの面白さで子供っぽくさえなっている自分がむき出しになっていることを発見したとき、伸子は自分とモスクワとを、抱きしめた。モスクワでのすべての印象は、日本の生活でそうであったようにせまい漏斗で伸子の内面にばかりたまりこまなかった。伸子の主観でつつまれるにしては、事件にしろ見聞にしろその規模が壮大であり、複雑であり、それ自身としての真面目な必然と意義をもっていた。旧さと新しさが異様に交りあったモスクワ生活の歴史的な立体性は、伸子の全知識と感覚をめざましく活動させ、なお、もっともっとと、生きる感興を誘い出しているのであった」。
13. A typical example is critical commentary on the photograph of Emperor Hirohito and General Douglas MacArthur taken right after the surrender of Japan in 1945. Emperor Hirohito, a short man with a strained face, stands in an upright posture while General MacArthur, a tall, solid man in a military uniform, assumes a relaxed posture.

14. 「モスクワに、そろそろ白夜がはじまった。自分のするべきことは何だろう。思いつめて、伸子は、自分は日本へ帰るべきだ、と考えるようになった。素子とつれだって伸子がそこから出て来た日本ではなく、モスクワの三年で、伸子に新しい意味をもって見られるようになって来た、その日本へ。それは佐々のうちのものの知らない日本であった。百万人の失業者があり、権力に抵抗して根気づよくたたかっている人々の集団のある日本へ、伸子は全くの新参として帰ろうと決心した。〔中略〕しかし、そこに伸子の生活の現実がある。そして、伸子が心を傾けて歌おうと欲する生活の歌がある。
    伸子は、きつく両手を握りあわせながら、自分のデスクの前に立ちつくした。伸子は、帰る。けれども、その言葉を声に出していうことはおそろしかった」。
15. For more recent discussions on late modernism, see Esty (2003), Tyrus Miller (1999) and Thomas Saverance Davis (2015).
16. For a recent discussion on the 'inward turn' in the Great Depression in the United States, see Morris Dickstein (2009).
17. 「リン博士のすんなりとした胸のなかには、そこをひらくと深い愛につつまれながら幾百幾千の中国の人々が、黒いおかっぱ頭を肩に垂らした女学生もこめて、生きている。それにくらべて、自分の白いブラウスの胸をさいて見たとして、そこから何が出て来るというのだろう。先ず、わたし。それから佃や動坂の一家列。しかもそれが、幾百幾千の人々の運命と、どうつながっているというのだろう」。

Bibliography

Aoyama, T. (2015), 'Yoshiko & Yuriko: Love texts, and camaraderie', in R. Barraclough, H. Bowen-Struyk and P. Rabinowitz (eds), *Red Love Across the Pacific: Political and Sexual Revolutions of the Twentieth Century*, New York: Palgrave Macmillan, pp. 123–39.

Cullen, J. (2010), 'A comparative study of tenkō: Sata Ineko and Miyamoto Yuriko', *The Journal of Japanese Studies*, 36: 1, pp. 65–96.

Daugherty, B. R. (2006), '"You see you kind of belong to us, and what you do matters enormously": Letters from readers to Virginia Woolf', *Woolf Studies Annual*, 12, pp. 1–19.

Davis, T. S. (2015), *The Extinct Scene: Late Modernism and Everyday Life*, New York: Columbia University Press.

Dickstein, M. (2009), *Dancing in the Dark: A Cultural History of the Great Depression*, New York: W. W. Norton.

Dobson, J. (2017), 'A "fully bloomed" existence for women: Miyamoto [Chūjō] Yuriko in the Soviet Union, 1927–1930', *Women's History Review*, 26: 6, pp. 799–821.

Dobson, J. (2016), 'Imagining the modern city: Miyamoto [Chūjō] Yuriko in Moscow and London, 1927–1930', *Japan Forum*, 28: 4, pp. 486–510.

Esty, J. (2003), *A Shrinking Island: Modernism and National Culture in England*, Princeton, NJ: Princeton University Press.

Friedman, S. S. (2005), 'Paranoia, pollution, and sexuality: Affiliations between E. M. Forster's *A Passage to India* and Arundhati Roy's *The God of Small Things*', in L. Doyle and L. Winkiel (eds), *Geomodernisms: Race Modernism, Modernity*, Bloomington: Indiana University Press, pp. 245–61.

Gan, W. (2009), 'Solitude and community: Virginia Woolf, spatial privacy and *A Room of One's Own*', *Literature & History*, 18, pp. 68–80.

Hicks, G. (1997), *The Comfort Women: Japan's Brutal Regime of Enforced Prostitution in the Second World War*, London: W. W. Norton.

Ikeda, K. (2015), 'Haikyo to gunyō doro: Miyamoto Yuriko *Banshū Heiya* ni okeru higai to kagai no jūsōsei' 廃墟と軍用道路――宮本百合子『播州平野』における被害と加害の重層性 [The ashes and the military roads: The ambivalent representation of war criminals in Yuriko Miyamoto's *The Plains of the Banshū*], *Fensuresu* フェンスレス [Fenceless], 3, pp. 23–39.

Jameson, F. (2005), *Archaeologies of the Future: The Desire Called Utopia and Other Science Fictions*, London: Verso.

Kamuf, P. (1982), 'Penelope at work: Interruptions in *A Room of One's Own*', *Novel: A Forum on Fiction*, 16: 1, pp. 5–18.

Kang, J. (2014), 'Miyamoto Yuriko *Banshū Heiya* niokeru sengo nippon' 宮本百合子「播州平野」における戦後日本 [Postwar Japan in Yuriko Miyamoto's *The Plains of the Banshū*], *Kenkyū Ronshū* 研究論集 [Research Journal of Graduate Students of Letters of Hokkaido University], 14, pp. 71–81.

Karlsson, M. (2011), 'United front from below, the Proletarian Cultural Movement's last stand, 1931–34', *The Journal of Japanese Studies*, 37: 1, pp. 29–59.

Marcus, J. (1987), *Virginia Woolf and the Languages of Patriarchy*, Bloomington: Indiana University Press.

Miller, T. (1999), *Late Modernism: Politics, Fiction, and the Arts between the World Wars*, Berkeley: University of California Press, 1999.

Miyamoto, Y. (2000–4 [1924–51]), *Miyamoto Yuriko Zenshū* 宮本百合子全集 [The Complete Works of Yuriko Miyamoto], 33 vols, Tokyo: Shin Nihon Shuppansha.

Oksala, J. (2016), 'Affective labor and feminist politics', *Signs: Journal of Women in Culture and Society*, 41: 2, pp. 281–303.

Ophir, E. (2014), '*A Room of One's Own*, ordinary life-writing, and *The Note Books of a Woman Alone*', *Woolf Studies Annual*, 20, pp. 25–40.

Shi, S.-M. (2001), *The Lure of the Modern: Writing Modernism in Semicolonial China, 1917–1933*, Berkeley: University of California Press.

Snaith, A. (2000a), *Virginia Woolf: Public and Private Negotiations*, Basingstoke: Palgrave Macmillan.

Snaith, A. (2000b), 'Wide circles: The *Three Guineas* letters', *Woolf Studies Annual*, 6, pp. 1–12.

Spivak, G. C. (2003), *Death of a Discipline*, New York: Columbia University Press.

Stevenson, C. (2014), '"Here was one room, there another": The room, authorship, and feminine desire in *A Room of One's Own* and *Mrs Dalloway*', *Pacific Coast Philology*, 49: 1, pp. 112–32.

Wall, K. (1999), 'Frame narratives and unresolved contradictions in Virginia Woolf's *A Room of One's Own*', *Journal of Narrative Theory*, 29: 2, pp. 184–207.

Williams, R. (1977 [1958]), *Culture and Society 1780–1950*, New York: Penguin.

Williams, R. (1988 [1976]), *Keywords: A Vocabulary of Culture and Society*, London: Fontana.

Williams, R. (1989 [1958]), 'Culture is ordinary', *Resources of Hope: Culture, Democracy, Socialism*, London: Verso.

Woolf, V. (2000 [1929/1938]), *A Room of One's Own/Three Guineas*, ed. M. Barrett, London: Penguin.

16

Rooms of Their Own: A Cross-Cultural Voyage between Virginia Woolf and the Contemporary Chinese Woman Writer Chen Ran

Zhongfeng Huang

Introduction

OVER THE PAST THREE DECADES, Virginia Woolf has assumed an iconic position in China. As many of her works have been translated into Chinese and become accessible to more Chinese readers, and as better translations have appeared, Woolf's popularity has increased to a level unmatched by any other foreign woman writer in China. These trends have also substantially promoted academic research on Woolf in China, and an increasing number of articles and manuscripts on Woolf have been published from a variety of perspectives.[1]

The increasing popularity of Woolf's works also shows her wider and deeper influences – especially her feminism and poetics – on modern and contemporary Chinese fiction writers, particularly women writers such as Chen Ran (1962–),[2] who regard Woolf as her literary mother. As a contemporary Chinese avant-garde feminist writer and essayist who won the first Contemporary China Female Creative Writer's Award (1998), Chen Ran is most famous for her individualised, subjective and introspective writing, which is best exemplified by her most acclaimed novel *A Private Life* (*Siren Shenghuo*, 1996). It was translated into English in 2004 and has won critical acclaim around the world. Sofia Tangalos (2004), Allison Block (2004), Larissa N. Heinrich (2005), Kay Schaffer and Song Xianlin (2006), and Xin Yang (2011) have all discussed different aspects in *A Private Life*.

Chen Ran's major works were published in the 1990s. This decade is viewed as a pluralist era that witnessed the increasing economic opening of China, more opportunities for women's education, rapid urbanisation and commercialisation, the introduction of western literary theories, and communication with the outside world, all of which contributed to a fruitful environment for the publication of Chen Ran's works. Her exploration of the female self and subjectivity is in line with the sexualising trend in China in the 1990s. According to Jiang Hongyan, the rapid commercialisation and marketisation that occurred in China strongly contributed to the interest of women writers in exploring women's sexual identity, which also became a popular strategy to capture readers' attention (1997: 30).

Chen Ran's works share an unmistakably distinctive trait, as most of her protagonists are young, urban, educated Chinese women who are often estranged from their families, alienated from the bustling world and disturbed by the drastic changes in society. As a result, they retreat into their 'rooms', where their personal and sensual experiences of being young modern Chinese women are given full and vivid expression. Although independent and free, these women are often besieged and invaded by an overpowering sense of loneliness and emptiness. Unable to find satisfaction or fulfilment with men, they often turn to women with whom they establish strong bonds, and sometimes express homoerotic desire towards women. The ready-made expression 'sisterly affection' is employed by Chen Ran to characterise sisterhood as well as female sexual desire. It is through sisterly affection that these women finally attain sexual awakening as well as distinct self-identity. Chen Ran's exploration of Chinese women's sexuality, spirituality, body and self-identity undoubtedly establishes her as a unique and important female voice among the many prominent contemporary Chinese women writers, which paradoxically isolates her from mainstream Chinese literature.[3] The Chinese literature scholar Zhang Yiwu (1962–) contends that Chen Ran 'seems to wander outside the mainstream culture with no orientation' (Zhang 1993: 50). In a similar vein, the renowned Chinese feminist critic Dai Jinhua (1959–) comments, 'To a certain extent, Chen Ran's writing is always individualised, but her writing via individualisation makes her and her works increasingly hard to identify' (Dai 1996: 56). As the translator John Howard-Gibbon succinctly states in the preface to *A Private Life*: 'Throughout her writing career, she has been a kind of disturbance on the perimeter of mainstream Chinese literature, a unique and important female voice' (Chen 2004: xii). Chen Ran addresses issues of same-sex bonding and the possibility of homoeroticism between women. She emphasises the complexity of women's issues in the inner world after they achieve their independence and freedom in modern China. As a central figure in individualised writing, Chen Ran occupies a prominent position in a distinctively Chinese women's literary tradition.

Focusing on their similar views on gender and women's writing, this chapter studies Woolf's influences on Chen Ran from three perspectives. First, Woolf's idea of a room of one's own lays the theoretical and metaphorical feminist basis for Chen Ran's works. Next, Woolf's idea of androgyny inspires Chen Ran's concept of 'gender-transcendent consciousness'. Third, Woolf's call for women's writing – in particular her expression 'Chloe liked Olivia' (*AROO*: 106) – becomes the literary source and inspiration for Chen Ran's notion of sisterly affection, which turns out to be an excellent example of gender-transcendent consciousness. Meanwhile, Woolf's call for women's writing is exemplified by Chen Ran's vivid and detailed presentation of women's subjective and introspective experiences, in particular their bodies and sexual desires. Woolf's ideas of a room of one's own and of androgyny form the theoretical basis for Chen Ran's works. Strongly influenced by Woolf, Chen Ran has created many new images of Chinese women with rebellious and insightful outlooks such as the perspectives of Yun Nan from 'Breaking open' (2002) and Ni Niuniu of *A Private Life*.

Woolf's *A Room of One's Own* and Chen Ran's 'a room of one's own'

As Chen Ran openly acknowledges, she is a disciple of Woolf, whose notion of a room of one's own lays a firm feminist basis for the pioneering women characters in her works. Chen Ran shows her admiration for and identification with Woolf in a 1995 interview:

> She is a woman I really appreciate. I've read many of her notes and articles[4] which are beautifully written. In particular we share the same women's psychological perspective, which builds a very close correspondence between our ideas. For example, she says that if a woman wants to write fiction, she must have some money and a room of her own. (Chen 2000: 198)[5]

Chen Ran appreciates Woolf's talent as a feminist woman writer. She finds resonance in Woolf and her works, in particular their shared opinions about gender and women's writing. Chen Ran is largely inspired and encouraged by Woolf's feminist manifesto that a woman writer must be financially, spatially and spiritually secure before she can write.

Woolf's idea of a room of one's own can be understood as a creative space, in both a literal and metaphorical sense, that represents women's experiences. While Woolf emphasises the significance of a physical space, financial stability, privacy and freedom for a woman writer, she also stresses the importance of the interiority of the room:

> The rooms differ so completely; they are calm or thunderous; open on to the sea, or, on the contrary, give on to a prison yard; are hung with washing; or alive with opals and silks; are hard as horsehair or soft as feathers. (*AROO/TG*: 114)

Woolf suggests that women furnish and decorate their room according to their likes, which generate infinite possibilities. As pointed out by Sheheryar B. Sheikh, Woolf's concept of room 'appear[s] simultaneously abstract and concrete' (2018: 24), which is a combination of 'negotiable physical space as well as negotiable head-space' (2018: 29). 'Room' is clearly a more complicated term than it appears to be and rejects one simple definition. According to Wendy Gan, Woolf's concept of room engages different negotiations between the private and the public. Her preference for a 'room' rather than a 'study' indicates her need for 'exclusion and inclusion, solitude and community' (2009: 69). In other words, the rooms in a Victorian home had a gendered purpose in accordance with the structuring of society. A study, for instance, which enables 'isolation and privacy', is often coded as a masculine space, while women often maintain power over the more 'social and open' space of the drawing-room (Rosner 2005: 64). As a symbol of political and cultural space, the room free from interruption also implies women's intrusion into space previously occupied by men (Goldman 2007: 71).

Similarly, Chen Ran reiterates that her 'understanding of a room is not limited to a room only; it is also a symbol of safety, independence and a guarantee of life' (Chen 2000: 198).[6] Both Chen Ran and Woolf's concept of 'room' encompasses physical, spiritual and psychological aspects. It is a spiritual and symbolic space free of a man's powerful voice, discourse, and overwhelming consciousness. In this private room, women are able to contemplate their private experiences, review the past and look forward to the future. In other words, if Woolf's room symbolises a necessary guarantee for a writer who needs freedom and privacy to create, then Chen Ran's room is a symbol that can be extended to every woman and man who needs private space and freedom of their own.

Chen Ran continues by saying that it is her long-cherished dream to 'read, write and complete the daily brain-to-heart conversation ... and have some freedom unnoticed and hindered by others in the room of her own described by Woolf' (1995: 359).[7] While Woolf's room seems to be for women writers as well as those who have not had opportunities to write, Chen Ran's room is of great importance to any woman who is an independent thinker. Six decades later, Chen Ran places Woolf's room in another context and endows it with new significance.

For instance, as noted above, homoerotic desires figure prominently in Chen Ran's works, which reflect China's tolerant attitude towards homosexuality throughout most of the nation's history. It was not until after the founding of the new China in 1949 that homosexuality was viewed as pathological. From the 1950s to the 1970s, Chinese homosexuals underwent a period of heightened political persecution (Wu 2003: 117). From 1978 on, China's reform and opening-up policy made it possible to undertake research on Chinese homosexuals and homosexuality. After 2001, when the third edition of the *Chinese Classification of Mental Disorders* (CCMD-3) was published, the classification of 'ego dystonic homosexuality' as a 'disease' was removed.

Woolf's Concept of Androgyny and Chen Ran's Gender-Transcendent Consciousness

In *A Room of One's Own*, Woolf's notion of androgyny aims to solve the problems of strong personal feelings such as anger and intense sex-consciousness that pose a threat to the creativity of both women and men artists.[8] Woolf maintains that 'It is fatal to be a man or woman pure and simple; one must be woman-manly or man-womanly' (*AROO/TG*: 136). Woolf employs the terms 'man-womanly' and 'woman-manly' to suggest the possibility and significance of a creative mental stance that has some attributes of the opposite sex yet remains in accordance with the writer's biological sex (*AROO/TG*: 128). In other words, writers should adopt a spiritually androgynous and detached state of mind to ward off the negative influences attendant upon their personal resentments and prejudice. This is how Woolf situates Jane Austen, whom she praises: 'she wrote as a woman, but as a woman who has forgotten that she is a woman, so that her pages were full of that curious sexual quality which comes only when sex is unconscious of itself' (*AROO/TG*: 121). Therefore, from Woolf's perspective, only when writers reach the state of sex-unconsciousness can their gender traits be conveyed without impediment.

Woolf's notion of androgyny becomes the primary literary source for Chen Ran's concept of gender-transcendent consciousness. Chen Ran first used this term in her speech titled 'Gender-transcendent consciousness and my creative writing' delivered at Oxford University, London University, Edinburgh University and elsewhere throughout the course of 1994. As Chen Ran acknowledges, she takes inspiration from Woolf's concept of androgyny:

> In *A Room of One's Own*, Woolf borrows Coleridge's words 'Great minds are androgynous'. In my opinion, this sentence does not merely mean that only when a writer spiritually unites qualities from both the male and the female can he/she transmit emotions and ideas without any impediment. Moreover, I think it also

embodies another layer of meaning: a person with great personality is first of all someone who sees others' qualities free from their sex. Their appreciation of people is gender transcendent. It is too superficial to judge others simply as a man or a woman. (1994: 107; 1998: 35)⁹

From the above quotation, it is clear that Chen Ran is influenced by Woolf's idea of 'androgyny', which is understood as a spiritual combination of qualities from both sexes to reach the most propitious creative state and best display the writer's creative talent. Although Chen Ran's new term gender-transcendent consciousness is derived from 'androgyny', it can also be employed in interpersonal communication. As Chen Ran notes, unlike the writer's creative state characterised by sex-unconsciousness, gender-transcendent consciousness should also be used as a fair standard of treating and appreciating people.

In the same article, Chen Ran also firmly asserts that 'genuine love transcends gendered sex just as pure literature transcends politics to achieve independence' (1994: 106).¹⁰ As she explains,

love, or emotional love, and making love, or sexual love, are two different things. Emotional love exceeds carnal love, as the former includes heart and soul, thought and the physical body. This is the most thrilling of all human sentiments and is what would really excite a modern woman's entire body and spirit. (1994: 106)¹¹

According to Chen Ran, there is a distinction between emotional love and sexual/physical love, with the former assuming greater significance because it involves the spiritual and is what deeply arouses a woman's physical and spiritual feelings.

It is worth noting that, in a 2007 interview, Chen Ran again references the quotations from Coleridge, but with some modification:

Woolf once mentioned in *A Room of One's Own* that 'Great minds are androgynous'. ... This does not mean that women's qualities will be reduced or hidden. Quite on the contrary, I think this expands and promotes our glories as women. (2007: 26)¹²

The last two sentences show her positive understanding and affirmation of Woolf's notion of an androgynous mind, which exhibits the writer's distinctive sexual traits and qualities.

Inspired by Woolf's idea of androgyny, Chen Ran uses the concept of gender-transcendent consciousness to elucidate the existence of same-sex friendship, or simply sisterly affection, which is defined as a type of female bonding that accommodates both intimate female friendship and female same-sex desire. In other words, gender-transcendent consciousness lays the theoretical foundation for the existence of sisterly affection, which then proves the possibility of genuine love between females. As Chen Ran explicitly contends, 'My thoughts are: genuine love transcends gender. ... Can we understand it this way: it is difficult for a profound thinker to seek the opposite sex with understanding and spiritual fulfillment' (Chen 1994: 106–7).¹³ According to Chen Ran, genuine love is built upon mutual love, appreciation and respect. It has little to do with one's gendered sex. Same-sex bonding, hence, becomes another important source of love for both women and men.

Consequently, she declares that 'human beings have the right to choose their love in accordance with their psychology and constitution. This is true humanitarianism! This is truly human!' (Chen 1994: 107).[14] That is, psychological intimacy as well as spiritual communication and understanding should be the primary concerns in choosing love. On similar grounds, in another article, Chen Ran argues, 'Truly excellent artists and writers will not be easily perplexed and seduced by the opposite sex or same sex. They have their own emotional pursuit and independent artistic exploration' (1994: 107).[15] In Chen Ran's view, for outstanding artists seeking emotions and pursuing artistic endeavors outweigh intimate relationships with people of any gender.

Chen Ran's gender-transcendent consciousness contrasts with gender consciousness. In this formulation, consciousness transcends the gender boundaries strictly prescribed by society and forcefully imposed upon men and women, and advocates for love that is free from the strict stipulations of heterosexual love: 'The hegemony of heterosexuality will eventually collapse, and from its ruins, gender-transcendent consciousness will arise' (Chen 1994: 107).[16] Chen Ran predicts that when women have better control over their bodies, when their reproductive freedom and economic independence represent a further stage in women's liberation, when genuine love is built upon mutual appreciation and understanding, the conventional norm of heterosexuality will end, opening up a space for gender-transcendent consciousness.

In short, the notion of androgyny for Woolf is a multifarious term that pursues 'a hybrid intermix of qualities', such as gender and sexuality (Kaivola 1999: 256). It calls for 'a recognition of the other within the self' (Kaivola 1999: 256) to display forthrightly all writers' sexual and gendered qualities. It offers both men and women writers equal opportunities for artistic creations as a man or a woman. Similar to Woolf, Chen Ran's concept of gender-transcendent consciousness does not aim at a clean elimination of gender or sex consciousness. Quite the contrary, it is built upon a clear recognition of gender consciousness. As Chen Ran asserts, 'I no longer care about gender, nor do I care about the "minority" close by me, which I don't think is "abnormal"' (2002: 235).[17] Chen Ran's concept of gender-transcendent consciousness provides contemporary women writers and the general public with a new starting point and angle from which to build women's own discourse without being fully assimilated into male discourse. More importantly, gender-transcendent consciousness calls on the general public to transcend gender in their everyday life.

Thus, with an emphasis on the spiritual cooperation of mental qualities from both genders, Woolf advises writers to adopt an androgynous and detached mind during the process of creation to eschew the negative influences of intense personal emotions and strong sex-consciousness. By contrast, Chen Ran's notion of gender-transcendent consciousness possibly draws upon the attributes of *yin yang* in ancient Chinese philosophy, which features harmony between females and males in general. As a fundamental principle, *yin yang* refers to the idea that all things in nature exist harmoniously as complementary and interdependent opposing sets, such as female and male, darkness and light, negative and positive, inaction and action. Chen Ran believes that although everyone is governed by powers from both genders, true gender-transcendent consciousness can be realised only when people adopt a state of mind that is not attendant upon their gendered sex but is instead based on being human. Hence, she proposes the diminution of gender consciousness and the blurring of sexual differences to reach gender equality. Furthermore, Chen Ran argues that the most ideal love is built upon both spiritual understanding and physical intimacy, regardless of gender. Chen Ran is well-read in Western writers and has travelled around the world.[18] She is conscious of the rights of the marginalised social groups such as homosexuals. She asserts, 'I understand, respect and uphold the rights of homosexuality in all civilisations of the world, just as I maintain the rights of heterosexuals of all civilisations' (Chen 2007: 25).[19] Therefore, Chen Ran uses Woolf as a way to resist heteronormativity in 1990s China.

Woolf's Call for Women's Writing and Chen Ran's Sisterly Affection and Women's Subjectivity

In *A Room of One's Own* and 'Women novelists' Woolf asserts that women's writing should be expressive of their particular experiences and thoughts. Woolf explains that women have different experiences and viewpoints, which lead to different focuses and styles in their writing (*AROO*: 96; Woolf 1965: 26–7). In other words, a woman writer is encouraged to compose what would take 'the natural shape of her thought without crushing or distorting it' (*CE* 2: 145) and to 'differ from men without fear and express their difference openly' (*D* 2: 342) with an emphasis on women writers' potential, capacity and capability to write differently from men writers. Woolf reiterates the possibility and significance of women writing differently from men by saying:

> It would be a thousand pities if women wrote like men, or lived like men, or looked like men, for if two sexes are quite inadequate, considering the vastness and variety of the world, how should we manage with one only? Ought not education to bring out and fortify the differences rather than the similarities? (*AROO*: 114)

According to Woolf, because language and male-centred literary traditions are antagonistic to women's experiences and views, women writers should construct a type of writing that is expressive of their unique minds and experiences.

Regarding the proper subject of women's writing, Woolf encourages women writers to write about things pertaining to women:

> And since a novel has this correspondence to real life, its values are to some extent those of real life. But it is obvious that the values of women differ very often from the values which have been made by the other sex; naturally, this is so. Yet it is the masculine values that prevail. Speaking crudely, football and sport are 'important'; the worship of fashion, the buying of clothes 'trivial'. And these values are inevitably transferred from life to fiction. This is an important book, the critic assumes, because it deals with war. This is an insignificant book because it deals with the feelings of women in a drawing-room. (*AROO*: 95–6)

Woolf claims that the values in life determine the values in fiction. While there is great disparity between masculine and feminine values, it is always the masculine values that are prevalent because it is the dominant social group, namely men who assign values to things. They identify 'football and sport' and 'war' as masculine values and 'the worship of fashion, the buying of clothes' and 'the feelings of women' as feminine values, with the former accorded much more significance and importance than the latter (*AROO*: 96). Both in life and literature, women's lives, experiences and voices are excluded and devalued. Woolf appeals to women writers to record in literature '[a]ll these infinitely obscure lives' (*AROO*: 116).

In 'Professions for women', the narrator expresses her desire to write about sexuality, which she fears would meet great challenges from society, and above all men, as she writes:

> To speak without figure she had thought of something, something about the body, about the passions which it was unfitting for her as a woman to say. Men, her reason told her, would be shocked. The consciousness of – what men will say of a woman who speaks the truth about her passions had roused her from her artist's state of unconsciousness. She could write no more. (*CE* 2: 287–8)

The narrator is eager to explore and examine female body and their sexual desires, but the fear of society, in particular men's discouragement and disapproval, stops her from that endeavour.

Also, in *A Room of One's Own*, Woolf writes: 'Chloe liked Olivia. They shared a laboratory together. . . . For if Chloe likes Olivia and Mary Carmichael knows how to express it she will light a torch in that vast chamber where nobody has yet been' (*AROO/TG*: 108–9). It is worth noting that the two women, Chloe and Olivia, work together in the same laboratory, which is suggestive of women's exposure to a wider and different 'room' from their domestic 'room'. Women's intriguing yet unrepresented experiences in that lab room, in particular the unrecorded and much repressed intimacy and love between women, is invested with revolutionary significance. The fact that the two women share a lab room that is an experimental work space instead of a domestic space may suggest that it is a form of testing new relationship. Moreover, as insightfully observed by Brenda Helt,

> that fact [Chloe and Olivia like each other] does not preclude their liking men as well, a point Woolf makes explicit. Olivia has two children and a husband, and leaves Chloe at the lab to go home to be with them. . . . Women's love for other women is a highly desirable and empowering emotive force common to most women, and not an identifying characteristic of a rare sexual type. (2016: 119)

Thus, 'Chloe liked Olivia' is Woolf's metaphorical expression of an exploration of women's relationship with women, including lesbian relationships, a field that remained to be fully explored by women writers, at least in 1990s China. This metaphorical expression challenges the traditional prevailing portrayal of women as mothers, wives and daughters, transforming conventional gender norms and values. It also critiques male writers' entrenched yet prejudiced representations of women as either angels or monsters. It opens up the imaginative possibility of a whole world of sharing and understanding among women. Women are seen and represented in relation to each other rather than as submissive and gentle angels in the house. Women's interpretations and re-evaluations of their own experiences are important steps towards a reconstruction of a distinctive voice and an identity of their own that can be recognised and identified.

There are strong echoes in Chen Ran from Woolf's appeal to future women writers to represent women as they are rather than who they are supposed to be. With an understanding of Woolf's expression 'Chloe liked Olivia', Chen Ran coins the term sisterly affection as a familiar expression to represent women's experiences and feelings such as friendship and intimacy, in relation to women, which is more inclusive than the ready-made term lesbian relationship. Moreover, there are two other reasons for Chen Ran's preference for sisterly affection over 'lesbianism'. First, lesbianism is a Western term. The current Chinese homosexual community generally uses the term *tongzhi* to refer to homosexuals. *Tongzhi* originally referred to the revolutionary comrades in both the Communist and the Nationalist Parties. In Chinese, *tong* literally means 'same/home', while *zhi* means 'ideal', 'ambition', 'will' and 'spirit'. The literal translation of homosexuals in Chinese is *tongxinglian*. This term became popular mainly because of its 'positive cultural references, gender-neutrality, de-sexualizing of the stigma of homosexuality, its politics beyond the homo-hetero binarism, and its indigenous cultural identity for integrating the sexual into the social' (Chou 2001: 28). Second, long-lived intimacy and affection between women stem from trust, support and strong emotional ties. Women in such relationships have much to share in terms of their similar experiences such as pregnancy, childbirth, marriage, rearing children, mother-in-law and daughter-in-law relationships, abandoned ambitions, worries and happiness, and troubles and successes. These shared experiences help women to forge a community of congenial companionship, friendship and affection. To a large extent, such relationships focus on emotional attachment rather than female same-sex desire. In today's Chinese society, there is a special word – *guimi* – to describe that kind of sisterly affection. *Gui* refers to the boudoir of Chinese women in traditional society, and *mi* refers to secrets or intimacy. Therefore, *guimi* means the most intimate type of female friends who are willing to share anything with each other such as their sorrows, joys, emotional and sex lives, and physiological changes. There seems to be no taboos in their conversations.

As a more inclusive term, gender-transcendent consciousness lays the theoretical basis for sisterly affection, which is illustrated in Chen Ran's compelling argument that 'love transcends gender'. Sisterly affection is represented in her story 'Breaking open' (2002), regarded by Dai Jinhua as 'the true manifesto for Chinese feminist literature' (qtd in Chen 2000: 70).[20] The two protagonists in 'Breaking open', the first-person narrator Dai Er and her close friend Yun Nan, are two independent, modern and educated Chinese women. Dai Er is a writer, while Yun Nan is 'an outstanding and sharp art critic' (Chen 2002: 232). The name Yun Nan is an unusual one for a woman; yun in Chinese means 'perish' or 'die', and nan shares the same pronunciation with the Chinese word for 'man'. Dissatisfied with gender discrimination and prejudices, and determined to fight against sexual hostility and negligence, these two women intend to establish a women's association called 'Breaking open'. This association is free of gender discrimination, and the question of gender is replaced by the question of humanity, as Yun Nan maintains:

> The dilution of gender consciousness should be regarded as an advance of human civilisation. We are first of all humans, and then women. . . . The greatest war will arise because of the divide between the sexes for the future generations. (Chen 2002: 231–2)[21]

Here, Chen Ran reiterates the great significance of gender-transcendent consciousness, which she predicts will greatly contribute to a peaceful future.

Dai Er and Yun Nan pursue female identity through their mutual sisterly affection, admiration, respect and support. Yun Nan even suggests that the adjective 'female' before animal names, such as 'she' in 'she-wolf', be discarded because it is suggestive of gender prejudice and is often closely associated with or equated with negative terms such as stupidity, weakness, passivity and incompetency (Chen 2002: 228). In Chinese, the word 'female' (in Chinese pinyin, *mu*) is often used as a sex-indicative prefix for female domesticated animals. Consistent with their reformist intention, the characters resolutely refuse to adopt 'The Second Sex' as the title of their women's association because that is an affirmation and support of the prescribed norms established by the first sex (Chen 2002: 236). The term 'second sex' parallels Woolf's notion of the 'Outsiders' Society' consisting of 'daughters of educated men', which experiments 'with private means in private' to achieve 'freedom, equality, peace' (*AROO/TG*: 320–1). Dai Er and Yun Nan's preference for 'Breaking open' over 'The Second Sex' for the title of the women's association does not necessarily involve a rejection of Simone de Beauvoir's notion of *The Second Sex*. Rather, 'Breaking open' (*Pokai* in Chinese) literally means 'breaks into two halves', signifying the author's keen desire to establish equality between women and men. The title might also allude to the Chinese philosophical principle of *yin yang*, which implies all things have a *yin* aspect and a *yang* aspect, contradictory yet complementary at the same time. With the ambitious aim to 'shatter the long-standing, well-established, and exclusively male rules and standards in life, culture and art' (Chen 2002: 236),[22] the establishment of such an association endeavours to pursue true gender equality and gender-transcendent consciousness without boasting of 'feminism'. Similarly, Woolf also contends in *Three Guineas* that the term 'feminist', which is 'a vicious and corrupt word that has done much harm in its day and it now obsolete', should be discarded and destroyed for its narrow and limited definition alienates men from fighting for the same cause (*AROO/TG*: 302).

Dai Er reflects upon her abandonment of socially prescribed gender construction in favor of a female companion:

> Later, I discarded the gender specification; I believed that the concept that a woman can or must only expect a man is an age-old but compulsory convention. To survive in this antagonistic world, a woman must choose a man to join the 'majority' to become 'normal', which is a choiceless choice. However, I don't think so. I prefer to put a person's gender behind their quality. . . . I think that an affinity between two people does not only exist between a man and a woman, but that it is indeed also a kind of latent vital potential that has long been neglected amongst us women. (Chen 2002: 235)[23]

When there are no longer institutional pressures on women to be heterosexual, when gender is not the first and foremost concern in interpersonal relationships, women will finally be free to develop close and sustainable attachments with other women, which might include sexual intimacy.

Dai Er comments upon the intimate relationship between herself and Yun Nan: 'I believe that the sisterhood between me and Yun Nan is of a higher and more intense quality than that of love' (Chen 2002: 239).[24] Yun Nan agrees that 'there is no gender question when we are together' (2002: 242)[25] and then continues to say that 'that question . . . seems to have retreated to an unimportant position' (2002: 242).[26] To test their friendship, Dai Er hypothetically asks Yun Nan what she would do if there were a plane crash. Yun Nan answers that 'I would say I love you very much'[27] and 'I would kiss you' (2002: 250).[28] It is a sexual kiss, which is subtly implied by Dai Er who says, 'There are no shackles for people at our age. This is a time of glass, as many rules will be demolished by the footsteps marching forward' (2002: 250),[29] which suggests the topic borders on the then still sensitive issue of homosexuality. They later reach a tacit agreement that 'only women most understand and sympathise with women' (2002: 254).[30] Chen Ran depicts a clear preference for same-sex rapport, trust and empathy over heterosexual relationships by suggesting that '[t]he closeness between a same-sex couple is a kind of spiritual relationship, which is more concise and simpler' (Chen et al. 1996: 92).[31] Similarly, Chen Ran contends that

> emotional love can also originate between the same sex as well as between the opposite sexes. . . . Sometimes it is easier for a same-sex couple to reach a tacit understanding, following the same natural laws as the fish to water, and humankind to air. (Chen 1994: 106)[32]

In Chen Ran's view, women possess the tendency to nurture emotional and spiritual love between women, which is of a higher quality than physical and sexual love. Her concept of sisterly affection indicates that there is more affinity between women than between man and woman, which can be regarded as another form of long-term relationship with vital potential. Chen Ran addresses questions of female–female intimacy and partnership, female sexuality and desire that are related to a modern Chinese woman's sexual awakening and self-identity. 'Breaking open' and *A Private Life* portray modern Chinese intellectual women's sexuality and identity and serve as an urgent call for the legitimacy of women's emotional and physical sexual desires, which are incompatible with traditional heterosexual and coercive reproduction norms.

A Private Life also illustrates gender-transcendent consciousness in the form of sisterly affection. The woman protagonist Ni Niuniu, whose given name means 'stubborn', forms an emotional, physical, intellectual and intimate relationship with Widow He,[33] with whom she finds solace, security and strength as she is undergoing turbulent life changes. Ni Niuniu's intimate relationship with He is evident in Ni's contemplation:

> [Widow He] . . . was a light in my otherwise dull inner life. In her I found a warm and amiable friend, a special woman who could be my surrogate mother. When she was by my side, even if she was silent, a warm feeling of safety, softness and gentleness enclosed me. It was a kind of intangible light that enveloped and brightened my skin. It was powerful enough to transcend the barriers between us. (1996: 98–9)[34]

Ni Niuniu often goes to Widow He for consolation and peace of mind, especially after experiencing emotional turmoil and suffering due to oppression by her father. Ni regards Widow He as a trusted friend and a surrogate mother, in whom she not only finds care, love and understanding but also relief and sympathy. Ni develops close ties with Widow He, who is a key figure in Ni's extended female network, aiding Ni in 'her struggle for identity and autonomy' (Smith-Rosenberg 1975: 17). Ni even regards Widow He as an accomplice, a partner in her own development of her self.

One highly symbolic incident in the novel occurs when Ni rebelliously cuts one of the legs off of her father's cherished grey pants to show her intense resentment against his dominance. Ni's mother (both the father and the mother are unnamed) is ordinarily gentle, submissive and fearful in the face of her violent and overbearing husband. However, she screams when she sees Ni cut off the leg of her father's pants, but she does not blame Ni for her action because both women are victims of the father's brutality and tyranny. The pants incident provokes a big fight between Ni's parents. Nevertheless, Ni's mother shows full understanding towards her daughter as if this incident had never happened. She spends the whole day repairing the pants, but by using black stitches she makes the repair prominently visible. Though Ni's mother tries hard to appease and please her husband, her efforts seem futile.

After the incident, unable to find an outlet to release the complicated emotions and feelings of abandonment inside her after her defiant behaviour, Ni enters the home of Widow He, whose 'wonderful, enchanting voice' has a magical effect upon Ni's turbulent inner world. In Widow He's arms, Ni's 'perturbation began to subside' and 'an unknown feeling of complicity arose from the soles of [her] feet' (1996: 49).[35] Later, when Ni breaks up with her first boyfriend Yin Nan, she is eager to share her deeply tense emotions with Widow He. She knows that 'no matter what happens, as long as she can turn to Widow He, all her agitation and confusion will disappear. Widow He is forever a most intimate and tacit accomplice' (Chen 1996: 173).[36]

Widow He is not a realistic figure; she is a too-perfect embodiment of womanhood. Chen Ran remarks in an interview: 'The most ideal woman is Widow He in *A Private Life*' (2000: 9).[37] Widow He's sudden and tragic death has a traumatic impact on Ni, whose body and mind are almost paralysed for months (Chen 1996: 216). Whether alive or dead, Widow He holds a central position in Ni's heart. She reflects upon Widow He's particular position in her life by saying that 'Widow He is a house made of mirrors in my heart. I can summon myself from any angle' (Chen 1996: 154).[38]

For Chen Ran's women characters, their genuine love derives from genuine appreciation and mutual understanding, as well as 'woman-identified experience', which could be extended to 'the sharing of a rich inner life, the bonding against male tyranny, the giving and receiving of practical and political support' (Rich 1980: 648–9). According to Chen Ran, gender-transcendent consciousness shatters the bondage of conventional sexual relationships and emancipates women from the reproductive values closely associated with heterosexuality and traditional gender norms. Women are therefore enabled to choose love 'according to their psychological tendencies and constructions' (1994: 107).[39] This type of relationship is centred on a union of the physical and emotional love that transcends the prescribed gender roles and concomitant stereotypes. According to Chen Ran, it is during women's same-sex friendships that they attain emotional and sexual awakening, which also marks an emotional journey to womanhood, women's self-realisation and rebirth.

A Private Life is also about Ni Niuniu's progress towards emotional and sexual awakening as she matures from a girl to a woman. Chen Ran aims to reveal that, for women, sexual desire is a breakthrough in achieving women's self-identity. Ni frequently examines her body and often in the mirror. Towards the end of the novel, Ni's narcissistic infatuation with her own body in the bathtub is a plain description of a woman who can only retreat into her inner world for strength and identity:

> There is a large mirror opposite the bathtub. From the mirror, I saw a young woman lying on her side in a small swaying white boat. I looked at her. The lines on her face were very soft, her skin was smooth and delicate, with a head of soft hair draping above the nape of her neck, like a cluster of thick, round, and fragrant flowers floating over the pool. The outline of her body was buried in a bundle of slender quilts in the water, light and warmth. (1996: 264)[40]

It is interesting to note that in this mirror scene, Ni finds the reflection of herself a stranger, which suggests her body is seen as an entity separate from her mind. The mirror allows her to view and examine her body from an observer's perspective. Fantasising herself first as Window He and then Yin Nan, Ni masturbates. Ni's sexual self-exploration and satisfaction suggests the fluidity of female sexuality and the possibility of female sexual self-fulfilment without men's presence.

Chen Ran calls for a type of female discourse that is expressive of women's unique bodies, experiences and thoughts. Her writing of the female body and experience echoes Hélène Cixous's *écriture féminine*. Cixous advocates for writing that aims to resist the dominant patriarchal order: 'Write your self. Your body must be heard. Only then will the immense resources of the unconscious spring forth' (1976: 880). For Cixous as well as Chen Ran, the female body becomes a powerful site of resistance to the dominant male discourse. Ni Niuniu cries out loudly that 'only my body itself is my language' (Chen 1996: 154).[41]

In Chen Ran's individualised writing, her female characters begin to assume agency over their bodies, of which they are now the owners. Their examination of their bodies is a starting point for a narrative that is distinct from the male writer's description of female bodies. This process is also one of creating a self-identity that has long been alienated from their selves. By depicting female bodies and their sexual desires, Chen Ran's female characters emancipate their bodies, which is a critical step in their sexual awakening.

Conclusion

Not only does Chen Ran detail the female body with particular care in her works, but she also presents female sexual desires. Women's self-reflexive appreciation of their own bodies is an important step by which they acquire female consciousness and assert agency over their female bodies, which have long been defined and controlled by men. In the short novel *A Toast to the Past*, Chen Ran employs the expressions 'the two beautiful flowers on her chest' (2001: 18) and 'the little bird that sings' (2001: 61) to describe metaphorically the young female protagonist Xiao Meng's sexual desires and pleasures.

In *A Room of One's Own*, Woolf pays close attention to women's, particularly educated women's, questioning of the traditional and entrenched thoughts of marriage as well as their struggles to break free of the society's expectation of them to be 'angels in the house'. Six decades later in a foreign land, the influential contemporary Chinese woman writer Chen Ran, who is keenly appreciative of Woolf's talent and insight as a champion of feminist ideas, becomes Woolf's devoted disciple to pursue a distinct voice that stands out bravely from the crowd. Chen Ran's notion of gender-transcendent consciousness is a localised manifestation of Woolf's concept of 'androgyny'. Through sisterly affection, Chen Ran's bold exploration of female sensual experiences revolts against the dominant discourse and patriarchal values. Chen Ran asserts that it 'is precisely the most personal and individual that is the most human' (Chen 2000: 181).[42] By writing about female issues, Chen Ran is also addressing the problems common to contemporary Chinese women. It is such a strong, articulate voice. It is the voice of a woman, by a woman, and for a woman. It is a voice of women's own – it is this echo that strongly connects the two women writers irrespective of their time and space.

Notes

1. Since the 1920s, when Woolf was first introduced to China, there have been more than 1,500 articles and theses published on Woolf, according to the China National Knowledge Infrastructure Database (CNKI) (n.d.), and around thirty monographs have been published on her. Through a study of Woolf's concept of 'other sexes', Lv Hongling contends that Woolf's understanding of the multiple features of gender and identity deconstructs the dualistic view of gender and reveals the complexity of identity (Lv 2005). Qi Liang maintains that the hybridity of Woolf's class and race identity weakens her critique of the imperialist national identity, which is featured with both 'a resistance to and a collaboration with imperialism' (2012: 76). Regarding the translations of Woolf works, her short story 'The mark on the wall' was translated by Ye Gongchao in 1932. The year 1935 saw the translation of *Flush* by Shi Pu. In the 1940s, *To the Lighthouse* and *A Room of One's Own* were translated by Xie Qingyao and Wang Huan respectively. Since the 1980s, more and better translations of Woolf works appeared. In 2001, four volumes of Woolf's *Collected Essays* were published by China Social Sciences Press. In 2003, twelve volumes of *Woolf Collected Works*, which include all Woolf's novels and most essays, were published by the People's Literature Publishing House.
2. Other modern and contemporary Chinese women writers, such as Tie Ning (1957–), Zhao Mei (1954–), Xu Xiaobin (1953–) and Hai Nan (1962–) have been influenced by Woolf. Tie Ning is the current chair of the China Federation of Literature and Art and chair of the Chinese Writers Association.
3. Popular highbrow literature in China in the 1990s focuses on ordinary everyday life, emphasises literature's function as entertainment and has a strong tendency to marketisation.
4. Apart from *A Room of One's Own*, it is difficult to identify other works by Woolf that Chen Ran has read. It is likely that she has read *To the Lighthouse*, *Mrs Dalloway* and some of Woolf's essays.
5. All works by Chen Ran cited in this chapter are written in Chinese. All translations are mine.这是我十分欣赏的女性,我读过她不少笔记、文章都非常漂亮,特别是我们共同的女性心理角度,使我们的许多想法格外贴近。比如,她说,一个女人如果要写小说,一定要有一些钱,有一间自己的屋子。
6. 我所理解的"屋子",已经不仅仅是屋子,而是一种安全,一种自立,一种生活的保障。
7. 拥有一间如伍尔夫所说的"自己的屋子",用来读书、写作和完成我每日必须的大脑与心的交谈...
8. Brenda Helt holds a different perspective of Woolf's idea of androgyny. In her view, Woolf first proposes the notion of androgyny but later gives it up because it is impossible for an artist to attain an androgynous mind 'precisely because of the social realities accompanying embodiment' (2016: 120). According to Helt, though it is 'currently impossible for women' to attain the state of androgyny since it is impossible for their mind to remain 'undivided', it

is possible for their mind to 'range freely and contemplate openly *all* desires, even those that are socially proscribed' to attain 'full intellectual and artistic freedom' (2016: 126, 127), which is the ultimate goal of an artist's androgynous state of mind. It is important to note that it is Woolf's early perspective on androgyny that appeals to Chen Ran, not the latter.

9. This quotation originally appears in her essay 'Firecrackers broke winter dreams' which appears in *Home Alone* (Chen 1998): 沃尔夫在《一间自己的屋子》里，曾借用柯勒瑞治的话说："伟大的脑子是半雌半雄的。"我认为，这话的意思不仅仅指一个作家只有把男性和女性两股力量融洽地在精神上结合在一起，才能毫无隔膜地把情感与思想传达得炉火纯青的完整。此外，我以为还有另外一层意思：一个具有伟大人格力量的人，往往首先是脱离了性别来看待他人的本质的。欣赏一个人的时候，往往是无性的。单纯地只看到那是一个女性或那是一个男性，未免肤浅。
10. 真正的爱超于性别之上，就像纯粹的文学艺术超于政治而独立。
11. 爱情、情爱与做爱、性爱是两回事。情爱远远高于性爱，它包含了心灵、思想以及肉体。这才是人类情感中最令人动心不已的东西，是真正能使一个现代女性全身心激动的东西。
12. 伍尔夫曾在《一间自己的屋子》里提到"伟大的脑子是半雌半雄的"，....这并不意味着缩减或隐藏我们作为女性的特质，恰恰相反，我以为这是更加扩展和光大了我们作为女性的荣光。
13. 我的想法是：真正的爱超于性别之上....是否可以这样理解：越是思想深刻的女性和男性，越是难于找到对等的异性伴侣。
14. 人类有权利按自身的心理倾向和构造来选择自己的爱情。这才是真正的人道主义！这才是真正符合人性的东西！
15. 真正优秀的艺术家、文学家，不会轻易被异性或同性所迷惑，她（他）有自己内心的情感追求和独立的艺术探索。
16. 异性爱霸权地位终将崩溃，从废墟上将升起超性别意识。
17. 我不再在乎男女性别，也不在乎身边"少数"，而且并不以为"异常"。
18. Chen Ran travelled to Australia, UK and Germany in the 1980s. She is well read in Western classics, such as those by Jorge Luis Borges, James Joyce, Vladimir Nabokov, Marguerite Yourcenar, William Faulkner, Michel de Montaigne, Søren Kierkegaard, Ludwig Wittgenstein and Carl Jung.
19. 我理解、尊重并维护世界上所有文明的同性恋的权利，正如同我维护所有文明的异性恋权利一样。
20. 这是中国女性主义文学的真正的宣言。
21. 性别意识的淡化应该说是人类文明的一种进步。我们首先是一个人，然后才是一个女人。...性沟，是未来人类最大的争战。
22. 打破源远流长的纯粹由男人为这个世界建构起来的一统天下的生活、文化以及艺术的规范和准则。
23. 后来我放弃了性别要求，我以为作为一个女人只能或者必须期待一个男人这个观念，无非是几千年遗传下来的约定俗成的带有强制性的习惯，为了在这个充满对抗性的世界生存下去，一个女人必须选择一个男人，以加入"大多数"成为"正常"，这是一种别无选择的选择。但是，我并不以为然，我更愿意把一个人的性别放在他（她）本身的质量后边...我觉得人与人之间的亲和力，不仅体现在男人与女人之间，它其实也是我们女人之间长久以来被荒废了的一种生命力潜能。
24. 相信我和我的朋友殒楠之间的姐妹情谊一点不低于爱情的质量。
25. ...我们在一起，好像都没有性别了。
26. 那个问题...好像已退居到不重要的地位。
27. 我会说我很爱你。
28. 我会亲你。
29. 活到我们这个份上，的确已没有什么是禁锢了，这是一个玻璃的时代，许多规则肯定会不断地被向前的脚步声噼噼啪啪地捣毁。
30. 只有女人最懂得女人，最怜惜女人。

31. 同性之间的亲近是一种心灵的关系，更简洁、更单纯一些。
32. 情爱来自何方？异性之间肯定会有，同性之间也可能出现。．．．．有时同性比异性更容易构成理解和默契，顺乎天性，自然而然，就像水理解鱼，空气理解人类一样。
33. 'He' is the widow's family name.
34. 禾．．．是我乏味的内心生活的一种光亮，她使我在这个世界上找到了一个温暖可亲的朋友，一个可以取代我母亲的特殊的女人。只要她在我身边，即使她不说话，所有的安全、柔软与温馨的感觉，都会向我围拢过来，那感觉是一种无形的光线，覆盖或者辐射在我的皮肤上。而且，这种光线的力量可以穿越我们俩之间的障碍物．．．
35. 忐忑便一步步安谧宁静下来。从我的脚底升起一股不知从何而来的与禾的共谋感。
36. 无论什么事，只要能够与她分担，所有的激动或困惑都会烟消云散。禾在我的心目中永远是一个心照不宣的最亲密的共谋者。
37. 最理想的女性是我的小说《私人生活》里的禾寡妇。
38. 禾，才是属于我内心的一座用镜子做成的房子，我在其中无论从哪一个角度，都可以照见自己。
39. 按自身的心理倾向和构造。
40. 浴缸的对面是一扇大镜子，从镜子中我看见一个年轻的女子正侧卧在一只摇荡的小白船上，我望着她，她脸上的线条十分柔和，皮肤光洁而细嫩，一头松软的头发蓬在后颈上方，像是漂浮在水池里的一簇浓艳浑圆的花朵，芬芳四散。身体的轮廓掩埋在水波一般的绸面被子里纤纤的一束，轻盈而温馨。
41. 只有我的身体本身是我的语言。
42. 恰恰是最个人的才是最为人类的。

Bibliography

Chen, R. (1994), 'Chaoxingbie yishi yu wode chuangzuo' 超性别意识与我的创作 [Gender-transcendent consciousness and my creative writing], *Bell Mountain*, 93, pp. 105–7.

Chen, R. (1995), *Qianxing Yishi* 潜性逸事 [The Potential Anecdote], Shijiazhuang: Hebei Education Press.

Chen, R. (1996), *Siren shenghuo* 私人生活 [A Private Life], Beijing: Writers Publishing House.

Chen, R. (1998), 'Baozhu Zasui Dongmeng' 爆竹炸碎冬梦 [Firecrackers broke winter dreams], in R. Chen, *Duzi zaijia* 独自在家 [Home Alone], Xi'An: Shanxi Normal University Press, pp. 33–43.

Chen, R. (2000), *Buke yanshuo* 不可言说 [Ineffable], Beijing: Writers Publishing House.

Chen, R. (2001), 'Yu wangshi ganbei' 与往事干杯 [A toast to the past], in R. Chen, *A Toast to the Past*, Beijing: Writers Publishing House, pp. 1–90.

Chen, R. (2002), 'Pokai' 破开 [Breaking open], in R. Chen, *Acciaccatura*, Beijing: New World Press, pp. 227–59.

Chen, R. (2004), *A Private Life*, trans. J. Howard-Gibbon, New York: Columbia University Press.

Chen, R. and S. Lin (2007), 'Chen Ran: Pokai? Yihuo hejie?' 陈染：破开？抑或和解？ [Chen Ran: Breaking open? Or reconciliation?], *Arts Criticism*, 3, pp. 24–7.

Chen, R., Z. Lin and H. Qi (1996), 'Nvxing geti jingyan de shuxie he chaoyue' 女性个体经验的书写和超越 [The writing and transcendence of women's personal writing], *Flower City*, 2, pp. 92–7.

Chen, R. and Xiao G. (萧刚) (1998), 'Lingyishan kaiqi de men' 另一扇开启的门 [An interview with Chen Ran – another door open], in R. Chen, *Home Alone*, Xi'An: Shanxi Normal University Press, pp. 237–64.

China National Knowledge Infrastructure Database (n.d.) Zhongguo zhiwang 中国知网, <http://www.cnki.net> (last accessed 20 June 2020).

Chinese Classification of Mental Disorders (CCMD-3) (2001), Zhongguo jingshen zhang'ai fenlei yu zhenduan biaozhun 中国精神障碍分类与诊断标准, Psychiatry Branch of the Chinese Medical Association, 3rd edn, Jinan: Shandong Science and Technology Press.

Chou, W.-S. (2001), 'Homosexuality and the cultural politics of *Tongzhi* in Chinese societies', *Journal of Homosexuality*, 40: 3–4, pp. 27–46.

Cixous, H. (1976), 'The laugh of the Medusa', trans. K. Cohen and P. Cohen, *Signs*, 1: 4, pp. 875–93.

Dai, J. (1996), 'Chen Ran: Geren he nvxing de shuxie' 陈染：个人和女性的书写 [Chen Ran: Individual and women's writing], *Contemporary Writers Review*, 13: 3, pp. 47–56.

Gan, W. (2009), 'Solitude and community: Virginia Woolf, spatial privacy and *A Room of One's Own*', *Literature and History*, 18: 1, pp. 68–80.

Goldman, J. (2007), 'The feminist criticism of Virginia Woolf', in G. Plain and S. Sellers (eds), *A History of Feminist Literary Criticism*, Cambridge: Cambridge University Press, pp. 66–84.

Helt, B. (2016), 'Passionate debates on "Odious Subjects": Bisexuality and Woolf's opposition to theories of androgyny and sexual identity', in B. Helt and M. Detloff (eds), *Queer Bloomsbury*, Edinburgh: Edinburgh University Press, pp. 114–31.

Jiang, H. (1997), 'Guanyu chaoxingbie de sikao' 关于'超性别'的思考 [On 'gender-transcendence'], *Wenyi zhengming* [Literature and Art Forum], 12: 5, pp. 25–30.

Kaivola, K. (1999), 'Revisiting Woolf's representations of androgyny: Gender, race, sexuality, and nation', *Tulsa Studies in Women's Literature*, 18: 2, pp. 235–61.

Lv, H. (2005), 'Woolf's "other sexes" and *The Waves*' 伍尔夫《海浪》中的性别与身份解读, *Foreign Literature Research* 28: 5, pp. 72–9.

Qi, L. (2012), 'Virginia Woolf's cultural imperialism' 民族身份的建构与解构－论伍尔夫的文化帝国主义, *Foreign Literatures*, 32: 2, pp. 67–76.

Rich, A. (1980), 'Compulsory heterosexuality and lesbian existence', *Signs*, 5: 4, pp. 631–60.

Rosner, V. (2005), *Modernism and the Architecture of Private Life*, New York: Columbia University Press.

Sheikh, S. B. (2018), 'The walls that emancipate: Disambiguation of the "room" in *A Room of One's Own*', *Journal of Modern Literature*, 42: 1, pp. 19–31.

Smith-Rosenberg, C. (1975), 'The female world of love and ritual: Relations between women in nineteenth-century America', *Signs*, 1: 1, pp. 1–29.

Woolf, V. (1965), 'Women novelists', in Woolf, *Contemporary Writers*, New York and London: Harvest, pp. 24–7.

Woolf, V. (1966), *The Collected Essays*, vol. 2, ed. L. Woolf, London: Hogarth Press.

Woolf, V. (1978), *The Diary of Virginia Woolf: Volume Two: 1920–1924*, ed. A. O. Bell, New York: Harcourt Brace Jovanovich.

Woolf, V. (2008 [1929/1938]), *A Room of One's Own/Three Guineas*, ed. M. Shiach, Oxford: Oxford University Press.

Wu, J. (2003), 'From "*long yang*" [male homosexuality] and "*dui shi*" [lesbianism] to Tongzhi: Homosexuality in China', *Journal of Gay & Lesbian Psychotherapy*, 7, pp. 117–43.

Zhang, Y. (1993), 'Huayu de bianzheng zhong de "hou langman": Chen Ran de xiaoshuo' 话语的辨证中的"后浪漫"－陈染的小说 [The dialectic 'post-romanticism' of discourse: On Chen Ran's fiction], *Wenyi zhengming* [Literature and Art Forum], 8: 3, pp. 50–3.

17

IN SEARCH OF SPACES OF THEIR OWN: WOOLF, FEMINISM AND WOMEN'S POETRY FROM CHINA

Justyna Jaguścik

> I want to write poetry
> I am a stubborn maker
> in my narrow room.
>
> (Wang Xiaoni 2017: 31)[1]

IN 2014 THE POET HUANG XI (1982–) published an essay that commemorated the sixteenth anniversary of the inception of the only unofficial[2] journal in the People's Republic of China (PRC) dedicated exclusively to female-authored poetry and criticism written from gender-aware or feminist positions. Huang's text opens with a long quotation from Virginia Woolf's *A Room of One's Own* that illuminates writing women's vulnerability to the influence of socio-cultural factors. The poet connected Woolf's observations to the history of female-authored poetry in China. In Huang's own words, even if almost 100 years have passed since the publication of Woolf's foundational text and women have finally entered the literary field for good, they nonetheless confront critical bias and patronising glances. Consequently, women writers have often been either ignored or essentialised by critics who see in them paragons of stereotypical feminine aesthetics (Huang 2014).

The opening of Huang's essay seems so natural because the spatial metaphor of Woolf's 'room' has accompanied the discourse of contemporary women's poetry in China from the mid-1980s. After 1976, the year of Mao Zedong's death, feminist sensibilities surfaced again[3] in literature as one of many new trends that marked the end of the aesthetic monopoly of socialist realism and revolutionary romanticism in cultural production. In the 1980s female academics began to question the real outcomes of the politics of socialist women's liberation. At the same time, a group of young female authors started experimenting with literary language in a search for a new vocabulary that would allow them to introduce their gender perspective into writing. The outburst of female creativity in literature and scholarship of the post-Mao era made it clear that while the Maoist version of the women's movement, with its core idea of liberating the female labour force, had granted women access to the workforce and public life and indeed encouraged them to enter these spheres on a previously unprecedented scale, it had never asked individuals who participated in this historical process to spontaneously express their genuine personal feelings that accompanied these revolutionary changes. Even less welcome was public critique of gendered social practices and relations.

This chapter opens with a brief outline of the journey of Woolf's writings, particularly of her *A Room of One's Own*, into twentieth-century China. It argues that shortly after the publication of the original text by Woolf, progressive intellectuals recognised its potential to inspire the local women's emancipation movement that was then already gaining momentum in China. Furthermore, it shows that *A Room of One's Own* has remained a recurrent point of reference in Chinese-language feminist theory and literature. Like no other feminist text from the West, it has influenced the language of different generations of scholars and authors in modern China.

Situating the appropriation of Woolf's ideas in the local socio-cultural context, I consider texts by female poets that echo Woolf's spatial metaphoric and her reflections on female authorship. In its concluding section the essay moves to the introduction of the independent journal *Yi* [Wings], which since 1998 has provided female poets, scholars and translators with 'a room of their own' or, in Huang Xi's words (2014), 'a utopian space' to publish and discuss their writings. This space harbours opportunities for development and cooperation that are often inaccessible to female authors in the official literary field, where the discursive power of male authors and critics remains unshaken.

Early Encounters

The birth of Chinese feminism was an 'event of global proportions' (Liu et al. 2013: 28) and the following anecdote is only one of many that demonstrate the cosmopolitan dimension intrinsic to the project of Chinese modernity. Scholars agree that Woolf's *A Room of One's Own* was for the first time discussed in China on the winter day of 17 December 1928 when the young but already well-known poet Xu Zhimo (1897–1931) gave a talk at a girl's middle school in the city of Suzhou.[4] Xu, who studied in America and Europe, was one of the chief propagators of the Anglo-American humanist tradition in Republican China (1912–49). He 'captured the hearts of his readers' (Wang D. 2011: 482) with romantic verse that fused English Romanticism and classical Chinese into a new form of vernacular poetry known in China as 'new poetry' (*xin shi*). On that day, however, Xu chose not to discuss romantic love, the all-pervasive subject that dominated large parts of cultural production of the early Republican China, but instead made female creativity and the emancipation of women the subjects of his lecture. Like many other enlightened male intellectuals of this period, Xu saw the inception of a gendered self, as well as a redefinition of gender roles, as crucial to the project of successfully imagining a modern Chinese nation.[5]

In his talk he draws upon his in-depth knowledge of English-language literature and, despite demonstrating extensive scholarship, still manages to retain a personal voice. He opens with a short paraphrase of a 'recently read essay by a famous English female novelist' (Xu 2009: 264), the author of which made two claims regarding conditions that make it possible for a woman to take up literary activities: a room and money of her own. Even though Xu does not mention the name of the 'novelist', there is no doubt that it must be Woolf.[6] Xu turns his brief summary of Woolf's essay into a point of departure for his own reflections on the necessary conditions for Chinese women's emancipation. Here Xu introduces a different train of thought from many of his counterparts who, as a rule, focus on a critique of the inferior position of women in premodern China – turning to foot-binding for the most recognisable signifier of severe restrictions put on women – and contrasting it with the progressive West. Xu, however, emphasises the recentness and incompleteness of the ongoing project of women's emancipation in the Western Hemisphere. In doing so, he foregrounds the universality of women's suffering under patriarchy and, by framing the local into a global context, encourages his young female auditors to fight for their rights and independence as English women were doing. Nevertheless, he still speaks in unison with the majority of his male contemporaries when he promotes these ideas not as ultimate goals in and of themselves but as women's particular contributions to the more general aim of accelerating social progress in China.

Xu must have been deeply impressed by Woolf's essay and while her ideas resonate throughout the entire text of his speech, the impact is most evident when it comes to the topic of female-authored literature. Significantly, in his discussion of women's writing, Xu does not simply repeat the names of writing women that appeared in Woolf's text; he also supplements her list with the names of Chinese female authors from different historical periods. Overall, Xu remains cautiously optimistic about the future progress of the women's emancipatory movement when he borrows Woolf's fictional character of Shakespeare's sister and declares that

> in the future there will be a female Shakespeare, Bacon, Aristotle, Rousseau, as there already were [female] monarchs such as Queen Elizabeth, the Empress Wu Zetian,[7] [female writers such as] the poets Browning, Rossetti, or the novelists Austen and the Brontë sisters. Even if today we do not dare to predict that one day women will finally surpass men, nevertheless we can fully trust that henceforth women's contribution to culture will grow boundlessly and nourish men's anxiety about one day being stripped of their power. (2009: 269)[8]

Only a two-month gap separates the publication of Woolf's essay in England from Xu's lecture in Suzhou. This short span demonstrates not only the poet's genuine interest and in-depth expertise in Anglophone literature but also his rare ability to create a productive dialogue with the newest literary trends from the West. From Xu's private correspondence we learn that during a short visit paid to his alma mater, the University of Cambridge, in late summer that same year, he also read Woolf's *To the Lighthouse* for the first time and was deeply moved by the new type of sensibility he found in the novel (Yang and Zhuo 2011: 112).

Xu was the first to discuss Woolf's writing in China and soon others followed his example. From 1929 onwards her works were regularly mentioned in journalistic essays and academic writing dedicated to modern English literature, and she became a household name in progressive intellectual circles. In 1932 Ye Gongchao (1904–81), another alumnus of Cambridge University, published the first Chinese translation of a Woolf story, 'The mark on the wall', appearing in the literary journal *Xinyue* [Crescent Moon].[9] Further renditions of Woolf's works followed soon after in Republican China. They mirrored the great excitement with which the literary scene welcomed the modernists' experiments with introspective narrative modes and new sensibilities. A translation of *Flush: A Biography* appeared in 1935, followed by 'Kew Gardens' (1936) and *To the Lighthouse* (1946). In 1947, nearly twenty years after Xu discussed *A Room of One's Own*, the full text was translated by the linguist Wang Huan (1915–2012) and published in Shanghai.[10]

One could say in conclusion that the eventual appearance of the formal translation of Woolf's essay marks the closure of a distinct literary epoch in China that began with the literary youths' rebellion against classical heritage and made writing in a vernacular language the vehicle of literary modernity (1915–19). This epoch was already in full bloom when Xu Zhimo delivered his enthusiastic lecture in praise of the new merits of individualism, gender equality and self-fulfilment. Nevertheless, not all his contemporaries identified with this canon of occidental modern values. On the contrary, it was propagated chiefly by members of a small group of mainly Western-educated urban bourgeoisie and as such was soon to be superseded by the Maoist vision of a very different type of new society to come.

Awakening

The establishment of the PRC in 1949 brought with it a centralisation and strict control of cultural production implemented with the help of surveillance mechanisms designed after the model of the Soviet Union. Mao Zedong, who had already formulated his programme for Chinese literature and art well ahead of his victory,[11] held writers in deep regard for their potential to take up the role of a 'cultural army' (DeMare 2015) in the revolutionary struggle. In his vision of the new society, literature and art were supposed to become parts of the war machine and target the political education of the masses, consisting of workers, peasants, soldiers and their cadres (Denton 1996: 462–84). While recent scholarship foregrounds the transnational and transcultural nature of the socialist project, its 'world-orientedness' (Volland 2017: 3) was nevertheless of a different kind than the Republican one. The collective as the agent of emancipation replaced the individual while the recently discovered female gendered self had to subordinate herself to the socialist women's movement that was orchestrated top-down by the ruling Communist Party. The aesthetic paradigm of socialist realism redefined literature as the 'creative labour of revolutionary writers . . . that shapes the raw materials found in the life of the people . . . into the ideological form of literature and art serving the masses' (Denton 1996: 472). While Western literature was not necessarily automatically banned, it simply became irrelevant to the needs of the revolutionary masses.

Consequently, translations of foreign literature from outside the socialist camp became scarce in Maoist China (1949–76) and, if published at all, they were mostly meant for internal circulation among higher party cadres. Accordingly, the only translation of Woolf's text to appear in this period was Zhu Hong's rendition of 'Mr Bennett and Mrs Brown'. It was published in the *Xiandai Ying Mei zichan jieji wenyi lilun wenxuan* [Selection of contemporary British and American bourgeois fiction and theoretical writings] in 1962, but the collection remained inaccessible to common readers (Yang and Zhuo 2011: 128).

Mao Zedong's death in 1976 concluded the Cultural Revolution and marked the beginning of a new epoch. His political successors opted for economic reforms and initiated a controlled opening to the West that put an end to the cultural autarky in China under late Mao. This long-awaited change in the political climate nourished new opportunities for aesthetic exploration and expression. Soon writers and academics left behind the aesthetic dogmas of the previous era, such as revolutionary romanticism or idealism, and published a large number of original works inspired by previously marginalised local cultural resources, as well as new and re-edited translations of Western theory and literature.

This great intellectual awakening was marked by an unusual simultaneity with which a colourful array of sometimes contradictory aesthetic trends and academic theories arrived in mainland China, be it in the original, in translation or in retellings. Not surprisingly, this post-revolutionary period has thus conventionally been referred to as 'feverish', pointing to the unusual state of agitation that intellectuals found themselves in throughout the decade of the 1980s (Wang J. 1996; Zhang X. 1997). The cultural frenzy of the 1980s brought with it an outburst of original literary works of various genres that were classified by scholars as modernist, avant-garde, nativist or feminist, to name just a few of the most widely used concepts (Chen 2009: 308–423). As this brief listing of attributes suggests, Woolf's writings were among the texts that regained favour and, again, caught the close attention of Chinese intellectuals. Since then, the perpetual flow of translations of her works has proved that this was indeed the case.

According to Gao Fen (2011), since 1979 academic interest in Woolf's texts has remained strongest within three theoretical fields of inquiry: those of literary form, the theory of fiction and feminist studies. The last one is the broadest and, particularly from the perspective of the history of Chinese gender and feminist studies, it can be claimed that Woolf's ideas had a formative influence on many of those who participated in the feminist revival of the post-Mao era. Even if the new publication of Wang Huan's translation of *A Room of One's Own* came out only in 1989, Woolf's contribution to Western feminist thought had been discussed in scholarly articles in China since 1981 (Yang L. 2009: 272). Consequently, many of her critical ideas regarding female authorship – such as 'Shakespeare's sister' (*AROO*: 70), 'a room of one's own' or 'think[ing] back through our mothers' (*AROO*: 114) – had already become common phrases to female intellectuals who came of age in that decade. Another factor also contributed significantly to the popularity of Woolf's text after it had been brought back into discussion. The ideas it presented corresponded well with the materialist outlook of many Chinese intellectuals from which the question of the existence of a certain material base as a necessary condition of female creativity could be easily comprehended. According to literary scholars (Yang L. 2009; Yang H. 2010), Woolf's famous metaphor of 'a room of one's own' turned into the inspiration and the main drive behind Chinese women's fight for an independent material and spiritual space.

Already Xu Zhimo's 1928 lecture demonstrates that Chinese intellectuals and writers have perceived Woolf's writing as potentially helpful for the articulations of local emancipatory politics. Not surprisingly, Virginia Woolf and her texts, next to the writings and life stories of Simone de Beauvoir, Sylvia Plath and Hélène Cixous,[12] figure prominently as inspirational role models for the budding feminist discourse of women's poetry in 1980s China. However, even in the case of these four authors it is impossible to claim that their works were the subject of a systematic academic inquiry in that period of intellectual upheaval. The process of translation typically resembled the mechanism of dissemination discussed in the previous section: original texts were summarised, retold to others and sometimes explained in a way that fitted the interpreters' agenda by those proficient in foreign languages, mostly by students who had experienced foreign education. At the same time, some old translations from the Republican era reappeared, closely followed by those that travelled in fragments from other parts of the Sinosphere, be it Taiwan or Hong Kong, due to the intensification of academic exchange within the region. Considering the channels through which foreign literature circulated, it is not by chance that Woolf's ideas first reverberated through creative texts by female students of the humanities from two prestigious universities in Shanghai. They were among the first groups of readers exposed to Western literature and foreign languages in the post-Mao era. Nevertheless, the impact of Western (female-authored) writing on contemporary Chinese poetry was indirect and should be understood as a broadening of the linguistic and imaginary horizon that clearly manifested itself in writings by a group of young female poets.

Zhang Zhen (1962–) and Lu Yimin (1962–) were both noticed for their poetic talent soon after they had enrolled at university, and they naturally entered unofficial poetry groups that flourished at many Chinese universities in the 1980s. Zhang, an undergraduate student in journalism, met her future husband, a Swedish visiting student, at the beginning of the 1980s in Shanghai. Soon after, the newly married couple set off on a journey to Europe. In 1983, in one of her first poems composed in Lund, Zhen imagines a female anarchist and quotes from Woolf in a premonition of the life far away from home that was ahead of her:

> Once you shouted at the centre of the market:
> as a woman, I have no country, nor religion.
> The metal ending of a policeman's baton tore at your uniform
> and little bells in your locks all shed their tears.
> Everyone could hear you. (Zhang 1998: 89)[13]

Woolf's reflections on the impossibility of female patriotism in a patriarchal state that would abandon a woman if she married a foreigner must have been an important point of reference for Zhen in the light of her then unusual situation. Her own personal decisions, for example returning to China as the wife of a Swedish diplomat or her latter pursuit of a doctorate in the United States, echo Woolf's claim that a women's country is the whole world (*TG*: 99). However, from the perspective of the history of Chinese feminism, the implications of the appearance of an anarcho-feminist figure in women's poetry go far beyond the documentation of the personal experience of a single poet. Most significantly, the poetic representation of a female anarchist creates a space for dialogue with an early twentieth-century trend in Chinese feminism, best represented by the works of He-Yin Zhen (He Zhen, 1884–c.1920), the founding editor of the first anarcho-feminist journal in the Chinese language. As this tradition was later marginalised by the national ideological project of Sino-Marxism, it is impossible that Zhang was consciously 'thinking through her mothers' when she wrote her poem.[14] On the contrary, this is another instance that shows that in the 1980s, Chinese female intellectuals had initially reconnected with feminist ideas in the course of an intense preoccupation with Western, mainly Anglophone and Francophone texts, before they began a gynocritical project of their own.

In addition, writing from a cosmopolitan, anarchist position challenges the previous local versions of feminism into a politically correct project authorised not only by the socialist state but also by many Republican intellectuals. That project was always already deeply rooted in the nationalist discourse that treated the emancipation of women as another helpful means in the struggle for the ultimate goal – the rejuvenation of the Chinese nation. Thus, the emergence of the anarcho-feminist rebel represents the search for alternatives in a feminist tradition by female intellectuals who no longer identify with the orthodox narrative that had entwined the destiny of women with that of the entire nation.

Zhang left China shortly before 1986, the year in which 'women's poetry' (*nüxing shige*) – written from a gendered point of view and often offering a feminist critique of social power relations – made a breakthrough into the official literary establishment.[15] As a matter of fact, since the beginning of the 1980s, a group of female authors, Zhang Zhen among them, had printed their works in various unofficial journals that were mostly short-lived and distributed only locally among small groups of friends. It was only in 1986 that Zhai Yongming (1955–), a young poet from the southern Sichuan province, had her works published for the first time in *Shikan* [Poetry Journal], a prestigious literary periodical of national range. Subsequently, literary critics coined the concept of 'women's poetry' in response to Zhai's official poetical debut and, soon after, it became one of the most innovative trends in Chinese avant-garde poetry of this period.

Searching for Imaginary Spaces of Their Own

Zhai Yongming and Lu Yimin were the first poets most commonly associated with the movement of women's poetry. Even though they came from different educational backgrounds and their poetic trajectories developed independently of each other,[16] they both stood at the avant-garde of budding feminist sensibilities in Chinese poetry. From a historical perspective, Zhai and Lu took on the topic of female subjectivity as it emerged at a time when previously hegemonic gender representations had become the subject of critique. Women of their generation consciously experienced the twilight of the Mao era in their youth and, as a consequence, they came of age feeling alienated from revolutionary symbolism. Neither could they relate to earlier representations of femininity nor to older female traditions in literature because these topics were marginalised in, or even entirely excluded from, the socialist literary education they received at school. As noted above the cultural opening to the West after Mao Zedong's death that incited a voracious appetite for foreign literature and translations of Western feminist texts became a point of departure for many female authors of that era. Not surprisingly, while women were searching for literary spaces of their own, Woolf's proposal became a tacit point of reference in much women's writing from that period.

Lu Yimin began writing poetry after she entered the Chinese Department of the Normal University in Shanghai. She completed her most accomplished poems between 1981 and 1993 before she gradually ceased writing for good. Critics most commonly describe her poetic style as 'elegant', 'controlled' (Cui 2015) and 'of the female gender' (Hu S. 2015). Lu's poetry is also perceived as representing a feminist or, at least, a distinctly gendered perspective, the origins of which has been traced back by commentators to the author's fondness for Woolf's writings (Hu L. 2015).

Lu's preoccupation with Woolf's ideas on women's writing is most straightforward in her only poetical manifesto: an essay that she originally wrote in 1989 for a special section dedicated to women's poetry in that year's *Shikan*. This issue is a collection of short opinion pieces by eleven female poets from different generations who all tackle the problematic omnipresence of the label 'women's poetry', the popularity of which skyrocketed between 1986 and 1989 within literary circles (Zhou 2007: 133–44). Authors invited to contribute to the section express strongly divergent opinions on the critical concept in question and, more often than not, they object to it as misleading. Some even contest the relevance of a gender-conscious perspective to the discussion of literary writing. The authors reveal their conflicted feelings towards their own position within the literary scene as they could neither fully identify with critical responses by literary authorities to their texts nor did they feel bound to any collective of female writers by virtue of their biological sex.

Lu Yimin's contribution to this discussion is entitled 'Shei neng lijie Fujiniya Wuerfu' [Who can understand Virginia Woolf?] (1989: 19–20). In this short text that considers female authorship, Lu's discussion echoes Woolf's ideas from the closing section of *A Room of One's Own*. In the poet's opinion, the crucial obstacle Chinese female authors confront is their own fear. Lu agrees with Woolf, that anxiety and a lack of gender consciousness hinder the majority of female authors from, in Woolf's words, 'writing exactly what we think' when viewing themselves in 'relation to reality' (*AROO*: 171). According to the poet, Virginia Woolf was not afraid of expressing her female point of view and other female authors should follow her example. The sad truth, Lu claims, is that many women poets often act as if they 'were afraid of Woolf's influence' (Lu 1989: 20) and the gender-conscious writing represented by her. Instead of challenging the marginalisation of women writers in literary tradition, they choose to hide behind conservative lyrical conventions of gentility and sentimentality or they narrow their focus to their personal bodily experiences. They dare neither to take critical positions nor to actively take responsibility for society or for themselves. Here, according to Lu, is how Chinese women's writing most differs from their Western counterparts: the former lags behind in terms of 'expressing critical self-consciousness, protesting against gender discrimination, discrediting opinions of women's natural weakness and sentimentality, ironising cheap romance, and opposing women who tend to sacrifice themselves or take revenge on others'[17] (Lu 1989: 20). From Lu's perspective, while the late twentieth century society promotes the ideals of gender equality and provides people with the same educational and professional opportunities, the biggest difference between female and male authors is that

> men have a clear gender consciousness and are very much aware of the privileges that have been traditionally granted to them only on the merit of their sex. Thus, male poets carry themselves with ease and full awareness of their superior position. (Lu 1989: 19)[18]

Women, on the contrary, remain bound by feelings of inferiority and, much too often, bow to their own fears.

Furthermore, Lu dismisses the biological determinism and essentialism often found not only in literary criticism but also in female-authored poetry. Consequently, Lu remains critical of the majority of female poets who, in her opinion, would rather perpetuate gender myths than courageously subvert stereotypes and experiment freely with transgressive poetic voices. According to Lu, male poets are, as a matter of fact, capable of composing verse as sentimental, refined and delicate as women's poetry and, consequently, the 'feminine style' in writing should be perceived as existing independently from the poet's actual biological sex.

In the light of Lu Yimin's contribution, one could argue that, in spite of occupying a very distant time-space, the difficulties female authors struggled with in 1980s China were not at all different from those Virginia Woolf had elaborated on in her essay. First, Chinese women poets were mostly ignorant of the existence of a female literary tradition in the past, as the names of their predecessors were marginalised in the official literary canon. Second, to express their perspective, they had first to invent a new poetical language of their own: one that would be different from the feminine style conventionally understood as gentle and weak, but that would not mimic the masculine language of power. These two conventional poetical dictions, feminine sentimentality and the masculine heroic, symbolically represent women's subordination to men in the androcentric socio-cultural order. While the first would only allow a female poet to admit that 'she is only a woman', the second would provide her no more help than showing that she is 'as good as a man' (*AROO*: 111). Chinese women poets distanced themselves from these literary conventions in their search for a language suitable for giving an account of the actual meaning of gender difference and undermining the previous ideologically overdetermined representations of femininity.

Creative Spaces of Poetic Agency

To find poetic agency and to renegotiate gender roles in the real world, Chinese women poets, starting in the late 1980s, had to set off on a journey of self-discovery and withdraw into imaginary spaces of their own. Women poets felt unfairly treated and perceived their voluntary retirement from the androcentric world as a radical negation of its social norms. Doing so would finally give them enough space for experimenting with alternative ways of expressing themselves. Consequently, one of the most common images in Chinese women's writing from the late 1980s is that of a solitary woman who enjoys the seclusion of a limited space 'of her own'.[19] In terms of novelty and its impact on poetic imaginary none of these rooms could be compared with the spatio-temporal metaphor of the 'black night' that emerged in an early text by Zhai Yongming.

Zhai originally completed the essay titled 'Black night consciousness' [Heiye de yishi] (1995) as a preface to her first series of poems entitled *Women*.[20] 'Black night', the first two characters of Chinese title of this short and obscure manifesto soon became essential to women writers who were in the process of emancipating female-authored poetry from the official literary tradition that had largely ignored their literary achievements. In 1985 Zhai imagined the black night as a women-only space, where women could learn to speak of their own experiences:

> Now is the moment when at last I've become powerful. Or perhaps I should say that now I've finally become aware of the world around me and of the implications of my place in it. An individual and universal inner consciousness – I call this Black Night Consciousness – has ordained that I be the bearer of female (*nüxing*) consciousness, beliefs, and feelings, and that I will directly take that charge upon myself, and put it into what I see as the best work I can do on behalf of that consciousness. Namely, poetry. (Zhai 2011: xiii)

According to Zhai, it was the space of a previously unmapped feminine imagination and creativity that could reveal an alternative world to the default masculine one:

> As one half of humanity, from the moment of her birth, a female faces a completely different world. Her very first glimpse of this world is of course coloured by her individual spirit and sensibility, and possibly even by a psychology of private resistance. (Zhai 2011: xiii)

In her literary debut, Zhai Yongming created an imaginary birthplace of the female consciousness of the post-Mao era.

Zhai's 'black night consciousness' was important for the consolidation of contemporary literary feminism in China for two reasons. First, it redefined the marginal position of women's poetry as a potential advantage. Being on the margins might give women a clearer vision, and they might no longer feel bound by literary conventions and taboos. Zhai turned the otherness of women's poetic imaginary into an enabling feature that could then help to question and eventually rewrite the literary tradition. Second, Zhai's writing revealed the existence of a suppressed female anger over the exclusion of female language from the official discourse that masks gender discrimination with its vocabulary of deliberate gender neutrality. Zhai describes her withdrawal into the space of the 'black night' as an important step towards female self-empowerment. Other poets took it from there and referenced imaginary spaces of female freedom and autonomy in later poems as necessary for the emergence of female creativity.

The short excerpt from Wang Xiaoni's (1955–)[21] poem quoted at very beginning of the essay points more directly to Woolf's spatial metaphoric. Here, the space desired by the female poet is no longer imaginary but literally a tiny room that belongs to the woman only. The female inhabitant of the small space feels full of creative powers, but to be able to make use of them to the utmost, she first asks her companion, perhaps her male lover, to leave her alone. The space does not belong to her from the very beginning, but has to be first reclaimed by the lyrical persona, and this only happens through certain personal sacrifices:

> I write the world
> and only then the world comes out with a lowered head,
> I write you
> and only then you take off your glasses to look at me,
> I write myself
> and see my hair pressed down under its own weight, it's time for a cut.
>
> Please twinkle your eyes
> and then don't look back and leave directly.
> I want to write poetry
> I am a stubborn maker
> in my narrow room. (Wang X. 2017: 31)[22]

Read in the most direct manner of a social commentary, this poem already offers some clues as to why, for Zhai and Wang's generation of women, the question of a space of their own was essential while the second of Woolf's conditions, a decent income, was not of similar importance. The poets discussed in these two sections grew up under the simple conditions of Maoist China, where living space was scarce and families often had to share cramped flats with others. The housing conditions were generally poor and left little privacy to individuals. At the same time, women entered the paid work force on a mass scale, so they, as a rule, had money at their own command.[23] In the post-Mao era these circumstances began to change in the course of China's socio-economic reforms and younger poets grew up in a period of gradual capitalist deregulation of state control over housing, labour and cultural production. In contrast to the generation of their mothers, they are no longer able to take a stable income for granted and have to compete for commodified living space on the growing real-estate market.

Wings: A Room of Their Own

When Zhai Yongming and others began to challenge the androcentric power structures that surrounded them, their texts met with mixed critical reactions. While some scholars admired the spirit of novelty that saturated women's poetry, others accused the authors of simply copying from the West. Furthermore, due to the focus on female bodily experience in early women's poetry, scholars often essentialised female-authored poetry as an extension of female bodily sensations.

It was not until the middle of the 1990s that the poet and scholar of Chinese literature Zhou Zan (1968–) observed that the field of official literature did not offer enough space for a systematic exploration of feminist writing. She concluded that, instead of maintaining their precarious existence on the margins of the official literary scene, female writers and critics should create an alternative literary room of their own. Subsequently, Zhou started *Wings*, the first unofficial literary journal dedicated to the discussion of women's poetry only. The first issue of the magazine was published in May 1998 in Beijing.

Wings began as an ambitious intellectual project aiming at a thorough investigation of the culturally and historically conditioned construction of the female voice in poetry. Besides featuring texts by Chinese poets, it has also introduced translations of women's poetry from other countries. The editors have actively encouraged independent scholarly exchange on the topic of women's poetry. To date, Zhou Zan remains the main driving force behind the inception of the journal, but she has also received support from Zhai Yongming, who co-edits the journal, and also from other younger poets and scholars.

The inception of *Wings* in the late 1990s may be regarded as the beginning of a new chapter in Chinese women's poetry. The journal radiated new energy as its editorial collective sought to offer a way out of a creative and theoretical impasse. In light of this point of departure, it is not surprising that in the early issues, which featured longer theoretical contributions, authors repeatedly reminded readers that women's writing is not only personal but also political, because it always targets unequal power relationships between genders. Created by academics and writers, *Wings*, as a theoretical endeavour, was inspired by Western feminist thought and Virginia Woolf figures prominently in the first issue of the journal. Zhou Zan in her programmatic 'Qianyan' [Introduction], the very first text published in *Wings*, declared the journal a 'room of our own' for female poets:

> When Virginia Woolf discerned society's impact on women's writing, from a different point of view, she actually confirmed that women have been long attracted to writing poetry. When we approach texts left to us by many talented female poets,

we should pay greatest attention to the wide range of topics that occupied them, as well as to their originality and exceptionality. Only in this way can we fully give justice to the abundance of meanings hiding in the history of literature. The beauty of modern women's poetry that we find in past and future works cannot be denied. It represents the essential power poetry has, the power to fly. Accordingly, the name we give this 'room of our own' is *Wings*. (Zhou 1998)[24]

The inspirational role Woolf's ideas played in shaping the feminist consciousness of a whole group of Chinese female poets is again confirmed in the text that closes the first issue of the journal. The poet Yu Lin (Zhang Yuling, 1975–) offers in her 'Houji' [Afterword] an explanation of the metaphorical meanings attached to the title of the journal. She argues that even if the word 'wings' originally did not carry a fixed connotation of any gender, it has since been used as a metaphor for a budding female consciousness that inspires women to transgress limitations traditionally associated with their sex. Accordingly, wings, on the one hand, symbolise the weight, or the extra burden, of gender on the lives and bodies of women. However, on the other hand, they are also a metaphor of power that allows female authors to fly away from literary conventions and overcome the limitations of a socially constructed female condition. Yu finds a suitable picture to illustrate the conflicted position that women occupy in fiction and history in the third chapter of Woolf's *A Room of One's Own*: 'It was certainly an odd monster that one made up by reading the historians first and the poets afterwards – *a worm winged like an angel*; the spirit of life and beauty in a kitchen chopping up suet' (*AROO* qtd in Yu L. 1998: 143; emphasis in original).

Female editors and poets behind *Wings* seek to empower not only female writers but also their readers and women in general. In spite of their different cultural background and literary tradition, many Chinese women can well identify with Woolf's observations on the deep chasm between male-authored representations of femininity in literature and the actual social position of women throughout history. Not only in the West but also in China, the 'woman' that emerges from historical sources is a 'queer, composite being. . . . Imaginatively she is of the highest importance; practically she is completely insignificant' (*AROO*: 66).

According to Zhou Zan and Yu Lin, the choice of 'wings' as the title of the journal represents their ambition to actively overcome the residual nature of the 'queer' position of women not only in literary circles but also, more generally, in social life as well. Interestingly, they did not consult each other when writing their programmatic pieces and the prominent position of Woolf in both of them was a sheer coincidence.[25] Zhou and Yu thought of the idea of 'a room of one's own' independently from each other as most suited to illustrating the feminist standpoint of the journal. This demonstrates that younger generations of female authors continue the dialogue with Woolf's writing and, moreover, that they appropriate her original ideas in a creative way for their own feminist purposes.

Conclusion

Virginia Woolf's texts have been a constant reference point in the literary exchange between China and the Western literary world. Even in times of greatest political restrictions, her writings did not entirely disappear and some members of the new cultural elites could read them as part of their education in the ways of the world beyond the Iron Curtain. From the very beginning, Woolf's writing travelled to China not only as the work of a gifted author but also as the words of a speaker for Western feminist thought. In both roles she proved equally inspiring to her readers who translated her ideas into Chinese literary texts and social practice. In today's China women's poetry occupies a place at the intersection of both these fields: it stands for avant-garde poetry written from a feminist standpoint. It carries with it the legacies of the inward turn of the late 1980s when female poets chose to withdraw into spaces of their own. In that moment, poets introduced a new vocabulary of private feeling and emotions, as well as of female bodily experiences, which had been excluded from Maoist literature. Later, however, these poets realised that it was time to end the self-imposed exile and turn to the social sphere. One of the reasons behind this shift of interest is that women felt left behind in the course of economic reform that since its beginning in the late 1970s wiped out some socialist guarantees such as full employment or equal pay regardless of gender. In an unexpected turn, for younger generations who come of age in the post-Mao era, having money and a room of one's own can no longer be taken for granted. Furthermore, younger generations must confront a conservative, Confucian backlash against women's emancipation. Zhai Yongming, for example, has repeatedly pointed out that current Chinese society needs feminist critique 'more than ever' due to the 'continuous existence of increasingly unfair social relations and the return of some [previously rejected] traditional views [on gender roles]' (qtd in Huang 2014).[26] In light of these changes, we can predict that throughout the twenty-first century Virginia Woolf will remain one of the most important feminist mother figures for subsequent generations of Chinese women writers.

Notes

1. *Wo yao xie shi le*
   Wo shi wo xia'ai fangjian li
   guzhi de zhizaozhe.
   我要写诗了
   我是我狭隘房间里
   固执的制造者。
   From Wang Xiaoni's poem 'Yinggai zuo yi ge zhizaozhe' [I should be a maker], first published in 1988. All translations are mine unless otherwise indicated.
2. Most widely, the term 'unofficial' (*fei guanfang* or *minjian*) indicates poetry written and disseminated independently of the publishing business that is officially administered by the state. Despite having its historical roots in the underground literary activities of the rusticated youth (*zhiqing*) during the Great Proletarian Cultural Revolution (1966–76), unofficial publishing should not be understood as necessarily dissident today. Unofficial literature covers a wide range of topics; furthermore, it relies on various channels of dissemination such as publications (recognisable by the lack of a book number but no longer inferior to official ones in terms of quality and aesthetics), readings and, the most recent development, social media and internet groups. It offers an important alternative not only to official state-controlled publishing but also to market-oriented popular content providers. The thin border between official and unofficial publishing is penetrable and many established authors reach to their readers through both channels. For more see Chapter 1 in Maghiel Van Crevel (2008).
3. The first wave of feminist writing surged in China in the 1920s. For more, see Amy D. Dooling and Kristina M. Torgesson (1998).

4. The talk was later published under the title 'Guanyu nüzi' [About women] in the literary journal *Xinyue* [Crescent Moon]; see Xu (1929). Since then, the essay has been included in several collections of Xu's works published later in the PRC. For more on Xu's 1928 lecture, see Gao (2011); Yang Lixin and Zhou Yan (2011).
5. In late nineteenth-century and early twentieth-century China the category of 'women' was an important site for the construction of the modern nation. Kang Youwei (1858–1927), Liang Qichao (1873–1929) and Chen Duxiu (1879–1942) were among the most influential male critics of the status of Chinese women. For more on the connections between women, writing and nationalism in modern China see Chapter 1 in Wendy Larson (1998).
6. Contemporary editions of Xu's essay reference directly Woolf's *A Room of One's Own* in a footnote attached to his recapitulation; see, for example, Xu (2009).
7. Wu Zetian (624–705) was the only empress in Chinese history; she rose to power during the reign of the Tang dynasty (618–907). She ruled effectively for many years, the last fifteen in her own name (690–705).
8. 'Jianglai de nüzi zi hui you tamen de Shashibiya, Peigen, Yalisiduode, Lusuo, zheng ru tamen de diwang zhong youguo Yilisabo, Wu Zetien, zai shiren zhong youguo Bailangning, Luoshadi, zai xiaoshuo zhong youguo Aosiding yu Bailongde meimei. Women suize bu gan yuyan nüxing jing keiyi wanquan chaoyue nanxing yi tian, dan women hen keyi fangxin de xiangxin cihou nüxing dui wenhua de gongxian bi xianzai zong keyi chaoguo wuliang peishu, dao nanzi yao danxin dao tade quanwei you yaodong de weixian de yi tian.'
'将来的女子自会有她们的莎士比亚、培根、亚理斯多德、卢梭，正如她们的帝王中有过依利萨伯、武则天，在诗人中有过白朗宁、罗刹蒂，在小说家中有过奥斯丁与白龙德姊妹。我们虽则不敢预言女性竟可以又完全超越男性的一天，但我们很可以放心的相信此后女性对文化的贡献比现在总可以超过无量倍数，倒男子要担心到他的权威有摇动的危险的一天。'
9. Ye Gongchao's translation appeared in 1932 in *Xinyue* [Crescent Moon].
10. For a detailed bibliography of Chinese-language translations of Woolf's works (up to 2011), see Yang Lixin (2009: 368–80) and Yang and Zhou (2011: 445–57).
11. See McDougall (1980).
12. For a detailed genealogy of the discourse of women's poetry and a discussion of its main features, see Zhang Jeanne Hong (2004). On the reception of de Beauvoir's works in China, see Dai Jinhua (2003) and Yu Zhongli (2015). For information on translations of Silvia Plath's poetry and their impact on early women's poetry, see Zhang J. H. (2004) and Jennifer Feeley (2017). The translation of Cixous's *écriture féminine* into China is discussed in Tani Barlow (2004) and Jaguścik (2018).
13. You yi ci ni dao jishi zhongyang hanguo:
nüren bu shuyu guojia he jiaohui
Nide haoyi bei jinggun shang de tieci guapo
Yi tiaotiao faliu shang man shi chuilei de lingdang
Suoyou ren dou tingjian le ni
有一次你到集市中央喊过：
女人不属于国家和教会
你的号衣被警棍上的铁刺挂破
一条条发绺上满是垂泪的铃铛
所有人都听见了你
14. Throughout the twentieth century He-Yin Zhen's contribution to feminist thinking fell into oblivion. The body of her work is given its fullest discussion in an English-language publication; see Lydia H. Liu et al. (2013).
15. Throughout the paper 'women's poetry' is used in this narrow sense as the English equivalent of *nüxing shige* and should not be confused with the entire corpus of female-authored poetry in Chinese language.

16. Zhai Yongming was born in Chengdu, Sichuan. Her education was interrupted during the Cultural Revolution and she spent time in the countryside as a rusticated youth during the 1970s. She graduated from the University of Electronic Science and Technology but quit her professional career shortly after graduation. Since then she has published several volumes of poetry and essays. Today Zhai is one of the most acclaimed Chinese poets. Lu Yimin was born in Shanghai. She became well known as a poet already during her time at university. She almost entirely stopped writing poetry in the latter half of the 1990s. Zhai and Lu began publishing poetry in the early 1980s and they were both associated with a trend that Chinese literary critics described as 'stream of consciousness' poetry (Lingenfelter 2008: 120).
17. 'Dan bing fei xiang xifang funü wenxue de shezuzhe nayang jiancha ziwo, liqing xianshi, dui shehui shang nannü bu pingdeng xianxiang zousou kangyi, dui ren wei funü nuoruo he ganqing shang shanggan de guyou xintiao you suo dihui, dui furen xiaojiemen aihao langman de jiqing you suo fengci, dui nüren ziwo xisheng huo jinxing baofu de xingwei you suo fouding.'
'但并非象西方妇女文学的涉足着那样检查自我、理清现实，对社会上男女不平等现象走索抗议，对人为妇女懦弱和感情上伤感的固有信条有所诋毁，对夫人小姐们爱好浪漫的激情有所讽刺，对女人自我牺牲或进行报复的行为有所否定。'
18. 'Nanxing shiren chongfen yishi dao ziji de xingbie yiji zhege xingbie zai chuantong yiyi shang de youyue diwei, zai shi zhong de yantan juzhi ye wu bu xianshi zhezhong youshi.'
'男性诗人充分意识到自己的性别以及这个性别在传统意义上的优越地位，在诗中的言谈举止也无不显示这种优势。'
19. For more examples, see Zhang J. H. (2004) and Wong Lisa Lai-ming (2006).
20. For an English translation of a selection of poems from Zhai Yongming's *Women*, see Zhai (2011: 2–11).
21. Wang Xiaoni shares similar generational experiences with Zhai Yongming: they both came of age during the Cultural Revolution, spent time in the countryside and were important contributors to the discourse of women's poetry in the late 1980s. In contrast to Zhai, Wang is known for her plain poetical language. For a collection of English translations of Wang's poems, see Wang X. (2014).
22. Wo xie shijie
    shijie cai ken chui tou xianxian.
    Wo xie ni
    ni cai zhaixia yanjing kan wo.
    Wo xie ziji
    toufa ya de hen di, yinggai jian le.

    Qing ni mi yixia yan
    ranhou bu yao huitou, zhijie zou yuan.
    Wo yao xie shi le
    wo shi wo xia'ai fangjien li
    guzhi de zhizaozhe.
    我写世界
    世界才肯睡着头显现。
    我写你
    你才摘下眼镜看我。
    我写自己
    头发压得很低，应该剪了。

    请你眯一下眼
    然后不要回头，直接走远。
    我要写诗了
    我是我狭隘房间里
    固执的制造者。

23. My assumptions were confirmed in personal conversation with Zhou Zan, a poet and editor of the journal *Yi* [Wings] (August 2018, Beijing). All women poets discussed in this essay received university education before they pursued professional careers, mostly in higher education and publishing. They took a regular income for granted, but they often struggled with poor conditions in student accommodations or communal housing provided by their work units.
24. 'Dang Fujiniya Wuerfu dongchale nüxing de shengcun huanjing duiyu nüxing xiezuo wenlei de yingxiang zhihou, ta shijishang shi cong ling yimian kendingle shige zhiyu nüxing chijiu de zhaohuan liliang. Jinru women yijing yongyou de yi dapi youxiu nüxing shiren de wenben zhong, tamen zai xiezuo zhong guanshe de zhuzhong mingti, qiaqia shi yi qi dutexing he jianzhi de gerenxing, huyingzhe wenxue yishu jincheng zhong fengfu de wenhuashi neihan. Yinzhi, nüxing shige de meili zai dangdai xiezuo zhong yiran he jijing chengxian de dou shi women de wenxueshi wufa guibide, shige benshen suo jubei de benzhixing de feixiang liliang. Zai zhe yi yiyi shang, women jiang zhe "yi jian wuzi" ming zhi wei "Yi".'
'当弗吉尼娅 尔夫洞察了女性的生存环境对于女性写作文类的影响之后，她实际上是从另一面肯定了诗歌之于女性持久的召唤力量。进入我们已经拥有的一大批优秀女性诗人的文本中，她们在写作中关涉的诸种命题，恰恰是以其独特性和坚执的个人性，呼应着文学艺术进程中丰富的文化史内涵。因之，女性诗歌的魅力在当代写作中已然和即将呈现的都是我们的文学史无法规避的、诗歌本身所具备的本质性的飞翔力量。在这一意义上，我们将这"一间屋子"名之为"翼"。'
25. Personal conversation with Zhou Zan (August 2018, Beijing).
26. 'Zhai Yongming shuo, youyu shehui bu gongping chixu ehua he fuxiu guannian zha fanqi, nage shidai duiyu nüxingzhuyi xiezuo de qiangdiao, dou meiyou xiang jintian zheyang poqie.'
'翟永明说，由于社会不公平持续恶化和腐朽观念渣泛起，哪个时代对于女性主义写作的强调，都没有像今天这样迫切。'

Bibliography

Barlow, T. (2004), *The Question of Women in Chinese Feminism*, Durham, NC: Duke University Press.

Chen, X. (2009), *Zhongguo dangdai wenxue zhuchao* 中国当代文学主潮 [Main Trends in Chinese Contemporary Literature], Beijing: Peking University Press.

Cui, W. (2015), 'Wenming de nü'er – guanyu Lu Yimin de shige' 文明的女儿–关于陆忆敏诗歌 [The cultivated daughter – on Lu Yimin's poetry], in Y. Lu (ed.), *Chumei ruxia: Lu Yimin shiji 1981–2010* 出梅入夏：陆忆敏诗集1981–2010 [The Rainy Season Ends with Summer: Collected Poetry by Lu Yimin, 1981–2010], Taiyuan: Northern Mountain Literature and Art Publishing House, pp. 122–41.

Dai, J. (2003), 'Traces of time: Simone de Beauvoir in China', *Bulletin de la Société Américaine de Philosophie de Langue Française*, 13: 1, pp. 177–91.

DeMare, B. J. (2015), *Mao's Cultural Army: Drama Troupes in China's Rural Revolution*, Cambridge: Cambridge University Press.

Denton, K. A. (1996), *Modern Chinese Literary Thought: Writings on Literature, 1893–1945*, Stanford, CA: Stanford University Press.

Dooling, A. D. and K. M. Torgesson (eds) (1998), *Writing Women in Modern China: An Anthology of Women's Literature from the Early Twentieth Century*, New York: Columbia University Press.

Feeley, J. (2017), 'Transforming Sylvia Plath through contemporary Chinese women's poetry', *Frontiers of Literary Study in China*, 11: 1, pp. 38–72.

Gao, F. (2011), 'Xin Zhongguo liu shi nian Wuerfu xiaoshuo yanjiu zhi kaocha yu fenxi' 新中国六十年伍尔夫小说研究之考察与分析 [Review and analyses of Woolf fiction studies in China over the past sixty years], *Journal of Zhejiang University (Humanities and Social Sciences)*, 41: 5, pp. 84–93.

Hu, L. (2015), 'Shei neng lijie Lu Yimin' 谁能理解陆忆敏 [Who can understand Lu Yimin?], in *Chumei ruxia: Lu Yimin shiji 1981–2010* 出梅入夏：陆忆敏诗集1981–2010 [The Rainy Season Ends with Summer: Collected Poetry by Lu Yimin, 1981–2010], ed. Y. Lu, Taiyuan: Northern Mountain Literature and Art Publishing House, pp. 1–6.

Hu, S. (2015), 'Ge yuan wangzhe renmen – lun Lu Yimin' 隔渊望着人们–论陆忆敏 [Looking at the humankind from the verge of an abyss – on Lu Yimin], *Chumei ruxia: Lu Yimin shiji 1981–2010* 出梅入夏：陆忆敏诗集1981–2010 [The Rainy Season Ends with Summer: Collected Poetry by Lu Yimin, 1981–2010], ed. Y. Lu, Taiyuan: Northern Mountain Literature and Art Publishing House, pp. 184–8.

Huang, X. (2014), 'Yi: Gei nüxing xiezuo yi feixiang de liliang' 翼：给女性写作以飞翔的力量 [Wings: Empowering women's writing to fly], *Nanfang dushibao wenhua fukan* [Southern Metropolis Daily, Cultural Supplement], 18 July, <https://site.douban.com/206010/widget/notes/12812056/note/374679443/> (last accessed 30 April 2019).

Jaguścik, J. (2018), 'From France to China's Internet – écriture *féminine chinoise*', in A. Malinar and S. Müller (eds), *Asia and Europe – Interconnected: Agents, Concepts, and Things*, Wiesbaden: Harrassowitz, pp. 253–78.

Larson, W. (1998), *Women and Writing in Modern China*, Stanford, CA: Stanford University Press.

Lingenfelter, A. (2008), 'Opposition and adaptation in the poetry of Zhai Yongming and Xia Yu', in C. Lupke (ed.), *New Perspectives on Contemporary Chinese Poetry*, New York: Palgrave Macmillan, pp. 105–20.

Liu, L. H., R. E. Karl and D. Ko (eds) (2013), *The Birth of Chinese Feminism: Essential Texts in Transnational History*, New York: Columbia University Press.

Lu, Y. (1989), 'Shei neng lijie Fujiniya Wuerfu' 谁能理解弗吉尼亚·伍尔夫 [Who can understand Virginia Woolf?], *Shikan* [Poetry Journal] 6, pp. 19–20.

McDougall, B. (1980), *Mao Zedong's 'Talks at the Yan'an Conference on Literature and Art': A Translation of the 1943 Text with Commentary*, Ann Arbor: University of Michigan Center for Chinese Studies.

Van Crevel, M. (2008), *Chinese Poetry in Times of Mind, Mayhem and Money*, Leiden and Boston, MA: Brill.

Volland, N. (2017), *Socialist Cosmopolitanism: The Chinese Literary Universe, 1945–65*, New York: Columbia University Press.

Wang, D. (2011), 'Chinese literature from 1841 to 1937', in K. Chang (ed.), *The Cambridge History of Chinese Literature*, vol. 2, Cambridge: Cambridge University Press, pp. 413–528.

Wang, J. (1996), *High Culture Fever: Politics, Aesthetics, and Ideology in Deng's China*, Berkeley: University of California Press.

Wang, X. (2014), *Something Crosses My Mind: Selected Poetry of Wang Xiaoni*, trans. E. Goodman, Brookline, MA: Zephyr Press.

Wang, X. (2017), *Haipa: Wang Xiaoni ji 1998–2015* 害怕：王小妮集 1998–2015 [Fear: Collected Writings by Wang Xiaoni, 1998–2015], Beijing: Writers Press.

Wong, L. L. (2006), 'Voices from a room of one's own: Examples from contemporary Chinese women's poetry', *Modern China*, 32: 3, pp. 385–408.

Woolf, V. (1929), *A Room of One's Own*, London: Hogarth Press.

Woolf, V. (2001 [1938]), *Three Guineas*, Oxford: Blackwell Publishers.

Xu, Z. (1929), 'Guanyu nüzi' 关于女子 [About women], *Xinyue* [Crescent Moon], 2: 8, pp. 21–38.

Xu, Z. (2009 [1929]), *Xu Zhimo sanwen jingxuan* 徐志摩散文精选 [Selected Prose Writings by Xu Zhimo], Wuhan: Yangtze River Art and Literature Publishing House.

Yang, H. (2010), 'Lun Wuerfu dui dangdai Zhongguo nüxing wenxue chuangzuo yingxiang' 论伍尔夫对当代中国女性文学创作影响 [Discussion of Woolf's influence on contemporary Chinese women's writing], *Journal of Zhengzhou Institute of Aeronautical Industry Management (Social Science Edition)*, 29: 6, pp. 89–90.

Yang, L. (2009), *20 shiji wentan shang de yinglun baihe: Fojiniya Wuerfu zai Zhongguo* 20 世纪文坛上的英伦百合：弗吉尼亚·伍尔夫在中国 [The Literary Lilies of the Twentieth Century: Virginia Woolf in China], Beijing: People's Publishing House.

Yang, L. and Zhuo, Y. (2011), *Wode he zai xiang ni benlai: 20 shiji yingyu nü zuojia zai Zhongguo* 我的河在向你奔来：20世纪英语女作家在中国 [My River Runs to Thee: Twentieth-Century English Women Writers in China], Nanjing: Nanjing University Press.

Yu, L. (1998), 'Houji' 后记 [Afterword], *Yi* [Wings], [Unofficial journal], 1, pp. 143–4.

Yu, Z. (2015), *Translating Feminism in China. Gender, Sexuality and Censorship*, London: Routledge.

Zhai, Y. (1995 [1985]) 'Heiye de yishi' 黑夜的意识 [Black night consciousness], in Q. Zhang (ed.), *Zhongguo xin shiqi nüxing yanjiu ziliao* 中国新时期女性研究资料 [Sources in Women's Studies from China's New Period], Jinan: Shandong Literature and Art Publishing House, pp. 70–2.

Zhai, Y. (2011), *The Changing Room: Selected Poetry of Zhai Yongming*, trans. A. Lingenfelter, Brookline, MA: Zephyr Press.

Zhang, J. H. (2004), *The Invention of a Discourse: Women's Poetry from Contemporary China*, Leiden: CNWS Publications.

Zhang, X. (1997), *Chinese Modernism in the Era of Reforms: Cultural Fever, Avant-Garde Fiction, and the New Chinese Cinema*, Durham, NC: Duke University Press.

Zhang, Z. (1998), *Meng zhong louge* 梦中楼阁 [Dream Loft], Louyang: Spring Wind Literature and Art Publishing House.

Zhou, Z. (1998), 'Qian yan' 前言 [Foreword], *Yi* [Wings], 1.

Zhou, Z. (2007), *Touguo shige xiezuo de qianwangjing* 透过诗歌写作的潜望镜 [Through the Periscope of Poetic Writing], Beijing: Social Sciences Academic Press.

18

Trans-Dialogues: Exploring Virginia Woolf's Feminist Legacy to Contemporary Polish Literature

Paulina Pająk

In Poland, Virginia Woolf has inspired the imaginations of contemporary feminist writers. In their fiction, she returns as a girl named Marianna living on the Baltic coast, becomes an incarnation of Sappho and even leads a queer afterlife as the lung of a Polish *flâneuse* in London. Woolf's works seem equally stimulating, as the authors rewrite or re-use her characters: 'Orlando' travels to Sri Lanka, a transgender monk joins a biographical wild-goose chase and 'Mrs Dalloway' hosts a farewell party in Warsaw. All these 'trans-dialogues' or transtextual encounters with Woolf have emerged in the pages of Polish authors. The aim of this chapter is to examine the significance of Woolf's legacy – as a vital part of planetary feminism[1] – to contemporary Polish feminist fiction. Twenty-first-century Polish feminism develops within transnational feminist networks, and many contemporary writers share – in Susan S. Friedman's phrase – the 'consciousness of the earth as a planet, not restricted to geopolitical formations', characteristic of planetary approaches (2018: 348). Thus, it is not only possible to trace Woolfian experiments in contemporary novels but also the presence of Woolf in recent biofictions.

Feminist rewritings of Woolf's oeuvre began to emerge after 1997, when the long-awaited publication of the first Polish translation of *A Room of One's Own*, one of the first works explicitly concerned with a gendered dimension of creativity, appeared. In the essay, Woolf shows that women need freedom to create art: both financial and intellectual freedom, which cannot be entirely stopped, even by cruel laws. As the multi-named, perambulating narrator,[2] who may be called 'Mary Beton, Mary Seton, Mary Carmichael' (*AROO*: 2), declares: 'there is no gate, no lock, no bolt that you can set upon freedom of my mind' (*AROO*: 64). At one point, while walking through the streets of London, this *flâneuse* talks with the fictitious Mary Carmichael and observes women: she is interested in their lives and seeks to render them in fiction:

> All these infinitely obscure lives remain to be recorded, I said, addressing Mary Carmichael as if she were present; and went on in thought through the streets of London feeling in imagination the pressure of dumbness, the accumulation of unrecorded life. (*AROO*: 77)

The persona searches for different kinds of roots, longing for women's heritage with a diverse 'genealogical tree', including subaltern and subversive voices. In an age of global literary networks, this dream of a feminist creative tradition has come true.

In Poland it has materialised in the works of Joanna Bator, Sylwia Chutnik, Marta Konarzewska, Renata Lis, Izabela Morska, Maria Nurowska and Olga Tokarczuk. These writers not only talk to Woolf, as her own essayistic personas were dialoguing with the multiple Marys, but also transform, rewrite and re-use her works in Central European cultural contexts. To understand the role Woolf plays in contemporary literature in Poland it will be useful, first, to reflect on her delayed reception and, second, to deploy Jessica Berman's 'trans critical optic' (2017; 2018) to read Polish textual dialogues with the writer. Berman's comparative approach allows to explore these innovative texts from transdisciplinary, transnational and transgender perspectives.

Woolf as a Feminist 'Icon' in Contemporary Poland

'As a woman, I have no country. As a woman, my country is the whole world' (*TG*: 206–7) – Woolf's proclamation in *Three Guineas* gains new meaning in the context of her increasingly global presence. Susan S. Friedman argues that Woolf embraces here 'cosmofeminism', an anarchist/pacifist perspective, 'situated in a feminist critique of the nation-state in wartime and a utopian longing for a peaceful world citizenship founded on justice and liberty' (2013: 23–4). Woolf's cosmofeminism resonates in numerous translations of her works (re)introducing feminist thought in the countries affected by political or religious regimes. It makes Woolf one of the central figures of world literature, as well as a replicable feminist 'icon', as captured by Brenda Silver, who associates Woolf's contemporary popularity with her 'uncanny ability to cross borders and reveal their arbitrary nature' (1999: 72). Analogous processes started in Poland in the mid-1990s after *Orlando* (1994) and *A Room of One's Own* (1997) were finally translated into Polish, inspiring feminist thinkers and grassroots activists. After that significant breakthrough, the popularity of Woolf's oeuvre substantially increased, as numerous publications have been translated and reissued, together with representative selections of her autobiographical writings and her hybrid fictional forms, including such major genre-fusing novels as the 'playpoem' *The Waves* (D 3: 203) or the 'play' *Between the Acts* (D 5: 356).[3]

Urszula Terentowicz-Fotyga, in the only published study of Woolf's reception in Poland from the 1920s to 2000s, tellingly titled 'From silence to a polyphony of voices', distinguishes its three phases (2002: 127–8). In the first period, which lasted until the late 1950s, Woolf remained relatively unknown, though highly valued by critics. After the end of the Second World War, Woolf was finally translated into Polish – her essay 'The patron and the crocus' was published in the magazine *Odra* in August 1945. The first Polish translation of Woolf's novels appeared in 1958, when *The Years* was published, followed by *Mrs Dalloway* and *To the Lighthouse* in the 1960s. There were further attempts at translating Woolf's essays, but they did not appear until 1977, when the collection *The Leaning Tower* won widespread critical acclaim. In the politically turbulent 1980s, *The Waves* was masterfully translated by Lech Czyżewski. Nonetheless, Woolf's feminist essays appeared only after the fall of Communism in Poland in 1989. Since the mid-1990s, more than forty of Woolf's works have been (re)published – most of them brilliantly and meticulously translated by Magdalena Heydel and Maja Lavergne.

Terentowicz-Fotyga suggests that this unexpected surge in Woolf's popularity was sparked by two simultaneous translations of *Orlando* (1994), and enhanced by Sally Potter's film adaptation (1992), as in this work 'we can find most issues that will prove crucial to Woolf's reception in the 1990s: autobiographical elements, feminist and lesbian themes and a widely defined question of transgression' (2002: 141). By contrast, Ewa Kraskowska argues that it was the publication of *A Room of One's Own* that changed the perception of Woolf, as it made her 'a canonical author in Poland', 'recognized as one of the first politically engaged feminist women writers' (2010: 2). However, it seems that Woolf has not become a traditional hypercanonical figure but rather one of the countercanonical '"contestatory" voices' (Damrosch 2006: 45), enthusiastically popularised by feminist scholars and diminished by conservative critics. For instance, when an anthology of Polish literary essays was published in 2017 by the prestigious publisher Ossolineum, the editor Jan Tomkowski neglected mentioning Woolf's essayistic oeuvre in his introduction, though 'ignoring Virginia is a feat that would not be attempted by anybody writing today about the history of essay around the world',[4] as Renata Lis ironically commented (2017a), using the author's first name to signal her own affinity with the modernist. In fact, Woolf's works have been voraciously read by feminist authors in Poland and consequently her iconic presence is visible in their writings. In contrast with numerous works on Woolf's legacy in North American and British literatures, there has been no research into Polish textual dialogues with this writer and hence this chapter seeks to fill this gap.

Why has Woolf become such an important figure for Polish feminist writers only at the turn of the twenty-first century? The first reason is her delayed reception caused by Poland's turbulent history. Some translations of Woolf's works entered Polish culture during the 'Thaw', a period following the death of Joseph Stalin and marked by a rise of civil liberties. However, few translators were able to perform such a challenging task, as many accomplished intellectuals who had introduced modernist literature into Polish culture either died during the World Wars, as did Tadeusz Boy-Żeleński (1874–1941), or were forced into immigration, as was Czesław Miłosz. Second, some intellectuals who have been engaged in popularising Woolf's oeuvre are central figures in Polish feminist culture. In fact, three feminists acted as midwives to the Polish translation of *A Room of One's Own*: Agnieszka Graff translated the essay, Renata Lis edited it and Izabela Morska wrote a foreword. Finally, the publishing company Sic!, managed by Lis and Elżbieta Czerwińska, issued the book. All of these writers frequently revisit Woolf's works in their own literary endeavours, enter into polemics with her over such issues as patriotism and transform her hybrid fiction and personal essays. Moreover, it seems that the popularity of Woolf among Polish feminist writers stems partially from the similarity between her opposition to Victorian patriarchal and capitalist society and their own resistance against a peculiar Polish mixture of radical Catholic conservatism and nationalism, manifested in 'bogoojczyźniany' ceremonies and rituals. 'Bogoojczyźniany' is an untranslatable pejorative epithet with ironic and critical overtones, which literally means 'god-and-country', but in actuality it is closer to 'jingoistic' and 'religiose', suggesting phoney patriotism and religiousness. Similar to the Western feminist thought that has become 'an inspiration that enabled Poles to think critically afresh about their own historical and psycho-cultural situation, but not as an infallible authority in itself' (Phillips 2013: 12), Woolf galvanises Polish writers and invites them into textual dialogues and experiments.

'Polish' Woolf(s) in a Trans Critical Optic

In Polish feminist literature, the most visible signs of Woolf's 'afterlives' are transtextual relations between contemporary works, numerous biographies of Woolf and her oeuvre. As a framework for my research, I apply Jessica Berman's 'trans critical optic', which is complemented with 'transtextuality' as theorised by Gérard Genette in *Palimpsests* (1997), and which is part of Rebecca L. Walkowitz's approach to translations, including her theory of 'born-translated' works (2017).

Since 2014, Berman has developed a new comparative approach that she called a 'trans critical optic' (2017; 2018). In an article titled 'Is the trans in transnational the trans in transgender?', alluding to the eponymous question of Kwame Anthony Appiah's 'Is the post- in postmodernism the post- in postcolonial?', Berman devotes her attention to a potential of the prefix 'trans' for enhancing communication across academic disciplines (transdisciplinary) and research on diverse kinds of 'texts' (transmedial). Since such an optic precludes the pairing of the prefix 'trans' with only one category of identity (transnational, transgender, etc.), Berman underlines that her perspective 'serves to decentre the "national tradition" as an object of inquiry, exploring texts in relation to other, transnational horizons of expectations, even while recognizing the importance of their local commitments' (2017: 220). Thus, a trans critical optic enables me to explore transnational, transgender and transtextual relationships between Woolf and Polish contemporary feminist authors who transform her legacy in Central European contexts.

Gérard Genette advances a broad understanding of transtextuality that encompasses 'all that sets the text in a relationship, whether obvious or concealed, with other texts' (1997: 1). In *Palimpsests*, he distinguishes five types of transtextual relationships, among which three are vital to the interpretation of Polish texts: intertextuality, paratextuality and hypertextuality.[5] Genette's definition of intertextuality is narrower than the one proposed by Julia Kristeva, who argues that 'any text is constructed as a mosaic of quotations; any text is the absorption and transformation of another' (1986: 37). Contrastingly, Genette formulates it as 'a relationship of copresence between two texts or amongst several texts: that is to say, eidetically and typically as the actual presence of one text within another' (1997: 1–2). Among various kinds of intertexts, quotations seem quintessential, since Genette defines intertextuality as practices and results of 'literal borrowing' (1997: 2). The second type of textual relations, paratextuality, comprises all 'allographic or autographic' signals, such as titles, subtitles, prefaces, forewords and notes (1997: 3). I analyse such paratextual relationships with reference to the first Polish edition of Woolf's *A Room of One's Own*. The last type, hypertextuality, creates new texts, 'hypertexts', through the intentional transformation of former texts, 'hypotexts' (Genette 1997: 5). The most complex hypertexts comprise many textual layers and create new meanings through rewritings of their hypotext(s): consequently, they resemble medieval 'palimpsests', which can reveal ancient texts obscured beneath the manuscript surface. In my analysis of Lis's *Lesbos* (2017), I attempt to undercover several layers of hypotexts hidden in its short fragment titled 'Amen' on Woolf and Jeanette Winterson.

Michał Głowiński underlines that a creative 'dialogue' emerges between a hypotext and a hypertext, allowing for different perspectives and polyphony (1986: 87). It is the polyphonic aspect of hypertextual work that draws the attention of neo-Bakhtinian feminist critics like Elaine Showalter and Patricia Yaeger, who work with Mikhail Bakhtin's theory of 'heteroglossia', or conflicting discourses, in their analysis of women's literature. As Showalter puts it, women's art is a double-voiced discourse that 'always embodies the social, literary, and cultural heritage of both the muted and the dominant' (1986: 263).[6] Such a fragmented and fractured discourse is in the core of Morska's novel *Absolutna amnezja* [Total Amnesia], in which the multi-voiced narration juxtaposes the voice of young Virginia Woolf with a depressed mother of two, a terrorist and an opera singer within just two pages (Filipiak [Morska] 2006: 205–6).[7] Yaeger claims that the polyphony of women's writing is a liberating form of resistance against patriarchal monologues, as well as the formal equivalent of diverse human experience: 'If a dominant discourse not only defines woman as *other* but becomes the source of her self-alienation, it is only in the act of appropriation that her own heteroglossia may be freed' (1984: 959). Thus, in Tokarczuk's novel *Dom dzienny, Dom nocny* (1998) (*House of Day, House of Night*, 2002) a transgender monk gains their own voice by appropriating the apocryphal story of Saint Kummernis. In this context, the polyphonic practices of Polish feminist authors who rewrite Woolf's works and biography have a liberating effect.

Translation and biofiction are two final literary endeavours that assume the utmost importance for Polish writers and could be considered Woolf's legacy to them, as she was both an author of 'auto/biografiction',[8] as well as a publisher and editor of translated books issued by the Hogarth Press.[9] Michael Lackey defines biofiction as 'literature that names its protagonist after an actual biographical figure' (2016: 4). Tracing how paradigm shifts have led to the rise of the postmodern biographical novel, he collates its diverse theories and creates a conceptual framework in relation to its fictional rather than biographical character. A similarly challenging task has been undertaken by Walkowitz who investigates the impact of translation on contemporary fiction and postulates that some literary works (particularly novels) are 'born translated', as 'they engage formally, thematically, and typographically with the theory and practice of translation. They are also self-translated: they participate from the start in several literary histories' (2017: 205). A case in point is an experimental short fiction 'Doti', written by Marta Konarzewska, in which she creates an English-Polish collage out of *The Waves*.

In my analysis of contemporary Polish feminist fiction, a particular focus will be placed on biofiction with Woolfian themes, intertextual echoes that enhance polyphonic effects, the functions of hypotexts written by Woolf in the text of Polish writers and other elements that allude to Woolf's legacy.

Woolf's Afterlives in Biofiction: Morska and Nurowska

The postmodernist rise of biofiction resulted in numerous narratives that focus on Woolf. The best known (through a film adaptation) is Michael Cunningham's *The Hours* (1998), which traces the creation of *Mrs Dalloway* and its impact on different generations of women. The novel – that opens with Woolf's drowning herself in the river Ouse – offers a vision of the artist struggling with her mental health. Cunningham rewrites Woolf's hypotext into the 1950s and 1980s landscapes, sometimes ironically, as when he turns embittered Miss Kilman into the queer activist Mary Krull, revealing unexpected similarities. Other biofictional authors include Susan Sellers exploring the relationship between Woolf and her sister in *Vanessa and Virginia* (2008), Alison Bechdel revisiting Woolf's diaries in *Are You My Mother?: A Comic Drama* (2012) that provides readers with a visualisation of the icon walking her dog in London and Maggie Gee's *Virginia Woolf in Manhattan* (2014) transporting the writer into contemporary New York and Istanbul. Similarly, Polish biofictional novels pose some challenging questions: Izabela Morska focuses on Woolf's relationship with her siblings and her life as a woman-artist in a patriarchal society while Maria Nurowska revisits *Mrs Dalloway*, gently mocking the surge in Woolf's popularity in Poland.

Morska (formerly Filipiak, 1961–), a writer and scholar, has published several books of prose, drama and poetry, as well as a monograph on postcolonial fiction, *Glorious Outlaws* (2016). She created the first Polish biofiction that (re)uses Woolf's life, entitled *Absolutna amnezja* [Total Amnesia] (1995), in which a child narrator, Marianna, speaks with different voices and travels in time. This vocal and temporal multiplicity allows Morska to explore two themes to which, as Maria Janion aptly delineates, 'European and Polish culture attaches special significance: a woman's madness and a woman's sacrifice' (2006: 320). In *Absoultna amnezja*, Morska deconstructs the myth of Iphigenia (Janion 2006: 332–40), critically examining gender oppression, power hierarchy and the absurdities of totalitarian states (Warkocki 2002: 106–7).

In her debut novel, Morska introduces Woolfian polyvocality, since she bestows on Marianna the ability to embody different perspectives. The girl gains insight into Woolf's mind while exploring the story of Woolf's half-sister Laura Stephen as a warning sign for 'rebellious women' in her school essay. Even though Morska is fully aware of the complex blended pattern of the Stephen family, as is visible in her essay 'Virginia Woolf, Orlando i stare Bloomsbury' [Virginia Woolf, Orlando and the old Bloomsbury] (Filipiak [Morska] 1998), she deliberately distorts the depiction of family relations by calling Woolf's half-brothers George and Gerald Duckworth 'Laura's brothers':

> In that future, my name is Virginia Stephen, and my sister is Vanessa Stephen. I will be a famous writer and my sister will paint. . . . [W]hen I was born, our sister Laura was separated from her siblings, because she was a poor student. And a few years later she was institutionalized, as she was a disobedient daughter. But her brothers stayed at home to torment us. Since then each of us knew what would happen if we were stupid enough to mock something that I oppose for the rest of my life. (Filipiak [Morska] 2006: 205)[10]

Explanations offered by the naive narrator inscribe the story of Laura, possibly a person on the autism spectrum, into another version of Iphigenia's sacrifice. The vicious circle of violence is unstoppable both within a family ('tormenting brothers') and on a larger societal scale ('institutionalisation'). Nonetheless, Woolf becomes here an ambiguous victim-rebel icon – haunted by sexual abuse, terrified by the prospect of being institutionalised, she spends her life opposing the unnamed patriarchal system ('something that I oppose'). For Marianna, Woolf embodies a female literary 'tradition' while also, paradoxically, she becomes the girl's 'future'.

Morska's foreword 'Własny pokój, własna twórczość' [Own room, own creativity], opening the first Polish edition of *A Room of One's Own*, offers an important context for Woolf's presence in *Absolutna amnezja*. Morska undertakes Woolfian narrative games with Polish readers, for example emphasising that the 1929 essay 'was both a unique and subversive book and its contents, which the Polish reader can easily find and perhaps, using their own mind, interpret in relation to the present, as they are still relevant' (Filipiak [Morska] 1997: 9).[11] She reverts to the question of women's creativity, perceiving it as an existential process guaranteed by personal and political liberties:

> Woolf is the closest to my heart, when she says: 'So that when I ask you to earn money and have a room of your own, I am asking you to live in the presence of reality, an invigorating life, it would appear, whether one can impart it or not'. . . . Fascinating means open. . . . Fascinating means all that has managed to melt a stiff barrier of fear. (Filipiak [Morska] 1997: 17–18)[12]

In Morska's text, the impact of translation is discernible – because the epithet 'invigorating' does not have a suitable equivalent, Graff translated this word as 'fascynujący' (fascinating). The Polish writer expresses the original in a series of parallels that broaden the meaning of 'fascinating'.

Furthermore, Morska enters into polemics with the second-wave feminist critique of Woolf's essay, succinctly captured by Kazimiera Szczuka as the fear 'whether this room of one's own is simply not a tomb, a single coffin' (2006: 22).[13] Rather, Morska juxtaposes the prison-like room of Elizabeth Barrett Browning in *Flush* and the painful 'homelessness' of many women-artists with a genuine creative freedom that enables them to transform a room into 'a railway station, a café, a lecture hall, a government headquarters, the UN building, a vast space in motion' (Filipiak [Morska] 1997: 18).[14] Morska's pretext is a tender and detailed introduction that allows Polish readers to discover some hypotexts hidden in Woolf's essay – including Radclyffe Hall's *The Well of Loneliness*, evoked by the ridiculed figures of its censors. Woolf's narrative persona asks her audience whether the magistrate, Chartres Biron, is not eavesdropping behind the curtains (*AROO*: 70) or if, by any chance, the Director of Public Prosecution, Archibald Bodkin, is not hiding in the cupboard (*AROO*: 96). Paradoxically, Morska, who 'has several biographies of Woolf' (1997: 16) on her shelves and vividly recreates the London literary scene, is not aware that Hall's novel was translated into Polish as early as 1933 (Pająk 2018). It is not surprising, as the forgotten history of Polish feminist movement and LGBTQ+ community has only started to be extensively explored at the turn of the twenty-first century.

It would seem that the bestselling writer of historical and crime novels Maria Nurowska (1944–) differs from the literary rebel Morska in all respects. Nonetheless, they both share a fascination with Woolf's life and oeuvre – clearly visible in Nurowska's novel with 'Wo(o)lfian' motives, titled *Requiem dla wilka* [Requiem for a Wolf] (2011). When answering an internet survey on 'the desks of Polish writers', Nurowska confesses that she has always wanted to create a biofiction on her 'two profound loves', Woolf and the Russian poet Marina Tsvetaeva, 'who had never met, lived in different countries, or even in different worlds. And yet, I have discovered that they have twin fates, including their childhood, artistic lives, love and death' (Nurowska 2016).[15] So far, she has not published such a work.

In *Requiem dla wilka*, Nurowska uses *Mrs Dalloway* and Quentin Bell's biography of Woolf as hypotexts. These hypotexts are read by Jerzy Glinicki, a film director, who after years of emigration comes back to Poland and settles in a mountain village. He undergoes an existential crisis and feels alienated in his 'homeland', where he complains: 'this Polish "god-and-country" air may have seeped into my lungs, I can barely breathe' (Nurowska 2011: 223).[16] In reaction, he immerses himself in various books found in a local library and a nearby bookshop. Jerzy is surprised by the rise of Woolf's popularity among her 'common readers':

> Recently I came across Virginia Woolf's *Biography* written by her cousin. I was surprised when I found such a book in a village library, but then I was truly astonished by what I heard from a librarian. . . . [Y]ou need to add yourself to a waiting list for this biography because of the huge public interest. . . . What a strange country is Poland! (Nurowska 2011: 34)[17]

Nurowska's efforts are supposed to expose Jerzy's ignorance about Woolf: he claims that he has not read any of her novels, the notation of Bell's book mistakenly suggests that it was written by Woolf and Bell is turned from a nephew into a 'cousin'.

Yet after Jerzy announces, 'On that day when Virginia Woolf with stones in her pocket entered river rapids, I reached my fourth birthday' (2011: 35),[18] Nurowska's masquerade is easy to see through, as Jerzy starts to betray a deeper knowledge of Woolf's life. First, when he discusses Woolf's farewell letter to Leonard, he does not follow Maja Lavergne's translation available in Bell's work but rather an alternative version (Nurowska 2011: 35; Bell 2004: 551). Second, while retelling the story of Woolf's sexual abuse by her half-brothers, Jerzy quotes from Woolf's letter to Ethel Smyth, in which the writer reveals that she was abused by Gerald Duckworth as a child. Here the quotation again does not follow the Polish translation of Bell's biography and is significantly longer (Nurowska 2011: 38; Bell 2004: 72). All these details suggest that the first-person narrator exceeds the character of Jerzy and has, at disposal, not only a village library but also a small collection of Woolf's works and her biographies.

In Nurowska's novel, Jerzy gradually discovers Woolf's works, identifies himself both with the writer and her character Clarissa and finally opens himself to unexpected love:

> Last night I dreamed about Mrs Dalloway. I was quarrelling with her, or maybe, I am not certain, with her creator, Virginia, with whom I have been debating for a long time. This novel is an active volcano of feelings and desires; always something flickers under the crust, something boils and falls down, but never erupts. So you wait, you reader, for the eruption, wait till the last page and stay in a strange bewilderment. (2011: 80)[19]

In this passage, Nurowska uses meta-literary strategies ('So you wait, you reader . . . '), again blurring the boundaries between auto/biography and fiction. Interestingly, even the very title of the novel *Requiem for a Wolf* is a play with the literal meaning of the surname 'Woolf', as Nurowska describes the extinction of wolves and woodlands in the Bieszczady Mountains.

'Born Translated' Collage: Konarzewska

In contrast to Nurowska's novel immersed in the local Polish context, Marta Konarzewska's (1977–) collage fiction 'Doti' (2012) on both formal and thematic levels belongs to 'born translated' literary works, re-using literary translations and inspired by the prospect of its simultaneous publication in Polish and English. This bilingual Polish–English text renders the synesthetic experience of London, combining British music and literary intertexts borrowed from Woolf. Konarzewska is a writer and journalist who has been engaged in many feminist and queer projects. After she came out as a lesbian by sending an open letter to the mass-circulation daily *Gazeta Wyborcza* in 2010, she lost her job as a teacher in a secondary school. In that same year she published, together with the journalist Piotr Pacewicz, the volume *Zakazane miłości. Seksualność i inne tabu* [Forbidden Loves. Sexuality and Other Taboos], a collection of reportage on LGBTQ+ people. Konarzewska is currently best known for her film scripts *Włast* and *Nina* (2018).

In the years 2009–12, Konarzewska was an editor of *Furia* (Fury), announced as 'a feminist-lesbian irregularzine'. The magazine was shaped by the editor-in-chief Anna Laszuk (1969–2012) and was characterised by its irregular frequency, a strikingly modern design and high expectations for both authors and readers. In the last issue of *Furia* (2012), with the theme of 'Queer dada!' running through all texts, Konarzewska published excerpts of her work-in-progress with a working title 'Dziewczyny z zawzięcia' [Girls by persistence]. One of these texts, titled 'Doti', is a postmodern medley, in which the writer renders Doti's experience of London, infiltrated through alternative rock music and Woolf's writing. It seems that Konarzewska was inspired by the forthcoming English issue of *Furia*.

The text opens with the narrator Doti, woken in the morning by the voices of her friends Angela and George; all three are hungover after being drugged in the club the night before. Readers soon learn that this is the last day of Doti's stay in London, as she is flying back to Warsaw the following day. Konarzewska's narrator bids farewell to the city, following the footsteps of Woolf's Clarissa Dalloway (the surname is misspelled, ironically suggesting the word 'doll'), which is signalled with laconic English–Polish phrases: 'Flowers, said Mrs Dolloway, flowers', and 'London, said Mrs Dolloway, London' (2012: 95).[20] The collage story renders the fragmentary nature of perception by juxtaposing Doti's experience of London with her memories of a relationship with her girlfriend Bee and brutal self-harm rituals, as well as intertextual elements, ranging from performative impressions of music videos to quotations from Woolf's works. The story reaches its climax in an embodiment of artistic liberty:

> The city pounds, pulsates, I breathe. I am walking. Walking. I do not need to gasp for air any more. I breathe with my whole body, I breathe Suede, I breathe Verve, I breathe Woolf, whom I carry like a lung, I breathe with the whole body of London. I breathe. I breathe. (Konarzewska 2012: 96)[21]

Here Woolf, mixed with alternative British music, leads a queer afterlife and becomes the lung of a narrative persona, enabling breathing and bringing much needed creative freedom to a Polish lesbian/queer writer.

Doti performs as a Woolfian *flâneuse*, and so accordingly Konarzewska incorporates fragments of *Mrs Dalloway* and *The Waves* into the text. Following Woolf's search for patterns in the ordinary experience, Doti buys a random book in a second-hand bookstore; not surprisingly, it turns out to be written by Woolf. In the final part of the story, Doti travels by underground to Bloomsbury Square and then reads her new book while sitting on a bench among trees and 'swallow[ing] the words like cool cherries' (Konarzewska 2012: 97):[22]

> [c] 'Those are white words', said Susan, 'like stones one picks up by the seashore'.
> 'They flick their tails right and left as I speak them', said Bernard . . .
> 'Those are yellow words, those are fiery words', said Jinny.
> [a] 'Stones are cold to my feet', said Neville.
> 'The back of my hand burns', said Jinny.
> [b] 'Run!' said Bernard. 'Run! . . . ' (Konarzewska 2012: 97; W: 5, 11, 14)[23]

Konarzewska cuts three excerpts (marked as c, a, b) from the Polish translation of Woolf's *The Waves* and then alters their original order, as in the novel they followed the a-b-c pattern, thus creating an intertextual collage within a larger Dadaistic collage of her prose. If her character Doti is in raptures over Woolf's fiction, Konarzewska manages to turn this very feeling into creating another (inter)textual world.

Trans/forming Woolf: Bator and Chutnik

Woolf's works offer inspiration to writers who question gender binarism or adopt a non-religious perspective – as in hypertexts created by Joanna Bator in *Wyspa Łza* [Isle Tear] (2015) and Sylwia Chutnik in *Cwaniary* [Sly Women] (2012). Nevertheless, their writings are also inspired by the socio-political contexts of feminism in Poland.

Agnieszka Graff, one of the leading Polish feminist scholars and activists, as well as the translator of Woolf's *A Room of One's Own*, argues that feminism in Poland falls outside the widely accepted 'waves' chronology: feminists fight for the 'second wave' demands, such as reproductive rights and workplace equality, but they use ironic and subversive camp strategies associated with the third wave. Polish feminism can be characterised by a series of paradoxes, since it

> began its growth by denying its own existence; it uses third wave tactics to achieve goals typically associated with the second wave of feminism; it exists in a cultural climate of backlash – but this backlash was not preceded by any feminist gains. (Graff 2003: 114)

Graff's bitter commentary casts some light on Woolf's popularity among contemporary writers. In the 2000s, reading Woolf offered Polish feminists a language and arguments to discuss the questions of gender, both in literary works and in public life. That is why Graff re-uses Woolf's *Orlando* and Sally Potter's film adaptation (1992) in her 2001 essay collection *Świat bez kobiet* [A World without Women] to explore an androgynous mind, same-sex unions and cross-gender identification: '*Orlando* – both the text, and the film – is a proposal for such an aesthetics and such an erotica, in which gender is mutable, temporary and misleading – and that makes it so attractive' (2008: 216).[24] Thirteen years later, commenting on her use of *Orlando*, Graff self-ironically states that her essay 'was an escape into literature' (2014: 207) and 'that is why in that book Orlando plays a gay, a lesbian and a transsexual – and this text was not political but rather poetic' (2014: 320).[25] Regardless of Graff's current dismissal of her essay, *Świat bez kobiet* has introduced a new generation of Poles to feminist views. In the 2000s, 'Orlando' became a part of cultural code on LGBTQ+ themes and, as such, it enters Joanna Bator's mock-reportage *Wyspa Łza* [Isle Tear] (2015).

Bator (1968–) is a writer and journalist who in 2013 won the prestigious Polish award Nike for her novel *Ciemno, prawie noc* [Dark, Almost Night] (2012). In *Wyspa Łza*, she alludes to works ranging from Woolf's *Orlando* through Potter's adaptation to Graff's hypertext on them. Bator borrows Orlando, a symbol of never-ending transformation, and her new Orlando closely resembles Tilda Swinton (the actor in Sally Potter's adaptation) and is the narrator's soulmate, a leftist intellectual:

> We say with Orlando: Barthes, Lacan, Mulvey, Žižek, like treasure hunters, who were digging the potato field behind my home in Warsaw. And when we found the common ground, we exchanged the stories about the childhood, parents, loves. . . . Lacanian therapy did not help him, maybe because the therapist was virtually silent. But the silence has made the film critic have gay dreams, like in a movie. Orlando is looking for himself and eating papayas. (Bator 2015: 235–6)[26]

In Bator's novel a re-used figure is brought into a contemporary landscape, similar to Cunningham's *The Hours*, though without the complexity of the latter.

Since its first translation into Polish in 1994, sixty-six years after its first publication, *Orlando* has captivated the imagination not only of writers like Bator but also of feminist common readers. This novel appears as the first on the shortlist of Woolf's most important works included in a review of *Jacob's Room* written by Sylwia Chutnik (1979–), another Polish author inspired by Woolf's artistic endeavour:

> I will never stop admiring Virginia Woolf. . . . For my generation of thirty-year-old feminists, Woolf was one of the most important teachers. She wrote, among other things, about an androgynous character (*Orlando*) that surpasses dull sexual dualism. She shared with us stream of consciousness (*The Waves*). And finally, she gave us *A Room of One's Own* – that is, a possibility of being an independent woman artist without feelings of guilt and shame. (Chutnik 2009)[27]

She refers to Woolf as a founding mother of feminist literary tradition; and not surprisingly, Woolf's formal and thematic legacy is visible in Chutnik's writing. A journalist and author of several novels, Chutnik is also the president of the MaMa Foundation, promoting mothers' rights. She has mastered Woolfian stream of consciousness, characterised by associations and synaesthesia.

In Chutnik's picaresque novel *Cwaniary* [Sly Women] (2012), female protagonists combine their efforts against cruel real estate developers to reclaim Warsaw. In the same way that *Mrs Dalloway* is a hymn to London, *Cwaniary* pays tribute to Warsaw, the city swept away during the Second World War and painstakingly rebuilt for many decades. One of central characters is Bronka, who, like Clarissa, wants to host a grand party. Initially, Woolf planned that the title character of her novel would commit suicide just after the gathering. Later that theme was developed into the tragic death of an ex-soldier, to whom Clarissa responds with a secular vision of existence:

> She had escaped. But that young man had killed himself.
> Somehow it was her disaster – her disgrace. It was her punishment to see sink and disappear here a man, there a woman, in this profound darkness, and she forced to stand here in her evening dress. (*MD*: 166)

In Chutnik's novel, Bronka throws a farewell party, as she is in the final stage of cancer and wants to die on her own terms. The reception ends in a euthanasia scene, portrayed in the poetics of magic realism. Nevertheless, Bronka's party, though brimming with existential concerns similar to those in Woolf's novel, is created with the use of camp aesthetics:

> And the mortally ill [Bronka] bought confetti, paper lanterns, balloons and little flags in the stationery warehouse. . . . The flat looked like a kids' party, a playschool. A village wedding, a day-care room or an apartment, decorated with kitschy wrappers.
> On the day of the ball she ordered Indian food, dressed in the most beautiful dress she had, and so she was waiting for her guests like a prom queen. (Chutnik 2012: 191)[28]

Bronka's guests roll around in the balloons, toss them up in the air and look through them into the light. It is not surprising that from time to time a balloon bursts and disappears:

> It could symbolize the life of many people, but these very people were cheerfully tossing up these blown-up delicacies, as they thought it was a feast – to dance and toss balloons.
> And it is open to an interpretation that, after all, these balloons go to heaven. That these are some souls imprisoned in the smelly rubber. But such stories are only for the people who believe in the soul; all others are not affected by symbols. (Chutnik 2012: 192)[29]

Chutnik replaces a subdued image of Clarissa, hopelessly watching people 'disappearing' at random, with a kitschy balloon scene. The story of the balloons' salvation ends with an ironic comment on patronising attitudes towards people who do not believe in an afterlife.

This scene shows that another source of Woolf's popularity among writers could be her 'humanism', or 'secular idealism',[30] present as well in Chutnik's *Cwaniary,* as Bronka has neither hope nor fear for an afterlife. Some interest into secular ethics is observed in Poland. For example, Maria Rogaczewska investigated secularisation trends (2015: 6), which can be attributed to the opposition to patriarchal views dominant in the Polish Catholic Church (2015: 175) and political life. Those Polish feminist intellectuals who do not belong to the Catholic majority and who advocate the separation of state and church find Woolf's writing particularly inspiring.

Woolfian Palimpsests: Tokarczuk and Lis

The last two Polish writers I consider in this chapter create complex hypertexts, referring to numerous hypotexts written by Woolf and other authors. The complexity of their fiction resembles palimpsests, whose surfaces hide former texts. While Olga Tokarczuk transforms Woolfian androgyny in her Lower-Silesian constellation novel, Renata Lis inscribes Woolf as a founder of feminist tradition into the myth of Sappho.

Tokarczuk (1962–), widely read and critically acclaimed as her 2018 Nobel Prize shows, is one of the few contemporary Polish writers who can be called global. Her fiction has been so far translated into forty-five languages and awarded with prestigious prizes. In 2018, together with the translator Jennifer Croft, Tokarczuk received the Man Booker International Prize for *The Flights*, an English translation (2018a) of her novel *Bieguni* (2008), consisting of 116 fragments united by the central themes of wandering and travels, farewells and returns, mortality and immortality. Her essayistic prose is frequently explored from ecocritical[31] and postcolonial perspectives.[32] In a thorough review of the scholarship on Tokarczuk, Agnieszka Kłos comments what she views to be the affinity between Woolf and the Polish writer: 'Woolf believed that women always wrote predominantly about themselves. Tokarczuk shares this view. The gift of her writing is the ability to juxtapose the everyday with the transcendent. Her women narrators possess remarkable intuition' (2012: 97).[33]

Despite Kłos's disputable statement on the writers' shared belief in an auto/biograficational character of women's works, there are interesting similarities between Woolf's and Tokarczuk's works, in which genre- and gender-crossing aspects come to the fore. Tokarczuk undertakes experiments with hybrid texts, as her essayistic fiction assumes the form of collage novels, comprising myths, essays and diaries. She herself calls them 'constellation novels' (Tokarczuk 2018b) and explains this striking cosmological metaphor, inscribing her prose in the realms of ritual practices:

> just as the ancients looked at stars in the sky and found ways to group them and then to relate them to the shapes of creatures or figures, so what she calls her 'constellation novels' throw stories, essays and sketches into orbit, allowing the reader's imagination to form them into meaningful shapes. (2018b)

Tokarczuk, a feminist and a psychotherapist well-read in Carl Gustav Jung's theory of androgyny, experiments in her prose with portraying transgender or androgynous characters, undermining the masculine/feminine binary.

Translated into English in 2002, her volume *House of Day, House of Night* (*Dom dzienny, Dom nocny*, 1998) combines formal hybridity with gender-questioning storytelling. The novel, set in the back of beyond in Lower Silesia, is seemingly the complete opposite of planetary *Flights*; it is rather its local 'twin', similarly constellational and transnational. In both novels all the embedded narratives are open-ended, fragmentary and retold by a sympathetic narrator, who perceives 'only the world in fragments, there won't be any other one' (Tokarczuk 2018a: 181), as the globe is in constant motion, 'yielding to me as I looked at it, constantly moving towards me, and then away, so first I could see everything, then only tiny details' (Tokarczuk 2002: 1). As the dream poetics enabled Woolf to travel across centuries in *Orlando*, Tokarczuk's oneiric prose in *House of Day, House of Night* echoes the cultural mosaics of the transnational borderlands of the Lower Silesia region: Austrian, Czech, German, Polish and Silesian.

House of Day, House of Night comprises more than 100 parts written in different modes and genres that are all tenuously connected. In its background it traces the history of a mysterious sect, 'Nożownicy', with radical views on the nature of the world that potentially undermine rational explanations. As in a dream, characters and their stories wander through fragmented parts of the novel, while elaborate schemes of embedded stories loop and overlap. Jerzy Jarzębski points out that the main frame of the novel plays with the autobiographical elements, as it is set in 'the heart of the writer's private homeland', and at the same time it creates its own 'fantastic reality that underlies . . . Olga's private world' (2008: 50).[34]

Tokarczuk explores transgender identity, most visibly in three characters: a banned gender-crossing Saint Kummernis, a transgender monk Paschalis and, finally, (a) mysterious androgynous character(s) of Agni who assume(s) shapes of women and men. Tokarczuk's understanding has been predominantly inspired by Jung's theory of androgyny, which holds that men have their (un)conscious feminine archetype called 'the anima' and women have their 'animus'. An interview with Tokarczuk sheds some light on possible Woolfian roots of her approach to gender identity. She underlines discrepancies and ambiguities between writers' biological sex and their gender: 'Is it visible that a book was written by a woman or by a man? In a questionnaire, Proust could have written "female" in the space provided, Virginia Woolf – "male"' (Tokarczuk 2000).[35] Interestingly, after referring to Woolf, Tokarczuk seems to echo *A Room of One's Own:* 'It is fatal to be a man or woman pure and simple; one must be woman-manly or man-womanly' (*AROO*: 90), as she explains:

> It seems to me that gender is a kind of continuum, reaching from femininity to masculinity. We all, men and women, are born with a certain configuration of features that situates us on this continuum. There are very 'manly' women and 'womanly' men. (Tokarczuk 2000)[36]

In *House of Day, House of Night*, Tokarczuk includes the apocryphal story of Saint Kummernis, a manly woman in the patriarchal fifteenth century who acts bravely and decisively. After she refuses to marry, Kummernis is kidnapped, but when one of her persecutors tries to rape her, she is bestowed with Christ's face and meets a martyr's death (Tokarczuk 2002: 52–67). Her story is reconstructed by the monk Paschalis, who longs 'to be a woman' (2002: 78) and represents the stereotypical features attributed to women in his times: he passively adjusts to expectations held by people, including three background characters: his devotee Celestyn, his Mother Superior and his lover Katka. Finally, in one of the embedded stories, an elusive character named Agni seduces and comforts a nameless couple called 'a he and a she' (2002: 249). This multiple androgyne reincarnates first as young man, then as a tomboy and eventually finally dissolves into thin air (2002: 255–73).

Tokarczuk complicates further the stories of Kummernis and Paschalis by blurring the hyper/hypotext binaries, thus leading readers to question who is the 'author' of Kummernis's apocryphal teaching, as when the saint's own texts, rewritten by Paschalis, are spoken aloud to a bishop:

> A sheet of paper filled with Paschalis's even handwriting fluttered on the floor.
> '. . . I belong to the sun and the moon, for I belong to You, I belong to the world of plants and animals, for I belong to You. When the moon stirs the blood within me each month I know that I am Yours, that You have invited me to Your table to taste the flavour of life.' (Tokarczuk 2002: 168–9)

Interestingly, the English translation omits here two sentences of Kummernis's teachings:

> When every autumn, my body gains weight and curves, I become like a wild goose, like a roe deer, whose body knows more about the nature of the world than the wisest of people. You bestow upon me a tremendous power to survive the night. (Tokarczuk 1998: 161)[37]

This excerpt represents ecofeminist views, which Tokarczuk espouses and which are open to transhumanist and ecocritcial interpretations. The image of a wild goose evokes the final scenes of Woolf's *Orlando,* possibly suggesting that the attempt of reconstructing the saint's life is a similar biographical wild-goose chase.

An even more daring biofictional endeavour is undertaken by Renata Lis (1970–), a writer and translator, in her essayistic *Lesbos* (2017b) that encompasses 120 years, from Oscar Wilde's imprisonment in Reading in 1897 to the refugee camps on Lesbos in 2017. In interviews following the publication, Lis underlines a transtextual character of her work by pointing to 'quotations interlaced into the text' and creates a self-image of a writer as a spinner: 'I weave various threads . . . but the fabric is mine and woven on the canvas of my sensitivity, imagination and energy' (2017c).[38] Lis published two other literary biofictions on Gustave Flaubert and Ivan Bunin, as well as numerous translations, including the works of Jean Baudrillard. In *Lesbos,* she creates a transnational collage of hypotexts on Sappho and other lesbian/queer artists, though she always writes the word 'lesbian' in inverted commas, and almost never uses the word 'queer'. As these words seem to her misleading and imprecise, Lis attempts to speak with her own voice, weaving the stories of 'women loving women' and 'women's love', thus adopting neither the language of the LGBTQ+ community nor of scholars.

Lis's persona travels (as the writer did) to the imaginary land of Sappho and finds Lesbos in the midst of a migrants' crisis. She declares her affinity with refugees, emphasising her constant feeling of otherness in Poland: 'I am a great-granddaughter and a granddaughter of refugees and I still travel on that train they were riding from Ural – "coming back" to their "homeland", which was a completely foreign country. Still not enough local, not enough Polish' (2017b: 192).[39] Lis locates herself as both a stateless person and a citizen of the world, for whom there is no possibility of 'coming back', as the word 'homeland' is deprived of meaning.

Finally, Lis reads Woolf's hypotext through Winterson's 1994 fiction *Art and Lies,* claiming that, for Winterson, Woolf becomes 'Sappho', a founding mother of the feminist art tradition:

> The author of *Mrs Dalloway* is her [Winterson's] Mistress not only in literary matters – she is as well her mentor, her authority, her model. When in *A Room of One's Own* Woolf addresses her female readers – now, then, always – Winterson becomes one of these engrossed women, a disciple who takes this Woolfian gospel to her heart. (Lis 2017b: 126)[40]

With the publication of *Lesbos* in 2017, Lis symbolically closes twenty years of textual dialogues with Woolf initiated by the Polish translation of *A Room of One's Own* in 1997.

New Paths

This chapter has focused on Woolf's presence in contemporary Polish feminist fiction as it is materialised in works of Morska, Nurowska, Konarzewska, Bator, Chutnik, Tokarczuk and Lis. As Terentowicz-Fotyga has pointed out, Woolf 'seems to write herself much better into the contemporary Polish context than other modernists' (2002: 127). In an age of world literature, a vital characteristic is Woolf's versatility. As Claire

Davison has said, this versatility is connected with her ability to work 'from a sense of *dislocation* – an outland or landscape gradually revealed to the mind that is neither homely and familiar, nor closed, alien, and unknowable' (2015: 73). As I have shown, Polish feminist intellectuals find Woolf inspiring because of the similarities between the patriarchal culture of interwar Britain and contemporary Poland.

The third edition of *A Room of One's Own*, published in 2019, has started a new pop cultural chapter in Woolf's reception in Poland. The essay, still based on Graff's masterful translation, is accompanied by a series of biographical interviews but it lacks notes providing cultural and socio-political contexts in the previous edition. The six interviews conducted by Chutnik and the journalist Karolina Sulej are not only marginally related to Woolf but also seem tenuously connected to each other, ranging from the rock singer Edyta Bartosiewicz (1965–), the writer Joanna Bator (1968–), the actress Magdalena Cielecka (1972–), the sculptor, installation and video artist Katarzyna Kozyra (1963–), the journalist and traveller Martyna Wojciechowska (1974–), to the therapist Ewa Woydyłło (1939–). However, Chutnik argues in her introduction that the interviewees 'seem to fulfil the last will of Virginia Woolf and to independently build their "own rooms" while providing others with inspiration' (Woolf 2019: 11).[41] The first part of the publication turns into a self-help book with passing mentions of Woolf – frequently introduced by the journalists themselves. As the publishing house OsnoVa is directly linked to the fashion lifestyle magazine *Vogue*, the essay was publicised by a book tour under the patronage of Soroptimist International, yet sponsored by car, cosmetics and hotel companies. Consequently, the third edition of *A Room of One's Own* seems to commercialise Woolf's rebellious text, while – nonetheless – spreading its feminist message. Time will tell whether these global trends of pop cultural readings and 'femvertising' take root in Poland, given the recent rise of conservative and antifeminist tendencies.

New research is needed in many areas of Woolf's studies in Poland, including her reception and legacy to feminist thinking and activism. Although Woolf appears in nonprofit magazines, and 'Manifa' (the annual Women's Day demonstrations) manifestos and zines, no studies examine her presence in an alternative culture. The question of women's creativity is too complex to describe it in terms of literary 'influence' and to provide a neat 'genealogical tree'. Rather, it is a never-ending creative transdialogue in which Woolf inspires new generations of writers and activists who in turn provide her works with new audiences and 'afterlives'.

Notes

1. The feminist writer and activist Robin Morgan invented the term 'planetary feminism' (1984). Some scholars criticised her proposal for its implied universalism (Mohanty 2003: 110–13) and consequent erasure of the intersections of racism and patriarchy, as elucidated by Kimberlé Williams Crenshaw (1991). The development of planetary studies by Spivak (2003) and the rising awareness of 'one single commonality [that] involves all those living on the planet: environmental deterioration' (Miyoshi 2001: 295) allows scholars to re-use this term critically, following Friedman's discussion of its epistemological grounds (2018: 7–8).
2. For the discussion of two identified narrators in *A Room of One's Own*, see, among others, Vara Neverow (2015: 199–200, n.1).

3. On Woolf and hybridity, see, among others, Anna Snaith (2002), Melba Cuddy-Keane (2003) and Max Saunders (2010).
4. 'pominięcie Virginii to wyczyn, na który nie zdobyłby się chyba nikt inny piszący dzisiaj o historii eseju na świecie'. All translations are mine unless otherwise indicated.
5. However, I do not apply within this text Genette's understanding of 'metatextuality'. I use the term 'metafiction' for prose writings self-conscious about their fictional status.
6. See also Graham Allen's outline of feminist transtextuality (2000: 133–73).
7. In an interview following the publication of her last novel *Znikanie* [Disappearing] (2019), Morska explained that she decided to legally change her name after a serious disease, placing her decision in the context of life changes imposed by the illness as discussed by Woolf in her essay 'On being ill' (Morska 2019).
8. For example, see Saunders (2010: 438–50).
9. See, among others, Davison (2014).
10. 'W tej przyszłości nazywam się Virginia Stephen, a moja siostra to Vanessa Stephen. Ja zostanę sławną pisarką, a moja siostra będzie malować . . . kiedy przyszłam na świat, nasza siostra Laura została odizolowana od rodzeństwa, bo źle się uczyła, i kilka lat później wysłana do zakładu zamkniętego, bo była nieposłuszną córką, chociaż jej bracia zostali w domu, by nas prześladować. I oto każda z nas wiedziała, co ją czeka, jeśli będzie na tyle głupia, żeby zakpić z tego, czemu i tak sprzeciwiałam się przez resztę życia.'
11. 'był książką tyle wyjątkową, co wywrotową i jej treści, które polski czytelnik łatwo może wyszukać i ewentualnie odnieść do teraźniejszości, używając do tego własnego rozumu, są wciąż aktualne'.
12. '"Kiedy więc każę Wam zarabiać pieniądze i zdobyć własny pokój, w istocie proszę Was o to, byście żyły świadome rzeczywistości, a więc wiodły żywot fascynujący, niezależnie od tego, czy uda wam się przekazać innym jego treść." . . . Fascynujące to znaczy otwarte. . . . Fascynujące to znaczy takie, które zdołało rozpuścić sztywną barierę lęku.'
13. 'czy ten pokój to nie jest po prostu grobowiec, taka jednoosobowa trumna'.
14. 'jakby ten własny pokój na chwilę stawał się dworcem kolejowym, kawiarnią, salą uniwersytetu, siedzibą rządu, budynkiem ONZ, wielką przestrzenią w ruchu'.
15. 'nigdy się nie spotkały, żyły w innych krajach, a nawet światach. A jednak odkryłam, że mają bliźniacze losy, poprzez dzieciństwo, twórcze życie, miłość i śmierć. O tym będzie moja książka.'
16. 'to polskie bogoojczyźniane powietrze chyba wsączyło mi się do płuc, ciężko mi się oddycha'.
17. 'ostatnio natrafiłem na *Biografię* Virginii Woolf napisaną przez jej kuzyna. Zdziwiłem się, że taka książka jest w zbiorach wiejskiej biblioteki, a już w prawdziwe zdumienie wprawiło mnie to, co usłyszałem od bibliotekarki: . . . na tę biografię trzeba się zapisywać, tak wielkie jest nią zainteresowanie. . . . Cóż za dziwny kraj ta Polska!'
18. 'Tego dnia, kiedy Virginia Woolf z kamieniami w kieszeniach wstępowała w nurt rzeki, ja obchodziłem swoje czwarte urodziny.'
19. 'Tej nocy przyśniła mi się pani Dalloway, byłem z nią w sporze, a właściwie już nie wiem, czy z nią, czy z jej twórczynią Virginią, z którą wiodę polemikę od dłuższego czasu. Ta powieść to niewygasający wulkan uczuć i namiętności, ciągle się tam coś tli pod tą skorupą, coś się kotłuje i przewraca, ale nie wybucha. Więc czekasz, czytelniku, na ten wybuch, czekasz do ostatniej strony i pozostajesz w dziwnym oszołomieniu.'
20. 'Flowers, powiedziała pani Dolloway, flowers'; 'Londyn, powiedziała pani Dolloway, Londyn.'
21. 'Miasto tętni, pulsuje, oddycham. Idę. Idę. Nie muszę już nawet łapać powietrza. Oddycham całym ciałem, oddycham Suede, oddycham Verve, oddycham Woolf, którą niosę jak płuco, oddycham całym ciałem Londynu. Oddycham. Oddycham . . . ' (translation mine). This story is not included in a special English issue of *Furia*. Though the English issue appeared with the same cover as *Furia* no. 5 in Polish, it – as Anna Laszuk and Rafał Majka explain – 'comprises translations of articles which were originally published in different issues of *Furia* (no. 1–5)' (2012: 4).

22. 'Połykam słowa jak chłodne wiśnie.'
23. ' – To są białe słowa – powiedziała Susan – jak kamienie zbierane nad brzegiem morza.
    – Machają ogonami w lewo i w prawo – powiedział Bernard. . . .
    – To są żółte słowa, to płomienne słowa – powiedziała Jinny.
    – Kamienie są chłodne – powiedział Neville.
    – Wierzch mojej dłoni płonie – powiedziała Jinny.
    – Uciekajmy – powiedział Bernard. – Uciekajmy! . . .'
24. '*Orlando* – i tekst, i film – to propozycja takiej estetyki i takiej erotyki, w której płeć będzie zmienna, zamienna, myląca, i właśnie przez to pociągająca.'
25. 'to była przecież ucieczka w literaturę'; 'Stąd ten Orlando, który robi w książce za geja, lesbijkę i transseksualistę – i to jest tekst poetycki, a nie polityczny'.
26. 'Mówimy z Orlando: Barthes, Lacan, Mulvey, Žižek, jak poszukiwacze skarbów dziabiący ziemię na kartoflisku za moim warszawskim domem, i ustaliwszy wspólny grunt, przerzucamy się na nim opowieściami o dzieciństwie, rodzicach, miłościach. . . . Nie pomogła mu w tym wszystkim terapia u lacanisty, może dlatego, że ten głównie milczał. Ale to milczenie sprawiło, że filmoznawca zaczął mieć gejowskie sny, filmowo wyraziste. Orlando szuka więc siebie, je papaje.'
27. 'Nigdy nie pozbędę się podziwu dla Virginii Woolf. . . . Dla mojego pokolenia trzydziestoletnich feministek Woolf była jedną z najważniejszych nauczycielek. Pisała, między innymi, o postaci androgyne (*Orlando*) przekraczającej nudny dualizm płciowy. Dzieliła się strumieniem świadomości (*Fale*). W końcu dała nam *Własny pokój*, czyli możliwość bycia niezależną artystką bez winy i wstydu.'
28. 'A śmiertelnie chora kupiła w hurtowni artykułów papierniczych konfetti, lampiony, baloniki i chorągiewki. . . . Mieszkanie wyglądało jak kinderbal, jak przedszkole. Jak wiejskie wesele, jak świetlica środowiskowa albo jak apartament ozdobiony kiczowatymi papierkami. W dzień balu zamówiła hinduskie jedzenie, ubrała się w najpiękniejszą sukienkę, jaką miała, i oczekiwała w niej gości jak jakaś królowa studniówki.'
29. 'Mógłby symbolizować życie wielu osób, ale one właśnie wesoło podrzucały te nadmuchane rarytasy, wyobrażając sobie, że to święto. . . . I ciśnie się interpretacja oto taka, że te balony lecą w sumie do nieba. Że to jakieś dusze uwięzione w śmierdzącej gumie. Ale takie opowieści to dla ludzi wierzących w duszę, całej reszty symbole nie dotyczą.'
30. A similar phenomenon appears in Sweden, though on a much larger scale. In their analysis of Woolf's reception, Nicola Luckhurst and Alice Staveley discuss Catherine Sandbach-Dahlström's research into Woolf's wide readership in Sweden. It turns out that her 'secular idealism' is well received in Swedish rural communities (2007: 234).
31. See, among others, Urszula Chowaniec (2015).
32. See, among others, Dorota Kołodziejczyk (2011).
33. 'Według Virginii Woolf kobiety zawsze pisały przede wszystkim o sobie. Ten punkt widzenia Tokarczuk jest bliski. Dar jej pisania polega przede wszystkim na zetknięciu z codziennością i czymś transcendentnym, a jej narratorki wyróżniają się intuicją.'
34. 'w samym centrum prywatnej ojczyzny autorki'; 'fantastycznej rzeczywistości, która podszywa . . . osobisty świat Olgi'.
35. 'Czy to widać, że jakąś książkę napisała kobieta lub mężczyzna? Proust mógłby mieć w dokumentach w odpowiedniej rubryce napisane "płeć żeńska", Virginia Woolf – "męska."'
36. 'Wydaje mi się, że płeć jest rodzajem kontinuum. Jednym biegunem jest żeńskość, a drugim męskość. Wszyscy, mężczyźni i kobiety rodzimy się z jakąś konfiguracją tych cech usytuowani gdzieś na tym kontinuum'. Są kobiety bardzo "męskie" i bardzo "kobiecy" mężczyźni.'
37. 'Kiedy każdej jesieni moje ciało okrągleje i przybiera, staję się jak dzika gęś, jak sarna, których ciało więcej wie o naturze świata niż najmądrzejszy z ludzi. Obdarzasz mnie wielką siłą, by przetrwać noc.' These sentences appear in all Polish editions – translation mine.

38. 'Używam do tego różnych nici . . . ale tkanina jest moja i trzyma się na kanwie mojej wrażliwości, wyobraźni i energii.'
39. 'Jestem prawnuczką i wnuczką uchodźców, i wciąż jadę tamtym pociągiem, którym oni jechali z Uralu – "wracali" nim do "ojczyzny", będącej dla nich zupełnie obcym krajem. . . . Wciąż nie dość swoja, za mało polska.'
40. 'Autorka *Pani Dalloway* jest jej [Winterson] Mistrzynią nie tylko w tym, co dotyczy literatury – jest również mentorką, autorytetem, osobistym wzorem. Kiedy we *Własnym Pokoju* Woolf zwraca się do swoich czytelniczek – teraz, wtedy, zawsze, – Winterson staje się jedną z zasłuchanych kobiet, uczennicą przyjmującą do serca tę Woolfiańską ewangelię.'
41. 'zdają się wypełniać testament Virginii Woolf i budować "własny pokój" niezależnością, stanowiąc równocześnie inspirację dla innych'.

Bibliography

Allen, G. (2000), *Intertextuality*, London: Routledge.
Bator, J. (2015), *Wyspa Łza* [Isle Tear], Kraków: Wydawnictwo Znak.
Bell, Q. (2004), *Virginia Woolf: Biografia*, trans. M. Lavergne, Warszawa: Twój Styl.
Berman, J. (2017), 'Is the trans in transnational the trans in transgender?', *Modernism/modernity*, 24: 2, pp. 217–44.
Berman, J. (2018), 'Practicing transnational feminist recovery today', *Feminist Modernist Studies*, 1: 1–2, pp. 9–21.
Chowaniec, U. (2015), *Melancholic Migrating Bodies in Contemporary Polish Women's Writing*, Newcastle upon Tyne: Cambridge Scholars Publishing.
Chutnik, S. (2009), 'Jakub od Virginii' [Jacob by Virginia], *Dwutygodnik* [Biweekly], 4, <http://www.dwutygodnik.com/artykul/114-jakub-od-virginii.html> (last accessed 30 July 2019).
Chutnik, S. (2012), *Cwaniary* [Sly Women], Warszawa: Świat Książki.
Crenshaw, K. W. (1991), 'Mapping the margins: Intersectionality identity politics, and violence against women of color', *Stanford Law Review*, 43: 6, pp. 1241–99.
Cuddy-Keane, M. (2003), *Virginia Woolf, the Intellectual, and the Public Sphere*, Cambridge: Cambridge University Press.
Cunningham, M. (1998), *The Hours*, New York: Farrar, Straus and Giroux.
Damrosch, D. (2006), 'World literature in a postcanonical, hypercanonical age', in H. Saussy (ed.), *Comparative Literature in an Age of Globalization*, Baltimore, MD: Johns Hopkins University Press, pp. 43–53.
Davison, C. (2014), *Translation as Collaboration: Virginia Woolf, Katherine Mansfield and S. S. Koteliansky*, Edinburgh: Edinburgh University Press.
Davison, C. (2015), 'Bilinguals and bioptics: Virginia Woolf and the outlandishness of translation', in J. Dubino, G. Lowe, V. Neverow and K. Simpson (eds), *Virginia Woolf: Twenty-First-Century Approaches*, Edinburgh: Edinburgh University Press, pp. 72–90.
Filipiak [Morska], I. (1997), Introduction, in V. Woolf, *Własny pokój* [*A Room of One's Own*], trans. A. Graff, Warszawa: Wydawnictwo Sic!.
Filipiak [Morska], I. (1998), 'Virginia Woolf, *Orlando* i stare Bloomsbury' [Virginia Woolf, *Orlando* and the old Bloomsbury], *Kresy* [Borderlands], 35, pp. 106–16.
Filipiak [Morska], I. (2006), *Absolutna amnezja* [Total Amnesia], Warszawa: Tchu Dom Wydawniczy.
Friedman, S. S. (2013), 'Wartime cosmopolitanism: Cosmofeminism in Virginia Woolf's *Three Guineas* and Marjane Satrapi's *Persepolis*', *Tulsa Studies in Women's Literature*, 32: 1, pp. 23–52.
Friedman, S. S. (2018), *Planetary Modernisms: Provocations on Modernity across Time*, New York: Columbia University Press.

Genette, G. (1997 [1982]), *Palimpsests: Literature in the Second Degree*, trans. C. Newman and C. Doubinsky, Lincoln: University of Nebraska Press.

Głowiński, M. (1986), 'O intertekstualności' [About intertextuality], *Pamiętnik Literacki* [Literary Memoir], 4, pp. 75–100.

Graff, A. (2003), 'Lost between the waves? The paradoxes of feminist chronology and activism in contemporary Poland', *Journal of International Women's Studies*, 4: 2, pp. 100–16.

Graff, A. (2008), *Świat bez kobiet: Płeć w polskim dyskursie publicznym* [A World without Women: Gender in Polish Public Discourse], Warszawa: W. A. B.

Graff, A. (2014), *Jestem stąd* [I am from here], interviewed by M. Sutowski, Warszawa: Wydawnictwo Krytyki Politycznej.

Janion, M. (2006 [1996]), *Kobiety i duch inności* [Women and the Spirit of Otherness], Warszawa: Wydawnictwo Sic!

Jarzębski, J. (2008), 'Realizm podszyty fantastyką' [Realism streaked with fantasy], *Teksty Drugie* [Second Texts], 6, pp. 44–53.

Kłos, A. (2012), 'Śmiertelni nieśmiertelni, nieśmiertelni śmiertelni. O pisarstwie Olgi Tokarczuk' [Mortal immortals, immortal mortals. About Olga Tokarczuk's writing], in J. Bierut, W. Browarny and G. Czekański (eds), *Rozkład jazdy: Dwadzieścia lat literatury Dolnego Śląska po 1989 roku* [A Timetable: Twenty Years of Upper Silesian Literature after 1989], Wrocław: Fundacja na Rzecz Kultury i Edukacji im. Tymoteusza Karpowicza, pp. 87–105.

Kołodziejczyk, D. (2011), 'The uncanny space of "lesser" Europe: Trans-border corpses and transnational ghosts in post-1989 Eastern European fiction', *Postcolonial Text*, 6: 2, pp. 1–19.

Konarzewska, M. (2012), 'Doti', *Furia*, 5, pp. 93–7.

Kraskowska, E. (2010), 'On the circulation of feminist discourse via translation (V. Woolf, S. de Beauvoir, J. Butler)', *Ruch Literacki* [Literary Movement], 1, pp. 1–14.

Kristeva, J. (1986 [1969]), 'Word, dialogue and novel', in T. Moi (ed.), *The Kristeva Reader*, New York: Columbia University Press, pp. 34–61.

Lackey, M. (2016) 'Introduction: Locating and defining the bio in biofiction', *a/b: Auto/Biography Studies*, 31: 1, pp. 3–10.

Laszuk, A., and R. Majka (2012), 'Editorial', *Furia: Special Issue*, pp. 4–5.

Lis, R. (2017a), 'Esej i kwanty' [The essay and the quanta], *Dwutygodnik (Biweekly)*, 224, <https://www.dwutygodnik.com/artykul/7480-esej-i-kwanty.html> (last accessed 30 July 2019).

Lis, R. (2017b), *Lesbos*, Warszawa: Wydawnictwo Sic!

Lis, R. (2017c), 'Pisać na głos' [Writing aloud], interviewed by A. Marchewka, *Dwutygodnik* [*Biweekly*], 219, <https://www.dwutygodnik.com/artykul/7346-pisac-na-glos.html> (last accessed 30 July 2019).

Luckhurst, N. and A. Staveley (2007), 'European reception studies', in A. Snaith (ed.), *Palgrave Advances in Virginia Woolf Studies*, Basingstoke: Palgrave Macmillan, pp. 227–52.

Miyoshi, M. (2001), 'Turn to the planet: Literature diversity, and totality', *Comparative Literature*, 53: 4, pp. 283–97.

Mohanty, C. T. (2003), *Feminism without Borders: Decolonizing Theory, Practicing Solidarity*, Durham, NC: Duke University Press.

Morgan, R. (1984), 'Introduction: Planetary feminism: The politics of the 21st century', in Morgan (ed.), *Sisterhood Is Global: The International Women's Movement Anthology*, Garden City, NY: Anchor Press/Doubleday, pp. 1–37.

Morska, I. (2019), 'Wymyśliła sobie pani chorobę' [Your illness is imaginary, Ms Morska], interviewed by D. Wodecka, *Wysokie Obcasy Extra* [High Heels Extra], 10: 89, <https://www.wysokieobcasy.pl/wysokie-obcasy/7,152731,25368039,wymyslila-sobie-pani-chorobe-wedrowka-po-labiryntach-systemu.html> (last accessed 6 September 2020).

Neverow, V. (2015), 'Multiple anonymities: Resonances of Fielding's *The Female Husband* in *Orlando* and *A Room of One's Own*', in J. Dubino, G. Lowe, V. Neverow and K. Simpson (eds), *Virginia Woolf: Twenty-First-Century Approaches*, Edinburgh: Edinburgh University Press, pp. 187–204.

Nurowska, M. (2011), *Requiem dla wilka* [Requiem for a Wolf], Warszawa: Wydawnictwo W. A. B.

Nurowska, M. (2016), 'Biurka polskich pisarzy: Maria Nurowska' [The desks of Polish writers: Maria Nurowska], interviewed by M. Buszkiewicz, <http://booklips.pl/biurka-polskich-pisarzy/biurka-polskich-pisarzy-maria-nurowska> (last accessed 30 July 2019).

Orlando (1992), film, dir S. Potter, Italy: Sony Pictures Classics.

Pająk, P. (2018) '"Echo texts": Woolf, Krzywicka, and *The Well of Loneliness*', *Woolf Studies Annual*, 24, pp. 11–34.

Phillips, U. (2013), 'Introduction', in U. Phillips (ed., asst. K. A. Grimstad and K. Van Heuckelom), *Polish Literature in Transformation*, Zürich: LIT Verlag, pp. 3–24.

Rogaczewska, M. (2015), 'Przemiany wzorów religijności w Polsce a mechanizmy uspołecznienia' [The impact of changing religious patterns on socializing mechanisms in Polish society], dissertation, University of Warsaw, UW Repository, <http://depotuw.ceon.pl/handle/item/1238> (last accessed 30 July 2019).

Saunders, M. (2010), *Self Impression: Life-Writing, Autobiografiction, and the Forms of Modern Literature*, Oxford: Oxford University Press.

Showalter, E. (ed.) (1986), *The New Feminist Criticism: Essays on Women, Literature and Theory*, London: Virago.

Silver, B. R. (1999), *Virginia Woolf Icon*, Chicago: University of Chicago Press.

Snaith, A. (2002), 'Of fanciers, footnotes, and Fascism: Virginia Woolf's *Flush*', *MFS: Modern Fiction Studies*, 48: 3, pp. 614–36.

Spivak, G. C. (2003), *Death of a Discipline*, New York: Columbia University Press.

Szczuka, K. (2006), 'Komplety u Kazimiery Szczuki' [Clandestine classes at Kazimiera Szczuka's], in A. Drotkiewicz and A. Dziewit (eds), *Głośniej!: Rozmowy z pisarkami* [Louder! Interviews with the Women Writers], Warszawa: Twój Styl, pp. 11–36.

Terentowicz-Fotyga, U. (2002), 'From silence to a polyphony of voices: Virginia Woolf's reception in Poland', in M. A. Caws and N. Luckhurst (eds), *The Reception of Virginia Woolf in Europe*, London: Continuum, pp. 127–47.

Tokarczuk, O. (1998), *Dom dzienny, Dom nocny* [House of Day, House of Night], Wałbrzych: Wydawnictwo Ruta.

Tokarczuk, O. (2000), 'O przyrodzie, literaturze, feminizmie, micie, życiu i śmierci' [About nature, literature, feminism, myth, life and death], interviewed by J. Korbel and M. Lelek, *Dzikie Życie* [Wild Life], 4: 70, <http://dzikiezycie.pl/archiwum/2000/kwiecien-2000/o-przyrodzie-literaturze-feminizmie-micie-zyciu-i-smierci-rozmowa-z-olga-tokarczuk> (last accessed 30 July 2019).

Tokarczuk, O. (2002) *House of Day, House of Night*, trans. A. Lloyd-Jones, London: Granta Books.

Tokarczuk, O. (2007), *Bieguni* [Flights], Kraków: Wydawnictwo Literackie.

Tokarczuk, O. (2018a), *Flights*, trans. J. Croft, New York: Riverhead Books.

Tokarczuk, O. (2018b), 'I was very naive. I thought Poland would be able to discuss the dark areas of our history', interviewed by C. Armitstead, *Guardian*, 20 April, <https://www.theguardian.com/books/2018/apr/20/olga-tokarczuk-interview-flights-man-booker-international> (last accessed 30 July 2019).

Walkowitz, R. L. (2017), *Born Translated: The Contemporary Novel in an Age of World Literature*, New York: Columbia University Press.

Warkocki, B. (2002), 'Poszukiwanie języka. O twórczości Izabeli Filipiak' [In a search for a language. About Izabela Filipiak's writing], *Teksty Drugie* [Second Texts], 6, pp. 92–112.

Woolf, V. (1977–84), *The Diary of Virginia Woolf*, 5 vols, ed. A. O. Bell and A. McNeillie, London: Penguin.

Woolf, V. (1997 [1929]), *Własny pokój* [A Room of One's Own], intro. I. Filipiak [Morska], trans. A. Graff, Warszawa: Wydawnictwo Sic!.

Woolf, V. (2001 [1929/1938]), *A Room of One's Own and Three Guineas*, London: Vintage.
Woolf, V. (2010 [1931]), *The Waves*, ed. M. Herbert and S. Sellers, Cambridge: Cambridge University Press.
Woolf, V. (2015 [1925]), *Mrs Dalloway*, ed. A. E. Fernald, Cambridge: Cambridge University Press.
Woolf, V. (2019 [1929]), *Własny pokój* [*A Room of One's Own*], interviewed and ed. S. Chutnik and K. Sulej, intro. Chutnik, trans. A. Graff, Warszawa: OsnoVa.
Yaeger, P. S. (1984), '"Because a fire was in my head": Eudora Welty and the dialogic imagination', *PMLA*, 99: 5, pp. 955–73.

19

Clarissa Dalloway's Global Itinerary: From London to Paris and Sydney

Monica Latham

Almost a century after its publication, Virginia Woolf's fourth novel, *Mrs Dalloway*, still haunts many readers and writers alike, provoking questions about its privileged canonical status. *Mrs Dalloway* has proved to have the literary and cultural power to endure as an influential text of modernist literature and continues to be a major source of inspiration for numerous contemporary international writers who engage in explicit dialogue with it[1] or are covertly influenced by it.[2] Indeed, *Mrs Dalloway* – as the novel in which the modernist author found a unique voice and signature, and with which she revolutionised the art of literature – constitutes the warp and weft of the fabric of many contemporary texts. Present-day writers around the world have been drawn to Woolf's novel for its aesthetic and cultural potential: they revive Dalloway-esque themes and methods, as well as modernist aesthetics, within a renewed spectrum of artistic, cultural and political contexts and expectations. *Mrs Dalloway* invites various stories with specific cultural resonances and thus enables contemporary authors to carry on a formidable tradition; however, these stories ultimately take on a life of their own and are inscribed in their own times and mores, displaying the authors' individual talents as well as their cultural and national specificities.

This chapter focuses on three contemporary women writers[3] who have authored recent novels in the wake of *Mrs Dalloway*. From direct, intended homages to Woolf's novel to more subtle influences, Anne Korkeakivi (b. ?) in *An Unexpected Guest* (2012a), Carole Llewellyn (1983–) in *Une ombre chacun* (2017b [A Shadow of One's Own]) and Gail Jones (1955–) in *Five Bells* (2012) have taken their own twenty-first-century Clarissa Dalloway to Paris and Sydney, each of the three authors having chosen a city with its topographic, historical and cultural specificities as the canvas of their characters' wanderings. Furthermore, in the process of dislocating the character to other chronotopes, they have also rewritten Woolf's masterpiece, and emulated and appropriated her 'Dalloway-isms'. Seymour Chatman (2005: 274) mainly sees Woolf's verbal, punctuation and syntactic characteristics as recognisable, repetitive 'tics'. I have extended his definition beyond these surface elements to include other stylistic, thematic and narrative qualities, ingredients, features or templates which intrinsically define Woolf's text, such as the fluidity and flexibility of the narrative voice, the multiplicity and intersection of subjective points of view, the shifts in perspectives, the piercing through different time strata, the alternations of interior/exterior events, the themes accentuated by Woolf during the process of creation of her novel (doubles, sanity/insanity, life/death), the creation of powerful moments of being and so on. However, I will not use Chatman's negatively connoted appellation 'Dalloway-ism' but will instead refer to the complex texture of Woolf's writing as 'Dalloway-esque'. These narrative, thematic, stylistic and syntactic Woolfian features are used, imitated, extended, transformed or updated by the three women authors who, as noted earlier, write in the wake of Virginia Woolf and whose prose is recognisably Dalloway-esque.

Just like their modernist predecessor, Korkeakivi, Llewellyn and Jones 'descend to the depth and investigate the crannies of [their characters'] consciousness' (*E* 3: 367) and rake up sensations and impressions from various strata of their minds. The reader is invited 'to follow these impressions as they flicker through [the characters'] mind[s], waking incongruously other thoughts and plaiting incessantly the many-coloured and innumerable threads of life' (*E* 3: 11). By plunging into their main characters' subjectivities, illuminating their minds and capturing their sensory impressions and minuteness of their private lives, these writers have put into practice a style that Woolf herself fashioned in *Mrs Dalloway*. Korkeakivi, Llewellyn and Jones weave into their prose fabric many such idiosyncratic Woolfian features, but they also make them new by adapting them to contemporary needs, settings and situations.

Parisian Variations on *Mrs Dalloway*

Anne Korkeakivi's circadian novel takes place on one April day in Paris. Echoes of *Mrs Dalloway* resonate in many ways through Korkeakivi's *An Unexpected Guest*. The author has openly acknowledged the kinship between Woolf's novel and her own:

> I recognized the similarity between the story forming in my head and how, in *Mrs Dalloway*, Virginia Woolf managed to talk so profoundly about post-WWI malaise while writing about something as seemingly commonplace as putting on a dinner party. So, yes, I felt privileged to be able to pay homage to that. Virginia Woolf was a genius. (Korkeakivi 2012b)

First and foremost, there are similarities between the names of the heroines, Clarissa and Clare; Korkeakivi has confessed in an interview that she carefully chose the name Clare Moorhouse to explicitly make reference to Clarissa Dalloway (Korkeakivi 2013). Clare, a forty-five-year-old American woman living in Paris, organises a last-minute dinner party crucial to her husband's career. On that day, she goes out to buy flowers for the party and spends the day shopping and preparing for it. Clare is the perfect wife, a gracious and efficient hostess who knows how to entertain her husband's important guests. Like Richard Dalloway, Clare's husband, Edward, is a politician, a British foreign servant in Paris who is deputy ambassador at the British Embassy, hoping to be named the new ambassador to Ireland. Clare sees her dinner party as a small domestic contribution to her husband's successful career and, by and large, to the big diplomatic relationships that are constantly changing between nations. The public, political background reflects the complexities of our contemporary age and is here given more weight than it is in *Mrs Dalloway*. Clarissa is quite indifferent to her husband's political meetings (for instance, access to Clarissa's interior monologue shows that she confuses Armenians and Albanians: 'He was already halfway to the House of Commons, to his Armenians, his Albanians, having settled her on the sofa, looking at his roses. . . . [N]o, she could feel nothing for the Albanians, or was it the Armenians?' [*MD*: 101]). Clare, in contrast, is attentive to the forming alliances and political permutations around her, and she contributes by organising dinners, which entail encounters between foreign diplomats and discussions about power shifts and business dynamics around her table. She is thus savvier than Clarissa, as she is aware that her actions participate to the global peace machinery.

Clare conceals her inner perspectives and she is perceived as a respectable 'middle-aged woman . . . well-groomed and confident, transformed by the mantle of respectability and societal stature' (Korkeakivi 2012a: 68). However, behind the perfect façade and the 'pomp and circumstance that surround a diplomatic family's daily life', the reader is given direct access to Clare's thoughts and fears, as she 'feel[s] the press of time, both past and present, on her' (2012a: 121). Woolf reveals Clarissa Dalloway's thoughts concerning her fears of death and anxieties of ageing: for example, when she is looking in the mirror and notes changes in her appearance, she muses on these fears: 'She feared time itself, and read on Lady Bruton's face, as if it had been a dial cut in impassive stone, the dwindling of life; how year by year her share was sliced' (*MD*: 26). Similarly, Korkeakivi reveals Clare Moorhouse's preoccupation with ageing as she observes changes in her body. Some considerations are triggered by looking at her hands, which become a metonymy for old age: 'an older woman's hands. Were they *her* hands? A touch of freckle sprayed across the top of the right one, the skin so thin the tendons were almost visible. The knuckles rose into a puckered ridge' (2012a: 20). Clare and Clarissa have similar personalities: Clare is described as being cool, reserved and aloof, as her husband's position of responsibility requires her to be: 'She was pale, beige, remote. She was cool, calm, efficient. She had molded herself into something perfect' (2012a: 169). Clarissa is also 'cold as an icicle' (*MD*: 68): Peter Walsh describes her as 'cold' and 'heartless', and he repeatedly refers to her 'coldness' and 'woodenness' (*MD*: 148) throughout the novel.

Like Clarissa who feels in her element while in Bond Street, Rue de Varenne is '[Clare's] street' (Korkeakivi 2012a: 32), and she perfectly 'fit[s] in here' (2012a: 33), as her husband once observed. 'Fitting' into a certain urban and social mould amounts to an erosion of her personality, of her former self, as she became the wife of a diplomat and has now adjusted to her husband's political environment:

> her development had been more like an act of erosion, a sanding away of all extraneous or undesirable elements, and this was how she felt more and more, as though each year were a grand wave washing away a little more of her. (2012a: 33)

Clare developed and cultivated a 'beige' personality from the moment she met Edward: 'He'd been admiring . . . the cool beige she'd begun using to cloak her own limbs and secret emotions, her ability to appear neutral at all times, at all costs, before anyone' (2012a: 37). Clarissa feels devoid of her feminine identity, being known as 'Mrs Richard Dalloway':

> She had the oddest sense of being herself invisible; unseen; unknown; there being no more marrying, no more having of children now, but only this astonishing and rather solemn progress with the rest of them, up Bond Street, this being Mrs Dalloway; not even Clarissa any more; this being Mrs Richard Dalloway. (*MD*: 9)

Likewise, Clare has become invisible or transparent, her identity being defined through her husband. Beige is her colour of invisibility, of camouflaging her feminine identity under the mask of respectability, domesticity and diplomacy. By adopting beige clothes, Clare thus blends in, in accordance with her social status and her husband's diplomatic expectations. Beige becomes a metaphor for conformity and erasure of her personality: 'She'd done everything in her power to make herself as unnoticeable as possible, swathing herself in beige cloth and neutral opinions' (Korkeakivi 2012a: 239). However, behind this 'neutrality' and 'diplomacy', behind this cool, imperturbable façade, Clare is tormented by a terrible political mistake she made in her youth which could now have repercussions in the present.

The minuteness and ordinariness of Clare's day as well as her inner turmoil as she moves in the streets of Paris from the flower shop to the very fashionable Le Bon Marché department store food hall is masterfully entwined with the global political anxieties and the intricacies of diplomatic life. Clare's street, situated in the seventh arrondissement, 'house[s] governmental offices or official residences' (2012a: 32) and the Rodin Museum is 'right down the street from her house'; it usually hums with tourists 'thanks to the Eiffel Tower and Les Invalides' (2012a: 40). The beauty of Paris is revealed under the changing light which is described in minute observations throughout the day. As in *Mrs Dalloway*, where Peter Walsh spots signs of the grandeur of the British Empire in London, in *An Unexpected Guest* Clare revels in these magnificent urban surroundings and is full of awe at the 'monumentality of Paris' (2012a: 150). But the Empire, just like Paris, is vulnerable in a postwar climate, and the two grand cities are no longer invincible.

Korkeakivi has stated that she intended to put the current serious, complex geopolitical situation at the heart of her story: 'I also wanted to explore ways in which feelings about terrorism, and even the definition of a terrorist, may have changed since 9/11 – which, I think, *is* central to Clare's story' (Korkeakivi 2013).[4] Indeed, Clare lives in a tense global climate, a post-9/11 political age marked by general trauma and fresh, painful scars of terrorism and assassinations. Thus, death and fear are constantly on her mind. During the day, she thinks of the most traumatic terrorist attacks of the past years: 'On 9/11 four years ago, and last summer on 7/7, the coverage had been inescapable – the hunted, haunted faces of people wandering Wall Street or emerging from the London Underground by Russell Square' (Korkeakivi 2012a: 105). Besides these major attacks imprinted in her heroine's memory, Korkeakivi interweaves other strands into the underlying political canvas: the Irish Republican Army's response to British actions, the Turkish defence of the Armenian catastrophe, political assassinations and young idealistic people like Clare's son, Jamie, protesting against war. These global political tensions and chaos are new, updated threats to the civilisation so much admired by Peter Walsh in *Mrs Dalloway*: 'there were moments when civilisation . . . seemed dear to him as a personal possession' (*MD*: 47). Similarly, Clare is thinking that '[t]errorism was too frightening, too inhuman. The utter breakdown of civilisation' (Korkeakivi 2012a: 132).

Clare's private thoughts that bring fragments of her past to the present are constantly interrupted by external events. J. Hillis Miller formulated the idea of the perpetual repetition of the past in the present in *Mrs Dalloway*, which can also apply to *An Unexpected Guest*: 'the weight of all the past moment presses just beneath the surface of the present, ready in an instant to flow into consciousness, overwhelming it with the immediate presence of the past' (1982: 184). In some interviews, Korkeakivi has commented on the way her character's past and present get superimposed within the circadian structure: 'Clare is a person who lives in the past and present simultaneously because of how the former haunts her, and the structure was designed from the get-go to reflect this' (Korkeakivi 2012b); 'On the day of the novel, Clare's complicated secret past comes, both literally and figuratively, knocking on her door' (Korkeakivi 2013). Indeed, just as in *Mrs Dalloway*, the reader is plunged into various layers of the past, which are brought together into this specific day when Clare's mind excavates those layers and brings memories to the surface: 'She'd buried the pivotal choices of her life, like the city of Troy, under layers of sediment, even as she carried the remembrance of it with her every minute' (Korkeakivi 2012: 239). As Clare walks the streets of Paris to run her errands, memories surface and we are given access to her interior life, secrets and guilt. These lengthy digressive memories, triggered by what she sees or does, expand in between short actions or quick verbal exchanges.

Dalloway-esque time in *An Unexpected Guest* is fluid and elastic. While clock time – with its chronological, mechanical regularity – punctuates the day unfolding inexorably towards the dinner party, time as filtered by Clare's individual, subjective inner life stretches and lingers oppressively, as Clare remembers again and again the mistake she made in her youth and the guilt with which she has lived ever since. Both clock time and psychological time are seen as burdens for Clare from the very start of the day. For instance, clock time governs the relentless progress of the day, marking the dwindling day leading to the party that Clare must quickly and efficiently organise and host. The clock in the kitchen is literally hanging above her, and symbolically time is repressively hanging over her head. The 'time on the clock' and the 'time in the mind' (*O*: 59), to borrow Woolf's concepts, set the dual movement of the novel: both move forward towards the evening of that day and backward towards Clare's illegal action of smuggling money from America into Ireland for the IRA when she was twenty. Clare's past actions on behalf of the IRA have repercussions on the present, as they now threaten her husband's impending ambassadorship.

Just as in *Mrs Dalloway*, when Sir William Bradshaw announces that his patient Septimus Warren Smith committed suicide, the subject of death is brought up at Clare's party. In *An Unexpected Guest* the news of a politician's assassination is the death to be avoided and contained, so as to 'maintain balance' (Korkeakivi 2012a: 87) in the diplomatic world. Despite the ominous and unpredictable terrorist attacks that bring trauma, shock and lasting fears, and wreak havoc in the political sphere, the dinner party goes on: 'But they would go on. That was the essential. One had to keep going' (2012a: 86). Thus, both novels are ultimately a celebration of life. Their specific days, with all the big and small events, are meaningful, as they allow the two women to bury the harrowing past and focus on the present moment. Although war-related deaths intrude upon the festivities in both novels, the protagonists decide to fully embrace life through their firm, soothing presence in the here and now of the party and their final, comforting sentences: 'For there she was' (*MD*: 165) and 'It's Clare here' (Korkeakivi 2012a: 277). As both women are acutely aware of living in a threatening world, the party itself becomes a strong statement that life should go on despite fears of death:

> They were proving that life would go on, could remain decent no matter what happened, despite the fact that someone could get up in the morning, go to work, and never come back again, because someone disagreed with their opinions, or race, or religion. (Korkeakivi 2012a: 215)

Clarissa repeats the soothing line from Shakespeare's *Cymbeline*, 'Fear no more', and she continues to endure, while Clare thinks that '[f]ear could be converted into a kind of terrorism of its own. She had to live in the world, for good of for bad. She had to be part of it' (Korkeakivi 2012a: 257). Both Clarissa and Clare momentarily retreat from their parties and after a few minutes of peaceful consideration, they go back to 'assemble' guests and the fragmented pieces of their lives into a whole.

As their days lead to the parties, both heroines re-examine their past and momentous choices, such as the decision to marry safe respectable men rather than the first men they loved, who in both novels unexpectedly come back into their lives on this specific day. In Clare's case, her first love is associated with her idealistic but foolish youthful political decisions and his presence threatens her honourable diplomatic life. Both women, albeit almost a century apart, live in a masculine world that stands for power and public, diplomatic authority, which is contrasted with their feminine, private domestic worlds in which they take refuge. Both novels thus read as a lament on the erosion of female identity, on how these women sand down their personalities to accommodate their husbands' and societal expectations.

However, *An Unexpected Guest* is not an exact replica of *Mrs Dalloway*; it goes beyond its original model and offers personal, contemporary variations. It has a life, or story, of its own, as the author herself stated in an interview:

> I realized early on that what I was attempting to do with my story – share the malaise of a certain moment in time through this one person's day – was what Woolf did so brilliantly in *Mrs Dalloway*. . . . After that initial acknowledgment, I let my story lead its own life. (Korkeakivi 2013)

As a post-9/11 *Mrs Dalloway*, *An Unexpected Guest* suggests that the political situation has acquired new dimensions, and Paris, despite its glory and magnificence, is a vulnerable city in a context of unpredictable global war, whose inhabitants are prey to terrorist attacks, unexpected violence and fear. With its urgent political sense and substance, Korkeakivi's novel reads very much like a political thriller in which action and plot are essential, unlike Woolf's lyrical narrative. Despite the digressive memories and incursions into the past, Korkeakivi creates suspense through dramatic revelations, twists, danger and intrigue, the pressure mounting with each passing hour within the novel's twenty-four-hour structural frame.

Writing in Woolf's Shadow

Carole Llewellyn's *Une ombre chacun* is also a direct homage to Woolf's *Mrs Dalloway* and is modelled on it. In an interview, Llewellyn has expressed her admiration for *Mrs Dalloway* and pondered how Woolf's character could be updated today. She has stated that we all have something of Clarissa Dalloway in us and live in a contradictory world, which Llewellyn wanted to explore in her own novel (see 'Au fil des livres' 2017). *Une ombre chacun* does not have *Mrs Dalloway*'s circadian scope, but there are obvious correlations in the portrayal and evolution of the two main characters named Clara and Seven, conceived as twins or shadows of each other, and in the way Woolf and Llewellyn sustain the parallels between their characters throughout the narration. Llewellyn signals her allegiance to *Mrs Dalloway* by adhering closely to Clarissa's and Septimus's personalities, traumas[6] and constant thoughts of death, and replicates

Woolf's design of her novel in the way she creates a balance between her pivotal themes of life and death, sanity and insanity.[7] She also offers the reader a Dalloway-esque ending insofar as Seven's suicide allows Clara to begin a new, more fulfilled life.

As is obvious, the very names of Llewellyn's main, dual characters, Clara de Hus and Seven Warren Smith, constitute a clear link to Clarissa Dalloway and Septimus Warren Smith. Septimus means seventh in Latin and Seven is his parents' seventh child. As explained in an interview, the author deliberately chose to name her characters after Woolf's, who remain her characters' *alter egos* (Llewellyn 2017a). Clara is an ordinary upper-middle-class thirty-year-old French housewife who lives with her wealthy banker husband in a spacious, luxurious apartment in the seventh arrondissement, one of the most elegant resident areas of Paris. Like Clarissa, she leads a sheltered, bourgeois life, spending her time shopping in Paris's fashionable Le Bon Marché, cooking, posting her creations on Instagram and entertaining guests. Her husband's aristocratic name, as well as the prime location of their apartment testify to their social class. Clara feels she is a commodity, as if her husband 'bought a wife to match his new apartment' (Llewellyn 2017b: 80).[8] Like her Woolfian counterpart, Clara laments her loss of individuality: by marrying Charles, she has become and is known as Madame Charles de Hus. Trapped in her golden cage and comfortable life, Clara is stifled by her domestic, marital life, even though she perfectly performs her obligations as a good wife and conforms to her husband's expectations, from preparing a perfect dinner to the prospect of carrying a perfect child. Her suicide seems to be the only personal choice she can make on her own. Similar to Clarissa, who, like a 'nun' (*MD*: 25) takes refuge in her room, Clara has her own, private, white, virginal room which Charles never enters. She often sits in this room during the day, where she experiences solitary, nun-like moments.

The reader is plunged into the ordinariness of Clara's life and the minute details she likes to pay attention to: she has a 'talent for an infinite number of trivial things' (Llewellyn 2017b: 103).[9] She lives an empty life, full of insignificant, unfulfilling tasks: her day starts by going out to buy fruit to make a tart for the dinner party she is hosting in the evening for her husbands' friends. This emptiness at the core of her life is filled with beautifully arranged Instagram photos. Clarissa wears a public disguise, and so does Clara. *Une ombre chacun* offers an updated vision of what this disguise entails: Clara reinvents an idyllic life for herself that she displays on social networks, where she has many followers who admire her lifestyle, the dishes that she cooks and presents, and the flawless decoration of her home. Instagram acts as a mask that hides Clara's real self and at the same time displays a fake perfection and carefully chosen poses through photographic filters. Indeed, Clara is constantly obsessed with 'finding the right filter on the right photograph' (Llewellyn 2017b: 276).[10]

Clara tweets her feelings and thoughts every day. Thus, the private, fleeting flow of consciousness becomes public, shared with numerous people and permanently inscribed on the internet: 'displayed on the public space of the Internet for eternity' (2017b: 54).[11] These verbalised thoughts are superficial, 'carefully staged' (2017b: 52),[12] theatrically arranged and fake: Clara craves to be admired for her perfect life, perfect marriage and perfect taste, and gives the impression of being an impeccable wife and hostess. However, her deep thoughts betray her inability to cope with everyday life after her abduction, a traumatic event that occurred when she was eleven years old. She thus fabricates a sanitised public image of perfection, as illustrated by the selfies she posts on social media. People around her see only a controlled, flawless projection of herself. However, behind the perfect façade displayed on social media, harrowing thoughts of death are constantly on her mind, thoughts about her own attempted death ('there are three hundred and sixty-four ways of committing suicide' [2017b: 11][13]) or other people's deaths: people she knew or innocent civilians killed in war or terrorist attacks. She finally decides to run away from home in order to find the right place and the right way to commit suicide. Charles tries to find her and hires Seven, an American ex-marine, to trace her.

Seven is conceived as Clara's double. His ordinariness is reflected in his very common surname, Smith. He served his country in Iraq, but is now weighted down by his daily routine, unsatisfactory job and superficial wife. He decides to leave everything behind him and to come to France to embark on a mission to find Charles's missing wife. This investigation gives a new impulse to his unfulfilled life. He follows Clara like a shadow throughout her European itinerary and journey of self-discovery, from Paris, through Marseilles, Savona, Lucca, Perugia, Ancona to Paros in Greece.

Clara's and Seven's stories alternate until they briefly intersect. Many echoes, symbolic bonds and affinities are created between the two main characters, such as Clara's 'obsession with detail' (2017b: 95)[14] and Seven's 'psychotic-like attention to minute details' (2017b: 115).[15] Their tortuous, troubled pasts cast a shadow over their present and prevent them from fully living their everyday lives and finding peaceful homes. Flashbacks reveal their psychological wounds and make their memories more traumatic, as they are relived again and again.[16] Like Woolf, who during the composition of *Mrs Dalloway* found her 'tunnelling' technique 'by which [she told] the past by instalments, as [she had] need of it' (*D* 2: 272), Llewellyn follows the meandering of her characters' thoughts, probes the past and brings meaningful 'instalments' to the surface.

Through the duality of the main characters, the author depicts two ways of dealing with the terror of death. Clara's trauma of the past, when she was abducted by a paedophile, resurfaces in the present. She miraculously escaped, but the incident left a vast shadow over her life and the man still haunts her dreams. This trauma was followed by a 'juvenile depression' (Llewellyn 2017b: 61)[17] that entailed hallucinations and obsessions. On the other hand, Seven Warren Smith is a war veteran who fought in Iraq and shows clear signs of post-traumatic stress disorder: he is traumatised by the war he survived, and the voice of his dead lieutenant colonel, Evans (named by Llewellyn after Septimus Warren Smith's own brother-in-arms), constantly resonates in his mind. Every single day he relives painful, vivid incidents and remembers the violence and chaos of war, the 'horror of the sand and the jihadi' (2017b: 108),[18] the odour of fresh corpses, the 'shreds of warm flesh' (2017b: 173)[19] on his face and the screams of dying soldiers and civilians. Seven almost died in a helicopter accident in Bagdad and saw his comrades dying around him. Back from war, he has no goal in life any longer. He is left out of the American society for which he heroically fought. He now has an empty family life and a useless, unfulfilling job selling mattresses. He is miserable and refuses to have a child, despite his wife's wishes, just like his Dalloway-esque counterpart Septimus in *Mrs Dalloway*, whose wife Lucrezia desperately wants a child: 'One cannot bring children into a world like this. One cannot perpetuate suffering, or increase the breed of these lustful animals, who have no lasting emotions, but only whims and vanities, eddying them now this way, now that' (*MD*: 77). Seven has no talent whatsoever for selling mattresses but feels he has the military and detective skills to find a missing woman: he is good at observing, learning from and understanding his environment and finding clues. Thus, searching for Clara momentarily allows him to find a new aim in life and feel useful again.

Death is the main and ultimate link between Clara and Seven: Clara wants to die but it is Seven who ends up committing suicide. However, before taking the plunge, their paths casually intersect one evening on the beach before diverging again: Clara will go on living (saved by Seven's gift, the child she is carrying), and Seven will unexpectedly put an end to his life. Clara continues her journey to her final destination, Beirut, where she is ready to start a new life with her yet unborn daughter, under her maiden name, Larvor. She thus detaches herself from Charles's oppressive influence and ultimately reclaims her former identity. As Clara's and Seven's fates intersect, the transfer of death operates from the former to the latter, as he takes the burden of death from her. Clara almost commits suicide by drowning but comes back to life after her confrontation with death. Like Septimus, Seven is a Christ-like saviour figure[19] who gives Clara his own life – both literally, since he actually commits suicide in her stead, and symbolically, through his child with whom she is now pregnant. As a result, she embraces the desire to continue living. Clara is finally able to find inner peace but Seven cannot. Llewellyn's ending thus follows Woolf's own design of *Mrs Dalloway*: during the process of creation,[20] Woolf changed her original plan in which Clarissa was meant to die and created the character of Septimus as Clarissa's surrogate in death.

Death is announced at the very beginning of Llewellyn's novel, through her epigraph echoing lines from *Mrs Dalloway*: 'Death was defiance. Death was an attempt to communicate; closeness drew apart; rapture faded; one was alone' (Llewellyn 2017b). The quotation thus anticipates the principal themes of Llewellyn's novel: couples growing apart, the impossibility of communication and death as the only escape from loneliness and suffering. The epigraph foreshadows Clara's emotional situation and her obsession to put an end to her life, leading the reader to believe that she will finally commit suicide in one of the 364 ways she systematically lists in her mind. The epigraph also invites the reader to keep *Mrs Dalloway* in mind as a permanent parallel and companion to the unfolding narrative. However, just like Korkeakivi, Llewellyn updates the theme of death to the post-9/11 world. For Clara and Seven, death is not only a personal matter but is also linked to the current global political situation, and past terrorist acts constantly occupy their thoughts. Fighting terrorism was Seven's former mission in Iraq, so when he gets to Paris, he inevitably thinks of the endless 'European 9/11' (Llewellyn 2017b: 52),[21] as he perceives this wounded city, just like his country, prey to a succession of terrorist attacks: the infamous massacres of Charlie Hebdo (7 January 2015), the Bataclan (13 November 2015) and the Stade de France (13 November 2015).

Llewellyn's ultimate homage to Woolf and *Mrs Dalloway* is to be found in a playful *mise-en-abyme* postmodernist literary trick. Clara reads Woolf's biography and annotates it. She intends to follow Woolf's example of drowning and commit suicide in a similar way; attracted by the sea, Clara finally finds the perfect place on the shore of a Greek island. Llewellyn thus brings several ontological levels together: her character Clara, based on Woolf's character Clarissa, reads about Woolf, the author who gave birth to Clara's fictional counterpart. Even more pertinently, Clara owns a copy of *Mrs Dalloway* in which she has underlined meaningful passages and which is later perused by Seven Warren Smith, ironically looking in it for clues about Clara's disappearance.

Mrs Dalloway casts a powerful and lasting literary 'shadow' over *Une ombre chacun*, but Llewellyn takes its original characters, themes and preoccupations further into the twenty-first century. She thus depicts a world in which nothing remains private. Clarissa's deep, personal moments of being are the equivalent of Clara's superficial, public moments of showing. All the characters are addicted to external news and events: round-the-clock TV news, Facebook updates, emails, text messages, Instagram and WhatsApp feeds. In our time and age of constant communication with new types of media, there is paradoxically little real communication and Clara's constant updates actually hide her real self, feelings and malaise. *Une ombre chacun* relies heavily on its Woolfian legacy, but the current volatile political context infuses the novel and reflects the French state of mind after the Paris terrorist attacks. Along with Woolfian characters and themes, Llewellyn also renews and popularises Woolf's writerly prose:[22] through the dual movement of the narrative, both forwards (Clara's progress towards her final destination and Seven's suspenseful and relentless quest for Clara) and backwards (through introspection and memories), the novel reads as a highly readerly combination of psychological thriller and metaphysical detective fiction, a genre which fulfils the expectations of the current mainstream readership. Unlike Woolf's *Mrs Dalloway*, Llewellyn's page-turner reflects the tastes of twenty-first-century readers for episodic structure, cliffhanger endings, suspense and dramatic effects.

A Haunted Day on Circular Quay

Gail Jones's *Five Bells* exhibits overt intertextuality, such as the main reference to Kenneth Slessor's poem 'Five Bells' and other intertextual fragments specifically included to reinforce central symbols in the narration. It also relies on an implicit dialogue with *Mrs Dalloway*, as its narrative traces the intersecting lives of characters who move around a busy city during the course of a single day. Dalloway-esque features – the passage of time, the workings of memory, the meaning of death, the traumatic haunting experiences that lead to diverging choices of life or death – make *Mrs Dalloway* a pervasive literary presence that is never mentioned explicitly but which clearly influenced Jones. As the author has explained in interviews: 'I have recently been re-reading Woolf's diaries and was fascinated by the architectural metaphors Woolf uses, about excavating the spaces behind the present' (Jones 2011: 30–1). Jones's novel has similar concerns: the characters' pasts 'balloon out as they take the familiar walk around the ferries and souvenir shops' (2011: 30–1).

The circadian structure of *Five Bells* marks the first notable similarity to Woolf's novel. It takes place on a bright, radiant day in Sydney, from the promising glorious morning to the recording of the characters' very last thoughts just before they fall asleep at night. During the day, four characters gravitate around and converge on Circular Quay, the site of the iconic Opera House and the Sydney Harbour Bridge. Their stories are told over the course of this single Saturday in January. Like Woolf, Jones uses the single-day format to reveal whole lives, as the four characters' pasts are summoned and resurface in the present. It is one 'haunted day' (Jones 2012: 173) for all of them, disrupted by the 'unbidden recall' (48) of past memories: the dead from their pasts 'hung around, insinuating [themselves] into the spaces that broke open between now and then' (2012: 173). The plot is relegated to secondary status in order to give the stream of consciousness expanding narrative space, which showcases the novelist's capacity to inhabit the minds of her characters and depict the torments of their inner worlds.

Jones's four characters all have distinguishable Woolfian traits. Ellie, for example, is reminiscent of Clarissa Dalloway from the very beginning of the novel when she steps out into sunlight, just like her Woolfian counterpart who plunges into the fresh June morning at the opening of *Mrs Dalloway*. Ellie is a literature postgraduate in her thirties who is trying to believe in 'unmediated joy' (2012: 3). She appreciates the 'pure morning sky' and is 'filled with corny delight and ordinary elation' (2012: 3): she feels 'the frisky vague euphoria of a new day in a new city' and revels in 'listening to the community of life around her and the mechanical and human sound that together, a rough orchestra, filtered through the streets of the city' (2012: 141). Ellie asks herself on arriving at Circular Quay, 'Why not be joyful against all the odds? Why not be child-like?' (2012: 4). Such musings recall Clarissa Dalloway's desire to be happy despite everything: 'For Heaven only knows why one loves it so ... life; London; this moment in June' (*MD*: 4). Ellie comes to Circular Quay that day to meet James DeMello, her school friend and unforgettable first lover from a Western Australian country town. Throughout the day, Ellie thinks of her past relationship with James and her father's death: 'Death, time, recollected acts of love-making – all together, simultaneous, ringing in her head' (Jones 2012: 141).

In Jones's novel, just like in Woolf's, 'the world [is] seen by the sane & the insane, side by side' (*D* 2: 207). For Ellie, Sydney is an exhilarating place of life and light; James, however, observes the city through a haze of prescription drugs. James is Ellie's double, insofar as he is 'pressed' or superimposed onto her mind and body: 'He was pressed into her life as they pressed together as fourteen-year-old lovers. Into her memory. Now and for evermore' (Jones 2012: 20). In contrast to Ellie, he is 'obstinately unjoyful' (2012: 4) as he grapples with past traumas and present depression, and tries to keep his overpowering feelings in check.[23] For many years, James has been in poor mental health and has recently been involved in a tragic incident in which one of his students accidentally drowned during a school trip he was in charge of. He feels guilty and wishes to tell Ellie everything about it. James and Ellie meet briefly during the day, but their reunion leaves James frustrated and despairing over his inability to communicate the truth of the event that has disrupted his life and his desire for connection. James would like to get rid of the burden he is carrying by communicating his grief and regrets: 'He must say something, so that he might be cured of the ordeal of his own history, of his failings, of his loss, of his disabling culpability' (2012: 106). As Septimus mutters in *Mrs Dalloway*, 'communication is health, communication is happiness' (*MD*: 79), but James is paralysed and unable to communicate his trauma and return to health.

During the day, James, like Ellie, thinks about their past relationship as well as death. Significantly enough, he is consumed by a multitude of visions and thoughts of people drowning: the young man at the reception of his hotel, his pupil and René Magritte's mother.[24] Throughout the day, James is prey to powerful visions and panic attacks. For instance, the Opera House precipitates visions of predatory white teeth. These invasive visions are obsessive and hindering, and he would like to find inner peace and be liberated from his torments: 'He wanted peace and quiet. He wanted not . . . this sense of failure and shame, but whatever he had felt when twenty years ago he first fell into [Ellie's] body' (Jones 2012: 75). The only physical and psychological comfort is linked to the memory of Ellie's welcoming and reassuring body, hence his desire to reconnect with her after twenty years.

As Septimus, and Woolf herself, were encouraged to worship 'proportion' (*MD*: 84), James is ill and is trying to find balance by resorting to drugs in order to forget and escape his guilt ('he took valium, then sleeping tablets, then uppers to stay awake in the morning' [Jones 2012: 149]) but he is unable to 'control his instability' (2012: 149). After the death of his pupil, he 'entered a kind of free fall' and was 'caught in a sensation of unreality and unbounded panic' (2012: 150). Since then, James has lived in a post-mortem world which inexorably will lead to his own death. Like Septimus, he looks and feels 'wounded', 'lost' (2012: 206) and 'disorientated' (2012: 74) in the city. He moves without direction and lets himself get carried away by anonymous wave-like crowds of people: 'James saw how they moved in urgent surges and breaking waves, the hiding place they offered, the self's liquefaction, the mad sense of being sucked inside a flexible organism' (2012: 32). During the day, he moves around in an aquatic-like atmosphere until he decides to let himself be 'sucked' inside the waters of the harbour. He finally enacts his thoughts and visions of drowning by committing suicide. He drinks whisky and takes pills, 'wanting the peaceful ruination of not having to remember' (2012: 207) before he plunges to his death in the embracing water of Sydney Harbour.

The third character in Jones's novel, Pei Xing, is also reminiscent of Woolf's Septimus Smith. Pei Xing was born in China into the intellectual elite condemned by Mao's Cultural Revolution, which killed both of her parents and subjected her to imprisonment and work camps. As a political prisoner, she was physically brutalised and after two years was sent to the countryside for 're-education' (2012: 8). She is now a 'nondescript grey-haired woman' (2012: 8), a survivor who, despite having fled to Australia, cannot escape the past, which resurfaces in the form of an encounter with an immigrant from China, a cruel camp guard who once tortured her and now wants forgiveness. Her parents, considered 'class traitor[s]' and 'running dog[s] of imperialists' (2012: 8) because of their education, were murdered by the new revolutionary powers. Pei Xing's Cultural Revolution, tinted with violence, oppression and death is the equivalent of Septimus's war. She vividly remembers the beatings, injuries, murders and destructions of the 'dark and volatile times' (2012: 82). However, unlike Septimus – and James – she 'has managed to sufficiently assimilate her trauma experience in order to achieve a state of resilience' (Mudie 2014: 18).

Catherine Healy, Jones's fourth character, is a thirty-three-year-old Irish journalist also running from the past. She is haunted by the loss of her brilliant, charismatic brother and best friend who was killed in a 'commonplace' (Jones 2012: 162) car crash at the start of a promising career. She has just arrived in Australia, hoping that this continent of new beginnings can give her a fresh start. For a long time, she was linked to her double, her beloved brother, and felt attached to him, like a 'derivative creature' (2012: 91). Thoughts of death occupy big spaces in her memories, infiltrating her very body: 'Brendan lay trapped in her atoms and in the folds of her brains, he had infiltrated, somehow, the way damp entered the clammy rooms of those stinky old flats in Dublin' (2012: 53). Her dead brother 'visits' her unexpectedly during the day: 'This is how Brendan haunted her, visiting at unexpected moments, falling over her, as if from the sky, smoothing her own definition' (2012: 58). After mysteriously intersecting with Catherine's path three times during the day, Pei Xing meets Catherine briefly at the police station, as they are both witnesses to a little girl's abduction.

Jones digs out 'beautiful caves' behind her characters, which confers them depth. Woolf used the cave metaphor while working on *Mrs Dalloway*:

> I have no time to describe my plans. I should say a good deal about The Hours, and my discovery: how I dig out beautiful caves behind my characters: I think that gives exactly what I want; humanity, humour, depth. The idea is that the caves shall connect and each come to daylight at the present moment. (D 2: 263)

Jones gives the reader a guided tour of these 'caves' and spotlights each character's memories of crucial episodes from their pasts, before resurfacing to the present time and place that they all share. Like Woolf, Jones alternates the points of view, using free indirect speech to access their inner tormented worlds and give voice to her characters. Although they are separated and alone during the day, their caves 'connect', as they observe or hear the same external stimuli and respond to them in their thoughts, in a very Dalloway-esque manner.

Although *Five Bells* includes big significant events from history, such as Pei Xing's experience of the Cultural Revolution and the characters' thoughts of ongoing wars, these external, political events are always subordinated to the small, trivial events that they live in their minds. This pattern is in keeping with Woolf's theory expressed in 'Modern fiction', where she strongly admonishes her contemporaries: 'Let us not take it for granted that life exists more fully in what is commonly thought big than what is commonly thought small' (E 4: 161). Both in *Mrs Dalloway* and *Five Bells*, the focus on the seemingly small but significant and life-altering 'moments of being' is mesmerising. Utmost narrative attention is conferred to minute details or 'atoms as they fall upon the [characters'] mind[s]' (E 4: 161). Just like her character James, who as a first-year medical student examines a slice of brain through the microscope, Jones's prose offers microscopic observations on the fluctuations of the characters' minds and memories. The small, past moments of being are powerful defining reminiscences that the characters 'return to again and again' (Jones 2012: 78) and that they cherish and preserve in their memories. At the same time, they all share an acute awareness of being in the 'dense here-now' (141), and while they experience it, they dissect and magnify it.

Time is arrested during these significant moments of being, but time is also running fluidly in a Dalloway-esque fashion during the day. Indeed, Jones updates the central Woolfian themes of time and water. Time is inscribed in the title of her novel (like Woolf's original title of *Mrs Dalloway*, 'The Hours'), 'five bells' being a nautical term that measures the passing of a four-hour watch on board the ship, as well as an allusion to Kenneth Slessor's famous poem, partially quoted in the epigraph of *Five Bells*. The image of the Clepsydra, a concept that James and Ellie's teacher taught them in high school, is central to the perception of time as fluid and continuous. Clepsydra, an ancient Chinese water clock, consists of vessels that leak time. Time is thus a process 'of emptying and filling, a fluent time-passing, not one chopped into pieces' (Jones 2012: 96). Time 'leaks' (2012: 214), dwindles away, or is 'stolen' – as the Greek etymology of the word clepsydra (*kleptein*, to steal) implies. However, the past is not irrevocably and completely lost; rather it oozes and resurfaces in personal memories brought back within a present historical time. As in Slessor's poem, memories of departed people return to the characters, visit them, infiltrate them and become part of them.

Finally, Jones updates and geographically displaces the Woolfian chronotope. Thus, Sydney, with its harbour, ferries and iconic sights such as the Opera House, the Harbour Bridge, Luna Park and Circular Quay is the place of interaction between characters and a canvas for their personal and public histories.[25] *Mrs Dalloway* is transposed to contemporary, cosmopolitan Sydney, which is a global cultural hub: it is the 'Sydney of mixed populations' (Jones 2012: 212) that Ellie admires. *Five Bells* echoes *Mrs Dalloway*'s fascination with the modern city and the way its topography shapes the characters' consciousness. It can thus be read as an ode to Sydney, a celebration of its vitality, modernity, lights, fragrance, colours and noises. For instance, the sound of the Aboriginal 'didgeridoo dissolv[ing] in the air, thick and newly ancient' (Jones 2012: 2) can be compared to the sound of Big Ben in *Mrs Dalloway* that recurs throughout the narration and functions as part of the urban soundscape as well as a reminder of the irrevocability of time.[26] Like her modernist predecessor, Jones gives a painterly attention to nuances of the colours of the sea and the sky as the day drifts away and the intensity of the light changes. The accumulation of such details composes a vast, vivid embroidery and contributes to her prose's rich texture.

Conclusion

Virginia Woolf's numerous admirers and indebted legatees continue to preserve and prolong her Dalloway-esque tradition and precepts of modernism today while updating and reimagining them. By doing so, the three women writers examined in this chapter depict specific present-day literary, feminist and political issues. Woolf's Clarissa Dalloway has become an 'everywoman', a global character who migrates and adapts to different geographical and cultural environments. As Carole Llewellyn stated in an interview, 'there is quite a bit of Clarissa Dalloway in all of us' ('Au fil des livres' (2017).[27] The character of Clarissa Dalloway has thus entered our collective knowledge and has acquired the status of an iconic universal literary figure. As a 'nebula whose borders are variable and imprecise' (Eco 2011: 106), she continues to diffuse her aura in other texts and engenders other versions of herself – characters who more or less resemble her and share her 'diagnostic properties' (2011: 105).[28] In the process of her migration across texts, the Woolfian character acquires new identities and is anchored in different narrative environments and literary trends.

The writers' 'improvisation on an existing piece of great [literature] from the past' (Cunningham 2003: 137) is quite obvious in *An Unexpected Guest* and *Une ombre chacun*. However, even when there is no onomastic bond left between Clarissa and her contemporary counterparts, when no umbilical cord or intertextual references connect Woolf's text to the contemporary improvisations, her essence somehow transpires in the DNA of other modern female characters. Even when the well-known Woolfian fabric wears thin, as in *Five Bells*, there are still invisible filaments and inherent Dalloway-esque characteristics that endure in order to perpetuate Woolf's legacy. The three authors – whether they engage in an explicit or implicit dialogue – invoke in many ways the prefigurative Woolfian text, which remains detectably present in their novels.

Like Janus, god of bridges, about whom Jones's character Ellie is thinking, their contemporary novels bridge past and present, looking at the past heritage of Woolf's *Mrs Dalloway* and drawing from it while facing the contemporary realities in which they are deeply anchored and offering new reading experiences.

With *An Unexpected Guest*, *Une ombre chacun* and *Five Bells*, Anne Korkeakivi, Carole Llewellyn and Gail Jones truly commemorate Virginia Woolf's *Mrs Dalloway*. The etymology of the verb 'to commemorate' enlightens this literary practice when considered in its double meaning: recalling and showing respect for someone's life and work, as well as paying homage by producing another piece of work to keep alive a predecessor's memory. The three authors' avowed aim, just like Michael Cunningham's, are clearly commemorative, as their purpose is not 'to lay any kind of direct claim to *Mrs Dalloway*, but to honour it and try to make other art out of an existing work of art' (Cunningham 2003: 137). These commemorative novels thus become part of Woolf's impressive and enduring legacy and contribute to the mythical aura glowing around *Mrs Dalloway*. They also consolidate the privileged canonic position that it still holds, almost a century after its publication, in our global literary and cultural pantheon.

Notes

1. Michael Cunningham has discussed the direct and deliberate links between his acclaimed novel *The Hours* and Woolf's *Mrs Dalloway*:

    What I wanted to do was more akin to music, to jazz, where a musician will play improvisations on an existing piece of great music from the past – not to reinvent it, not to lay any kind of direct claim to it, but to honour it and try to make other art out of an existing work of art. (2003: 137)

2. For instance, Zadie Smith has acknowledged the implicit influence Woolf had on her novel *NW*:

    I really did not give Woolf a second thought when I was writing the book, but when I finished it and read it over, it became obvious that she must've been in my mind somewhere, even just as a model. (qtd in Zipp 2012)

3. I have examined elsewhere male homages to *Mrs Dalloway*: Ian McEwan's *Saturday*, John Lanchester's *Mr Philips* and James Hynes's *Next*. See Latham (2015: 129–66) and Latham (2013).
4. Ian McEwan and James Hynes have also borrowed Dalloway-esque structures, themes and symbols as well as modernist tools to render their visions of the global and domestic socio-political situation in *Saturday* and *Next*, two post-9/11 novels situated at the intersection of historical, objective and subjective times contained in a circadian time frame. See Latham (2015: 137–56).
5. On representations of trauma in *Mrs Dalloway*, see DeMeester (1998) and Kathryn Van Wert (2012).
6. 'Mrs Dalloway has branched into a book; & I adumbrate here a study of insanity & suicide: the world seen by the sane & the insane side by side – something like that' (*D* 2: 207); 'I want to give life & death, sanity & insanity; I want to criticize the social system, & show it at work, at its most intense' (*D* 2: 248).
7. 'Charles avait acheté une femme pour aller avec son nouvel appartement.' All translations into English are mine unless otherwise indicated.
8. 'Clara était douée dans un nombre infini de choses inutiles.'

9. 'trouver toujours ... le bon filtre sur la bonne photo'.
10. 'étalés sur la place publique de l'Internet pour l'éternité'.
11. 'soigneusement mise en scène'.
12. 'Il existe trois cent soixante-quatre façons de mourir.'
13. 'obsession du détail'.
14. 'un souci presque psychotique de minutie'.
15. Roger Luckhurst argues that a traumatic event is 'persistently re-experienced – through intrusive flashbacks, recurring dreams, or later situations that repeat or echo the original' (2008: 1).
16. 'dépression juvénile'.
17. 'l'horreur du sable et des djihadistes'.
18. 'lambeaux de chair tiède'.
19. See Arthur F. Bethea (2010).
20. On the genesis of *Mrs Dalloway*, see Latham (2015: 16–61).
21. 'Les Européens avaient eu un 11-Septembre qui n'avait pas de fin.'
22. See Roland Barthes's distinction in *S/Z* between a readerly text (that demands no special effort to read and understand, the reader being a mere consumer of the text) and a writerly one (a challenging text, using an elaborate language and demanding a special effort from the reader to read and interpret).
23. On *Five Bells* belonging to the genre of 'trauma novel', see Robert Dixon (2012: 7–12). He argues that 'the stylistic innovations of modernist novels like *Mrs Dalloway* are regarded as foundational to the trauma aesthetic and trauma novel, especially free indirect discourse, prolepsis, and the flashbacks or analepsis' (2012: 9).
24. On James's interest in the visual arts, especially his obsession with the life and work of the Belgian Surrealist painter René Magritte, see Dixon, who states that 'James's obsession with Magritte is both an insistent restatement of his own wounds, the mental illness of his mother and the drowning of his student' (2012: 10).
25. On the representation of Sydney in *Five Bells*, see Sue Kossew (2016).
26. On the 'sound as a powerful trigger for recollection' and as a 'synchronising mechanism', see Ella Mudie (2014: 12–13). Jones has also commented on her novel as an 'acoustical novel' (Gaunt 2010: 43).
27. 'j'ai réalisé que nous avions pas mal de Mrs Dalloway en nous'.
28. The 'diagnostic properties' are dominant characteristics, aggregates of 'semes' or properties (physical or external, actantial, social and mental or internal), 'essential attributes' or 'cluster of traits' (Richardson 2010: 536); they are 'essential traits' (Margolin 1987: 116) of a character specified by the original text. They define the character's 'identity' or 'personality' (Richardson 2010: 527).

Bibliography

'Au fil des livres' (2017) [Leafing through books], blog, 24 April, <https://aufildeslivres-blogetchroniques.wordpress.com/2017/04/24/rencontre-avec-lauteur-carole-llewellyn> (last accessed 17 December 2018).

Barthes, R. (1990), *S/Z*, Oxford: Blackwell.

Bethea, A. F. (2010), 'Septimus Smith, the war-shattered Christ substitute in *Mrs Dalloway*', *The Explicator*, 68: 4, pp. 249–52.

Chatman, S. (2005), 'Mrs Dalloway's progeny: *The Hours* as second-degree narrative', in J. Phelan and P. J. Rabinowitz (eds), *A Companion to Narrative Theory*, Oxford: Blackwell, pp. 269–82.

Cunningham, M. (2000), *The Hours*, New York: Picador.

Cunningham, M. (2003), 'First love', in F. Prose (ed.), *The Mrs Dalloway Reader*, New York: Harvest, pp. 136–7.

DeMeester, K. (1998), 'Trauma and recovery in *Mrs Dalloway*', *MFS: Modern Fiction Studies*, 44: 3, pp. 649–73.
Dixon, R. (2012), 'Invitation to the voyage: Reading Gail Jones's *Five Bells*', *Journal of the Association for the Study of Australian Literature*, 12: 3, pp. 1–17.
Eco, U. (2011), *Confessions of a Young Novelist*, Cambridge, MA: Harvard University Press.
Gaunt, D. (2010), 'Author interview: Gail Jones on *Five Bells*', *Bookseller + Publisher Magazine*, 90: 5, p. 43.
Jones, G. (2011), 'Interview with Catherine Keenan', *Sydney Morning Herald*, 5–6 February, pp. 30–1.
Jones, G. (2012), *Five Bells*, London: Vintage.
Korkeakivi, A. (2012a), *An Unexpected Guest*, New York: Back Bay Books.
Korkeakivi, A. (2012b), 'An unexpected guest', interview with S. Dayson, 28 May, <https://parisimperfect.wordpress.com/2012/05/28/anne-korkeakivi/> (last accessed 17 December 2018).
Korkeakivi, A. (2013), 'A conversation with Anne Korkeakivi about *An Unexpected Guest*', interview with B. Wolfe, 27 October, <https://readherlikeanopenbook.com/2013/10/27/a-conversation-with-anne-korkeakivi-about-an-unexpected-guest/> (last accessed 17 December 2018).
Kossew, S. (2016), 'City of words: Haunting legacies in Gail Jones's *Five Bells*', in C. Sandten and A. Bauer (eds), *Re-inventing the Postcolonial (in the) Metropolis*, Leiden: Brill, pp. 277–89.
Latham, M. (2013), 'Clarissa Dalloway's itinerary: Narrative identity across texts', *E-rea* (Revue électronique d'études sur le monde anglophone), 10: 2, <http://journals.openedition.org/erea/4724> (last accessed 3 September 2018).
Latham, M. (2015), *A Poetics of Postmodernism and Neomodernism: Rewriting* Mrs Dalloway, London: Palgrave.
Llewellyn, C. (2017a), 'Le nom des gens' [People's names], <https://www.carolellewellyn.com/single-post/2017/03/04/Le-Nom-X-Les-Gens> (last accessed 17 December 2018).
Llewellyn, C. (2017b), *Une ombre chacun* [*A Shadow of One's Own*], Paris: Belfond.
Luckhurst, R. (2008), *The Trauma Question*, London: Routledge.
Margolin, U. (1987), 'Introducing and sustaining characters in literary narrative', *Style*, 21: 1, pp. 107–24.
Miller, J. H. (1982), *Fiction and Repetition: Seven English Novels*, Oxford: Blackwell.
Mudie, E. (2014), 'The synchronous city: Aural geographies in Gail Jones's *Five Bells*', *New Scholar*, 3: 2, pp. 11–22.
Richardson, B. (2010), 'Transtextual characters', in J. Eder, F. Jannidis and R. Schneider (eds), *Characters in Fictional Worlds: Understanding Imaginary Beings in Literature, Film, and Other Media*, Berlin: De Gruyter, pp. 527–41.
Van Wert, K. (2012), 'The early life of Septimus Smith', *Journal of Modern Literature*, 36: 1, pp. 71–89.
Woolf, V. (1981), *The Diary of Virginia Woolf: Volume 2: 1920–1924* ed. A. O. Bell, London: Penguin.
Woolf, V. (1986–2011), *The Essays of Virginia Woolf*, ed. A. McNeillie and S. N. Clarke, 6 vols, San Diego: Harcourt; London: Hogarth Press.
Woolf, V. (1998 [1925]), *Mrs Dalloway*, Oxford: Oxford University Press.
Zipp, Y. (2012), 'Two of September's biggest novels', *The Christian Science Monitor*, 20 September, <https://www.csmonitor.com/Books/2012/0920/Two-of-September-s-biggest-novels/NW-by-Zadie-Smith> (last accessed 17 December 2018).

20

VIRGINIA WOOLF AND FRENCH WRITERS: CONTEMPORANEITY, IDOLISATION, ICONISATION

Anne-Laure Rigeade

Introduction

Is THERE A 'FRENCH WOOLF', and if so, what are her characteristics? To this complex issue, there are two answers given in literary theory and criticism. The first one leads to a historical approach, inherited from Hans Robert Jauss's *Toward an Aesthetic of Reception* (1982). The starting point of Jauss's theory is the idea that a newly published work is read and understood from the perspective of the 'horizon of expectations' of the time, and this horizon of expectations consists of readers' current knowledge and presuppositions about literature (Jauss 1982). The newness of a work can be measured by the deepness and extension of the horizon of expectations' transformation: the more important and newer a literary work is, the more it will reshape the contemporary genres, themes and language. Such a study has not been carried out for Virginia Woolf in France. The second answer to the question of knowing how to describe Woolf's reception in France aims at drawing specific connections between writers, as Pierre-Éric Villeneuve does when he shows how Nathalie Sarraute, Simone de Beauvoir and Maurice Blanchot read Virginia Woolf (2002).

In this chapter I offer a third perspective: a typology of attitudes towards Woolf's work that lays the foundations of a theory of influence. Tiphaine Samoyault has stressed the fact that, when rewriting a text, one may show 'admiration' or, on the contrary, 'denegation', a form of critical distance (2001: 101–2, 102–3). Expanding on Harold Bloom's 'anxiety of influence' (1975), Samoyault shows that this positioning affects the tone and the style of the text; the psychological attitude has, therefore, stylistic and literary consequences. In my argument, I distinguish three categories of attitudes among French writers who write after Virginia Woolf, from the early 1920s to the beginning of the twenty-first century, and under Woolf's influence: contemporaneity, idolisation and iconisation. Examining each of these attitudes successively, I also consider the historical and intellectual conditions in which they emerge and how they interact with the spirit of their time and the horizon of expectations.

Contemporaneity

Nathalie Sarraute (1900–99), an important French writer of the New Novel group, was Virginia Woolf's contemporary in several senses. First, they had a shared sensibility. Second, Sarraute began to write her first text, *Tropismes*, in 1932, when Woolf was still publishing and writing. And above all, Sarraute was Woolf's contemporary in the sense Vincent Descombes gives to that word: two events, he suggests, are contemporary if, taking place at the same time, they interfere. In Descombes's formulation, the writer who is a contemporary is the one who wrote just before, the one to whom one can reply 'right away' (Descombes 1999–2000: 29).[1] This interference, adds Henri Meschonnic in *Modernité, modernité* (Modernity, Modernity), occurs in one's imaginary world more than in the actual historical facts: 'The Middle Ages, a romantic creation, is contemporary with Romanticism. ... The contemporary is ahistorical' (Meschonnic 1993: 136).[2] Although Romanticism developed more than three centuries after the Middle Ages ended, the belief in the existence of obscure and irrational forces at work, and the Gothic aesthetics that resulted from it, reappeared in the heart of the nineteenth century, against chronological laws. Thus, though living in the same period, Arthur Rimbaud and Lautréamont were not 'contemporaries', in the sense that Meschonnic gives to this concept, because their aesthetics were too dissimilar (1993: 137). If we refer to Meschonnic's definition of the notion, Sarraute's work can be said to be 'contemporary' with Woolf's for it establishes an intimate dialogue with Woolf's own literary projects.

Like Woolf, Sarraute chose to explore the thick darkness of an interior life concealed under the surface. As Naomi Toth has shown in *L'écriture vive* (Vivid Writing), a precise and extensive comparison of Woolf's and Sarraute's works, both authors share the 'same desire to make the sensitive obviousness tremble and to seize what comes out of it in its shadow, phantom, strange evanescent material' (2016: 102).[3] In 'Conversation et sous-conversation', Nathalie Sarraute places Virginia Woolf among the 'modern' writers, along with Marcel Proust, James Joyce and Franz Kafka, all of whom explore the 'dark places of psychology': with this phrase Sarraute quotes from Woolf's 'Modern fiction' (*E* 4: 162), while evoking her own field of exploration. A few pages further, she rephrases Woolf's words: writing about her own work Sarraute describes herself as 'this poor obstinate soul who ... still rummages at all costs the dark places with the hope to extract from it some plot of unknown material' (1996: 1589).[4] 'The dark places of psychology' have become 'the dark places', without inverted commas, and then, further in the essay, 'this secret darkness' (Sarraute 1996: 1589).[5] This process of appropriating Woolf's words attests to the way Sarraute reactivates Woolf's imaginary rather than her own historical contemporaries. In 1956, when Sarraute's essay was published, the 'engaged literature' ('littérature engagée') of Sartre and of de Beauvoir was being overshadowed by the 'New Novel' ('Nouveau Roman'), whose leader, Alain Robbe-Grillet, called for objective literature, vacated of any subjectivity. Sarraute's decision to claim the heritage of Virginia Woolf, the paragon of the psychological writer, seemed completely out of context: Woolf's intent to write in the style of the stream of consciousness and to evoke the subjective world of sensations clashes with this ideal of objective literature. Hence, when she refers to Virginia Woolf, Sarraute both draws on Woolf and pretends not to do so, adopting the ironic tone of a hypothetical young and trendy writer of the 1950s: 'Who would think today about taking seriously, or even reading, the essays, published a few years after the First World War, that Virginia Woolf wrote on the art of fiction?' (1996: 1587).[6]

If Sarraute adopts this tone, it is because her own reception mirrors that of the 1920s French reception of Virginia Woolf; to get back to Meschonnic's example, just as Romanticism is contemporary with the Middle Ages in its sensibility, Sarraute's view converges with what French readers in the 1920s perceived in Woolf's work. Virginia Woolf's reception as an experimental writer and a 'psychologist' goes back to the 1920s when she first appeared in the French literary landscape.[7] The first review of Woolf's work, published in 1925 in *La Revue politique et littéraire* (Political and literary journal), focuses on Woolf's talent to describe psychology and the 'elusive shades of characters' ('d'insaisissables nuances de caractère') (Logé 1925: 754), and is shortly followed by Charles Mauron's translation into French of Woolf's very experimental section from *To the Lighthouse*, 'Times passes', published in *Commerce*.[8] *Commerce*, an elite journal founded by Paul Valéry and Valéry Larbaud, and *La Nouvelle Revue Française* (The New French Review), where an interview with Virginia Woolf by Jacques-Émile Blanche was published in 1927, were two major journals at the forefront of the modern literary movement of the time. In other words, Virginia Woolf was introduced in France by the most eminent literary personalities, including Blanche and André Maurois, who shared her exploration of writing and subjectivity in fiction. Quoting the exact same page of 'Modern fiction' as Nathalie Sarraute, Maurois writes, in a 1929 review of *Jacob's Room* and *Mrs Dalloway*, that 'to become a great novelist, one must be able to understand the other's soul' (1929: 1).[9] Far from being an exception, Maurois, who stresses Woolf's psychological insight, exemplifies a strong tendency of the critics in the 1920s to read Woolf psychologically. The sensibility of the 1950s and 1960s shifts from the interior life and psychology to social and political concerns, which explains to an extent why French readers discover Woolf's feminism at that time. The translation of *A Room of One's Own* by Clara Malraux was released in 1951, in the aftermath of Simone de Beauvoir's *Le Deuxième Sexe* (1949, first translated into English in 1953 as *The Second Sex*) and explicitly refers to Virginia Woolf as an authority on the matter of woman's condition.[10] But Sarraute does not retain this interpretation. On the contrary, in the 1960s she emphasises the psychological dimension of Woolf's work predominant in the 1920s.

By doing so, Sarraute positions Woolf as a vanguard experimental writer of the 1960s. A year after a lecture Sarraute gave at Lausanne, 'Roman et réalité' (The novel and reality) (1959), in which she quoted a passage from Virginia Woolf's short story 'The moment',[11] the first issue of the journal *Tel Quel* (As It Is)[12] (1960) released a translation by Roger Giroux of this very story. In her lecture, Sarraute views Woolf's 'moment' as an echo in her own work, explaining that she herself tries to create a temporality – an 'expanded present' ('présent agrandi' [Sarraute 1996: 1655]) – that is close to Woolf's 'moment of being'. Sarraute intends to make the reader experience each vivid emotion as if it were ever present. Actualising Woolf's short story and philosophy of time explicitly expressed in 'A sketch of the past' (see *MB*: 72),[13] she turns Woolf into a 1960s writer. In fact, the translation of Virginia Woolf's 'The moment' in *Tel Quel* can be read as a way for Philippe Sollers, its founder, to integrate this Sarrautian sensibility at the price of a dehistoricisation of Woolf's work. The contributors to the first issue of *Tel Quel*, listed with Woolf, are Claude Simon and Jean Cayrol. *Tel Quel* was published by the new press, Les Éditions de Minuit, and printed works by the 'New Novelists', who were also listed as *Tel Quel*'s co-founders. The contributors to the first issue, listed with Woolf, are Claude Simon and Jean Cayrol. The last name in the table of contents is the major poet Francis Ponge, whose texts, being a reflection on language, appear as a paragon of the reflexive literature of the 1960s. The fact that Woolf's name appears in this list produces the illusion that she too is a 1960s writer, all the more so as the original date of publication of 'The moment' is not mentioned. Furthermore, this short story directly echoes the purpose of the journal, which is to show how we perceive 'the world as it is (TEL QUEL), the infinite extension of its richness and its possibilities' (*Tel Quel* 1960: 4).[14] This publication makes Woolf's contemporaneity to Sarraute visible and turns this intimate and subterranean dialogue into an external sign of a literary tendency of the time. However, as I suggested earlier, this reception does not entirely coincide with the historically dominant reception of Woolf's work in the 1960s in France.

Idolisation

Focusing on Woolf's views related to women's autonomy, this feminist wave generates another attitude, more broadly shared than contemporaneity: idolisation. If 'contemporaneity' names a privileged connection between two writers and two imaginary worlds, upsetting all types of chronology, 'idolisation' refers to a religious attitude of adoration, as exemplified by French writers, such as Viviane Forrester, Anne Bragance and Claudine Jardin, who were inspired by Woolf in the context of the rise of a feminist conscious. In the 1960s, the woman's liberation movement in France expanded and intensified its actions, resulting in the creation of the Mouvement de Liberation des Femmes (MLF) in 1968, and in various actions between 1960 and 1975, such as the 'Manifesto of the 343 sluts' in 1971, when famous as well as unknown women claimed they had abortions and asked for abortion to become a right ('Le "Manifeste"' [2007]). At the same time, Woolf's feminist texts began to circulate in French, from *A Room of One's Own*, translated in 1951 by Clara Malraux, to *Three Guineas*, translated in 1977 by Viviane Forrester, and *Les Fruits étranges et brillants de l'art* (*Women and Writing*) translated by Sylvie Durastanti in 1983. Biographical essays or fictions starring Virginia Woolf were also proliferating shortly after the publication of her *Writer's Diary* in French (*Journal d'un écrivain*, Le Rocher, 1958): *Virginia Woolf par elle-même* (Virginia Woolf by Herself) by Monica Nathan (Seuil, 1956); *Virginia Woolf* by Viviane Forrester (Maurice Nadeau, 1973); *Trois ou quatre choses que je sais d'elle* (Three or Four Things That I Know about Her) by Claudine Jardin (Hachette, 1973); *Une Vie à soi* (A Life of One's Own) by Cécile Wajsbrot (Mercure de France, 1982); and *Virginia Woolf ou la dame sur le piédestal* (Virginia Woolf or the Lady on the Pedestal) by Anne Bragance (Des Femmes, 1984).

Moreover, the translations as much as the biographies and biofictions undoubtedly bear the traces of this historical context. Forrester's translation of *Three Guineas* was published in 1977 by Les Éditions des Femmes (Women's Publishing House), founded in 1973 by the MLF's leading figure Antoinette Fouque. Fouque's explicit goal was to promote women's writing and advance an activist feminism. Forrester adds strong oppositions between a 'we-women' and a 'they-men', as in these examples: 'to an outsider' (Woolf 1977: 154) becomes 'à nous qui demeurons en marge' (literally: 'to us who remain at the margin') (Woolf 1977: 81); 'A woman's sense of values, he writes' (Woolf 1977: 198) becomes 'votre système de valeurs, écrit-il' ('your sense of values') (1977: 148). These translations of articles and pronouns clearly show that Forrester reads *Three Guineas* as a stage on which the war of sexes rages, which is quite different from what I believe to be the idea of community Woolf promotes in her essay.[15]

The militant feminism of Clara Malraux's[16] and Viviane Forrester's translations, like the biographies and biofictions of the time, rest on what I would call an attitude of idolisation, which I will try to describe since these publications have specificities that we do not typically find in the French academic field.[17] This attitude is characterised, first, by a religious adoration of Virginia Woolf's person and work. Anne Bragance's *Virginia Woolf ou la dame sur le piédestal* (1984) exemplifies this tendency. Bragance stages herself at her writing table, composing under Woolf's eyes and authority:

> Then I drew her – I who draw so badly, I who never wanted to draw a face. From a photograph, a few years ago, I made her portrait. Beside me, in this corner where I stand, my corner, where I write, on this wall that I could touch, if I stretched my hand, she is there, always. I frequently changed places and yet this wall, that I can feel when I'm sitting there, sitting and writing, is the same everywhere. I have not finished settling down somewhere that I have recreated my corner, hung on the wall elements of an unchanging and necessary decor: some work realized by my children in kindergarten and a charcoal portrait of Virginia Woolf, clamped between a rigid board and a glass plate. (1984: 14–15)[18]

The small 'corner' – the image above the writing table (like the crucifix above the bed), the proximity of the children's drawings, underlining the continuity between one love and another – converge to identify the charcoal portrait with the statue of an idol. Veneration takes on overtly religious overtones: Bragance largely borrows from the sacred lexicon when referring to Virginia Woolf, whether to describe a gesture of rejection – 'Everyone has once insulted his god and uttered against him sacrilegious words in the moment when he believed he was betrayed, abandoned, despised or excluded' (1984: 52)[19] – or one of adoration – 'So all you can do is to kneel. Genius is nothing but the hand that gently forces you to bow down' (1984: 54).[20]

This extensive use of religious metaphor can be understood in light of the displacement of worship from religion to art. In *The Glory of Van Gogh: An Anthropology of Admiration*, the sociologist Nathalie Heinich contends that, in the modern age, an artist like Van Gogh takes on some of the characteristics of the sainthood. Not at all recognised as a genius or an artist when he was alive, the consecration and the 'construction of the Van Gogh legend' (Heinich 1996: xi) followed three steps: first he was noted for his singularity, then he was admired for his greatness, and finally he was celebrated as a virtual saint. In Heinich's argument, the first step begins during Van Gogh's lifetime with the earliest reviews of Gabriel-Albert Aurier in the 1890s, and the next step in the 1930s with the creation of an idolatrised Van Gogh. Biographical hagiographies move the focal point from the work to the man: the artist is no longer just admired as the creator of a great work of art but is viewed as a person made great by suffering and, as such, comparable to a saint.

The twin pillars of admiration in modern art, in Heinich's formulation, are compassion and sacrifice. The first is a compassionate logic that responds to a heroised and sanctified pain, on which Bragance focuses. In Bragance's *Virginia Woolf ou la dame sur le piédestal*, we recognise some of the motifs that Heinich offers to illustrate how this compassionate logic works, such as the motifs of martyrdom and exceptionality. In alignment with Heinich's discussion of Van Gogh, Bragance alludes to Woolf's 'genius' and writes of Woolf: 'Her biography, that I read at once, informed me with a cruel brutality: it plunged me into mourning' (1984: 12).[21] The second pillar is sacrificial logic: according to Christian logic, as Heinich explains, a community turns the artist's suffering into guilt, and this collective guilt reintegrates the marginalised individual into the collective body; the price of redemption may require that readers or viewers buy the works or make a pilgrimage to the fetishised places previously inhabited by the dead artist. This analysis can apply, I believe, to the religious adoration that Woolf receives: from the French feminists' point of view, she was misunderstood and misread by the patriarchal society in which she was brought up. If the feminist idolater Viviane Forrester, for instance, can worship Woolf as a saint, it is precisely because feminists shift the focus from the work to the woman, who, 'exhausted in this world left to concentration hell, to Nazism fought by a society that contained its seeds' (Forrester in Woolf 1977: 30),[22] was sacrificed by patriarchal society. And the same question is raised, as in Van Gogh's death, of who is responsible for Woolf's suicide, of who is really guilty; when Viviane Forrester revises her biography of Virginia Woolf in 2009, after she published the first version in 1973, she explains this death not only by Woolf's depression or by the context (of the war) and the surrounding despair, but also by Woolf's doctor's attitude and by her husband's indifference.[23] In a word, it is because Woolf is seen by French feminists of the 1960s such as Forrester or Bragance as a victim of men (in the first rank of which is her husband, Leonard Woolf[24]) that Woolf can be idolised as an artist-saint.

One consequence of this idolisation is that it leads to a deadly fascination. In Cécile Wajsbrot's biofiction *Une Vie à soi* (A Life of Her Own), Anne, a young journalist, discovers Woolf's texts after she falls in love at first sight with Woolf's face ('the first time – it was a little bit like the story of an encounter' [Wajsbrot 1982: 11]).[25] Anne buys *A Room of One's Own*, and sees on the cover 'the unforgettable face of Virginia Woolf, her eyes with an unforgettable melancholic depth. Hypnotized by this look, she remained immobile' (1982: 11).[26] The fascination Anne feels, 'hypnotized' by the 'melancholic eyes', freezes her body, which is gradually invaded by Woolf's life, sensations and imagination. Seduced by this gaze, Anne reads compulsively Woolf's work and begins a paper on Woolf's life and death for her magazine. She goes to London, where she experiments with a dispossession of herself: 'Another will had taken possession of her: Clarissa Dalloway had made her follow her own itinerary and had wanted her to buy flowers for her reception of tonight' (Wajsbrot 1982: 31).[27] Later, listening to a concert at Albert Hall with a British friend, Jane, Anne suddenly feels projected into Woolf's body and time; withdrawing from the present moment, Jane comments: 'You are so absorbed, as you say, that you are confusing your life with hers' (1982: 66).[28] Fascination with her idol Virginia Woolf, glorified on posters and photos (1982: 11–14), leads Anne to become not only several of Woolf's characters but Virginia Woolf herself. This mechanism is described by the psychoanalyst Roland Meyer in his study on 'fascination' as 'a quest for the Same, the similar' (Meyer 1988: 10):[29] a destruction of the self in the other in order to reach a symbiosis, a confusion of identities. André Green has described this 'death narcissism', or 'negative narcissism' (2007: 41),[30] as an experience by which the subject turns against him or herself, and against his or her vital force since another takes possession of the self. Indeed, Anne disappears little by little, as if progressively invaded by Woolf's imaginary and interior life.

Not only is Anne invaded by Woolf's feelings and sensations, but she becomes trapped in Woolf's own words as her growing obsession leads her to rewrite Woolf's work and diary (Wajsbrot 1982: 204):

> When she saw the charcuterie platter, Anne felt that it would be impossible to taste it. Pink forms evoked human flesh ravaged, clusters of dissected cadavers. . . .Then she saw only [the] mouths, [a] huge machine that would knead the swollen flesh, wild carnivorous jaws hunting, terrible destroyer. Pushing her plate away, she got up, took a few steps stumbled and fell into unconsciousness. She was in a light unknown room. She saw Olivier and Veronique, leaning over her, and remembered. Food, disgust. . . . A date besieged her thoughts, 19 August 1925 (Wajsbrot 1982: 105–6).[31]

These lines allude to various fragments from Woolf's texts. The first sentence evokes Quentin Bell's comments upon Woolf's 'phobias about eating' (Bell 1972, vol. 2: 170) and that Leonard Woolf also mentions in *Beginning Again* (1964), in contrast to his own appetite during their honeymoon. He describes, for instance, the 'beef, mutton and lamb', and the 'enormous hams, cured by themselves and hanging from the rafters in the kitchen' (1964: 153), that were served at breakfast at the Plough Inn. The second sentence is a reference to *The Voyage Out*, in which the same metaphor of wildness and a reference to lions expresses St John Hirst's disgust at the well-fed men and women around him, as they rest after dinner:

> As every other person, practically, had received two or three plump letters from England, which they were now engaged in reading, this seemed hard, and prompted Hirst to make the caustic remark that the animals had been fed. Their silence, he said, reminded him of the silence in the lion-house when each beast holds a lump of raw meat in its paws. (*VO*: 198)

Finally, the third sentence in Wajsbrot's paragraph above – 'A date besieged her thoughts, 19 August 1925' – refers directly to Woolf's diary where, on 19 August 1925, she wrote about her fainting fit during Quentin's birthday: '[I] fell down in a faint at Charleston in the middle of Q's birthday party' (*D* 3: 38).

Anne's fascination and identification with her idol leads her to repeat Woolf's life and work: to die to herself, wanting to be who she is not, longing to kill her own identity so that she can become Woolf. If we change scale, the same conclusion can be drawn with regard to Cécile Wajsbrot's project with this novel. Wajsbrot, fascinated with Woolf's work, repeats it. If the logic of idolisation is at the centre of the fiction, it reflects the author's attitude. Thus, Wajsbrot, like her character Anne who struggles to imagine a life of her own, fails to create her own writing style. In a word, idolisation prevents Wajsbrot from really creating an original work and she remains trapped in the repetition of the same, unable to create a style of her own.

Iconisation

Iconisation differs from idolisation for it opens up a way of completely recycling Woolf's work and life. The phenomenon corresponds to a late reception, derived from the evolving understanding and reception of Woolf's work and life. As Brenda Silver has shown, it is because the term bears with it an entire period, as a fantasy or a powerful symbol, that an artist becomes an icon:

> occurring across the cultural terrain, whether in academic discourses, the intellectual media, or mass/popular culture, the proliferation of Virginia Woolf has transformed the writer into a powerful and powerfully contested cultural icon, whose name, face and authority are persistently claimed or disclaimed in debates about art, politics, sexuality, gender, class, the canon, fashion, feminism, race, and anger. (Silver 1999: 3)

Iconisation first broadens the reception: it marks a moment when Virginia Woolf moves beyond the framework of the intellectual or purely academic reception and enters the popular sphere. The second feature of iconisation, according to Silver, is its slippage from the work to the woman, her name and her face: 'Virginia Woolf acquired an iconicity that exists independently of her academic standing or literary signification' (Silver 1999: 9). After Edward Albee's *Who's Afraid of Virginia Woolf* (1962) was published and staged in the 1960s, after Quentin's Bell's biography (1972) was released in the 1970s, after a wave of fascination for the Bloomsbury Group blossomed in the 1970s and into the 1990s, Woolf's name and face continued steadily to grow in fame along with her work. The difference I see between idolisation and iconic transformation is that the latter is not a 'fascination': it gives space to create freely and does not trap the idolator in a dead gaze that condemns him or her to repetition.

While Silver focuses on the Anglo-American reception, a similar slippage can be observed in the French reception, from the academic sphere to pop culture and from the work to the iconic woman. Just as Woolf's image became a 'depersonalized sign' (Silver 1999: 142), like Andy Warhol's representation of Marilyn Monroe that reduces the star to a smiling face with its crown of blonde hair, Woolf's name was reduced to a charm, conjuring an epoch and a fantasised life. After Quentin Bell's version of Woolf in the 1970s, her name could evoke for some the image of 'a twentieth-century madwoman with a bedroom of her own – witty and malicious, yes, and productive, but ... delicate, ethereal, asexual, apolitical, etc.' (Silver 1999: 123). Quentin Bell's biography was translated into French in 1973, and had a large influence on the shaping of Woolf's public image. In the same year, Claudine Jardin published a portrait of Woolf, using Quentin Bell's book as a major source, and relaying this image of a fragile madwoman, comparing her to Proust and his illness:

> How could we not think of this other nervous patient who knew that happiness buried in the most beautiful days of his memory would only rebirth with them, when he would be able, thanks to his imagination, to ensure their revival. (Jardin 1973: 108)[32]

A small book published in 2002, *Virginia Woolf à Cassis: Roches et failles* (Virginia Woolf in Cassis: Rocks and Faults), is in line with such an iconic representation. Joelle Gardes wrote a brief text accompanying pictures of Cassis, both text and pictures constituting a 'daydream' ('une rêverie') based on Woolf's stays in Cassis between 1925 and 1929 (Gardes 2002: 9). Gardes develops the myth of the 'madwoman' as constructed by Quentin Bell: 'Absent, far from herself. Terrified that her family bonds, friendships, and bridges to the outer world were perhaps wrecked forever' (Gardes 2002: 66). Riding the wave of what Silver calls 'the 1996 Bloomsbury revival', Gardes's text-image book seems indeed to 'use' Woolf's name to 'sell the concepts and the goods' (Silver 1999: 189). Gardes barely quotes Woolf's work to concentrate on her biographical experience, and on an idealised depiction of the south of France: 'she spends only several weeks in Cassis, but they were weeks so dense and luminous they had the taste of eternity' (2002: 91). This comment that concludes the short bilingual text, in French and English, is a free interpretation of Woolf's evocation of her stays in Cassis.[33] Thus, Woolf's name and life becomes a product that helps to sell the region of Cassis and the work of a contemporaneous and local photographer, Christian Ramade. This work shows how much Virginia Woolf has penetrated popular and commercial culture in France.

However, the transformation of Virginia Woolf into a cultural icon is not only a capitalistic operation, nor, as Silver argues, is it a simple catalyst for fears and anxieties: it also opens up the way to a new reception and recycling of Woolf's life and work in France.[34] What I call the attitude of 'iconisation' is illustrated by Anne-James Chaton's *Elle regarde passer les gens* (She Watches People Passing), titled *Icônes* in its choreographic adaptation. In this creative biography, Chaton retraces the life of thirteen women he considers icons of the twentieth century,[35] among them Virginia Woolf, and draws his inspiration from the iconisation process itself.

The first characteristic of iconisation is that Chaton plays with our individual and collective memory since the reader has to guess who hides behind the third person subject of all verbs: Chaton never names the women talking; each sentence begins with an unidentified 'she'. Thus, the reader has to draw on his or her encyclopaedic knowledge to identify the thirteen women. For instance, a reader who knows Virginia Woolf's life will recognise the pivot between Isadora Duncan and Woolf when reading the first allusion to Vita Sackville-West: 'She receives a letter from Vita' (Chaton 2016: 69).[36] In the sentence that immediately precedes, 'She can no longer stay on the côte d'Azur' (2016: 69),[37] Chaton was still unfolding Isadora Duncan's life. But in the space of one sentence, he suddenly switches to the next icon, without explicitly notifying the reader. Iconisation relies on an operation of recognition: the reader is expected to recognise each icon because each is so well known. Thus we are led to wonder what we know of Virginia Woolf, and also what kind of collective memory of her life and work has been constituted through time. For instance, if one relates Woolf to Vita Sackville-West, one will immediately identify the 'she' in the above-quoted sentence; if not, the second clue maybe the key, if one recognises Woolf's address ('52 Tavistock Square' [2016: 70]), or the third (an allusion to Leonard), or the fourth, an allusion to *A Room of One's Own* (2016: 71), if one is familiar with Woolf's work but not with her private life.

The second characteristic of iconisation is its reinterpretation of our understanding of recent history. By retracing these women's lives, Chaton also changes the perspective on the events of the past century and thus their meaning. On a macro-level, Chaton evokes the most significant events through a woman's eyes, a woman who stands on the margins of history. In the Woolf section, for instance, the imminence of the Second World War and the Blitz are described from the point of view not of the male soldier or of the politician choosing a strategy but of the woman civilian living in the countryside at Rodmell, hearing of the war through the radio (Chaton 2016: 93, 97, 100, 102), and enduring the bombing (2016: 100–1) or suffering rationing (2016: 99). In his depiction of Woolf, the war is seen from its outside, far from the battlefields and from any kind of geopolitical analysis.

At the micro-level of the sentence, Chaton undermines the historical narrative by intertwining the biographical events with the historical events without giving any precedence to one over the other. Woolf's listening to Mussolini's voice is intermixed with more personal considerations:

> She listens to the radio. She hears Mussolini's voice. She is impressive. She follows his talk. She endorses the failure of the negotiations. She announces the invasion. She walks in the London streets. She reads the fascist inscriptions on the walls. She takes a bus. She goes to the publishing house. She cannot concentrate. She is distracted. She thinks about her book. (Chaton 2016: 93)[38]

The 'she' ('elle') opening all the sentences smelts together Woolf's daily preoccupations with the rise of fascism as if no hierarchy existed. First, the pronoun 'she' refers alternatively to Woolf and to the voice ('la voix') of Mussolini, as if no separation existed between the inside and the outside. Second, the sound of radio and the view of fascist inscriptions superimpose with Woolf's wandering in the streets of London and her creative process. Woolf's perceptions absorb exterior and interior reality, collective history and individual impulses and extraordinary events with daily life. In consequence, the historical reality loses its weight, diluted in an everyday life experience where historical events fade and recede into the background.

Finally, the third characteristic of iconisation is its intense intertextuality: as Brenda Silver puts it, 'the star image is always intertextual and always changing' (1999: 17), a factor which *Elle regarde passer les gens* exemplifies. This intertextuality intrinsic to iconisation operates, in Chaton's work, at two levels: when shaping Woolf's voice, Chaton solicits intensively Woolf's writings; when shaping Woolf's story, he incorporates diverse female destinies that echo hers.

Chaton literally rewrites Virginia Woolf's *Diary*, remaining very close to Woolf's syntax and images. Chaton's 'She works at her novel. She takes some notes. She won't try to tell a story' (2016: 73)[39] rephrases Woolf:

> Now about this book, The Moths. . . . Every morning, I write a little sketch, to amuse myself. I am not saying, I might say, that these sketches have any relevance. I am not trying to tell a story. (*D* 3: 229)

Chaton, at this level, does not interact with texts describing Woolf from the outside, as Silver would have defined intertextuality in the iconisation process, but with texts evoking her interior life through her own diary writing.

Also, Chaton sets Woolf's biography in a network of women's stories, either because he had interest in some that may have shaped her thought or because he finds underground links between his icons. Chaton inserts, for instance, a short biography of Antigone (2016: 90) just after the mention of Woolf's rereading Sophocles' play ('She will reread the classics. She begins with Antigone' [2016: 90])[40]: he selects elements linked to

Antigone's political resistance that Woolf herself will reuse in *Three Guineas*. When he then adds Jeanne d'Arc's narrative (Chaton 2016: 83–6) it may seem randomly connected to Woolf, since it appears as a digression when narrating Woolf's journey in France. But not only does this biography appear immediately before Chaton tells of Woolf's struggle to write Elizabeth Barrett Browning's biography, but Jeanne d'Arc's story echoes in many ways Woolf's life and feminist texts (Jeanne d'Arc's hearing voices echoing Woolf's own hallucinations, her conviction before a court composed of men echoing Woolf's arguments about patriarchy, etc.). This specific intertextuality, if slightly different from what Silver envisioned, reshapes and transforms Woolf's image: the echoes with Jeanne d'Arc link Woolf with a historical heroine. And the fact that her life story is connected with Isadora Duncan's stresses not only the role of southern France in Woolf's life but also her enjoyment of motor cars and speed. Indeed, when switching from Duncan to Woolf, Chaton makes the transition around their journeys in France: Isadora Duncan died driving her car in 1927 in Nice (the first six sentences), and Woolf stays with Vita at Fontcreuse, in 1928 (continuing from the seventh sentence):

> She speeds through La Croisette. She regains her suite at the Negresco. She spends her nights at the casino. She will soon regret it. She is ruined again. She cannot stay on the French Riviera any more. She receives a letter from Vita. She invites her to come to London. She could give lessons. She does not have a choice. She does not have any link with Paris any more. She must sell her apartment. She is not welcome in the Parisian hotels. She leaves Canne. She drives through France. She passes through Cassis. She stays at the Fontcreuse Castle. She sojourns there a few days. (Chaton 2016: 69)[41]

Woolf becomes an icon, as Chaton's work illustrates, because her work and her image can be articulated with a collective memory intertwining major historical events and central cultural figures, because Woolf could take place in a global collective imaginary of the twentieth century.

Conclusion

French writers interested in and influenced by Woolf's work have, over time, revealed three different attitudes towards her work. The first one, contemporaneity, illustrated by Nathalie Sarraute, can be defined as a subterranean and intimate link between two imaginary worlds that exist beyond historical periodisation. The second, idolisation, flourished in France with the feminist reception of Woolf and an identification between Woolf's destiny and the woman artist's martyrdom. The worship of her person, driven to commit suicide by a patriarchal society in Viviane Forrester's reading, takes place in a double context, offering a denunciation of the patriarchal values of the 1970s and, more broadly, a shift from religion to art, as described by Nathalie Heinich. Finally, iconisation consists of questioning the very process of reception, the impact of a work on our individual and collective memory. One may object that these three attitudes are not specifically French. And, indeed, they are not. Nevertheless, what is specifically French is, first, the local context that explains the emergence of each perspective, and, second, the specific form each response takes within each logic explored in this chapter.

Notes

1. 'sur le champ'. All further translations are mine unless otherwise indicated.
2. 'Le Moyen-Âge, création romantique, est contemporain du romantisme.... Le contemporain est anhistorique.'
3. 'même désir de faire trembler l'évidence sensible et de saisir à vif ce qui s'en échappe comme ombre, spectre, étrange matière évanescente'.
4. 'malheureux obstiné qui, insoucieux de l'indifférence ou de la réprobation qui l'attendent, s'acharne à fouiller encore les régions obscures dans l'espoir d'en extraire quelques parcelles de matière inconnue'. Maria Jolas translates this sentence as, 'However, the unfortunate die-hard who, being unconcerned by the indifference and reproval awaiting him, persists nevertheless in digging in these dark regions, in the hope of extracting from them a few particles of an unknown substance' (Sarraute 1963: 81).
5. 'ces ténèbres secrètes'. Jolas translates this phrase as 'these secret recesses' (Sarraute 1963: 82).
6. 'Qui songerait aujourd'hui à prendre encore au sérieux ou seulement à lire les articles que Virginia Woolf, quelques années après l'autre guerre, écrivait sur l'art du roman?' Jonas's translation is, 'Who today would dream of taking seriously, or even reading, the articles that Virginia Woolf wrote, shortly after the First World War, on the art of the novel?' (Sarraute 1963: 77).
7. For instance, Louis Gillet writes that Woolf inherits from Joyce the transformation of the novel in a 'sort of film that had to record in its completeness, during a day, the succession of phenomena that compose what we call the conscience of an individual' ('espèce de film qui devait enregistrer dans sa totalité, pendant le cours d'une journée, la succession de phénomènes qui composent ce qu'on appelle la conscience d'un individu' [1929: 221]). On the same year, Jacques-Émile Blanche writes that Woolf has 'a creation of her own: a feminine psychology with no kinship with anything' ('une création bel et bien à elle: psychologie féminine sans parenté avec quoi que ce soit' [1929: 9]).
8. The title of the journal *Commerce* refers to the social skills of having polite, cultured conversation, but also refers to exchanges between countries and tradition, and is an allusion to the concepts of Montaigne, among others.
9. 'Pour devenir un grand romancier, il faut être capable de comprendre les âmes des autres.'
10. In *The Second Sex*, Simone de Beauvoir quotes *A Room of One's Own* and concludes: 'In England, Virginia Woolf notes women writers always engender hostility' (2011: 124).
11. In her essay, Sarraute quotes 'The moment', but approximatively: 'it is largely composed of visual and of sense impressions' (Woolf 1948: 3) becomes '[e]ach moment is an overflowing atom, she said, made of a combination of thoughts and sensations' ('Chaque instant est un atome plein à craquer, disait-elle, d'une combinaison de pensées et de sensations' [Sarraute 1996: 1650]). The substitution of 'visual impression' with 'thoughts' ('pensées') shows how Sarraute reappropriates Woolf's work.
12. 'Tel quel' is a pun that refers to the idea of not modifying reality but showing reality as it is.
13. In *Moments of Being*, and more specifically 'A sketch of the past', Woolf expresses this idea of the relivable present of the trauma: she feels a shock at moments of high intensity, 'moments of being', that tear apart the continuity of time, and thus insert another temporality, close to Sarraute's 'expanded present' (*MB*: 72).
14. 'le monde TEL QUEL, l'étendue de sa richesse et de son possible'.
15. See Rigeade (2017).
16. See Rigeade (2014).
17. See Rodier (2002).

18. 'Alors je l'ai dessinée, moi qui dessine si mal, moi qui n'ai jamais eu envie de dessiner un visage. A partir d'une photographie, il y a quelques années, j'ai fait son portrait. Près de moi, dans cet angle où je me tiens, qui est mon coin, celui où j'écris, sur ce mur que je toucherais pour peu que je tende la main, elle est là, toujours. J'ai souvent changé de lieux et pourtant ce mur-là, celui que je peux toucher quand je suis assise là, assise à écrire, est partout le même. Je n'ai pas fini de m'installer quelque part que j'ai déjà recréé mon coin, accroché sur ce mur les éléments d'un décor immuable, nécessaire: quelques travaux que mes enfants réalisèrent en classe maternelle et le portrait au fusain de Virginia Woolf, pincé entre un carton rigide et une plaque de verre.'
19. 'Chacun a un jour insulté son dieu et proféré contre lui des paroles sacrilèges dans le moment où il s'est cru trahi, abandonné, méprisé ou exclu.'
20. 'Alors il ne reste qu'à s'agenouiller. Le génie n'est rien d'autre que cette main qui vous force doucement à vous prosterner.'
21. 'sa biographie consultée sur-le-champ me renseigna avec une cruelle brutalité: elle m'endeuilla'.
22. 'Epuisée dans ce monde livré à l'enfer concentrationnaire, au nazisme combattu par une société qui en contenait les germes' (my translation).
23. 'he does not see her any more, seems to be tired of her' ('il ne la voit plus, semble lassé d'elle') (Forrester 2009: 315).
24. In the portrait she draws of Virginia Woolf before her suicide, from a 1973 essay, Viviane Forrester writes that she was 'exhausted, once again left alone with her madness in this world dominated by men, where her husband, for a final gesture, has strained her, with the hope of appeasing her crisis, a rag, so that, becoming again a normal woman, she dusts these very books she was afraid not to know how to write any more' ['épuisée, livrée une fois de plus à la folie dans ce monde dominé par les hommes, où son mari, pour dernier geste, lui a tendu, dans l'espoir d'apaiser sa crise, un chiffon, afin que, redevenue femme normale, elle poussette ces livres qu'elle redoutait de ne plus savoir écrire'] (Forrester in Woolf 1977: 30, my translation).
25. 'La première fois – c'était un peu comme l'histoire d'une rencontre.'
26. 'Elle avait découvert le visage inoubliable de Virginia Woolf, ses yeux d'une inexprimable profondeur mélancolique. Hyptnotisée par ce regard obstinément fixé ailleurs, elle était restée immobile.'
27. 'une autre volonté l'avait prise: Clarissa Dalloway lui avait suivre son propre itinéraire et avait voulu lui faire acheter des fleurs pour sa réception du soir'.
28. 'Tu es tellement absorbée, comme tu dis, que tu es en train de confondre ta vie et la sienne.'
29. 'La Fascination existe toujours d'abord sans réciprocité, mais est recherche de la réciprocité. C'est là le leurre. La recherche du même, du pareil' ['Fascination exists always at first without any reciprocity, but seeks reciprocity. That is the lure. The quest of the Same, the similar'].
30. 'le narcissisme de mort' or 'le narcissisme négatif'. Green's work was originally published in English in 2001.
31. 'Lorsqu'elle vit le plateau de charcuterie, Anne sentit qu'elle qu'il lui serait impossible d'y goûter. Les formes roses lui évoquaient une chair humaine défaite, des amas de cadavres disséqués.... Puis elle ne vit que leur bouche, énorme machine à pétrir les chairs tuméfiées, gueule sauvage de carnassiers en chasse, effroyable destructrice. Repoussant son assiette, elle se leva, fit quelques pas en titubant et sombra dans l'inconscience. Elle se trouvait dans une chambre claire inconnue. Elle aperçut Olivier et Véronique, penchés au-dessus d'elle, et se souvint. La nourriture, son dégoût.... Une date assiégeait sa pensée, 19 août 1925.'
32. 'Comment ne pas songer à cet autre malade nerveux, qui savait que le bonheur enfoui dans les beaux jours de sa mémoire ne renaîtrait qu'avec eux, quand il serait capable, par l'imagination, d'en assurer le retour.'

33. In her *Diary*, for instance, Virginia Woolf concludes her description of Cassis with these words:

    > But L. & I were too, too happy, as they say; if it were now to die &c. Nobody shall say of me that I have not known perfect happiness, but few could put their finger on the moment, or say what made it. Even I myself, stirring occasionally in the pool of content, could only say But this is all I want. (*D* 3: 8–9)

    Joelle Gardes claims that Cassis was a moment of intense happiness for Woolf, though these lines suggest that, even if Woolf did appreciate her stay in the south of France, no one but herself could identify precisely these moments of intensity.
34. Brenda Silver explains, for instance, the success of Sally Potter's adaptation of *Orlando* and Garland's adaptation of *A Room of One's Own* by the fact that 'they raise some of the most hotly debated issues of our time' (Silver 1999: 214).
35. In *Elle regarde passer les gens*, the thirteen icons Anne-James Chaton engages with are: Camille Claudel, Mata Hari, Rosa Luxembourg, Isadora Duncan, Virginia Woolf, Lucie Schwob (Claude Cahun), Frida Kahlo, Marilyn Monroe, Jackie Kennedy, Janis Joplin, Silvia Kristel, Margaret Thatcher and Lady Diana.
36. 'Elle reçoit un courrier de Vita.'
37. 'Elle ne peut plus rester sur la côte d'Azur.'
38. 'Elle écoute la radio. Elle entend la voix de Mussolini. Elle est très impressionnante. Elle suit son allocution. Elle entérine l'échec des négociations. Elle annonce l'invasion. Elle marche dans les rues de Londres. Elle lit des inscriptions fascistes sur les murs. Elle monte dans un bus. Elle se rend à la maison d'édition. Elle a du mal à se concentrer. Elle a l'esprit ailleurs. Elle pense à son livre.'
39. 'Elle travaille à son roman. Elle prend quelques notes. Elle ne racontera pas d'histoire.'
40. 'Elle relit les classiques. Elle commence par Antigone.'
41. 'Elle file à toute allure sur la Croisette. Elle retrouve sa suite du Negresco. Elle passe ses soirées au casino. Elle le regrettera bientôt. Elle est à nouveau ruinée. Elle ne peut plus rester sur la Côte d'Azur. Elle reçoit un courrier de Vita. Elle l'invite à Londres. Elle pourrait y donner des cours. Elle n'a pas vraiment le choix. Elle n'a plus d'attaches à Paris. Elle a dû vendre son appartement. Elle est malvenue dans les hôtels de la capitale. Elle quitte Canne. Elle traverse la France. Elle passe par Cassis. Elle est logée au château de Fontcreuse. Elle y séjourne quelques jours.'

Bibliography

Bell, Q. (1972), *Virginia Woolf: A Biography*, 2 vols, London: Hogarth Press.
Blanche, J.-É. (1929), 'Un nouveau roman de Virginia Woolf' [A new novel by Virginia Woolf], *Nouvelles littéraires*, 16 February, p. 9, <https://gallica.bnf.fr/ark:/12148/bpt6k6450513w/f10.item> (last accessed 22 January 2020).
Bloom, H. (1975), *The Anxiety of Influence: A Theory of Poetry*, London: Oxford University Press.
Bragance, A. (1984), *Virginia Woolf ou la dame sur le piédestal* [Virginia Woolf or The Lady on the Pedestal], Paris: Éditions des Femmes.
Chaton, A. J. (2016), *Elle regarde passer les gens* [She Watches People Passing], Paris: Verticales.
de Beauvoir, S. (1949), *Le deuxième sexe*, Paris: Gallimard.
de Beauvoir, S. (2011 [1953]), *The Second Sex*, trans. C. Borde and S. Malovany-Chevallier, London: Vintage Books.
Descombes, V. (1999–2000), 'Qu'est-ce qu'être contemporain?' [What is it to be contemporary?], *Le Genre humain*, 35, pp. 21–32.
Forrester, V. (2009 [1973]), *Virginia Woolf*, Paris: Le Livre de poche.

Gardes, J. (2002), *Virginia Woolf à Cassis: Roches et failles* [Virginia Woolf in Cassis: Rocks and Faults], photographs C. Ramade, trans. C. Carsten, Marseille: Images en manœuvre.
Gillet, L. (1929), 'L'*Orlando* de Mme Virginia Woolf' [Mrs Virginia Woolf's *Orlando*], *La Revue des deux mondes*, 1 September.
Green, A. (2007 [1983]), *Narcissisme de vie, narcissisme de mort*, Paris: Éditions de Minuit, 'Reprise'.
Heinich, N. (1996), *The Glory of Van Gogh: An Anthropology of Admiration*, trans. P. L. Browne, Princeton, NJ: Princeton University Press.
Jardin, C. (1973), *Virginia Woolf, trois ou quatre choses que je sais d'elle* [Virginia Woolf, Three or Four Things I Know about Her], Paris: Hachette Littérature.
Jauss, H. R. (1982), *Toward an Aesthetic of Reception*, trans. T. Bahti, Minneapolis: University of Minnesota Press.
'Le "Manifeste"' (2007), 'Le "Manifeste des 343 salopes" paru dans le *Nouvel Obs* en 1971' ['The "Manifesto of the 343 Sluts" appeared in the Nouvel Obs in 1971'], *L'Obs*, <https://www.nouvelobs.com/societe/20071127.OBS7018/le-manifeste-des-343-salopes-paru-dans-le-nouvel-obs-en-1971.html> (last accessed 22 January 2020).
Logé, M. (1925), 'Quelques romancières contemporaines' [Some contemporary novelists], *Revue Politique et Littéraire*, 21 November, pp. 753–6.
Maurois, A. (1929), 'Première rencontre avec Virginia Woolf' [First meeting with Virginia Woolf], *Les Nouvelles littéraires*, 327, 19 January, p. 1, <https://gallica.bnf.fr/ark:/12148/bpt6k64505090/f1.item.r=woolf> (last accessed 22 January 2020).
Meschonnic, H. (1993 [1988]), *Modernité, modernité* [Modernity, Modernity], Paris: Gallimard.
Meyer, R. (1988), 'La Fascination: Essai psychanalytique' [Fascination: The psychoanalytic essay], dissertation, Lille University.
Rigeade, A. L. (2014), '*A Room of One's Own*, Un Cuarto propio, Une Chambre à soi: Circulations, déplacements, réévaluations' [A Room of One's Own, A room of your own, A room of your own: Circulations, displacements, re-evaluations], *Ticontre. Teoria Testo Traduzione* [Ticontre. Theory Text Translation], 2 <http://www.ticontre.org/ojs/index.php/t3/article/view/36/0> (last accessed 23 February 2020).
Rigeade, A. L. (2017), '*Three Guineas/Trois Guinées* ou la question de la traduction' [Three Guineas/Three Guineas or the question of the translation], in C. Davison and A.-M. Smith-Di Biasio (eds), *Trans-Woolf, Thinking across Borders*, Perugia: Morlacchi University Press, pp. 165–84.
Rodier, C. (2002), 'The French reception of Woolf: An état présent of études Woolfiennes', in M. A. Caws and N. Luckhurst (eds), *The Reception of Virginia Woolf in Europe*, London: Continuum, pp. 39–53.
Samoyault, T. (2001), *L'intertextualité: Mémoire de la littérature* [Intertextuality: Memory of Literature], Paris: Nathan.
Sarraute, N. (1963), *The Age of Suspicion: Essays on the Novel*, trans. M. Jolas, New York: George Braziller.
Sarraute, N. (1996), *Œuvres complètes* [Complete Works], ed. J.-Y. Tadié, Paris: Gallimard.
Silver, B. R. (1999), *Virginia Woolf Icon*, Chicago: Chicago Press University.
Tel Quel (1960), 1.
Toth, N. (2016), *L'écriture vive: Woolf, Sarraute, une autre phénoménologie de la perception* [Vivid Writing: Woolf, Sarraute, Another Phenomenology of Perception], Paris: Classiques Garnier.
Villeneuve, P.-É. (2002), 'Virginia Woolf among writers and critics: The French intellectual scene', in M. A. Caws and N. Luckhurst (eds), *The Reception of Virginia Woolf in Europe*, London: Continuum, pp. 19–38.
Wajsbrot, C. (1982), *Une Vie à soi* [A Life of Her Own], Paris: Mercure de France.
Woolf, L. (1964), *Beginning Again: An Autobiography of the Years 1911–1918*, London: Hogarth Press.

Woolf, V. (1938), *Three Guineas*, London: Hogarth Press.
Woolf, V. (1948 [1941]), *The Moment and Other Essays*, New York: Harcourt Brace Jovanovich.
Woolf, V. (1976). 'A sketch of the past', ed. J. Schulkind, *Moments of Being*, New York: Harcourt Brace Jovanovich, pp. 61–137.
Woolf, V. (1977), *Trois Guinées*, trans. V. Forrester, Paris: Éditions des Femmes.
Woolf, V. (1980), *The Diary of Virginia Woolf: Volume 3: 1925–1930*, ed. A. O. Bell, London: Hogarth Press.
Woolf, V. (1992 [1915]), *The Voyage Out*, Oxford: Oxford University Press.
Woolf, V. (1994), *The Essays of Virginia Woolf: Volume 4: 1925–1928*, ed. A. McNeillie, London: Hogarth Press.

21

THE DREAM WORK OF A NATION: FROM VIRGINIA WOOLF TO ELIZABETH BOWEN TO MARY LAVIN

Patricia Laurence

VIRGINIA WOOLF FEARED THAT THE 'loudspeaker' voice of war would drown the personal voice of the writer in 1940 (*DM*: 244). Surrounded by the wartime blare of megaphones, radio, films, newspapers, posters and magazines that glorified soldiers at the battlefront, she knew the capacity of nationalist bombast and fascist hectoring to mute other voices – particularly women's – in the build-up to the Second World War. '"Hitler!" The loudspeakers cry with one voice. Who is Hitler? What is he? Aggressiveness, tyranny, the insane love of power made manifest, they reply' (*DM*: 245). Addressing educated men in her polemic, *Three Guineas,* Woolf charges that with 'the sound of guns in your ears you have not asked us [women] to dream' (*TG*: 163). Women who do dream and write in the personal voice in times of national conflict, she asserts, are not heard.

Woolf imagines a different kind of society for men and women, and she inspires other women writers around the globe to listen not to the rush of loudspeakers that trumpet violence and war but to 'a recurring dream that has haunted the human mind since the beginning of time; the dream of peace, the dream of freedom' (*TG*: 163). Such a dream emerges from an enlightened notion of the capacity of men and women – as individuals and in family, community and nation – to change. These dreams are inscribed in *Three Guineas*, where she advocates the advancement of women's lives through education and careers and a rethinking of their social position and political participation. She urges women to dream.

In addition, Woolf reconsiders kinds of writing and explores why women's writing with its concern over so-called 'small' subjects is often ignored or suppressed during times of national conflict. In 'Modern fiction', she advises that modern writers not take it for granted that 'life exists more fully in what is commonly thought big than what is commonly thought small' (*CR 1*: 154–5). In doing so, she creates a new ground for 'the proper stuff of fiction' (*CR 1*: 154), challenging the notion that the 'large' or 'big' events of war, conflict or bellicose rhetoric (that often surface in the male tradition in wartime or heightened nationalism) are more important in fiction and history than the 'small' events or contretemps that figure in women's stories and novels. In *A Room of One's Own*, she also dreams and makes a plea for more education for women and the material conditions – money and a room of one's own – that would enable them to write. Dreams of how women's lives might be different surface in her characters from

To the Lighthouse: the artist, Lily Briscoe, stands at her easel with Mr Tansley whispering in her ear 'Women can't paint, women can't write' (*TL*: 75) and she dreams of a time when women artists would not be taunted. Mrs Ramsay, consumed with '[a]ll the being and the doing' as a charitable mother of eight with a difficult husband, feels the need 'to be silent, to be alone' (*TL*: 95).

Partha Chatterjee, a postcolonial critic, extends Woolf's thinking and writes of the 'new woman' in nineteenth- and twentieth-century India who, like British women writers, had to cope with dominant male voices during periods of colonialism, anti-colonial nationalism and after. Women's writing was distinguished, according to Chatterjee, in 'the way in which the very themes of disclosure of self remains suppressed under a narrative of changing times, changing manners, and customs and changing values' (1993: 138). His analysis of women's position, like other postcolonial critics – Gayatri Chakravorty Spivak and Susan Stanford Friedman – has comparative implications as the personal voice of the woman writer is drowned not only by the loudspeaker of war as in Britain but also during periods of surging national conflict and nationalism in modern states. This expands our global canvas as we think about and reason across different cultures finding 'the transnational condition that informs any local formations' (Friedman 1998: 111), with the condition being the suppression of the personal voices of women writers in times of conflict through the devaluation of their stories that are revelatory of the inner life of self, family and community. This chapter then is not only about women and wartime writing but also considers how and what women can or are allowed to write in times of heightened national conflict and nationalism.

Virginia Woolf reconsidered the traditional literary model in her essays and provided a path for our reading of such women around the world. As examples, this chapter proposes a rereading of two Irish women writers in generations following Woolf: the Anglo-Irish writer Elizabeth Bowen (1899–1973) and the Irish-American writer Mary Lavin (1912–96). Both wrote with a divided self and consciousness about having grown up in two countries – Bowen in Ireland and the UK, and Lavin in the US and Ireland – and they both attracted interest as hybrid Irish writers of a new generation. Bowen was touched by the Easter Uprising, the Irish War of Independence (1919–21) and 'the Troubles'. Lavin arrived in Ireland from America, a year after the establishment of the Irish Free State in 1922, living through the neutrality of the Second World War and later, the time of the Troubles. As Janet Egleson Dunleavy has perceptively noted, 'one generation of Irish writers already had achieved international recognition, a second was emerging, and everywhere editors and publishers were courting new Irish voices in literature. It was a time to be proud of being Irish' (1983: 72).

Both women lived through the Second World War – Bowen enduring the Blitz in London and Lavin outside of it in neutral troubled Ireland. Though their worlds were in political turmoil, they withdrew from the centre of these national conflicts and became 'outsiders', 'educated men's daughters' whose first oath would be 'not to fight with arms' and to assess the meanings of country and patriotism *(TG*: 122–3). They were drawn to the literary and cultural perspectives that Woolf describes in *Three Guineas*, *A Room of One's Own*, 'Thoughts on peace in an air raid' (*DM*: 243–8) and 'Modern fiction' (*CR 1*: 150–8), among other works. Though retreating from the centre of national conflict as a subject, Bowen and Lavin critique their societies from the sidelines and, in so doing, enlarge the landscape of wartime and nationalist literature, mainly mapped up to then by male authors. They offer a new way of telling the story of a nation that includes social criticism and a vision of a future in which women 'fight with the mind' without firearms (*TG*: 244). They do the dream work of a nation.

In addition, the lives of Woolf, Bowen and Lavin touched one another. Letters reveal that Woolf became a treasured friend of Elizabeth Bowen, introduced to her in 1932 by Ottoline Morrell. They had critical discussions and joyful meetings at both Bowen's Court and Monk's House. Mary Lavin was also enthralled with Woolf and was a graduate student writing a PhD dissertation about her at University College Dublin when Woolf was just beginning to be a subject for study by prescient authors like Winifred Holtby (1932) and Ruth Gruber (1935). It was 1938, just at the time that Woolf was completing *Three Guineas*. According to writer and critic Belinda McKeon, Lavin revealed in an interview that an elderly woman, when informed of her dissertation on Woolf, remarked, 'Oh fancy that, I had tea with her [Woolf] just yesterday' (McKeon 2012). This remark was a catalyst for Lavin's own writing: 'I went home and took my thesis and I tore it, I turned it upside down' (McKeon 2012). She wrote her first short story, 'Miss Holland', on the reverse page of the thesis and published it in *Dublin Magazine* in 1939, abandoning her thesis and dedicating herself to writing short fiction.

Woolf's ideas provided a model for these women writers living through historical periods of conflict. Living in England on the verge of the Second World War, Woolf and Bowen heard warplanes and buzzing bombs overhead, witnessed daily scenes of the destruction and dislocation of people on the streets of London and also suffered the bombing of their own homes before and during the Second World War. Lavin lived through the violent aftermath of the Irish War of Independence in 1919–21, Ireland's neutrality in the Second World War, and the period of the Troubles from the 1960s into the 1990s. Their art – written amid national and international conflict – reveals their struggle to rescue and preserve small segments of their own experiences and perspectives on the nations in which they live. Yet their writing is often devalued as personal, subjective and trivial, and is subsumed under the rubric of domestic or home-front fiction by mainstream critics. Such judgements limit their scope and impact. Diana Trilling, for example, is part of this critical stream beginning mid-century that devalues the work of some of the most talented women writers of the day because they were perceived as focused on the internal and subjective, ignoring so-called external reality (Trilling 1949: 254). Male writers of the period, on the other hand, were and are still viewed as deeply engaged with 'big' issues like politics, identity, history and 'reality' in the wider society and the world. Yet Woolf asserts,

> It is obvious that the values of women differ very often from the values which have been made by the other sex; naturally, this is so. Yet is it the masculine values that prevail. Speaking crudely, football and sport are 'important'; the worship of fashion, the buying of clothes 'trivial'. And these values are inevitably transferred from life to fiction. This is an important book, the critic assumes, because it deals with war. This is an insignificant book because it deals with the feelings of women in a drawing-room. (*AROO*: 76–7)

This chapter illuminates how Lavin and Bowen, bolstered by Woolf's values and writing, use their own sharp and subtle observations to highlight the importance of the minimal or small subject alongside the maximal. Elizabeth Bowen's perspective and writing is treated more briefly to deepen Woolf's stance; the main focus is on Mary Lavin's stories that have been critically devalued, as have those by other women writers, and consigned to private, domestic or unworldly domains. Both Bowen and Lavin, nevertheless, write the kind of fiction Woolf calls for, where 'the accent falls differently; the emphasis is on something hitherto ignored' (*CR 1*: 157). They enter women's consciousness and employ female narrators to challenge established values and reassess women's roles and relations with men and other women. They critique their societies through fiction, exposing the hypocrisies in characters and fissures in communities and institutions. This is their dream work.

'The private and the public worlds are inseparably connected': Virginia Woolf

Woolf provides the backbone for three important arguments that transform our reading of women's writing during times of war or national conflict and struggle. First, Woolf creates a new ground for 'the proper stuff of fiction' (*CR 1*: 154). She rethinks the use of the words 'small' and 'large' in criticism and fiction, advising that 'life' as represented in women's writing has often been evaluated as being unimportant and 'small' compared to the 'big' worldly issues dealt with in the male tradition of writing (*CR 1*: 154–5). Second, she attacks 'unreason' in private and public life in the shape of fascism by creating links between domestic and the public 'tyranny' in *Three Guineas* (*TG*: 162). Third, she offers a model for reading women authors along the lines echoed by Chatterjee who, as noted earlier, discusses the cultural practices of women writing under periods of nationalism and during times of flux and conflict. Chatterjee asserts that 'the inner spaces of community life' (1993: 147) are what truly matter in the life of a nation; nevertheless, he demonstrates that the writing of women is often marginalised or repressed under the banner of nationalism. It is then, he asserts in line with Woolf, the duty of women to hold fast to and preserve private, family and community beliefs, concerning religion, spirituality and otherwise. Woolf and Chatterjee challenge and re-evaluate what has been considered the 'proper stuff' of women's writing, especially during times of national disorder.

In recasting the relationship between the private and the public, Woolf challenges claims of critics who assert that women writers do not engage with or link their fiction to the wider society, the nation and the world. Woolf sidelines critics who have socialised readers into outworn ideologies that diminish the import of women's lives and, subsequently, the stories they tell and write. The reading model proposed in this chapter urges critics to acknowledge that this literary dialogue takes place in a field of power in which the national narrative or so-called worldly writing of men is the dominant power. But as Chatterjee asserts, 'dominance here cannot exhaust the claims of subjectivity, for even the dominated must always retain an aspect of "autonomy", as "power" is always a relation and a struggle' (1993: 137). Woolf's thinking is transformative in *Three Guineas* as she outlines the struggle and asserts that the 'the public and the private worlds are inseparably connected; that the tyrannies and the servilities of the one are the tyrannies and the servilities of the other' (*TG*: 162). She observes that the same social and political systems that make it possible for women to fight for education enables them to actively resist war. She urges women to participate in the systems constructed by 'educated men' and to fight against the Fascist and Nazi forces that threaten freedom (*TG*: 62). There is a potential unity between the sexes, she asserts, in a mutual effort to end patriarchy in the home, paternalism in institutions like the church and fascism, a movement on the rise in Europe. She presents her dream work, urging the building of a college to admit and grant degrees to women and proposes that the Civil Service offer exams that would lead to women's certification in the professions enabling them to earn an income (*TG*: 42–3). Women with independent incomes and opinions would then be empowered to speak and act against war (*TG*: 47). The 'recurring dream' of peace and freedom, she asserts, might then be realised; yet she decries the 'educated men who have not asked us to dream' (*TG*: 163).

Both Woolf's critical essays and fiction reveal this connection between the private and public worlds. The impact of the First World War hovers over Woolf's *To the Lighthouse*, as she tells the story of the Ramsay family and their house ravaged by time and war. The house, empty for ten years, partly during the war, is linked to family deaths: Mrs Ramsay, Prue and Andrew. 'The house was left; the house was deserted. It was left like a shell on a sandhill' (*TL*: 206), with the shell both a natural object on a beach and an allusion to the military explosive that results in Andrew's death in the war: '[A shell exploded. Twenty or thirty young men were blown up in France, among them Andrew Ramsay, whose death, mercifully, was instantaneous]' (*TL*: 201). Andrew's death is conveyed not with sensationalist loudspeaker rhetoric about honour and glory, as might have appeared in the media, but with a small 'thud of something falling' (*TL*: 201); it is a death, nevertheless, devastating. Woolf here demonstrates a new cultural narrative about war by focusing on the small, the individual and the family.

Woolf's posthumous novel, *Between the Acts*, also spotlights war *between* the acts of Miss La Trobe's literary pageant performed in a country house that is distanced from the war in the period between the First World War and the impending Second World War. In September 1940, Woolf writes of the fighter battles going on over Rodmell as well as Lewes, Sissinghurst and London, where their former home on Tavistock Square was destroyed and their residence in Mecklenburgh Square that housed the Hogarth Press was damaged (*D* 5: 428). The violence war inflicts on the domestic is reflected in her novel where the harmony of nature and human voices is shattered by the droning military flights overhead. Interruptions and disjointed rhythms enter as the Reverend Streatfield pleads, '"So that each of us who has enjoyed this pageant, still has the opp . . ." The word was cut in two. A zoom severed it. Twelve airplanes in perfect formation like a flight of wild duck came overhead' (*BA*: 193).

Writing for Woolf is an act of saving the fragments of art – like Miss LaTrobe's. It is part of her dream work for the nation to assert her own fiction between the First World War and the impending Second World War, as well as to provide a woman's perspective and critique of war as 'an outlet for manly qualities' (*TG*: 10).

'Glimpses between the battles': Elizabeth Bowen

In *Between the Acts*, the sounds of war tear through the events of the day and interrupt the acts of a play that celebrates English history; similarly, Elizabeth Bowen focuses on things that happen between battles in her twelve wartime stories, *Ivy Gripped the*

Steps (1946). In the preface, she explains that they are not war stories as traditionally understood, since there are no accounts of battles, 'action' or even 'air raids'. Rather, these stories are

> more, studies of climate, war-climate, and of the strange growths it raised. I see war (or should I say feel war?) more as a territory than as a page of history; of its impersonal active historic side I have, I find, not written. (1946: viii)

Bowen reminds us that the narratives of nation found in sensational media, propaganda or official histories neglect the 'feeling war' that she attempts to capture in her wartime writing. They are 'between-time stories – mostly reactions from, or intermissions between, major events' (Bowen 1946: xii). One of the best-known stories in this collection, 'Mysterious Kor', is about a soldier on furlough for a night and his lover who wander through the bright moonlit night in London, unable to find a place to make love. Bowen illuminates the personal loss and effects of war on people and their relationships without a grandiose anti-war statement. In the title story of the collection, Bowen focuses on a wartime house where people struggle to 'save bits of themselves' from the ruins of war and, afterwards, assemble fragments of who they were from remembered stories and poems or from what they remembered of one another (1946: xiv). In her story 'The demon lover', characters in hallucinatory states preserve 'bits' of themselves from remembered experiences. Kathleen Drover in flight from the London Blitz returns to her bombed house to recover some familiar things for her family; instead she finds a fragment of her old self. She discovers a letter addressed to her from her fiancé written during the First World War, when he was planning to come home to her, but he had since died. The date on the letter matches the date in which she is living, causing the two world wars to collapse in her mind. The doubleness and irony of her situation are perceptively captured as she flees in horror, pursued by the psychic demons of war. Bowen highlights here a character, a feeling, a mood and, importantly, a narrative sense of slow time. In her preface to these stories, Bowen underlines how important the personal story or small gesture is in preserving the self in the midst of war, the 'flying particles of something enormous and inchoate that had been going on. They were sparks from experience – an experience not necessarily my own' (1946: viii). She says of her technique, 'I cannot paint or photograph', but instead 'I have isolated, I have made for the particular, spotlighting faces or cutting out of gestures' (1946: xi). Just as Virginia Woolf retreats from the loudspeaker voice reverberating on the streets of London to the personal voice of the writer, Bowen seeks to save the fragments of individual identity and patches of experience in her wartime stories.

Bowen also creates a bridge between the private home and the public world in her family history, *Bowen's Court*, begun in 1939 and echoing Woolf's *Three Guineas*, published the year before. In her family history, Bowen confronts her Anglo-Irish heritage and compares the forces of domination at play in their lives with those that took place in world history. She asserts that the English colonisation of Ireland, beginning with Cromwell's settlements in the seventeenth century that included the establishment of Bowen's Court, was built upon 'an inherent wrong' (1979: 453). Anglo-Irish families like the Bowens who had colonised Ireland – seizing the land, establishing feudal farms and establishing big houses – were 'in subjection to fantasy and infatuation with the idea of power' (1979: 454), a toxicity that would also erupt in fascist Germany and Italy. Bowen continues, 'the private cruelty and the world war both have their start in the heated brain' (1979: 455) of a Cromwell, a Hitler or a Mussolini. Woolf similarly indicted the barbarism and tyranny of fascist leaders like Hitler and Mussolini in *Three Guineas*. England's colonisation of Ireland and the unhappy role of Anglo-Irish families like the Bowens share in Hitler and Mussolini's will to domination.

'What is commonly thought small': Mary Lavin's Short Stories

Mary Lavin does not take for granted Woolf's assertion 'that life exists more fully in what is commonly thought big rather than what is commonly thought small' (*CR 1*: 155). She herself compares writing a short story to examining a slide under a microscope. 'A microscope magnifies', she noted in a 1979 interview; 'A snowstorm', she said, 'can be an immensely impressive sight, but a single snowflake under a magnifying glass shows a complexity of design that has its own intensity' (Lavin and Murphy 1979: 223). She is attuned to Woolf's fictional re-evaluation of a 'small' subject that expands into national or global values. If Lavin is restoring the individual voice or selfhood in a time of national Troubles, then what she and other women writers are doing is 'big'. She sidesteps the overtly political and spotlights individual men and women and their family dramas in her stories: these domestic spaces are, nevertheless, part of the systemic class, gender, religious and social inequities in the nation. It is important to note the capacity of her fiction to expose the fissures in Irish society allowing discordant, marginal and critical views of relations between the sexes, classes and the institution of the church (Chatterjee 1993: 136). Kathleen MacMahon, the writer and granddaughter of Mary Lavin, recently wrote of the inattention to the weight of such topics in Lavin's stories written between the 1940s and the 1980s that

> chronicle the sinister pathologies that run through families: jealousy and treachery among women, abusive and sometimes subtle bullying by men, small-town snobbery, bigotry and savagery. In the story 'Asigh', a young woman is maimed by a violent father. 'In the middle of the fields' features a young widow faced with an unwelcome advance from a neighbouring farmer. 'Sarah' is about a country woman who bears three children by three different men and ends up dead in a ditch with her baby. If Ireland found these subjects quiet, Ireland needed its hearing adjusted. (2020)

Lavin, like Bowen, rarely wrote directly about Irish history and, as Colm Toíbín asserts, she need not fulfil the idea 'that it is the job of writers to write their nation' (Toíbín 2013: 2). But one story, 'The patriot's son', stands out. In this story Lavin focuses on individuals – two young Irishmen, Sean Mangon and Matty Conerty – and links their personal story to the public world and the future of the Irish nation. Sean and Matty hold contrasting views, at least initially, of the Fenians, the radical movement that began in the nineteenth century and spearheaded the Irish drive for independence from England. Matty is the son of a domineering mother who opposes Irish nationalism in all of its forms – the Gaelic league as well as the Fenian movement – and demonstrates her loyalty to the British by, for example, selling food from her country store to the Royal Irish Constabulary, a British government police force that kept the Irish under surveillance. She warns her son about the movement's ominous 'drilling in the hills again' (Lavin 1956: 17). She also infantilises him 'as a child still' and, since his grandfather had been a Fenian, fears that this bitterness may be 'a disease that's passed down from father to son' (1956: 8). Meanwhile, Sean Mangan, a young Fenian in the neighbourhood, passionately works against this view in an effort for independence and targets the burning of the barracks of the Constabulary. In spite of his mother's efforts, Matty unwittingly becomes involved in Sean's violent plot; 'feeling a spirit of elation' (1956: 10) run through him, he liberates himself from his overbearing mother to make his own political decisions. Despite this last-minute support that Matty provides for him, Sean's political venture fails, and he is wounded in the conflict. Matty's mother, realising her son's participation in the plot, labels him 'a gob' (a foolish person) in the last line of the story. Lavin here has engraved part of the history of the Independence movement into a family drama that portrays both a personal entrance into manhood (a boy's first challenge to the matriarchal power in family life in Ireland) and a dawning political awareness of a movement to liberate Ireland from the tyranny of oppressive England. As Woolf observed in *Three Guineas*, the tyrannies of patriarchy enter the home, linking the private and the public realms. In Lavin's story, Matty's mother dominates her son's life and the same link is established between domestic tyranny and the political tyranny of the English in Ireland that the Fenians opposed.

As Heather Ingman has rightly argued, Lavin is concerned, as we see in this story, with the oppressed lives of men as well as women in Ireland (2013: 30–48). Lavin exposes the different ways in which men are diminished, and in other stories portrays male shopkeepers such as those in the Grimes family saga who struggle with meagre incomes, deadening routines and romantic illusions. But Lavin does not forget the women married to these men, who surrender their own ambitions and endure the poverty and depression of men unrealised in their daily work and nationalist political goals. Again the failures in the national realm filter into private family life. In the tradition of James Joyce's *Dubliners* (1914), Lavin writes, at times, of the paralysis in private lives that parallel the oppressive colonial context. In her story, 'At Sallygap', she presents the destructiveness of romantic illusions and marital conventions that bind a young man to a deadening relationship and place. Bound for Paris with his band of musician friends who had tired of unappreciative 'Dublin jackeens' (worthless fellows) (Lavin 1971: 28), Manny boards a boat for a new life. Seeing, however, the sadness in the eyes of his intended, Annie, standing on the shore, he leaps off the boat, his violin tossed after him and 'broken to smithereens' (Lavin 1971: 22). This return to land leads him to a life of quiet stagnation with a materialistic wife who cannot bear his kindness. One 'reckless' night (1971: 33), he arrives home late, having found peace on a country walk. He resolves that nature and country living are the balm of life in Ireland. Here, as elsewhere, Lavin explores the challenges to masculinity from sharp-tongued wives and domineering mothers who suffer through a historical period when both Irish masculinity and the nation are threatened by the public tyranny of English colonialism on another scale.

Irish women were historically and culturally marginalised in a country focused for many decades on men's nationalist struggle against the British with marginal involvement of women. Widows of men who died in civil conflict or travelled with the Irish Republic Army (IRA) absorbed the national tremors of a constitution that culturally circumscribed their roles. Following the establishment of the Republic in 1919 and the Irish Free State in 1922, violence continued to erupt in daily life not only against the British but also among the Irish themselves – namely, between those who supported and those who opposed the Treaty with the British. When Lavin was writing her stories, women were assigned to be in the home according to Article 41.2 of the Irish Constitution written in 1937 (later amended):

1. In particular, the State recognises that by her life within the home, woman gives to the State a support without which the common good cannot be achieved.

2. The State shall, therefore, endeavour to ensure that mothers shall not be obliged by economic necessity to engage in labour to the neglect of their duties in the home. ('Article 41.2' 2018: 4)

Women's access to education, employment, careers and an independent income – posited as the *sine qua non* of egalitarianism – as discussed earlier in *Three Guineas*, had little force at that time in Irish culture. Lavin attends to the lives of these widows in which loneliness, hardship and the care of children figure. She presents the lives of women circumscribed not just by economics but by the inequities in the institution of marriage, middle-class social codes and class structures that diminished women servants. Chatterjee's belief in the value and intimacies of community (1993: 163–7) are present in Lavin's stories and reverberate from the larger society. Social safety nets had yet to be spread for women in Ireland, and that concerned Lavin who was a widow herself. There were no grants such as those that exist today – for example, the Widowed or Surviving Civil Partner Grant (2011) – to provide needed assistance with funeral expenses and financial support for families.

Though life's disappointments and sharp social observations suffuse Lavin's writing, her writing has a lyricism. In her story 'Happiness', a woman recalls a time when her husband was dying and she gathered armfuls of joyful daffodils, the flowers he loved, from the front yard to bring to his hospital bedside. When she arrives, however, she is confronted by a life-denying nun who scolds, 'Where are you going with those foolish flowers you foolish woman? . . . Don't you know your husband is dying?' (1971: 400). After his death, the widow continues to reflect on the clergy, including Father Hugh, a caring friend of the family who drops in to comfort her and her family. Her daughter, the narrator, referring to her own family, observes that he 'did not know there was a cavity in his own life, much less that we would fill it' (1971: 402). The daughter implicitly questions the Church that asks a man to surrender the comforts of family as a part of his priestly vows, and the mother herself states that 'celibacy was never meant to take all the warmth and loneliness out of their lives' (Lavin 1971: 402). In highlighting a woman's thoughts on male clergy, Lavin reveals fissures and discordancies in the institution of the church, which is so powerful a force in Irish society. There is also a hint of suspicion about the economic support of priestly vanity.

In 'The great wave', Father Kane, an egotistical bishop, is drawn towards pomp, and his beautiful vestments are funded by scarce town and diocese funds (Lavin 1971: 314). In this story, Jineen (who becomes Father Kane) remembers a past youthful sea venture with a friend, Seoineen, who is home in his fishing village on a short leave from the novitiate. Despite being under 'the yoke' (1971: 315) of his mother's care, Seoineen decides to join the other fishermen who are out on a dangerous day that yields the best catch of the year. His mother tries to put a brake on his venture – as do many of the mothers in Lavin's fiction – out of a fear that 'steals into the heart of every priest's mother thinking of the staying power that a man needs to reach to the end', his ordination (Lavin 1971: 317). Jineen recalls his youth as he reflects on the incident when, despite having only an ill-prepared currach (an Irish boat constructed with a wooden frame and animal skins), he launched it with Seoineen. In the adventure, Seoineen asserts his own manhood, refuting the views of the other men who 'think because of the collar, I haven't a man's strength about me anymore' (Lavin 1971: 327). The descriptions of the bodies of the men exercised in the rigour of throwing and pulling in the net, their hands bleeding, is a kind of sensuous glory in counterpoint to Seoineen's earlier reflections. Uncharacteristically, Seoineen yells orders and curses, and Jineen drags 'the net over the side where it emptied and spilled itself into the bottom of the boat. [The fish] came alive then all right! Flipping and floundering, some of them flashed back into the sea' (1971: 340). The friends are inebriated by the physical challenge of the swelling sea and the hauling in of the enormous catch. Nevertheless, despite their spirit and physical endurance, the great waves destroy their currach and seize their bounty of fish, sweeping away the other fisherman and all of the currachs from the town itself in an almost supernatural tragic event that claims all except for the two friends who survive.

In 'The nun's mother', the vocation of sisterhood in a convent is viewed with ambivalence. The deprivations of Angela, who is entering the order, are expressed through her parents. Luke Lattimer, the novitiate's father, views her vocation as 'unnatural, abnormal – abhorrent' (Lavin 1974: 44). He wonders if his wife has informed their daughter Angela of what she would be missing in life with her decision to enter the novitiate; has she told Angela about men and women's bodies; has Angela ever been kissed? The mother, however, feels triumph instead of grief and loss about her daughter's vocation. Women, she feels, have 'a curious streak of chastity no matter how long they were married or how ardently they had loved' (1974: 44).[1] When a young girl enters 'cloisters ivied over by centuries', the mother reflects, 'these young girls would be going away gladly, without once looking backward to where, behind them on summer lawns, and sunny river banks, others, with lovers lay dallying' (1974: 44). Nevertheless, when the mother sees her daughter on her last day home stripping the movie star posters from the walls of her room and giving away her favourite velvet toque, her postcards and theatre programmes, she thinks 'a vow of poverty would surely be a kind of little death in life' (1974: 52).

Despite the subtle social, political and religious critique in Lavin's stories, she is placed in the 'domestic' rather than the 'public' realm by Toíbín (2013: 2). The individual experiences in family and community reverberate with the national during times of political and social unrest like the Troubles. As Woolf asserted, 'the private and public worlds are inseparably connected'. Human relationships change under the pressure of the times, and men in covert political roles like IRA relate differently to the women who assist or resist them; more women become widows during times of violence and war; neighbours who live on opposite sides of the street turn away from others in the community or ally with other neighbours of the same political stripe; the prime minister, the Parliament, the Royal Irish Constabulary and the Church respond differently to guerrilla fighting, militarism and the presence of British troops. Despite Toíbín's private and public classification, he finds that Lavin's work moves 'to a level that is beyond the personal' (2013: 2) and does not remain in the linguistic eddies of the personal and domestic space, which is a historically devalued space. Toíbín slips into outmoded vocabulary when he states that Lavin was more interested in a character she had invented in all its strangeness and individuality than she was in the wider society; she was more interested in families than politics; she was more interested in the drama around the solitary figure than the drama around Irish history, or large questions of identity. (2013: 1)

However, he overlooks her dream work and the cultural impact of the 'small' subject on the wider society that Woolf and Bowen articulated and that Chatterjee conceptualised as the intimacies of community. Woolf and Bowen attend to the social and national ripples from stories of a solitary character, family or community and highlight the 'minimal' rather than the 'maximal' rhetoric of nationhood. Though Lavin's stories may not directly address the Troubles surrounding her in Ireland, seemingly moving away from the nationalist and public call of politics, there is a cultural and political dimension in her stories.[2]

Inspired by Woolf and in accord with Bowen, Lavin creates an art that is not separate from but contributes to the shape of a nation. She illuminates the 'small' events and drama of individuals, families, communities and institutions, creating ripples in the reader's mind from the private to the public. She does not ignore the wider society or the nation, as some claim, but shows the impact of the Troubles, gender iniquities, patriarchy, class discrimination, church paternalism and poverty on the society in her stories. Like many women writers, she redirects the attention of readers to society and the impact of its dehumanising institutions and public policies without overt messages. Lavin, though focused on individuals – beleaguered widows, loyal wives, enfeebled husbands, rebel daughters, obedient sons and needy clergy in Irish society – illuminates the problems and fissures in her Ireland. It is left to readers like ourselves to reject the devaluation implicit in the language of critics and attune ourselves to the philosophic and cultural patterns of Woolf's thinking that inspire women writers like Mary Lavin and Elizabeth Bowen to attend to the personal voice of the writer during times of deafening political rhetoric and national conflict, to attend to feeling and dreaming. The vocabulary of Bowen and Lavin underlines Woolf's proposal for the 'small' subject as the ground for fiction. Bowen said her wartime stories were 'between-time' stories (1946: xii) that happened away from the battles of the war and Lavin said her short stories were 'written under a microscope' (Lavin and Murphy 1979: 223) – that they are close-ups – away from the Troubles. The intimate lives and communities imagined in their stories and novels are not outside of politics and history and the world, as critics often claim, but are a part of the social and political history of the times. These women writers present a resistance to dominant views of conflict, war and social institutions that offer rich possibilities for a future of communities of peace, thus performing the dream work of a nation.

Notes

1. This notion of chastity is present in Woolf's character, Clarissa Dalloway: 'So the room was an attic; the bed narrow; and lying there reading, for she slept badly, she could not dispel a virginity preserved through childbirth which clung to her like a sheet (*MD*: 36).
2. This is separate from the nationalist call for 'patriotic' Irish literature that surfaced in the decades after the Irish War of Independence. Sean Ó'Faoláin claimed that Elizabeth Bowen's *Last September* (1929) was subject to the criticism that it was not 'Irish enough' (1937).

Bibliography

'Article 41.2 of the Constitution of Ireland' (2018), June, <https://www.ihrec.ie/app/uploads/2018/07/IHREC-policy-statement-on-Article-41.2-of-the-Constitution-of-Ireland-1.pdf> (last accessed 9 March 2020).

Bowen, E. (1946), *Ivy Gripped the Steps and Other Stories*, New York: Knopf.

Bowen, E. (1979 [1942]), *Bowen's Court*, New York: Ecco Press.

Bowen, E. (2000 [1929]), *The Last September*, New York: Anchor.

Chatterjee, P. (1993), *The Nation and Its Fragments: Colonial and Postcolonial Histories*, Princeton, NJ: Princeton University Press.

Dunleavy, J. E. (1983), 'The subtle satire of Elizabeth Bowen and Mary Lavin', *Tulsa Studies in Women's Literature*, 2: 1, pp. 69–82.

Friedman, S. S. (1998), *Mappings, Feminism and the Cultural Geographies of Encounter*, Princeton, NJ: Princeton University Press.

Gruber, R. (2005 [1935]), *The Will to Create as a Woman*, New York: Carroll and Graf.

Holtby, W. (1978 [1932]), *Virginia Woolf: A Critical Memoir*, Chicago: Cassandra.

Ingman, H. (2013), 'Masculinities in Mary Lavin's short stories', in E. D'hoker (ed.), *Mary Lavin*, Kildare, Ireland: Irish Academic Press, pp. 30–48.

Lavin, M. (1956), *The Patriot Son and Other Stories*, London: Michael Joseph.

Lavin, M. (1971), *Mary Lavin, Collected Stories*, Boston, MA: Houghton Mifflin.

Lavin, M. (1974), *The Stories of Mary Lavin*, vol. 2, London: Constable.

Lavin, M. and C. Murphy (1979), 'Mary Lavin: An interview', *Irish University Review*, 9: 2, pp. 207–24.

McKeon, B. (2012), 'An arrow in flight: The pleasures of Mary Lavin', *Paris Review*, 12 June, <https://www.theparisreview.org/blog/2012/06/12/an-arrow-in-flight-the-pleasures-of-mary-lavin/> (last accessed 15 May 2015).

MacMahon, K. (2020), 'Irish women writing fiction were dismissed as "quiet". Ireland wasn't listening', *Guardian*, 30 July, <https://www.theguardian.com/books/2020/jul/30/irish-women-writers-described-as-quiet-ireland-sally-rooney-women-writers> (last accessed 2 August 2020).

Ó'Faoláin, S. (1937), 'Letter to Elizabeth Bowen, 22 April 1937', Bowen Collection, 11.6, Harry Ransom Center, University of Texas at Austin, 1923–75, <https://norman.hrc.utexas.edu/fasearch/findingAid.cfm?eadid=00015> (last accessed 11 July 2020).

Spivak, G. C. (1988), 'Can the subaltern speak?', in C. Nelson and L. Grossberg (eds), *Marxism and the Interpretation of Culture*, Chicago: University of Illinois Press, pp. 271–313.

Toíbín, C. (2013), Foreword, in E. D'hoker (ed.), *Mary Lavin*, Kildare, Ireland: Irish Academic Press, pp. 1–4.

Trilling, D. (1949), 'Fiction in review', *The Nation*, 26 February, pp. 254–5.

'Widowed or Surviving Civil Partner Grant' (2011), Department of Employment Affairs and Social Protection, <http://www.welfare.ie/en/Pages/Widowed-or-Surviving-Civil-Partner-Grant.aspx> (last accessed 15 May 2019).

Woolf, V. (1955 [1927]), *To the Lighthouse*, New York: Harcourt Brace Jovanovich.

Woolf, V. (1942), *The Death of the Moth and Other Essays*, New York: Harcourt Brace and Company.

Woolf, V. (1953 [1925]), *The Common Reader*, New York: Harcourt, Brace and World.

Woolf, V. (1957 [1929]), *A Room of One's Own*, New York: Harcourt, Brace and World.

Woolf, V. (1969 [1941]), *Between the Acts*, New York: Harcourt Brace Jovanovich.

Woolf, V. (1986 [1938]), *Three Guineas*, London: Hogarth Press.

22

Great Poets Do Not Die: Maggie Gee's *Virginia Woolf in Manhattan* (2014) as Metaphor for Contemporary Biofiction

Bethany Layne

In *A Room of One's Own* (1929), Woolf famously wrote of Judith Shakespeare that 'great poets do not die; they are continuing presences; they need only the opportunity to walk among us in the flesh' (*AROO*: 131). In *Virginia Woolf in Manhattan* (2014), Maggie Gee (1948–) offers that opportunity to Woolf herself, imagining what might transpire if she were to be resurrected in twenty-first-century New York. Virginia is conjured by the fictitious novelist Angela Lamb, who is visiting the Berg Collection in preparation for a keynote address at an international Woolf conference. Alternating between the perspectives of Virginia, Angela, and Angela's thirteen-year-old daughter Gerda, marooned at a Hampshire boarding school, the novel details the women's romp through the horrors and delights of modernity, taking in television, hamburgers and Google. Their exploits are funded by the proceeds of a copy of *To the Lighthouse*, signed posthumously by Virginia. With Angela, Virginia makes the plane journey that Woolf never managed in life, in a section titled, appropriately enough, 'Time passes'. She then, in the novel's third section, touches down in Istanbul for a guest appearance at her own conference. Gerda, who has escaped from Bendham Abbey to pursue her mother across two continents, delights in the idea of 'the actual writer, telling all the academics and people like my mother where they are going wrong' (Gee 2015: 45). Angela, however, forewarns Virginia that 'some modern scholars think authors don't know anything about their work. . . . It's "The Death of the Author". It's – well, it's French'. Virginia retorts, 'But I'm the living embodiment of that. I'm a dead author' (2015: 317). In such moments, Angela is tempted to conclude that 'the Virginia Woolf I was writing about was so much less trouble than the one I was with' (2015: 139).

By resurrecting a 'dead author', Gee's story acts as a metaphor for the subgenre of biofiction, defined in adversarial fashion by Jonathan Dee as a derivative form of 'literary graverobbing' (Dee 1999). In David Lodge's more measured account,

> the novel which takes a real person and their real history as the subject matter for imaginative exploration, using the novel's techniques for representing subjectivity rather than the objective, evidence-based discourse of biography – has become a very fashionable form of literary fiction in the last decade or so, especially as applied to the lives of writers. (2007: 8)

Yet while Lodge correctly locates the upsurge in biofiction's popularity around the turn of the twenty-first century, intriguing antecedents for Woolf-inspired biofiction can be found in the subject's own theory and practice of life writing. In 'The new biography' (1927), a review of Harold Nicolson's *Some People* (1927), Woolf details the advances made by the eponymous movement towards the more accurate transmission of the subject's personality. These include a levelling of the relationship between the subject and the biographer, who is now 'raised upon a little eminence' where formerly he 'toil[ed] even slavishly in the footsteps of his hero' (Woolf 1960: 152). This change in perspective was judged to enable selection and synthesis, producing a poetic précis of the subject rather than a cradle-to-grave account of every stage of his life. The most suggestive development, however, is the revelation that 'one can use many of the devices of fiction in dealing with real life' (1960: 134), which appears to 'wave ... a hand' (1960: 155) in the direction of biofiction. Yet despite observing that 'a little fiction mixed with fact' was able 'to transmit personality very effectively', Woolf concluded that the two were 'antagonistic; let them meet and they destroy each other' (1960: 154–5). The essay's final hints at the incompatible nature of fact and fiction are reiterated in 'The art of biography' (1942), Woolf's final word on the subject. Perhaps informed by her 'donkey work' and 'sober drudgery' on *Roger Fry* (1940) (*D* 5: 133), Woolf ultimately rejected the marriage of fact and fiction: 'no one, the conclusion seems to be, can make the best of both worlds; you must choose, and you must abide by your choice' (*DM*: 124).

Yet despite Woolf's 'insistent characterisation of biography as suspended between the poles of fact and fiction' (Gualtieri 2000: 355), she herself, as Anna Snaith points out, 'has been enacting in her writing just such a complex negotiation [between fact and fiction] throughout her life' (2000: 104). We witness this negotiation in *Orlando* (1928), Woolf's joke-biography about Vita Sackville-West, as well as in *Flush* (1933), her biographical novel about Elizabeth Barrett Browning's spaniel. Even if *Roger Fry* appears to reinstate the 'impassable binary', this is, perhaps, because a novelistic biography is less easily accomplished than a biographical novel (Gualtieri 2000: 360–1). For Hermione Lee, Woolf's essays on modern fiction provide further evidence for the interplay of truth and invention by portraying 'fiction as a form of life-writing' (2005: 44). Thus the essays' emphasis on the creation of character in fiction finds a parallel in the foregrounding of 'personality' over 'actions' and 'works' in 'The new biography' (Woolf 1960: 150). Biofiction about Woolf, then, while symbolically prohibited in her essays on biography, finds its authority in her wider oeuvre.

In this chapter, I read Gee's character Angela, a contemporary novelist who recalls her subject to life, lends her clothing and helps her to sign her name, as symbolic of the real-life novelists who recreated Woolf in their own image and reinterpreted her works in line with their respective versions. Angela faces problems similar to those with which her real-life counterparts have grappled. Her frustrations at sightseeing with Virginia reveal feelings of authorial belatedness, the sense that 'I could have thought of all those things. But because she got there first, I didn't' (Gee 2015: 106–7). The 'patch of darkness' that Virginia leaves on photographs symbolises anxieties that biofiction will have an emptiness at its heart, will leave readers asking, 'Where's Virginia?' (2015: 345). And Angela's question, 'would she have – *liked* me?' (2015: 11), indicates the discomfort that attends on such an intimate engagement with a writer who so valued privacy. It is my contention, then, that this recent manifestation of Woolf-inspired biofiction may be read successfully as an extended metaphor for the twenty-year-old subgenre, originating with Sigrid Nunez (1998) and Michael Cunningham (1998), and extending to recent work by Priya Parmar (2014) and Norah Vincent (2015). I first examine issues of content, focusing on Gee's presentation of Virginia's suicide and sexuality. I then expand the discussion to think both critically and broadly about Woolf-inspired biofiction, particularly the ethical issues attendant on its invasion of the subject's privacy.

The popular fascination with Woolf's suicide is established early in Gee's novel when Angela makes her archival visit to the New York Public Library to consult 'all those famous manuscripts, *Orlando*, *The Waves*, *To the Lighthouse*' (Gee 2015: 14). Excited 'to get my hands on her', Angela is disappointed to learn that the documents are only available on microfilm, which she judges 'hardly the same' (2015: 17). Whereas the original documents are hidden from view, 'the walking stick she carried on that final day' is conspicuously displayed in a 'heavy glass case' (2015: 17). Angela is ambivalent about this preservation: 'it looked – cursed. I'm allergic to suicide. And yet, it was a link to her' (2015: 18). Together with the concealment of Woolf's manuscripts, the memorialisation of her walking stick suggests that the sensationalised narrative of her suicide has come to eclipse her work. The novel also implies that Woolf's writings are 'so valuable' in part *because* of the manner of her death, invoking the link between suicide and genius that has long frustrated Woolf scholars (2015: 17). This link is reinforced by Angela's daughter Gerda's recollection of her introduction to Sylvia Plath in school: 'the teacher said, in a special solemn voice, "She is a great poet, who took her own life", as if the two things were actually connected' (2015: 152). (To Gerda, this is a false relation: 'what sense does it make to kill yourself? If she'd stayed alive, she'd have written more poems' [2015: 153]). The relevance of Plath to Woolf soon becomes apparent in a scene in a Barnes and Noble, where the salesman claims to 'associate [Woolf's] poetry with Sylvia Plath . . . because they're both a little dark. Woolf's poems are dark, wouldn't you say?' 'Dark, not to say unknown,' thinks Angela, reflecting bitterly on the popular conflation of these 'two strange women who killed themselves' (2015: 176–7).

One of the originators of this way of reading was Julia Kristeva, for whom Woolf's suicide, like Plath's, was caused by following 'the call of the mother' and rendered in highly poetic terms: 'I think of Virginia Woolf, who sank wordlessly into the river, her pockets weighted by stones' (1988: 39). In her survey of the diffuse biographical explanations for Woolf's death, Catherine Sandbach-Dahlström also cites obsession with both mother and father, as well as with death itself, borne out by her fiction (2011: 171–3, 176–80). Yet as Holly Laird argues, such 'othering' of 'Virginia Woolf (and suicidal people like her)' undermines both 'the complex circumstances within which she managed to live a relatively long and extraordinarily productive life' and the 'nuanced representations of and diversified struggles with suicide in her writing' (2007: 277).

Such complexity was flattened in Stephen Daldry's film adaptation, *The Hours* (2002), of Michael Cunningham's novel *The Hours* (1998). The popular representations challenged by Angela and Gerda are reflected in the film's fetishisation of suicide and spurious linkage of the death drive and the creative impulse. In his novel, Cunningham dispensed with the image of Woolf 'walking into the river with a stone in her pocket' in a few pages of his Prologue (1999: 152). Having staged the death of the author as an embodied person, Cunningham then showed Woolf surviving through her textual remains by virtue of his intricate engagement with *Mrs Dalloway*. The film, conversely, was bookended by the suicide, a 'doubled framing' that, as Heather Levy complained, served to 'pathologize ... Woolf's life' (2003: 47). Lee similarly protested the establishing of

> a life story which is moving inexorably towards that death. In the next moment that we see her, she is starting to write *Mrs Dalloway*, so that to a casual audience the two things – her writing of the novel and her suicide – might seem to be going on at the same time. (2005: 40)

Given that the subtitle 'Sussex, 1941' was not repeated in the film's final scene, Lee raises the legitimate concern that the common reader could misunderstand the chronology of Woolf's life, and assume that her suicide followed immediately upon the completion of *Mrs Dalloway*. And even for the more knowledgeable reader, there remains the troubling conflation of the moment of creativity with the suicidal impulse and the implication, in Gerda's terms, that 'the two things were actually connected' (Gee 2015: 153).

More recent biofictions have differed in how they negotiate the fact of Woolf's suicide. Priya Parmar avoids the issue entirely by focusing on her subjects' early years in *Vanessa and Her Sister* (2014), while the other joint biofiction, Susan Sellers's *Vanessa and Virginia*, is historically grounded in Woolf's falling in a dyke on 18 March 1941 but invents a corresponding suicide attempt for Vanessa, impelled by Duncan Grant's 'confess[ion] that he could never be [her] lover again' (2008: 147). Sellers presents Vanessa's unsuccessful and Virginia's successful attempts as responses to extreme circumstances rather than manifestations of a pre-existing tendency. Like Leonard Woolf in his autobiography, for whom 'Virginia's death' was a 'catastrophe' rather than 'either a journey or an arrival', Sellers engages in productive de-mythologising (Laird 2007: 247). Most recently, in *Adeline*, Norah Vincent represents Woolf's death-drive as a separate entity, a ghostly version of the adolescent Adeline Virginia Stephen. Having 'never recovered' from her experiences of 'unbearable loss' (2015: 144), Adeline's only hope of release is in Virginia's death, and when her adult self steps into the Ouse, Adeline responds with 'radiant satisfaction' (2015: 276). From one perspective, this separate characterisation emphasises that the mature Virginia was more than the sum of her suicidal impulses. However, like Daldry's film, the characterisation also results in a teleological interpretation of Woolf's life as a journey, with death as the point of arrival.

In Gee's *Virginia Woolf in Manhattan*, the subject cannot, at first, remember her suicide, which detail serves to emphasise that it was not her defining moment. The conceit of a resurrected Woolf then enables a simple message:

> I myself never wanted to die. The self I knew, the self I owned, that loved the sunlight on the spine of the downs, loved Leonard, loved my Nessa.
> Of course I didn't want to die. It was just the illness, the cloud of darkness, something outside me, tracking me. (2015: 332)

The 'cloud of darkness' is indicative of Woolf's depression, always attendant on her finishing a novel, and linked biographically to her completion of *Between the Acts* (Sandbach-Dahlström 2011: 169–71). Its location 'outside me' externalises and contains the suicidal impulse, in the same spirit as Vincent's *Adeline* but with far less sensationalism. In a moment of telling symbolism, a bookseller's morbid rumination about Woolf's 'dark' poetry is then interrupted by 'the real author, back from the dead', 'smiling, clutching a carrier-bag of her books' (Gee 2015: 177). The smiling Virginia, Rizzoli bag in hand, recalls a diary entry in which Woolf describes shopping on Oxford Street as 'a fairly specimen day' (*D* 4: 195). Gee's echo serves a valuable function, reminding us, as Christie Mills Jeansonne points out, that Woolf's 'life was not one of daily miseries' (2014: 97).

As well as challenging expectations of her dourness, the resurrected Virginia is also able to query the popular preoccupation with her body, stating baldly that 'I'm not a virgin. Do my readers expect me to be a virgin?' (Gee 2015: 383). Angela, however, remains horrified at the prospect of girl-talk with Virginia, invoking her idol's image as a 'sexless Sappho' (Barrett 1997: 6). She exclaims, 'How could I talk about sex to *her*! She wasn't a girlfriend! She was . . . Virginia! Famously chaste, traumatised! What was that passage in "Professions for Women"? She said women couldn't write about the body' (Gee 2015: 381). Angela's construction bears striking resemblance to the one summarised by Lee: 'a chaste, chill, sexually inhibited maiden: Virginia the virgin' (1997: 244). Writing fifteen years after Lee, Patricia Morgne Cramer confirms that this 'most egregious of sexual categories', one extreme of the '"virgin–whore" dichotomy', has lost none of its force, remaining 'pervasive in conceptions about Woolf and sexuality' (2012: 136). The assumption of Woolf's frigidity, if not her virginity, originates in gossip circulated by Vanessa and Clive Bell. In a now notorious letter to her husband, Vanessa Bell described how her sister 'still gets no pleasure at all from the act, which I think is curious' (1993: 132). Gee nods to this letter in her honeymoon scene, in which Leonard's 'eye shone, desperate, staring, mad, and then it was over, and I had felt nothing, just hard dry friction and loneliness' (Gee 2015: 438).

Bell's letter went on to playfully assert her own 'sympath[y] with such things' as 'orgasm' and 'sexual passion in men', bolstering her own sexuality through opposition to 'the Goat's coldness' (V. Bell 1993: 132). This dualistic representation proved adhesive in popular culture, producing a shorthand that Diane Gillespie summarises deftly:

> It serves the purposes of Virginia Woolf and Vanessa Bell, or their later biographers and critics, to think of the virginal, barren woman versus the sensual, maternal one; the domestically inept versus the practical and competent; the dependent versus the independent; the conversationalist versus the silent listener; the mentally unstable versus the sane. (1998: 5)

Gee's Virginia seems wise to this aspect of her popular representation: 'because I was clever', she notes wryly, 'they had to gloat that I was not a proper woman. Yes, they were glad I could not be a mother' (2015: 193). Yet she goes on to characterise her relationship with Vanessa in the same oppositional terms, noting that while she 'bested' her sister 'in the competition for our father's love . . . at words . . . at Greek', there remained an area in which she could not hope to compete:

> The secret heart of us. The womanly part, the making part, whence children, passion, the river flowed. There I was dead, and the river passed by, leaving me writing, dry, on the bank, while she struck out into the centre and swam, surrounded by

men, admirers, in the morning; flanked by children, the water-babies I also loved, but could not possess; flesh in the sun, rosy, easy; once I had so longed for them; I waved across: was an aunt: was nothing. (2015: 399)

This passage symbolically opposes Gillespie's 'virginal, barren woman', left 'writing, dry, on the bank', to the 'sensual, maternal one', who is 'flanked by children' and 'surrounded by men'. In this instance, Virginia proves unable to see past the reified constructions that vex discussion of the sisters' relationships.

Yet scattered fragments from across the novel enable the reader to piece together a counter-narrative, one that recasts the sisters as points on a sexual continuum. Elsewhere, Virginia notes that

> they thought I was cold, but what did they know of the way my love and I lay together? On summer nights. Those summer nights . . . even if I failed him. In the ultimate place. He was my love. We lay together. Is one caress better than another? (2015: 193)

By emphasising the intimacy inherent in non-penetrative, even non-sexual displays of affection, Gee contributes to a process of fictional intervention initiated by Sigrid Nunez and Susan Sellers, both of whom revealed Virginia to have an admirable physical life. In *Mitz: The Marmoset of Bloomsbury* (1998), Leonard is witnessed 'put[ting] his arm around Virginia' and 'nuzzl[ing] Virginia's cheek' to entice the animal down from a tree (Nunez 2007: 33), while in *Vanessa and Virginia*, a similar game of 'mongooses and mandrills' involves grooming, licking, and nuzzling (Sellers 2008: 92). Such instances of 'affectionate cuddling and play' testify, for Lee, that '[t]his is not an a-sexual marriage' (1997: 333), and the relationship is watched with envy by Sellers's Vanessa, who thinks of her own 'solitary bed' (Sellers 2008: 107). Gee's novel similarly emphasises that the Woolfs' married love outlasted Vanessa's 'voluptuous abandon' (DeSalvo 1989: 87). Engaging in a spot in internet research, Virginia discovers

> from the Hades of the laptop that [Vanessa's] life after I died had been long, and hard, that Duncan loved boys into his dotage, that her goddess good looks grew dry and worn and our family sadness fell upon her like hoar frost. (Gee 2015: 282).

Like Louise DeSalvo before her, Gee bridges the gap between the sisters by emphasising that celibacy defined the longest periods in their lives (DeSalvo 1989: 87). Gee is then able to offer a different perception of Woolf as a body by imagining a fulfilling sexual life for her in Istanbul. Calling by Virginia's room to solicit last-minute feedback on her conference paper, Angela is troubled at the enigma presented by 'a large black shoe on the floor' and a Muslim maid without her headscarf, who is unwilling to admit her to the room (2015: 423). Unable to sleep, Angela ponders the possible solutions to this riddle, including the explanation that

> Virginia was a lesbian. (As her husband summarised it, after her death.) When she talked about her 'feelings' for men, in the café, it was a smokescreen.
> But . . . the shoe I had glimpsed on the carpet by the bed, sturdy, black and shiny, was a man's. Or a lesbian shoe? Did it belong to the maid? (2015: 424)

The rapidity with which Angela moves on from this explanation can be connected to the unease felt among some readers about 'the term "lesbian"', which Cramer connects to 'queer distrust of identity labels of any kind' (2012: 131).¹ Angela subsequently arrives at a more 'mind-boggling explanation. [Virginia] had gone to bed with a woman and a man' (Gee 2015: 424). She then supplants this with a convoluted story of how the maid, 'a small person with very big feet', is simply 'looking after a guest', and has removed her shoes 'out of respect' and taken off her veil because the guest is female. While Angela pretends to believe this explanation, all the while criticising herself for being 'censorious' (2015: 425), the text favours the previous intimation of a bisexual liaison. It is patently obvious that the shoe belongs to Muhsin, a Turkish man whose liaison with Virginia is recounted from her own perspective:

> a long croon of ecstasy began, somewhere in the room a cat's voice unspooled through octaves of sound, a cat in bliss – and as it abated, the ebb-tide of blood warmed every abandoned cell of my body, finally freeing, unfastening me. . . . I realised the deep-throated sound was my own, a ribbon of happiness thrown from nowhere: my body singing its own lost song. (2015: 440)

The moment is followed by Virginia's revelation that 'the night of love was not yet over' (2015: 442), a coded reference to her encounter with the maid. Crucially, it is preceded by her recognising 'feelings I haven't had for some time. Some time before I died, that is. One hadn't felt – desire – in ages' (2015: 381). By linking this climactic scene to feelings experienced by Virginia in life, Gee unsettles popular perceptions of Woolf's frigidity. Or, in Virginia's own words, she queries the assumption that 'I am not "up for it". If that is what you modern women say' (2015: 383).

The description of Virginia's orgasm is interpretable as a homage to, perhaps even a pastiche of, the match-burning-in-a-crocus passage in *Mrs Dalloway*:

> It was a sudden revelation, a tinge like a blush which one tried to check and then, as it spread, one yielded to its expansion, and rushed to the farthest verge and there quivered and felt the world come closer, swollen with some astonishing significance, some pressure of rapture, which split its thin skin and gushed and poured with an extraordinary alleviation over the cracks and sores! Then, for that moment, she had seen an illumination; a match burning in a crocus; an inner meaning almost expressed. But the close withdrew; the hard softened. It was over – the moment. (*MD*: 80)

Gee rehearses Woolf's use of the extended sentence while also reprising the structure of her passage, in which full immersion in the sensual moment is succeeded by narratorial extrapolation about the moment's significance. Gee's passage is also reminiscent of a moment from Rhoda's perspective in *The Waves*:

> Now my body thaws; I am unsealed, I am incandescent. Now the stream pours in a deep tide fertilizing, opening the shut, forcing the tight-folded, flooding free. To whom shall I give all that now flows through me, from my warm, my porous body? I will gather my flowers and present them – Oh! to whom? (*W*: 44)

Gee's Virginia's 'ebb-tide of blood' recalls Rhoda's 'deep tide fertilizing'; what 'free[s]' and 'unfasten[s]' Virginia, 'open[s] the shut' and 'forc[es] the tight-folded' for Rhoda. Yet while Rhoda is stopped short by the question of 'whom' to 'present' her 'flowers' to, Virginia experiences a moment of oneness, conceived as 'my body singing its own lost song' (Gee 2015: 440). Gee's passage might therefore be interpreted as a critical intervention, which serves to remind us of Woolf's own vivid depictions of female sexuality in her writing. This is valuable given that Lytton Strachey's famous dismissal of her writing as 'an exquisite arabesque' is grounded in the supposed absence of 'copulation' (Strachey qtd in Holroyd 1994: 569). For Clive Bell, worse still, this textual absence is indexed to sexual failure on Woolf's part. As she noted in her diary, Bell grounded his criticism 'upon the theory that I can't feel sex: have the purple light cut off' (D 3: 275). By rendering a passage in which Virginia emphatically does 'feel sex' in imagery redolent of Woolf's own, Gee refutes both aspects of Bell's facile theory. She insists that, in the words of Leena Kore-Schröeder, 'Woolf is *not* guilty of ignoring the body. . . . [B]odily experience determines nothing less than her very use of metaphor itself' (2000: 15). Gee, then, contributes to Woolf's own project of 'eroticis[ing] the female body as . . . a rich resource of ecstasy, transcendence, and illumination' (Cramer 2012: 135).

For many readers, Gee's reimagining of her subject's sexual life might feel uncomfortably intimate. But so too are the gossipy letters exchanged between Vanessa and Clive Bell; so too is the 'secret bestiary of names' Angela recalls from the *Diaries*, of whose author, she admits, 'I knew too much, we knew too much' (Gee 2015: 85). While Gee makes speculative additions to this material, rather than simply rehearsing it, she highlights an ethical concern that pertains to real-world Woolf scholars regarding our untrammelled access to private documents. In the novel, Angela worries about how to tell Virginia that 'I'd read her diaries. That everyone at the conference would have read them', thereby contravening 'her clear instructions: destroy my papers' (2015: 244). Later, in Istanbul, she interrupts Virginia's recounting of her youthful impressions of the city on the grounds of over-familiarity:

> of course, as ever, it was in the *Diaries*, that secret passage so many of us had crept down without her knowledge or consent.
> And yet, the writing, the writing. . . . [W]hat a loss if Leonard had obeyed her! Her description of Aya Sophia . . . (2015: 291)

The image of readers accessing the 'secret passages' of an unknowing, unconsenting subject is redolent of the abuse Woolf suffered at the hands of the Duckworth brothers, figuring the publication of autobiographical writing as a symbolic violation. Yet the alternative pulls Angela up short by forcing her to contemplate the inevitable loss to Woolf's textual corpus. The passage thus eloquently opposes Woolf as an embodied person, whose right to privacy the *Diaries* contravened, with Woolf as a writer, a legitimate object of attention.

In her essay, 'Virginia Woolf's diaries and letters', Susan Sellers is similarly attentive to 'the issue of trespass', asking, 'are we justified in reading a set of essentially private journals at all?' (2000: 114). Though the evidence marshalled to justify the 'trespass' varies, several readings converge in questioning whether the diaries were, in fact, private. As Mills Jeansonne reminds us, 'even when a diarist writes with the intent that it later be destroyed, there is a consideration of audience – the future readers it seeks to deny' (2014: 98). Deborah Martinson highlights the presence of contemporaneous, as well as future, readers: the father who read Woolf's adolescent journal, the husband who occasioned the diaries' performance of sound mind and good health, and the Bloomsbury friends whose habitual secret-sharing put the document 'at public risk' (2003: 96–8). As Sellers herself points out, the absence of 'the real Virginia' serves to query the status of the diaries as inviolable: they make limited reference to Woolf's instances of illness, her impending suicide and her affair with Vita Sackville-West (2000: 110). While Woolf rejected the idea of full publication on the grounds that the diaries were insufficiently condensed and revised, this seeming reluctance to embrace them as a wholly private space hints at her acceptance that excerpts might be published following her death. In a passage from which Sellers quotes and paraphrases, Woolf asks,

> But what is to become of all these diaries, I asked myself yesterday. If I died, what would Leo make of them? He would be disinclined to burn them; he could not publish them. Well, he should make up a book from them, I think; & then burn the body. I daresay there is a little book in them: if the scraps & scratches were straightened out a little. God knows. (D 3: 67)

Woolf's belief that 'there is a little book in them' lends symbolic licence to the publication of *A Writer's Diary* (1953), though the subsequent five volumes that were published a quarter of a century later travesty her belief that 'the body' would be burned. If the complete *Diary* is to be justified in Woolf's own terms, it is, perhaps, 'on the grounds of [her] feminism': 'Woolf was acutely aware of the need for female role models' (Sellers 2000: 116). Thus while her injunction to 'destroy all my papers' condemned the diaries to the same fate as Judith Shakespeare's secret writings, hidden or 'set fire to' (*AROO*: 55), the publication of the 'precursors' (Martinson 2003: 26) to Woolf's novels is a major contribution to the 'unsolved' problem of 'women and fiction' (*AROO*: 4).

The *Diary* also, however, provided raw material for the biographies, described by Angela as 'so thick, so intimate, so many' (Gee 2015: 74). Together, the diaries 'told us more than anyone should know about another human being, unless they are their parent, sibling, child' (Gee 2015: 84). As Lee writes of the *Diary* on which they drew, the biographies encourage readers 'to call [Woolf] Virginia, and speak proprietorially about her life' (1997: 4). Accordingly, in *Virginia Woolf in Manhattan*, the eponymous subject is disgusted at how Angela 'said my name, that first time, as if I belonged to her' (Gee 2015: 21). Anne Olivier Bell describes an earlier chain of influence whereby the popular interest in Woolf revived by *A Writer's Diary* was fuelled by the auto/biographical writings by Leonard Woolf and Quentin Bell that followed (A. O. Bell 2002: 23). Similarly, the complete *Diary*, and its companion publication, the *Letters*, enabled a multitude of further biographies, which produced both the audience and the sense of ownership needed to recuperate Woolf into fiction. When the *Letters*, *Diary* and biographies are then cited within that fiction, they serve to muddy the ontological waters. This is seen most clearly in *Vanessa and Her Sister*, whose five sections are demarcated by extracts from published letters exchanged within the Bloomsbury Group.[2] The effect of these letters is to legitimate the surrounding prose. When combined with Parmar's adapt ventriloquism, the letters produce the risk that invented material will be mistaken for historical data. This risk is exacerbated by the form of the novel, a diary. Like *Vanessa and Virginia*, which takes the form of a letter, Parmar's novel in the form of a journal makes for a symbolic addition to Woolf and Bell's biofictional corpus.

Gee, in her Acknowledgements, takes steps to preserve the distinction between fact and invention that is endangered by this citation of historical data within imaginative works. She emphasises that '[t]hough most references to Woolf's real nineteenth and twentieth-century life are based at least loosely on her writings or on the biographies, her thoughts and feelings are mostly my imaginings', and goes on to illustrate the novel's boldest inventions (2015: 474). Yet in the novel that the reader of her Acknowledgements has just consumed, Gee imagines the consequences of such authorial ventriloquism. Virginia struggles to interact with the physical world, so requires Angela's assistance to sign the first edition of *To the Lighthouse* that the two of them then sell. Gee uses this moment to confront the implication that biofiction effectively puts words in the subject's mouth:

> I sat beside her on the bed, with the books open on my bedside table, slipped my hand over the back of hers – cool, bony, the veins making ridges like water-contours in hard sea-sand – and with my hand pressing hers, it worked, the familiar writing, clear and bright, and my heart jumped as I read what she'd written. (2015: 110)

The irony of this, of course, is that Angela is effectively reading what she herself has had a hand in writing. While Virginia's signature is unlikely to have been altered by the process, the scene serves as a metaphor for the biofiction or biopic writer's broader substitution of their own words for Woolf's. Roberta Rubenstein articulates the consequences of such substitution in Stephen Daldry's film *The Hours*, suggesting that 'the real Woolf' risks being reduced to 'Virginia Woolf lite' (Rubenstein qtd in Lee 2005: 110). In other words, there is the danger that the appropriation will misrepresent Woolf's writing, or even negate the need for a direct encounter with her work. In the case of Daldry's film *The Hours*, the treatment of the following passage from *Mrs Dalloway* serves to justify the fears of misrepresentation:

> Did it matter then, she asked herself, walking towards Bond Street, did it matter that she must inevitably cease completely; all this must go on without her; did she resent it; or did it not become consoling to believe that death ended absolutely? but that somehow in the streets of London, on the ebb and flow of things, here, there, she survived. (*MD*: 7)

These lines are spoken in voice-over by Nicole Kidman's Virginia and intercut with a scene of the pregnant Laura Brown, played by Julianne Moore, reading the published novel in a hotel room, bottles of sleeping pills at her side. However, the original text is truncated after 'death ended absolutely', and the remainder of the passage substituted by the phrase 'it is possible to die. It is possible to die' (*The Hours* 2003). Whereas Cunningham's novel attributes this revelation to Laura, who 'thinks, suddenly, of how she – how anyone – can make a choice like that', the film misleadingly attaches Laura's morbid conclusion to Woolf's text, thereby perverting the passage's emphasis on the survival of a transcendent soul (Cunningham 1999: 151). Yet the film also, as Lee notes, 'sent readers back in droves, not only to Cunningham's novel but also to *Mrs Dalloway*, which for a short time became the number 1 paperback on Amazon's sales list, the first time the book had ever been a best-seller' (2005: 57). The film, then, inspired numerous readers to approach *Mrs Dalloway* directly, when any misconceptions could, one hopes, be revised in light of first-hand knowledge of Woolf's work.

Similar optimism about the immortality of Woolf's writing imbues one of Gee's final scenes, which imagines ventriloquism of a happier sort than the business with Virginia's signature. Deciding to abandon her prepared conference paper and ad-lib, Angela struggles to recall a passage from *A Room of One's Own*. Gerda, having finally tracked down her mother in Istanbul, is on hand to supply and read this aloud:

> Her voice was nervous, at first, yes, she went too fast, but as she spoke, it steadied, strengthened; the words carried her, the words became her, they walked confidently, gracefully through the hall, they were Virginia Woolf, alive and with us (*where was Virginia, I thought, briefly?*) – they were Shakespeare, too – and Shakespeare's sister. (Gee 2015: 457)

This passage acts as an inverse of the autograph sequence. There, Angela was speaking through Virginia; here, Woolf is speaking through Angela's daughter as she reads the passage. Significantly, Virginia fades in and out of view while Woolf's words are being read, symbolising the ephemeral nature of any one biographical representation when compared to the 'real thing'. For as Lee would have it, while Woolf 'continues to be reinvented – made up, and made over – with every new adaptor . . . there is no owning her' (2005: 61). Gee corroborates the limitations of such reinventions, acknowledging that 'Virginia is a phantasm . . . always and only my own' (2015: 475). What remains, however, when the phantasm dissolves are Woolf's works and the people who read them, their interpretations inevitably informed by the concerns of the gateway text. In the case of Gee, popular perceptions of Woolf's suicide, her sexuality and her practice as a diarist are put on trial, encouraging Woolf's readers to take none of these representations as a given in their future encounters with her works. *Virginia Woolf in Manhattan* functions, then, both as a text in its own right and as a guiding intermediary between Woolf and her readers, ensuring that 'a new generation of young women will reinvent and reappraise her' (Alvarez qtd in Lee 2005: 59). Gerda is prototypical of this new generation; by reading Woolf's works she will 'help Virginia go on into the future' (Gee 2015: 446).

Notes

1. Cramer does, however, note that twentieth-century critics referred to Woolf as '"Sapphic" and "lesbian" . . . with an ease that disappeared under the influence of queer theories in the late 1980s to the present' (2012: 129). Eileen Barrett, writing in her Introduction to *Virginia Woolf: Lesbian Readings*, went some way towards reclaiming the term, citing Bonnie Zimmerman's observation that it would be indefensible to suggest 'that current definitions of marriage should not be applied to the work of modernist heterosexual writers' (Barrett 1997: 7). The changing critical reactions to Woolf as lesbian find a parallel in the current reluctance to link her to the term 'feminism', which suggests an unwillingness to over-specify, compounded by association with a writer who 'wanted to avoid all categories' (Lee 1996: 490). Notwithstanding these reservations, some common terminology remains necessary to indicate how, in Diana L. Swanson's terms, 'Woolf's feminism and lesbianism are key to her narrative experimentation and restructuring of the novel' (2007: 199).
2. See also the first volume of Woolf's letters (*L* 1).

Bibliography

Barrett, E. (1997), 'Introduction', in E. Barrett and P. M. Cramer (eds), *Virginia Woolf: Lesbian Readings*, New York: New York University Press, pp. 3–9.
Bell, A. O. (2002), 'Editing Virginia Woolf's diary', in J. M. Haule and J. H. Stape (eds), *Editing Virginia Woolf: Interpreting the Modernist Text*, Basingstoke: Palgrave Macmillan, pp. 11–24.
Bell, V. (1993), *Selected Letters of Vanessa Bell*, ed. R. Marler, London: Bloomsbury.
Cramer, P. M. (2012), 'Virginia Woolf and theories of sexuality', in J. Goldman and B. Randall (eds), *Virginia Woolf in Context*, Cambridge: Cambridge University Press, pp. 129–46.
Cunningham, M. (1999), *The Hours*, London: Fourth Estate.
Dee, J. (1999), 'The reanimators: On the art of literary graverobbing', *Harper's Magazine*, June, pp. 76–84, <https://harpers.org/archive/1999/06/the-reanimators/> (last accessed 4 August 2016).
DeSalvo, L. (1989), *Virginia Woolf: The Impact of Childhood Sexual Abuse on Her Life and Work*, London: The Women's Press.
Gee, M. (2015), *Virginia Woolf in Manhattan*, London: Telegram Books.
Gillespie, D. F. (1998), *The Sisters' Arts: The Writing and Painting of Virginia Woolf and Vanessa Bell*, New York: Syracuse University Press.
Gualtieri, E. (2000), 'The impossible art: Virginia Woolf on modern biography', *The Cambridge Quarterly*, 29: 4 pp. 349–61.
Holroyd, M. (1994), *Lytton Strachey: The New Biography*, New York: Farrar, Straus and Giroux.
The Hours (2003), film, dir. S. Daldry, USA: Miramax.
Kore-Schröeder, L. (2000), 'Virginia Woolf and the body: Corporeality metaphor, and the in-between', *Virginia Woolf Bulletin*, January, pp. 15–20.
Kristeva, J. (1988 [1977]), *About Chinese Women*, trans. A. Barrows, London: Boyars.
Laird, H. (2007), 'Reading "Virginia's death": A (post)traumatic narrative of suicide', in S. Henke and D. Eberly (eds), *Virginia Woolf and Trauma: Embodied Texts*, New York: Pace University Press, pp. 247–69.
Lee, H. (1997), *Virginia Woolf*, London: Vintage.
Lee, H. (2005), *Virginia Woolf's Nose: Essays on Biography*, Princeton, NJ: Princeton University Press.
Levy, H. (2003), 'Apothecary and wild child: What lies between the acts of 'The Hours' and *Mrs Dalloway*', *Virginia Woolf Bulletin*, 13, pp. 40–9.
Lodge, D. (2007), *The Year of Henry James*, London: Penguin.
Martinson, D. (2003), *In the Presence of Audience: The Self in Diaries and Fiction*, Columbus: Ohio State University Press.
Mills Jeansonne, C. (2014), 'Identity and trauma in the diaries of Plath and Woolf: Rhetorical modes of revelation and silence in recovering the self', *European Journal of Life Writing*, 3, pp. 82–102.
Nunez, S. (2007), *Mitz: The Marmoset of Bloomsbury*, New York: Soft Skull Press.
Parmar, P. (2015), *Vanessa and Her Sister*, New York: Ballantine Books.
Sandbach-Dahlström, C. (2011), '"In my end is my beginning": The death of Virginia Woolf', in S. Helgesson (ed.), *Exit: Endings and New Beginnings in Literature and Life*, Amsterdam: Rodopi, pp. 161–86.
Sellers, S. (2000), 'Virginia Woolf's diaries and letters', in S. Roe and S. Sellers (eds), *The Cambridge Companion to Virginia Woolf*, Cambridge: Cambridge University Press, pp. 109–26.
Sellers, S. (2008), *Vanessa and Virginia*, Ross-shire Scotland: Two Ravens Press.
Snaith, A. (2000), '"My poor private voice": Virginia Woolf and auto/biography', in A. Donnell and P. Polkey (eds), *Representing Lives: Women and Auto/Biography*, Basingstoke: Macmillan, pp. 96–104.
Swanson, D. L. (2007), 'Lesbian approaches', in A. Snaith (ed.), *Palgrave Advances in Virginia Woolf Studies*, Basingstoke: Macmillan, pp. 184–208.

Vincent, N. (2015), *Adeline*, London: Virago.
Woolf, V. (1943 [1942]), *The Death of the Moth and Other Essays*, London: Hogarth Press.
Woolf, V. (1960 [1927]), 'The new biography', in *Granite and Rainbow*, London: Hogarth Press, pp. 149–55.
Woolf, V. (1975), *The Letters of Virginia Woolf: Volume 1: The Flight of the Mind, 1888–1912*, ed. N. Nicolson and J. Trautmann, London: Hogarth Press.
Woolf, V. (1977–84), *The Diary of Virginia Woolf*, 5 vols, ed. A. O. Bell and A. McNeillie, London: Hogarth Press.
Woolf, V. (1996 [1925]), *Mrs Dalloway*, London: Penguin.
Woolf, V. (1998 [1931]), *The Waves*, ed. G. Beer, Oxford: Oxford University Press.
Woolf, V. (2004 [1929]), *A Room of One's Own*, London: Penguin.

23

THE WOOLF GIRL: A MOTHER–DAUGHTER STORY WITH VIRGINIA WOOLF AND LIDIA YUKNAVITCH

Catherine W. Hollis

Inside everything I have ever written, there is a girl.
(Lidia Yuknavitch, *The Small Backs of Children*, 2015)

The image that comes to my mind when I sit and think of this girl is the image of a fisherman lying sunk in dreams on the verge of a deep lake with a rod held out over the water.
(Virginia Woolf, 'Professions for women', 1931 [*E* 6])

'WE THINK BACK THROUGH OUR MOTHERS if we are women'; for Virginia Woolf, this meant thinking back through the legacy of her literary foremothers as an inheritor of their legacy (*AROO*: 79). Taking up Woolf's claim, feminist literary critics have shown how relationships between literary foremothers and daughters are characterised as much by affiliation as by differentiation, such as when Woolf criticises Charlotte Brontë's *Jane Eyre* for its flashes of undisguised anger (*AROO*: 73). By critiquing Brontë's approach, Woolf makes space for herself as a woman writer.[1] Similarly, contemporary feminist writers think back in turn through Woolf; her legacy is profound, ongoing and global, as the many contributors to this volume attest. But perhaps some feminist writers are ambivalent about Woolf's influence: 'I am not Virginia Woolf', an unnamed character declares in Lidia Yuknavitch's novel *The Small Backs of Children* (2015). This character, a woman writer burdened with a traumatic past, continues: 'A woman must have money and a room of her own if she is to write fiction. What a crock. Fuck you, old girl, old dead girl' (Yuknavitch 2015c: 7). Through these opening lines, Yuknavitch expresses a debt to Woolf with brash ambivalence, attesting to the shaping influence of Woolf on contemporary women writers. Inevitably, we think back through Virginia Woolf if we are women writers.[2] In the twenty-first century, however, it is not enough to think *back* through our literary foremothers; we must also think *forward* through the literary work currently being done by Woolf's global progeny.

In his poem, 'My heart leaps up when I behold', William Wordsworth claims that the 'Child is Father of the Man': it is the contention of this essay that the girl is mother of the woman. In the work of Virginia Woolf and Lidia Yuknavitch, the figure of the girl is simultaneously the wounded source of the woman artist's creativity and the bearer of her biographical and historical trauma. Although this chapter focuses on the intergenerational dynamic within and between Woolf and Yuknavitch, other contemporary global writers like Bhanu Kapil (1968–), Akwaeke Emezi (1987–) and Eimear McBride (1976–) similarly deploy the body of their girls as registers of sexual, political and ethnic trauma.[3] Woolf's symbol of the girl fishing in 'Professions for women' (1931) serves as a vivid source image for both the creative potential of the girl as a young artist and the trauma (the 'smash') that shapes her art:

> She was letting her imagination sweep unchecked round every rock and cranny of the world that lies submerged in the depths of our unconscious being. Now came the experience, the experience that I believe to be far commoner with women writers than with men. . . . And then there was the smash. There was an explosion. . . . The imagination had dashed itself against something hard. The girl was roused from her dream. She was indeed in a state of the most acute and difficult distress. (*E* 6: 482)

Woolf's pairing of creative pleasure and traumatic knowledge ('she had thought of something, something about the body' [*E* 6: 482]) is often seen, quite rightly, as 'heteronormative censure' (Lemaster 2012: 89) or silencing of the creative and erotic potential of the adolescent girl. I argue however that contemporary writers like Kapil, Emezi and McBride recognise that sexual violence against girls and women is sadly more the norm rather than the exception. As tragic as the statistics on global sexual violence are,[4] these writers are not permanently silenced by trauma, whether witnessed or experienced. Instead, each of these adult writers reaches back to her 'girl' as the matrix for her own creative work: the girl as mother to the woman writer.

Attention to the figure of 'the girl' in Woolf's oeuvre is surprisingly limited, often analysed through specific characters, or through the more general lens of childhood.[5] For example, Elizabeth Abel's reading of the character Cam in *To the Lighthouse* positions her as an unwilling inheritor of a patriarchal tradition: 'through Cam, Woolf dramatizes the narrative dilemma of the daughter who thinks back through her father' (1989: 46). Lois Gilmore discusses Bloomsbury's inheritance of Lewis Carroll through a 1930 costume party, when Woolf dressed up as the March Hare, which demonstrates the 'possibility of the adult who can participate in the fantasy of childhood' (2018: 123). These critical formulations of Woolf's depiction of childhood portray it as either a prison to be escaped from or a fantasy world returned to, but in each case, childhood is a world apart from the retrospective position of the adult writer. By contrast, Tracy Lemaster offers a compelling and original interpretation of the figure of the girl in Woolf's writings through the lens of Girls' Studies, a third-wave feminist branch of the social sciences that focuses on female adolescence. Girls' Studies challenges feminism's focus on adult women by seeking to explore and analyse the adolescent girl as a feminist figure in her own right (Lemaster 2012: 82). Lemaster's argument tracks how Woolf 'uses the term "women" when *theorizing* the state of female authorship, but "girls" when *fictionalizing* scenes of this authorship' (2012: 78). In Lemaster's reading, Woolf depicts the writer as a girl in fictionalised scenes in order to emphasise the birth of the woman author; she is 'a girl sitting with a pen in her hand' or 'an unknown girl writing her novel in a bed-sitting-room' in 'Professions for women' and *A Room of One's Own*, respectively (2012: 85). Lemaster's depiction of Woolf's 'girl' as a writer lends itself fruitfully to Yuknavitch's portrait of the girl as a young artist: both Woolf and Yuknavitch are invested, I argue, in developing aesthetic representations of girls as practicing artists, not as passive victims of childhood circumstance.

'Inside everything I have written, there is a girl' is a line from Lidia Yuknavitch's *The Small Backs of Children* that may serve as a key to her life and work (2015: 8). Both this novel and Yuknavitch's earlier memoir, *The Chronology of Water: A Memoir* (2011), depict the experience of giving birth to a stillborn daughter as the central autobiographical trauma of Yuknavitch's life, one which has become a powerful source for her subsequent art. A North American writer, Yuknavitch (1963–) is known for her wild, rollicking, sometimes violent narratives rooted in the somatic, bodily experiences of girls and women.[6] Rebecca Solnit's cover blurb for the first edition of *The Small Backs of Children* describes Yuknavitch as an inheritor of the countercultural tradition of American writers like Henry Miller, Charles Bukowski and Jack Kerouac, minus their misogyny (Yuknavitch 2015c). Indeed, Yuknavitch began her writing life as a member of Ken Kesey's University of Oregon writing class (1987–8), when the group collaboratively wrote the novel *Caverns* under the pseudonym O. U. Levon (1990). Although this framework positions Yuknavitch as the inheritor of a male narrative tradition, she situates her own writing in alliance within an international community of women writers, including, significantly, Virginia Woolf.

The relationship between Yuknavitch's and Woolf's writing is compound and multidirectional. In one respect, Woolf is the literary foremother whom Yuknavitch 'thinks through' in her writing: Woolf as influence and mentor. Yuknavitch, however, not only follows in Woolf's footsteps but creates new pathways in turn that build on the problems of literary form that engaged Woolf, especially concerning the representation of female bodily existence. As Woolf herself notes in 'Professions for women': 'telling the truth about my own experiences as a body, I do not think I solved. I doubt that any woman has solved it yet' (*E* 6: 483). By developing a methodology Yuknavitch calls 'corporeal writing', she actively develops Woolf's legacy with regards to the bodily experience of girls and women, a somatic record that inevitably registers the violence and damage done to their bodies under patriarchy (Yuknavitch n.d.).

This chapter begins by examining the figure of the girl in Yuknavitch's memoir *The Chronology of Water*, the award-winning book that first brought Yuknavitch public acclaim. My analysis contrasts Yuknavitch's autobiographical 'girl', which refers both to herself as a girl and to her stillborn daughter, with Woolf's representation of her own girlhood in 'A sketch of the past'. Both writers, I argue, locate the source of their creativity in childhood moments of 'shock', to use Woolf's word for the impact of violence on the child. Yuknavitch's novel *The Small Backs of Children* builds on her memoir by further developing the figure of the girl as an artist through both explicit and implicit references to Woolf. In the second half of this chapter, I contrast *Small Backs* with *Three Guineas* to compare Woolf's representation of children injured or killed during war with Yuknavitch's response to Woolf's question in that text: 'how . . . are we to prevent war?' (*TG*: 5). The answer, for Yuknavitch, lies in helping children gain artistic agency to represent their own experiences. In both her memoir and novel, Yuknavitch develops the notion of the girl as witness to violence and subsequent creator of art, a theme implicitly present in Woolf's 'Professions for women', 'A sketch of the past' and *Three Guineas*.

In Yuknavitch's memorable phrasing, Woolf is the ultimate 'old dead girl' haunting her work (Yuknavitch 2015c: 7). Although this might sound like an expression of anger or rejection, I argue that Yuknavitch uses the phrase to express a complex range of affiliations. The old dead girl can refer to the adult woman writer who calls upon her own girlhood to create a relationship between childhood perception and mature reflection in her work, or it can also refer to the haunting presence of girls whose lives were cut short by violence. Intergenerationally, the old dead girl refers to women writers from the past, like Woolf, whose example provides inspiration or provocation across decades or centuries, especially with regards to their depiction of childhood trauma. Throughout the essay, I argue that the generative figure of this girl is muse, matrix and mother to the contemporary woman writer.

A Mother–Daughter Story

Virginia Woolf's 'A sketch of the past' and Lidia Yuknavitch's *The Chronology of Water* both use memoir to document the process of becoming a writer, and both reflect on how childhood trauma plays into that process. The relationship between the adult writer and her origin as a 'girl' is pivotal for both memoirs. For Woolf, drawing a lineage between the 'I now, I then' (*MB*: 75), as an adult retrospectively writing about herself as a child, functions as a methodology for memoir, or what Evelyne Ender calls 'an alignment between a remembering self and a remembered self' (2005: 47). In Ender's formulation, memoir is created retrospectively by the adult 'rememberer'; the 'remembered' girl is fashioned through the adult's act of reflection (2005: 186). Alison Light proposes a more dynamic intertextual relationship between child and adult selves by comparing the function of Woolf's diaries and memoirs. In Light's argument, Woolf's diary – particularly the early volumes, beginning in 1897 when Woolf was fifteen – composes an adolescent self by documenting the 'ongoingness'[7] of the present moment: 'the diary was a lifeline, a way of creating and sustaining an ego' (2007: 5). For Light, the memoir serves a similar function, only retrospectively: 'in the memoirs, Woolf went back over her origins in order to incorporate an account of how she became a writer, of how she fashioned an identity for herself. The memoirs allowed her to invent her self again' (2007: 19). If Woolf's diaries were 'note taking for some future revision', then her late memoir is that revision anticipated by the young diarist (*MB*: 154). Following Light and Lemaster, the relationship between Woolf's early diaries and late memoir is seen in this chapter as a dynamic collaboration over time between the girl writing and the woman writer.

If 'A sketch of the past' uses the 'I now, I then' as a 'platform' to move between the present and the past, then *The Chronology of Water* uses 'the girl I was and the girl I had' (2011: 292) to create a more circular temporal movement. The girl haunting Yuknavitch's writing is twofold; she is both the girl Lidia was and the stillborn daughter she gives birth to as college student. Although Yuknavitch's memoir is about many things – an abusive childhood, competitive swimming, addiction, grief, violence and sex – the 'born dead' girl (2011: 28) is at the heart of the nonlinear pieces of life-writing that make up *The Chronology of Water*. Indeed, this girl functions narratively as both story (Yuknavitch's tale of trauma and healing) and plot (the structure of the memoir itself). The very first sentence of the memoir invokes the narrative paradox of giving birth to 'my dead girl' (2011: 25), for what should be the beginning of a life (and a memoir) is instead a death and an ending. This paradox is stated more explicitly in the novel *The Small Backs of Children*, when a character recollects holding her stillborn daughter: 'I was holding life and death – those supposed opposites, those markers of narrative worth; a beginning, an ending – all at once in my arms' (2015c: 20). What kind of linear chronology is possible after the catastrophe of a stillbirth? *The Chronology of Water* thus narrates the slow and painful process of a young woman learning to make art from the ashes of her dead daughter. In the process, Yuknavitch names her literary 'foremothers' as helpers, including Woolf, whose work provided a life-line.

Like 'A sketch of the past', *The Chronology of Water* foregrounds the writerly process of structuring the memoir. Where Woolf discovered 'a possible form for these notes' by using the present moment 'as platform to stand upon' (*MB*: 83–4), Yuknavitch's temporal scheme reflects the fragmentary perceptual experience of trauma. The first sentence of the memoir begins, 'the day my daughter was stillborn', positioning this event as central to the life represented there; but rather than a beginning or an ending, this trauma is experienced and represented as the centre of a circle of expanding waves.

> I thought about starting this book with my childhood, the beginning of my life. But that's not how I remember it. I remember things in retinal flashes. Without order. Your life doesn't happen in any kind of order. . . . It's all a series of fragments and repetitions and pattern formations. Language and water have this in common. (2011: 28)

Early on, Yuknavitch's representation of grief is nearly wordless, a 'strange space' (2011: 26) that she calls 'the white' (2011: 106) to indicate the blankness of dissociative grief. In 'the white', time and space are not linear but nonetheless patterned:

> Lie all the baby clothes that have been given to you as scripts or gifts on the floor in lines. Sit with the tiny clothes and your rocks and think of nothing at all. Have endless patterns and repetitions accompanying your thoughtlessness. (2011: 33)

Using the second person and the imperative voice allows Yuknavitch to express the sensation of grief, creating distance between the narrating self and the traumatised self. The narrating self tries to establish order, to lay down baby clothes and smooth river rocks in orderly rows on the floor, like words on a page, while the traumatised self thinks 'of nothing at all'. Making patterns with objects is soothing, suggesting that one day, making patterns with words, or 'scripts', will also be healing. This scene is significant for its emphasis on the making of something, anything, even a simple mark or a line, out of the inarticulate experience of grief. This scene, as we will see, also resonates with the opening pages of *The Small Backs of Children*, when a traumatised girl makes her mark by urinating on wolf's blood in the snow. Indeed, there are many metaphorical and narrative patterns that circulate between Yuknavitch's memoir and her novels; throughout Yuknavitch's oeuvre, making a mark on the blank 'white' of trauma signifies healing.

Thematically, Yuknavitch's pattern-making impulse echoes Woolf's statement in 'A sketch of the past' that 'the shock-receiving capacity is what makes me a writer' (*MB*: 72). When 'shocks' fragment the developing self, 'putting it into words' offers the lifelong satisfaction of 'putting the severed parts together' (*MB*: 72). For Woolf, this idea begins as a childhood perception in response to moments of both violence and beauty and includes, significantly, a sense of futurity. For example, when Woolf describes her insight that a flower in its garden bed is 'a part of the earth', she also describes how her childhood self puts the thought 'away as being likely to be very useful to me later' (*MB*: 71). The child's anticipatory perception of a future self who will make use of this insight is then recollected, in 'A sketch of the past', as a source for the adult writer's later creative vision. While Ender argues that the mental architecture of memory produces Woolf's description of the flower as a 'retrospective projection' on the part of the adult memoirist (2005: 186), I want to argue that Woolf depicts her childhood self as engaged in a more active conversation with the writer she will eventually become. In other words, the child who banks on her perceptual experiences as 'something I should go back [to], to turn over and explore' (*MB*: 71) is already planting the seeds for a collaboration with her future writer self. Of course, the adult narrator shapes this scene as we read it in 'A sketch of the past', but Woolf is at pains to locate the foundation of her creativity in this childhood 'intuition' that has 'given its scale to my life ever since I saw the flower in the bed by the front door at St Ives' (*MB*: 72).

Woolf's late experiment in memoir is the development of a creative theory that links the girl she was to the writer she becomes, an insight that she only expresses towards the end of her life. For Yuknavitch, the reverberation between girl and woman shapes her work, in both memoir and fiction, from the very beginning. This difference between the two writers stems in part from the different ways they draw upon autobiographical material in fictional works. Where Woolf saw 'granite and rainbow', fact and fiction, as a constitutive tension informing the relationship between auto/biography and fiction (*E* 6: 478), Yuknavitch refuses to recognise such generic distinctions. For Yuknavitch, the relationship between autobiography and fiction is always porous: 'they inform, deform, and reform one another' she says in an interview (Yuknavitch 2015b). Dispensing with the so-called 'autobiographical pact',[8] the conventional memoirist's adherence to accurately representing events and facts, Yuknavitch prioritises the emotional truth of a scene over and above its representation of specific facts. In doing so, Yuknavitch's work attests to Timothy Dow Adams's idea that autobiography is not 'meant to be taken as historically accurate but as metaphorically authentic' (1990: ix). While details shift between *The Chronology of Water* and *The Small Backs of Children*, their central metaphors remain consistent: the stillborn girl who gives life to her mother's art and water as metaphor for memory and time.

Indeed, two parallel scenes that represent a funeral ritual for Yuknavitch's stillborn daughter suggest the differing compensations of fact and fiction. In the memoir, Lidia goes with her family – her husband, sister and parents – to release the ashes of her baby into the ocean at Heceta Head on the Oregon coast:

> Philip and I took the little pink box which I had been clutching in my hand hard enough to nearly crush it and walked over to where the river joins the ocean. That's why I'd picked that spot. . . . I don't know if I was crying – my face was wet with ocean and rain. . . . All the waters of a life met at that tiny nexus. (2011: 91–2)

But the cross-current in the intermixture of salt and fresh waters keeps forcing the pink box back in to shore no matter how many times they throw it in, and Lidia and Philip, the baby's father, begin laughing hysterically. Eventually Lidia opens the box and tears open the plastic bag of ashes with her teeth; she walks into the water fully dressed in her red coat:

> I wave walked until I was up to my abdomen. The water felt ice cold on my stitches. Numbed the hurt there. I dumped the nearly weightless contents of my daughter into my right hand. . . . And then I let my right hand lower into the water, and I let go. (2011: 93)

The factual elements of this scene are precise: her right hand, her red coat, the pink box and Heceta Head. The emotional details feel truthful as well: the hysterical laughter indistinct from sobbing and how the ice of the water numbs the sting of the stitches from her labour. Water is also a key metaphorical element here: the place where the waters meet, river and ocean, fresh water and salt, is the place where life and death mingle.

The metaphorical symbolism of life and death intermingling persists from memoir to novel, but in the novel it further evolves through the use of fairy-tale imagery. In *The Small Backs of Children*, the dead body of the writer's daughter is rescued from the hospital's morgue by her friend, a poet, while a little pig is sent to the crematorium instead. The writer then takes her daughter's body and goes alone to 'a place where a river empties into a sea' (2015c: 20). There she sings to her daughter and builds a funeral pyre out of kindling, sage and her own hair; after the fire burns out, the writer takes her daughter's ashes into the sea 'so there was a moment when we were together in the same waters' (2015c: 21). I would argue that the critical difference between these two scenes is that in the novel the narrator is already a writer; in the memoir, Lidia is not yet a writer. As a writer, the narrator of the novel has the tools to recast her daughter's death into the language of fairy tale – the substitution of pig for baby and the building of the funeral pyre – to recreate the scene as a foundational myth. Reimagining the baby's sea burial in this way turns the blunt somatic grief of memoir into art: this is how the writer would choose to mourn her daughter.

The repetition of scenes between the memoir and novel speaks to the healing mythology that Yuknavitch creates: the woman writer is born from the ashes of her dead girl. The midwives for this metaphorical birth are the women writers who have come before, particularly Woolf. As Yuknavitch acknowledges in *The Chronology of Water*, using the second person again, 'you were never, in the end, alone' (2011: 201). She goes on to list a constellation of literary doulas, beginning with Marguerite Duras and ending with Virginia Woolf, and along the way including Emily Dickinson, Hélène Cixous, Jean Rhys, Leslie Marmon Silko, Toni Morrison and Anne Carson among others, each of whose writing touched the young Lidia, trapped in the expressionless 'white' of her trauma: 'whatever else there was or is, writing is with me' (2011: 203). Significantly, Woolf is the final helper in Yuknavitch's catalogue of life-saving writers: she is imagined going on a 'long walk' with 'you', 'a walk that will last all day' (2011: 203). Woolf and 'you' stand arm in arm: 'at your backs will be history. In front of you, just the ordinary day, which is of course your entire life. Like language. The small backs of words' (2011: 203). The 'you' here is deliberately inclusive of both the memoir's narrator and the reader; part of Yuknavitch's writerly mythology is that, as expressed in her 2016 TED talk and subsequent book *The Misfit's Manifesto* (2017), '"sometimes telling the story IS saving your own life"' (2017: 62). Reading Woolf or any of the other writers that Yuknavitch mentions reminds us that we are not alone and that healing occurs when we are able to tell the story of 'our girl' in our own words. 'In every book I have ever written there is a girl. And there always will be' (2017: 48).

I have been arguing that one significant result of Woolf's late experiment in memoir is the development of a creative theory that links the girl she was to the writer she becomes and that this creative theory both informs and is exceeded by Yuknavitch's own experiments in memoir and fiction. Such an argument also supports Leigh Gilmore and Elizabeth Marshall's recent scholarship on life-writing and the figure of girl as witness. In autobiographies stretching back to Harriet Jacobs's *Incidents in the Life of a Slave Girl* (1861) and as recently as the testimonies from female athletes abused by Larry Nassar, Gilmore and Marshall argue that women writers return to the scene of girlhood trauma to 'accompany' their girl as witness: 'the child in these texts is positioned to testify to experience rather than to suffer it passively' (2019: 5). Their notion of authorial 'accompaniment' suggests, as I have argued, that the adult memoirist actively collaborates with her girlhood self: 'the adult interrupts the narrative of girlhood to accompany and protect the younger, narrated self' (2019: 62). When Woolf returns to her earliest memories in 'A sketch of the past', or when Yuknavitch writes and rewrites the story of her daughter's stillbirth, they stand arm in arm with their younger selves, much as Woolf does for Yuknavitch on their imagined walk together. Yuknavitch ends *The Chronology of Water* by gesturing towards a double reading of the girl: the girl is both Lidia and her stillborn daughter, 'the girl I was and the girl I had' (2011: 292). Both girls, the abused daughter and her stillborn baby, are brought back to literary life by 'the small backs of words' (2011: 203) that the adult writer draws upon to document their brief and tender existence. 'Arrang[ing the] pieces' (2011: 203) of traumatising experiences provokes the young girl, in both Yuknavitch and Woolf, into becoming an artist.

Portrait of the Artist as a Girl

The work of accompaniment and testifying to childhood trauma is often the work of a lifetime, which may explain why many of the metaphorical patterns in Yuknavitch's *The Chronology of Water* re-emerge in *The Small Backs of Children*. An experimental novel that defies generic conventions, *Small Backs* takes as its subject the impact of war and violence on the bodies of children and women, themes also central to Woolf's *Three Guineas*. *Small Backs* is narrated by multiple artist-characters who are never named but who are referred to by their chosen medium: a writer, a poet, a playwright, a photographer and a performance artist are all drawn into a story about a girl, injured by a bomb blast in an unnamed Eastern European country. Indeed, the first lines of the book instruct the reader to 'picture your image of Eastern Europe' (2015c: 3) as a setting for its opening scene in which the six-year-old girl survives the explosion that kills her family and destroys their home, and who then runs into the stark winter woods to hide.

Yuknavitch's puzzling command to the reader to imagine 'Eastern Europe' bears further consideration. As Adam F. Kola points out, a blurring of the 'semi-peripheries' of Eastern and Central Europe make for a 'convenient intellectual counterpoint' (2015) that erases specific regional and linguistic differences, as well as different historical contexts. In fact, Yuknavitch seems to have had a specific Eastern European country and conflict in mind; in an interview, she discusses how family photographs sent to her from Lithuania prompted her thoughts about this book. 'My great uncle . . . had apparently been a photographer, and he had taken some photos of a massacre that took place at a Lithuanian hospital' (Yuknavitch 2015a). In this interview, Yuknavitch reports that her great uncle was subsequently imprisoned in a Soviet gulag. Certain Lithuanian words and place names also appear in *Small Backs*, including the word *vilkas* or wolf. Yuknavitch thus blends specific fragments of Lithuanian language and culture into the novel's more universal imagery of war and violence. The problem of war is at once both specific and general, as in *Three Guineas*, when Woolf refers to images of children wounded or killed in the Spanish Civil War, but embeds the specifics of that conflict within a larger argument about violence and patriarchy.

The opening pages of the novel create a fantastic, gory and almost fairy-tale like atmosphere. Like Red Riding Hood, the injured girl meets a wolf in the woods, but this wolf is wounded, its leg caught in a hunter's snare. After watching the wolf gnaw off its own leg to free itself from the trap, the girl squats and urinates on top of the bloody stain the wolf has left in the snow. 'What is a girl but this?' the narrator asks, 'This obscene and beautiful *making* against the white' (2015c: 6). These are metaphorical repetitions that we saw earlier in this chapter's analysis of *The Chronology of Water*. Here, the blank 'white' page of snow is stained with a palimpsest of wolf's blood and girl's urine, suggesting Yuknavitch's main theme that art and creativity can and do emerge from violence and carnage. The girl's feral actions suggest animality; by urinating on the spot of the wolf's trauma, she claims the wolf's blood as a part of her own territory. Yuknavitch thus draws a symbolic lineage between the wolf/*vilkas*/Woolf and the girl, creating a hybrid creature we might think of as the Woolf girl, whose resistance to the violence done to bodies is expressed via a corporeal and symbolic '*making*'. Both the girl and the wolf will survive, leaving traces of their wounds on the page: '[the wolf] runs three legged, like all damaged creatures, across the snow' (2015c: 5).

Immediately after the scene between the girl and the wolf, the narration switches to the first person, as the character known only as the writer begins speaking. Her opening monologue extends and develops the wolf/Woolf connection from the previous scene and is worth quoting in full.

> A woman must have money and a room of her own if she is to write fiction.
> What a crock. Virginia, fuck you, old girl, old dead girl.
> I am in a midnight blue room. A writing room. A room of my own making – with its rituals and sanctuary. I can see my husband and son in the next room fiddling with a video camera. Looking at them together makes my heart feel crushed like a wad of paper. I reach down below my desk and pull up a bottle of scotch. My scotch. Balvenie. Thirty year. I pour myself a shot. I drink. Warm lips, throat. I close my eyes. I am not Virginia Woolf. Do you know how many women can't afford the room, or have no help, or scratch away at things in bars, buses, closets? I much prefer a different line of yours, anyway: Arrange whatever pieces come your way. Or this: Someone has to die in order that the rest of us should value life more.
> I know something about death. (2015c: 7–8)

Yuknavitch's depiction of Woolf as an 'old dead girl' has been previously discussed. The subsequent references to Woolf in this passage speak to her persistence as a source of influence. *A Room of One's Own* is, of course, directly quoted in the first lines the writer character speaks, suggesting that she, or indeed any contemporary woman writer, speaks through Woolf's example in order to speak at all. To make space for herself – to mark her own territory – the writer curses at Woolf like a rebellious daughter, even though Woolf is difficult, if not impossible, to reject or ignore. She can be argued with, however, as the writer does when she directly addresses Woolf, pointing to her privileged economic position compared to writers who cannot afford the luxury of a study. 'I am not Virginia Woolf', Yukanvitch's writer says, even though she too has managed to obtain a room of her own.

The next quotation from Woolf, 'arrange whatever pieces come your way', which the writer says she prefers, is from Woolf's diary, recounting a mental and physical collapse during the process of drafting *To the Lighthouse* (D 3: 39). Yuknavitch also quotes this line in *The Chronology of Water*, citing it as 'a line of hers that keeps me well: Arrange whatever pieces come your way' (2011: 203). As a writer's manifesto, this quotation suggests that we have no control over the events that happen to us, the 'pieces' of our ordinary lives; we only have the power of arrangement, of taking these pieces and creating patterns of meaning. Woolf's words thus form part of the metaphorical pattern that Yuknavitch draws upon across her work in memoir and fiction. The last quotation attributed to Woolf in the writer's monologue is not a direct quote from Woolf at all but rather a line that the character of Virginia Woolf speaks in David Hare's screenplay of *The Hours* (2002), based on Michael Cunningham's novel of the same name. In Hare's screenplay, Virginia utters the line, 'someone has to die in order that the rest of us should value life more', after she has decided to kill off 'the poet, the visionary' in her manuscript of *The Hours* (Hare 2002: 111). This is not something Virginia Woolf the author ever wrote, although countless online sources misattribute it to Woolf herself. Woolf scholars have previously enumerated the problematic slippage between the biographical Woolf and her representation in the film version of *The Hours* (see Chapter 22 by Bethany Layne in this volume); but in this case the slippage also suggests a generative interpretation of the evolving figure of the girl in Yuknavitch's work.

In *Small Backs*, this idea of a sacrificial character resonates with the figure of the girl as creative muse. For example, the writer immediately follows her address to and quotations from Woolf with this passage:

> Inside everything I have ever written, there is a girl. Sometimes she is dead, and haunts the story like a ghost. Sometimes she is an orphan of war. Sometimes she is just wandering. Maybe the girl is a metaphor, or maybe she is me, or maybe a character who keeps coming. (Yuknavitch 2015c: 8)

Although these lines are delivered by a fictional character, they parallel the autobiographical details of Yuknavitch's own life, as portrayed in *The Chronology of Water*; both writers, the autobiographical Yuknavitch and her fictional stand-in, suffer from the stillbirth of a daughter and turn towards writing as a survival strategy. As companion texts, both memoir and novel formally accrete around the loss of this girl, who persists as a muse for the mother-artist, 'inside everything I have ever written'. Like

Yuknavitch's girl, Virginia Woolf haunts the narrative of *The Small Backs of Children* as she was herself haunted by the deaths of those she loved. For both Yuknavitch and Woolf, the greatest autobiographical trauma – those 'shocks' or 'blows' as Woolf called them in 'A sketch of the past' – re-emerge as complex sources of creativity.

The theme of art as a survival strategy suggests a further parallel between *The Small Backs of Children* and Woolf's *Three Guineas*. Both of these texts question the ethics of visually representing injured or dead children through photography; both also question the ethical responsibilities of those who make or reproduce these images. In *Small Backs*, the girl who survives the initial bombing is photographed by a journalist at the instant of the explosion; the image of the girl is described 'as if she is coming out of fire, her eyes bullets heading for the lens' (2015c: 38). The photographer, a woman who is a former lover of the writer's, wins a prestigious award for capturing this powerful image of a child caught up by violence; she sends a framed copy of the image to the writer with a short message: '*this is the girl*' (2015c: 39). Although the writer hangs this black and white image of a weaponised girl ('her eyes bullets') in her home, she also condemns the photographer for taking pictures instead of actively helping the child. This argument occurs by telephone on the night of the prize ceremony, and the writer's critique troubles the drunken photographer, who thinks about Woolf: 'remember what Virginia Woolf said: Give back the awards, should you be cleverly tricked into believing they mean something' (2015c: 48). This indirect quote from *Three Guineas* – in Woolf's words, 'if we are offered honours and degrees for ourselves we can refuse them' (*TG*: 46) – suggests its intellectual resonance with *Small Backs* and shows how Yuknavitch herself is, once again, thinking back through Virginia Woolf.

Yuknavitch's echo of *Three Guineas* suggests that Woolf's question – 'how in your opinion are we to prevent war?' (*TG*: 5) – is a necessary and ongoing one; significantly, both Yuknavitch and Woolf broach the question through the photographic representation of children injured or killed by war. Woolf initially asks the question after viewing pictures of 'dead bodies' in the Guernica bombing: 'those certainly are dead children' (*TG*: 14). Woolf's choice not to include any of these photographs in *Three Guineas* is deliberately made. Sarah Cole and Emily Dalgarno, among others, have analysed Woolf's decision as an ethical and aesthetic one: Cole's view is that 'we are guided by Woolf to feel the outrage of war in her terms, to see the pictures, almost literally, through her eyes. They become literary, rather than visual testaments' (2012: 56–7). Both Woolf and Yuknavitch find words a more nuanced medium through which to discuss the origins of war in the gendered violence that plays out on the bodies of women and children. In Dalgarno's reading, Woolf's choice to verbally 'represent . . . rather than reproduce' the Spanish photographs encourages the reader to question the use of documentary photography in contemporary newspapers; when newspapers like *The Times* censor the depiction of dead bodies in the Spanish Civil War, they may tacitly encourage a policy of non-intervention in the conflict (Dalgarno 2001: 151, 172). In other words, it might be easier to ignore the violence of war when it is not visually and viscerally documented in the newspaper. So which choice is the ethical one? Can a photograph of a wounded child help prevent future violence?

The answer, it seems, depends upon who takes the picture of the child. Initially, the novel suggests that the photographer commits an act of representational violence when she transforms an injured girl into an object of art, framed and hung on the writer's wall. This reading is supported by the writer's collapse into a suicidal depression after placing the child's photograph in her home; her passive complicity in the objectification of the child's injury is symbolised through her depressive paralysis. The writer is subsequently hospitalised after she stops speaking, eating or drinking; her artist-friends gather in the hospital and don't, at first, connect her collapse with the arrival of the photograph of the girl. It soon becomes clear however that the girl's photograph has triggered the writer's trauma at having, years earlier, lost a baby girl in a stillbirth. Among the writer's friends, it falls to the poet to make out the metaphorical connection between the stillborn baby and the girl in the photograph; while at the writer's hospital bed, the poet reflects on 'grief and trauma, how they can hide out inside a woman, how they can come back' (2015c: 88). Subsequently, the writer's friends embark on an international search for the girl in the photograph; they determine that they must save this girl and bring her to the writer in order to cure her renewed grief from the loss of her daughter. The trauma of the earlier stillbirth can only be psychologically integrated by the writer if she has the chance to help this girl, injured by war.

As has been previously noted, the imagery of stillbirth is one of those porous metaphorical patterns that shape both this novel and Yuknavitch's earlier memoir. Both texts refer to the grief of losing a child as 'the white' (Yuknavitch 2011: 130) and further define the 'white' as a period of time 'when a soul has to leave the body' (Yuknavitch 2015c: 106; Yuknavitch 2011: 130). In *Small Backs,* the writer's depression symbolically mirrors the dissociative state of the girl in its opening pages, as the girl stumbles through the mute white snowfield after the bomb blast. After the writer loses her voice to 'the white', the rest of the novel is collectively narrated by her artist-friends as they search for the girl in the photograph. Yuknavitch uses different literary forms to reflect the art practice of each character, such as a play, poem or duet between the writer and the girl. These different mediums suggest one way of resisting the social violence of war. Art, or more simply 'making', plays an active role in the healing of both writer and girl, as does being a member of a close-knit community of artists and lovers. Making art about war is a form of activism, and activism is a form of healing.

Thus, to answer Woolf's question on war, Yuknavitch suggests that we must bravely enter 'the white', the nothingness that symbolises both trauma and the blank page or canvas, to make and remake ourselves through whatever medium lies at our disposal (blood, urine, ink, paints, film). Whereas *Three Guineas* asks what adults can do to prevent war, Yuknavitch's solution involves the girl, and by extension, children more generally. Future violence will not be prevented by a photograph of a wounded girl, unless the girl herself can document her experiences; *Small Backs* suggests the girl must have the agency and tools to represent herself, rather than being represented by the adults around her. We see the girl's art-making impulse from the beginning, when she marks the bloody snow with her urine: over the course of the novel, the girl moves from being the object of art to becoming a maker of her own.[9] Towards the end of *Small Backs,* the writer and the girl are united, and the girl moves into the writer's home, where she is provided with a room of her own and plenty of art materials. In her room, the girl learns to paint canvases that reflect her own experience of the world, with some documenting graphic violence and others painted with her own blood. The girl's art represents the violence that she herself has experienced up to this point in her life. After the girl begins making art, the writer as a character disappears from the text. The girl's perspective, her own thoughts and images, shape the chaotic play of images that close the novel, as the 'mother' gives way to the 'daughter', who finds her own voice through making art. 'This, reader, is a mother-daughter story', the writer tells us in the beginning of the novel (2015c: 11). It culminates in the portrait of the young girl, mothering her future self into becoming an artist.

Conclusion

In *A Girl's Story*, French writer Annie Ernaux (1940–) confronts the persistent voice of the 'girl of '58', who is herself at eighteen, a voice she recognises as the 'perpetually missing piece, always postponed' throughout her oeuvre (Ernaux 2020: 13). Ernaux, writing in the first person as a woman in her seventies, documents the voice of this girl in the third person and 'dreams of a sentence that would contain them both, seamlessly, by way of a new syntax' (2020: 56). Ernaux, like Woolf in 'A sketch of the past', seeks a platform through which to link the 'I now, I then' (*MB*: 75), the mature woman writer and her adolescent self. Similarly, Ernaux's turn to the voice of her girl occurs near the end of a long and distinguished writing career. This sets Woolf and Ernaux apart from Yuknavitch, who builds her work around the figure of the girl from the beginning. That all three of these writers are haunted by the voices of girls suggests a growing awareness that the lives of girls, or even more broadly, the thoughts and feelings of children, may offer significant psychological and political insights for adults.

For example, the creative potential that Woolf locates in the girl of 'A sketch of the past' extends beyond the formation of the individual artist to the larger global community. Violence and war continue to 'shock' and 'deform' the bodies of children worldwide, which troubles both Woolf and Yuknavitch even as they remain dedicated to art as resistance: 'I feel that by writing I am doing what is far more necessary than anything else' (*MB*: 73). Here too the figure of the girl offers an insight into Woolf's pacifism. Among the three childhood 'moments of being' that Woolf documents in 'A sketch of the past', only one – the flower and its connection to the earth – offers a feeling of satisfaction. The first moment of 'violent shock' Woolf documents is not so easily resolved:

> I was fighting with Thoby on the lawn. We were pommelling each other with our fists. Just as I raised my fist to hit him, I felt: why hurt another person? I dropped my hand instantly, and stood there, and let him beat me. (*MB*: 71)

This experience produces a feeling of 'hopeless sadness', of 'powerlessness' and of a 'horribl[e] depression' (*MB*: 71). The 'horror' and 'passiv[ity]' (*MB*: 72) occasioned by it are the opposite of the experience with the flower. And yet despite or because of these uncomfortable feelings, the unresolved question 'why hurt another person?' that the child asks ultimately gives birth to the adult writer of *Three Guineas*, who also asks 'Why fight?' (*TG*: 9). The girl's choice to '[drop] my hand' (*MB*: 71) is an active and ethical choice that serves as the foundation of Woolf's mature pacifism.

The choice not to fight suggests an important difference between Woolf's work and Yuknavitch's. While both writers suggest that violence is a foundational aspect of girlhood, Yuknavitch's work can seem to suggest that violence is necessary for creativity to manifest. As she acknowledges in *The Misfit's Manifesto*: 'not all misfits are born up and through violence, but large numbers of us are' (2017: 7). In Yuknavitch's work, art is an activist remedy for resisting this violence, often through graphic and visceral details depicting it. For Woolf, non-violence is an active choice that the child makes despite further harm ('I dropped my hand . . . and let him beat me') that serves as the foundation for a mature ethical and aesthetic vision. For both writers, the testimony of the girl who is witness to violence is echoed by the adult writer in a nonlinear collaboration between child's perception and adult's narration. Woolf's formulation of the 'I now, I then' suggests that the girl and the woman are engaged equally in the process of 'arranging the pieces'. Yuknavitch's variations on a stillbirth imply that a mother–daughter story between 'the girl I was and the girl I had' may take a lifetime, and multiple genres, to work out. But in both cases, 'making' something out of the experience offers a path forward.

This chapter has argued that the figure of the Woolf girl is a dynamic source of creativity for Lidia Yuknavitch and other contemporary global writers. Moreover, this collection of essays as a whole demonstrates that Woolf's example guides not only creative writers but literary critics worldwide. Woolf is in many respects our collective foremother, an eminent figure that we as writers and critics read, emulate and quarrel over. But she is also the girl whose childhood experiences and perceptions demanded their expression in prose; the girl who gave birth to Virginia Woolf, the writer. Where Woolf found herself blocked from further development ('telling the truth about my body, that I do not think I did'), Yuknavitch and many other writers have continued the work of representing the somatic lives of the bodies of girls and women. Here it is worth repeating that the terms I have used in this chapter, 'girl' and 'woman', may be understood as open terms that extend equally to the somatic experiences of trans- and non-binary persons. Telling the truth about our bodies, in all the shapes and forms they take over a lifetime, is an act of social justice. That Woolf only began the process of representing the bodily lives of girls and women at the end of her life shows the importance of the work contemporary women writers continue to do.

Notes

1. Jane Marcus pioneers the affiliative approach in 'Thinking back through our mothers' (1981). Marianne Hirsch documents the generational process of 're-vision' and 're-making' between literary foremothers and daughters in her discussion of Adrienne Rich's critique of *A Room of One's Own* (Hirsch 1989). Molly Hite discusses Woolf's ambivalence towards her literary foremothers in a chapter titled 'Not thinking back through our mothers' (2017).
2. I wish to acknowledge that my use of the limited term 'woman writer' can and should be extended to trans- and non-binary individuals who are influenced by Woolf and recognise themselves in her work.
3. Examples include Bhanu Kapil's *Ban and Banlieu* (2015), Akwaeke Emezi's *Freshwater* (2018) and Eimear McBride's *A Girl is a Half-Formed Thing* (2013).
4. United Nations' statistics estimate that 35 per cent of women worldwide have experienced physical or sexual violence. 'Of the 87,000 women who were intentionally killed in 2017 globally, more than half . . . were killed by intimate partners or family members' (UN Women 2018).
5. In addition to Abel (1989) and Gilmore (2018), see also Susan Rae Belle Bowers (1981), Elizabeth Anne Ford (1989) and Elizabeth Goodenough (1994).
6. See especially Garth Greenwell's review, 'The wild, remarkable sex scenes of Lidia Yuknavitch' (2015).

7. The phrase 'ongoingness' comes from Sarah Manguso's experiments in diary keeping (2015).
8. Phillipe Lejeune's term, 'the autobiographical pact', refers to the expectation of the reader that an autobiography is true and that its narrator is understood to be identical with the author (Marcus 2018: 3).
9. We might think of current projects where children caught in global crises are given materials to write and draw their traumatic experiences. See John Knefel (2015) on Syrian children and art therapy.

Bibliography

Abel, E. (1989), *Virginia Woolf and the Fictions of Psychoanalysis*, Chicago and London: University of Chicago Press.
Adams, T. D. (1990), *Telling Lies in Modern American Autobiography*, Chapel Hill: University of North Carolina Press.
Bowers, S. R. B. (1981), 'The child as mother of the woman: Virginia Woolf's female *Bildungsromane*', dissertation, University of Oregon: Proquest Dissertations Publishing, 8201807.
Cole, S. (2012), *At the Violet Hour: Modernism and Violence in England and Ireland*, Oxford: Oxford University Press.
Dalgarno, E. (2001), *Virginia Woolf and the Visible World*, Cambridge: Cambridge University Press.
Ender, E. (2005), *Architexts of Memory: Literature, Science, and Autobiography*, Ann Arbor: University of Michigan Press.
Ernaux, A. (2020 [2016]), *A Girl's Story*, trans. A. Strayer, New York: Seven Stories Press.
Ford, E. A. (1989), *Nursery Tea: Child Characters in the Novels of Virginia Woolf and E. M. Forster*, dissertation, Kent State University: Proquest Dissertations Publishing, 8920470.
Gilmore, L. (2018), '"Where childhood's dreams are twined": Virginia Woolf and the literary heritage of Lewis Carroll', in J. de Gay, T. Breckin and A. Reus (eds), *Virginia Woolf and Heritage*, Liverpool: Clemson University Press and Liverpool University Press, pp. 121–6.
Gilmore, L. and E. Marshall (2019), *Witnessing Girlhood: Toward an Intersectional Tradition of Life Writing*, New York: Fordham University Press.
Goodenough, E. (1994), '"We haven't the words": The silence of children in the novels of Virginia Woolf', in E. Goodenough, M. Heberle and N. Sokoloff (eds), *Infant Tongues: The Voice of the Child in Literature*, Detroit, MI: Wayne State University Press, pp. 184–201.
Greenwell, G. (2015), 'The wild, remarkable sex scenes of Lidia Yuknavitch', *The New Yorker*, 25 August, <https://www.newyorker.com/books/page-turner/the-wild-remarkable-sex-scenes-of-lidia-yuknavitch> (last accessed 14 July 2020).
Hare, D. (2002), *The Hours: A Screenplay*, New York: Hyperion Press.
Hirsch, M. (1989), *The Mother/Daughter Plot: Narrative, Psychoanalysis, Feminism*, Bloomington: Indiana University Press.
Hite, M. (2017), *Woolf's Ambiguities: Tonal Modernism, Narrative Strategy, Feminist Precursors*, Ithaca, NY: Cornell University Press.
Knefel, J. (2015), 'How art therapy is being used to help Syrian children in Lebanon', *The Nation*, 5 August, <https://www.thenation.com/article/archive/how-art-therapy-is-being-used-to-help-syrian-children-in-lebanon/> (last accessed 11 July 2020).
Kola, A. F. (2015), 'The politics of the archive in semi-peripheries', in *The 2014–2015 Report on the State of the Discipline of Comparative Literature*, <https://stateofthediscipline.acla.org/entry/politics-archive-semi-peripheries> (last accessed 25 March 2020).
Lemaster, T. (2012), '"Girl with a pen": Girls' Studies and Third-Wave feminism in *A Room of One's Own* and "Professions for women"', *Feminist Formulations*, 24: 2, pp. 77–99.
Levon, O. U. (1990), *Caverns*, New York: Penguin.

Light, A. (2007), *Composing One's Self: Virginia Woolf's Diaries and Memoirs*, Southport: Virginia Woolf Society of Great Britain.
Manguso, S. (2015), *Ongoingness: The End of a Diary*, Minneapolis: Grey Wolf Press.
Marcus, J. (1981), 'Thinking back through our mothers', in J. Marcus (ed.), *New Feminist Essays on Virginia Woolf*, Lincoln: University of Nebraska Press, pp. 1–30.
Marcus, L. (2018), *Autobiography: A Very Short Introduction*, Oxford: Oxford University Press.
UN Women (2018), *Facts and Figures: Ending Violence Against Women*, <https://www.unwomen.org/en/what-we-do/ending-violence-against-women/facts-and-figures> (last accessed 25 February 2020).
Woolf, V. (1957 [1929]), *A Room of One's Own*. New York: Harcourt Brace Jovanovich.
Woolf, V. (1980), *The Diary of Virginia Woolf: Volume Three: 1925–1930*, ed. A. O. Bell, New York: Harcourt Brace Jovanovich.
Woolf, V. (1985), *Moments of Being*, ed. J. Schulkind, New York: Harcourt Brace.
Woolf, V. (2006 [1938]), *Three Guineas*, New York: Harcourt, Inc.
Woolf. V. (2011), *The Essays of Virginia Woolf: Volume Six: 1933–1941*, ed. S. N. Clarke, London: Hogarth Press.
Wordsworth, W. (2008) 'My heart leaps up when I behold', in *William Wordsworth: The Major Works including* The Prelude, Oxford: Oxford University Press, p. 246.
Yuknavitch, L. (n.d.), *Corporeal Writing*, <http://www.corporealwriting.com/> (last accessed 25 February 2020).
Yuknavitch, L. (2011), *The Chronology of Water*, Portland, OR: Hawthorne Books.
Yuknavitch, L. (2015a) 'Beautiful and wonderful and really terrifying: An interview with Lidia Yuknavitch', by Liz Wyckoff, *Covered with Fur: A Strange Object*, September, <http://www.astrangeobject.com/cwf/beautiful-and-wonderful-and-really-terrifying-an-interview-with-lidia-yuknavitch-liz-wyckoff/> (last accessed 25 February 2020).
Yuknavitch, L. (2015b), '"I had zero allegiance to realism": An interview with Lidia Yuknavitch', by T. Carroll, *Vol. 1 Brooklyn*, 20 July, <http://vol1brooklyn.com/2015/07/20/i-had-zero-allegiance-to-realism-an-interview-with-lidia-yuknavitch/> (last accessed 25 February 2020).
Yuknavitch, L. (2015c), *The Small Backs of Children*, New York: Harper Perennial.
Yuknavitch, L. (2017), *The Misfit's Manifesto*, New York: TED Books.

Index

Abdulkareem, Fareeda, 216n39
Abel, Elizabeth, 413, 425n5
Abu-Lughod, Lila, 180n4
Acevedo-Leal, Anabella, 269
Achebe, Chinua, 207, 212
Adams, Bert N., 207
Adams, Timothy Dow, 417
Addison, Joseph, 137
Adichie, Chimamanda Ngozi, 199, 213
Aeschylus, 120, 122, 154
aesthetics, 4, 10, 153, 155, 156, 157, 158–60, 161, 268, 314, 326n2, 341, 343, 354, 372
affect, affect studies, 153, 155, 158–60, 161
affection, 404
affection (sisterly), 298, 301–10
Africa, 2, 4, 6, 7, 9, 11, 92n26, 199–216, 261
   sub-Saharan, 6, 9, 11, 199–216
   see also individual countries
Agamben, Giorgio, 97–8, 106
Agrachev, Dmitry, 139
Ahmed, Leila, 180n4, n5
Aksakov, Sergey, 137
Aidoo, Ama Ata, 210
Al-Amir, Ayman, 166
Al-Asadi, Tawfiq, 168
Albee, Edward, 106, 107, 138, 211, 248, 378
Aleramo, Sibilla, 194n2
Allan, Tuzyline Jita, 201, 202
Allen, Judith, 97
Allen, Mary Cecil, 73
Alonso, Mariângela, 254
Al-Qalamawy, Saheir, 168

Al-Samman, Ghada, 166–7
Al-Zumur, Murad, 167
America, American *see* United States
Anderson, Sherwood, 27
Andringa, Els, 152, 159
Anedda, Antonella, 186
anger, 90, 153, 155, 159–61
Anikst, Alexander, 135
Animal Studies, 12, 267–78
Aoyama, Tomoko, 283
Appiah, Kwame Anthony, 335
Arabic, 4, 5, 9, 11, 19–21, 166–79, 179n1, n2, 180n3, n8, n10, n11
Arendt, Erich, 128n4
Argentina, Argentinian, 2, 4, 7, 8, 11, 13n3, 14n17, 15n20, 79–81, 86, 89, 90, 91n14, 170, 225, 226, 227, 229, 233, 240n1, 258, 259
   Buenos Aires, 87, 91n3, 92n29, 92n32, 225, 226, 277, 229, 233, 240n1
Arnés, Laura A., 87
Aromanian, 44
Arrojo, Rosemary, 179
Astvatsaturov, Andrey, 144
Atarova, Ksenia, 137
Auden, W[ystan] H[ugh], 119
Auerbach, Erich, 37, 132
Augustine (Saint), 162n4
'Aurora Leigh', 58n16
Austen, Jane, 90, 137, 155, 186, 215n27, 262, 300, 316
Austria, 15n20, 26, 35–6, 344
   Vienna, 36–7
Australia, 1, 4, 5–7, 10, 12, 13n3, 15n21, 62–76, 208, 311n18, 364, 365

Australian English Association, 68
Avery, Simon, 277–8n3
Ayandele, Emmanuel A., 215n23

Babatunde, Rotimi, 211
Bachmann, Ingeborg, 124
Badenas, Guillermo, 86–7
Badenhausen, Ingeborg, 7
Bakhtin, Mikhail, 125, 335–6
Baleeta, Margaret, 212
Ballista, Serena, 193
Barcelos, Sergio da Silva, 257
Barlow, Tani, 327n12
Barnaby, Paul, 14n13
Barnes, Djuna, 156, 231
Barrett, A. Igoni, 199
Barrett, Eileen, 409n1
Barrett, Michèle, 213n3, 403
Barrett Browning, Elizabeth, 12, 35, 36, 268, 270–7, 277–8n3, 278n9, 338, 381, 400
Barthes, Roland, 98, 342, 349n26, 369n22
Batchelor, Kathryn, 172
Bator, Joanna, 333, 341–2, 346–7
Beach, Sylvia, 6, 90n1, 91n3, 226
Beardsley, Aubrey, 189
Beasley, Rebecca, 162n3
Beauvoir, Simone de, 157, 162n2, 306, 318, 327n12, 371–3, 382n10
Bechdel, Alison, 337
Becker, Jurek, 128n4
Beckett, Samuel, 47
Beeber, Matthew, 79
Beer, Gillian, 92n26
Belgium, 14n17, 68
Bell, Anne Olivier, 407
Bell, Clive, 37n1, 63, 69, 74, 236, 403, 406
Bell, Julian, 12, 119, 128, 235, 259
Bell, Quentin, 12, 14n8, 96, 128n8, 177, 235, 338–9, 348n17, 377–9, 384, 407–8
Bell, Vanessa, 52, 53, 54, 59n22, 65, 72, 92–3n41, 189, 199, 235–6, 337, 348n10, 402–3, 406
Bellamy, Suzanne, viii, 1, 5, 10, 15n21, 62–78, 208
Benetti, Piera, 193–4
Benhabib, Seyla, 162n2

Benjamin, Walter, 32, 178
Bennett, Arnold, 67, 119, 136
Benson, Stella, 65
Bent, Maria, xiii, 5, 11, 132–51
Bergson, Henri, 8
Berman, Jessica, 6, 81, 154–5, 246–7, 333, 335
  trans critical optic 333, 335
Bermann, Sandra, 178–9
Bertolone, Gloria, 193–4
Bespalova, Larisa, 139
Between the Acts, 20, 39n25, 48, 71, 116, 127, 139, 144, 229, 333, 391, 402
Beza, Marcu, 44–5
Bhabha, Homi, 5
Bibbò, Antonio, 187
Biermann, Wolf, 117
biofiction, 332, 336–9, 346, 375, 376, 399–409
Bizé, Paul, 8
Black, Naomi, 213n6
Black Lives Matter (BLM), 1
Blake, William, 231
Blanche, Jacques-Émile, 7, 107, 111–12n18, 373, 382n7
Blanchot, Maurice, 99, 371
Blixen, Carena, 231, 238, 239
Block, Allison, 297
Blok, Alexander, 133
Bloom, Harold, 371
Bloomsbury group, 63, 69, 73–5, 132, 134, 142–3, 158, 177–8, 209, 288, 337, 378–9, 407, 413
Blum, Beth, 212–13
Blyth, Ian, 85, 92n22
Boas, Eliana Garcia Vilas, 257
Bode, Katherine, 63
Bolchi, Elisa, viii, 4, 11, 183–98
Bombal, María Luisa, 231
Borges, Jorge Luis, 38n16, 86–7, 92n29, n30, 152–3, 160, 170, 226, 228, 230, 232, 241n3, n4, 311n18
Botez, Demostene, 45
Botswana, Botswanan, 210, 215n22
Bowen, Elizabeth, 6, 13, 387–90, 391–3, 397, 397n2
Bowen, Marjorie, 202–3
Boxall, Nelly, 2
Bradshaw, David, 169

Bradu, Fabienne, 269
Bragance, Anne, 12, 374–6
Brassard, Geneviève, 152–4
Braun, Volker, 128n4
Brazil, 10, 12, 21, 96, 98, 104–6, 111n16, 246–64
  Arquivo Público Municipal Cônego Hérmogenes Cassimiro de Araújo Brunswick (Sacramento), 257
  Brazilian Academy of Letters, 250, 259
  favelas, 255–7
  Federal University of Minas Gerais, 257
  Hilda Hilst Institute / Casa do Sol (Campinas), 260–1
  Minas Gerais, 257
  Petrópolis, 96, 98, 104–5
  Rio de Janeiro, 96, 98, 104, 105, 249, 251, 258, 261
  São Paulo, 249, 256
  University of Campinas, 260
Brazilian modernism, 250, 252, 259
Britain, British, British Isles, 43
  see also United Kingdom
Brecht, Bertolt, 125
Brezhnev, Leonid, 115, 136
Bronstein, Michaela, 208
Brontë, Charlotte, 90, 137, 155, 262, 316, 412
Brontë, Emily, 137, 262, 316
Browning, Robert, 268, 275, 277n3
Bukowski, Charles, 414
Bulawayo, NoViolet, 199
Bulgaria, Bulgarian, 58n10, 110–11n9
Bunin, Ivan, 133, 144, 147n26, 154, 346
Burova, N., 139
Busia, Kofi Abrefa, 207
Butcher, Ellis, 267
Butler, Judith, 162n2
Butler, Samuel, 44
Büchner, Georg, 118
Byatt, A. S., 186
Byrne, Anne, 75, 76

Caba, Olga, 43–4
Calle Orozco, Jhonny Alexander, 170
Calvino, Italo, 186
Camara, Elizabeth Vieira, 253
Cameron, Julia Margaret, 52

Campos, Paulo Mendes, 6, 10, 96, 98, 104–9, 111n15, n16
Camus, Albert, 156
Canada, 7, 8, 9, 13n3, 15n22, 142
Caramagno, Thomas, 180n12
Carluccio, Cristina, ix, 4, 6, 10, 79–95
Carrer, Chiara, 193
Carroll, Lewis, 427
Carson, Anne, 418
Carson, Susan, 71
Carter, Angela, 231
Carter, David, 63
Cary, Joyce, 228
Castillo, Debra A., 269
Catalan, 7, 92n28
Caughie, Pamela, 268
Caws, Mary Ann, 7, 152
Călin, Vera, 48–51, 56
Ceaușescu, Nicolae, 10, 42–3, 47–8, 50–1, 58n9, n11
Cecchi, Emilio, 185
Celenza, Giulia, 185
censorship, 4, 5, 42–3, 46–54, 56–7, 59n18, n19, 64, 67, 72, 105, 117, 123, 127, 134–6, 138, 140, 156, 162n6, 233–4, 251, 260, 338, 422
  self-censorship, 5, 10, 47, 49, 50, 52, 53, 56, 59n19, 405
Cesar, Ana Cristina, 246, 258–9, 261, 262–3
Chakava, Henry, 215n28
Chamberlain, Lori, 180n14
Chatman, Seymour, 354–5
Chaton, Anne-James, 379–81, 384n35
Chatterjee, Choi, 157
Chatterjee, Partha, 388, 390, 393, 395, 397
Chekhov, Anton, 137, 143
Chen, Duxiu, 327n5
Chen, Xiaoming, 318
Chesterman, Andrew, 178
Chesterton, G. K., 230
Chikiar Bauer, Irene, 92n25
Chile, 14n17, 15n20
China, Chinese, 3, 12, 13n3, 21, 98–9, 235, 259, 282, 292–3, 297–310, 314–26, 326n3, 327n5, n12, 365, 379
Chinese (language), 3, 4, 7, 12, 305–6, 310n5, 315, 316, 319, 327n10, n15
Chou, Wah-Shan, 305
Chukovsky, Korney, 133

Chutnik, Sylwia, 333, 341, 342–3, 346, 347
'The cinema', 58n16, 141, 145
Cixous, Hélène, 109–10, 112n31, 125, 129n22, 177, 239, 255, 309, 317n12, 318, 418
Clarke, Stuart N., 52, 147n34
  see also Kirkpatrick, B. J. and Stuart N. Clarke
Claudel, Camille, 384n35
Cliff, Michelle, 14n6, 201, 214n9
Coborca, Liliana, 42–3, 46, 47, 50
Coisson, Josefina, 86–7
Cole, Sarah, 422
Coleridge, Samuel T., 300, 301
Colette, 262
Collett, Marcie, 72
Colón Vale, Laila, 268, 275
colonialism, decolonialism, neocolonialism, postcolonialism, precolonialism, re-colonialism, 3, 5, 6, 11, 14n6, 62–4, 66, 69, 73, 74, 76, 110n7, 111n14, 167, 177, 200–10, 214n18, 215n21, 240n1, 246–7, 259, 272, 273, 286, 335, 337, 344, 388, 394
The Common Reader, 93n52, 97, 137, 138, 141, 145, 152, 155, 162n4, 168, 195n7, 253, 294n8
The Common Reader, Second Series, 69, 138, 141, 145, 195n7, 294n8
  see also individual essays
Conrad, Joseph, 25, 26, 133, 208, 225
Constantinople, 51, 54, 58n14
  see also Istanbul
conversation, 10, 69, 82–4, 86, 96–112, 121, 145, 169, 232, 251, 254, 300, 305, 329n23, n25, 372, 382n8, 417
Cordery, Lindsey, ix, 3, 11, 92n26, 225–45
Corelli, Marie, 214n11
Cornell, Drucialla, 162n2
Cortés, Hernando, 271
Cosi, Francesca, 187–8
cosmopolitanism, 10, 12, 65, 66, 80, 81, 89, 91n11, 153, 154–5, 161
Cossington Smith, Grace, 73–5
Costa, Demetrio, 189
Costa, Júlia da, 262
Coutinho, Edilberto, 111n16
Coutinho, Sônia, 246, 261
Covid-19, 1, 15n27
Cramer, Patricia, 268, 403, 405, 409n1

Crenshaw, Kimberlé Williams, 347n1
Creția, Petru, 48
Crick, Joyce, 116
Cristea, Valeriu, 50
Croft, Jennifer, 344
Cuddy-Keane, Melba, 81, 91n10, 184, 203
Cunha, Helena Parente, 250
Cunningham, Michael, 142, 234, 242n23, 336–7, 342, 367, 368, 368n1, 401, 408, 421
Curtis Brown agency, 10, 25, 26, 32, 35, 36
Czech (language), 7, 14n12, 344
Czechoslovakia, 47, 58n10
Czyżewski, Lech, 333

Dai, Jinhua, 298, 305, 327n12
Dalcastagné, Regina, 257
Daldry, Stephen, 142, 226, 234, 235, 401–2, 408
Dale, Leigh, 63–4, 65
Dalgarno, Emily, 154, 162n3, 422
Dalmagro, Maria Cristina, 232
Damrosch, David, 4, 334
Dangarembga, Tsitsi, 211
Danish (language), 7
Dark, Eleanor, 70–1, 76
Darwin, Charles, 92n26, 225, 238, 242n36, 278n5
Daugherty, Beth R., 216n41, 294n8
'David Copperfield', 137
Davis, Lloyd, 58n12
Davison, Claire, 154, 155, 161, 346–7
  outlandishness, 155
De Angelis, Giulio, 186
The Death of the Moth and Other Essays, 162n4, n5, 195n7
De Beer, Gabriella, 269
Dee, Jonathan, 399
Defoe, Daniel, 187
Delattre, Floris, 7–8
DeMare, Brian James, 317
DeMeester, Karen, 268, 368n5
Demurova, Nina, 132
Denmark, 14n17
Denton, Kirk A., 317
De Quincey, Thomas, 137
Derrida, Jacques, 99, 270
Desai, Anita, 186
Descombes, Vincent, 372

Detloff, Madelyn, 2, 111n14
DeWald, Rebecca, 87, 92n30
Diana, Lady, 384n35
Diary, 1, 2, 4, 5, 14n8, 27, 52, 59n18, 73, 82, 92n22, 97, 102–3, 110, 119, 121, 152, 202, 214n8, 225, 229–30, 234, 303, 333, 361, 364, 366, 368n6, 377, 380, 384n33, 391, 400, 403, 406, 407, 415, 421, 426n7
Dibia, Jude, 199
Dickens, Charles, 27, 43, 57n1, 137
Dickinson, Emily, 105, 258, 418
Dickinson, Violet, 236
Dinesen, Isak, 202, 205–7, 214n19
Dixon, Robert, 64, 369n23, n24
Dneprov, Vladimir (Volf Reznik), 139
Dobson, Jill, 282, 284
dogs, 3, 12, 35, 36, 260–1, 267–78, 286, 337
  see also *Flush: A Biography*
Dojčinović-Nešić, Biljana, 153
Domenella, Ana Rosa, 269
Dostoevsky, Fyodor, 100, 137, 154
Dreadnought hoax, 202, 214n10
Duarte, Constância Lima, 249, 250
Dubino, Jeanne, ix, 1–24, 93n52, 199–222, 278n5
Duckworth, George Herbert, 337, 406
Duckworth, Gerald, 337, 339, 406
Duder, C. J. D., 214n14, n18
Duffy, Julia, 58n12
Duncan, Isadora, 379, 381, 384n35
Dunleavy, Janet Egleson, 388
DuPlessis, Rachel Blau, 155
Duras, Marguerite, 227, 238, 241n5, 242n38, 418
Durastanti, Sylvie, 374
Dutch, 159
Dzhamankulova, Cholpon, 147n33

Eagleton, Terry, 208
Eberly, David, 268
Eco, Umberto, 367
Eddy, Elizabeth McKee, 8
Egypt, 166–80
  Cairo, 167, 168, 169
Eichholz, Anita, 118
Einaudi (Giulio Einaudi Editore publishers), 184, 186–7
Eldershaw, M. Barnard, 70–1
Eliot, George, 215n27, 262

Eliot, T[homas] S[tearns], 66, 97, 107, 110n6, 112n20, 134, 135, 156, 208, 228, 253
Elizabeth I, 51, 58n14
Emecheta, Buchi, 210
Emezi, Akwaeke, 413, 425n3
Ender, Evelyne, 415, 417
England see United Kingdom
Ermoshin, Fyodor, 140–1
Ernaux, Anne, 424
Estonia, 11, 152–62
Estonian (language), 4, 6, 11, 152, 153, 155–8, 159, 160, 161, 162n2, n8
Esty, Jed, 291
Europe, 3, 4, 7, 8, 10, 11, 14n12, 15n21, 42, 44, 47, 48, 58n11, 63, 68, 74, 79, 86, 87, 89, 91n4, 119, 121, 132, 152, 153, 157, 177, 183, 188, 201, 202, 206, 207, 209, 210, 214n18, n20, 215n21, n22, 225, 226, 227, 246, 250, 252, 284, 288, 289, 291, 315, 319, 333, 335, 337, 361, 391
  Central Europe, 157, 333, 335, 419–20
  Eastern Europe, 153, 157, 289, 419–20
  Western Europe, 284, 289
  see also listings for individual countries
Evaristo, Conceição, 257
'Evening over Sussex: reflections in a motor car', 141
Even-Zohar, Itamar, 153, 162n1

Farid, Maher Shafik, 174, 180n7, n8
Faris, Wendy B., 268
Farsi see Persian
fascism, fascist, anti-fascism, anti-fascist, 4, 46, 68–70, 79, 82, 84, 88, 92n39, 105, 119, 128n13, n16, 167, 185, 229, 268, 380, 387, 390, 391, 393
Faulkner, William, 26, 35, 47, 156, 228, 311n18
Federeci, Eleonora, 170, 171
Feeley, Jennifer, 327n12
Feldbach, Inna, 156
feminism, feminist studies, 2–6, 32, 63, 66, 68, 70, 71, 72, 75–6, 81, 82, 84, 87, 91n13, 97, 110n6, 111n10, 152–5, 157–8, 159, 160, 161, 200, 246, 247, 249–51, 253, 255, 257, 260, 263, 332–4, 335–6, 338, 340, 341–3, 344, 346–7, 347n1, 367, 407, 412

in Brazil, 11–12, 246, 249–51, 255, 257
in China, 12, 17, 297–9, 306, 309–10, 314–29
cosmopolitan feminism, 5, 6, 153–5, 160, 161
in East Germany, 10, 116, 118, 121, 125–6, 129n20, n23
ecofeminism, 346
e-feminism, 210
in Estonia, 11, 153, 157–8, 159, 161
in France, 12, 129n3, 373, 374–81,
in Germany, 32
international feminism, 81, 282, 284
in Italy, 184, 185, 190, 193
in Japan, 282, 285
lesbianism and feminism, 409n1
in the Middle East, 11, 166–79
planetary feminism, 332, 347n1
in Poland, 12, 335, 336, 338, 340, 341–4, 343, 344, 346–7
in Russia, 140, 143, 145, 148n57,
third-wave feminism, 55, 167, 250, 286, 294n9, 341, 413
transnational feminism, 2, 255, 259, 263
in Uruguay, 226, 231, 241n3, n16
see also feminist translation studies *under* translation studies; Girls' Studies
Feracho, Lesley, 256
Feuerstein, Anna, 268
Filipiak, Izabela *see* Morska, Izabela
Finke, Ilse, 8
Finland, 15n20
Finţescu, Traian Grigore, 42, 45, 46, 57n7
Fischer, Bermann, 37
   see also S[amuel] Fischer Verlag
Fischer, Samuel, 27, 36
   see also S[amuel] Fischer Verlag
Fitzgerald, Zelda, 262
Flaubert, Gustave, 229, 237, 241n11, 346
flâneuse, 200, 289, 332, 340
Fleißer, Marieluise, 124
Flesher, Erika, 53, 56, 58n16, 59n20
Floresta, Nísia Brasileira Augusta, 249
Flotow, Luise von, 171–2, 173
Flush: A Biography, 12, 35–6, 58n12, n16, 69, 139, 168, 185, 209, 261, 267–78, 310n1, 316, 338, 400
Focşeneanu, Veronica, 48
Foley, John Miles, 215n37

Forna, Aminatta, 211
Forrester, Viviane, 12, 374–6, 381, 383n23, n24
Forster, E. M., 226
Foucault, Michel, 99
France, 6, 7, 8, 9, 12, 13n3, 14n12, n17, 15n20, n22, 25, 43, 44, 96, 98, 110n7, 111n8, 152, 215n22, 227, 259, 282, 292, 361, 371–84, 391
   Grenoble, 28
   Paris, 6, 10, 12, 74, 96, 98, 110–11n9, 227, 283, 284, 288, 293, 354–63, 381, 384n41, 394
Franco, Jean, 269
Franklin, Miles, 62, 71
Fraser, Nancy, 162n2
Freedman, Morris, 208
Freire, Paulo, 257
French (language), 2, 4, 5, 7, 9, 10, 12, 14n11, n12, 26, 27, 28, 30, 32, 45, 82, 98, 110n7, 112n30, 129n22, 152, 154, 160, 161, 177, 195n6, 207, 226, 360, 371–84, 399, 424
French, Marilyn, 177
Freud, Sigmund, 154, 269
Friani, Stefano, 190
Friedan, Betty, 250
Friedman, Susan Stanford, 2, 4, 5, 80, 81, 91n9, 203, 284, 332, 333, 347n1, 388
Frisch, Efraim, 38n21
Frost, Natasha, 202
Froula, Christine, 201, 213n7
Fry, Roger, 69, 73–5, 147n33
Fryer, Peter, 200
Fusini, Nadia, 186, 187, 190
Füger, Wilhelm, 26, 30, 32, 34, 36, 37, 37n10
Fühmann, Franz, 128n4
Füredi, Frank, 200

Galsworthy, John, 25, 119, 136, 289
Gan, Wendy, 288, 299
Gao, Fen, 318
Gardes, Joelle, 378–9, 384n33
Garibaldi, Giuseppe, 225, 242n35
Garrity, Jane, 202
Gaskell, Elizabeth, 137, 262
Gee, Maggie, 5, 13, 337, 399–409
Genette, Gérard, 172, 237, 335, 348n5

Genieva, Ekaterina, 132, 137–8, 141
'George Eliot', 176
George H. Doran (publisher), 6, 14n8
Gerhardt, Renate, 118, 126
German (language), 4, 5, 7, 8, 10, 14n12,
    19–21, 25–39, 117–18, 122, 124, 126–7,
    128n8, 152, 194–5n6, 214n18, 285, 344
  Low German dialect, 33
Germany, 8, 9–10, 10–11, 14n17, 15n20,
    n22, 25–39, 43, 115–27, 152, 210,
    234, 311n18, 393
  Berlin, 5, 25, 27, 30, 32, 34, 36, 37n1, 116,
    117–18, 128n8, 129n24, 283, 284, 293
  Bremen, 30
  Federal Republic of Germany, West
    Germany, 34, 35, 38n25, 115, 117,
    118, 126, 127
  German Democratic Republic, East
    Germany, 5, 10–11, 32, 38n25, 58n10,
    115, 116–17, 126, 127, 128n5, 128n7,
    129n24
  Goethe- und Schiller-Archiv (Weimar), 5,
    27, 30, 37n3
  Hamburg, 28, 141
  Leipzig, 27, 29, 30, 32, 33, 117
  (Greater) German Reich, Nazi Germany,
    26, 36, 39n36
  Munich, 32, 118, 229
  Weimar, 27, 30, 37n3, 128n6
Ghana, 207, 215n22
Gheorghiu-Dej, Gheorghe, 47, 58n9
Giammarco, Emanuele, 190
Gide, André, 45
Gillespie, Diane F., 58n16, 403–4
Gillet, Louis, 7, 382n7
Gilman, Charlotte Perkins, 71
Gilman, Claudia, 241n13
Gilmore, Leigh, 419, 425n5
Gilmore, Lois J., 214n9, 413
Girls' Studies, 6, 413–15
Girnus, Wilhelm, 126
Githae-Mugo, Micere, 206
global, global studies, 1–6, 8–9, 10, 11, 13, 26,
    27, 37, 63, 65, 80–1, 86, 91n10, 143, 157,
    170, 178, 199, 200, 203, 207, 212–13,
    215n35, 246–7, 249, 257, 263, 288, 291,
    315, 316, 332, 333, 343, 347, 356, 357,
    359, 362, 367, 368, 368n4, 381, 388, 393,
    412, 413, 424, 425, 425n4, 426n8

Godard, Barbara, 169, 172, 173
Goethe, Johann Wolfgang von, 27, 29
Gorbachev, Mikhail, 138
  see also perestroika
Gordimer, Nadine, 210
Gorla, Paola Laura, 38n16
Gotlib, Nádia Battella, 264n5
Goulimari, Pelogia, 247
  transtemporal, 247, 263
Göske, Daniel, ix–x, 5, 9–10, 25–41
Graff, Agnieszka, 156, 334, 338, 341–2, 347
Gramuglio, María Teresa, 91n3
Great Britain *see* United Kingdom
Greece, 14n17, 15n20, 118, 121–2, 188,
    361, 362, 366–7
  Lesbos, 346
Greek (language), 7, 19–21, 97, 102, 106,
    122, 123, 126, 154, 162n3, 269, 403
Green, André, 376, 383n30
Greene, Graham, 226, 228
Greshnykh, Vladimir, 142–3
Grimm Brothers (Jacob Ludwig Carl and
    Wilhelm Carl), 33
Groth, Helen, 71
Gruber, Ruth, 8, 15n19, 389
Gualtieri, Elena, 119, 400
Gumilyov, Nikolay, 133

Hai, Nan, 310n2
Hall, Radclyffe, 59n18, 64, 260, 338
Haraway, Donna, 270
Hardy, Thomas, 107
Haskins, Mabel, 103
Hausman, Bernice L., 79, 83
Hayot, Eric, 3
Head Bessie, 210
Heathcote, Christopher, 74
Heidegger, Martin, 226
Heine, Heinrich, 27
Heinich, Nathalie, 375–6, 381
Heinrich, Larissa N., 297
Heise, Ursula, 5
Helt, Brenda, 304, 310–11n8
Hemingway, Earnest, 228
Henke, Suzette, 268
Hentze, Margaret (Margot), 10, 62–3,
    68–70, 76
Herlitschka, Herberth Egon, 35–7, 38n17,
    39n32, n35, n36

Herlitschka, Marlys, 35–7, 39n32, 39n35, n36
Hermelin, Stephan, 128n4
Herrmann, Anne, 116, 125
Heurck, Jan van, 126, 129n22
Heydel, Magdalena, 333
He-Yin, Zhen, 319, 327n14
Heym, Stefan, 128n4
Hicks, George, 292
Hilst, Hilda, 246, 260–1, 264n13
Hilzinger, Sonja, 127
Hind, Emily, 269
Hirohito, Emperor, 294n13
Hirsch, Marianne, 425n1
Hite, Molly, 155, 425n1
Hitler, Adolf, 70, 88, 92n39, 234, 242n22, 387, 393
Hochschild, Adam, 200
Hoffmann, Hans-Joachim, 116–17, 128n3, 129n24
Hofmannsthal, Hugo von, 27
Hogarth Press, 5, 6–7, 10, 14n8, n10, 25, 26, 27, 31, 36, 37n6, 51, 54, 59n18, 62–5, 67, 69, 75–6, 144, 154, 189, 195n16, 209, 226, 336, 391
Holden, Stephen, 214n18
Hollis, Catherine W., x, 1–23, 213, 412–27
Holtby, Winifred, 389
Homer, 122, 125
hooks, bell, 257
The Hours see Daldry, Stephen
'Hours in a library', 192
'How should one read a book?', 137, 184, 212–13, 216n41
Howarth, R[obert] G[uy], 63, 68, 70, 72–3
Hsieh, Lili, 155, 159, 160
Hu, Liang, 320
Hu, Sang, 320
Huang, Xi, 12, 314, 315
Huang, Zhongfeng, x, 3, 12, 297–313
Hudson, W. H., 225
Humm, Maggie, 2, 36, 54, 58n16, 59n22, 98
Hungarian (language), 7
Hungary, 58n10,
hunger, *hambre*, 10, 79–81, 84, 91n4
Huopalainen, Astrid, 270
Hussey, Mark, 1, 119

Hussein, Jeylan W., 211–12
Huyssen, Andreas, 81
Huxley, Aldous, 7, 27, 35, 43, 57n1, 68, 79, 134, 135
Huxley, Elspeth, 202, 205, 206, 207
hybridity, 5, 256, 302, 310n1, 333, 334, 344, 348n3, 388, 420
Hynes, James, 368n3, n4
hypertextuality, 335–6, 338, 341–2, 343–6
 see also Genette, Gérard

Iceland, 158
Ikeda, Keigo, 282
Ikheloa, Ikhide R., 199
India, 8, 15n20, 388
Ingman, Heather, 394
Insel Verlag, 26–7, 28–32, 34, 35–6, 37n3, 38n24–6, 117, 128n6
 see also Kippenberg, Anton; Kippenberg, Katherina
internet (web), 8, 9, 19–21, 139, 161, 184, 191, 210, 213, 215n33, n37, 231, 326n2, 338, 360–1, 369n10, 399, 404
Iraq, 168, 169, 361, 362
 Baghdad, 169
interruption, 83–4, 90, 101, 108–10, 194, 288, 299, 391
intertextuality, 33, 335–6, 340–1
 see also Genette, Gérard
Ireland, Irish, 6, 13n3, 15n22, 75, 214n16, 355, 357, 358, 365, 388–9, 392–7
Irigaray, Luce, 125
Isherwood, Christopher, 119
Israel, 8, 15n20, n22
Istanbul, 337, 399, 404, 406, 409
 see also Constantinople
Italy, Italian, 4, 7, 9, 11, 14n17, 15n20, 82–4, 119, 170, 183–96, 236, 242n35, 267, 268, 271, 273, 274, 275, 277, 393
 Florence, 12, 275
 Milan, 191, 193, 196n25
 Rome, 15n26, 82, 84, 191
Italian (language), 4, 7, 11, 72, 83, 152, 160, 170–1, 183–96
Ittner, Jutta, 268

Jacobs, Harriet, 419
Jacob's Room, 8, 14n12, 19, 48, 67, 69, 102–3, 121, 139, 140, 142, 144, 262, 342, 373
Jaguścik, Justyna, x, 3, 12, 314–31
Jaillant, Lise, 184, 188
James, Henry, 44, 139, 228
James I, 51, 58 n14
Jameson, Fredric, 288
'Jane Austen', 137, 146n18
'Jane Eyre', 137, 146n18
Janion, Maria, 337
Jankowsky, Karen H., 126, 129n23
Japan, 3, 8, 9, 12, 14n10, 15n20, 142, 282–95
  Tokyo, 7, 283, 284, 294
Japanese (language), 3, 7, 9, 12, 19–2, 282–95
Jardin, Claudine, 374, 378
Jauss, Hans Robert, 371
Jeanne d'Arc, 381
Jesus, Carolina Maria de, 3, 246, 255–8
Jewish, 2, 36, 39n36, 91n11, 214n16, 238, 253
Jiang, Hongyan, 297
Jiang, Hua, 259
Johnson, Jamie, 268, 275
Jones, Danell, 200
Jones, Gail, 3, 12, 354, 355, 363–8, 369n26
Joplin, Janis, 384n35
Joyce, James, 7, 26, 28, 30, 34, 37n4, 43, 47, 57n1, 66, 68, 70, 110n6, 117, 128n5, n7, 134, 135, 156, 166, 186, 208, 228, 259, 263, 311n18, 372, 382n7, 394
Jung, Carl Gustav, 226, 311n18, 344, 345

Kabanova, Irina, 141
Kafka, Franz, 47, 50, 372
Kahane, Claire, 268
Kahlo, Frida, 384n35
Kaivola, Karen, 302
Kalliney, Peter J., 208
Kamal, Hala, x, 5, 11, 166–82
Kamal, Izabel, 168
Kamuf, Peggy, 288
Kang, Jeonho, 282
Kang, Youwei, 327n5
Kantorowicz, Alfred, 32

Kapil, Bhanu, 413, 425n3
Karamzin, Nikolay, 138
Karlsson, Mats, 282
Karp, Maria, 139, 140, 146n23
Keller, Evelyn Fox, 162n2
Kellner, Dora Sophie, 32, 38n19
Kennedy, Jackie, 384n35
Kenya, 11, 200, 202–13, 214n18, 215n21, n22, n24
Kerouac, Jack, 414
Kesey, Ken, 414
'Kew Gardens', 156, 225, 316
Key, Ellen, 285
Keynes, Maynard, 69
Kharitonov, Vladimir, 132
Khrushchev, Nikita, 136
Kierkegaard, Søren, 311n18
Kingsley, Mary, 124
Kipling, Rudyard, 230
Kippenberg, Anton, 27–33, 34, 38n15, n17, n26
  see also Insel Verlag
Kippenberg, Katherina, 27–33, 38n17
  see also Insel Verlag
Kirkpatrick, B. J. and Stuart N. Clarke, 14n12, n15, 14–15n17
Kirsch, Sarah, 128n4
Knauer, Elizabeth, 268
Knipp, Thomas R., 205
Kola, Adam F., 419–20
Konarzewska, Marta, 333, 336, 339–41, 346
Kore-Schröeder, Leena, 406
Korkeakivi, Anne, 3, 12, 354, 355–9, 362, 368
Koteliansky, Samuel S., 144, 146n23, 154, 162n3
Kraskowska, Ewa, 334
Krause, Henrike, xi, 5, 10, 115–31
Kristel, Silvia, 384n35
Kristeva, Julia, 6, 10, 96, 98–101, 104, 107, 108, 109, 110n7, n8, n9, 162n2, 177, 335, 401
Kunert, Günter, 128n4

La Bruyère, Jean de, 160
Lacan, Jacques, 342, 349n26
Lackey, Michael, 336
'The lady in the looking-glass', 45–6
Laird, Holly, 401, 402

Langford, Jean M., 267–8, 270
Lanoire, Maurice, 32
Laplanche, Jean, 269
Larbaud, Valéry, 373
Larreta, Antonio, 11, 233–7,
Lascelles, Henry George Charles, 51
Latham, Monica, xi, 3, 5, 12, 63, 354–70
Latin America, Latin American, 79–93, 170, 225–8, 230, 237, 255, 256, 258
  see also individual countries
  see also South America
Latvian (language), 7
Laurence, Patricia, xi, 6, 13, 259, 387–98
Lautréamont, 372
Lavergne, Maja, 333, 339
Lavin, Mary, 6, 13, 388–90, 393–7
Lawrence, D. H., 7, 26, 27, 28, 35–6, 68, 134, 135, 154, 208
Lawrence, Frieda (Frieda von Richthofen), 36
Layne, Bethany, xi, 5, 13, 399–411, 421
'The leaning tower', 154, 333
Leavis, F[rank] R[aymond], 62, 63–4, 68, 76n1, 208–9, 215n27
Leavis, Q[ueenie] D., 208–9, 215n27
Lebanon, 166–9
  Beirut, 167, 169, 362
Lee, Hermione, 1, 52–3, 111n13, 400, 402, 403, 404, 407, 408–9, 409n1
Lemaster, Tracy, 413–14, 415
Lenin, Vladimir, 133, 134
Leonardi, Vanessa, 153, 170–1
Leopold II (King), 200
Lerbs, Karl, 5, 30–4, 35, 36, 38–9n26, 39n32
le Roux, Elizabeth, 209, 212, 215n28, n29, 216n40
Levine, Robert M., 256
Lewis, Andrea, 203
'Lewis Carroll', 132, 136, 137
Levy, Heather, 402
Liang, Qichao, 327n5
Light, Alison, 415
Lilienfeld, Jane, 268
Linati, Carlo, 7, 194n2
Lindsay, Claire, 269
Lingenfelter, Andrea, 328n16
Lins, Álvaro, 254
Lis, Renata, 333, 334, 343, 346
Lispector, Clarice, 3, 231, 238, 240, 242n38, 246, 250, 253–5, 262–3, 263n5, 264n6

Liu, Na'ou, 292
Livergant, Alexander, 138, 143, 145
Llewellyn, Carole, 3, 12, 354–5, 359–63, 367, 368
Llewelyn Davies, Margaret, 119
Lobo, Luiza, 250, 251
Lodge, David, 399–400
Logé, Marc, 373
Lojo Rodríguez, Laura M., 7, 79, 80, 86, 87, 90n1, 91n3
Lohmüller, Gertrud, 8
Lo Liyong, Taban, 207
London, Jack, 25
Loriye, Maria, 139
Lotman, Maria-Kristiina, 160, 161
Lóper-Pérez, Lourdes, 191, 196n23
López, Irma M., 269, 275, 277n2
Lu, Yimin, 319, 320–2, 328n16
Luckhurst, Nicola, 7, 81, 152, 158, 183, 349n30
Luckhurst, Roger, 269, 369n15
Lukács, Georg, 117, 128n5
Lukashkina, Maria, 141
Lunacharsky, Anatoly, 133
Lunardi, Adriana, 246, 261–2
Lutz, Bertha, 250
Luxembourg, Rosa, 384n35
Lv, Hongling, 310n1
Lyon, Jane, 2
Lyons, Joseph, 70
Lyotard, Jean-François, 269–70
Lypka, Celiese, xi, 13n1, 213

Mabel see Haskins, Mabel
MacArthur, Douglas, 294n13
McBride, Eimear, 413
MacDermott, Gladys, 75–6
MacDonald, Ramsay, 290
McEwan, Ian, 368n3, n4
Macgoye, Marjorie, 210
Machilar, Antonio, 7
McKeon, Belinda, 389
MacMahon, Kathleen, 393
Macmillan, Harold, 207
MacNeice, Louis, 119
Magenau, Jörg, 117
Maggio, Paula, 216n42
Magritte, René, 364, 369n24
Mahfud, Abd al-Karim, 168

Makotsi, Ruth L. and Lily K. Nyariki, 209, 212
Majstorovic, Gorica, 80, 91n3
Malory, Thomas, 189
Malraux, André, 226
Malraux, Clara, 373–5
Malyugin, Oleg, 136
Manguso, Sarah, 426n7
Mann, Klaus, 30
Mann, Thomas, 30, 31, 35, 37, 38n14, 117
Mansfield, Katherine, 65, 154, 228, 238, 242n38, 258, 261, 262
Mansi, Girgis, 167–8
Mao, Zedong, 99, 314, 317, 318, 319, 320, 323, 324, 326, 365
Marcus, Jane, 2, 71, 93n52, 201, 288, 425n1
Marcus, Laura, 25, 26, 35, 36, 154, 426n8
Margolin, Uri, 369n28
Marian, Nora, 46
Markham, Beryl, 202, 205, 206, 207
Marling, Raili (Põldsaar, Raili), xi, 6, 10, 11, 152–65
Marshall, Elizabeth, 419
Marshik, Celia, 59n18
Martinson, Deborah, 407
Mass, Nuri, 15n21, 62–3, 65, 68, 72, 76
Mata Hari, 384n35
Matsumoto, Hogara, xii, 3, 7, 12, 282–96
Mauer, Mare, 162n2
Mauriac, François, 27
Maurois, André, 27, 30, 45, 373
Mauron, Charles, 14n11, 373
Mayakovsky, Vladimir, 146n8
Mbae, Justus G., 212
Meihy, José Carlos Sebe M., 256
Mejía-Pérez, Marcelo, 269
Melnikov, N. G., 141–2
Melrose, Fiona, 199
Melville, Herman, 101
Mepham, John, 1
Mermin, Dorothy, 277–8n3
Meschonnic, Henri, 372
metamorphosis, 49–50, 56
Mexico, 12, 225, 267, 268, 269, 271–7
  Mexico City, 12, 225, 268, 272, 273, 276
Meyer, Roland, 376
'Middlebrow', 141, 184, 294n8
Miethe, Kaethe, 30, 32, 37n10
Migdal, Alicia, 11, 226–7, 237–40, 241n5, 242n40, 243n44

Mikhalskaya, Nina, 135–6
Miller, Henry, 226, 414
Miller, J. Hillis, 357
Mills Jeansonne, Christie, 403, 406
Milton, John, 162n6, 208
Miroiu, Mihai, 48
Mirsky, D. S. (Dmitry Svyatopolk-Mirsky), 69, 132, 134
'Miss Mitford', 176
Mistral, Gabriela, 85, 88, 92n23, n24
Mits, Krista, 156, 158
Miyamoto, Yuriko, 3, 12, 282–95
'Modern fiction', 45, 109, 110n6, 121, 135, 136, 137, 144, 145, 156, 168, 366, 372, 373, 387, 388
'The Modernist Archives Publishing Project' (MAPP), 14n10, 209
Modjeska, Drusilla, 63, 66
Mohanty, Chandra Talpade, 246–8, 257, 347n1
  solidarity, 248, 257
'The moment', 373–4, 382n11
The Moment and Other Essays, 162n4, 195n7
Moments of Being, 44, 96, 101–4, 145, 156, 158, 237, 382n13, 415–17, 424
  see also 'A sketch of the past'
Moncrieff, C. K. Scott, 154
Mondadori (Arnoldo Mondadori Editore), 11, 183, 185–6, 189, 194n5, n6
Mondadori, Alberto, 185, 194n5
Mondadori, Arnoldo, 185
Monday or Tuesday, 6, 14n8, 65, 169, 189
Monegal, Emir Rodríguez, 227–30, 241n7, n8
Monnier, Adrienne, 91n3
Monroe, Marilyn, 378, 384n35
Montaigne, Michel de, 107, 112n20, 146n18, 311n18, 382n8
Monye, Ambrose Adikamkwu, 211
Moore, Nicole, 64
Moran, Patricia, 268
Moraru, Christian, 3
Morel, Edmund, 200
Moretti, Franco, 3–4, 6
Morra, Umberto, 7, 183, 194n2
Morrison, Toni, 418
Morska, Izabela, 333, 334, 336–8, 346, 348n7
Moser, Benjamin, 254
Moura, Maria Lacerda de, 250

'Mr Bennett and Mrs Brown', 66–7, 137, 141, 144, 145, 317

Mrs Dalloway, 7, 12, 14n12, 15n24, 19, 26, 27, 28–30, 32, 34, 35, 37n1, n9, 44, 47, 48, 51, 57, 67, 69, 71, 92n28, 116, 117, 121, 127n1, 128n6, 132, 133, 135, 136, 137, 139, 142, 144, 156, 168, 185, 186, 193–4, 196n27, 199, 226, 227, 231, 234, 237, 240, 242n22, 243n45, 252–3, 254, 262, 264n13, 310n4, 332, 333, 336, 337, 338–9, 340, 342, 346, 348n19, 350n40, 354–69, 373, 397n1, 402, 405, 408–9

'Mrs Gaskell', 176
Mudie, Ella, 365, 369n26
Mulindwa, Gertrude Kayaga, 209
Mulvey, Laura, 342, 349n26
Muraro, Rosie Marie, 250
Musicò, Raffaella, 191
Mussolini, Benito, 82–4, 380, 384n38, 393
Mutti, Cecilia, 189
Mutzenbecher, Theresia, 28–9, 32, 36, 38n17
Müller, Heiner, 128n4
Mwaniga, Gloria, 211

Nabokov, Vladimir, 226, 311n18
Nadotti, Anna, 186–7
Nagaty, Laila Othman, 169
Namibia, 9
  Ndonga (language), 9
Naoot, Fatimah, 169, 171, 179n2, 180n7
Nathan, Monica, 374
Năstase, Adrian, 47
Ndlovu-Gatsheni, Sabelo J., 207, 208
Nelson, Cynthia, 180n4
neocolonialism *see* colonialism, decolonialism, postcolonialism, precolonialism, re-colonialism
Netherlands, 15n20, 142
Neverow, Vara, xii, 9, 13n1, 15n25, 213, 347n2
New Zealand, 7
Ngugi, Mukoma wa, 209
Ngũgĩ, wa Thiong'o, 203, 207, 208, 210
Nicolson, Harold, 25, 27, 30, 400
Nigeria, Nigerian, 199, 207, 210, 211, 212
Night and Day, 6, 19, 46, 48, 72, 73, 92–3n41, 97, 132, 140
Nilin, Alexander, 139

Nixon, Richard, 115
North America, North American, 4, 225, 334, 414
  see also Canada; Mexico; United States
North, Marianne, 225
'The novels of Turgenev', 137, 146n18
Novillo-Corvalán, Patricia, 81, 86, 92n26
Nunes, Aparecida Maria, 254
Nunez, Sigrid, 401, 404
Nurowska, Maria, 333, 336, 337, 338–9, 346
Nünning, Ansgar and Vera Nünning, 8, 26, 37, 118
nüxing shige [women's poetry], 314–26, 327n15
Nwapa, Flora, 210
Nwaubani, Adaobi Tricia, 212
Nyariki, Lily K.
  see Ruth L. Makotsi and Lily K. Nyariki

Ocampo, Victoria, 4, 10, 79–93, 225–6, 228–9, 258–9, 264n10
Ogunlesi, Tolu, 211
Okri, Ben, 199
Olden, Anthony, 209
Oliveira, Hilda Gouveia de, 246, 262
Oliveira, Maria A. de, xii, 3, 6, 11–12, 246–66
Olvera-Lobo, María Dolores, 191, 195n23
Onetti, Juan Carlos, 227, 231, 238, 239
Ophir, Ella, 294n8
Opitz-Wiemers, Carola, 124
Orlando: A Biography, 5, 7, 9, 14n12, 19, 27, 29, 30–2, 35–6, 37n11, 38n15–16, 38n20, 38n22–3, 38n26, 39n27, 42, 43, 47, 48–57, 58n12–14, n16, 59n18, n20–4, 67, 69, 71, 87, 89, 92n28–30, n32, 96, 105, 106, 108–9, 112n22, n25, n27, 121, 129n4, 139–40, 144, 152, 154, 156, 158, 168, 170, 183, 185, 192, 193, 194n2, 226, 230–3, 234, 238, 241n4, n18, 242n36, 247, 248–9, 252, 260, 261, 294n5, 332, 333, 337, 341–2, 344, 346, 349n24–7, 358, 384n34, 400, 401
  'Preface', 48, 50
  images, 43, 48, 51–7, 58n16, 59n20–2
Orlando (film) *see* Potter, Sally
Ortega y Gasset, José, 85, 91n3, n5

OsnoVa Publishing, 347
Ossolineum, publishing house, 334
Ostle, Mary Geraldine, 294n8
Out of Africa (film), 214n18
Owuor-Anyumba, Henry, 207
Oyeyemi, Helen, 199, 213
Ó'Faoláin, Sean, 397n2

Pająk, Paulina, xii, 1–22, 213, 332–53
Palmer, Nettie, 10, 62, 65–7, 70, 71, 76, 78
Papadache, Frieda, 48
Paraschivescu, Radu, 48
paratextuality, 11, 31, 36, 153, 157–8, 159, 166–79, 335, 337–8
  see also Genette, Gérard; 'Preface'
Parker, Dorothy, 261
Parks, Tim, 154
Parmar, Priya, 401, 402, 407–8
Parra-Lazcano, Lourdes, xii, 3, 12, 267–81
Parrott, Fiona G., 86, 89
Partridge, Ralph, 14n8
'The patron and the crocus', 333
Paul, Georgina, 122
Pereira, Lucia Miguel, 246, 252–3
perestroika, 138–40, 142, 146n20
Peri Rossi, Cristina, 11, 227, 237–8, 240
Perosa, Sergio, 7, 15n26, 183
Persian (language), 9
Pessoa, Fernado, 106
Pfeiffer, Erna, 269
Pinho, Davi, xii, 6, 10, 96–114
Pitman, Thea, 269
Pizer, John D., 4
Plate (river), 11, 225, 226, 234, 238, 240n1
Plath, Sylvia, 258, 262, 318, 327n12, 401
Plato, 112n24
Plescia, Iolanda, 190
Pleynet, Marcelin, 110n8
Plomer, William, 14n10
Poe, Edgar Allan, 230
Poland, Polish, 6, 14n17, 15n20, n24, 58n10, 153, 156, 332–50
  Baltic coast, 332
  Bieszczady Mountains, 339
  Lower Silesia, 343–4
  Świętokrzyskie Mountains, 2
  Warsaw, 332, 340, 342
Polish (language), 2, 4, 12, 15n24, 152, 332–50

Porter, Katherine Anne, 228
Portugal, 9, 15n20, 21, 215n22, 142
Portuguese (language), 4, 109, 152, 207, 248
post-Soviet culture, 11, 145, 153, 157, 161
  see also Soviet
postcolonialism see colonialism, decolonialism, neocolonialism, precolonialism, re-colonialism
Potter, Sally, 192, 334, 341–2, 384n34
Põldsaar, Raili, see Marling, Raili
precolonialism see colonialism, decolonialism, neocolonialism, postcolonialism, re-colonialism
Preston, Margaret, 73–5
Proctor, Thea, 73–5
'Professions for women', 89, 119, 146n18, 304, 403, 412, 413, 414
Proletkult-ism, 46, 58n8
Proust, Marcel, 28, 139, 154, 252, 259, 263, 345, 349n35, 372, 378
Puga, María Luisa, 3, 12, 267–78

Qi, Liang, 310n1
queer, queer studies, 4, 50, 111n14, 143, 158, 325, 332, 336, 338, 340, 341, 346, 405, 409n1
Queiroz, Rachel de, 250
Quijano, Carlos, 227

Ralian, Antoaneta, 48, 50
Rama, Ángel, 228, 230, 233
Ramadan, Aqila, 168
Ramadan, Somaya, 168, 173, 174–6, 177–8, 180n11
Rampello, Liliana, 185, 190
Ran, Chen, 3, 12, 297–312
Raterman, Jennifer, 154, 155
Raverat, Jacques, 103
Rähesoo, Jaak, 156, 158, 162n4
Reckley, Alice, 269
re-colonialism see colonialism, decolonialism, neocolonialism, postcolonialism, precolonialism
Reinhold (Bushmanova), Natalya, 134, 137, 138, 140, 141, 142, 143, 144–5, 147n40, 164
Repossi, Alessandra, 187–8

Rhys, Jean, 418
Ribeiro, Djamila, 257
Rice, Thomas Jackson, 7–8, 14–15n17
Richardson, Brian, 369n28
Richardson, Dorothy, 7, 44
Riddell, Florence, 202–5, 214n14, n16
Rigeade, Anne-Laure, xiii, 5, 12, 14n11, 371–86
Rilke, Rainer Maria, 27, 154
Rimbaud, Arthur, 372
Robins, Elizabeth, 52
Roger Fry, 58n12, 400
Rogers, Gayle, 5, 63, 79, 81, 82, 86, 91n3, n13, n20
Romania, 10, 15n20, 42–59
   Cluj (Cluj-Napoca), 44
   Bucharest, 44
Romanian (language), 4, 5, 7, 10, 42–59, 156
A Room of One's Own, 2, 11, 12, 19, 48, 68, 69, 71, 72, 73, 82, 88, 90, 90n1, 92n29, 93n49, 97, 99, 101, 107, 108, 116, 118, 119, 122, 123, 126, 129n4, 137–8, 140, 141, 145, 153, 155, 156, 157–60, 161, 162n4, 167, 168, 170–80, 193, 194n2, 195n7, 196n23, 199–222, 226, 239, 240, 214n3, 246, 253–4, 255, 257–9, 260, 262, 263, 269, 282–96, 298–312, 314–16, 318, 321, 322, 325–6, 327n6, 332, 333–4, 335, 337–8, 341, 342, 345, 346, 347, 374n2, 373, 374, 376, 379, 382n10, 384n34, 387, 388, 389, 399, 407, 409, 412, 413, 421, 425n1
   see also Shakespeare, Judith
Rosner, Victoria, 299
Ross, Johanna, 157
Rubenstein, Roberta, 408
Rudomino, Margarita, 133, 137
Rusca, Luigi, 185, 194n4
Russia, Russian, 5, 9, 13n3, 14n17, 132–49, 282, 283, 284, 289, 291, 292, 338
   Moscow, 133, 136, 137, 138, 145
   St Petersburg, 138
Russian (language), 2, 4, 11, 132–49, 154, 162n3, 338
'The Russian point of view', 135, 137, 143, 154
Ryan, Derek, 268, 270

Sackville-West, Edward Charles, 25
Sackville-West, Vita, 25–6, 32, 34, 37n1, 39n27, 51, 53, 59n19, 108, 193, 247, 379, 400, 407
Il Saggiatore (publishing house) *see* Mondadori, Alberto
Sahkai, Heete, 162n2
Salmerón, Julia, 87
Saloman, Randi, 119–20
Samoyault, Tiphaine, 371
S[amuel] Fischer Verlag, 25, 26, 27, 34–7
   see also Fischer, Bermann; Fischer, Samuel
Sandbach-Dahlström, Catherine, 349n30, 401, 402
Sandoval-Cervantes, Iván, 271–2
Santos, Leandra Alves dos, 261
Sappho, 125, 332, 343, 346, 403
Sarker, Sonita, 203
Sarraute, Nathalie, 5, 12, 371–4, 381, 382n4–6, n11, n13
Satama, Suvi, 270
Saxton, Ruth, 209–10
Sánchez, María, 227, 240
Sbârcea, George, 46
Scalero, Alessandra, 183, 185, 194n3, 194–5n6
Schaffer, Kay, 297
Schaffer, Talia, 52, 59n19
Schiller, Friedrich, 27
Schmidt, Rita Terezinha, 255
Schneider, Rolf, 128n4
Schulz, Georg-Michael, 128n17
Schwob, Lucie (Claude Cahun), 384n35
Scotti, Massimo, 189–90
Scutts, Joanna, 199
Segura, Celia, 8
Selitrina, Tamara, 145
Sellers, Susan, 337, 402, 404, 406–7
'The sentimental journey', 137
Serbian, 153
sexuality, 50, 119, 158, 231, 233, 289, 298, 300–9, 337, 339, 342, 403–4, 406, 413, 425n4
Séllei, Nóra, 124
Shaaban, Buthaina, 166–7, 180n9
Shakespeare, Judith, 97, 101, 122, 140, 158, 200–1, 202, 253, 254, 316, 318, 399, 407, 409
   see also A Room of One's Own

Shakespeare, William, 90, 104, 111n11, 208, 359, 409
Shalash, Ali, 166
Shaw, Carolyn Martin, 206
Shaw, George Bernard, 105, 133, 134, 289
Sheikh, Sheheryar B., 299
Shi, Shu-Mei, 292
Shiach, Morag, 247
Showalter, Elaine, 239, 336
Shuhua, Ling, 259
Sic! Publishers, 334
   Czerwińska, Elżbieta, 334
   see also Lis, Renata
Sicherman, Carol, 208
Sikk, Merilin, 162n2
Silakova, Svetlana, 141
Silesian, 343–4
Silko, Leslie Marmon, 418
Silver, Brenda R., 1–2, 152, 155, 159, 215n34, 247, 248, 263, 333, 378–81, 384n34
'Sir Walter Scott', 137, 146n18,
Siskind, Mariano, 80, 86
'A sketch of the past', 13, 44, 96, 98, 101, 103, 108, 233, 237, 373, 382n13, 414–7, 419, 422, 424
   see also Moments of Being
Slaughter, Joseph R., 3
Slessor, Kenneth, 363, 366–7
smaller languages, 6, 152
Smith, Craig, 268
Smith, Lesley, 214n20
Smith, Sidonie, 214n19
Smith, Zadie, 368n2
Smith-Rosenberg, Carole, 308
Smyth, Ethel, 339
Snaith, Anna, 128n13, 268, 275, 287–8, 294n8, 400
Snir, Reuven, 171
Socrates, 112n24
Solar, Xul, 80
Solberg, Helena Collett, 254
Sollers, Philippe, 99, 110n8, 373
Solnit, Rebecca, 414
Solovyova, Elena, 144
Solzhenitsyn, Aleksandr, 156
Somers, Armonía, 11, 230–3, 237, 240
Sonbol, Amira, 180n4
Sophocles, 122, 380

South Africa, 7, 199, 209, 212, 215n22
South America, South American, 4, 10, 79–93, 111n14, 225, 227, 241n6, 255
   see also listings for individual countries
South Korea, South Korean, 9, 13n3, 142, 282
Southworth, Helen, 75–6
Soviet Union, post-Soviet Union, Soviet, 11, 42, 46, 47, 50, 58n10, 118, 133–9, 145, 146n8, n20, 153, 156–7, 162n6, n7, 259, 283–4, 288, 290–1, 293, 317, 420
Spain, Spanish, 7, 14n17, 15n20, n22, 90, 91n14, 119, 158, 225, 229, 233, 237, 242n35, 271
   Bilbao, 229
   Madrid, 91n3
   Spanish Civil War, 91n13, 119, 242n35, 420, 422
Spanish (language), 4, 7, 14n17, 38n16, 68, 80, 85, 86, 87, 92n28, n41, 93n43, 152–3, 160, 170, 225–6, 227, 228, 230, 232, 235, 239, 240n1, n8, n10, 259, 269, 271, 272, 277n1, n2, 422
Spark, Muriel, 137
Spender, Stephen, 107, 112n18, 119
Spivak, Gayatri Chakravorty, 3, 99, 247–8, 257, 286, 347n1, 388
Squier, Susan, 268
Sri Lanka, 332
Stalin, Joseph, 136, 334
Stansky, Peter, 202, 214n10
Staveley, Alice, 349n30
Stead, Christina, 62, 71, 76
Stein, Gertrude, 66, 156
Stephen, Laura, 337
Stephen, Leslie, 52, 228–9, 236
Stephen, Thoby, 103
Stephen, Vanessa *see* Bell, Vanessa
Sterne, Laurence, 43, 57n1
Stevenson, Robert Louis, 186
Stoenescu, Ștefan, 48
Stone, E. Kim, 211
Storer, Richard, 208
Stott, Rebecca, 277–8n3
Strachey, Lytton, 69, 141, 406
Strange, Nora K., 202–5, 214n16
'Street haunting: A London adventure', 141, 185
Strong, Archibald T., 65

Suber, Peter, 212
Subiha, Ahd, 168, 173, 174, 175–6
Suhrkamp, Peter, 34, 36
Sulej, Karolina, 347
Sur, 80, 81, 85, 87, 91n3, 92n29
   Editorial Sur, 80, 92n29
Surits, Elena, 132, 139, 140
Sütiste, Elin, 160, 161
Swanson, Diana L., 409n1
Sweden, Swedish, 14n17, 15n20, n22, 349n30
   Stockholm, 37
Swedish (language), 7, 14n12,
Swinton, Tilda, 342
   see also Potter, Sally
Switzerland, 14n12, 26, 36
   Basel, 30
Syria, 166, 168, 169, 173, 174 , 426n9
   Damascus, 169

Taha, Taha Mahmoud, 166
Talvet, Malle, 156, 157, 159–60, 161, 162n4, n10
Tamura, Toshiko, 285
Tangalos, Sofia, 297
Tarozzi, Bianca, 186
Tauchnitz (publisher), 8, 27
Teffé, Tetrá de, 246, 251–2
Telles, Lygia Fagundes, 246, 259–60, 262–3, 264n10
Temkina, Anna, 157
Terentowicz-Fotyga, Urszula, 152, 153, 333–4, 346
Thatcher, Margaret, 384n35
Thierry, Raphaël, 209
Thoreau, Henry David, 162n4
'Thoughts on peace in an air raid', 2, 141, 388
Three Guineas, 2, 10–11, 58n12, n16, 66, 69–72, 81, 82, 88, 91n13, 92n40, 115–29, 144, 154, 155, 158, 159, 171, 185–6, 190, 209, 246, 306, 333, 374, 381, 387, 388, 389, 390, 392–3, 394, 395, 414, 419, 420, 422, 423, 424
   see also Spanish Civil War
'Three pictures', 141
Tie, Ning, 310n2
Tismăneanu, Vladimir, 46, 50
Tobin, Jean, 209–10
Tocqueville, Alexis de, 162n4
Toíbín, Colm, 393, 396
Tokarczuk, Olga, 12, 333, 336, 343–6, 349n33
   constellation novel, 343–4
   see also hybridity
To the Lighthouse, 7, 14n11, n12, 15n24, 26, 27, 29, 32–4, 35, 37, 37n1, 39n27, 43–4, 48, 64–5, 66–7, 69, 71, 74, 92n28, 116, 117, 121, 128n6, 132, 136, 139–40, 144, 145n1, 156, 166, 167–8, 185, 186, 187, 191, 193, 195n9, 226, 227, 234, 252–3, 262, 310n1, n4, 316, 333, 373, 388, 391, 399, 401, 408, 413, 421
Tolstoy, Leo, 137, 139, 142, 145n2, 186
Toth, Naomi, 372
Tõnnov, Anu, 162n2
Transeurasian, 12, 283, 284, 287, 292, 293
translation, translation studies, 5, 6, 9–11, 12, 14n11, 25–39, 42–59, 80, 85–7, 92n28–9, n41, 152–62, 225–30, 241n3, 253, 294n5, 305, 310n1, 316–18, 327n9, n12, 328n20, 332–4, 336, 338, 339, 341, 342, 344–7, 373–4
   feminist translation studies, 87, 166–79
transnational, transnational studies, 2–6, 12, 63, 74, 79, 91n9, 152, 154, 155, 246–8, 255, 259, 263, 292–3, 317, 332–3, 335, 344, 346, 388
   see transnational feminism under feminism, feminist studies
transcultural studies, 246–7, 263, 317
trauma, 3, 12, 240, 241n6, 267–78, 308, 357, 358, 360–1, 365, 368n5, 369n15, n23, 382n13, 403, 412–16, 418, 419–20, 422–3, 426n9
Trilling, Diana, 389
Trías, Fernanda, 227, 237, 240, 243n45
Troncotă, Tiberiu, 42, 47, 58n9
Trump, Melania, 199
Tsvetaeva, Marina, 96, 100, 101, 338
Turgenev, Ivan, 137
Turkey, Turkish, 9, 188, 247, 357
Turkish (language), 9, 405

Uganda, 215n24
Ukraine, 44, 253
Ulbricht, Walter, 128n5

United Kingdom (UK), 2, 4, 6, 7, 8, 9, 11, 25, 27, 29, 30, 32, 34, 35, 36, 42, 43, 44, 45, 48, 50, 51, 54, 62, 63, 64, 65, 68–70, 79, 80, 81, 85, 89, 91n11, 109, 110n1, 132, 133, 134, 136, 137, 138, 140, 141, 142, 143, 144, 145, 146n23, 154, 160, 162n3, 168, 169, 176, 177, 188, 199–213, 214n10, 215n22, 225, 226, 227, 230, 232, 234, 235, 236, 237, 239, 247, 249, 250, 253, 258, 259, 262, 267, 268, 269, 270–5, 277, 282, 285, 286, 288, 289–90, 291, 292, 311n18, 317, 334, 340, 347, 355, 357, 376, 388, 389, 391, 392, 393–6
  Edinburgh, 236
  London, 25, 29, 30, 32, 44, 64, 67, 68, 69, 74, 79, 82, 84, 146n23, 162n3, 187, 199–200, 206, 209, 213, 236, 237, 239, 262, 267, 268, 269, 271–5, 277, 283, 284, 287, 288, 289, 293, 300, 332, 337, 338, 340, 342, 357, 364, 376, 380, 381, 388, 389, 391, 392
United Nations, 250, 425n4
United States (US), 2, 3, 6, 8, 9, 13, 14n8, 15n20, n21, 25, 27, 48, 51, 52, 64, 79, 115, 118, 142, 145, 169, 177, 184, 199, 201, 202, 209, 214n10, 216n42, 225, 226, 228, 230, 249, 274, 282, 291, 292, 295n16, 315, 317, 319, 334, 358, 361, 388, 292, 319, 378, 388, 414
  New York, 9, 12, 13, 37, 91n3, 283, 293n2, 337, 399–409
  Washington, DC, 253
Ural, 346, 350n49
Urrutia, Carlos, 277n2
Uruguay, 3, 11, 225–43
  Montevideo, 226–9, 232–4, 239, 240, 240n1
Usova, Nina, 140

Vakhrushev, Vladimir, 140
Valéry, Paul, 27, 373
van der Wiel, Reina, 268
Van Gogh, Vincent, 375–6
Vanita, Ruth, 268
Van Wert, Kathryn, 368n5
Varga, Adriana, xiii, 5, 10, 13, 42–61
Vasiliyeva, Natalya, 139
Venezuela, 230

Venuti, Lawrence, 173
Verrall, Arthur Woollgar, 162n3
Vilariño, Idea, 227
Villeneuve, Pierre-Éric, 7, 371
Vincent, Norah, 401–3
Vittorini, Elio, 189
Viviani, Paola, 171, 179n2
Vladimirova, Natalia, 143
Voigt-Goldsmith, Margaret, 25–6
Volland, Nicolai, 317
Volzhina, Natalia, 138
Vorontsova, Tatiana, 134
The Voyage Out, 6, 14n8, 67, 72, 73, 86, 92n26, 140, 142, 155, 193, 225, 377

Wagenseil, Hans, 25
Wagenseil, Kurt, 25, 37n1
Wahab, Atta Abdel, 167, 168
Wahl, François, 110n8
Wajsbrot, Cécile, 12, 374, 376–7, 385
Wales, 271
Walker, Alice, 200–1
Walker, Rebecca, 294n9
Walkowitz, Rebecca L., 3, 5, 63, 91n11, 154–5, 335–6
  'born-translated', 335–6, 339–41
Wall, Kathleen, 288
'Walter Sicket: A Conversation', 69, 109, 110n4
Wang, David, 315
Wang, Huan, 310n1, 316, 318
Wang, Jing, 318
Wang, Xiaoni, 314, 323, 326n1, 328n21
Ward, Mrs Humphry, 214n11
Warhol, Andy, 378
Watson, Peggy, 157
Waugh, Evelyn, 228
The Waves, 1, 15n24, 48, 71, 93n52, 98, 100, 121, 129n24, 139, 156, 166, 167, 186, 187, 193–4, 194n2, 227, 234, 240, 252, 258, 262, 333, 336, 340–1, 342, 380, 401, 405
Weidner, Eva, 8
Weisgerber, Leo, 148n45
Weiß, Christian, xiii, 5, 9–10, 25–41
Weldon, Fay, 137
Wells, H[erbert] G[eorge], 44, 68, 119, 133, 134, 136, 228
Wenger, Étienne, 190–1, 191–2

Wheatley, Phillis, 200–1
White, Eric Walter, 30
White, Patrick, 70
Whitman, Walt, 105
Wicht, Wolfgang, 35, 38n25, 117, 128n5–7
Wild, Friedrich, 7
Wilde, Oscar, 133, 346
Wilder, Thornton, 35
Wilkinson, Kate, 212
Williams, John F., 74
Williams, John K., 199
Williams, Raymond, 290
Willis, John H., 6–7, 64
Willison, I[an] R., 14n15
Wilson, Patricia, 228, 241n4
Wilson, Edmund, 253
Wilson, Evelyn, 294n8
Wilson, Nicola, 27, 64
Wings see Yi [Wings] (journal),
Winterson, Jeanette, 335, 346, 350n40
Wittgenstein, Ludwig, 311n18
Wollstonecraft, Mary, 177, 249, 285
Wolf, Christa, 5, 10–12, 115–29
Wolf, Gerhard, 115, 117, 118, 119, 128n9
Wolfe, Cary, 270
'Women and fiction', 246, 284, 293
'Women novelists', 303
Woolf, Leonard, 2, 6, 14n10, 25, 26, 48, 59n18, 62, 64, 72–3, 75–6, 86, 87–8, 91n11, 92n26, n35 103, 109, 162n3, 185, 189, 195n15, 200, 213n3, 229, 235–6, 242n30, 339, 376, 377, 379, 402, 403, 404, 406, 407
Woolf, Virginia, works *see* individual listings
Wordsworth, William, 412
A Writer's Diary, 73, 87–8, 141, 193, 226, 229, 374, 407
Wu, J., 300
Wulfman, Clifford, 268
Wussow, Helen, 58n16
'Wuthering Heights', 137
Wu Zetian (empress), 327n7, n8, 316
Wylie, Dan, 268

Xavier, Elódia, 250
Xi, Huang, 314

Xianlin, Song, 297
Xie, Liuyi, 292
Xie, Qingyao, 310n1
Xu, Xiaobin, 310n2
Xu, Zhimo, 315–18, 327n4, n6

Yaeger, Patricia, 336
Yamakawa, Kikue, 285
Yang, Hua, 318
Yang, Lixin, 316, 317, 318
Yang, Xin, 297
Yanovskaya, Galina, 142–3
Ye, Gongchao, 310n1, 316, 327n9
The Years, 15n24, 35, 36, 48, 69, 116, 119, 135, 140–1, 154, 187, 209, 252, 333
Yeats, W. B., 35
Yelin, Louise, 71
Yi [Wings] (journal), 315, 324–5, 329n23
yin yang, 302, 306
Young, John K., 14n10
Young, Kevin, 202
Yourcenar, Marguerite, 153–4, 311n18
Yu, Dafu, 292
Yu, Lin, 325
Yu, Zhongli, 327n12
Yuknavitch, Lidia, 6, 13, 412–27

Zamorano, Ana, 87
Zamyatin, Yevgeny, 133
Zdravomyslova, Elena, 157
Zell, Hans, 209, 215n29
Zhai, Yongming, 12, 320, 322–4, 326, 328n16, n20, n21, 329n26
Zhang, Jeanne Hong, 327n12
Zhang, Xudong, 318
Zhang, Yiwu, 298
Zhang, Yuling, 325
Zhang, Zhen, 319–20
Zhantieva, Dilyara, 135–6
Zhao, Mei, 310n2
Zhou, Zan, 321, 324–5, 329n23, n25
Ziarek, Ewa Plonowska, 155, 159, 161
Zimmerman, Bonnie, 409n1
Zimmerman, Tegan, 210
Žižek, Slavoj, 342, 349n26

EU representative:
Easy Access System Europe
Mustamäe tee 50, 10621 Tallinn, Estonia
Gpsr.requests@easproject.com

www.ingramcontent.com/pod-product-compliance
Lightning Source LLC
Chambersburg PA
CBHW060333010526
44117CB00017B/2816